DEFINING DOCUMENTS
IN AMERICAN HISTORY

Civil War
(1860-1865)

DEFINING DOCUMENTS
IN AMERICAN HISTORY

Civil War
(1860-1865)

Editor
James M. McPherson

Volume 2

SALEM PRESS
A Division of EBSCO Information Services
Ipswich, Massachusetts

GREY HOUSE PUBLISHING

Library of Congress Cataloging-in-Publication Data

Civil War (1860-1865) / [editor, James M. McPherson]. -- [1st ed.].

  2 v. : ill., maps ; cm. -- (Defining documents in American history)

 Includes bibliographical references and index.
 ISBN: 978-1-4298-3746-0

  1. United States--History--Civil War, 1861-1865--Sources. 2. Confederate States of America--History--Sources. 3. Speeches, addresses, etc., American. I. McPherson, James M.
 973.7

Cover photo: Abraham Lincoln's Gettysburg Address Speech Notes ©Bettmann/CORBIS

E464 .C58 2014

Table of Contents

Volume 1

THE APPROACHING STORM   1

DISUNION: THE SECTIONAL CRISIS   107

THE POLITICS OF WAR   150

War Stories   256

Volume 2

The Home Front   321

THE HOME FRONT

Much as the narratives of individual soldiers give depth to the political and military maneuvers of the Civil War, the experience of civilians in the path of conflict also provides an important perspective. Since the war took place on American soil, the home front in the South was also often the battlefield, and Confederate women recorded violence and deprivation, as well as resistance and service. The North was not exempt from a full share of the cost of war, and most families experienced loss. Those who worked near the front lines, particularly those who tended the wounded, described scenes of suffering to their families back home. Soldiers and civilians, men and women, all were engaged in the war, and looked to their leaders, and to their religious faith, to make meaning of their sacrifice.

The three Confederate women whose words are recorded here provide a detailed record of the difficulty of providing for themselves and their families during the blockades and occupation. Food was exceptionally scarce, as was cloth and other household goods, and labor that had traditionally been provided by "servants" (the word "slave" is not used in these narratives to describe household labor), was now left to women accustomed to a life of leisure. Judith Brockenbrough McGuire bemoaned her inability to weave and spin to provide clothing for her family. Food and supplies were also in constant danger of being taken by soldiers, and indeed, Cornelia Peake McDonald, mother of eighteen children, defended her house against a mob that smashed her windows and stole her food. She would

have lost her house completely if it were not for the intervention of a sympathetic officer. Children, both young and liable to get sick or into trouble, and older and likely to be killed or captured, proved a constant source of anxiety. McDonald saw one of her young sons imprisoned for refusing to relinquish a snowball. Two others lit off small pipe bombs in the back yard while playing, drawing the unwelcome attention of Union soldiers. Mary Jeffreys Bethell, more than the other two, took great comfort in her religious belief. Her Christianity may have also influenced her belief that the abolition of slavery would be a benefit to the South, while the other two writers believed that former slaves had been misled and were better off with their masters.

American poet Walt Whitman described to his family the terrible suffering he witnessed while serving in military hospitals in Washington, and also gave a glimpse of the changing role of African Americans as the war progressed. Within a decade after Dred Scott was found by the Supreme Court to be ineligible for citizenship on account of his race, Whitman watched black troops march past President Lincoln as he saluted. Black soldiers played an important part in the Union victory, and distinguished themselves in battle. They hoped that this would encourage the nation to grant them full citizenship at the war's end. In his final speech on the eve of his assassination, Lincoln agreed, and set the stage for Reconstruction.

Bethany Groff

THE GETTYSBURG ADDRESS

DELIVERED
BY
ABRAHAM
LINCOLN
NOV. 19 1863

AT THE
DEDICATION
SERVICES
ON THE
BATTLE FIELD

Fourscore and seven years ago our fathers brought forth on this continent a new nation, conceived in liberty, and dedicated to the proposition that all men are created equal. ✶ ✶ ✶ Now we are engaged in a great civil war, testing whether that nation, or any nation so conceived and so dedicated, can long endure. ✶ ✶ We are met on a great battle-field of that war. ✶ We have come to dedicate a portion of that field as a final resting place for those who here gave their lives that that nation might live. ✶ ✶ It is altogether fitting and proper that we should do this. ✶ ✶ But in a larger sense we cannot dedicate, we cannot consecrate, we cannot hallow this ground. ✶ The brave men, living and dead, who struggled here, have consecrated it far above our poor power to add or detract. The world will little note, nor long remember, what we say here, but it can never forget what they did here. ✶ ✶ It is for us, the living, rather to be dedicated here to the unfinished work which they who fought here have thus far so nobly advanced It is rather for us to be here dedicated to the great task remaining before us, that from these honored dead we take increased devotion to that cause for which they gave the last full measure of devotion; ✶ that we here highly resolve that these dead shall not have died in vain; that this nation, under God, shall have a new birth of freedom, and that the government of the people, by the people, and for the people, shall not perish from the earth

The Gettysburg Address. Document on the Gettysburg Address appears on page 363. Source: Library of Congress, Prints & Photographs Division, LC-USZ62-5438.

■ "Luxuries Have Been Given Up Long Ago"

Date: November 29, 1862–April 24, 1865
Author: McGuire, Judith White Brockenbrough
Genre: diary

"How all this happened—how Grant's hundreds of thousands overcame our little band, history, not I, must tell my children's children. It is enough for me to tell them that all that bravery and self-denial could do has been done."

Summary Overview

During the Civil War, Judith White Brockenbrough McGuire, a Southern white woman and loyal Confederate, kept a diary of the events in her own life as well as those that affected her family, community, and nation, though she initially intended the diary to be read only by her "children's children." This excerpt from her book *Diary of a Southern Refugee during the War* (1867) details her experiences and thoughts between November 29, 1862, and April 24, 1865, shortly following the surrender of General Robert E. Lee at Appomattox. Her words allow the reader a keen insight into the thoughts and feelings of a white Confederate woman thrown into uncertainty as the war progressed and the Confederacy went into decline.

Defining Moment

At the time of McGuire's birth, the United States was just recovering from the War of 1812 against Great Britain, a conflict that allowed the young nation to display its perseverance and fortitude. But as McGuire aged, arguments over slavery and its effect on the economy began to grow, until the country spiraled toward rupture. This culminated in the secession of South Carolina on December 20, 1860, a little more than a month after Abraham Lincoln had been elected president. Ten other states seceded following South Carolina, leading to the creation of the Confederate States of America. Jefferson Davis, a native of Kentucky, was elected president of the Confederacy, with Georgia's Alexander H. Stephens serving as his vice president.

Between April 1861 and April 1865, the Civil War raged throughout the United States, drawing battle lines through families and friendships. Those within the Confederacy and in the border states faced a situation unlike that of their Union counterparts: the war was brought into their backyards. It may be argued that the South provoked the war, so battles were brought to them. However, the people of the Confederacy would have argued quite differently. As they saw it, they were fighting for their homeland, to protect their values and way of life, their homes and families.

Author Biography

Judith White Brockenbrough McGuire was born on March 5, 1813, to William and Judith White Brockenbrough in Virginia, where her father served in the state house of delegates and as a judge in the Virginia Supreme Court of Appeals. In 1846, McGuire married the Reverend John Peyton McGuire, a rector who later became the principal of a high school in Alexandria, Virginia.

McGuire and her family lived in Alexandria until 1861. Her diary begins on May 4, 1861, not long before the McGuires fled their home, fearing that federal troops might occupy the city. They stayed in Winchester, Virginia, for the duration of 1861, then moved to Richmond, the very heart and capital of the Confederacy, in February 1862. It was here that McGuire kept the larger portion of her wartime diary. Written in a frank and passionate manner, McGuire's diary catalogues the sorrows and tribulations that she and her white neighbors faced during the war, as well as their desperate feelings of uncertainty and disbelief as the Confederacy crumpled. Her excerpted entries mention pivotal events in the war, such as General Lee's surrender at Appomattox and the assassination of Abraham Lincoln. McGuire's initial purpose for keeping the diary was to keep a record of events for "members of the family who are too young to remember these days," as she writes in the preface, rather than for the public at large. Her diary thus reveals much of the vulnerability she felt at the time of the surrender—a vulnerability she may not have been at liberty to share openly. In light of the tragedy she saw as a result of the war, McGuire's diary may be used to glean insight into experiences common to many Southern white women during this time. Not only did many of their men not come home, but for many, the war destroyed the very home that sheltered them.

McGuire did not merely stay at home during the war and write; she also worked as a clerk in the Confederate Commissary Department. An army's commissary department is responsible for the appropriation and distribution of food to soldiers. On the Confederate side, given the Union blockade of Southern ports and the coast enforced by President Lincoln on April 19, 1861, this was an unenviable office in which to work, especially during the later parts of the conflict. In performing this post, McGuire differed from most women who wanted to take an active part in the war effort. The majority of women who did participate in the war effort were consigned to roles in such areas as nursing, sewing, and fundraising.

Following the war, McGuire and her husband operated a school in Essex County, Virginia, which McGuire continued to run after her husband died in 1869. McGuire's diaries were published in 1867, with additional printings later on. In 1873, she published a second book, *General Robert E. Lee, the Christian Soldier*. McGuire passed away on March 21, 1897. Her writing has played a vital part in preserving the history of those left behind when Confederate soldiers left for the front. For those who clashed with Union forces, the women and children at home symbolized all they fought to save.

HISTORICAL DOCUMENT

November, 1862

29th.—Nothing of importance from the army. The people of Fredericksburg suffering greatly from the sudden move. I know a family, accustomed to every luxury at home, now in a damp basement room in Richmond. The mother and three young daughters cooking, washing, etc.; the father, a merchant, is sick and cut off from business, friends, and every thing else. Another family, consisting of mother and four daughters, in one room, supported by the work of one of the daughters who has an office in the Note-Signing Department. To keep starvation from the house is all that they can do; their supplies in Fredericksburg can't be brought to them—no transportation. I cannot mention the numbers who are similarly situated; the country is filled with them. Country houses, as usual, show a marvellous degree of elastic-

ity. A small house accommodating any number who may apply; pallets spread on the floor; every sofa and couch *sheeted* for visitors of whom they never heard before. If the city people would do more in that way, there would be less suffering. Every cottage in this village is full; and now families are looking with wistful eyes at the ballroom belonging to the hotel, which, it seems to me, might be partitioned off to accommodate several families. The billiard-rooms are taken, it is said, though not yet occupied. But how everybody is to be supported is a difficult question to decide. Luxuries have been given up long ago, by many persons. Coffee is $4 per pound, and good tea from $18 to $20; butter ranges from $1.50 to $2 per pound; lard 50 cents; corn $15 per barrel; and wheat $4.50 per bushel. We can't get a muslin dress for less than $6 or $8 per yard; calico $1.75, etc. This is no great hardship, for we will all resort to homespun. We are knitting our own stockings, and regret that we did not learn to spin and weave. The North Carolina homespun is exceedingly pretty, and makes a genteel dress; the only difficulty is in the dye; the colours are pretty, but we have not learned the art of *setting* the wood colours; but we are improving in that art too, and when the first dye fades, we can dip them again in the dye.

October, 1864.

28*th.* . . . An officer from the far South was brought in mortally wounded. He had lost both legs in a fight below Petersburg. The poor fellow suffered excessively; could not be still a moment; and was evidently near his end. His brother, who was with him, exhibited the bitterest grief, watching and waiting on him with silent tenderness and flowing tears. Mr. —— was glad to find that he was not unprepared to die. He had been a professor of religion for some years, and told him that he was suffering too much to think on that or any other subject, but he constantly tried to look to God for mercy. Mr. —— then recognized him, for the first time, as a patient who had been in the hospital last spring, and whose admirable character had then much impressed him. He was a gallant and brave officer, yet so kind and gentle to those under his control that his men were deeply attached to him, and the soldier who nursed him showed his love by his anxious care of his beloved captain. After saying to him a few words about Christ and his free salvation, offering up a fervent prayer in which he seemed to join, and watching the sad scene for a short time, Mr. —— left him for the night. The surgeons apprehended that he would die before morning, and so it turned out; at the chaplain's early call there was nothing in his room but the chilling signal of the empty "hospital bunk." He was buried that day, and we trust will be found among the redeemed in the day of the Lord. This, it was thought, would be the last of this good man; but in the dead of night came hurriedly a single carriage to the gate of the hospital. A lone woman, tall, straight, and dressed in deep mourning, got quickly out, and moved rapidly up the steps into the large hall, where, meeting the guard, she asked anxiously, "Where's Captain T.?" Taken by surprise, the man answered hesitatingly, "Captain T. Is dead, madam, and was buried to-day." This terrible announcement was as a thunderbolt at the very feet of the poor lady, who fell to the floor as one dead. Starting up, oh, how she made that immense building ring with her bitter lamentations! Worn down with apprehension and weary with travelling over a thousand miles by day and night, without stopping for a moment's rest, and wild with grief, she could hear no voice of sympathy—she regarded not the presence of one or many; she told the story of her married life, as if she were alone—how her husband was the best man that ever lived; how everybody loved him; how kind he was to all; how devoted to herself; how he loved his children, took care of, and did every thing for them; how, from her earliest years almost, she had loved him as herself; how tender he was of her, watching over her in sickness, never seeming to weary of it, never to be unwilling to make any sacrifice for her comfort and happiness; how that, when the telegraph brought the dreadful news that he was dangerously wounded, she never waited an instant nor stopped a moment by the way, day nor night, and now "I drove as fast as the horses could come from the depot to this place, and he is dead and buried!—I never shall see his face again!" "What *shall* I do?"—"But where is he buried?" They told her where. "I must go there; he must be taken up; I must see him!" "But, madam, you can't see him; he has been buried some hours." "But I must see him; I can't live without seeing him; I must hire some one to go and take him up; can't you get some one to take him up? I'll pay him well; just get some men to take him up. I *must* take him home; he must go home with me. The last thing I said to his children was, that they must be good children, and I would bring their father home, and they are waiting for him now! He must go; I can't go without him; I can't meet his children without him!" and so, with her woman's heart, she could not be turned aside—nothing could alter her purpose. The next day she had his body taken up and embalmed. She watched by it until every thing was ready, and then carried him back to his own house and his children, only to seek a grave for the dead father close by those he loved, among kindred and friends in the fair sunny land he died to defend.

Many painfully interesting scenes occur, which I would like so much to write in my diary, but time fails me at night, and my hours of daylight are very closely occupied.

April, 1865

Thursday Night [April 13, 1865].—Fearful rumours are reaching us from sources which it is hard to doubt, that it is all too true, and that General Lee surrendered on Sunday last, the 9th of April. The news came to the enemy by telegram during the day, and to us at night by the hoarse and pitiless voice of the cannon. We know, of course, that circumstances forced it upon our great commander and his gallant army. How all this happened—how Grant's hundreds of thousands overcame our little band, history, not I, must tell my children's children. It is enough for me to tell them that all that bravery and self-denial could do has been done. We do not yet give up all hope. General Johnston is in the field, but there are thousands of the enemy to his tens. The citizens are quiet. The calmness of despair is written on every countenance. Private sorrows are now coming upon us. We *know* of but few casualties.

✳ ✳ ✳

Sunday Night [April 16, 1865].—The Episcopal churches being closed, we went to the Rev. Dr. Hoge's church. The rector was absent; he went off, to be in Confederate lines; but the Rev. Dr. Read, whose church is in ruins, occupied the pulpit.

Strange rumours are afloat to-night. It is said, and believed, that Lincoln is dead, and Seward much injured. As I passed the house of a friend this evening, she raised the window and told me the report. Of course I treated it as a Sunday rumour; but the story is strengthened by the way which the Yankees treat it. They, of course, know all about it, and to-morrow's papers will reveal the particulars. I trust that, if true, it may not be by the hand of an assassin, though it would seem to fulfil the warnings of Scripture. His efforts to carry out his abolition theories have caused the shedding of oceans of Southern blood, and by man it now seems has his blood been shed. But what effect will it have on the South? We may have much to fear. Future events will show. This event has made us wild with excitement and speculation.

General Lee has returned. He came unattended, save by his staff—came without notice, and without parade; but he could not come unobserved; as soon as his approach was whispered, a crowd gathered in his path, not boisterously, but respectfully, and increasing rapidly as he advanced to his home on Franklin Street, between 8th and 9th, where, with a courtly bow to the multitude, he at once retired to the bosom of his beloved family. When I called in to see his high-minded and patriotic wife, a day or two after the evacuation, she was busily engaged in her invalid's chair, and very cheerful and hopeful. "The end is not yet," she said, as if to cheer those around her; "Richmond is not the Confederacy." To this we all most willingly assented, and felt very much gratified and buoyed by her brightness. I have not had the heart to visit her since the surrender, but hear that she still is sanguine, saying that "General Lee is not the Confederacy," and that there is "life in the old land yet." He is not the Confederacy; but our hearts sink within us when we remember that he and his noble army are now idle, and that we can no longer look upon them as the bulwark of our land. He has returned from defeat and disaster with the universal and profound admiration of the world, having done all that skill and valour could accomplish. The scenes at the surrender were noble and touching. General Grant's bearing was profoundly respectful; General Lee's as courtly and lofty as the purest chivalry could require. The terms, so honourable to all parties, being complied with to the letter, our arms were laid down with breaking hearts, and tears such as stoutest warriors may shed. "Woe worth the day!"

✳ ✳ ✳

W., 24th.—On Saturday evening my brother's wagon met us at the depot and brought us to this place, beautiful in its ruins. We have not been here since the besom of destruction swept over it, and to us, who have been in the habit of enjoying its hospitality when all was bright and cheerful, the change is very depressing. We miss the respectful and respectable servants, born in the family and brought up with an affection for the household which seemed a part of their nature, and which so largely contributed to the happiness both of master and servant. Even the nurse of our precious little J., the sole child of the house, whose heart seemed bound up in her happiness, has gone. It is touching to hear the sweet child's account of the shock she experienced when she found that her "mammy," deceived and misled by the minions who followed Grant's army, had left her; and to see how her affection still clings to her, showing itself in the ardent hope that her "mammy" has found a comfortable home. The army had respected the interior of the house, because of the protection of the officers. Only one ornament was missing, and that was the likeness of this dear child. Since the fall of Richmond, a servant of the estate, who had been living in Washington, told me that it was in the possession of a maid-servant of the house, who showed it to him, saying that she "looked at it every day." We all try to be cheerful and to find a bright side; and we occupy the time as cheerfully as we can. The governess having returned to her home in Norfolk, I shall employ myself in teaching my bright little niece here and the dear children at S. H., and feel blessed to have so pleasant a duty.

GLOSSARY

Fredericksburg: a city in Virginia along the Rappahannock River; the site of Civil War battles

General Johnston: Joseph E. Johnston, a Confederate general who surrendered to General Sherman in late April 1865

lamentations: cries, sorrows

likeness: a picture of a person, possibly a photograph

mammy: an African American woman serving as a white child's nurse and caretaker

Norfolk: a city on the southeastern coast of Virginia

pallets: small stowaway beds.

Petersburg: a city in Virginia along the Appomattox River; the site of a siege during the Civil War

Richmond: a city in Virginia; the capital of the Confederacy

Seward: William H. Seward, Lincoln's secretary of state

Document Analysis

This excerpt from Judith McGuire's diary opens on November 29, 1862, roughly nineteen months after the hostilities began. While many historians agree that the Confederate Army held the upper hand in this part of the war, the South already found itself dealing with increasingly difficult hardships, particularly rising food prices. Four days after President Lincoln's call for volunteers on April 15, 1861, a blockade of the Southern coast was enacted, closing vital Confederate ports to supplies from abroad. The prices of various goods, from foodstuffs to shoes, steadily rose, and as a result, Confederate money lost value. Because of McGuire's location in the Confederate capital, supplies in her area were more plentiful than for those living further south, but she and her neighbors could not escape from rising prices. She writes, "Luxuries have been given up long ago, by many persons. Coffee is $4 per pound, and good tea from $18 to $20; butter ranges from $1.50 to $2 per pound; lard 50 cents; corn $15 per barrel; and wheat $4.50 per bushel." It is telling that she considered these food staples to be luxuries; the simple act of making a pot of coffee was then left to the very wealthy, if they could even procure the coffee at all. In the later years of the war, South Carolina resident Emma Le Conte and her family dined on "rancid salt pork and stringy beef," compared to the "beef, . . . cornbread, potatoes, and hominy" they ate earlier in the conflict (Mintz 129). The same year as this entry, "meat and grain had begun to disappear from many plates, and by 1864 one Confederate official informed Jefferson Davis that in Alabama, at least, civilian 'deaths from starvation have absolutely occurred'" (Faust 1212).

Material for clothes was also among the scarce items that McGuire lists. With such prohibitive prices, Southerners were reduced to repeated mending, and after mending no longer sufficed, many produced their own homespun material. Soon the wearing of homespun symbolized the wearer's commitment to the Confederacy, much like their Revolutionary War predecessors who wore their own homespun rather than buying British imported materials.

While coffee, tea, sugar, and lace may indeed have been luxuries Southerners could have gone without, the blockade also impeded their access to necessary items such as plows. The blockade, especially as it tightened during the war, held the Southern states in a siege. Confederate troops fighting on the front lines could not give their all while knowing their families back home were starving. In short, not only did the blockade threaten starvation, it also made a major impact on morale.

Confederate Women on the Home Front

Confederate women on the home front did what they could to aid the war effort. Some wrote poetry to hearten those who supported and fought for the Confederacy. Others held relief parties to collect money for their troops. Most typically, however, Southern women's war efforts included nursing and sewing. Sewing and knitting circles served multiple purposes. First, they provided soldiers with clothing and gear, such as underclothes, scarves, and even pillowcases. This type of work gave women the chance to create items that would directly assist the soldiers fighting for their protection. It also gave them a sense of purpose, while allowing them to remain "within the code of feminine virtue and support" (Brown 769).

The second vital purpose of Confederate women's sewing circles and similar organizations was community. The women of the Confederacy turned to their female communities for support to help them endure wartime deprivations and losses that only increased as the conflict persisted. Though Southern white women of the nineteenth century typically lived in gender-segregated spheres, the war brought different facets of white society together. In his modern evaluation of the Confederacy legacy, Tony Horwitz estimates that "one in four Southern men of military age died in the War"

(26). Such numbers would have made it difficult to find a household not connected with the conflict. It is highly understandable, therefore, that Confederate women bonded together and gave each other moral support; they knew too well the sacrifices and hardships others had endured.

As the war raged on, long past the few months many in the South expected it would take to beat the Northern army, white Confederate women were often left in charge of their households. In many instances, this was at odds with the societal norms in which they were raised. Southern white women who had previously performed small duties in the household—or, if they were of the upper classes, had performed more leisurely activities while supervising the work of enslaved women within the house—were now compelled to perform those chores executed by men, both free and enslaved, as well. This transformation of Southern white women's lives, as described by Alexis Girardin Brown, included managing slaves, deciding which crops to plant, and producing clothing and food (766).

As demonstrated by the scene documented by McGuire in her October 28, 1864, entry, there was one sacrifice some Confederate women were unwilling to make: forgoing proper burials for their dead. It is not known exactly how McGuire came to learn about the woman who arrived too late to see her dying husband before his hasty burial; however, the scene is illustrative of how Confederate women were committed to honoring their fallen family members and friends. McGuire records the widow's words, writing, "'I *must* take him home; he must go home with me. The last thing I said to his children was, that they must be good children, and I would bring their father home, and they are waiting for him now! He must go; I can't go without him; I can't meet his children without him!' and so, with her woman's heart, she could not be turned aside—nothing could alter her purpose." Women like this widow felt they could not fail their husbands or other family members in this final act. According to the widow, her husband had honored her throughout their married life, taken care of her and their children, and provided everything they required. She had to be allowed to bring him back home and give him a proper burial; it was all she could do in return, to honor him as he had her. This is a sentiment examined by Drew Gilpin Faust: "While men at the front hurried their slain comrades into shallow graves, women at home endeavored to claim bodies of dead relatives and to accord them proper ceremonies of burial. Woman's role was not simply to make sacrifices herself but also to celebrate and sanctify the martyrdom of others" (1214). Sadly, there were a great number of women who were not able to similarly honor their loved ones, as numerous soldiers from both sides of the conflict were buried in mass and unmarked graves.

McGuire wrote her entry for April 13, 1865, between two historically vital moments. Her entry captures the first of these events, rumor of the Confederate surrender: "Fearful rumours are reaching us from sources which it is hard to doubt, that it is all too true, and that General Lee surrendered on Sunday last, the 9th of April." To McGuire, the rumor was inconceivable, one that defied belief. She wanted to ignore it, but her words reveal her fear, which turned out to be justified, for the rumor was true: General Robert E. Lee had surrendered to General Ulysses S. Grant at Appomattox on April 9, 1865. Lee had long been struggling with depleting troops and vanishing supplies, while the North remained strong, with new immigrants joining the ranks. Lee had done well, but there was not much more he could have accomplished.

Though McGuire did not hear of it for another couple of days, the nation was shaken on April 14, 1865, by the shooting of President Abraham Lincoln at Ford's Theatre while he watched *Our American Cousin* with his wife, Mary Todd Lincoln. Mortally wounded by Confederate actor John Wilkes Booth, Lincoln died the following day, a little more than a month after his second presidential inauguration. On April 16, McGuire wrote, and with some foreboding: "It is . . . believed . . . that Lincoln is dead. . . . I trust that . . . it may not be by the hand of an assassin, though it would seem to fulfil the warnings of Scripture. . . . It now seems . . . his blood been shed. But what effect will it have on the South? We may have much to fear. Future events will show." Though there were those in the South who felt a degree of satisfaction at the loss of Lincoln, McGuire herself was very much aware of the repercussions of such an action, and she was right to worry.

The end of the war was followed by Reconstruction, whereby the former Confederacy was rigidly structured by martial law. It also made Southerners confront the changed status of African Americans; the passage of the Thirteenth Amendment ended slavery, while the Fifteenth Amendment enfranchised black men. The legacy of the fallen Confederacy lives on today in the South, in some places to a high degree.

Essential Themes

There is a distinctly resounding theme of pure disbelief in McGuire's last two excerpted entries. In this, she was not unusual among Confederate civilians. This particular line is imbued with her passion: "How all this happened—how Grant's hundreds of thousands overcame our little band, history, not I, must tell my children's children. It is enough for me to tell them that all that bravery and self-denial could do has been done. We do not yet give up all hope."

Though Lee had already surrendered by this point, it is clear that neither McGuire nor her compatriots were ready to do so. Everything about the end of the war—the end of everything they knew and sought to protect—sent fear and sadness into her heart, particularly at the loss of the servants of a house that she used to visit and to which she had returned: "We miss the respectful and respectable servants, born in the family and brought up with an affection for the household which seemed a part of their nature, and which so largely contributed to the happiness both of master and servant." In McGuire's view, the estate's servants—it is not clear whether or not they were enslaved—were part of the family. McGuire seems to think that the esteem that she had for the estate's servants was mutual; hence her disbelief over their departure. The nursemaid who left was, in McGuire's opinion, "deceived and misled by the minions who followed Grant's army"; a maidservant took a "likeness," or picture, of a child from the house and, according to another servant, "looks at it every day." Although McGuire may have considered these signs of the servants' affection for the family who lived on the estate, it is important to remember that the diary is her record, not the servants'. She might describe their words and actions, but probably not their true feelings or thoughts.

The departure of estate's servants was especially hard for the children who, having always known a nursemaid, now found that cherished person had left them, such as the child mentioned in the final entry. McGuire's words reveal a significant degree of incredulity that servants would leave the family. McGuire was clearly saddened by the servants' departure; for her, as for so many Southern white women, it brought home the reality of the Confederacy's demise.

Jennifer L. Henderson, PgDip

Bibliography

Brown, Alexis Girardin. "The Women Left Behind: Transformation of the Southern Belle, 1840–1880." *Historian* 62.4 (2000): 759–79. Print.

David, Shannon Clark. "Confronting the Reality of Changed Lives: Love and Loss for Women in Civil War America." *Voces Novae: Chapman University Historical Review* 1.2 (2010): 3–10. Web. 8 Apr. 2013.

Faust, Drew Gilpin. "Altars of Sacrifice: Confederate Women and the Narratives of War." *Journal of American History* 76.4 (1990): 1200–1228. Print.

Horwitz, Tony. *Confederates in the Attic: Dispatches from the Unfinished Civil War.* New York: Vintage Departures, 1999. Print.

Kerber, Linda K. "Separate Spheres, Female Worlds, Woman's Place: The Rhetoric of Women's History." *Journal of American History* 75.1 (1988): 9–39. Print.

McGuire, Judith White Brockenbrough. *Diary of a Southern Refugee, during the War.* 3rd ed. Richmond: Randolph, Print. 1889.

McPherson, James M. *Battle Cry of Freedom: The Civil War Era.* Oxford: Oxford UP, 1988. Print.

Mintz, Steven. *Huck's Raft: A History of American Childhood.* Cambridge: Harvard UP, 2004. Print.

Norton, Mary Beth. *Liberty's Daughters: The Revolutionary Experience of American Women, 1750–1800.* Boston: Little, 1980. Print.

Ott, Victoria E. *Confederate Daughters: Coming of Age during the Civil War.* Carbondale: Southern Illinois UP, 2008. Print.

Smith-Rosenberg, Carroll. "The Female World of Love and Ritual: Relations between Women in Nineteenth-Century America." *Signs* 1.1 (1975): 1–29. Print.

Additional Reading

Clinton, Catherine. *The Other Civil War: American Women in the Nineteenth Century.* New York: Hill, 1984. Print.

Farnham, Christie Anne. *The Education of the Southern Belle: Higher Education and Student Socialization in the Antebellum South.* New York: New York UP, 1994. Print.

Faust, Drew Gilpin. *Mothers of Invention: Women of the Slaveholding South in the American Civil War.* Chapel Hill: U of North Carolina P, 1996. Print.

Jabour, Anya. *Scarlett's Sisters: Young Women in the Old South.* Chapel Hill: U of North Carolina P, 2007. Print.

Stowe, Steven M. *Intimacy and Power in the Old South: Ritual in the Lives of the Planters.* Baltimore: Johns Hopkins UP, 1987. Print.

■ The Military Hospitals in Washington

Date: March–May 1864
Author: Whitman, Walt
Genre: letter

> *"There were, I should think, five very full regiments of new black troops, under Gen. Ferrero. They looked and marched very well. It looked funny to see the President standing with his hat off to them just the same as the rest as they passed by."*

Summary Overview

In the spring of 1864, the poet Walt Whitman wrote a series of letters to his family, including three addressed to his mother, Louisa Van Velsor Whitman, and one to his brother, Thomas Jefferson Whitman, known as Jeff within the family. The letters, poignant in their honesty—a trait displayed by Whitman throughout his literary career—bring the reader directly inside the makeshift hospitals set up in Washington, DC, as the poet recounts the scenes of despair among the wounded while championing the fighting spirit of the men who lay before him. The personal nature of these eyewitness accounts of wounded Civil War soldiers provides a unique perspective of the illustrious writer that shows a man wholly disgusted by war and desperate for the alleviation of the soldiers' suffering.

Defining Moment

A quote from one of the letters is striking in its frank mention and positive appraisal of African American soldiers: "There were, I should think, five very full regiments of new black troops, under Gen. Ferrero. They looked and marched very well. It looked funny to see the President standing with his hat off to them just the same as the rest as they passed by." Whitman's word usage may convey a misunderstanding: he saw the event not as amusing but rather as amazing. It is vital to remember that less than ten years before Whitman witnessed these uniformed men marching past the president of the United States, Dred Scott, a slave from Missouri, had sued for his right to freedom following the death of his owner, and the case had found its way to the Supreme Court. Ultimately, the court upheld his slave status; because slaves were not considered citizens according to the law at the time, Scott could not bring legal suit.

Keeping the example of Scott in mind, modern readers can understand the amazement felt by Whitman, and others of his ilk, when seeing President Abraham Lincoln saluting the black regiment as they marched past. The president did not alter his salute from that bestowed on the white troops; all soldiers were treated with equal respect.

Author Biography

As the United States found its footing during the nineteenth century, strengthening its stance during and after the War of 1812, cultural icons so familiar and commonplace today began to find their voices, contributing their skills and art to the identity of the growing nation. Born May 31, 1819, in West Hills, New York, Whitman is a primary symbol of American poetry. Evocative, sensual, emotive, and at times controversial, Whitman's work changed people's perspectives on poetry.

He began his life in Long Island, the second son of a large family headed by Walter Whitman and Louisa Van Velsor. His family included his five brothers, three of whom were named after prominent Americans—Jesse, Edward, Andrew Jackson, George Washington, and Thomas Jefferson—and his two sisters, Mary and Hannah. Both during and after his lifetime, rumors about Whitman's sexuality abounded; some historians insist he was homosexual, while others maintain otherwise. Like many others of history, this debate continues without any clear evidence pointing toward a resolution.

Whitman's career, most notable for his poetry collection *Leaves of Grass* (1855), was not solely within the literary realm. He spent a few years teaching in various parts of Long Island, though it was not a position in which he wished to continue; nor did he have any desire to take up his father's career in agriculture, despite his father's wishes. Aside from his forays into teaching and journalism, Whitman was a poet, and he shall be most remembered for his stirring work, especially those poems focused on the Civil War, its valiant soldiers, and Lincoln. Whitman died on March 26, 1892, in Camden, New Jersey.

HISTORICAL DOCUMENT

WASHINGTON, March 2, 1864.

DEAR MOTHER—You or Jeff must try to write as soon as you receive this and let me know how little Sis is. Tell me if she got entirely over the croup and how she is also about George's trunks. I do hope he received them; it was such a misfortune; I want to hear the end of it; I am in hopes I shall hear that he has got them. I have not seen in the papers whether the 51st has left New York yet. Mother, I want to hear all about home and all the occurrences, especially the two things I have just mentioned, and how you are, for somehow I was thinking from your letters lately whether you was as well as usual or not. Write how my dear sister Mat is too, and whether you are still going to stay there in Portland avenue the coming year. Well, dear mother, I am just the same here nothing new. I am well and hearty, and constantly moving around among the wounded and sick. There are a great many of the latter com- ing up the hospitals here are quite full lately they have [been] picking out in the hospitals all that had pretty well recovered, and sending them back to their regiments. They seem to be determined to strengthen the army this spring to the utmost. They are sending down many to their reg'ts that are not fit to go in my opinion then there are squads and companies, and reg'ts, too, passing through here in one steady stream, going down to the front, returning from furlough home; but then there are quite a number leaving the army on furlough, re-enlisting, and going North for a while. They pass through here quite largely. Mother, Lewis Brown is getting quite well; he will soon be able to have a wooden leg put on. He is very restless and active, and wants to go round all the time. Sam Beatty is here in Washington. We have had quite a snow storm, but [it] is clear and sunny to-day here, but sloshy. I am wearing my army boots anything but the dust. Dear mother, I want to see you and Sis and Mat and all very much. If I can get a chance I think I shall come home for a while. I want to try to bring out a book of poems, a new one, to be called "Drum-Taps," and I want to come to New York for that purpose, too.

Mother, I haven't given up the project of lecturing, either, but whatever I do, I shall for the main thing devote myself for years to come to these wounded and sick, what little I can. Well, good-bye, dear mother, for present write soon. WALT.

✳✳✳

WASHINGTON, March 29, 1864.

DEAREST MOTHER—I have written to George again to Knoxville. Things seem to be quiet down there so far. We think here that our forces are going to be made strongest here in Virginia this spring, and every thing bent to take Richmond. Grant is here; he is now down at headquarters in the field, Brandy station. We expect fighting before long; there are many indications. I believe I told you they had sent up all the sick from front. [The text here is difficult to read but appears to describe the arrival of over six hundred sick and wounded soldiers on a train.] I could not keep the tears out of my eyes. Many of the poor young men had to be moved on stretchers, with blankets over them, which soon soaked as wet as water in the rain. Most were sick cases, but some badly wounded. I came up to the nearest hospital and helped. Mother, it was a dreadful night (last Friday night) pretty dark, the wind gusty, and the rain fell in torrents. One poor boy this is a sample of one case out of the 600 he seemed to be quite young, he was quite small (I looked at his body afterwards), he groaned some as the stretcher bearers were carrying him along, and again as they carried him through the hospital gate. They set down the stretcher and examined him, and the poor boy was dead. They took him into the ward, and the doctor came immediately, but it was all of no use. The worst of it is, too, that he is entirely unknown there was nothing on his clothes, or any one with him to identify him, and he is altogether unknown. Mother, it is enough to rack one's heart such things. Very likely his folks will never know in the world what has become of him. Poor, poor child, for he appeared as though he could be but 18. I feel lately as though I must have some intermission. I feel well and hearty enough, and was never better, but my feelings are kept in a painful condition a great part of the time. Things get worse and worse, as to the amount and sufferings of the sick, and as I have said before, those who have to do with them are getting more and more callous and indifferent. Mother, when I see the common soldiers, what they go through, and how everybody seems to try to pick upon them, and what humbug there is over them every how, even the dying soldier's money stolen from his body by some scoundrel attendant, or from some sick ones, even from under his head, which is a common thing, and then the agony I see every day, I get almost frightened at the world. Mother, I will try to write more cheerfully next time but I see so much. Well, goodbye for present, dear mother. WALT.

✳✳✳

WASHINGTON, April 26, 1864.

DEAREST MOTHER—Burnside's army passed through here yesterday. I saw George and walked with him in the regiment for some distance and had quite a talk. He is very well; he is very much tanned and looks hardy. I told him all the latest news from home. George stands it very well, and looks and behaves the same noble and good fellow he always was and always will be. It was on 14th St. I watched three hours before the 51st came along. I joined him just before they came to where the President and Gen. Burnside were standing with others on a balcony, and the interest of seeing me, etc., made George forget to notice the President and salute him. He was a little annoyed at forgetting it. I called his attention to it, but we had passed a little too far on, and George wouldn't turn round even ever so little. However, there was a great many more than half the army passed without noticing Mr. Lincoln and the others, for there was a great crowd all through the streets, especially here, and the place where the President stood was not conspicuous from the rest. The 9th Corps made a very fine show indeed. There were, I should think, five very full regiments of new black troops, under Gen. Ferrero. They looked and marched very well. It looked funny to see the President standing with his hat off to them just the same as the rest as they passed by. Then there [were the] Michigan regiments; one of them was a regiment of sharpshooters, partly composed of Indians. Then there was a pretty strong force of artillery and a middling force of cavalry many New York, Pennsylvania, Massachusetts, R.I., etc., reg'ts. All except the blacks were veterans [that had] seen plenty of fighting. Mother, it is very different to see a real army of fighting men, from one of those shows in Brooklyn, or New York, or on Fort Greene. Mother, it was a curious sight to see these ranks after rank of our own dearest blood of men, mostly young, march by, worn and sunburnt and sweaty, with well-worn clothes and thin bundles, and knapsacks, tin cups, and some with frying pans strapt over their backs, all dirty and sweaty, nothing real neat about them except their muskets; but they were all as clean and bright as silver. They were four or five hours passing along, marching with wide ranks pretty quickly, too. It is a great sight to see an army 25 or 30,000 on the march. They are all so gay, too. Poor fellows, nothing dampens their spirits. They all got soaked with rain the night before. I saw Fred McReady and Capt. Sims, and Col. Le Gendre, etc. I don't know exactly where Burnside's army is going. Among other rumors it is said they [are] to go [with] the Army of the Potomac to act as a reserve force, etc. Another is that they are to make a flank march, to go round and get Lee on the side, etc. I haven't been out this morning and don't know what news we know nothing, only that there is without doubt to be a terrible campaign here in Virginia this summer, and that all who know deepest about it are very serious about it. Mother, it is serious times. I do not feel to fret or whimper, but in my heart and soul about our country, the forthcoming campaign with all its vicissitudes and the wounded and slain I dare say, mother, I feel the reality more than some because I am in the midst of its saddest results so much. Others may say what they like, I believe in Grant and in Lincoln, too. I think Grant deserves to be trusted. He is working continually. No one knows his plans; we will only know them when he puts them in operation. Our army is very large here in Virginia this spring, and they are still pouring in from east and west. You don't see about it in the papers, but we have a very large army here . . . WALT.

✳ ✳ ✳

WASHINGTON, Monday forenoon, May 23, '64.

DEAR BROTHER JEFF—I received your letter yesterday. I too had got a few lines from George, dated on the field, 16th. He said he had also just written to mother. I cannot make out there has been any fighting since in which the 9th Corps has been engaged. I do hope mother will not get despondent and so unhappy. I suppose it is idle to say I think George's chances are very good for coming out of this campaign safe, yet at present it seems to me so but it is indeed idle to say so, for no one can tell what a day may bring forth. Sometimes I think that should it come, when it must be, to fall in battle, one's anguish over a son or brother killed would be tempered with much to take the edge off. I can honestly say it has no terrors for me, if I had to be hit in battle, as far as I myself am concerned. It would be a noble and manly death and in the best cause. Then one finds, as I have the past year, that our feelings and imaginations make a thousand times too much of the whole matter. Of the many I have seen die, or known of, the past year, I have not seen or heard of one who met death with any terror.

Yesterday afternoon I spent a good part of the afternoon with a young man of 17, named Charles Cutter, of Lawrence city, Mass., 1st Mass, heavy artillery, battery M. He was brought in to one of the hospitals mortally wounded in abdomen. Well, I thought to myself as I sat looking at him, it ought to be a relief to his folks after all, if they could see how little he suffered. He lay very placid in a half lethargy with his eyes closed. It was very warm, and I sat a long while fanning him and wiping the sweat. At length he opened his eyes quite wide and clear and looked inquiringly around. I said, "What is it, my dear? do you want anything?" He said quietly, with a good natured smile, "O nothing; I was only looking around to see who was with me." His mind was somewhat wandering, yet he lay so peaceful, in his dying condition. He seemed to be a real New England country boy, so good natured, with a pleasant homely way, and quite a fine looking boy. Without any doubt he died in course of night.

There don't seem to be any war news of importance very late. We have been fearfully disappointed with Sigel not making his junction from the lower part of the valley, and perhaps harassing Lee's left or left rear, which the junction or equivalent to it was an indispensable part of Grant's plan, we think. This is one great reason why things have lagged so with the Army. Some here are furious with Sigel. You will see he has been superseded. His losses [in] his repulse are not so important, though annoying enough, but it was of the greatest consequence that he should have hastened through the gaps ten or twelve days ago at all hazards and come in from the west, keeping near enough to our right to have assistance if he needed it. Jeff, I suppose you know that there has been quite a large army lying idle, mostly of artillery reg'ts, manning the numerous forts around here. They have been the fattest and heartiest reg'ts anywhere to be seen, and full in numbers, some of them numbering 2000 men. Well, they have all, every one, been shoved down to the front. Lately we have had the militia reg'ts pouring in here, mostly from Ohio. They look first rate. I saw two or three come in yesterday, splendid American young men, from farms mostly. We are to have them for a hundred days and probably they will not refuse to stay another hundred. Jeff, tell mother I shall write Wednesday certain (or if I hear anything I will write to-morrow). I still think we shall get Richmond. WALT.

GLOSSARY

Burnside: Ambrose Burnside, a general in the Union Army

Capt. Sims: Samuel Harris Sims, a captain in the Fifty-First New York Volunteer Regiment

Col. Le Gendre: Charles Le Gendre, a colonel in the Fifty-First New York Volunteer Regiment

furlough: a leave of absence, usually associated with military life

Gen. Ferrero: Edward Ferrero, a general in the Union Army

George: George Washington Whitman, one of Whitman's brothers

Jeff: Thomas Jefferson Whitman, another of Whitman's brothers

Mat: Martha E. Whitman, Jeff's wife

vicissitudes: unpleasant changes or variations

Document Analysis

Whitman's letters, all penned in the spring of 1864, about a year before the end of the war, present emotions of worry over his family and anxiety and desperation over the depravity of war and. Whitman suggests that he will feel a sense of surprise and self-abasement if his family comes out of the war unscathed while hundreds of thousands of families mourn the loss of sons, husbands, or brothers. Whitman's words to his mother are fearful and genuine, but he is also at pains to assure her that future letters will have more cheer despite all he sees:

> Mother, when I see the common soldiers, what they go through, and how everybody seems to try to pick upon them, and what humbug there is over them every how, even the dying soldier's money stolen from his body by some scoundrel attendant, or from some sick ones, even from under his head, which is a common thing, and then the agony I see every day, I get almost frightened at the world. Mother, I will try to write more cheerfully next time but I see so much.

In 1864, Whitman was in his forties, yet he was unabashed in sharing his apprehensions with his mother. Beyond these family cares, though, he shares military news and was present to watch a regiment of African Americans march past President Lincoln, who saluted them just as he had the white soldiers. This was enough of a moment for the poet that he had to include it in his letter to his family. Though history has greatly benefited from more formal documents, informal missives such as these letters allow the modern reader a far more personal view of history. Whitman did not spend time at makeshift hospitals writing to his mother in the hopes of posterity, nor did he share these details for the same reasons. This candid view provides a true window to the past.

As historical documents, letters hold a special place. Like diaries, letters are typically, though not always, written without publication in mind; therefore, the writer did not foresee the especial need for applying final polishes to the product. Letters are in essence private communication with the intended recipients, a reaching out in the distance, no matter the reason. When examining history through any document, it is important to consider the following before making conjectures: who wrote it, for whom was it written, and why was it written? In the case of these four letters, the questions are easily answerable. Whitman, while away from the family home in New York, kept in touch with his mother and brother Jeff and kept them informed of exactly what was happening in the nation's capital during the final years of the war. In writing to his family, there is genuine emotion for how his family fared, including Jeff's wife, Martha, whom Whitman refers to as Mat. While some documents may require a reading between the lines, Whitman's letters do not appear to sanction such a reading.

Based on the beginning of the first letter to his mother in March 1864, Whitman feels anxious about his ill sister and wonders if his brother George received his trunks. During the Civil War, postal service could be delayed for any number of reasons, and the shipment of goods to camps and hospitals carried the risk of theft. Luckily for George Whitman, according to a letter catalogued on the Whitman Archive, his trunks did arrive safely; this is mentioned in a letter by George to his mother, dated March 6, 1864, just four days after his brother's inquiry: "I found my trunk up at Fort Schuyler all right the morning I left home."

George Washington Whitman, one of Whitman's illustriously named younger brothers, has been well documented by countless historians as the indirect catalyst for bringing his brother Walt's attention to the plight of wounded Civil War soldiers. Fourteen years younger than his literary brother, George served in New York's Fifty-First Regiment. Whitman made great haste to the site of the Battle of Fredericksburg, fought during the second week of December 1862, after reading in a newspaper article that his brother had been seriously injured. As it happened, George only suffered a minor wound, but Whitman stayed with him, living like a soldier; he soon became afflicted by the sight of the wounded soldiers in his brother regiment.

Military Hospitals

During the Civil War, medicine was comparatively primitive; full knowledge of the benefits of sterilization and the use of anesthesia was not yet commonplace, and many times the treatment was worse than the ailment. Some men did benefit from the alleviating effects of chloroform and ether, the former of which had seen a rise in popularity in the previous decade, particularly after its much-publicized use by Queen Victoria during childbirth. The hospitals themselves did not necessitate a specialized building but could be a simple

tent set up in a field or a nearby house. Robert Roper, in his article, "Collateral Damage," states, "These hospitals—hard to distinguish from foul charnel houses, especially early in the war, before a reformist surgeon general began to clean them up—were where the casualties of Antietam and Chancellorsville and Gettysburg ended up, and where thousands died of their wounds or of hospital-borne infections" (77). William Morton has been noted by N. H. Metcalfe, a writer for the Center for the History of Medicine in Birmingham, England, as more than likely the first anesthesiologist of the American military, having used his knowledge on the soldiers at the Battles of Fredericksburg and the Wilderness; coincidentally, George Whitman fought in both of these battles.

Medical treatment on the battlefield was comparable to an assembly line; men were moved from a stretcher to a table for examination and then to a bed. When the men died, their bodies were removed, and the bed was filled again. With sterilization not yet commonplace and cleaning limited—not to mention the questionable availability of materials to do so—each new deposit of a wounded soldier brought with it more germs and cross-contamination. Although he makes no specific mention of these conditions or of painkillers, Whitman, after approximately three years tending to the soldiers, was not reconciled to what he saw:

> One poor boy . . . seemed to be quite young, he was quite small . . . he groaned some as the stretcher bearers were carrying him along. . . . They set down the stretcher and examined him, and the poor boy was dead. They took him into the ward, and the doctor came immediately, but it was all of no use. The worst of it is, too, that he is entirely unknown there was nothing on his clothes, or any one with him to identify him, and he is altogether unknown. Mother, it is enough to rack one's heart such things. Very likely his folks will never know in the world what has become of him. Poor, poor child, for he appeared as though he could be but 18.

For the men and boys tended to affectionately by Whitman, the care they received was in equal measure to the respect felt by Whitman toward them for their sacrifices for their country. Historian Stanley Plumly cites another Whitman quote involving his desire to be of service to the soldiers:"I try to give a word or trifle to everyone without exception . . . I make regular rounds among them . . . I give all kinds of sustenance, blackberries, peaches, lemons . . . shirts & all articles of clothing" (15). Whitman's role as a Civil War nurse seems to have been the turning point in his poetry, ignited by his emotion.

Walt Whitman and Post-Traumatic Stress Disorder

Historical research, while not glamorous, is not without its moments of intrigue. Questions are important in research because they help historians formulate their arguments and lead to examination of documents. Therefore, it is vital that history is read with at least a small degree of skepticism. One historian may expound on a topic of which their counterparts have made no mention; in these cases, especial attention needs to be given to the sources used. One researcher, David Hsu, has deduced that Whitman possibly suffered from post-traumatic stress disorder (PTSD), a modern diagnosis most commonly associated with soldiers in combat and individuals who have experienced violent encounters.

Hsu, a medical doctor, focuses on PTSD in his article "Walt Whitman: An American Civil War Nurse Who Witnessed the Advent of Modern American Medicine." He maintains that Whitman "began to show signs of post-traumatic stress disorder . . . with associated psychosomatic illness. Nightmares, triggers, and hypervigilance are evidenced in his writing" (238). While historians take multiple sources into account during investigations, Hsu's focus relies on his interpretations of Whitman's writings and his background in medical knowledge. He continues, "Whitman frequently re-experienced the traumatic event in his mind, as evidenced by his vivid memories, distressing dreams, and seeing of 'ghosts.' . . . He avoided thoughts, feelings, activities, and even symbolic representations of his experiences, such as his notebook pages, which would trigger spurts of emotional pain" (238). Although it is possible Whitman did suffer from PTSD, a definitive diagnosis requires the dedication of further research and would certainly create a new direction for the study of Whitman and his poetry.

Essential Themes

The marching of the black regiment past President Lincoln, while Whitman watched from the crowd, was a momentous occasion for Whitman, for the troops, and for the country at large. African Americans had only been in active combat since the year before. The most widely known regiment of black soldiers was the Fifty-Fourth Regiment Massachusetts, headed by Bostonian Robert Gould Shaw; their modern notoriety was enhanced in part by the 1989 film *Glory*, though this film is mildly inaccurate. It should be noted that there existed "contraband" troops made up of black men before this; however, official organizations of black regiments did not begin until 1863.

Although it is entirely unknown if Whitman came into contact with members of black regiments, historian Jane E. Schultz, researching the challenges women faced as nurses on the front lines, found writings of a nurse who cared for soldiers of the Fifty-Fourth after their regiment was nearly wiped out at Fort Wagner in July 1863. On discovering the theft of items meant for the soldiers, Esther Hill Hawks writes, "The fowl which I had obtained for the sick were all eaten by those in the office. *Not* one was ever cooked for a patient. . . . A box of luxuries sent out to the 54th wounded . . . was disposed of in the same way. . . . I endeavored with my whole heart, to make this dreary hospital life, as homelike as possible" (qtd. in Schultz 383–84). Whatever her personal feelings may have been toward black soldiers, Hawks demonstrated her desire to give the men of the Fifty-Fourth the best treatment, and she was furious with the open disregard of her superiors. Women like Hawks fought for African Americans as they had, in turn, fought for her; to use Whitman's phrase, it is "funny" that that which had recently seemed incomprehensible—black men in sanctioned military uniforms—had become integral to the Union war effort.

Jennifer L. Henderson Crane, PgDip

Bibliography

Bradford, Adam. "Recollecting Soldiers: Walt Whitman and the Appreciation of Human Value." *Walt Whitman Quarterly Review* 27.3 (2010): 127–52. Print.

Folsom, Ed, and Kenneth M. Price. "Walt Whitman." *Walt Whitman Archive*. Ctr. for Digital Research in the Humanities at the U of Nebraska-Lincoln, n.d. Web. 5 Apr. 2013.

Hsu, David. "Walt Whitman: An American Civil War Nurse Who Witnessed the Advent of Modern American Medicine." *Archives of Environmental and Occupational Health* 65.4 (2010): 238–39. Print.

Metcalfe, N. H. "Military Influence upon the Development of Anaesthesia from the American Civil War (1861–1865) to the Outbreak of the First World War." *Anaesthesia* 60.12 (2005): 1213–17. Print.

Plumly, Stanley. "Whitman's Compost." *Virginia Quarterly Review* 88.2 (2012): 13–16. Print.

Price, Angel. "Whitman's Drum Taps and Washington's Civil War Hospitals." *American Studies at the University of Virginia*. University of Virginia, n.d. Web. 5 Apr. 2013.

Roper, Robert. "Collateral Damage." *American Scholar* 78.1 (2009): 75–82. Print.

Schultz, Jane E. "The Inhospitable Hospital: Gender and Professionalism in Civil War Medicine." *Signs* 17.2 (1992): 363–92. Print.

Whitman, George Washington. Letter to Louisa Van Velsor Whitman. 6 Mar. 1864. *Walt Whitman Archive*. Ctr. for Digital Research in the Humanities at the U of Nebraska-Lincoln, n.d. Web. 9 Apr. 2013.

"Wound Dresser." *Revising Himself: Walt Whitman and Leaves of Grass*. Lib. of Cong., 16 Aug. 2010. Web. 5 Apr. 2013.

Additional Reading

Alcott, Louisa May. *Civil War Hospital Sketches*. Mineola: Dover, 2006. Print.

Kurant, Wendy. "'Strange Fascination': Walt Whitman, Imperialism, and the South." *Walt Whitman Quarterly Review* 29.2/3 (2012): 81–95. Print.

Loving, Jeremy. *Walt Whitman: The Song of Himself*. Berkeley: U of California P, 2000. Print.

Reynolds, David S. *Walt Whitman's America: A Cultural Biography*. New York: Knopf, 1995. Print.

Roper, Robert. *Now the Drum of War: Walt Whitman and His Brothers in the Civil War*. New York: Walker, 2008. Print.

Whitman, Walt. *Drum Taps*. Miami: HardPress, 2010. Print.

---. *Leaves of Grass*. New York: Simon, 2013. Print.

■ "The Shadows Are Darkening . . . Jackson Is Certainly Dead"

Date: September 26, 1862–May 15, 1863
Author: McDonald, Cornelia Peake
Genre: diary

"He spoke gaily and enthusiastically of the life in the camp. . . . I did not like to be a prophet of evil, and tell him about the dark side of war that I had seen."

Summary Overview

War has always left family behind to worry and agonize over the fate of loved ones. The American Civil War saw thousands upon thousands of women left at home while their husbands, sons, brothers, and fathers fought for liberty, and such was the case of Cornelia Peake McDonald. Confederate women, including McDonald, faced a far different experience than their Northern counterparts did, especially in consideration of the blockade imposed along the Southern coastline in the early days of the war. This affected the supply of not just foodstuffs, but also medicines, cloth, and munitions. The diary entries below, composed in the middle years of the war, are emotional and vivid and present the modern reader with a grim view of life amid such a pivotal moment in America's past; while the early days of the war are glossed with romance, McDonald's words emphasize just how quickly that glamour vanished.

Defining Moment

By the time of McDonald's diary entries, the war had already raged on for approximately a year and a half and showed no signs of ending. Already the privations of the blockade were felt, and cemeteries throughout the Confederacy held countless soldiers who had fallen while fighting for the Southern cause. Bower's Hill in McDonald's hometown of Winchester, Virginia, had

been the site of battle (the First Battle of Winchester) only months before these entries; given her proximity to the hostilities, it is highly probable that she herself witnessed the more gruesome details of war.

In the entry dated October 13, 1862, McDonald describes meeting "a little soldier from the Maryland camp came this evening—a mere boy, but with his eyes full of fire, eagerness to join the flag." The boy, never specifically named, had just come from France and declared that "his father wished him to come; did not think it honourable to remain in a foreign land while Maryland struggled for her freedom. His mother was not so anxious." It is evident that the boy, not just his father, felt himself honor-bound to return to fight, a sentiment McDonald appears reluctant to dampen by relating her wartime experiences to him. For McDonald, a mother of a large family (composed of both her children and stepchildren) as well as a wife with a husband off at the front, there is pity and sadness at the boy's joviality at the prospect of entering the fray himself: "He spoke gaily and enthusiastically of the life in the camp, and the battles he expected to take part in; and I did not like to be a prophet of evil, and tell him about the dark side of war that I had seen." The boy was not alone, and many youths like him marched off to war, both to fight and to serve as drummers, age being no protection from the dangers of war.

Author Biography

Cornelia Peake McDonald began life on June 14, 1822, in Alexandria, Virginia. She was born to Dr. Humphrey and Anne Lane Peake, parents of a large retinue of children. The Peake family moved several times during Cornelia's childhood and youth, finally settling in Hannibal, Missouri, in the late 1830s. By a twist of fate, her destiny followed that of her sister Susan, who met and married Edward C. McDonald. On May 27, 1847, the twenty-four-year-old Cornelia married Edward's brother, Angus McDonald III, a widower in his late forties with nine children from his previous marriage.

By April 1861, when the firing upon Fort Sumter along the South Carolinian coast signaled the start of the Civil War, the McDonalds had nine children together and had returned to Virginia. With the outbreak of war, Angus McDonald left his law practice and, as a Confederate colonel serving in the Seventh Regiment of the Virginia Cavalry, participated in General Thomas "Stonewall" Jackson's Shenandoah Valley Campaign during the spring of 1862. Wounded and captured in June 1864, he spent several months as a prisoner of war in Wheeling, Virginia (now West Virginia).

Not long after Angus's release, Cornelia McDonald became a widow in December of 1864, little more than two years after the loss of her three-year-old daughter, Bess; it is this young child's death that McDonald describes in the first entry below. McDonald did not merely send her husband and the father of her children off to war only to sit idly and await his return. Rather, she faced severe challenges herself throughout the war years, endeavoring to save the family home from confiscation by the Union forces and her children from danger. In these respects, she was only partially successful, eventually being forced to evacuate Winchester and to see her sixteen-year-old son Harry off to war as well. All told, McDonald lost her husband, her brother-in-law, and her stepson C. W. McDonald as a result of the war, and two McDonald children were wounded and became prisoners of war.

Despite the travails of this tumultuous time, McDonald and her surviving children endured. She lived an exceptionally long life, dying months before her eighty-seventh birthday and nearly fifty years after the start of the Civil War, on March 11, 1909, in Louisville, Kentucky.

HISTORICAL DOCUMENT

Sept. 26th—Two months since I wrote a line, and oh! the sorrow they have left me. They have taken away my flower. My sweet blue-eyed has left me forever. I saw her fading out but never dreamed that she was dying. Though for many nights I have sat with her in my arms soothing her restlessness, the day time would come and bring smiles and happy looks, and I had not a thought of danger.

> After a time the smiles were all gone,
> and the little face was sad and grave.
> Just as if her soul had tasted
> Drops of death's mysterious wave.

Her head drooped and her little round limbs grew thin, and her eyes followed me wherever I went. Then I held her night and day and I clung to her as if I could not give her up.

One evening as the sun was going down I held her in my arms, and as she breathed out her little life her eyes were fixed in my face with the shadow of death over them. The children stood around sobbing. The little breast heaved and panted, one long sigh and all was still; her eyes stilled fixed in my face. Ah that fearful shadow! How I saw it flit over that lovely countenance, withering all its bloom and leaving its own ashen grey to remain forever. . . .

For days after she left me I felt as if my heart was dead. Nothing could interest me and it was vain to try to occupy myself with any thing. All seemed unreal, as if it was slipping rapidly away. The world was a dream, and a troubled, sorrowful one. Eternity appeared so near that earth and its concerns were being absorbed in its light.

On Tuesday night, August 26th, after she was buried, I was lying in bed with a feeling only indifference to everything, a perfect deadness of soul and spirit. If I had a wish it was the world, with its fearful trials and sorrows, its mockeries and its vanishing joys, could come to an end. Suddenly the house was shaken to its foundations, the glass was shivered from the windows and fell like rain all over me as I lay in bed; a noise, terrific as of crashing worlds, followed, prolonged for some fearful moments. . . . Then a cry, and my room door was burst open. "The town is on fire!" screamed Betty, rushing in. I got up and running across the hall to where the windows look towards the town, and then saw the whole eastern sky lighted by the blaze of burning buildings, a long line of which was in one huge conflagration. We learned the next day that the enemy had evacuated during the night, and had fired the depot, and the building where were government stores and army supplies, many other buildings having taken fire, a large hotel among them. Their great magazine had been blown up, which had caused the fearful noise. . . .

✳✳✳

October 13th—A little soldier from the Maryland camp came this evening—a mere boy, but with his eyes full of fire, eagerness to join the flag. He had just come from Paris, France, where his family are living, to join the Maryland line. He said his father wished him to come; did not think it honourable to remain in a foreign land while Maryland struggled for her freedom. His mother was not so anxious.

He spoke gaily and enthusiastically of the life in the camp, and the battles he expected to take part in; and I did not like to be a prophet of evil, and tell him about the dark side of war that I had seen. So he talked on about Maryland, and I asked him what he would do if, when the Confederacy was established, Maryland was left in the hands of his enemies.

"They cannot keep her," he said. "No peace will be made that leaves her with the North."

✳✳✳

December 26th—All day distress and misery. As soon as I was up, and before I was dressed, some officers came to search the house. They found poor Harry's gun which, with his toy pistol, they took of course.

That was scarcely over and we were about to sit down to breakfast, when the house was surrounded by men who, with their fists began to break in the windows, and

also threatened to come in and break up the furniture if breakfast was not immediately given them. I rushed to the front of the house, and shut and locked the hall door, but on opening the study door found that they had entered there by breaking in the windows, and were carrying off the few stores I had which had been put there instead of the usual place for safe-keeping. I locked that door, shutting them off from the rest of the house, leaving the things there to their mercy, and returned to the other part of the house where were assembled at least a hundred desperate and furious men. We fastened down the windows and tried, Sue and I, to keep them from coming in at the door. In the midst of it all a deputation of surgeons arrived and there was a pause in the havoc for a while. They came to inform me that they should that day take the house for a hospital, and would give me a few hours to find quarters elsewhere.

I stood in the door, and they around it, with fierce, resentful faces. Not a look of kindliness or pity did I see on a face in the group. All around were the soldiers, impudent and aggressive, and not one word was said by any one of them, who no doubt thought themselves gentlemen as they wore shoulder straps, to remonstrate with the men for their behaviour, or to interfere in behalf of a helpless woman and a young girl.

I asked them as calmly as I could why they must take my house. They replied that it was a good "location" and that they would have the best places for their men who were sick, they would not allow them to occupy places that had before been used as hospitals while rebel women and children slept under comfortable roofs, and in clean beds. . . .

As the surgeons departed a rush was made for the dining room where Sue and I were with the children. A hundred heads looking over each other seemed to be clustered about the door. I told Sue if she would try to keep them out, I would, as a desperate venture, go in town and see the commanding officer. I went, and met Mr. Williams near there, and he went with me to see Cluseret. At first he was indisposed to listen to me, but Mr. Williams kindly helped me to lay the case before him. He was very polite, listened to the end, and taking his cap requested me to lead the way to the scene of commotion. When he arrived at the house, he looked around at all the havoc and destruction, knitted his brows, and told a man to disperse the crowd, and send a guard. That was done and we were once more left in peace. When I left, Sue told me, the crowd continued to push in, and that for some time she, with Kenneth's assistance, small as he is, was able to keep them out by standing in the door and holding to the sides of it. Even they were not brutal enough to push her away, but presently she saw a powerful man with a pipe in his mouth pushing his way through the crowd, and elbowing his way up to her, and with oaths and curses declaring his determination to enter in spite of her. Then she cried aloud, "Is there not one man in that crowd that will keep that Dutchman away from me?" One tall fellow seized him from behind, another, and then another, and between them they turned him around and put him out on the porch. The rest then quieted down a little, and she maintained her position till I arrived with Cluseret. Tonight, thank our Father, we have a shelter left.

✳✳✳

January 20th—It is a great effort to bring myself to write to overcome the listlessness and want of interest in things that sometimes tempts me to give up the task I have undertaken. Our victories at Vicksburg and Murfreesboro are confirmed. A few Northern papers seem to be violent against the Lincoln Administration, and it is said go so far as to demand Lincoln and his cabinet shall be hung. The draft has aroused their ire, it has just begun to hurt them, this war, and they want it stopped. The Government is accused of fraud and dishonesty as well as crimes of every description. The Fort Wayne (Indiana) Sentinel is especially bitter against the administration. I had one this morning, procured by an accident. The thought of peace seems to be entertained by them very seriously. Governor Seymour seems to promise well. If all the Western Governors act as he says he will do, the power of Lincoln's administration will soon be broken.

To day the walls of Mr. Mason's house were pulled down; they fell with a crash; the roof had gone long ago. The house has disappeared now, and the place which knew it will know it no more. I suppose if I were not in this house it would share the same fate. Every outbuilding is gone, the carriage house was pulled down over the carriage, and crushed it of course. Nothing is left of them all but heaps of logs which the Yankees carry away for fire-wood; and I, I can scarcely tell it, help them to burn it, for they have taken all our wood and we can get no other supply, but they graciously permit us to share with them, and my boys and the Yankee soldiers stand side by side cutting up the logs and boards of the houses; and I sit by the fire, and though I know that the crackling walnut logs are from my own hen and turkey houses, I must say I enjoy the cheerful blaze. They have taken the stones of Mr. Mason's house as well as many of our stone fences to build their fortifications. Snowing all day and could not take my walk.

✳✳✳

March 17th—A Federal officer was struck in the street by a snowball today, as he was passing a group of boys, among whom was Harry. As Harry had one in his hand the officer concluded he had thrown it, and walking up to him peremptorily ordered him to throw it down. This Harry refused to do at his order, and he was immediately arrested, hurried off to the Provost Marshall's and thence to the guard house. He had been there long enough for his wrath to cool, a little, and to begin to feel very homesick and downhearted, when the officer put his head in the door to ask him if he would do what he told him another time. "No," shouted Harry, "I will not for you had no right to make me put it down." Maj. Quinn came about bed time and effected his release.

I have to be constantly on the watch for fear of my boys doing something to provoke the persecution of the Yankees. Not long since I heard an explosion in the yard loud enough to create some alarm, and on hurrying out saw a squad of soldiers approaching the scene of action, thinking it was an alarm. The noise proceeded from a battery the boys had erected on the top of the cistern and had supplied it with guns they had manufactured out of musket barrels cut into lengths of eight or nine inches, and bored for a touch hole, then mounted on carriages of their own make. I had noticed them very busily engaged about the yard for some time but never dreamed what they were after.

✳✳✳

May 15th—The shadows are darkening around us in the devoted town. Jackson is certainly dead. There is no longer room to doubt it. To say that it is a personal calamity to each and every individual is to say little. "The Mighty has fallen," but he carries to his grave the hopes, and is followed by the bitter tears of the people in whose defense he lost his life, and who lived him with grateful devotion. No loss could be felt as his will be. In every great battle fought in Virginia he has been a leader, and has never known defeat. Success crowned his every effort. Especially was Winchester the object of his care and solicitude. Last spring when he was driving Banks out, as he rode through the town, the people poured out of their houses giving vent to their joy and exultation, he was heard to say, "A noble old town. It and its people are worth fighting for." Even the Yankee papers accord to him the praise that was justly his. One, the New York Tribune, the greatest enemy the South has, speaks of him as "A great General, a brave soldier, a pure man, and a true Christian," but adds that they are glad to be rid in

any way of so terrible a foe. He needs not their praise to add to the lustre of his great name. His place will be forever in the hearts of the Southern people. Not only the Hero's laurels bind his brows, but a crown incorruptible has been placed on it by the great Captain whose he was and whom he served. The people in town feel very despondent about being relieved from their bondage now that the Champion of the Valley is no more.

Well may they sigh for relief, for the tyrant's hand becomes every day heavier; besides there are indications, it is said, of a dreadful disease breaking out in the camps. Eight hundred of the soldiers are sick in the town, besides many dying, and in town there is scarcely a house where there is not sickness, mostly of young persons. Notice was given Dr. Boyd that he must vacate his house and give it up for a hospital, and tomorrow he and his family must go, and become wanderers like so many others. Of course, they will be sent out of the lines. . . .

GLOSSARY

Banks: Nathaniel P. Banks (1816–94), a former governor of Massachusetts who, serving as a Union general, had fought at the First Battle of Winchester on May 25, 1862

Cluseret: Gustave Paul Cluseret (1823–1900), a native Frenchman who served as a general for the Union Army

Governor Seymour: Horatio Seymour (1810–86), the Democratic governor of New York, who opposed the Union draft and was seen as sympathetic to the South

Jackson: Thomas "Stonewall" Jackson (1824–63), a formidable Confederate general who was mortally wounded by friendly fire following the Battle of Chancellorsville, in Fredericksburg, Virginia

magazine: arsenal, storehouse usually associated with ammunition

Winchester: Cornelia Peake McDonald's hometown; a city located in north central Virginia where two Civil War battles were fought

Document Analysis

Primary source documents, contemporary evidence of a person and/or a historical event, are always highly prized when conducting research. They provide vital details and contextual information, as well as a first person account of what transpired. As with any document, including a letter, newspaper, or speech, the historian must, when analyzing what lies therein, take into account the writer and intended audience. At face value, a diary's writer and audience may be the same person.

Diary entries, such as those written by Cornelia Peake McDonald, are personal communications and may not have a specific readership in mind. However, this is not always the case. McDonald's entries are highly descriptive and very emotive and read as though retelling a narrative meant to be saved. While she may indeed have simply written for herself, one historian credits her writing with other motives.

In her article "Women at War: The Civil War Diaries of Floride Clemson and Cornelia Peake McDonald,"

Clara Juncker contends that these diaries were, in fact, kept so as to keep her husband apprised of the goings-on at home, and furthermore, McDonald later had them printed and bound to hand out to each of her surviving children (98). However, Juncker does not provide further substantiation of McDonald's intentions, whether by way of scholarly citation or indication of original, firsthand research. Although McDonald led an extraordinary life in extraordinary times, just like so many of her Confederate counterparts, few historians have taken an in-depth look into her life, so there are but few sources to cross reference such particulars.

Women on the Front Lines

With her husband off at the war, McDonald was left to be father and mother, husband and wife, homemaker and home defender. Historian Jennifer Lynn Gross, in her essay "'Good Angels': Confederate Widowhood in Virginia," writes, "During the war, the absence of fathers and husbands from the home front allowed or forced many women to experience expanded opportunities for autonomy. For the war's duration, wives regularly assumed the role of household head" (135).

Just as World War II would later radically alter what could be termed "women's work," after so many women performed well in the factories and various other previously male-dominated roles, the Civil War also had the same effect. As Jennifer Lynn Gross states, "the postbellum period was a period in which everything, including gender roles, was up for debate" (145). This is especially so as it cut across societal lines. Southern women of the middle and upper classes were raised quite differently from those further down the social scale and therefore faced a steeper learning curve. Minrose Gwin, in her introduction to McDonald's published diary, provides some clues as to Cornelia Peake McDonald's own socioeconomic position. According to Gwin's description, it appears the Peake family was relatively well to do: Cornelia's father was a medical doctor; despite being indebted, the family owned slaves; and young Cornelia read a great deal from her father's library. Clara Juncker notes that the adult Cornelia not only married a lawyer who owned and hired slaves, but also became acquainted with the Confederate elites. Such a background presumably made the wartime experience all the more harrowing for her. Not only did women deal with the everyday ordeals of childcare and household management, but

they were also required to safeguard the homestead when necessary. In this, McDonald proved to be as stalwart a soldier as her husband was, as the time for such action arose frequently.

One such incident was recorded in the entry for September 26, 1862, recounting the events of the previous month, shortly following the burial of her young daughter, Bess. McDonald recalls:

> Suddenly the house was shaken to its foundations, the glass was shivered from the windows and fell like rain all over me as I lay in bed; a noise, terrific as of crashing worlds, followed, prolonged for some fearful moments. . . . Then a cry, and my room door was burst open. . . . I got up and running across the hall to where the windows look towards the town, and then saw the whole eastern sky lighted by the blaze of burning buildings . . . We learned the next day that the enemy had evacuated during the night, and had fired the depot, and the building where were government stores and army supplies, many other buildings having taken fire, a large hotel among them. Their great magazine had been blown up, which had caused the fearful noise.

It is left to individual imagination the terror McDonald felt on this occasion. It is more palpable when her home was invaded by Union soldiers demanding breakfast and attempting to turn her and her children out so the family home could be used as a Union hospital. It sat in a prime area and the Union soldiers, wanting "the best places for their men who were sick . . . would not allow them to occupy places that had before been used as hospitals while rebel women and children slept under comfortable roofs, and in clean beds." While McDonald successfully fought against those incursions, it could not have been the outcome of every similar incident.

As the war continued, it began to ravage the patriotic fervor that had originally fueled McDonald. In another diary entry, the McDonald family has been transplanted from their family home in Winchester to Lexington, Virginia. There is a marked difference in her tone from the earlier entries (such as those above):

How often I wished then that of all the land their father had owned, I had only a few acres on which I could live with my children and try to make a living. That would have been independence, and none of us would have shrunk from labour . . . It almost broke my heart. Others worked, the first young men of Virginia went cheerfully to the plough; but the land was their own, the farms they had been born and bred on, and that was so different. (qtd. in Gross 140)

Whatever her fears, show, privately or publicly, she soldiered on and saw the war through with her eight surviving children.

New York City Draft Riots

Given Juncker's contention that the diary entries were written to keep McDonald's husband informed of everything at the family home, it is thought-provoking that McDonald chose to include her opinions on issues facing the North during the months leading to the pivotal summer of 1863, which would see the Battle of Gettysburg, the turning point in the war, that July. There are many questions regarding how she got her news, as well as which newspaper carried the information and how partisan that particular paper was. While she did not put those answers in her writing, her topic of choice is worth closer inspection and raises the question of how this event was spun in the South. Surely, reports of unrest and anarchy within the Union would have provided a badly needed morale boost to the Confederacy, implying an inward social collapse—and possible upheaval—in the North.

The diary entry dated January 20, 1863, describes the discussion of a draft in the North that had already begun to stir up trouble. She writes, "A few Northern papers seem to be violent against the Lincoln Administration, and it is said go so far as to demand Lincoln and his cabinet shall be hung. The draft has aroused their ire, it has just begun to hurt them, this war, and they want it stopped."

This draft would have devastating consequences for the city of New York in the summer, leading to the deaths of approximately 105 people (Bernstein 5). While war posed the threat of conscription, such a prospect did not see fruition until the late winter and early spring of 1863. The battlefield losses from injury and disease

forced the move as "the federal government became desperate for more soldiers" (Peterson 223–24). Although discontent about the federal draft was evident early on, as noted by McDonald in her diary, authorities could not anticipate that the implementation of the National Conscription Act, which decreed that "all male citizens . . . between the ages of twenty and thirty-five were to be enrolled in the military" (224), would lead to massive violent riots in New York City. The morning of July 13, 1863, saw the start of hostilities, initially aimed at government officials charged with selecting draftees and at law enforcement personnel. Over the course of the day, however, the mood within the largely white, working-class mob shifted, and the city's wealthy elites, Republicans, and African Americans—all of whom the rioters associated with the unpopular war—became the primary targets of violence.

As evidenced by the riots, the Union, contrary to modern assumptions, was not populated exclusively with abolitionists, and not all Northern men were quick to join the fight, seeing the war as placing an unfair financial and physical burden on them for the benefit of others. Likewise, not all Southerners approved of the institution of slavery; many fought for their homeland, though not necessarily to keep African Americans enslaved. Cornelia McDonald could perhaps have been counted among this latter group. In her retrospective "Recollections of the year 1861," not reproduced here, McDonald expresses similar sentiments, stating, "I never in my heart thought slavery was right. . . . I could not think how the men I most honored and admired, my husband among the rest, could constantly justify it" (247).

"Jackson Is Certainly Dead"

McDonald's diary is especially poignant with her description of General Jackson, showing just how idealized and respected he was by contemporaries. His death by friendly fire was truly tragic, and no doubt lends itself then, as even now, to the plethora of "what-ifs" in Civil War history. There is unmistakable bitterness in her realization that Jackson, no matter how admired in the North as a skilled general, was nonetheless killed, his talent as a leader lost to the Confederacy: "One, the New York Tribune, the greatest enemy the South has, speaks of him as 'A great General, a brave soldier, a pure man, and a true Christian,' but adds that they are glad to be rid in any way of so terrible a foe."

McDonald's strong pride, evident in the passage,

may have resulted from a combination of factors: her soldier husband, her association with the state of her birth, or simply a community feeling. Whatever the particular reason, Jackson's death was a blow to her and her brethren, and reading the reports of his death, from a Union newspaper, must have been all the more hurtful. Again, how McDonald came to possess a Northern newspaper remains a mystery. However she came by it, the writer sparked the heated pride of this Southern wife, who felt it necessary to reaffirm her allegiance to the Confederacy.

Essential Themes
Cornelia Peake McDonald, blood mother to nine children and stepmother to an additional nine, literally stood along the lines of war, whilst trying to balance the lives of her children with a semblance of normality. Although there was another motive to keep her diaries during the Civil War, she devoted her time in recording it, and it now belongs to historians and the modern history students.

Jennifer L. Henderson Crane, PgDip

Bibliography
Bernstein, Iver. *The New York City Draft Riots: Their Significance for American Society and Politics in the Age of the Civil War*. New York: Oxford UP, 1990. Print.

Gross, Jennifer Lynn. "'Good Angels': Confederate Widowhood in Virginia." *Southern Families at War: Loyalty and Conflict in the Civil War South*. Ed. Catherine Clinton. Cary: Oxford UP, 2000. 133–54. Print.

Gwin, Minrose. Introduction. *A Woman's Civil War: Reminiscences of the War, from March 1862*. By Cornelia Peake McDonald. Madison: U of Wisconsin P, 1992. 3–18. Print.

Juncker, Clara. "Women at War: The Civil War Diaries of Floride Clemson and Cornelia Peake McDonald." *Southern Quarterly* 42.4 (2004): 90–106. Print.

McDonald, Cornelia Peake. *A Woman's Civil War: Reminiscences of the War, from March 1862*. Ed. Minrose C. Gwin. Madison: U of Wisconsin P, 1992. Print.

McDonald, William N. *A History of the Laurel Brigade*. Ed. Bushrod C. Washington. Baltimore: Sun Job, 1907. Print.

Peterson, Carla L. *Black Gotham: A Family History of African Americans in Nineteenth-Century New York City*. New Haven: Yale UP, 2011. Print.

Additional Reading
Clinton, Catherine, and Nina Silber, eds. *Divided Houses: Gender and the Civil War*. New York: Oxford UP, 1992. Print.

Faust, Drew Gilpin. *Mothers of Invention: Women of the Slaveholding South*. Chapel Hill: U of North Carolina P, 2004. Print.

Floyd, Claudia. *Maryland Women in the Civil War: Unionists, Rebels, Slaves and Spies*. Charleston: History P, 2013. Print.

Ott, Victoria E. *Confederate Daughters: Coming of Age during the Civil War*. Carbondale: Southern Illinois UP, 2008. Print.

Schultz, Jane E. "The Inhospitable Hospital: Gender and Professionalism in Civil War Medicine." *Signs* 17.2 (1992): 363–92. Print.

Silber, Nina. *Gender and the Sectional Conflict*. Chapel Hill: U of North Carolina P, 2009. Print.

State Committee Daughters of the Confederacy, ed. *South Carolina Women in the Confederacy*. Columbia: State, 1903. Print.

■ The Draft Riots

Date: July 14, 1863
Author: *New York Times*
Genre: article

*"Elated with success, the mob, which by this time
had been largely reinforced, next formed themselves
into marauding parties and paraded through
the neighboring streets, looking more like
so many infuriated demons."*

Summary Overview

Early in the morning of Monday, July 13, 1863, riots began in New York City that rocked the metropolis for five days. A reaction against the conscription lottery that had begun two days before, these so-called draft riots reflected the racial, political, and economic tensions between the city's largely Democratic, low-income immigrant population and those that they both feared and opposed: the Republican federal government and the African American population that, by this point in time, it sought to emancipate as part of the Civil War. The draft riots spread quickly from their initial military and government targets in what was a direct reaction against perceived unfair conscription laws to redirect toward the city's substantial free black community. Homes and businesses belonging to blacks, and even the Colored Orphan Asylum, were attacked in the mayhem; nearly a dozen black men had been lynched by the time the riots ended on Friday, July 17, following the arrival of federal troops on Thursday afternoon.

Defining Moment

During the early months of the Civil War, the Union Army was composed entirely of volunteers. As the war dragged on, however, the number of enlistments failed to keep pace with the need for new soldiers. In early

July of 1862, President Abraham Lincoln called for the expansion of the Union military by 300,000 troops, but Northern enthusiasm for the conflict had waned such that the practical response to that call was insufficient. Several days later, the US Congress passed the Federal Militia Act. This law established, among other clauses, the right of African Americans to enlist in the army and the right of the president to require state governments to conscript their citizens into state militias in order to meet ever-growing federal troop demands. The Militia Act thus set up a scenario in which governments could force white male citizens to serve in the Civil War, but African Americans—who lacked status as citizens under the pre-war Supreme Court decision in *Dred Scott v. Sandford* (1857)—need serve only by choice.

Unsurprisingly, the act was not universally popular. Copperheads , those who wished to end the Civil War through diplomatic negotiation with the Confederacy rather than armed conflict, particularly opposed the draft. Despite some resistance, states did successfully begin drafting new soldiers. By the spring of 1863, however, the federal government had decided to bypass the state-level drafts and simply carry out conscription at the federal level. Congress passed the first true federal draft law, the Enrollment Act, in early March of 1863. This sweeping law made all male citizens between the ages of twenty and thirty-five, along with unmarried male citizens between the ages of thirty-five and forty-five, eligible to serve in the Union military. Draftees were chosen by lottery, but not all chosen men had to serve. They had the option of having a substitute to serve in their stead or of paying the government three hundred dollars—a substantial sum—to avoid service. Well-off citizens could therefore opt out of service, but poor men lacked this luxury.

In the weeks before the first draft lottery took place on July 11, 1863, a dozen Copperhead newspapers and government leaders in New York, a city with a relatively high level of sympathy for the South, lashed out against the draft. The city had long-standing economic ties to the South thanks to the lucrative trade in cotton. It was also home to a large working-class immigrant population that believed the emancipation of black laborers would create untenable competition for available jobs as freed slaves moved to Northern cities. Further, New York already claimed one of the largest urban free black populations in the nation.

Author Biography

The *New York Times* was a relatively young but already influential publication by the time of the city's draft riots. Established in 1851 with the aim of reporting the news objectively rather than in the sensationalist or passionate styles preferred by the contemporary *New York Herald* and *New York Tribune*, the daily nevertheless reflected the politics of its cofounder and editor, Henry Jarvis Raymond. Both journalist and editor, Raymond had served as a Whig representative in the New York State Assembly and as the state's lieutenant governor during the 1850s. In 1856, he helped form the new Republican Party, becoming a delegate to its national convention in

1860. Thus, the *Times* supported Republican aims, including the active execution of the Civil War to restore the Union and, for the most part, the administration of President Lincoln. It did so with a dispassionate and measured tone, however, which helped it grow its circulation to some seventy-five thousand in the early 1860s, making it the city's second most popular newspaper.

The Civil War only increased the newspaper's importance. Its Charleston, South Carolina, reporter relayed the news of growing secessionist feeling in the city throughout 1860 and was returned to the North as a Union spy after secession. In July 1861, Raymond himself covered the First Battle of Bull Run, the war's opening encounter, although he initially mischaracterized the battle as a Union victory. The *Times*'s war correspondents were effective ones with a deep understanding of the South; they were so successful that the newspaper relayed the news of the Union victory at Franklin, Tennessee, in November 1864 even before the War Office had been officially informed.

During the draft riots of 1863, the newspaper's Republican leanings made it a target for violence along with the city's other leading Republican outlet, the *New York Tribune*. Its offices were attacked and damaged by the mob, but the *Times* was willing to fight back. Three Gatling guns that had been gifted to the paper by the Lincoln administration were placed on the premises, and rifles were handed out to the newspaper's staff. Raymond also fought against the mob in the newspaper's pages, declaring that he would not give in to what he characterized as blackmail and calling for its defeat. After the riots had ended and the city began to attempt to make sense of their events, the *Times* had no reluctance to point its finger firmly at the inflammatory stories printed by the Democratic press.

HISTORICAL DOCUMENT

The Mob in New York

The initiation of the draft on Saturday in the Ninth Congressional District was characterized by so much order and good feeling as to well nigh dispel the foreboding of tumult and violence which many entertained in connection with the enforcement of the conscription in this City. Very few, then, were prepared for the riotous demonstrations which yesterday from 10 in the morning until late at night; provided almost unchecked in our streets. The authorities had counted upon more or less resistance to this measure of the Government after the draft was completed, and the conscripts were required to take their place in the ranks, and at that time they would have been fully prepared to meet it, but no one anticipated resistance at so early a stage in the execution of the law, and, consequently, both the City and National authorities were totally unprepared to meet it. The plotters of the riot knew this, and in it they saw their opportunity. We say plotters of the riot, for it is abundantly manifest that the whole affair was concocted on Sunday last by a few wire-pullers, who, after they saw the ball fairly in motion yesterday morning prudently kept in the background. Proof of this is found in the fact that as early as 9 o'clock, some laborers employed by two or three railroad companies, and in the iron foundries on the eastern side of the City, formed in procession in the Twenty-second Ward, and visited the different workshops in the upper wards, where large numbers were employed, and compelled them by threats in some in instances, to cease their work. As the crowd augmented, their shouts and disorderly demonstrations became more formidable. The number of men, who thus started out in their career of violence and blood, did not probably at first exceed three-score. Scarcely had two dozen names been called, when a crowd, numbering perhaps 500, suddenly made an irruption in front of the building, (corner of Third-avenue and Forty-sixth street,) attacking it with clubs, stones, brickbats and other missiles. The upper part of the building was occupied by families who were terrified beyond measure at the smashing of the windows, doors, and furniture. Following these missiles, the mob rushed furiously into the office on the first floor, where the draft

was going on, seizing the books, papers, records, lists, &c., all of which they destroyed, except those contained in a large iron safe. The drafting officers were set upon with stones and clubs, and, with the reporters for the Press and others, had to make a hasty exit through the rear. They did not escape scatheless, however, as one of the enrolling officers was struck a savage blow with a stone, which will probably result fatally, and several others were injured. . .

Soon after the rioting began Superintendent KENNEDY hurried to the scene in a carriage, and as he alighted a portion of the crowd recognized him, greeting him at first with uncomplimentary epithets and afterwards with blows. A score or more of the ruffians fell upon him, and dealt heavy blows upon his head, face, and body, injuring him severely. They doubtless would have killed him outright had not a strapping fellow in the crowd felt some compunction at the brutality of the rest and dashed in to the rescue. By vigorous blows, he kept a clear space about Mr. Kennedy's prostrate body until two policemen gathered up their Chief and removed him to a place of safety. In addition to his painful cuts and bruises, Mr. KENNEDY was also a sufferer in the loss of his watch, spectacles and gold-beaded cane. The ruffians in this as in many other instances made plunder a part of their programme.

The rioters soon betook themselves to other places apparently with no concerted plan but bent on fresh depredations. . . .

At 11 A. M., word reached the Park Barracks of the disturbances and Lieut. RIED and a detachment of the Invalid corps immediately reported to the scene of the riot. They went by the Third avenue route, the party occupying one car. On the way up, crowds of men, women, and children gathered at the street corners hissed and jeered them, and some even went so far as to pick up stones, which they defiantly threatened to throw at the car. When near the scene of the disturbance, Lieut. RIED and command alighted, and formed in company line, in which order they marched up to the mob. Facing the rioters the men were ordered to fire which many of them did, the shots being blank cartridges, but the smoke had scarce cleared away when the company which did not number more than fifty men, if as many, were attacked and completely demoralized by the mob, who were armed with clubs, sticks, swords and other impediments. The soldiers had their bayonets taken away and they themselves were compelled seek refuge in the side streets. But in attempting to flee thither, several it is said were killed, while those that escaped did so only to be hunted like dogs, but in a more inhuman and brutal manner. They were chased by the mob. Who divided themselves into squads, and frequently a single soldier would be caught in a side street with each end blocked up by the rioters. The houses and stores were all closed (excepting a few liquor shops which had the shutters up but kept the back door open,) no retreat was, therefore, open for him, and the poor fellow would be beaten almost to death, when the mob becoming satiated and disgusted with their foul work, he would be left sweltering in blood, unable to help himself.

Elated with success, the mob, which by this time had been largely reinforced, next formed themselves into marauding parties and paraded through the neighboring streets, looking more like so many infuriated demons, the men being more or less intoxicated, dirty and half-clothed. Some shouted, "Now for the Fifth-avenue Hotel—there's where the Union Leaguers meet!" Others clamored among themselves for the muskets, which they had taken from the soldiers. The streets were thronged with women and children, many of whom instigated the men to further work of blood, while the injured men left the crowd, and found seats up the street corners, at one of which the reporter heard the following conversation, between an intoxicated youth, who was badly wounded in the hand, and an elderly excited woman, probably his mother.

Youth—"An' bedad, if it hadn't been for this lick, which the son of a — guy me, I'd a belabored him 'aior this. And bedad I wud."

Woman—"Musshantulusha, ye betters mind yer own biserniss."

Youth—"No, if SAM. GARRIGAN [or Galligan—REP.] had a 'dun the business browner, it wud be all right."

From this may be inferred that the Sam Garrigan, or Galligan, mentioned in the conversation above, is the ringleader, of which there can be little doubt, as the reporter frequently heard Garrigan's or Galligan's name cheered and called the "Bully boy." Garrigan, or Galligan, we believe is a well known wire-puller of the ward, and from conversations between the men, we gleaned the following which may be taken for what it is worth. That Garrigan or Galligan is the ringleader. That the mob, numbering about 500 men, assembled this morning at Central Park, armed and equipped, i.e. with clubs and sticks, and from there went to the Draft Office where they commanded all else. . . .

The Orphan Asylum for Colored Children was visited by the men about 4 o'clock. This institution is situated on Fifth-avenue, and the building, with the grounds and gardens adjoining, extended from Forty-third to Forty-fourth street. Hundreds, and perhaps thousands of rioters, the majority of whom were women and children, entered the premises, and in the most excited and violent manner they ransacked and plundered the building from cellar to garret. The building was located in the most pleasant and healthy portion of the City. It was purely a charitable institution. In it there are on an average 600 or 800 homeless colored orphans. The building was a large, four-story one, with two wings of three stories each.

When it became evident that the crowd designed to destroy it, a flag of truce appeared on the walk opposite, and the principals of the establishment made an appeal to the excited populace, but in vain. . . .

✳ ✳ ✳

The Riots Yesterday

It has long been declared by the rebel journals, and also by the European journals in the interest of the rebels, that the Conscription act could not be enforced, and that this would compel a discontinuance of the war. The anti-war journals here in the North, while they in general have not ventured to recommend violent resistance to the Conscription, have yet studied to excite against it every unreasoning passion and prejudice. Malignants, too, of the Vallandigham type, have for months been doing their best, by artful harangues, to foment a spirit of resistance. These men understood their work thoroughly. Their business was to bring about violence; and ANTONY himself never managed that business more skillfully. Ever discerning man saw what it would end in—the mob in the street taking upon themselves all the risks, these gentry in their closets rejoicing in the fray in which they dared not mingle. The Government could not blind itself to this flagitious course of action. It made some effort to defeat it; but it was found that this only armed these public enemies with new power for they turned it to their advantage by pretending that it was now a question of freedom of speech, and gained new influence by setting themselves up as its champions. Thus the dangerous element has been continually growing. It has spread more or less through every part of the North. It has reached all the baser portions of society everywhere, and made them restless, and ready for almost any violence. In most communities this spirit is effectually kept under by superior public opinion. But there are localities where this public sentiment has no such force. This has been shown in the rural districts by the outbreaks which have already occurred in Ohio and Indiana. It is now being shown amid a city population, where the passions of men are far more inflammable, and where the facilities for effective organization are far greater. What its real strength is no man can yet measure; but yesterday's demonstrations sufficiently attest that it is quite strong enough to be formidable and dangerous.

The practical question now is, how this spirit of resistance is to be met. Is it to be done by discussing the merits and the necessities of the Conscription act? Decidedly No! it will be a fatal mistake for the friends of the Government to suspend their action on the turn of any such question. No man who is at heart for the war, by which alone the Government can be sustained, has a serious doubt about either the constitutionality, of the justice, or the propriety, or the necessity of this resort for replenishing the national armies. Even where it otherwise—were the measure actually one that could be reasonably questioned, it would not affect present duties one tittle. The one sole fact that must determine the action of our public authorities against these demonstrations is, that the Conscription act stands on the National Statute Book a law. It was enacted by the two bodies in which, under the Constitution, "all legislative powers" are granted, and it was "approved" by the President. There has never been in this Republic a law of more absolute validity, or more perfect sanction. Until it is repealed, or pronounced by the highest Court unconstitutional and null, it must stand, and its requirements must be satisfied. The administrators of law have no alternative but to enforce its provisions, without fear or favor. Come what may, they are shut up to that line of action. And it is the duty of every law abiding man to sustain them in it. The official or the citizen who falters is treacherous to every civil obligation.

The issue is not between Conscription and no-Conscription, but between order and anarchy. The question is not whether this particular law shall stand, but whether law itself shall be trampled underfoot. Is this City to be at the mercy of a mob? Have the statutes of the land to await the approval of all the Jack Cades of society before they can attain any binding force? Nobody ever imagined that this conscription act would suit either rebels in the South, or rebel-sympathizers in the North. No valuable law is ever passed that has the favor of the evil-minded. Yield to them the ratification of our public legislation, and you will speedily be reduced to the condition of being without any law whatever. There is not a man's life in this City that is safe, nor a dollar's worth of property, if the spirit which dominated this City yesterday is to be left to its own working. It is as fatal to our whole civil and social organization as the plague is to the physical constitution of man. To give way before it is simply to invoke destruction. Our authorities, we perfectly understand, have been taken at a great disadvantage. These riots have been precipitated upon them at the very time when they were least able to meet them with promptitude. It has proved to have been a great mistake to suffer our city to be so completely stripped of its military defenders. But it is idle now to repine over this. There are yet available means enough, if seasonably and properly taken in hand, to crush, before another twenty-four hours, this twin hydra of the rebellion utterly, beyond all possibility of its ever writhing again. But it will require boldness, decision, nerve of no ordinary character. The responsibility is practically with Gov. SEYMOUR and Mayor OPDYKE. Men in their positions never were confronted with more stupendous duties.

GLOSSARY

brickbat: a piece of brick used as a weapon

epithets: insults

flagitious: extremely criminal or wrong

hydra: mythical multiheaded beast

manifest: obvious, apparent

rebel journals: Confederate newspapers

scatheless: unharmed

score: quantity of twenty

tittle: very small bit

ward: a division of a city used for governance

Document Analysis

The *New York Times*'s contemporaneous description of the city's multiday draft riots combines the newspaper's signature dispassionate reporting style with a clear condemnation of the rioters and those who may have incited them, a stance in keeping with the publication's advocacy of Republican policies in general and the actions of the Lincoln White House in particular. Throughout its coverage of the riots, the *Times* consistently presents the rioters as senselessly brutal and thoroughly unpatriotic for their drive to not just oppose what the *Times* characterizes as a legal and necessary draft but also to inflict physical harm on the persons and property of their fellow New Yorkers. "The issue is not between Conscription and no-Conscription, but between order and anarchy," proclaims the *Times*. The publication's own position on that issue clearly informs its writings on the riots that stemmed from it.

The cover article, "The Mob in New York," opens with a purposefully dramatic contrast between the apparent civility of the draft when it began in New York City on Saturday, July 11, and the outbreak of violence on Monday morning; the article's internal chronology suggests that it was written on Tuesday, July 14, even as violence raged on in the city. The *Times* does, however, acknowledge that the draft was far from universally popular, noting that authorities expected some

type of visible opposition—but not, it seems, until the time that draftees were actually to be required to formally join with the military. The draft was an exception rather than the rule in US military practice. State-level militias had occasionally used the draft somewhat inconsistently in earlier conflicts and in the preceding months of the Civil War, but the conscription lottery that sparked the New York draft riots was the first application of a true nationwide draft in the United States. Government and military leaders thus had no prior experience on which to draw to anticipate what kind of resistance was likely to come from opponents and unwilling draftees, and the *Times* argues, the "plotters of the riot knew this, and in it they saw their opportunity" to wreak havoc unchecked by adequate police or military forces.

For the *Times* was apparently certain that the riots were no spontaneous demonstration by the men unwillingly tapped for military service. Instead, it argues, the outbreak had been planned and launched by a small behind-the-scenes group. As proof of this allegation the *Times* points to incidents in which a small number of industrial workers traveled from workplace to workplace Monday morning, demanding that the workers there stop their regular duties and, presumably, join with their small but growing band. Modern historians generally disagree with this view, instead categorizing the draft riots as a popular uprising fomented largely within the white working-class New York community that took part in the violence. Although the *Times* believes all to have been quiet in the city on the weekend preceding the riots, modern scholars instead believe that those who incited the riot on Monday morning had spent much of Sunday feeding their rising anger with cheap liquor and heated talk. The riots may have erupted rapidly on Monday, but they were not, as the *Times* suggests, entirely without warning.

In fact, officials were aware that some people were planning to resist the draft in the Ninth Congressional District, and a small group of troops was sent to the draft office early Monday. The draft lottery was set to resume that morning, and it was at the draft office at Third Avenue and Forty-Sixth Street that the first violent incidents of the riots began. Although the *Times* estimates the early crowd at perhaps sixty ranging up to five hundred people, later estimates suggest that the mob may already have reached several thousand by the time that it paraded from a nearby vacant lot, where draft opponents had been giving speeches to rouse the crowd further. By mid-morning, the growing mob had reached the draft office, and as officials began to announce the names of those who were first selected, the angry rioters were attacking the draft office. Rioters damaged parts of the building, destroyed whatever draft records they could find, and began to assault the draft officers responsible for conducting the lottery, who fled out the back of the building. Some of these men were injured, at least one severely, the *Times* reports. The draft office itself was set on fire.

The mob took out a greater part of its anger on Metropolitan Police superintendent John Kennedy. By this time, Kennedy had received numerous telegrams and other notices of troubles throughout the city, and he had sent additional men to threatened draft offices; however, rioters had been destroying telegraph lines as they proceeded through the city, effectively cutting police and military communications with each other and with the outside world. The superintendent then decided to visit the site of the riots himself, traveling by carriage to the troubled draft office. He was unprepared for the reception that he received, however. Despite being unarmed and in plainclothes, the sixty-year-old officer was soon recognized by some members of the crowd and physically attacked. The *Times*—perhaps loathe to give credit to a Democratic politician—notes that an anonymous "strapping fellow . . . dashed in to

the rescue." This man was, in fact, a Democratic official of the local ward and longtime acquaintance of Kennedy, John Eagan, who managed to keep the crowd at bay until two police officers who had accompanied Kennedy removed the gravely injured man from the scene. The *Times* claims that Kennedy's savior accomplished this through physical resistance, but the majority of historians agree that Eagan actually held off the crowd by convincing them that the much-beaten man was already as good as dead. To show how insult was added to injury, the *Times* lists a number of items stolen from the superintendant by the "ruffians" of the mob. In this story, the mob is clearly the villain while the Republican representative of the government—and, by association, the draft—is the victim; furthermore, the mob is portrayed as petty and heartless. The *Times* has no sympathy for their cause or their methods.

Although the riots began by focusing on military offices connected with the draft lottery, they quickly expanded throughout the city as the mob spread out "apparently with no concerted plan but bent on fresh depredations." By now numbering several thousands, the mob contained not just men but also a large number of women and children. Some sources suggest that women were among the loudest and most enthusiastic voices in condemning the draft. This teeming mob was increasingly met but not controlled by a growing police presence. The rioters managed to destroy numerous telegraph lines and thus impede communications, but precincts sent out detachments to places where they had received reports were under attack by the mob or where officials believed threats were likely to take place. The *Times*'s reporting of the resulting encounters leaves no doubt as to which group it saw as the aggressors. In describing an altercation between security forces under the leadership of a Lieutenant Ried and the mob, the *Times* presents the police and the limited soldier presence affiliated with the draft as a noble, if thoroughly inadequate, force. The soldiers, under orders, shoot harmless blanks at the mob; the rioters, in response, set on them with any weapon on which they could lay their hands, chasing soldiers into side streets, beating and killing the forces of law, and hunting down those who attempted escape in a way even "more inhuman and brutal" than might be expected of hunters on the trail of animals.

The power of the mob obviously outstripped that of the law. The *Times* describes the beleaguered troops as "completely demoralized," and indeed the inability of police and military forces to deal with the rioters runs through the entire account. Kennedy had escaped death at the hands of the mob only by the timely intervention of another. The forces under Ried had no such benefactor, and many, the *Times* claims, were killed as a result. In contrast, the mob is presented as a strong, almost irrepressible mass capable of organizing themselves into effective squads to locate and attack their targets. The language that the *Times* uses to describe the rioters reinforces this characterization. The mob is alternatively "satiated and disgusted with their foul work" and "elated with success" but never controlled, calculating, or possessed of any particular goal. Frenzied and apparently propelled by heavy drinking, the mob pressed on into the afternoon "like so many infuriated demons," readily suggestible for more ways to cause destruction upon those it perceived as enemies.

Among those that the mob saw as opponents were the members of the Union League Club, formed by the city's Republican elite to support the cause of the Union and work against all those that may have been considered disloyal to its cause. The mob moved toward the club's headquarters, allowing the *Times*'s reporter an opportunity to eavesdrop on some of the on-the-ground conversations between mob members. The rendering of the dialect used by the two quoted rioters certainly indicates their lower-class status and suggests the Irish tenor of the mob's composition, as does the name of Sam Garrigan or Galligan that the *Times* reporter identifies as a likely ringleader. Although no further details of this supposed mob leader appear to be recorded in history, certainly some members of the mob acted to incite others, leading them from place to place and making inflammatory speeches.

Later on the first day of the riots, the mob reached the Orphan Asylum for Colored Children, more commonly known as the Colored Orphan Asylum. Founded in the late 1830s by white philanthropists, the orphanage provided room, board, and basic labor training for more than 230 children at the time of the riots; the *Times*'s estimate of "600 or 800" charges vastly exceeded the founder's own numeration of her charges, as historian Barnet Schecter reports.

The organization was an obvious example of the African American presence in the city and of white charity toward that community, making it an easy target for the rioters' antiblack wrath. As the mob reached the area where the orphanage was located, several hundred members of the group broke off from the mass and

invaded the building, setting fires as "they ransacked and plundered the building from cellar to garret." The property was a large one, but its destruction took as little as twenty minutes; the efforts of city firefighters under Chief Engineer John Decker were insufficient to prevent fire from consuming the premises.

Remarkably, the orphans, who fled the building as the rioters set to destroying it, managed to escape without significant personal harm. Although the mob was not deterred from destroying the property, the orphanage's staff was able to lead the children out of the premises and through the crowd safely. Some white protectors apparently within the mob who spoke up in defense of the orphans were less fortunate; at least one Irishman who yelled at the mob to leave the children alone himself became the victim of mob attacks. Although the orphans managed to survive the riots in the security of a police precinct station house, the intent of the rioters was readily apparent. They rejected the presence of African Americans and the notion of white support for black lives and well-being; further, the economic connections of the asylum, which trained orphans as manual laborers and even sent them out as indentured servants, may suggest that the rioters were also expressing their anger over the competition for low-wage working-class jobs presented by free black labor. The incident at the Colored Orphan Asylum was the first and one of the largest-scale actions against the city's black community, but it certainly was not the last. Attacks on individual African American persons, homes, and businesses continued throughout the course of the riots, particularly against black dock workers. Just as the mob had attacked the white Irishman who condemned them for not helping the black children, rioters targeted white New Yorkers who fraternized with African Americans, rented them housing, employed them, or otherwise supported their presence in the city over the following days of the riots. The mob may have lashed out against the hated conscription laws on the surface, but an obvious and violent racism boiled just beneath.

The *Times* dedicates the latter paragraphs of "The Riots Yesterday" to a discussion of the nature of the riots and the necessity of crushing them in the interests of the Union and of American patriotism. Vital to this discussion was a strong defense of the draft law and, at a deeper level, the Republican method of waging the Civil War; nearly as vital was a condemnation of those publications that had spoken out against the conscription law. Such newspapers and various discontents as influential Ohio Copperhead Clement Vallandigham, the *Times* accuses, had worked for months to generate public opposition to the draft and even to incite just the kind of violence that had in fact erupted in New York City. Wise thinkers—and, naturally enough from this Republican-leaning newspaper, officials of the sitting Republican government—saw the dangers of speaking against the cause of the Union and had sought to end it, presumably a reference to Vallandigham's arrest by Union soldiers two months previously for giving an antiwar speech that the government saw as treasonous. The Ohio politician had based his defense partially on the right of freedom of speech, and the Democratic press had united behind him; his conviction and banishment to the Confederacy generated sufficient media coverage that his ideas likely reached a much broader audience than they would otherwise have. This the *Times* sees as a mistake. Antiwar speech served only to create anger and mayhem, as could be seen in the riots that had taken place across the nation, from Ohio and Indiana to the major metropolis of New York. Resistance, readers are warned, was thus "formidable and dangerous."

The article concludes by framing the riots in a broader perspective: not as a question of draft, but as a question of whether citizens had a duty to follow the law. This question likely resonated with readers more than two years deep into a civil war over the issue of national government authority over state government and individual citizens alike. Firm public action against the belligerent rioters was fully warranted, according to the *Times*, because the conscription law was just that—a law passed by the US Congress and signed by the US president in full accordance with the provisions of the nation's Constitution. As such, it demanded not only adherence but protection by the federal government. "The official or the citizen who falters is treacherous to every civil obligation," asserts the *Times*, clearly implicating the rioters in this statement. That, like most laws, the draft law had not enjoyed complete bipartisan support is dismissed by a publication that strongly supported the ruling Republican regime as simply "the favor of the evil-minded," tying objections to the draft to a rejection of the overall cause of the Union. Finally, the article issues a call to action to the state and local authorities overseeing New York to work to "crush . . . this twin hydra of the rebellion utterly," bringing both the riots and the resistance to the draft—and thus the war—to a close.

Essential Themes

In the short term, the draft riots failed to make much of a difference in the requirements placed upon the city's working class men. The draft went on, albeit in a reduced form. New York's governor persuaded Lincoln to require the state to provide fewer men for the federal army and sought to limit the overall number drafted by counting as many late enlistments as possible. When New York City ran its second lottery on August 19, ten thousand federal troops were present in the city to prevent a repeat of the previous month's riots. Tammany Hall also sought to ease working-class concerns by promising to help anyone drafted who did not wish to serve; to live up to this promise, the resulting County Substitute and Relief Committee found just over one thousand substitutes for unwilling local draftees. New York, however reluctantly, thus gave its men to the Union Army.

The riots did, however, highlight the social and racial tensions that ran through New York and indeed many parts of the North during this time. Black New Yorkers left in droves, with many settling in the Williamsburg neighborhood of Brooklyn—a city separate from New York until 1898—and across the river in New Jersey. By 1865, fewer than ten thousand African Americans remained in New York City proper, a decrease of about twenty-five hundred from the city's 1860 black population and the lowest level in four decades. Those that remained faced continued discrimination and the threat of violence from those that harbored antiblack sentiments. Black workers found it hard to go back to their jobs and even harder to find new ones; many black residents had also lost their homes and accumulated property, thus facing not only an economic but also a political setback due to the state's property requirements for black voters. Nevertheless organizations such as the Union League Club and the Committee of Merchants for the Relief of Colored People run by the city's Republican elite worked to assist those African Americans affected by the riots.

Yet despite the racism of some Democratic newspapers and white working-class residents in the city, the first African American regiment in New York organized and marched out of the city in March of 1864. African American soldiers from across the nation fought bravely in high-profile war battles, helping improve public perception of black people both as soldiers and as potential citizens. Yet the antiblack racism evidenced by the draft riots remained in force for many decades to come, particularly among the same white working class that had launched the 1863 riots and that continued to see free black labor as a threat to its economic livelihood.

Vanessa E. Vaughn, MA

Bibliography

Bernstein, Iver. *The New York City Draft Riots: Their Significance for American Society and Politics in the Age of the Civil War.* New York: Oxford UP, 1990. Print.

Harris, Leslie M. *In the Shadow of Slavery: African Americans in New York City, 1626–1863.* Chicago: U of Chicago P, 2003. 279–88. Print.

Heidler, David S., and Jeanne T. Heidler, eds. *Encyclopedia of the American Civil War: A Political, Social, and Military History.* 5 vols. New York: Norton, 2000. Print.

Mindich, David T. Z. "Raymond, Henry Jarvis." *American National Biography Online* (2010): 1. *Biography Reference Center.* Web. 2 Apr. 2013.

Schecter, Barnet. *The Devil's Own Work.* New York: Walker, 2005. Print.

Additional Reading

Barnes, David M. *The Draft Riots in New York, July, 1863: The Metropolitan Police, Their Services during Riot Week, Their Honorable Record.* New York: Baker, 1863. Print.

McCague, James. *The Second Rebellion: The Story of the New York City Draft Riots of 1863.* New York: Dial, 1968. Print.

McKay, Ernest A. *The Civil War and New York City.* Syracuse: Syracuse UP, 1990. Print.

Werstein, Irving. *The Draft Riots: July 1863.* 1957. New York: Messner, 1971. Print.

■ "There Has Been a Great Deal of Sickness in My Neighborhood"

Date: July 29, 1863–December 1865
Author: Bethell, Mary Jeffreys
Genre: diary

"I expect that slavery will be abolished in a few years,
I think it will be better for us."

Summary Overview

Mary Jeffreys Bethell, a Confederate woman, made her life with her family in Rockingham County, North Carolina, where she spent many years keeping a diary. The diary in its entirety spans twenty years, from 1853 until 1873; her record, therefore, includes entries written during the Civil War, from a July 29, 1863, entry through December 1865, eight months after the surrender of General Robert E. Lee at Appomattox. Bethell used her writing to document many aspects of her life: her sons' wartime experiences, her charitable and neighborly activities within the community, and, most poignantly throughout, her unwavering devotion to God and her faith. Bethell's relationship with God played a large role in providing the solace she needed while the war raged around her, and it was a relationship she desired her children to build as well. Though she believed in the Confederacy, she placed her faith and hopes in God and the Bible, not the battlefield.

Defining Moment

Slavery has long been the presumed cause of the Civil War, though the exact cause was, in fact, a combination of factors. For the Confederacy, states' rights were a major factor; the issue of slavery, for the Union, came later. Bethell's diary makes few references to the institution, and, from them, she does not seem to be too concerned about its probable abolishment following the war; she even expressed approval: "I expect that slavery will be abolished in a few years, I think it will be better for us." Although not expressly stated in her diary, Bethell's writing and her religious views indicate that she was against slavery, believing it better for the South to not rely on slaves for its prosperity.

Unlike other Confederate women who documented their experiences of life on the home front, Bethell comes across as matter-of-fact regarding the ongoing events in the South, including the surrender of General Lee, which was devastating to many. Her faith in God sustained Bethell through these "trials," as she terms them, and she therefore placed the future in God's hands.

Author Biography

Primary sources such as Bethell's diary are valuable resources and provide important insight into the past. Though a rich source of historical information on the daily life of a Confederate woman, her writing does not include much biographical information. Bethell was born in 1821 and married her husband at the age of nineteen. The couple raised a family, which included at least three children, sons George and Willie, who both served in the war, and a daughter, Mary Virginia. Bethell's life, as was the case with most nineteenth-century women, was driven by her family, religion, and community. As a married woman, Bethell's sphere was within the home, the nursery, and the church, as well as out in the community assisting other women through traditionally female tasks and rituals, often related to either birth or death.

Bethell lived her life according to the standards of her time, and, from reading her words, it is clear she took much joy from it: "I love to visit the sick because God has commanded us to do it." While some women may have contributed their time and energy out a sense of necessity or a sense of reciprocity, Bethell gave herself up to her religious teachings and embraced her participation in the community. The religious welfare of her children is also a recurring topic within the diary entries. As a mother, she felt it one of her sacred duties to foster in them a strong sense of faith; she no doubt wished to see all of her children give their lives to God's teachings and carrying out those teachings within their communities. She wrote:

> My dear daughter has professed religion, speaks of joining the Episcopal church, I am sorry, it grieves me to think of it. I would be glad for her to be with me and join the Methodists, but I pray that the Lord's will may be done.

Bethell did no more than what was expected of Southern women, and in this she was a testament to her faith and her upbringing.

HISTORICAL DOCUMENT

July 29, 1863

There has been a great deal of sickness in my neighborhood. I have been visiting the sick, and I carry them something nice to eat, lightbread and rice. I love to visit the sick because God has commanded us to do it. I have been to Mrs. Griffith's, four of her family down sick with bloody flux, while I was there Sally Ann died, and I assisted in shrouding her. Lizzy died on Monday, Sally Ann on the day before. May the Lord bless that afflicted family. Old Mr. DeJarnette died last Saturday, I am sorry for his daughters left by themselves. May the Lord take care of them.

We have had an overflow from the river, we will lose half our crop of corn.

There has been a battle at Gettysburg, Pennsylvania, great many killed on our side, we heard that Julius Ferguson, N. Strader were killed, Charlie Watkins lost his leg, Peter Scales died from his wounds. Green Daniel slightly wounded and a prisoner, my dear son George was taken prisoner. I thank my Saviour that it was no worse, I pray that God may save his life and grant that this trial may be the means of making him a christian. Man's extremity is God's opportunity, 'tis my daily prayer that God may convert his soul. I have examined my heart and I find that I do love God, and believe that I am his child, and he is my Father. I delight in doing the will of God. I take great pleasure in reading my bible and in secret prayer, but after I have done all that is commanded, I feel that I am an unprofitable servant, and only done my duty, I deserve nothing, and I have nothing but what I have received from God. I have peace and comfort, I rejoice in the Lord, my soul is happy, hallelujah. I will praise the Lord for his wonderful goodness to me and mine, I have faith to believe that God will bless all my children. I want to be kept humble and resigned to my Father's will.

August 18

No tidings yet from my dear children. I live by faith in the Son of God. I have so many answers to prayer, I feel encouraged to pray. The Lord comforts me, I will praise him.

September 16

We have heard that our dear George was taken prisoner and carried to Johnson's island, which is on Lake Erie in the state of Ohio. I thank the Lord 'tis no worse. I hope the Lord will watch over him, bless him and bring him back to his home and Parents.

We heard that our daughter and her husband Mr. Williamson were taken prisoners, but we will still look to God and beg him to save them. If I know my heart, I do love God with all my heart, soul, mind and strength, and have the witness of the spirit, with it I am the child of God. I feel that I am on my way to my home in Heaven, hallalujia! Praise ye the Lord!

I have been to see Mrs. Watson, a poor widow lady, her husband died in the army. I tryed to comfort her.

I went to see Sophia and Bettie De Jarnette, poor orphan girls, I pray that God may bless and take care of them. I shall try and visit Mrs. Mitchell a poor widow-lady, her daughter died a few days ago, she is afflicted. May the Lord help and bless all the poor of my neighborhood. I feel more resigned to God's will than I ever did, and I want to do his will.

I have been to see poor old Mrs. Mitchell, she was sad, she has lost her youngest child. I tryed to comfort her, she seemed grateful for my visit.

October 7

We received a letter from our dear George, he is at Johnson's Island, he wrote that he was getting well. I do thank the Lord for taking care of George. No tidings from my dear Mary Virginia and Willie. I beg the Lord to bring me a letter from them very soon.

My health is feeble, I have fallen off, was very sick Sunday night with pain in my stomach and bowels, indigestion. I have been living on milk and mush. I pray the Lord to spare me to see my dear George, Willy, and Mary Virginia come home. The waves of trouble nearly go over me, I am in trouble and distress, but I will look to God and call on him to have mercy upon me, and comfort my poor sorrowful soul. I have often thought that I would trust in God as long as I live, and in every extremity, yes I do trust in him, and I believe he will come to my help.

April 1864

It has been some time since I wrote in my diary, owing to the scarcity of writing paper.

My dear Willie started to the army two weeks ago, he left the 7th of this month to join Gen. Lee's army near Orange C. House, it was a trial to me, but I committed him into the hands of my Saviour. God is my refuge in every trouble. I pray that his life may be preserved.

I have not heard from George and Mr. Williamson since Feb they were well. We are looking for them home as there will be an exchange of prisoners. I thank the Lord for his goodness to my dear sons in the army.

My dear daughter has professed religion, speaks of joining the Episcopal church, I am sorry, it grieves me to think of it. I would be glad for her to be with me and join the Methodists, but I pray that the Lord's will may be done.

The Lord permits me to pass through many trials, I hope that I am growing in grace. I intend to labor for my Lord and Master . . .

May 9th 1864

I intend to point my children and servants to the Lamb of God that taketh away the sin of the world, it is my prayer that God would make me holy in heart and life.

I went to Union a few days ago to hear our dear Minister, brother Gannon, he is an able preacher. Oh how it grieves me that I cannot hear him, I am so deaf in one ear. I am the child of affliction. I have lately passed through a fiery trial, it was my constant prayer that God would give me grace to bear with meekness and patience all that he might see fit for me. I have been greatly tempted and cast down for many days, but 'tis all for the best. My Saviour designs to make me holy I give myself into his gracious hands, and pray that I may be able to do his blessed will.

I was 43 years old last Sunday, the Lord has spared my life, I hope for some good. Goodness and mercy have followed me all the days of my life, though I have had some fiery trials, and passed through deep waters, yet I have always found God's grace sufficient for every extremity, he has always been with me, and comforted me in all my trials. I will praise him for his wonderful goodness to me, who am so unworthy. I was greatly blessed in my childhood, for I had a good pious Father who led me in the way to Heaven. I had the advantage of a good christian education, eternity will show the great blessing of a pious parents.

I was converted and joined the church when I was 16 years old. I have grown in grace, God has given me strong faith, he has answered my prayers. I thank and praise him. Hallelujah for the Lord will reign 'til all enemies are put under his feet.

May 9th 1864

We have received two letters from Willie since he left for the army, he was doing well. I received a letter from George who is at Johnson's island, he was quite well. Mr. Williamson was well, thank the Lord for all his mercies.

June 28th

Since I last wrote we have had a death in our family. Mollie Weldon, my little grandaughter died on the 2nd of June, her bowels and lungs were diseased, she was about 9 months old, a bright and lovely babe, one of the sweetest buds of promise. We miss her, but we have another angel in Heaven to praise God, our blessed Saviour. May the Lord help us all to meet Mollie Weldon in Heaven.

Last Sunday was my birth day, I was 43 years old, and now as I enter my 44 year I will renew my covenant with God. I now consecrate myself and all that I have to his service. I am the Lord's and he is my Saviour. I will love and serve him as long as I live, hope to praise him in Heaven.

July 9th

Last Saturday and Sunday was our meeting at Union, on Sunday we commemorated the death and suffering of our Saviour by partaking of the Holy sacrament. I did enjoy it and the Lord blessed me, soul and body, my soul was refreshed, 'twas a comfort to me. Brother Gannon preached for us, he came home with us and spent the night, he is our minister, may the Lord bless him abundantly. My health is good now, thank the Lord. I will praise the Lord for his goodness to me, my children all tolerable well.

Tuesday 2nd of May 1865

I have not written in my diary in some time. I have had a good deal of company, over one hundred soldiers have stopped here to get something to eat, they were on their way from the army. Gen. Lee's army surrendered to the Yankees, also Gen. Johnston's army has surrendered also to Sherman. I think the war has closed, and we will perhaps go back to the Union. I feel thankful to God for his great goodness. I hope that we will have some rest now.

The war lasted four years, thousands of men were killed. I expect that slavery will be abolished in a few years, I think it will be better for us.

My dear George arrived home safe from Johnson's Island, where he had been a prisoner about 20 months. I felt so thankful to God for his goodness in bringing him back to me, his health is good. My dear Willie arrived home safe a week ago from the army, he is in fine health. Mary Virginia's health is better, I have all of my dear children at home with me now. The Lord is good. My health has been quite feeble this spring, suffered much with constipation of the bowels, and sometimes a weakness about my womb, I have been low spirited. The desolation of some part of our country by the cruel enemy. I have many little trials, my hearing is bad which causes me to feel lonesome, but I will look to my Saviour for comfort. I have been greatly afflicted by fiery trials, my Heavenly Father only knows what I have suffered. I have been sick and feeble for some time, besides many other trials. I have been brought very low. I feel very humble, the Lord permits it all for my good. I will kiss the rod, for whom the Lord loveth he chastiseth. My precious Saviour has been with me in all my trials, his arm of love underneath me, he has kept me from sinking, blessed be his holy name. My soul doth magnify the Lord my spirit hath rejoiced in God my Saviour, in all my troubles I run to the Lord and his ear is open unto my cry, he helps he comforts me, it is a great trial to be deaf, but I know it has worked out for my good, it causes me to think more on Heavenly things, and I am praying without ceasing. I will now renew my covenant with God, I am his and he is my Saviour. I offer up myself and my husband and children, my talents, my property and every thing I possess. Oh! that I may do his will, and suffer with meekness and resignation all that I have to pass through. I feel like God is my Father and heaven my home, my soul is resting upon Jesus.

August 7th 1865

I will write this morning as I have an opportunity. I feel sad when I look at the church, almost desolate, some of the members have died, and some backslidden, nearly all of the rest worldly minded, prayer meetings, class meetings, Sunday school, all are broken up because iniquity abounds. The love of many has waxed cold, all are selfish and seeking their own. I feel like I am stript, but is all for my good to make us seek our rest and happiness in God alone. There is a good deal of trouble and some confusion about the servants, they are all free and good many have left. 14 of ours have left, but all of them left with our consent except 2 who ran away. I hope they will get homes and become christians. I hope they are on the road to Heaven. I do pitty them and pray for them. The war is over, but still there is much trouble and a great deal of wickedness, if the people don't repent I expect they will have some more judgments sent upon them, I look for it. Some of our prominent members of the church to all appearances look cold, lifeless, and backslidden. I sigh and grieve on account of it. Oh Lord pitty and save us from eternal death, there is none good, no not one, none but God, he alone is perfect. There is not a just man on earth but what sins, for my part, I feel myself an unprofitable servant.

I look back upon my life as having come far short of my duty, many times done wrong and been foolish and disobedient, if the Lord were to stab iniquity I would not stand. I feel weakness, imperfection, I'm poor and frail, tending to the grave, every day I say Lord forgive me. I feel sad and repent every day. The Lord Jesus is my righteousness, he is become my salvation. I search the scriptures and pray every day, it strengthens me. I am constantly looking to God to help me, I have given myself to him, he is my Saviour, I bless his holy name. I have had many remarkable answers to prayer. Thanks be to him for his condescension and goodness to poor, unworthy me. I will praise him forever!!!! Bless the Lord Oh! my soul, and all that it within me bless his holy name.

My dear George is not a christian, I do pray to God to convert his soul. 3 of my children are in the Church, I hope they are all christians. I pray to my Heavenly Father to bring them all in and make them happy christians.

I have entered my 45 year. I give myself to the Lord. Oh! Father make me what I ought to be, help me to suffer with meekness and patience all my sorrows and afflictions for thy sake who suffered the loss of all things for me.

Aug. 7th 1865

Our armies have surrendered to the Federals, the war is over. The slaves are set free. I hope the poor negroes will be learned to read the Bible and be enlightened and become christians. A great many slaves have left their homes and perished for want of food and shelter. 14 of ours have left, the most of those left here are doing well. Since I last wrote some more of our servants have left, 24 in all, one woman has died that left us, Dellah.

Nov. 13th 1865

My husband left home today for Memphis, Ten. will be gone a month. Mary Virginia, Robert and George are with me, my dear Willie was 21 years old yesterday, he has a lovely wife, suits him so well. I feel thankful.

I have a great deal to do since the servants left, but I have two women to help me. I can get along by hiring out my sewing. My children are in good health, my own health is better, I have strengthened some. I go to the Lord every day for prayer, I look to him and trust in him. I can say Lord be merciful to me a sinner. I give myself into his hands, and pray for strength to do and suffer his will, and be resigned to all my sufferings.

Dec. 1865

I have been married 25 years, the Lord has been good to me, he has been with me in all my troubles, he has comforted me, bless the Lord Oh! my soul, and all that is within me bless his holy name.

I have been a member of the church 28 years, and I am not tired of serving God. I am rooted and grounded in the faith of Jesus Christ. I have grown up into Christ, my living head. I expect to get to Heaven. I love my Saviour with all my heart, soul, mind and strength.

My husband is in Memphis, he has been gone near a month. I have been in great temptations, greatly tried and troubled since he left, many cares pressing upon me, sick in body, but I continued to call on God, he heard and has helped me, comforted me, he has showed me how weak and vile I am. I repent, I feel low in the valley of humility. I am nothing but weakness and infirmity. Oh! how frail, can do nothing. God is my strength and righteousness, he is my salvation, he is my Father, brother, and every thing to me.

My family are all well, all of our servants have left us but 4, they are all free.

GLOSSARY

backslidden: relapsed, regressed

Battle of Gettysburg: fought from July 1–July 3, 1863; incurred the most casualities of any battle during the war

bloody flux: dysentery, a disease that affected the bowels

Gen. Johnson: Joseph E. Johnson, a Confederate general

Johnson's Island: a prisoner-of-war camp near Sandusky Bay in Ohio

Sherman: General William T. Sherman, a commander of the Union Army

Document Analysis

This excerpt of Mary Jeffreys Bethell's diary opens on July 29, 1863—four weeks after the first volleys were fired during the Battle of Gettysburg. The Bethell household was only one of many to know men killed or wounded at Gettysburg, and the first entry presents names of those she had heard about. After making this list, Mary notes that her George was taken prisoner and that she was taking solace in her faith: "I thank my Saviour that it was no worse, I pray that God may save his life and grant that this trial may be the means of making him a christian."

Bethell's diary was kept for her own records and reflections, not necessarily for the sake of history or posterity. She wrote for herself, not for an audience. More than just providing insight into her daily life, the diary entries also provide the rare opportunity to study the emotional state of the writer—to learn how she felt about her life and the world around her. By studying Bethell's writing, readers can gain an in-depth picture of a middle-class woman and mother from that time. The personal use of such a journal as Bethell's, especially with her catalog of her faith and religious convictions, establishes it as a genuine primary resource for historians. With it, a better and more candid firsthand experience of Civil War–era Americans like her can be understood.

Southern Women and Religion

Religious faith was tightly interwoven with the era's ideal of a proper Southern woman, and piety was considered an important trait in a wife. A slip in a woman's devotion could tarnish her honor and place in her community. To women like Bethell, therefore, it was vital to remain chaste and devout, rather than risk losing their religious purity.

Visiting and tending to the sick were activities not only done for community and friendship's sake; this outreach was also a part of carrying out God's work. Bethell took this seriously, and enjoyed doing so: "There has been a great deal of sickness in my neighborhood. I have been visiting the sick, and I carry them something nice to eat . . . I love to visit the sick because God has commanded us to do it." The same entry also details the other rounds she has made, which also included the laying out of two neighbors for burial, another ritual often conducted by women. While she was saddened by the losses, Bethell's description demonstrates that she was a woman accustomed to such responsibilities; from her writing it is apparent that assisting her neighbors with a shroud was a part of life.

Bethell's dairy indicates that she was a woman who frequently struggled with the safety of her children. She worried about the fate of George in captivity, despite her promise of leaving it to the will of God: "I have faith to believe that God will bless all my children. I want to be kept humble and resigned to my Father's will." Typically, historians see Gettysburg as a turning point in the Civil War, especially for the Union as the victors in the fight. The Battle of Gettysburg holds the tragic distinction of having the most casualties of any other battle during the war. Feelings of uncertainty about the Confederacy's fate must have been growing in Bethell's community, enough to shake her confidence that Providence would deliver her children home unharmed.

Prisoners of War

Bethell's entry for September 16, a little over two months since news last reached her of her children, reveals that her son George was imprisoned in the Johnson's Island military prison on Lake Erie in Ohio. Johnson's Island was a new prison, built expressly for the Civil War in 1861. As an island prison, Johnson's Island was relatively safe from Southern forces, yet still accessible to Northern forces for resupply and staffing needs. Confederate prisoners such as Bethell's son who were held on the island were given adequate food and shelter, even comparable to that of the prison's guards. Life for captured Southerners at Johnson's Island stood in stark contrast to conditions at the Confederate's Andersonville Prison.

For the North, the Confederacy's Andersonville Prison, located near Andersonville, Georgia, came to symbolize the utmost cruelty. Union soldiers imprisoned at Andersonville were left with inadequate shelter, often made from no more than sticks and blankets or other cloth; there were no barracks at the site. The poor conditions of the prison and the lack of care for the prisoners resulted in many deaths, most often due to exposure, malnutrition, and disease. The ever-rising numbers of the dead—estimated at around thirteen thousand—outraged many Americans.

As a result of the spread of news about such treatment of Union soldiers, the situation at Johnson's Island was altered. At their own prison for captured Confederates, the Union reduced food rations and cut items like coffee and sugar altogether. Prisoners were not allowed to purchase food or even receive it from their families at home. Even with its low food rations, on hearing that her son George was at Johnson's Island, Bethell wrote, "I thank the Lord 'tis no worse."

Due to what Bethell referred to as a "scarcity of writing paper"—though not specified, this was more than likely due to the blockade along the Confederacy's coastline and ports—her diary entries jump from October of 1863 to April 1864. Here, she wrote that she had not received any recent news of either her son George or her son-in-law, Mr. Williamson, who was also a prisoner of war. Bethell noted that she hoped and prayed for an "exchange of prisoners." Sadly, prisoner exchange was no longer practiced by the Union by that time. In the summer of 1863, the same time George was captured, the United States began sending African American troops into battle; the Fifty-Fourth Massachusetts Regiment, led by Bostonian Robert Gould Shaw, was

the best known of these. In response to the African American troops, Confederacy announced plans to reenslave or execute any black soldiers, as well as their officers. Union's War Department then suspended their practice of prisoner exchange; in doing so, they were effectively holding Confederate soldiers hostage in the hopes of protecting regiments such as the Fifty-Fourth.

The War's End

Bethell's diary then jumps ahead once again, from July 9, 1864, to May 2, 1865. The war had ended by this time, and Bethell describes how her community came to be filled with soldiers making their journeys homeward. The May 2 entry is one of the few where there is specific mention of war events aside from news associated with the fate of her sons. In her diary Bethell recorded the surrender of Generals Robert E. Lee and Joseph E. Johnston—Lee on April 9, 1865, at Appomattox, Virginia, to General Ulysses S. Grant; and Johnston surrendered seventeen days later to General William T. Sherman outside of Durham, North Carolina. The Confederacy was now defunct, but Bethell's entries continue with an even tone; again, to her, what happened to her sons and the outcome of the Civil War were the will of God. While this could perhaps be interpreted as unpatriotic, Bethell was simply a woman who put her faith and religion above the Confederacy. She trusted that whatever happened was already ordained by Providence and therefore, she submitted to her circumstances.

This same entry, May 2, 1865, also brings the news that her son George arrived home safely after his twenty months of imprisonment at Johnson's Island; her other son, Willie, and her son-in-law returned safely as well. Indeed, Mary was a very lucky woman. As Confederate soldiers, her sons and son-in-law were more likely to die in the Civil War than their Union counterparts, and to have them return safely from both battle and the prisoner-of-war camps would have been seen by Bethell as a blessed event. On their return, she notes: "My precious Saviour has been with me in all my trials, his arm of love underneath me, he has kept me from sinking, blessed be his holy name."

The same entry that cataloged her answered prayers also shared Bethell's belief that slavery would be abolished, and that the act of ending slavery would be a positive one for the country at large. Such a statement largely goes against contemporary assumptions about those who lived in the Confederacy, but, in Bethell's case, her sentiment regarding slavery's end may be interpreted as having more to do with her religious leanings. She evidently did not view the holding of human beings, created in God's image, by others as a Christian act.

As Bethell's diary entries approach the end of December 1865, the conclusion of the excerpt, she offers repeated expressions of gratitude for both her health and the health of her family, as well as the sadness of losing cherished servants. She made note of the African Americans freed after the war, saying that "14 of ours have left, the most of those left here are doing well" and adding that more continued to leave. Bethell also prays for their spiritual salvation: "I hope the poor negroes will be learned to read the Bible and be enlightened and become christians." It is telling that Bethell hopes that freed slaves will learn to read; some Confederate states held severe laws against the literacy of slaves, as well as the teaching of them. Such a stance sets Bethell apart from many assumptions about nineteenth-century Southern women. She saw value in all people both within and without the community, and did not exclude any due to race.

Essential Themes

The recurring theme of religion throughout Bethell's entries speaks of her commitment to Christianity as a major aspect of her life. Of God, she wrote: "My precious Saviour has been with me in all my trials, his arm of love underneath me, he has kept me from sinking." For her, faith and prayers were not solely a matter of Sunday observance, relegated to the church; rather, her religion was a constant, daily devotion. There is a sharp division between Bethell's discussion of the war, and its potential outcomes, and that of other Confederate women. Although both her sons survived the war, it can be inferred from Bethell's writings with little doubt that, had George or Willie been lost, she would have accepted it with the aid of her religion as God's will. She left these judgments to God.

Bethell did not waver in her beliefs, even when she discussed her own mortality. In her entry for May 9, 1864, she wrote, "I was 43 years old last Sunday, the Lord has spared my life." Based on the life expectancy of the nineteenth century, Mary had already lived most of her life. Given her assistance to neighbors in times of death and disease, as well as the limited medical

knowledge of the time, Bethell was well aware of how quickly life could end. She therefore reminded herself in her diary—God having spared her life another year was also mentioned once she reached the age of forty-four the following year—how thankful she ought to be, as she was still among her family and had her health.

Jennifer L. Henderson Crane, PgDip

Bibliography

Brown, Alexis Giradin. "The Women Left Behind: Transformation of the Southern Belle, 1840–1880." *Historian* 6.4 (2000): 759–77. Print.

Elder, Robert. "A Twice Sacred Circle: Women, Evangelicalism, and Honor in the Deep South, 1784–1860." *Journal of Southern History* 78.3 (2012): 579–614. Print.

Faust, Drew Gilpin. "Altars of Sacrifice: Confederate Women and the Narratives of War." *Journal of American History* 76.4 (1990): 1200–1228. Print.

Horwitz, Tony. *Confederates in the Attic: Dispatches from the Unfinished Civil War.* New York: Vintage, 1998. Print.

McPherson, James. *Battle Cry of Freedom: The Civil War Era.* Oxford: Oxford UP, 1988. Print.

Smith-Rosenberg, Carroll. "The Female World of Love and Ritual: Relations between Women in Nineteenth-Century America." *Signs* 1.1 (1975): 1–29. Print.

Additional Reading

Chestnut, Mary Boykin. *A Diary from Dixie: A Lady's Account of the Confederacy During the American Civil War.* Driffield, England: Leonaur, 2010. Print.

Clinton, Catherine, and Nina Silber, eds. *Divided Houses: Gender and the Civil War.* Oxford: Oxford UP, 1992. Print.

Faust, Drew Gilpin. *Mothers of Invention: Women of the Slaveholding South in the American Civil War.* New York: Vintage, 1997. Print.

Jabour, Anya. "'Grown Girls, Highly Cultivated': Female Education in an Antebellum Southern Family." *Journal of Southern History* 64.1 (1998): 23–64. Print.

---. *Scarlett's Sisters: Young Women in the Old South.* Chapel Hill: U of North Carolina P, 2009. Print.

Kerber, Linda. "Separate Spheres, Female Worlds, Woman's Place: The Rhetoric of Women's History." *Journal of American History* 75.1 (1988): 9–39. Print.

■ Gettysburg Address

Date: November 19, 1863
Author: Lincoln, Abraham
Genre: speech

> *"We here highly resolve that these dead shall not have died in vain, that this nation under God shall have a new birth of freedom, and that government of the people, by the people, for the people shall not perish from the earth."*

Summary Overview

On November 19, 1863, four months after one of the most brutal (and pivotal) battles of the Civil War, President Abraham Lincoln stood on the same battlefield for two purposes. The first was to commemorate the fallen and "consecrate" the land as a national cemetery. The second was to inspire the nation, which remained at war, to continue to fight for the democratic principles on which the United States was founded. The speech was extremely short—less than three hundred words in length—but was nonetheless extremely impactful, using powerful and poetic language. Despite its brevity, the Gettysburg Address, as it is called, stands as one of the greatest speeches in American history.

Defining Moment

In the spring of 1863, General Robert E. Lee led the Confederate States Army into Pennsylvania, having proven successful in repelling Union advances into Virginia. Lee was pursuing two goals: the abundant supplies of the Pennsylvania farmland and a push away from Virginia and into the North. The Union Army of the Potomac, led by General George Gordon Meade, marched north and west in order to protect Washington, DC, from Lee's army, which organized fully in Gettysburg, awaiting the oncoming Union counterattack.

From July 1 through July 3, the two armies clashed violently on this hilly region of eastern Pennsylvania. More than 160,000 men took part in a series of bloody attacks and counterattacks, with both sides gaining and losing ground during the battle's many engagements. Finally, on the battle's third day, a twelve-thousand-man Confederate charge up Cemetery Ridge—the infamous "Pickett's Charge"—was repelled by the Union's cannons and guns, forcing Lee and his men to disengage and begin the long march back to Virginia. More than fifty thousand Union and Confederate men were killed, wounded, or captured during this bloody battle.

Four months later, President Lincoln arrived on the battlefield to commemorate the Union victory, honor the dead, and dedicate a large portion of the battlefield as the Soldiers' National Cemetery. Fifteen thousand people came to witness the ceremony. Boston professor, diplomat, and statesman Edward Everett, who was known for his brilliant oratory skills, was invited to deliver the ceremony's keynote address. Everett's address to the crowd was two hours long, illustrating the countless details of the battles and drawing comparisons between the Gettysburg combatants to the warriors of ancient Greece.

Lincoln had a number of important tasks to accomplish during his speech. First, he attempted to comfort the American people who had witnessed the bloody battle. He also needed to honor the dead—Union and Confederate alike—who had taken part in the campaign. Third, he needed to move the country forward; because the Civil War was far from over, he needed to inspire the American people to continue to follow his lead in defeating the Confederacy. Finally, he needed to make a statement to the Confederacy as well, reminding the South that the North would not yield in its efforts to reunite the Union as one nation.

Following Everett's brilliant (if verbose) speech, Lincoln's brief, two-minute speech surprised the crowd and left them silent for several moments; the audience had expected the American president to say more. Nevertheless, Lincoln's Gettysburg Address was highly influential, accomplishing Lincoln's goals and inspiring the country to move forward toward ending the Civil War.

Author Biography

Lincoln was born on February 12, 1809, near Hodgenville, Kentucky, to Thomas Lincoln and Nancy Hanks. His mother died when he was only nine years old. Lincoln and his father moved several times after Nancy's death, first to Indiana and then to Illinois. Living on the frontier and moving frequently, Lincoln was afforded a minimal childhood education (his school in Indiana was a log cabin, and his father assisted in his education at home), although he quickly developed a love for literature, with particular interest in the law.

In 1832, while he was in his twenties, Lincoln joined the army as a volunteer during the Black Hawk War. He quickly rose through the chain of command, elected captain of his unit within months of joining. After the war, Lincoln was involved in a number of business activities, including work on a riverboat and in a store, before he set up a law practice in New Salem, Illinois. He was initially defeated in a campaign for the Illinois state legislature, but he continued to practice law (and also held a number of local government positions) before successfully campaigning again for the state legislature in 1834. He was reelected three times before retiring from the legislature and returning to practicing law in Springfield. In 1847, he was elected, as a member of the Whig Party, to the US House of Representatives, a post he held for one term.

In 1855, Lincoln ran unsuccessfully for the US Senate. He tried again in 1858, this time as a Republican; the unsuccessful campaign included the famous debates with his opponent, Stephen A. Douglas. During the same year, he married Mary Todd, with whom he would have four children (although only one survived childhood). In 1860, Lincoln, undaunted by his previous electoral defeats, ran for president on the Republican ticket. This time, he was successful. He was reelected in 1864.

President Lincoln's 1861–65 presidential tenure was marked by not only his Civil War accomplishments, but also his role in building the Republican Party, unifying the northern Democrats, bringing an end to slavery, and even improving relations with the Indians on the American frontier. After the war, he led the effort to reconcile the nation's relationship with the secessionist South. However, he was unable to complete his work as president—in 1865, while attending a play at Ford's Theatre in Washington, DC, he was assassinated by John Wilkes Booth. After three days of being laid in state in the Capitol Rotunda, he was interred at Oak Grove Cemetery in Springfield, Illinois.

HISTORICAL DOCUMENT

Fourscore and seven years ago our fathers brought forth on this continent a new nation, conceived in liberty and dedicated to the proposition that all men are created equal. Now we are engaged in a great civil war, testing whether that nation or any nation so conceived and so dedicated can long endure. We are met on a great battlefield of that war. We have come to dedicate a portion of that field as a final resting-place for those who here gave their lives that that nation might live. It is altogether fitting and proper that we should do this. But in a larger sense, we cannot dedicate, we cannot consecrate, we cannot hallow this ground. The brave men, living and dead who struggled here have consecrated it far above our poor power to add or detract. The world will little note nor long remember what we say here, but it can never forget what they did here. It is for us the living rather to be dedicated here to the unfinished work which they who fought here have thus far so nobly advanced. It is rather for us to be here dedicated to the great task remaining before us—that from these honored dead we take increased devotion to that cause for which they gave

the last full measure of devotion—that we here highly resolve that these dead shall not have died in vain, that this nation under God shall have a new birth of freedom, and that government of the people, by the people, for the people shall not perish from the earth.

GLOSSARY

consecrate: to declare a property (such as land or a church) sacred ground

fathers: predecessors

fourscore: eighty

hallow: to make holy

Document Analysis

The Gettysburg Address was written only a day before President Lincoln arrived at the Gettysburg battlefield. Although the keynote address by Everett was the most highly anticipated of the presentations during the ceremony, Lincoln's presence was nonetheless expected to be significant. His comments needed to be both comforting and inspiring. Despite the fact that it was only two minutes long, Lincoln's Gettysburg Address met these expectations, at least in the years that followed his delivery.

The Battle of Gettysburg had occurred only a few months before, which meant that the commemoration of the Soldiers' National Cemetery would be an emotional experience. After all, only months before, on that very field, thousands of bodies sat rotting in the hot summer sun, emitting a foul odor and leaving a stain on the ground that likely remained when the crowd gathered for Lincoln and Everett's ceremony.

There is a common myth that Lincoln quickly jotted down the speech on the back of an envelope while on the train from Washington, DC, to Gettysburg. This story might account for the short length of the speech. The fact that the speech was written on Lincoln's official White House stationery, however, casts doubt on this legend. In all likelihood, historians believe, Lincoln was working on this speech for weeks before leaving on the train. Although this speech was exceptional in terms of its brevity, it was reflective of Lincoln's style. His speeches were frequently short (his second inau-

gural address was only seven hundred words in length, for example) and filled with language and imagery that were typically his (as opposed to speeches that were inspired by classical literature and religious ideals). Lincoln's address, therefore, was presented in this manner because he wanted to effectively meet the lofty goals the speech demanded.

The tasks at hand for Lincoln were to honor the dead and inspire the living. This challenge was all the more difficult for the president because of the conditions at hand. The Civil War was by no means over. In fact, although the Gettysburg campaign sent Lee and his troops back to Virginia, the war continued to rage onward. The country remained divided and in danger of becoming even more fractured to a point that it would completely disintegrate. Given the political circumstances, Lincoln would need to speak not only to the bloody battle that had just occurred only months earlier, but also to the country's direction going forward from this point in history. Convincing the audience of the value of moving forward in the war against the South would be difficult—Lincoln needed to make the point that the unconscionable violence that occurred on the very ground on which they all stood was necessary, and future, similar bloodshed would also be needed to protect the nation.

Lincoln's address begins by speaking to the foundations of what Alexis de Tocqueville called "the great experiment" that is the United States. "Four score and seven years ago" (eighty-seven years), he states, the

United States pronounced itself a new nation through the Declaration of Independence. This new nation would be based on the personal liberties and equality of all.

Likely standing on a stage on Cemetery Hill (where Pickett's Charge hastened the end of the battle), Lincoln chose to begin his address by referencing the founding of the country to remind Americans of what was at stake in the Civil War. The United States became unified under the principles of liberty and freedom, which would apply to all Americans. The war was endangering both those principles and the fabric of the relatively young nation.

The next sentence of the address speaks directly to this threat. The war, which was three years old at the time of Lincoln's speech, had already stretched the fabric of the United States. As Lincoln says in his speech, the war was a test of the durability of the liberty and freedom the nation's founders had brought into being. Lincoln even broadened the significance of this battle beyond American borders—when referring to this "test," he questions whether or not any nation founded on the same principles could withstand a civil war such as that which was occurring in the United States. (Implicit in his statement is the fact that many other nations adopted constitutions and democratic principles not long after the American Revolution.)

Indeed, Lincoln understood the international stakes if the Confederacy was successful in its attempts to permanently fracture the United States. The economic promise of opening commercial relations with the resource-rich Confederate States of America was a great incentive for recognizing the region's legitimacy. The Confederate government in Richmond understood this fact and therefore petitioned both France and Great Britain to recognize it. It also looked to these countries to provide financial and other forms of assistance. Should any foreign governments get involved in the war, the advantage could tilt to the South. Gettysburg helped the Union regain its footing—Lincoln did not want to lose the momentum that had barely been established after battle. By including other democratic countries in the Gettysburg Address, Lincoln was linking the United States to foreign governments, ideally discouraging them from helping the Confederacy and encouraging them to stay out of the Civil War.

Lincoln's point was that the country was "conceived" in the notions of liberty and freedom. These principles were on the minds and in the hearts of every American in 1776, making the establishment of a new nation based on such concepts an absolute priority during that period. The onset of a true civil war that threatened to completely disintegrate the United States of America, however, proved that a great number of Americans had lost sight of this priority. Lincoln begins his speech, therefore, by reminding the audience, and indeed the entire nation, of this once top priority and the value of continuing the fight to preserve the Union.

If the Civil War continued in this brutal fashion, Lincoln states, it is possible that the war would eventually destroy the ideals set forth in the Declaration of Independence. The Battle of Gettysburg was the battle with the greatest number of casualties, and it represented a major turning point in the war, as the Union Army was able to turn around Lee's forces. For this reason, Gettysburg was, in Lincoln's view, "a great battlefield" worthy of recognition.

In light of the significance of the Battle of Gettysburg, Lincoln says, it was appropriate to honor the soldiers who gave their lives so "that that nation might live." Because of this sacrifice, it was "altogether fitting and proper" to turn a portion of the battlefield into a national cemetery. Lincoln's speech underscores this point for the audience by not placing the president in a position to consecrate the cemetery himself. Instead, his speech shows outright humility and respect for the fallen. In reality, the president says, those who stood on this commemorative site were not in a position to dedicate or consecrate this hallowed ground. Rather, he says, the living and the dead who fought at Gettysburg a few months earlier had already done so through their struggles, and those in attendance at the ceremony— Lincoln included—possessed the "poor power to add or detract" to the consecration of the site.

Lincoln was known for his writing and public-speaking prowess, and the Gettysburg Address serves as a showcase for both talents. Lincoln's use of contrasts, for example, was particularly effective for connecting with the audience's emotions. For example, he refers to both the living and the dead, connecting the fallen at Gettysburg to those who survived and those who would benefit from the sacrifices of the dead.

Another example of Lincoln's use of contrasts can be found in his statement on the deeds of the fallen. Lincoln states that the "world will little note nor long remember" the words that were spoken at the Gettysburg commemoration ceremony. Although these words will be forgotten, he says, the world will forever remember the deeds committed on this battlefield. The contrast between what will be remembered and forgotten resonates, as it reminds the audience of the value of mere rhetoric in comparison to action. After all, he says, the acts of the Union soldiers at Gettysburg, who were risking (and in the case of thousands, giving) their lives to protect the American way of life, could be connected to similar actions by the Founding Fathers, who took similar risks to establish this nation.

In this regard, Lincoln not only honors the fallen of Gettysburg but also issues an imperative for the American people. What happened at Gettysburg (and indeed, what was happening on every battlefield during the Civil War) involved American troops fighting with zeal to protect the Union. By reminding his audience of their actions, Lincoln is telling every American that they too must join him and the rest of the American government to fight the notion of Southern secession.

President Lincoln's call for action becomes far more direct when he calls upon the American people to continue the work performed by those who participated in the Battle of Gettysburg. He implies that the people should continue what American soldiers began during this battle. "It is for us the living," he says, "to be dedicated here to the unfinished work which they who fought here have thus far so nobly advanced." Using such language, Lincoln is directly linking the success of the Union troops to the rest of the United States.

Lincoln appeals to the emotions of his audience in this regard, adding that the American people were linked not only to the Union Army's success at Gettysburg, but also to the loss of life there. He professes that the people should take note of the devotion demonstrated by those who died. Based on the example of those who fell in battle, he says, Americans should show similar devotion to their country by fighting for the Union. Lincoln asserts that if Americans come together in this manner, those who died during the Battle of Gettysburg shall not have died in vain.

Lincoln finishes his address by once again harking back to the founding principles of the Declaration of Independence. With the active support of the American people, the aforementioned threat to the principles of liberty and freedom may be averted. As stated earlier, Lincoln was afraid that the country that was borne from the Declaration of Independence may have become lost over the course of less than a century. However, if the people take up the cause to which the partici-

pants of Gettysburg were dedicated, a new nation, with a "government of the people, by the people, [and] for the people" would be reborn in its place.

Furthermore, if the American people took up the mantle of the fallen of Gettysburg, they would not only be responsible for ensuring the survival of the democratic government found in the United States, but also their success in bringing about a favorable end to the Civil War would protect the liberty and freedom espoused by other governments. At risk in this war, Lincoln implies, was the notion of democracy, and with the end of the war, such institutions would not cease to exist on Earth.

As mentioned earlier, Lincoln's speech was initially received with surprise, primarily because of the fact that it was over almost as soon as it began. The crowd at hand responded with a smattering of applause, which famed historian Shelby Foote described in *Civil War: A Narrative—Volume Two* (1963) as "barely polite." While the brevity of Lincoln's speech played a major role in the initial response from the crowd, when the speech was later reviewed by the media, it became clear that the politics of the time would also play a role in Americans' response. The *Chicago Times*, a longtime critic of Lincoln, skewered the speech as little more than "silly, flat and dishwatery utterances" (Edwards). On the other hand, the Republican-leaning (and therefore pro-Lincoln) *New York Times* showered the address with compliments. Lincoln clearly understood the political landscape—and that not all Americans were firmly behind their president—when he wrote the speech.

Given the politics at hand, Lincoln is said to have had his own doubts about how the speech should have been written and how it would be received. Although he was correct in his initial assessment, the speech would find nearly universal favor after the war's end and throughout postwar American history.

Essential Themes

Four months after the three-day Battle of Gettysburg, President Lincoln arrived on the battlefield in eastern Pennsylvania to commemorate the site as a national cemetery. Although Lincoln was not supposed to give a major speech (that responsibility fell to Everett), his comments were expected to be poignant and inspiring, especially in light of the significance of the event. At less than three hundred words, Lincoln's Gettysburg Address surprised the crowd of fifteen thousand as a result of its brevity, but those words were nonetheless momentous.

There were two major themes present in Lincoln's speech. The first was paying homage to the soldiers, both living and dead, who fought bravely and risked (and even gave) their lives to preserve the Union. The commemoration of the national cemetery would serve as the vehicle for this homage. Lincoln carefully crafted his words in such a way that he avoided assuming any power over such a task. Instead, he says in his speech, the men who took part in this battle (particularly those who lost their lives) had already consecrated the land. His choice of language in this capacity appealed to the emotions of both the audience members and those who would read it later. Lincoln's point was that those who died on the battlefield paid the ultimate price to defend the Union.

The second major theme in the speech was its appeal to Americans to continue the fight begun by the fallen soldiers. Lincoln uses a connection to the Declaration of Independence and the American Revolution. He reminds the audience of the passion the Founding Fathers (and all Americans) had for liberty and freedom, suggesting that the Civil War came into being because many of the people had forgotten the values of early America. By the summer of 1863, the war had had taken a turn in favor of the secessionists. Gettysburg was a victory against the Confederacy, but Americans, in the words of Lincoln, needed to build on that victory by continuing to fight until the war was over.

Lincoln's Gettysburg Address is considered one of the greatest speeches in American history. Brief but powerful, the speech provided both comfort and inspiration to the audience. It inspired them to appreciate what had occurred at Gettysburg and to take part in the reunification and reconciliation of the fractured United States.

Michael Auerbach, MA

Bibliography

Beschloss, Michael, and Hugh Sidey. "Abraham Lincoln." *White House*. White House Historical Assn., 2009. Web. 15 Feb. 2013.

Edwards, Owen. "Gettysburg Address Displayed at Smithsonian." *Smithsonian*. Smithsonian, Dec. 2008. Web. 18 Feb. 2013.

"Gettysburg." *Civil War Trust*. Civil War Trust, 2013. Web. 15 Feb. 2013.

"The Gettysburg Address Text." Visit-Gettysburg.com. 2013. Web. 15 Feb. 2013.

"Lesson 3: The Gettysburg Address (1863)—Defining the American Union." *National Endowment for the Humanities*. National Endowment for the Humanities, n.d. Web. 15 Feb. 2013.

"Lincoln, Abraham." *Biographical Directory of the United States Congress*. Biographical Directory of the United States Congress, n.d. Web. 15 Feb. 2013.

Additional Reading

Barone, Michael, and Gerald Parshall. "Who Was Lincoln?" *US News and World Report* 27 Sept. 1992. Web. 3 Apr. 2013.

Boritt, Gabor. *The Gettysburg Gospel: The Lincoln Speech That Nobody Knows*. New York: Simon, 2008. Print.

Sears, Stephen W. *Gettysburg*. Boston: Mariner, 2004. Print.

Wills, Garry. *Lincoln at Gettysburg: The Words That Remade America*. New York: Simon, 2006. Print.

■ Reception to the Enlistment of Black Soldiers

Date: July 17, 1863; November 15, 1865
Author: *Liberator* (Boston, MA); *North American* (Philadelphia, PA)
Genre: article

> *"All thinking men have at last been convinced that the moral struggle in which we are engaged required us to use all the legitimate means within our power to crush a rebellion which else will crush us."*
> —*Liberator,* "Enlistment of Colored Regiments"

> *"Your services, offered in the early part of the war, were refused, but when the struggle became of life and death, then the country gladly received you, and, thank God, you nobly redeemed all you promised."*
> —*North American,* "Reception of Colored Troops
> —Speech of General Cameron"

Summary Overview

Although the onset of the American Civil War was inextricably linked with the practice of race-based slavery in the states that became the Confederacy, African Americans were prohibited from serving in the conflict during the war's early years. The war, argued Union leaders, was being fought to restore the Union, not to end slavery. As the war progressed, however, the need for soldiers increased, and the tone of the conflict became more antislavery. With the issuance of the Emancipation Proclamation in 1863 came the decision to recruit African American soldiers from both the North and the South for the Union Army. From 1863 onward, African American volunteers enlisted in great numbers, wishing both to aid efforts to abolish slavery and to encourage the restored United States to grant them full citizenship rights. Despite initial reservations, many military leaders came to welcome their contributions to the struggle.

Defining Moment

When the Civil War erupted in 1861, free African Americans in both the Union and the Confederacy sought to answer the call to serve. African American soldiers had served in the Revolutionary War and the War of 1812, and the Civil War seemed even more relevant to these Americans' pursuit of life, liberty, and happiness. Yet the free African Americans in the North who attempted to join the Union Army were unsuccessful. A 1792 federal law barred African Americans from service in the US military—a law conveniently ignored during the War of 1812—and black men were equally forbidden service in state militias. Some African Americans continued efforts to join nevertheless, with one group in Massachusetts beginning drill exercises and repeatedly petitioning for a change in the discriminatory laws. In Massachusetts and throughout the North, the answer was always a firm no. The war, leaders argued, was based on the stability of the Union rather than the issue of slavery, and as such, it was not one of especial concern to the nation's African American population. This contention aimed to assure border slave states such as Maryland and Kentucky that their continued loyalty to the Union posed no threat to the continuation of the institution of slavery within their borders, but it gave little comfort to the free blacks rejected by their national and state governments.

Contrary to early expectations, however, the war was not quickly or easily won. Levels of white enlistment dropped off, and in 1862 Union leaders began to reconsider the viability of black units. In July of 1862, Congress passed the Second Confiscation Act and the Militia Act, which freed those African Americans enslaved by owners who were fighting for the Confederate Army and encouraged the Union Army to take on freed slaves as fighters and support workers. As the Emancipation Proclamation took effect in 1863, Northern recruitment of black soldiers began apace. Although many African Americans were initially reluctant to volunteer, leaders such as Frederick Douglass urged enlistment, believing that a strong showing of African American service for the Union cause would help secure black citizenship rights after the war ended. Enlistments increased, and in the spring of 1863 the Bureau of Colored Troops was created to oversee black soldiers. In time, some 179,000 African Americans enlisted in the army and about 19,000 in the navy. African American troops fought in combat, served behind the lines, and proved valuable as scouts and spies.

Author Biography
Liberator
Unquestionably the leading antislavery publication in the United States, the *Liberator* was founded as a weekly newspaper in Boston in 1831 by abolitionist William Lloyd Garrison. Intensely opposed to slavery, Garrison was among the first and was certainly the loudest voice to call for complete and immediate abolition throughout the nation. He commenced publication of the *Liberator* with a strong statement supporting the equality of all people, including enslaved African Americans, as expressed in the Declaration of Independence. Over the next several decades of the fight against slavery, Garrison never backed down from this stance, earning a reputation as arguably the most radical of the abolitionist figures operating in the United States at that time. Under his guidance, the *Liberator*, although boasting a paid circulation of just three thousand, became widely recognized as influential well beyond its nominal readership.

During the Civil War, Garrison called not only for emancipation and a constitutional amendment abolishing slavery throughout the United States, but also for the inclusion of African American soldiers in the Union Army, with pay equal to that of white soldiers. With the passage and ratification of the Thirteenth Amendment to the US Constitution, which abolished slavery in 1865, Garrison considered the work of the *Liberator* complete. It ceased publication with a declaration of victory on December 29, 1865.

North American
In contrast, the *North American* was a mainstream publication founded in Philadelphia in 1839. Through a merger with the competing *American Daily Advertiser*, the *North American* could lay claim to connections with the oldest daily newspaper in the United States. Unlike the *Liberator*, the *North American* had no particular antislavery agenda and as late as the 1850s offered only tempered support for the Republican Party. Unlike Garrison, the editors of the *North American* largely supported the Civil War as a method to restore the divided Union, not as a moral crusade to obtain liberty and civil rights for African Americans.

HISTORICAL DOCUMENT

Enlistment of Colored Regiments

HEADQUARTERS SUPERVISORY COMMITTEE ON COLORED ENLISTMENTS, 1210 Chesnut St., June 27, 1863—The Supervisory Committee on Enlistments for Colored Regiments ask that cooperation of their fellow citizens in an undertaking which they deem of the most importance to the successful prosecution of the war against rebellion.

Authority has been given by the War Department to recruit in Pennsylvania colored regiments for three years, or the war. These troops, when raised, will be credited to the quota of Pennsylvania under the next draft. The Government receives and rousters them in at Camp William Penn, at Chelton Hills, and all previous expenses of recruitment, subsistence and transportation must be provided by the public.

It will be seen that funds to a considerable extent will be required to prosecute successfully and energetically the enterprise which has been entrusted to us. Without bounties of extra allowance for the men, each regiment recruited in this vicinity will not cost less than ten thousand dollars. Yet, to accomplish all that we hope to do, we must look beyond the limits of our immediate neighborhood. In 1800, the colored male population of Pennsylvania was only 25,878; and if one in four of those is able to bear arms, we have for our field of operations only six or seven thousand men, of whom four hundred have already, through our own negligence, been abstracted for the benefit of Massachusetts. Our field, therefore, should not be limited by the narrow boundaries of our own State, and this will necessarily entail increased expenditure. The Massachusetts regiments, obtained by a system of agencies extending from St. Louis to Philadelphia, cost about $25,000 each, exclusive of the $50 bounty per man. The funds for this had, with a wise forethought, been appropriated by the State.

We must rely upon private liberality. The same machinery which was so successfully employed for Massachusetts is at our command, and the extent of funds placed at our disposal. If large, we can make this the centre of recruitment for the colored population of all the States where such enlistments are not permitted by the State authorities.

But it is not only pecuniary aid that we look for at your hands. Our labors can be materially assisted by your influence and sympathy. Whether encouraged or not, the events of the past fortnight have shown that there is sufficient spirit and patriotism in our colored population to insure a reasonable response to our invitation to enlist; but the extent of that response can be vastly increased by individual efforts, and by the appreciation which the community at large may manifest of the patriotic self devotion of the negro to a country which has thus far given him but a stepmother's affection.

Six months since, had we appealed to you, we should have felt it necessary to argue the propriety and expediency of negro enlistments. That time, however, has passed. All thinking men have at last been convinced that the moral struggle in which we are engaged required us to use all the legitimate means within our power to crush a rebellion which else will crush us. It has been recognized that the severest blow which can be inflicted upon the slave oligarchy must come from the institution of slavery itself; and while we were thus turning upon the rebels the arms which they had been using against us, it would be folly longer to deny to the free colored men of the North the opportunity which they had earnestly desired of offering themselves as a sacrifice, not only to their race, but the country. Since volunteering can no longer fill the ranks of our armies, and recourse to conscription becomes necessary, unreasoning prejudice only can be blind to the fact that every colored recruit nets as an unpurchased substitute for a white man. If, forgetful of past experience in our two wars with England, many of us believe that the colored race could not face the white man in battle, the generous self-sacrifice of the noble spirits who fell at Fort Hudson and Milliken's Bend has effectually dissipated the prejudice. If too, we hesitated to place arms in the hands of a race degraded by centuries of servitude, lest their ungovernable fury should repay upon the innocent and unprotected the long arrears of wrong, the result has shown how baseless were these fears. We have seen, that while the negro can exhibit unsurpassed courage on the field, he is thoroughly amenable to discipline, and that, when properly trained and officered, he may be implicitly relied on to observe the rules of honorable warfare.

The last objection has thus been removed, and no loyal citizen can hesitate to aid in every practicable mode a movement which must prove most efficient in quieting the rebellion. To all classes, therefore, we appeal, with full confidence that we shall receive for the undertaking the active support, both moral and pecuniary, of a community which has never yet failed in its response to every call made in the name and for the cause of the Union.

Contributions can be sent to the office of the Finance Committee, at Messrs. E. W. Clark & Co., No. 35 South 3d-st.

Applications for positions in the regiment should be transmitted through Henry Samuel, Esq., Corresponding Secretary of the Executive Committee, at the headquarters, No. 1210; Chesnut street. Authority to recruit will be given by Maj. Stearne, No. 1210 Chessnut street.

MEN OF COLOR! At length the opportunity is offered for which you have waited so long and so patiently. A gigantic contest, in which the interests of your race are so largely involved, threatens with destruction the land which for centuries has been your home. At the very commencement of the struggle, you eagerly offered your services. They were rejected for reasons which, whether well or ill-founded, were all-powerful at the time. Those reasons exist no longer, and your country now invites you to arms in her defense.

Men of color! We speak to you of your country, of the land where God in his mysterious providence has placed you to work out his inscrutable purposes. Yet you have been strangers in a land of strangers, and it is now for you to decide whether that land shall be to you and your children more in the future than it has been in the past. We can make no promises, but we have an abiding faith that the Almighty has not visited us with tribulation in wrath, but in mercy; that you and we, thus tried in the fiery furnace, if true to ourselves and to Him, shall emerge purified and redeemed from the sins and the wrongs of the past. . . .

Reception of Colored Troops—Speech of General Cameron

HARRISBURG, Nov. 15—The reception of the colored troops in this city today was a success throughout. Early in the morning the sidewalks of the city were crowded with delegations from a distance, and at the hour when the line of march was commenced not less than six or seven thousand colored people accompanied their soldier brethren over the route.

The reception of these troops was as it should be, respectful and honorable by the great mass of the people of Harrisburg, and many a fair white hand did not shrink from waving a kerchief in welcome of those who escaped the perils of a contest in which they risked their lives, in defense of the national honor and support of the constitutional authorities. As the troops passed over the line of march they halted before the mansion of General Cameron, on Front street, for the purpose of saluting that gentlemen, who was among the very first in the land to insist on recognizing the ability of the colored men to be of service in aiding to suppress the slaveholders' rebellion.

General Cameron appeared and welcomed the troops in the following language:

I cannot let the opportunity pass without thanking the African soldiers for the compliment they have paid me, but more than all to thank them for the great service which they have rendered to their country in this terrible rebellion. I never doubted that the people of African descent would play a great part in this struggle, and am proud to say that all my anticipations have been more than realized. Your services, offered in the early part of the war, were refused, but when the struggle became of life and death, then the country gladly received you, and, thank God, you nobly redeemed all you promised. . . . Like all other men, you have your destinies in your own hands, and if you continue to conduct yourselves hereafter as you have done in this struggle, rights you ask for—all the rights that belong to human beings. . . . I can only say again that I thank you—I thank you from my heart for all that you have done for your country, and I know the country will hold you in grateful remembrance. I cannot close without saying that there is at the head of me the national government a great man, who is able and determined to deal justly with all.

I know that, with his approval, no State that was in rebellion, will be allowed to return to the benefits of the Union without having first a constitutional compact which will prevent slavery in this land for all time to come; which will make men equal before the law; which will prescribe no distinction of color on the witness stand

and in the jury box; and which will protect the honor and the domestic relations of all men and all women. He will insist; too on the repudiation of all debts contracted from the support of the war of the rebellion. Remember, when this war began there were four millions of slaves in this country protected by law. Now, all men are made free by the law. Thank God for all this, for He alone has accomplished the work.

Major General Kiddoe, Brig. General James S. Brisbin, who organized the colored troops of Kentucky, Captain Patterson, Provost Marshal of this district, and other distinguished gentlemen were on the steps of General Cameron's mansion, and participated by their presence in the welcome to the colored troops. The procession moved up Front street to the Capitol grounds, where an organization was effected by electing Stephen Smith, of Philadelphia, as President, supported by a large number of Vice Presidents and Secretaries.

Rev. John Walker Jackson addressed the Throne of Grace. His prayer was an eloquent rehearsal of the wrongs of the black man, a thrilling appear for aid from that source whence the downtrodden can only look for redress, and a beautiful acknowledgement of the services which the black man rendered in the struggle for American nationality, civilization and freedom.

A number of letters were then read from distinguished gentlemen, including Gen. Butler, Gen. Meade, Senator Samner and others, acknowledging invitations, and assigning reasons why they could not be present.

The orator of the occasion, Prof. Wm. Howard Day, of New York, was then introduced, and proceeded at length to discuss the attitude of the colored man before and during the war, and the prospect which lies before him for personal improvement, social elevation, and acquirement of those great political right which would place him on an equality among the governed as well as those who govern in the United States. Professor Day's oration will not admit of condemnation, and can only be referred to telegraphically as an effort of great fairness, eloquence, and accuracy in its statement of facts.

The proceedings of the day will be continued this evening by a meeting, in the Court-house, which will be addressed by distinguished men of color now in the city. A grand ball, with all the paraphernalia and display of such an affair, will terminate the events of the reception of the colored troops of Pennsylvania in the State capital.

GLOSSARY

abstracted: removed; in this case, enlisted

brethren: brothers

compact: agreement

contest: war, conflict

fortnight: two weeks

pecuniary: financial

providence: action by God to shape human lives and activities

repudiation: rejection

Document Analysis

The Civil War was a time of great change for African Americans, not only because it led to the abolition of slavery throughout the nation but also because it set the stage for a brief period of time during which African Americans made significant strides in legal and political equality. In the closing days of the conflict and Reconstruction, for example, African Americans were fully emancipated from slavery; given legal citizenship rights equal to those of white Americans; granted the franchise on equal footing with white men; successfully elected to representative office at the local, state, and federal levels; and, through the efforts of the Freedmen's Bureau, slowly propelled along a path toward economic advancement through education and training. Although the promise of Reconstruction was not fully realized due to its abrupt end in 1877, those rights that had been granted constitutionally could not be entirely revoked. Slavery in particular could not be restored. Yet these changes required a level of public support in order to be successfully enacted, even in the Republican-dominated legislature of the Civil War era. Before the war, many Northerners opposed the extension of slavery, and a smaller but growing number had come to support the idea of nationwide emancipation; whether that emancipation should be immediate or gradual and whether those who gained liberty should attain suffrage remained unsettled questions. Over the course of the war, however, sufficient support for African American rights spread through the North and enabled these changes to take place.

One important factor in achieving these reforms in the North was the dedicated military service of African Americans in the Union Army. Although African Americans were initially believed to make poor soldiers and were thus rejected for service, changing needs and the enactment of the Emancipation Proclamation in 1863 meant that free blacks in the North and emancipated blacks in the South could be recruited for service in the Union military. This force in transforming white Northern public opinion of the value of their African American neighbors as possible citizens can thus be traced through the appeals to African American recruits in the 1863 *Liberator* article and the celebration of black military service in the 1865 *North American* article reprinted here. In 1863, white acceptance of black soldiers was growing due to the valor of the earliest black troops in battle; by 1865, white respect for those soldiers' contributions had only grown, helping African Americans throughout the nation work toward the goals of liberty and equality. African American military service was thus inextricably linked with emancipation.

The Liberator

Formal calls for that service rang loudly by mid-1863, when the abolitionist weekly the *Liberator* published an article encouraging support for recruitment efforts in Pennsylvania. Along with providing the details of the service expected of recruits, the article calls on readers to offer financial support to help cover the great burden of paying for such efforts; tax revenues in these pre–income tax days were too low to cover the costs of fielding a large fighting force for an extended period, and Pennsylvania lacked the needed monies to pay for its planned African America militia. It also lacked sufficient men, the article argues, calling for the expansion of recruitment efforts outside the state's borders following a model similar to that used by Massachusetts. Some Union states retained the institution of slavery, and these states were obviously reluctant to organize their own African American militias. Yet free African Americans did live in these states and provided a possible body on which other states could draw.

The article then moves to stir its readers' "influence and sympathy" for the cause and value of African American soldiers. The respect of the white community, the author argues, gave black soldiers an additional incentive to enlist in the army of a nation "which has thus far given [them] but a stepmother's affection"—affection that is unwilling and inadequate, thanks to the oppression of both free and enslaved blacks in the North and South. The article then calls strongly for the recruitment of African American soldiers to oppose the rebellion and reminds the reader of the contributions of black soldiers throughout US military history. Americans, the article notes, may have become "forgetful of past experience in [their] two wars with England"—that is, the American Revolution and the War of 1812, both conflicts in which black soldiers fought as members of the American military. Thus, the article suggests, many Americans may have equally forgotten that African American soldiers were more than capable of challenging white soldiers on the battlefield.

Yet the "generous self-sacrifice" of black soldiers in the Civil War battles of Fort Hudson and Milliken's Bend, the author argues, served to reverse that forgetfulness. The battle of Fort Hudson (more commonly known as the Siege of Port Hudson) was one of the first major altercations to involve some of the Union's newly recruited African American soldiers, in this case the first and third Louisiana regiments. Both regiments, known as the Native Guard, were made up mostly of freedmen—the Emancipation Proclamation had freed slaves held within rebelling states at the beginning of the year—and the First Regiment was particularly well known, having formed under free African American officers in New Orleans. As part of the overall campaign against the hotly contested city of Vicksburg, Mississippi, Union forces launched an attack on the Confederate outpost at Port Hudson in late May of 1863. Among the first Union troops to lead the assault against the heavily defended stronghold were the black Louisiana regiments, who fought with great bravery and distinction despite failing to carry the day. One African American officer, historical accounts report, continued to rally his men even after his own arm had been shattered by munitions fire. Like the *Liberator*, white publications throughout the North hailed the black soldiers for their "unsurpassed courage" in this battle, beginning the shift in opinion and expectations of African American troops.

On June 7, 1863, black soldiers fighting in enemy territory again showed their valor. Recently recruited regiments of freedmen successfully repelled a Confederate attack on the Union outpost at Milliken's Bend, a point on the Louisiana side of the Mississippi River not far from Vicksburg. Milliken's Bend had been used as a supply stop and medical center, and many of the troops stationed there were African Americans with little training or battle experience. A force of Confederate troops estimated at about 1,500, under the command of Brigadier General Henry E. McCulloch, attacked the outpost before dawn. Despite suffering heavy casualties, the Union force managed to resist the attack until the arrival of two gunboats helped chase away the Confederate forces in earnest. Particularly notable in the battle was the bravery of the untested black regiments, whom leaders on both sides of the conflict acknowledged as especially effective soldiers. Indeed, the African American soldiers of the Ninth Regiment took the heaviest casualties of the Union forces; 62 of the regiment's men were killed and 130 wounded out of a total force of 285. Because of the high numbers of African American casualties in this and other battles, scholars have speculated that Confederate troops may have specifically targeted black Union soldiers or even killed them after they had surrendered—an action that

violated military ethics. Some black soldiers were taken prisoner by the Confederate forces, and later reports indicated that these men had been enslaved in Texas and not freed until the war's end. In contrast, the *Liberator* claims that "when properly trained and officered, [the African American solider] may be implicitly relied on to observe the rules of honorable warfare." African American soldiers, the article suggests, were not just competent and brave; they were, in fact, more valiant and reliable than the white soldiers of the Rebel army.

The actions of the black troops at Milliken's Bend helped dispel commonly held conceptions within the military and the civilian populace that African American soldiers simply would not fight as diligently or as well as white ones. Military leaders who oversaw the Vicksburg campaign stated that the African American troops had proven themselves, and the assistant secretary of war, Charles Dana, declared that the bravery of the troops at Milliken's Bend had completely changed the way that all black soldiers were viewed at all levels of command. Thus, as the *Liberator* notes, "the last objection" to black recruitment was "removed, and no loyal citizen [could] hesitate to aid in every practicable mode a movement which must prove most efficient in quieting the rebellion." The article's sentiment is clear: no one could reasonably oppose the enlistment of black soldiers for the Union cause, for no logical objection to their efforts existed. This is consistent with the *Liberator*'s ongoing message during the conflict, that African American soldiers must be recruited and deserved pay equal to that of the white soldiers with whom they fought.

Backed by these claims of African American valor and fitness for fighting to both restore the Union and end slavery, the *Liberator* article concludes with a call to moral and financial action in support of the enlistment of black soldiers. The article notes that the publication's readers are certain to support this cause, for it aids the Union at large, a goal obviously compatible with the aims of a group opposed to slavery and the oppression of African Americans.

Reprinted in the article is a standard recruiting message used by the Union Army. Proclaiming itself a message to "men of color," the advertisement notes the delay in recruiting African American soldiers but asserts that the "well or ill-founded" reasons on which that delay was based were no longer considered valid. Instead, the advertisement uses persuasive language and reasoning that seeks to convince the reader to enlist. The Civil

War, it points out, was a conflict concerning issues of great interest to African Americans as well as one that endangered the continuation of a country that had been inhabited by people of African descent for centuries. This country, the advertisement asserts, "now invites [African Americans] to arms in her defense"—a clear call to enlist in the Union Army.

That the black residents of North America had overwhelmingly arrived unwillingly and in chains in the bellies of slave ships was apparently not considered relevant to this patriotic argument, although the advertisement does acknowledge that the experience of African Americans had often been at minimum a difficult and troubled one. The United States, the messages argues, is the place to which for reasons unknown and incomprehensible to humankind, God drew people from their African homes. The conflation of God with human slave traders does not necessarily seem likely to appeal to free African American men who may have been born into slavery, but the comparison does serve to support black racial pride and confidence to an extent. If God was the ultimate force driving Africans to the Americas, then their presence there was divinely ordained and morally proper. If the US government was now acknowledging this propriety, the often-discussed plan to relocate native-born African Americans to colonies in West Africa was at last being accepted as a poor solution to the question of managing the nation's black population. The advertisement attempts to draw in possible troops by suggesting that service in the "fiery furnace" of military conflict could cleanse both white and black Americans of "the sins and the wrongs of the past," allowing a future to emerge in which the nation's African American residents and their descendents might enjoy a more just and equitable stature. This language allowed the advertisement's white authors to admit guilt in the oppression of their readers subtly without condemning the society that they so fervently hoped to sustain in part through African American military action. Black military service, according to those who sought to recruit, thus allowed African Americans both to fulfill their patriotic duty to a country that now acknowledged having treated them unfairly and to prove to the same country that they deserved to be accepted as its legitimate children.

The North American

African Americans in both the Union and the Confederacy responded to that call, largely joining the Union Army in segregated units commanded by white officers. The extent to which the bravery and patriotic spirit of these African American soldiers managed to reshape white opinion of black abilities—at least in the North—is evident in the tone of the 1865 *North American* article reporting on the warm welcome given to African American militia members during a victory march in Harrisburg, Pennsylvania. According to the article, several thousand African American noncombatants joined the returning soldiers on their parade. The author hails the reception of the troops as being "as it should be, respectful and honorable." This language obviously expresses approval of the crowd's welcome of the African American soldiers, affirming that the respect and honor given to these troops was proper and befitting their status as US soldiers.

The next portion of the *North American* article focuses on the congratulatory speech given by Simon Cameron, who had served as secretary of war in Lincoln's cabinet at the outset of the conflict. Cameron had argued for the recruitment of free African Americans as early as 1861; in October of that year, for example, he had authorized military leaders in South Carolina to employ fugitive slaves in their forces. Cameron's tenure in office was short, however, and he was replaced by Edwin Stanton in early 1862, several months before serious consideration of arming black soldiers began. In his speech, Cameron reiterated the bravery and patriotism demonstrated by African American troops in battle, which he declared had "nobly redeemed all [they] promised." He affirmed the idea that African American military service was likely to lead to increased civil rights and hailed black soldiers as having the same claim to self-determination as all other humans. Such language reflected the growing acceptance of African Americans as humans rather than subhuman slaves.

Cameron then briefly outlined the plan for Reconstruction proposed by "a great man . . . able and determined to deal justly with all," President Andrew Johnson. Johnson's plan for Reconstruction was similar to that proposed by his predecessor, Abraham Lincoln, in that it offered a relatively easy path for rejoining the Union to the rebellious states but required them to affirm certain rights and freedoms for their black residents. Among these requirements was the ratification of the Thirteenth Amendment, which outlawed slavery, and a series of measures that eventually became part of the Fourteenth Amendment: equal protection under the law and the right to due process of law, both widely denied to African Americans by state and federal law in the years leading up to the war. Cameron then hailed the emancipation of African Americans, tying this action to the will of God. Just as the 1863 Union military recruitment advertisement claims that God had caused Africans to come to the Americas as slaves, so did the 1865 US military spokesman credit God with ending that institution.

The *North American* article concludes by detailing the formal celebrations that honored the Pennsylvania soldiers' war contributions. A number of military leaders hailed the troops, and the event's religious speaker praised the work done by African Americans "in the struggle for American nationality, civilization and freedom" despite their history of oppression by the country. The keynote speaker expanded upon these recurring themes and again argued for the political and social advancement of the nation's black population as a result of their countrymen's military service. Formal support and respect for the contributions of those soldiers whose offer to enlist had been rejected just four years previously had grown so greatly that the article mentions "distinguished men of color," a concept previously foreign to many in the United States, and the state government hosted a grand ball to honor its soldiers. Truly, African American military service had brought about what decades of antislavery action had failed to achieve: full emancipation and, for a time, increased popular support for black equality.

Essential Themes

The enlistment of African American soldiers in the Union Army both reflected the changing nature of the war and helped encouraged the ultimate Northern victory. Slavery had been a political, economic, and social fact of life in the United States since the earliest colonial era; the majority of white Americans, regardless of whether they supported the expansion of slavery, believed that African Americans were naturally inferior to whites. When the war began, its stated purpose was not to end slavery or enfranchise repressed free blacks but rather to force the rebellious Confederate states to accept the validity of the US federal government. Lincoln and the moderate Republicans opposed the expansion of slavery but not its continuation in the places where it already existed, a stance that allowed them, they believed, to retain the loyalty of those border states that permitted slavery but remained part of the Union. Although the question of slavery was the obvious spark for the conflict, US leaders avowed that the war itself was not fought based on issues of race or slavery.

This stance changed dramatically as the war progressed. A war to maintain the status quo—particularly one as politically contentious as slavery had been since the time of the nation's founding—did little to arouse Northern vigor as the conflict proved a long, costly, and bloody one. Lincoln's decision to issue the Emancipation Proclamation and extend African Americans the opportunity to fight for the Union altered the tenor of the conflict. It was no longer simply a political war fought for the power of one government over another; instead, it was a moral crusade to promote the American ideals of liberty, equality, and democracy. The inclusion in the Union military of African American soldiers, who enlisted despite the knowledge that they were likely to be brutally abused or even killed if captured by Confederate troops in battle, helped carry this wave of sentiment forward. It also provided practical assistance to a military sorely challenged by the Southern forces. The nearly 200,000 African Americans who served in the Northern military—some 10 percent of the total Union Army—were vital to the war effort. African American regiments went on to contribute significantly to battles in Louisiana, Virginia, Tennessee, and South Carolina, among other efforts. During the war, a number of African American soldiers were awarded the Medal of Honor in recognition of their service.

The many African Americans who enlisted in the war effort found their service rewarded during Reconstruction. The so-called Reconstruction amendments went far beyond what might have been expected when the Civil War began in 1861. Slavery was abolished throughout the country. Birthright citizenship and equal protection under the law were extended to all Americans regardless of race. Black men gained the right to vote. Yet racism and discrimination, including in the US military, endured for many decades to come.

Vanessa E. Vaughn, MA

Bibliography

Hargrove, Hondon B. *Black Union Soldiers in the Civil War.* Jefferson: McFarland, 1988. Print.

McPherson, James M. *The Negro's Civil War: How American Black Felt and Acted during the War for the Union.* New York: Vintage, 2003. Print.

Smith, John David, ed. *Black Soldiers in Blue: African American Troops in the Civil War Era.* Chapel Hill: U of North Carolina P, 2002. Print.

Weigley, Russell F., et al. *Philadelphia: A 300-Year History*. New York: Norton, 1982. Print.

Additional Reading

Blackerby, H. C. *Blacks in Blue and Gray: Afro-American Service in the Civil War*. Tuscaloosa: Portals, 1979. Print.

Cornish, Dudley Taylor. *The Sable Arm: Black Troops in the Union Army, 1861–1865*. Lawrence: U of Kansas P, 1987. Print.

Glatthaar, Joseph T. *Forged in Battle: The Civil War Alliance of Black Soldiers and White Officers*. New York: Free, 1990. Print.

Hansen, Joyce. *Between Two Fires: Black Soldiers in the Civil War*. New York: Watts 1993. Print.

Quarles, Benjamin. *The Negro in the Civil War*. Boston: Little, 1969. Print.

■ Abraham Lincoln's Last Public Address

Date: April 11, 1865
Author: Lincoln, Abraham
Genre: speech

> *"Let us all join in doing the acts necessary to restoring the proper practical relations between these states and the Union."*

Summary Overview

Two days after the surrender of General Robert E. Lee and his Confederate States Army, President Abraham Lincoln stood at the White House and addressed a tremendous crowd that had come to hear the president's thoughts on the end of the Civil War. Lincoln shared with the throng his ideas for postwar reconstruction of the South. He also discussed his thoughts on the next course of action to reconcile the differences between the North and South, which included bringing Louisiana back into the Union. Furthermore, Lincoln made a controversial statement on his preference for giving black Americans the right to vote. Lincoln's speech, particularly his comments on black suffrage, was not well received by his opponents, including John Wilkes Booth, who was on hand during the speech and who would assassinate Lincoln in only a matter of days.

Defining Moment

On April 9, 1865, the Union Army had effectively cut off General Lee from the rest of the Confederate Army, having driven him out of Richmond, Virginia, the Confederate capital. Lee and his twenty-eight thousand troops, constantly harassed by the pursuing Union Army and lacking food and supplies, had no choice but to surrender. Lee and his Union counterpart, Ulysses S. Grant, met inside Appomattox Court House, just east of Lynchburg, Virginia. After hearing and agreeing to Grant's terms, Lee and his men were given a meal and were allowed to return to the South as private citizens

once more. Grant turned to his officers and told them, "The war is over. The Rebels are our countrymen again."

The surrender of Lee and his men understandably caused great jubilation across the nation, as four years of violence, bloodshed, and fear had come to an end. It also turned a page in American history, as the attention of the American people turned to reconciliation with the former secessionist Confederate states. President Lincoln was in the unenviable position of both welcoming the joy of the war's end and planning for the immediate next steps with regard to the South. As word quickly spread of Lee's surrender, attention turned to the president and his plans for the reunited country.

On the morning of April 11, two days after the events at Appomattox, the loud reports of celebratory cannon fire from the Washington Navy Yard attracted a crowd of revelers. The rapidly growing crowd, carrying six large cannons with it, moved through the muddy streets of the city. The group approached the White House, anticipating Lincoln's first public words since the surrender. Lincoln came to the window above the main doors of the White House and offered his thoughts on both reconciliation with and the reconstruction of the South.

Lincoln's address to the celebrants who gathered on the White House lawn included some policies he was developing, with regard not only to the South but also to the recently emancipated slaves. These proposals would not sit well with people such as Confederate sympathizer Booth. Lincoln told the audience that another, more formal announcement on the ideas he had just introduced would be coming shortly. After Lincoln's speech, Booth told Lewis Powell, a coconspirator, "That is the last speech he will ever make."

Author Biography

Lincoln was born on February 12, 1809, near Hodgenville, Kentucky, to parents Thomas Lincoln (a farmer and frontiersman) and Nancy Hanks (who died when Abraham was only nine years old). Lincoln and his father moved through the frontier several times after Nancy's death, first to Indiana and later to Illinois. Lincoln's childhood education was basic, a product of his upbringing in the rural areas of the Midwest. For example, his school in Indiana was a log cabin. His father assisted in Lincoln's education. Although his education was limited, young Lincoln developed a love for literature that continued throughout his life. As he grew older, he also gained a strong interest in law.

In 1832, the twenty-three-year-old Lincoln joined the army as a volunteer during the Black Hawk War. He was elected captain of his unit within months of joining and remained involved until the end of the conflict. After the war, Lincoln explored a number of business activities, including work on a riverboat and at his father's store, before he set up a law practice in New Salem, Illinois.

Lincoln soon pursued elected office. He was defeated in his first campaign for the Illinois state legislature. He remained involved in government until his next cam-paign opportunity, holding a number of local appointed positions, such as surveyor and postmaster. He also continued to practice law from his own office. In 1834, he successfully campaigned for the state legislature and was reelected three times thereafter. After retiring from the state legislature, he returned to Springfield, Illinois, where he had established a new law practice after passing the Illinois bar. In 1842, he married Mary Todd, with whom he would have four children, although only one would survive into adulthood.

In 1847, Lincoln was elected, as a member of the Whig Party, to the US House of Representatives, a post he held for one term. In 1855, he ran unsuccessfully for the US Senate. He tried again in 1858, this time as a Republican. In 1860, undaunted by his previous electoral defeats, Lincoln ran successfully for president on the Republican ticket. He was reelected in 1864.

President Lincoln's 1861–65 tenure was marked not just by his Civil War accomplishments. He also helped build the Republican Party, unify the Northern Democrats, bring an end to slavery, and improve relations with the Indians on the American frontier. During his second term, he led the effort to reconcile the nation's relationship with the secessionist South. However, he was unable to complete his work as president: On April 14, 1865, while attending a play at Ford's Theatre in Washington, DC, he was assassinated by John Wilkes Booth. After three days of lying in state in the US Capitol rotunda, he was interred at Oak Grove Cemetery in Springfield.

HISTORICAL DOCUMENT

We meet this evening, not in sorrow, but in gladness of heart. The evacuation of Petersburg and Richmond, and the surrender of the principal insurgent army, give hope of a righteous and speedy peace whose joyous expression can not be restrained. In the midst of this, however, He, from Whom all blessings flow, must not be forgotten. A call for a national thanksgiving is being prepared, and will be duly promulgated. Nor must those whose harder part gives us the cause of rejoicing, be overlooked. Their honors must not be parcelled out with others. I myself, was near the front, and had the high pleasure of transmitting much of the good news to you; but no part of the honor, for plan or execution, is mine. To Gen. Grant, his skilful officers, and brave men, all belongs. The gallant Navy stood ready, but was not in reach to take active part.

By these recent successes the re-inauguration of the national authority—reconstruction—which has had a large share of thought from the first, is pressed much more closely upon our attention. It is fraught with great difficulty. Unlike the case of a war between independent nations, there is no authorized organ for us to treat with. No one man has authority to give up the rebellion for any other man. We simply must begin with, and mould from, disorganized and discordant elements. Nor is it a small additional embarrassment that we, the loyal people, differ among ourselves as to the mode, manner, and means of reconstruction.

As a general rule, I abstain from reading the reports of attacks upon myself, wishing not to be provoked by that to which I can not properly offer an answer. In spite of this precaution, however, it comes to my knowledge that I am much censured for some supposed agency in setting up, and seeking to sustain, the new State Government of Louisiana. In this I have done just so much as, and no more than, the public knows. In the Annual Message of Dec. 1863 and accompanying Proclamation, I presented *a* plan of re-construction (as the phrase goes) which, I promised, if adopted by any State, should be acceptable to, and sustained by, the Executive government of the nation. I distinctly stated that this was not the only plan which might possibly be acceptable; and I also distinctly protested that the Executive claimed no right to say when, or whether members should be admitted to seats in Congress from such States. This plan was, in advance, submitted to the then Cabinet, and distinctly approved by every member of it. One of them suggested that I should then, and in that connection, apply the Emancipation Proclamation to the theretofore excepted parts of Virginia and Louisiana; that I should drop the suggestion about apprenticeship for freed-people, and that I should omit the protest against my own power, in regard to the admission of members to Congress; but even he approved every part and parcel of the plan which has since been employed or touched by the action of Louisiana. The new constitution of Louisiana, declaring emancipation for the whole State, practically applies the Proclamation to the part previously excepted. It does not adopt apprenticeship for freed-people; and it is silent, as it could not well be otherwise, about the admission of members to Congress. So that, as it applies to Louisiana, every member of the Cabinet fully approved the plan. The Message went to Congress, and I received many commendations of the plan, written and verbal; and not a single objection to it, from any professed emancipationist, came to my knowledge, until after the news reached Washington that the people of Louisiana had begun to move in accordance

with it. From about July 1862, I had corresponded with different persons, supposed to be interested, seeking a reconstruction of a State government for Louisiana. When the Message of 1863, with the plan before mentioned, reached New-Orleans, Gen. Banks wrote me that he was confident the people, with his military co-operation, would reconstruct, substantially on that plan. I wrote him, and some of them to try it; they tried it, and the result is known. Such only has been my agency in getting up the Louisiana government. As to sustaining it, my promise is out, as before stated. But, as bad promises are better broken than kept, I shall treat this as a bad promise, and break it, whenever I shall be convinced that keeping it is adverse to the public interest. But I have not yet been so convinced.

I have been shown a letter on this subject, supposed to be an able one, in which the writer expresses regret that my mind has not seemed to be definitely fixed on the question whether the seceded States, so called, are in the Union or out of it. It would perhaps, add astonishment to his regret, were he to learn that since I have found professed Union men endeavoring to make that question, I have *purposely* forborne any public expression upon it. As appears to me that question has not been, nor yet is, a practically material one, and that any discussion of it, while it thus remains practically immaterial, could have no effect other than the mischievous one of dividing our friends. As yet, whatever it may hereafter become, that question is bad, as the basis of a controversy, and good for nothing at all—a merely pernicious abstraction.

We all agree that the seceded States, so called, are out of their proper practical relation with the Union; and that the sole object of the government, civil and military, in regard to those States is to again get them into that proper practical relation. I believe it is not only possible, but in fact, easier, to do this, without deciding, or even considering, whether these states have even been out of the Union, than with it. Finding themselves safely at home, it would be utterly immaterial whether they had ever been abroad. Let us all join in doing the acts necessary to restoring the proper practical relations between these states and the Union; and each forever after, innocently indulge his own opinion whether, in doing the acts, he brought the States from without, into the Union, or only gave them proper assistance, they never having been out of it.

The amount of constituency, so to speak, on which the new Louisiana government rests, would be more satisfactory to all, if it contained fifty, thirty, or even twenty thousand, instead of only about twelve thousand, as it does. It is also unsatisfactory to some that the elective franchise is not given to the colored man. I would myself prefer that it were now conferred on the very intelligent, and on those who serve our cause as soldiers. Still the question is not whether the Louisiana government, as it stands, is quite all that is desirable. The question is "Will it be wiser to take it as it is, and help to improve it; or to reject, and disperse it?" "Can Louisiana be brought into proper practical relation with the Union *sooner* by *sustaining*, or by *discarding* her new State Government?"

Some twelve thousand voters in the heretofore slave-state of Louisiana have sworn allegiance to the Union, assumed to be the rightful political power of the State, held elections, organized a State government, adopted a free-state constitution, giving the benefit of public schools equally to black and white, and empowering the Legislature to confer the elective franchise upon the colored man. Their Legislature has already voted to ratify the constitutional amendment recently passed by Congress, abolishing slavery throughout the nation. These twelve thousand persons are thus fully committed to the Union, and to perpetual freedom in the state—committed to the very things, and nearly all the things the nation wants—and they ask the nations recognition, and it's assistance to make good their committal. Now, if we reject, and spurn them, we do our utmost to disorganize and disperse them. We in effect say to the white men "You are worthless, or worse—we will neither help you, nor be helped by you." To the blacks we say "This cup of liberty which these, your old masters, hold to your lips, we will dash from you, and leave you to the chances of gathering the spilled and scattered contents in some vague and undefined when, where, and how." If this course, discouraging and paralyzing both white and black, has any tendency to bring Louisiana into proper practical relations with the Union, I have, so far, been unable to perceive it. If, on the contrary, we recognize, and sustain the new government of Louisiana the converse of all this is made true. We encourage the hearts, and nerve the arms of the twelve thousand to adhere to their work, and argue for it, and proselyte for it, and fight for it, and feed it, and grow it, and ripen it to a complete success. The colored man too, in seeing all united for him, is inspired with vigilance, and energy, and daring, to the same end. Grant that he desires the elective franchise, will he not attain it sooner by saving the already advanced steps toward it, than by running backward over them? Concede that the new government of Louisiana is only to what it should be as the egg is to the fowl, we shall sooner have the fowl by hatching the egg than by smashing it?

Again, if we reject Louisiana, we also reject one vote in favor of the proposed amendment to the national constitution. To meet this proposition, it has been argued that no more than three fourths of those States which have not attempted secession are necessary to validly ratify the amendment. I do not commit myself against this, further than to say that such a ratification would be questionable, and sure to be persistently questioned; while a ratification by three fourths of all the States would be unquestioned and unquestionable.

I repeat the question. Can Louisiana be brought into proper practical relation with the Union *sooner* by *sustaining* or by *discarding* her new State Government?

What has been said of Louisiana will apply generally to other States. And yet so great peculiarities pertain to each state; and such important and sudden changes occur in the same state; and, withal, so new and unprecedented is the whole case, that no exclusive, and inflexible plan can safely be prescribed as to details and collaterals. Such exclusive, and inflexible plan, would surely become a new entanglement. Important principles may, and must, be inflexible.

In the present "*situation*" as the phrase goes, it may be my duty to make some new announcement to the people of the South. I am considering, and shall not fail to act, when satisfied that action will be proper.

GLOSSARY

agency: the ability to exert or the exertion of power

apprenticeship: first introduced by British colonists, a policy of "training" freed slaves to be a part of society by performing simple jobs with low wages

elective franchise: the privilege or right to vote

emancipation: a term applied to the policy of liberating slaves in the Confederate states

proselyte: proselytize; to seek the conversion of others to one's own faith or ideals

Document Analysis

Lincoln begins his speech by speaking directly to events that had unfolded only a few days earlier. General Grant's troops were successful in driving the Confederates from Richmond and Petersburg, Virginia, cornering General Lee's men and forcing them to surrender. Lincoln says that he was near the front, witnessing firsthand the Union Army's campaign and transmitting the news to the rest of the United States. However, he insists, he played no part in the army's accomplishments at Appomattox. The honors and recognition, he states, must be bestowed upon Grant and his men.

Lincoln says that what occurred at Appomattox warrants a national celebration, and that the crowd at the White House was there "in gladness of heart" for this accomplishment, for it brought about a quick and "righteous" end to the conflict. This success, he says, deserves a "joyous expression" that cannot be understated. In fact, he says, a national day of thanksgiving was being planned and would soon be established.

Although the Appomattox surrender warranted a national celebration, Lincoln adds, a much more difficult task was at hand in the wake of the war's end. The end of the war reestablished the government in Washington, DC, as the "national authority." This "re-inauguration" of the federal government's authority over the whole country was to be focused on the reconstruction of the United States. However, how Reconstruction (which came to be used as a proper noun to refer to the whole postwar period) was to proceed was a major challenge. Reconciliation with the South had been on the minds of Lincoln and his leadership team since the war began, he says, but now that the war had come to a close, the government needed to act quickly on this issue.

The task of reconciliation and reconstruction was particularly daunting to the American government because there had never before been a conflict like the Civil War, Lincoln says. Independent warring nations were always able to reconcile using treaties, he adds, but there was no vehicle for the US government to use to bring back into the Union the former Confederate states. It would be enough of a challenge to convince the Southern states (and their citizens) to give up their rebellion. There was no single approach, nor a single entity with which to engage on the subject of reconciliation. Lincoln says that the government would need to deal with each entity on an individual basis. If that approach was successful, it could be used as a model for addressing other Southern entities.

Compounding the issue, Lincoln says, was the fact that not every Northern leader had the same ideas about how to address Reconstruction. There would almost certainly be a diversity of views on how to proceed, and Lincoln says that it is no "small additional embarrassment" that the country's leaders are not in agreement on the issue. His argument was not based on a desire to control the nation's policy on Reconstruction. Rather, he is speaking to what he sees as divisive political forces that may actually undermine the entire process.

One major area where Lincoln saw political difficulties was the subject of Louisiana. As he states in the speech, many states and regions in the postwar South would require a different approach for reconciliation. In 1863, Lincoln—in his Proclamation of Amnesty and Reconciliation—had offered the Southern states an opportunity to reintegrate. If 10 percent of the voters in each state followed the rules of emancipation and took an oath of allegiance to the Union, their respective states could be reinstated in the United States, with a full pardon to all its residents. Louisiana, however, had already taken the oath and emancipated its slaves, giving that state a large number of free black citizens under a Unionist government. Seeking to solidify Louisiana's support for the Union during the war, Lincoln reached out to Governor Michael Hahn to broach the subject of allowing black suffrage.

The fact that Lincoln made this move set off a backlash in the North. Many in Congress (including South-friendly members of Lincoln's own Republican Party) bristled at his overtures, deciding that it was best to wait until after the war before returning to this hot-button issue. With the war's end, the divisive rhetoric returned, and the Louisiana issue took center stage.

Lincoln is defensive of his actions during the war, stating that his proposal to Hahn was not made in secret. In fact, he says, when he was presenting his ideas for Reconstruction to Congress in 1863 (referring to the Proclamation of Amnesty and Reconciliation), he "distinctly stated that this was not the only plan which might possibly be acceptable," adding that the executive would not interfere in any way in the states' congressional elections. Furthermore, he states, Louisiana made the decision to emancipate its slaves and follow the guidelines of the proclamation on its own accord. Meanwhile, Lincoln's own cabinet approved of the proclamation, and, he adds, many members of Congress commended Lincoln's proposal.

Furthermore, Lincoln says, there were a number of cabinet and congressional leaders who offered what they deemed improvements to the proclamation—modifications that would have both given more power to Lincoln and applied the Emancipation Proclamation—the landmark declaration bestowing freedom to the slaves of the rebellious Southern states—to states such as Louisiana and Virginia. Put simply, the well-intentioned suggestions of these leaders would likely have generated more controversy than what Lincoln had initially offered. The controversial suggestions were not integrated, but Louisiana continued its policy of emancipation. In fact, Louisiana had gone further than the Emancipation Proclamation had: the new state constitution in Louisiana unilaterally declared emancipation and did away with mandatory apprenticeships for former slaves as well.

Lincoln's comments on Louisiana underscore the hazards of eliminating the practice of slavery. The Emancipation Proclamation did not grant unlimited freedom to all slaves, nor did it provide any sort of guidance for the integration of freed slaves into society. Lincoln says that much of the responsibility for addressing the issue of freed slaves fell to the states that reintegrated. Louisiana simply granted their slaves freedom in the constitution they sent to Washington, DC. In fact, the constitution included another major omission: it was, as Lincoln states, "silent" on the subject of former slaves' right to vote. Lincoln tells the crowd that, despite this omission, Congress approved the constitution, with some members even forwarding commendations for the document's language.

Despite the fact that Louisiana took it upon itself to emancipate its slaves in this manner and that Congress overwhelmingly approved that state's constitution, Lincoln continued to receive criticism. He continued to communicate with the government of Louisiana during that state's reconstruction. Lincoln says he had his doubts about the sincerity of Louisiana's convictions and the viability of its plan, but he refrained from interceding further. Nevertheless, Congress and other leaders, faced with the reality that the state had chosen its own course and potentially allowed for black suffrage, chose to criticize Lincoln for his continued communication with Louisiana's government.

Next, Lincoln speaks to the question of how the states that seceded before and during the war could be reintegrated into the Union. He tells his audience that he was criticized in a letter from a citizen for his stance (or rather his lack thereof) on how and if the states were to be returned to the United States. The issue had long been simmering in Washington, DC. Some believed that the former Confederate states should follow the example of Louisiana, establishing a system of self-government that was both loyal to and represented by the federal government. Others, however, argued that the seceded states should be placed under strict federal control, with all aspects of social services and the economy in the hands of the federal government.

With regard to this question, Lincoln insists that he has no set opinion on the specific form of government the former Confederate states should establish. He clearly understands that there are political motivations for asking this question and states that he finds such a question irrelevant at the time. In the future, the question of the federal government's role in these reintegrated states will be worthy of exploration, he says. However, he adds, the at this early stage of the postwar period, asking such a question only creates divisions in state and federal government and is "good for nothing at all."

Lincoln's refusal to definitively answer the question of the states' relationship with the federal government was in line with the ongoing question of the states' overall status as members of the Union. He says that there is no disagreement that the seceded states had come "out of their proper practical relation with the Union" and that the role of every level of government is to bring these states back to the fold. Here he is echoing the comments he made a month earlier during his second inaugural address: the government should be focused on welcoming back the former Confederate states. At one point in the future, the federal government might explore the nature of the federal-state relationship. However, Lincoln says, the most important pursuit at this stage was to make sure the states were "safely at home," not to ask "whether they had ever been abroad." This action called for the collective effort of all involved.

Lincoln maintained this stance when referring to the Louisiana question. He says that it would be more favorable if the number of people living and voting in that state totaled as much as fifty thousand rather than twelve thousand. The black residents of Louisiana played an integral role in this pursuit, he adds. Regardless of whether Louisiana's government took the shape preferred by Lincoln, Congress, or anyone else, Lincoln says, is irrelevant. The more pressing question at hand, he states, is whether Louisiana can sooner be brought back into "practical relation" with the Union by allowing it to keep or discard its current form of government.

Lincoln continues to underscore his point by describing how Louisiana has progressed since opting to return to the Union. The state, he said, had twelve thousand voters agree to swear allegiance to the United States. It also adopted a viable constitution, held elections, established a government, and gave the proper authority to that government. Louisiana also decided to offer both the same public school benefit to black residents that it gave to white citizens and to extend suffrage to black residents, and it ratified the recently passed constitutional amendment to abolish slavery nationwide. Put simply, Lincoln said, the people of Louisiana had done everything that was expected of them in order for the state to be considered a committed member of the United States. The state looked to the federal government both for recognition of its commitment and for assistance.

If the federal government rejected the Louisiana mode of government, Lincoln says, in effect, it would be turning its back on a loyal member of the Union. Such a course of action would send that state into disarray, undermining its ability and willingness to return to the Union. However, Lincoln says, if the federal government recognizes and encourages Louisiana's reintegration, all twelve thousand residents of that state would commit fully to (and even fight for) the nation. The black population of Louisiana would also be "inspired with vigilance, and energy, and daring" if the nation showed its support for Louisiana's freed blacks. Furthermore, if the federal government pushed away Louisiana's state government, Lincoln warned, the Union would lose one vote for the proposed constitutional amendment to fully abolish slavery in the United States (since the amendment, it was at first proposed, would need to be ratified by three-fourths of the states that had not seceded, as opposed to three-fourths of *all* the states; ultimately it was submitted for ratification to all the states). Ratification might be still be possible, he says, but there would remain questions and doubts about the legitimacy of that ratification if not all of the states voted in favor.

Therefore, Lincoln poses the question: Can Louisiana be brought back into the Union with greater expediency if the federal government approves or disapproves of the state government? This question could be applied to any state, he says. Lincoln's Republican leanings are apparent here, as he suggests that each state should be allowed to devise its own government framework. Each state, after all, will have its own "peculiarities" and immediate priorities to address. It would be imprudent to impose a general and "inflexible" plan on the states, particularly in light of the fact that there was no historical precedent to guide the nation on post–Civil War reconstruction.

Lincoln emphasizes that any exclusive, inflexible plan imposed on the governments of reintegrating states would only create new problems for Reconstruction. He stresses that the important democratic principles of the US government should be upheld and, therefore, remain inflexible aspects for reintegration. Beyond that, however, the federal government should be respectful of the nuances and special features of state governments, particularly as long as those details do not run counter to the values of the United States.

Lincoln's address was designed as a relatively informal speech. Speaking before a celebratory crowd, he provided in broad terms his opinions on the nation's next course of action. Lincoln completed his address by stating that more formal announcements and policies would be coming soon, as the government began the difficult task of postwar reconstruction. Unfortunately, there would be no more addresses on this or any other subject from Lincoln. Three days after his last public address, he was shot, and he died the next day, April 15. The responsibility of postwar reconstruction would fall to Lincoln's successor, Andrew Johnson, and Congress.

Essential Themes

Lincoln's last public address was an informal speech prepared as a large crowd, which gathered in the southeast section of Washington, DC, marched in celebration of the surrender of General Lee and the Confederate forces. Indeed, Lincoln himself was relieved that the end of the war had come. He had been near the front where the Union Army had chased Lee's Confederate troops, and he says during this address that he was immediately made aware of the goings on at Appomattox Court House. Therefore, he had great cause for celebration, but he had already moved past the jubilation for the end of the war and into deep thought about the next steps to take regarding the seceded states. As the crowd gathered in front of the White House, Lincoln shared the generalities of his proposals, all of which were still being developed. Formal announcements on Lincoln's policies concerning Reconstruction, he promised, would be coming in the near future.

Reconstruction was a topic given great consideration while the war continued to rage. The general consensus was that, if seceded state governments made formal declarations of loyalty to the Union and adhered to the general principles of the United States, they would be allowed to reenter the Union. Among the expectations for these states was adherence to the ideals of the Emancipation Proclamation. However, the proclamation was interpreted differently by Louisiana, one of the first states to seek reintegration. This state fully freed its slaves and even explored the idea of black suffrage (its leaders sharing their ideas with Lincoln during his wartime communications with the Louisiana governor).

Lincoln's opinions about emancipation, coupled with his Republican ideologies (which favored states rights over a strong central government), made him an easy target for rival Democrats and pro-Southern Republicans. In his last public address, Lincoln defiantly stated that the federal government should give returning states some flexibility in the creation of state governments loyal to the federal government. Furthermore, he added, the most pressing matter was not low-priority "peculiarities" in the draft constitutions sent to Washington, DC, for approval. There was no historical precedent or set of guidelines to be used for Reconstruction, a fact that led Lincoln to believe that the federal government should be flexible with regard to the foundation of state governments. According to Lincoln, the top concern was the full restoration of the United States. This pursuit, he argued, required the concerted efforts of the president, Congress, and the state governments. He completed his speech by calling upon all Americans to work collectively on the issue of reconciliation and reconstruction. Lincoln was never able to work on these formal policies; one of the audience members would assassinate him only a few days after this public address.

Michael Auerbach, MA

Bibliography

Beschloss, Michael, and Hugh Sidey. "Abraham Lincoln." *White House*. White House Historical Association, 2009. Web. 15 Feb. 2013.

Burton, Vernon. "Lincoln's Last Speech." *College of Liberal Arts and Sciences, University of Illinois*. University of Illinois Board of Trustees, May 2009. Web. 20 Feb. 2013.

"Lincoln, Abraham." *Biographical Directory of the United States Congress*. Biographical Directory of the United States Congress, n.d. Web. 15 Feb. 2013.

"Louisiana and Black Suffrage." *Mr. Lincoln and Freedom*. Lincoln Institute, 2002–13. Web. 20 Feb. 2013.

Additional Reading

Carter, Dan T. *When the War Was Over: The Failure of Self-Reconstruction in the South, 1865–1867*. Baton Rouge: Louisiana State UP, 1985. Print.

Carwardine, Richard. "Lincoln and Emancipation: Black Enfranchisement in 1863 Louisiana." *OAH Magazine of History* 21.1 (2007): 45–46. Web. 4 Apr. 2013.

Foner, Eric. *Reconstruction: America's Unfinished Revolution, 1863–1877*. New York: Harper, 2002. Print.

Holzer, Harold, Edna Greene Medford, and Frank J. Williams. *The Emancipation Proclamation: Three Views (Conflicting Worlds)*. Baton Rouge: Louisiana State UP, 2006. Print.

■ Selections from *Drum Taps* by Walt Whitman

Date: October 1865
Author: Whitman, Walt
Genre: poetry; literature

*"The hospital service, the lint, bandages
and medicines,*

*The women volunteering for nurses, the work begun
for in earnest, no mere parade now;"*

"From the stump of the arm, the amputated hand,

*I undo the clotted lint, remove the slough, wash off
the matter and blood..."*

Summary Overview

In 1865, the Civil War was four years along on its destructive and divided path. Walt Whitman, the author of this document, was keenly involved with the war effort and used his poetry to convey the pride, pain, and horrors which he felt and experienced to the public. Whitman was not of an age to enlist, but he supported the soldiers, and his own friends, by visiting the wounded in hospitals and relating their stories to others. From his unique perspective, that of a published author and wordsmith, Whitman created the following document in which he was able both to convey his pride and patriotism concerning the soldiers that were marching off to fight for the North, and also his sadness at the loss felt by every person who saw a father, husband, brother, or son killed in the fierce fighting that split the country. The theme of military hospitals in this work shows Whitman's own contributions to the war effort and his need to reveal the darker aspects of fighting for one's country.

Defining Moment

Walt Whitman's poems and whole body of work have been used to find beauty in the poet's own surroundings and the events that occurred during his lifetime. But even more than finding beauty, Whitman tried to find truth through his work—truths about life, living, the human condition, and, in the case of this document, *Drum Taps*, about the immeasurable suffering which is ever the companion of war. Much of Whitman's work was not appreciated by the public, at first, owing to the raw quality of the descriptions, which in earlier times tended to be buried by observers/authors in metaphor and ambiguity. But Whitman's fearless portrayal of life gives a modern audience the ability to understand the Civil War in a way that a more traditional understanding of the sequence of events simply cannot.

This document contributes, in other words, to the social understanding of the Civil War. While there are several documents from the era that allude to or even speak plainly about the atrocities that happened during the battles of the Civil War, few are so eloquent on the topic as Whitman's poetry. In the opening poem, "First O Songs for a Prelude," the main feeling stressed is the movement and anticipation felt by Whitman himself and his fellow citizens heading into a fight which he, and they, found to be just and necessary. As the quote above shows, the nurses are prepared to go into battle, but the carnage and the toll of human casualties has not yet been fully understood. In the second quote, however, Whitman has gone to the front lines and spent significant time in military hospitals, tending to the wounded and trying to alleviate their suffering in any way he is able. His later poems, such as "The Wound-Dresser" and "Dirge for Two Veterans," show the growing grief which is a by-product of the war. By examining the differences between the tones of the poems and the material which is his focus, Whitman's distaste for the war and need to help those injured by it comes into focus, showing how war is so much more than the march of booted feet and the beating of drums.

Author Biography

Walt Whitman was born in 1819 in Long Island to a working class family. He had four brothers and two sisters and spent much of his young life moving around New York, while his father speculated on real estate, attempting to turn a profit. Although Whitman is considered to be one of the greatest American poets, his basic schooling was rudimentary at best. Clearly overcoming this lack of fundamental education, Whitman, as a boy, spent many hours in museums and libraries, learning as much as he could, all of which influenced his later works, which are marked by the experiences of his youth. These experiences included becoming a la

borer at age eleven and eventually becoming an apprentice in the printing trade.

Later in his life, Whitman was both a schoolteacher and an author of short fiction stories, which seems unlikely in a man so famous for his poetry. His main career, however, was that of a journalist, which he pursued throughout the 1840s. During this time, he began to write poetry, and, in the early 1850s, published *Leaves of Grass,* one of his most famous and enduring works. After several editions of *Leaves of Grass* were published, Whitman's life was radically altered by the outbreak of the Civil War, with which he became heavily involved, even though, being over 40, he was too old to enlist. He began by visiting wounded friends in the hospital and progressed into becoming a nurse, moving from New York to Washington, D.C., and eventually heading to the battlefield of Fredericksburg. Here, while he was intent on finding out the condition of his brother, he came face to face with the horrors of battle in the 1800s—including the witnessing of amputations and disfigurements as occurred on the battlefield. During this time, Whitman ran errands for wounded soldiers and did anything he could in order to help them to regain some hold on their rapidly changed lives. He continued his work when he returned to Washington, D.C. and it was during these times that he began to write *Drum Taps.* His need to express all aspects of the war created a monumental work highlighting the driving forces behind the Civil War and all its consequences.

Whitman wrote many more poems and was involved in numerous projects after the end of the Civil War. He continued working on *Leaves of Grass* and even helped to have his own biography written by Richard Maurice Bucke, entitled *Walt Whitman.* He continued to be close to his family throughout his life, even living with his brother, George, for some time. After a long and colorful career, Whitman died in 1892 after months of illness which started with a stroke and left him partially paralyzed.

HISTORICAL DOCUMENT

FIRST O SONGS FOR A PRELUDE.

First O songs for a prelude,
Lightly strike on the stretch'd tympanum pride
and joy in my city,
How she led the rest to arms, how she gave the
cue,
How at once with lithe limbs unwaiting a moment
she sprang,
(O superb! O Manhattan, my own, my peerless!
O strongest you in the hour of danger, in crisis! O
truer than steel!)
How you sprang—how you threw off the cos-
tumes of peace with indifferent hand,
How your soft opera-music changed, and the
drum and fife were heard in their stead,
How you led to the war, (that shall serve for our
prelude, songs of soldiers,)
How Manhattan drum-taps led.

Forty years had I in my city seen soldiers parading,
Forty years as a pageant, still unawares the lady of
this teeming and turbulent city,
Sleepless amid her ships, her houses, her incalcu-
lable wealth,
With her million children around her, suddenly,
At dead of night, at news from the south,
Incens'd struck with clinch'd hand the pavement.

A shock electric, the night sustain'd it,
Till with ominous hum our hive at daybreak pour'd
out its myriads.

From the houses then and the workshops, and
through all the doorways,
Leapt they tumultuous, and lo! Manhattan arming.

To the drum-taps prompt,
The young men falling in and arming,
The mechanics arming, (the trowel, the jack-
plane, the blacksmith's hammer, tost aside with pre-
cipitation,)
The lawyer leaving his office and arming, the judge
leaving the court,
The driver deserting his wagon in the street, jump-
ing down, throwing
the reins abruptly down on the horses' backs,
The salesman leaving the store, the boss, book-
keeper, porter, all leaving;

Squads gather everywhere by common consent
and arm,
The new recruits, even boys, the old men show
them how to wear their
accoutrements, they buckle the straps carefully,
Outdoors arming, indoors arming, the flash of the
musketbarrels,
The white tents cluster in camps, the arm'd sen-
tries around, the sunrise cannon and again at sunset,
Arm'd regiments arrive every day, pass through the
city, and embark from the wharves,
(How good they look as they tramp down to the
river, sweaty, with their guns on their shoulders!

How I love them! how I could hug them, with
their brown faces and their clothes and knapsacks
cover'd with dust!)
The blood of the city up--arm'd! arm'd! the cry
everywhere,
The flags flung out from the steeples of churches
and from all the public buildings and stores,
The tearful parting, the mother kisses her son, the
son kisses his mother,
(Loth is the mother to part, yet not a word does
she speak to detain him,)
The tumultuous escort, the ranks of policemen
preceding, clearing the way,
The unpent enthusiasm, the wild cheers of the
crowd for their favorites,
The artillery, the silent cannons bright as gold,
drawn along, rumble lightly over the stones,
(Silent cannons, soon to cease your silence,
Soon unlimber'd to begin the red business;)

All the mutter of preparation, all the determin'd arming,

The hospital service, the lint, bandages and medicines,

The women volunteering for nurses, the work begun for in earnest, no mere parade now;

War! an arm'd race is advancing! the welcome for battle, no turning away;

War! be it weeks, months, or years, an arm'd race is advancing to welcome it.

Mannahatta a-march--and it's O to sing it well!
It's O for a manly life in the camp.

And the sturdy artillery,
The guns bright as gold, the work for giants, to serve well the guns,
Unlimber them! (no more as the past forty years for salutes for courtesies merely,
Put in something now besides powder and wadding.)

And you lady of ships, you Mannahatta,
Old matron of this proud, friendly, turbulent city,
Often in peace and wealth you were pensive or covertly frown'd amid all your children,
But now you smile with joy exulting old Mannahatta.

✳✳✳

THE WOUND-DRESSER.

1

An old man bending I come among new faces,
Years looking backward resuming in answer to children,
Come tell us old man, as from young men and maidens that love me,
(Arous'd and angry, I'd thought to beat the alarum,

and urge relentless war,
But soon my fingers fail'd me, my face droop'd and I resign'd myself,
To sit by the wounded and soothe them, or silently watch the dead;)
Years hence of these scenes, of these furious passions, these chances,
Of unsurpass'd heroes, (was one side so brave? the other was equally brave;)

Now be witness again, paint the mightiest armies of earth,
Of those armies so rapid so wondrous what saw you to tell us?
What stays with you latest and deepest? of curious panics,
Of hard-fought engagements or sieges tremendous what deepest remains?

2

O maidens and young men I love and that love me,
What you ask of my days those the strangest and sudden your talking recalls,
Soldier alert I arrive after a long march cover'd with sweat and dust,
In the nick of time I come, plunge in the fight, loudly shout in the rush of successful charge,
Enter the captur'd works--yet lo, like a swift-running river they fade,
Pass and are gone they fade--I dwell not on soldiers' perils or soldiers' joys,
(Both I remember well-many the hardships, few the joys, yet I was content.)
But in silence, in dreams' projections,
While the world of gain and appearance and mirth goes on,
So soon what is over forgotten, and waves wash the imprints off the sand,
With hinged knees returning I enter the doors, (while for you up there,
Whoever you are, follow without noise and be of strong heart.)

Bearing the bandages, water and sponge,
Straight and swift to my wounded I go,

Where they lie on the ground after the battle brought in,
Where their priceless blood reddens the grass the ground,
Or to the rows of the hospital tent, or under the roof'd hospital,
To the long rows of cots up and down each side I return,
To each and all one after another I drawn near, not one do I miss,
An attendant follows holding a tray, he carries a refuse pail,
Soon to be fill'd with clotted rags and blood, emptied, and fill'd again.

I onward go, I stop,
With hinged knees and steady hand to dress wounds,
I am firm with each, the pangs are sharp yet unavoidable,
One turns to me his appealing eyes-poor boy! I never knew you,
Yet I think I could not refuse this moment to die for you, if that would save you.

3

On, on I go, (open doors of time! open hospital doors!)
The crush'd head I dress, (poor crazed hand tear not the bandage away,)
The neck of the cavalry-man with the bullet through and through I examine,
Hard the breathing rattles, quite glazed already the eye, yet life struggles hard,
(Come sweet death! be persuaded O beautiful death!
In mercy come quickly.)

From the stump of the arm, the amputated hand,

I undo the clotted lint, remove the slough, wash off the matter and blood,
Back on his pillow the soldier bends with curv'd neck and side-falling head,
His eyes are closed, his face is pale, he dares not look on the bloody stump,
And has not yet look'd on it.

I dress a wound in the side, deep, deep,
But a day or two more, for see the frame all wasted and sinking,
And the yellow-blue countenance see.
I dress the perforated shoulder, the foot with the bullet-wound,
Cleanse the one with a gnawing and putrid gangrene, so sickening, so offensive,
While the attendant stands behind aside me holding the tray and pail.
I am faithful, I do not give out,
The fractur'd thigh, the knee, the wound in the abdomen,
These and more I dress with impassive hand, (yet deep in my breast a fire, a burning flame.)

4

Thus in silence in dreams' projections,
Returning, resuming, I thread my way through the hospitals,
The hurt and wounded I pacify with soothing hand,
I sit by the restless all the dark night, some are so young,
Some suffer so much, I recall the experience sweet and sad,
(Many a soldier's loving arms about this neck have cross'd and rested,
Many a soldier's kiss dwells on these bearded lips.)

GLOSSARY

coterie: a group of people who associate closely

delicatesse: delicate or dainty; a French word, now out of use

gangrene: necrosis or death of soft tissue due to obstructed circulation

jack-plane: a plane for rough surfacing; used for general smoothing of edges

lint: a soft material for dressing wounds, usually made from treated linen cloth

loth: unwilling; reluctant (Middle English form); now loath

nimbus: a cloud, aura, atmosphere; halo

rude: rough in manners or behavior; harsh; ungentle

slough: cast-off skin; a mass of dead tissue separating from an ulcer

tympanum: a drum or similar instrument; a stretched membrane forming a drumhead

Document Analysis

In the numerous poems that make up Walt Whitman's *Drum Taps*, several are devoted specifically to the suffering of soldiers and those selfless individuals who are their caregivers. Furthermore, while the wounded may not be specifically referred to in each poem, the theme of military aid and the wounded carries through the compilation of the separable poems in order to express fully the magnitude and depth of Whitman's own experiences. By focusing an analysis on two poems from *Drum Taps*, "First O Songs for a Prelude" and "The Wound-Dresser," readers are able to understand how Whitman's views of the war changed steadily as he became more aware of the hardships and tragedies which are associated with battle. The glory and pride demonstrated in the first poem of *Drum Taps* are replaced by disgust for the pain of the wounded and hatred for the battles which caused them.

"First O Songs for a Prelude"

In Whitman's opening poem, "First O Songs for a Prelude," he begins with an uplifting and proud image of a city coming to life in order to defend the values of its citizens and not submitting to the injustices, as they saw them, committed by the Confederacy. Whiteman here describes Manhattan, or New York City, as leading the rest of the country into war—springing into action and being strong in the face of danger and adversity. All of which sounds wonderful, for a city fighting for its beliefs and for freedom strikes a poignant chord with readers of all times and generations. Patriotism was not less known to those of Walt Whitman's time than it is to modern readers. The ability for a city to throw off its normal daily routine in order to face some unknown difficulty ignites pride in those who learn of the sacrifice. As Whitman states, the high culture—the "opera-music"—was given up for the fight—the "drum and fife." The movement shown in the first stanza of the poem leads Whitman and his readers into war, standing as an opening act to what is to come.

The next stanzas continue the set tone—a city hurdling toward war. Whitman describes the soldiers as "parading" and the whole affair as a "pageant"—strong images, but still overwhelmingly positive in their usage. The horrors that these soldiers, and even the civilians, would soon see have little place in this poem. The city and her inhabitants were galvanized by the actions of the South, and Whitman catches that somewhat frenetic movement in his poetry. The people do not just rise to the occasion, they run at it full force. Little of the poem is dedicated to the darker aspects of war, although he does use such phrases as "ominous hum" and "loth is the mother to part." The main attitude is concentrated on the overwhelming force that the city has created and pushes toward the front lines.

Whitman spends many lines of the poem paying homage to those who walked away from their lives in order to become soldiers—everyone from cart drivers to judges. The young men are tutored by the old, and droves of men come together in order to form a fighting force. Whitman states that he loves them, each and every one, and here he is most likely presenting the attitude of most of the Union citizens, supporting the army with positive thoughts and prayers. He even spends several lines to praise those who act in supporting roles—specifically, nurses—little knowing that he himself would soon join their ranks. It is in this stanza that he speaks to the fact that from this point on war will no longer be pretty parades and simple drum beats: "...the work begun for in earnest, no mere parade now." In the last few lines, praise mixes with trepidation, for he knows that not all the boys and men will be returning home and even those who do will never be the same.

"The Wound-Dresser"

This poem is essentially Walt Whitman's personal account of his time in a battlefield hospital. The very title, "Wound-Dresser," is more than probably a reference to the role that Whitman himself filled many times during battles and in the bloody aftermath. The most essential idea of this poem is in its comparison to the opening poem of *Drum Taps*, "First O Songs for a Prelude." Unlike the forward movement evoked by that poem, "The Wound-Dresser" has a feeling of unrelenting despair and a lack of movement similar to being caught and held by the pain of those around him. Even though many years are referenced and the opening lines speak of a man growing old, there is no change in his life, just the pain of those with whom he sits.

As he says, battles come and go, but something that is every changing, and something that must be learned by the young and inexperienced, is that pain and death are the companions of war, far more so than bravery and heroism. The second stanza focuses on the fleeting nature of the battle itself, the charge and the rush of the fight fade quickly and only the bad things, "many the hardships," are remembered by the survivors. The wound-dresser speaks of his more prominent role, not as a fighter but as an aid to those wounded, possibly drastically or even fatally, in battle. He invites his audience to follow him into the hospitals, but warns that

a "strong heart" is necessary to look upon the carnage with which he now deals.

Beginning with the wound-dresser carrying in bandages, Whitman's descriptions are poetic but do not dive straight into the horrors that he saw. It is a slow build—first, the soldiers lying on the battlefield after the fighting has ceased, unable to move under their own power, their blood flowing into the grass. Second, a more horrifying scene—the rows upon rows of injured soldiers in battlefield hospitals, pails used to dispose of bloody rags and anything else employed. Then, the more personal descriptions of pain and suffering begin. The soldier who pleads with eyes for some end. The soldier who has lost his sense from the blows to his skull. The member of the cavalry who knows he is dying but is not ready yet to give up and leave the world, even though death is now more merciful than life. Then begin the descriptions of the amputations, the gangrene, the shattered bones— even if the soldiers live through their wounds and the terrible conditions of their sick beds, even then their lives will no longer be the same.

The wound-dresser, Whitman himself, does his best to take care of these men who are dependent upon him, and others like him, for their lives. He is sickened by what he sees, but he is also "impassive," for he has to become immune to the suffering or else empathy would destroy him as well. He would not be able to help those who are in such a desperate need if he could not push down his reactions and simply do what needs to be done. This does not mean that he feels nothing—"yet deep in my breast a fire, a burning flame." He clearly cares about these men, or he would just go home. Whitman went to the battlefield in order to check on his brother, but this short errand turned into something much more complex—a need to stay and do whatever he could for the wounded soldiers.

These experiences marked him for the rest of his life. He even writes in his last stanza that in his dreams he returns to the battlefield and continues to wipe the brows of the injured. He sees the dying faces of young boys and remembers how he tried to comfort them in their darkest moments or just before they passed. While he never displays any contempt for the wounded, his disgust, while not emphasized in the poem, is rightly placed with the war that brought the wounded so low. No parade or victory makes up for the lost limbs and lost lives. At best, it allows their sacrifice not to be in vain. Whitman uses his experiences to show his audience the true cost of war and to honor those with whom he interacted, whether they survived or not.

The differences in tone and wealth of experience between "First O Song for the Prelude" and "The Wound-Dresser" highlight Walt Whitman's experiences during the Civil War. At the conclusion he was no longer the wide-eyed, hopeful, and slightly naïve man who wrote the opener for *Drum Taps*. Through his experiences he became almost imbued with the need to help those who suffered and was not able to turn his back on them. While this was not a trait unique to Whitman, he expressed it in a more eloquent manner than many would be able to pen. War for him, and for many others, was no longer the beating of drums and the push to right the wrongs committed by the South, but a thing of pain, suffering, and death which scarred the nation and had a profound effect on every individual—soldier, noncombatant, or civilian.

Essential Themes

War is too often thought of as the heroic actions of individuals and the glorious victories of generals. This is especially true when the horrors of war become overshadowed by the ultimate triumphs, which in the Civil War are remembered mainly as the emancipation of the southern slaves and returning the Confederate states to the fold of a united America. Walt Whitman, having experienced all aspects of war first hand, thought to expose not only the positive aspects of the Civil War—the patriotism and the fight for freedom felt by so many—but also the carnage and the destruction. In order that the public was able to absorb his experiences, by proxy, he used his poetry to highlight reasons to avoid war and how it affects soldiers and all other noncombatants. Soldiers suffered bullets and shrapnel wounds, limbs broken by cannon fire and other projectiles, and, possibly the most horrifying, amputation without truly proper medical care and conditions. But soldiers were not the only ones to suffer. In such a war, where family member could fight family member, families were torn apart, lands were destroyed and drowned in blood, and the survivors were forever haunted by what they had seen and done to survive. While Whitman couches these horrors in the softer form of poetry, he is able to bring light to these dire straits, in that manner for which he is revered. Even now, over a hundred and fifty years later, readers may look upon Whitman's work and see not the idealized view of war, which is too often portrayed, but a gritty and true-to-life portrayal, from which lessons can be learned and, possibly, lives saved.

Anna Accettola, M.A.

Bibliography

Folsom, Ed, and Kenneth M. Price. *"Walt Whitman."* The Walt Whitman Archive, n.d. Web. 21 Aug. 2013.

Whitman, Walt. *Drum Taps*. New York: Grosset and Dunlap, 1865. Print.

Additional Reading

Bucke, Richard Maurice. *Walt Whitman*. D. McKay, 1883. Print.

Buinicki, Martin T. *Walt Whitman's Reconstruction: Poetry and Publishing between Memory and History*. Iowa City: U of Iowa P, 2011. Print.

Morris, Roy. *The Better Angel: Walt Whitman in the Civil War*. Oxford: Oxford UP, 2000. Print.

Roper, Robert. *Now the Drum of War: Walt Whitman and His Brothers in the Civil War*. New York: Walker, 2008. Print.

"The Walt Whitman Archive." *Center for Digital Research in the Humanities*. Ed. Ed Folsom and Kenneth M. Price. U of Nebraska, Lincoln. Web.

Walt Whitman. Public Broadcasting Service. New York: Films Media, 2008. Electronic Resource.

"Walt Whitman at Chatham." *National Park Service*. U.S. Department of the Interior, Web.

■ "The Conclusion of the Battle of Gettysburg"

Date: July 6, 1863
Author: Wilkeson, Samuel
Genre: article; editorial; report

"...more marvelous to me than anything I have ever seen in a war—are a ghastly and shocking testimony to the terrible fight of the Second corps that none will gainsay."

Summary Overview

This document, which is a description of the finale of the Battle of Gettysburg, was written not only to detail and narrate the scenes which Samuel Wilkeson had been sent to report upon, but also to communicate his own pain, caused by the brutal death of his son at the same battle. Even though his pain is apparent in the document, his pride at his countrymen and distaste for such a gruesome affair also shine through. The quote above defines his own feelings toward the battle—not that it is something to be praised, but that it is so horrible that he can barely comprehend its magnitude, nor will anyone else be able to do so either. While there were many reports of Gettysburg, this is perhaps the only one written with ink infused with so much heart and sorrow of the journalist.

Defining Moment

The subject of this document was clearly the Battle of Gettysburg, which took place in Gettysburg, Pennsylvania from July 1, 1863 through July 3, 1863. In this battle, which is infamous for having the highest number of casualties in any battle of the Civil War, Major General George Gordon Meade led the Union troops against the Confederates, led by General Robert E. Lee. This was the second attempt by General Lee to invade the North. This three-day battle ended with Lee's forces being turned back and a victory for the Union. Further-

more, General Lee and the Confederate forces did not plan any more offensive maneuvers against the North. Since that time, the Battle of Gettysburg has been the subject of much fascination by historians, both professional and amateur. And while not considered a particularly important battle at the time, it is now regarded as a pivotal moment in the Civil War.

This document was written by Samuel Wilkeson as part of his job reporting for *The New York Times*. As such, his audience was any subscriber to his newspaper during the time period in which the report was published. It contributed to both the social and political feeling of the time. Because the newspaper was the only way in which contemporary people could learn about the events of the war, reporters had significant influence over the population. Through their reports they could highlight the horrors of war, incite passion and patriotism for the cause and the troops, and even sway public opinion. There were many reports from the Battle of Gettysburg, for forty-five reporters were sent in to the town in order to gather information. The styles of these reports varied by the individual reporters' backgrounds and personal influences. One such reporter was Thomas Morris Chester of the *Philadelphia Press*, who was the first black reporter in the Civil War to work for a major newspaper. Many of his reports had a distinct trend toward reporting the events as they concerned African American troops, which would clearly show his own personal interests. Likewise, while doing his duty to report the facts about the battle, Samuel Wilkeson was also able to express his horror at the bloodshed and his own grief from the loss of his son. Such intricacies set him, and other reporters, apart from any simpler, dry recitation of the events.

Author Biography

The life story of Samuel Wilkeson has been somewhat obscured by time, but his work for the *New York Times* during the Civil War has insured his name in history. Born in 1817, he is best known for his work with the *Times* and for his reporting on the Battle of Gettysburg during the Civil War. One of 500 correspondents who were assigned and embedded with the soldiers fighting in the Civil War, Samuel Wilkeson was also one of forty-five reporters who reported directly on the Battle of Gettysburg.

Wilkeson was from a wealthy and affluent family, his father, also Samuel Wilkeson, helped to found the city of Buffalo. He was married to Catherine Cady, sister of the famous social activist Elizabeth Cady Stanton.

They had several sons. Samuel had been assigned to cover the events in which the Army of the Potomac was involved, including the Battle of Gettysburg. Overcoming his own personal loss at the death of one of his sons, Lieutenant Bayard Wilkeson, at the Battle of Gettysburg, who was nineteen years old at the time, Samuel managed to complete his assignment and published the following report on the battle.

A year after this battle, his younger son, Frank Wilkeson, ran away from home to join the military, lying about his age, as he was only fourteen years old at the time. Samuel Wilkeson lived long enough to see this same son, having survived his time spent fighting in many battles in the Civil War, follow in his father's footsteps and being a journalist for the *New York Times*. While not much more is known about Samuel Wilkeson, his name and the names of his family members have an indelible place in United States history. Samuel Wilkeson died in 1889, but his work continues to shed light on one of the most infamous and bloody battles of the Civil War.

HISTORICAL DOCUMENT

Who can write the history of a battle whose eyes are immovably fastened upon a central figure of transcendingly absorbing interest—the dead body of an oldest born, crushed by a shell in a position where a battery should never have been sent, and abandoned to death in a building where surgeons dared not to stay?

The battle of Gettysburgh! I am told that it commenced, on the 1st of July, a mile north of the town, between two weak brigades of infantry and some doomed artillery and the whole force of the rebel army. Among other costs of this error was the death of Reynolds. Its value was priceless, however, though priceless was the young and the old blood with which it was bought. The error put us on the defensive, and gave us the choice of position. From the moment that our artillery and infantry rolled back through the main street of Gettysburgh and rolled out of the town to the circle of eminences south of it. We were not to attack but to be attacked. The risks, the difficulties and the advantages[?] of the coming battle were the enemy's. Our[s] were the heights for artil-

lery; ours the short, inside lines for manoeuvering and reinforcing; ours the cover of stonewalls, fences and the crests of hills. The ground upon which we were driven to accept battle was wonderfully favorable to us. A popular description of it would be to say that it was in from an elongated and somewhat sharpened horseshoe, with the toe to Gettysburgh and the heel to the south.

Lee's plan of battle was simple. He manned his troops upon the east side of this shoe of position, and thundered on it obstinately to break it. The shelling of our batteries from the nearest overlooking hill, and the unflinching courage and complete discipline of the army of the Potomac repelled the attack. It was renewed at the point of [sic] the shoe—renewed desperately at the southwest heel—-renewed on the western side with an effort consecrated to success by Ewell's earnest oaths, and on which the fate of the invasion of Pennsylvania was fully put at stake. Only a perfect infantry and an artillery educated in the midst of charges of hostile brigades could possibly have sustained this assault. Hancock's corps did sustain it, and has covered itself with immortal honors by its constancy and courage. The total wreck of Cushing's battery—the list of its killed and wounded—the losses of officers, men and horses Cowen [sic] sustained-and the marvellous outspread upon the board of death of dead soldiers and dead animals—of dead soldiers in blue, and dead soldiers in gray—more marvellous to me than anything I have ever seen in war—are a ghastly and shocking testimony to the terrible fight of the Second corps that none will gainsay. That corps will ever have the distinction of breaking

the pride and power of the rebel invasion.

For such details as I have the heart for. The battle commenced at daylight, on the side of the horse-shoe position, exactly opposite to that which Ewell had sworn to crash through. Musketry preceded the rising of the sun. A thick wood veiled this fight, but out of its leafy darkness arose the smoke and the surging and swelling of the fire, from intermittent to continuous, and crushing, told of the wise tactics of the rebels of attacking in force and changing their troops. Seemingly the attack of the day was to be made through that wood. The demonstration was protracted—it was absolutely preparative; there was no artillery fire accompanying the musketry, and shrewd officers in our western front mentioned, with the gravity due to the fact, that the rebels had felled trees at intervals upon the edge of the wood they occupied in face of our position. These were breastworks for the protection of artillery men.

Suddenly, and about 10 in the forenoon, the firing on the east side, and everywhere about our lines, ceased. A silence as of deep sleep fell upon the field of battle. Our army cooked, ate and slumbered. The rebel army moved 130 guns to the west, and massed there Longstreet's corps and Hill's corps, to hurl them upon the really weakest point of our entire position.

Eleven o'clock-twelve o'clock-one o'clock. In the shadow cast by the tiny farm house 10 by 20, which Gen. Meade had made his Headquarters, lay wearied staff officers and tired reporters. There was not wanting to the peacefulness of the scene the singing of a bird, which had a nest in a peach tree within the tiny yard of the whitewashed cottage. In the midst of its warbling, a shell screamed over the house, instantly followed by another, and another, and in a moment the air was full

of the most complete artillery prelude to an infantry battle that was ever exhibited. Every size and form of shell known to British and to American gunnery shrieked, whirled, moaned, whistled and wrathfully fluttered over our ground. As many as six in a second, constantly two in a second, bursting and screaming over and around the headquarters, made a very hell of fire that amazed the oldest officers. They burst in the yard—burst next to the fence on both sides, garnished as usual with the hitched horses of aids[sic] and orderlies. The fastened animals reared and plunged with terror. Then one fell, then another—sixteen lay dead and mangled before the fire ceased, still fastened by their halters, which gave the expression of being wickedly tied up to die painfully. These brute victims of a cruel war touched all hearts. Through the midst of the storm of screaming and exploding shells, an ambulance, driven by its frenzied conductor at full speed, presented to all of us the marvelous spectacle of a horse going rapidly on three legs. A hinder one had been shot off at the hock. A shell tore up the little step of the Headquarters Cottage, and ripped bags of oats as with a knife. Another soon carried off one of the two pillars. Soon a spherical case burst opposite the open door—another lipped through the low garret. The remaining pillar went almost immediately to the howl of a fixed shot that Wentworth must have made. During this fire the houses at twenty and thirty feet distant, were receiving their death, and soldiers in Federal blue were tom to pieces in the road and died with the peculiar yells that blend the extorted cry of pain with horror and despair. Not an orderly—not an ambulance—not a stragger [sic] was to be seen upon the plain swept by this tempest of orchestral death thirty minutes after it commenced. Were not one hundred and twenty pieces of artillery, trying to out from the field every battery we had in position to resist their purposed infantry attack, and to sweep away the light defences behind which our infantry were waiting? Forty minutes—fifty minutes—counted on watches that ran! Oh so languidly. Shells through the two lower rooms. A shell into the chimney that daringly did not explode. Shells in the yard. The air thicker and fuller and more deafening with the howling and whirring of those infernal missiles. The chief of staff struck—Seth Williams loved and respected through the army, separated from instant death by two inches of space vertically measured. An Aide bored with a fragment of iron through the bone of the arm. Another, out with an exploded piece. And the time measured on the sluggish watches was one hour and forty minutes.

Then there was a lull, and we knew that the rebel infantry was charging. And splendidly they did this work-the highest and severest test of the stuff that soldiers are made of. Hill's division, in line of battle, came first on the double-quick. Their muskets at the "right-shoulder-shift." Longstreet's came as the support, at the usual distance, with war cries and a savage insolence as yet untutored by defeat. They rushed in perfect order across the open field up to the very muzzles of the guns, which tore lanes through them as they came. But they met men who were their equals in spirit, and their superiors in tenacity. There never was better fighting since Thermopyalae than was done yesterday by our infantry and artillery. The rebels were over our defenses. They had cleaned cannoniers and horses from one of the guns, and were whirling it around to use upon us. The bayonet drove them back. But so hard pressed was this brave infantry that at one time, from the exhaustion of their ammunition, every battery upon the principal crest of attack was silent, except Crowen's. [sic] His service of grape and cannister was awful. It enabled our line, outnumbered two to one, first to beat back Longstreet, and then to charge upon him, and take a great number of his men and himself prisoners.

Strange sight! So terrible was our musketry and artillery fire, that when Armistead's brigade was checked in its charge, and stood reeling, all of its men dropped their muskets and crawled on their hands and knees underneath the stream of shot till close to our troops, where they made signs of surrendering. They passed through our ranks scarcely noticed, and slowly went down the slope to the road in the rear.

Before they got there the grand charge of Ewell, solemnly sworn to and carefully prepared, had failed.

The rebels had retreated to their lines, and opened anew the storm of shell and shot from their 120 guns. Those who remained at the riddled headquarters will never [forget] the crouching, and dodging, and running, of the Butternut-colored captives when they got under this, their friends, fire. It was appalling to as good soldiers even as they were.

What remains to say of the fight? It staggled [sic] warily on the middle of the horse shoe on the west, grew big and angry on the heel at the southwest, lasted there till 8 o'clock in the evening, when the fighting Sixth corps went joyously by as a reinforcement through the wood, bright with coffee pots on the fire.

I leave details to my excellent friend and associate Mr. Henry. My pen is heavy. Oh, you dead, who at Gettysburgh have baptized with your blood the second birth of Freedom in America, how you are to be envied! I rise from a grave whose wet clay I have passionately kissed, and I look up and see Christ spanning this battlefield with his feet and reaching fraternal and lovingly up to heaven. His right hand opens the gate of Paradise—with his left he beckons to these mutilated, bloody, swollen forms to ascend.

GLOSSARY

battery: two or more pieces of artillery used for combined action

bayonet: a daggerlike steel weapon attached to or at the muzzle of a gun and used for stabbing or slashing in hand-to-hand combat

breastworks: a defensive work; usually breast high

cannister: now called canister shot; similar to grapeshot but the balls were smaller and more numerous

cannoniers: a person who manages, or fires, a canon

Ewell: Richard Stoddert Ewell, United States Army officer and a Confederate General

gainsay: to deny, dispute, or contradict

grape: also called grapeshot; not one solid element, but a mass of small metal balls or slugs tightly packed in a canvas bag

hock: the joint in the hind leg of a horse, cow, etc.

Reynolds: John Fulton Reynolds, United States Army officer and a Union General

straggled: to stray from the road, course, or line of march; to spread or be spread in a scattered fashion

stragger: to move or stand unsteadily

Thermopyalae: also spelled Thermopylae; mainly known for the Battle of Thermopylae where Greek, including Spartan, and Persian forces met for one battle of the Greco-Persian Wars

Document Analysis

This document reports the details of the Battle of Gettysburg from the point of view of a spectator, but not just any spectator, that of a trained professional journalist working for the *New York Times* who had lost his son in that same battle, simply a day before he arrived on the scene. From the first sentence, Samuel Wilkeson shows his dedication to his son and his overwhelming grief for his violent and brutal death. His apparent confusion about how to do his job while in the throes of such depression is infused into every word. This is the aspect of Wilkeson's article that most sets his report apart from other descriptions of the Battle of Gettysburg—his blatant grieving for his son mixed with his ability still to recount the details of the battle and strategies of each side of the conflict. Wilkeson truly shows his merit as a writer, however, by using poetic language and descriptions to enrich his descriptions and paint for his audience the landscape of the battle.

Expressions of Grief and the Details of the Battle

Wilkeson's first paragraph clearly gives a voice to the pain which was so overwhelming to him. With the words "in a position where a battery should never have been sent," Wilkeson both shows a parent's hate for the battle and conditions surrounding a child's death and criticizes the battle strategy. But by acknowledging his loss, and then putting that pain aside momentarily, Wilkeson is able to describe for his audience the events of the battle. Beginning with a description of the start of the battle, he then proceeds to outline the strategy of the Confederate leaders. These sentences may reveal that he did not approve of the strategy which was used by the Union generals, although it did lead to a victory for the Union. The geographical placement of the Battle of Gettysburg was more one of chance than true planning, with delays and issues with leadership obstructing General Robert E. Lee's attempt to move his army to the north against the Union. The actual placement of troops almost entirely favored the Northern side of the conflict, with men, such as Wilkeson's son, placed on hilltops and in strategic and defensively sound areas. But, as with any battle, men on both sides were injured and killed. Unfortunate though it was, bad luck had more to do with Wilkeson's son being hit by a mortar shell and dying of shock than any poorly placed battlement.

As Wilkeson states, beginning in the second paragraph, the battle commenced on the 1st of July and General Lee was immediately faced with several issues that led to the Union gaining an upper hand that they would not relinquish for the rest of the battle. Even though Wilkeson reports that "Reynolds," whose full name and title is Union General John Fulton Reynolds, was killed in the initial skirmish, before the full force of the Union troops could arrive, Lee was not able to do more than move into the weak position that his troops occupied for the remaining of the fighting. Wilkeson spends the rest of the paragraph describing the land upon which the battle was fought—its disadvantages for the Confederate troops and the advantages for the Union soldiers. Wilkeson continues by describing the movement of Lee's army, his use of shelling, and the Union troops who, valiantly in his opinion, held off the barrage.

The end of the third paragraph, however, has a slightly different tone than a strict report of the details of the battle. As is highlighted in the quote above, Wilkeson describes the losses suffered by the Union infantry and artillery on account of the continuous shelling by the Confederates as "more marvelous to me than anything I have ever seen in war." This editorializing enlivens his report from a dry retelling of the facts, which could be done by anyone who saw the battle and had a basic understanding of battle tactics and strategy. Because Wilkeson knew there was more to journalism than a simple recitation of events, he was able to create a narrative which brought the far-away scene of the battle home to those who could only learn of it through his article. Mothers, fathers, wives, husbands, and children all had to wait for journalists to give them the details about those battles which took their family members away from them and into danger. A soulless recitation of events only gives information detached from experience, but in order to be able to comprehend the war which the country had been embroiled in for so long, personal reactions were also necessary.

The Poetry of the Battle

He takes his article to another level of beauty, however, when Wilkeson begins to describe the battle scene using poetic rhetoric. When he writes the fourth paragraph of his report, Wilkeson begins to expand on his basic descriptions using more flowery terms in order to convey the dramatic effect of the battle. With such phrases as "out of the leafy darkness" and "a silence as of deep sleep" color the description of one push of the battle so that it is no longer in the realm of dry retelling. By using such language, Wilkeson was able to aid his readers in becoming a part of the scene and better understanding the tension, pain, and bleakness that haunts a battlefield. Without his ability to weave so eloquent a narrative, much of his contemporary audience would not have been able to identify with those who fought, were injured, and died upon that piece of ground.

Wilkeson continues his narration with juxtaposition of peace and destruction. The quiet and still morning was broken by the sound of a bird, warbling from its perch. This idyllic scene is then shattered by the commencement of Confederate shelling. Later, Wilkeson relates the image of a horse running on three legs, the "hinder one having been shot off at the hock." Where a running horse should inspire a lightness of spirit and awe at natural beauty and grace, this one only inspires horror. By using such imagery, Wilkeson uses common events—the singing of a bird and the running of a horse—to show his audience the battle and give them something to which they could relate. While many of his readers would never have seen a battle or known the shock of a wounded soldier firsthand, they would all know the morning call of a bird in a tree or how a horse looks pulling a carriage or running through a field.

The last section of Wilkeson's article is devoted to the ending of the battle, the fierce fighting and the eventually defeat of the Confederate forces. While not as poetic as the preceding sections, his pride in the Union troops and their ability to hold their ground against such an onslaught of Confederate soldiers is apparent in his descriptions of their fighting. Interestingly, he is also positive in his descriptions of the southern troops, describing them as having "perfect form" in their charge and strong in their fighting. His loyalty to the Union won out, however, as he states that they are "equal in spirit, and their [the Confederates'] superiors in tenacity." While his poetry is not as apparent in these last passages, his heart still is—an attribute which gives his readers the ability to experience his pain and the turmoil of the battle.

With his final paragraph, Wilkeson blends the elements of his writing which have been discussed—the grief, the reporting of facts, and the poetry. When he states that "my pen is heavy" and turns over the remaining reporting to his associate Mr. Henry, his grief for his own child and all who fell at Gettysburg is evident, as is his belief that the work of broadcasting the details to the public must continue. He then describes the clay in which his son is buried and creates the fanciful image of Christ leading the fallen into Paradise, a clear demonstration of his poetic talents. But even through all of this pain, Wilkeson ends on a positive note, declaring the fallen to be envied and that through their sacrifice "the second birth of Freedom in America" has come. While somewhat ahead of his time, as the war would not end for some years to come, this announcement seemed moderately prophetic of the eventual victory of the Union and the freedoms promised to its citizens.

Essential Themes

This document shows the Battle of Gettysburg in a way that few battles have able to be recorded, with a mix of emotion and professional detachment. And it is brought together by the author's poetic flair which elevates it to something far beyond a sketch of a battle plan or even a recitation of the death of a son. While this article was written with the short-term purpose of fulfilling an assignment and passing information to the public, it had the long-term effect of preserving the firsthand experience of one of the most infamous battles in the Civil War. Furthermore, this account gives life to a battle that for most people is simply a piece of history, tragic but completed. Wilkeson gives personalities to the faces of the dead, names to the bodies, and serves himself as a poignant reminder of all that is lost in battle, for those who fall and those who remain.

There are many historians who, today, declare the Battle of Gettysburg to be a defining moment in the tide of the Civil War. It has been said that once the Union had won that decisive victory, the South was es sentially on a downward trend until the end of the war. But even if that is true, and it is consistently debated even to the present day, those who witnessed the battle or fought in it or even led it had no idea that they were participating in something so pivotal. One of the only things they knew for certain, as it is well known to-day also, was that Gettysburg was one of the bloodiest battles in American history—horrifying in its destruction and loss of life—a fact which anyone who reads a firsthand account, such as that of Samuel Wilkeson, is unlikely to forget.

Anna Accettola, M.A.

Bibliography

McElfresh, Earl B. "Fighting on Strange Ground." *Civil War Times* 52.4 (2013): 31-36. Print.

Shahid, Sharon. "In News History: The Lone Black Reporter of the Civil War." *Washington DC News Museum*. N.p., n.d. Web. 25 Aug. 2013. http://www.newseum.org/news/2011/02/thomas-morris-chester.html.

"The Civil War and Gettysburg: The Correspondents' Perspective." *Gettysburg National Military Park*. Gettysburg Foundation, n.d. Web. 25 Aug. 2013.

Wilkeson, Samuel. "Samuel Wilkeson: "The Conclusion of the Battle of Gettysburg"" California State University Pomona, n.d. Web. 24 Aug. 2013.

Additional Reading

Cutler Andrews, J. *The North Reports the Civil War*. [Pittsburgh]: U of Pittsburgh P, 1955. Print.

DeAngelis, Gina. *The Battle of Gettysburg: Turning Point of the Civil War*. Mankato, MN: Bridgestone, 2003. Print.

Perry, James M. *A Bohemian Brigade: The Civil War Correspondents, Mostly Rough, Sometimes Ready*. New York: Wiley, 2000. Print.

Starr, Louis Morris. *Reporting the Civil War: The Bohemian Brigade in Action, 1861-65*. New York: Collier, 1962. Print.

"The Battle of Gettysburg." Civil War Trust, n.d. Web. 25 Aug. 2013.

■ Letters of a Transport Nurse

Date: 1862
Author: Wormeley, Katherine Prescott
Genre: letter; report; memoir

"Yesterday I came on board this boat, where there are thirty very bad cases, — four or five amputations."

"Instances of such high unselfishness happen daily that...I feel myself strengthened in my trust in human nature..."

Summary Overview

This document is a compilation of letters written by Katherine Prescott Wormeley during her time working for the Sanitary Commission and as a transport nurse and administrator during the Civil War. By examining elements of a few letters, the details of how the injured were administered to and the interactions of noncombatants in the war show the involvement of all people without making distinction for race, wealth, status, or gender. Katherine Wormeley, along with many other high-class women, dove into the war effort in an attempt to alleviate some of the suffering and pain of those who fought for the Union, despite the existing taboo of women involving themselves in such gruesome work or, as Wormeley came to do, managing men in an official capacity. The complete book of these letters was published years later in order to show how women and nurses participated in the war and is justly titled *The Other Side of the War with the Army of the Potomac.*

Defining Moment

This document is a valuable piece of the historical record as it chronicles one upper-class woman's time in the Civil War. This was not just any woman, however, but a woman who gave up the comforts of her high-society life to become an integral part of the nursing force which cared for the wounded soldiers, both in the field and in permanent hospitals and medical facilities. This same woman also became one of the first women ever to be given direct command of men—an impressive feat considering the nearly crippling ideas of the time period concerning the inferiority of women and their "place" in the household. An analysis of the entire book *The Other Side of the War with the Army of the Potomac* would reveal aspects of many parts of life in the 1860s, including social standards, race relations, gender relations, conditions of medical facilities in the Civil War, and even grammatical and diction tendencies of upper-class women from Rhode Island; but in this particular analysis the concentration is on the how the wounded were seen by those who aided them, as well as the reactions of Wormeley herself to her situation and the soldiers' suffering.

This document mainly contributes to the social context of the Civil War, for Wormeley is one of several dozen high-society women who walked away from their lives of leisure in order to aid soldiers in the Civil War. They did not do this for praise or for thanks, but because they were driven to do so by a powerful internal need to help the war effort, even though no such aid work had been done previously. Wormeley's book of letters gives an inside look into the life she choose to lead and a perspective which was captured the moment it happened, not as a memoir written later in life when the sights and memories were dulled and softened by time, but when everything was still sharp and painful. By reading these letters, modern audiences are able to take away a feeling of presence—that they too are in the hospitals, standing next to the wounded and dying soldiers, doing their absolute best to try to help, in any way they might be able.

Author Biography

Katherine (or Katharine) Prescott Wormeley was born in 1830 in England to an English father, who held the rank of rear-admiral in the British Navy, and an American mother. The family later immigrated to the United States. With the beginning of the Civil War, Katherine Wormeley decided to take up the cause alongside the soldiers who went to war and the civilians who geared their efforts toward supporting them. Her main goals were to gather supplies which would be necessary to soldiers, but she was not the only one to do so. In fact, she worked with many other women, beginning with a meeting of other women held in her mother's home. This society was named the "Woman's Union Aid Society," and it became a springboard for Wormeley's later work, after she served as its president and continued to serve as an administrator.

In approximately this same period, 1861-62, Wormeley strove for a new type of work, in which she was able to procure a contract with the military to provide shirts to the army. These shirts were hand made by the men and women whom Wormeley was working to help, poorer civilians who felt the need to support the war effort and needed the money to survive. This contract was set to expire in April 1862. Almost immediately after this, the United States Sanitary Commission was created and, soon after, Wormeley was recognized as an impressive and capable leader and administrator, taking charge of not only the sick and wounded being cared for after battles, but also men, in a time when such action by a woman, especially an unattached and relatively young woman, was unheard of.

Katherine Wormeley, like nearly every other woman who worked in the service of the Sanitary Commission, eventually succumbed to the incredible demands of her job, sickening with fever and being forced by her health to remove herself from this aid work. But after returning home for a short while, she once again took up a place as a superintendent, until once again she was forced to retire due to her health. This time it was final. But she did not entirely give up on her work. She published letters and details of her time serving as a nurse and administrator in the Civil War, allowing more people to understand the horrors she witnessed and the necessity of such aid, both for the men they helped and for the women who were able to contribute. Wormeley spent much of the end of her life translating works by French authors, becoming much distinguished for her abilities.

She passed away on August 4, 1908 at her home.

HISTORICAL DOCUMENT

[aboard] "Wilson Small,"
May 13 [1862].

Dear Mother, — Yours of the ninth received. The mails come with sufficient regularity. We all rush at the letter-bag, and think ourselves blighted beings if we get nothing. Yesterday I came on board this boat, where there are thirty very bad cases, — four or five amputations. One poor fellow, a lieutenant in the Thirty-second New York Volunteers, shot through the knee, and enduring more than mortal agony; a fair-haired boy of seventeen, shot through the lungs, every breath he draws hissing through the wound; another man, a poet, with seven holes in him, but irrepressibly poetic and very comical. He dictated to me last night a foolscap sheet full of poetry composed for the occasion.

His appearance as he sits up in bed, swathed in a nondescript garment or poncho, constructed for him by Miss Whetten out of an old green table-cloth, is irresistibly funny. There is also a captain of the Sixteenth New York Volunteers, mortally wounded while leading his company against a regiment. He is said to measure six feet seven inches, — and I believe it, looking at him as he lies there on a cot, pieced out at the foot with two chairs.

I took my first actual watch last night; and this morning I feel the same ease about the work which yesterday I was surprised to see in others. We begin the day by getting them all washed, and freshened up, and breakfasted. Then the surgeons and dressers make their rounds, open the wounds, apply the remedies, and replace the bandages. This is an awful hour; I sat with my fingers in my ears this morning. When it is over, we go back to the men and put the ward in order once more; re-making several of the beds, and giving clean handkerchiefs with a little cologne or bay-water on them, — so prized in the sickening atmosphere of wounds. We sponge the bandages over the wounds constantly, — which alone carries us round from cot to cot almost without stopping, except to talk to some, read to others, or write letters for them; occasionally giving medicine or brandy, etc., according to order. Then comes dinner, which we serve out ourselves, feeding those who can't feed themselves. After that we go off duty, and get first washed and then fed ourselves; our dinner-table being the top of an old stove, with slices of bread for plates, fingers for knives and forks, and carpet-bags for chairs, — all this because everything available is being used for our poor fellows. After dinner other ladies keep the same sort of watch through the afternoon and evening, while we sit on the floor of our state-rooms resting, and perhaps writing letters, as I am doing now.

Meantime this boat has run up the York River as far as West Point (where a battle was fought on Thursday), in obedience to a telegram from the Medical Director of the Army, requesting the Commission to take off two hundred wounded men immediately. A transport accompanies us. But we pay little heed to the outside

world, and though we have been under-way and running here and there for hours, I have only just found it out. Don't fret if you do not hear from me. I may go to Washington on a hospital transport, or — to Richmond with the army! and you may not hear of me for a week. Let no one pity or praise us. I admit painfulness; but no one can tell how sweet it is to be the drop of comfort to so much agony.

***

[aboard] "S. R Spaulding,"
Off Headquarters, Army of the Potomac,
White House, May 18 [1862].

Dear A., — My date will excite you. Yesterday, after getting off the "Knickerbocker" with three hundred sick on board, we transferred our quarters to this vessel, and started to run up the Pamunky. It was audacious of us to run this big ocean-steamer up this little river, without a chart and without a pilot. In some places we brushed the trees as we passed, for the water is said to be fifteen feet deep a yard from the shore. "What a garden land it is! Such verdure of every brilliant shade lining the shore, and broken into, here and there, by little creeks running up through meadow-lands into the misty blue distance. We anchored for the night off Cumberland, — the limit of my aspirations; and I went to sleep in the still lingering twilight, listening to the whippoorwill. In the morning when I came on deck Mr. Olmsted called me forward into the bows: and what a sight was there to greet us! The glow of the morning mist, the black gunboats, the shining river, with the gleam of the white sails and the tents along the shore, made a picture to be painted only by Turner. We ran up to the head of the fleet, in sight of the headquarters of the army, to the burned railroad bridge, beyond which no one could go.

After breakfast we went ashore, where General Franklin met us and took us through part of his command, — through trains of army-wagons drawn by four mules; through a ploughed field across which mounted officers and their staffs were galloping at full speed; through sutlers' tents and commissary stores, and batteries and caissons. It was like a vast fairground. We met one man eating six pies at once, and not a man without one pie! I wished intensely to stop at General Headquarters as we passed it. But to-day General McClellan is overborne by business: the army arrived here on the 16th; twelve scouting-parties are now out, some coming in every hour; McClellan himself is not able to speak an unnecessary word; a council is to be held this evening, to arrange the last details for the move to-morrow, — so we felt we ought not even to wish to see him.

General Franklin took us to the White House, — a house and estate just quitted by the family of a son of

General Lee, whose wife was a Custis. I copied the following notice, written in a lady's hand on a half sheet of note-paper, and nailed to the wall of the entrance: —

> Northern soldiers! who profess to reverence the memory of Washington, forbear to desecrate the home of his first married life, the property of his wife, and now owned by her descendants.
>
> *A Granddaughter of Mrs. Washington.*

Underneath was written (in the handwriting, as I was told, of General Williams, Adjutant-General of the army): —

> Lady, — A Northern soldier has protected this property within sight of the enemy, and at the request of your overseer.

And so it was. On reaching the spot, General McClellan would not even make his headquarters within the grounds. Guards were stationed at the gates and fences, on the lawns and the piazzas. Within, all was beautiful, untrodden, and fresh, while without was the tumult and trampling of war. Already the surrounding country was a barren and dusty plain. We walked through the grounds, across the peaceful lawns looking down upon the river crowded with transports and ammunition barges. We went through the house, which is a small cottage, painted brown, and by no means a *white house*. The carpets and a great part of the furniture had been removed, but enough remained to show that modern elegance had adorned the quaint old place. Washington never lived in the present house, which has been built on the site of the one in which he spent his early married life.

General Franklin allowed me to gather some ivy and some holly. We stayed nearly an hour, sitting on the piazza and talking to him. He struck me as an officer of *power*, — large, with square face and head, deep-sunk, determined blue eyes, close-cropped reddish-brown hair and beard. He told us that the battle of Williamsburg was full of anxiety from first to last, and that it took much to decide the final fortunes of the day; but at West Point, after the men

were landed, he was not for a moment uneasy, the game was in our hands from the beginning. He feels, confident that the enemy will make a great resistance before Richmond; if not, it will be a virtual surrender of their cause, which he thinks they are far from making. Everything, he said, depended on the strength of our army, and he told us that McDowell was at last coming down on our right wing, which is to be extended to meet him. He spoke with the deepest confidence in McClellan, who, he said, was in good spirits, though fearfully overworked.

As we were leaving White House, General Fitz-John Porter came to meet us, and walked with us to our wharf, where we met General Morell; and they all came on board and stayed half an hour. I felt great interest in General Porter, who commands one *corps d'armee*, General Franklin commanding another. General Morell is also an interesting man; looks like dear father, but wears a long white beard. He received the command of a division yesterday. General Porter spoke of McClellan just as we all feel, — as a patriot as well as a general, as a man who wisely seeks to heal, as well as to conquer. There is a fine spirit in General Porter. He probably has less power than General Franklin, is more excitable and sympathetic; but there is an expression of devotion about him which inspires great confidence. They were all very guarded, of course, in what they said of the future; but two hours' talk with such men in such places teaches much.

This afternoon General Seth Williams, Adjutant-General, came on board to pay his respects to Mrs. Griffin. His visit gave us all great pleasure. I am told that if any man possesses in an equal degree the respect and attachment of others, he does; and yet his quiet, modest manner and plain appearance would hardly instruct a stranger as to his position in the army. These gentlemen were accompanied by many young officers, all spurs and swords and clanking. They were thankful for some of our private stores, —needles, buttons, and linen thread were as much prized as beads by an Indian; and even hairpins were acceptable to General Porter, one button of whose cap was already screwed on by that female implement.

I am happy to say that there is no immediate chance of my being anywhere but here. "We came up for medicines and general information; the result is that Mr. Olmsted finds such a state of disorganization and sixes-and-sevenness in the medical arrangements that he has determined to make his headquarters here for the present. Mr. Knapp has therefore just started in the tug for Yorktown to bring up the supply-boats, and leave orders for our hospital fleet to follow us up the river as they arrive from the North.

The state of affairs is somewhat this: when the march from Yorktown began, and the men dropped by thousands, exhausted, sick, and wounded, the Medical Department, unprepared and terribly harassed, flung itself upon the Sanitary Commission. When it became known that our transports were lying in the river, the brigade-surgeons made a business of sending their sick on board of them; and the Medical Director sanctioned the practice. The hospitals at Yorktown, Fortress Monroe, and Newport News are full; the Commission has therefore been forced to take these men to the North. Nothing, of course, is more desirable for those who are seriously ill or badly wounded; but every man who falls exhausted from the ranks is sent to us. This will prove in the end actually demoralizing to the army if not checked. The men will come to think that illness, real or shammed, is the way to get home. Already suspicious rheumatic cases have appeared. Mr. Olmsted remonstrates against the system, but of course he has to act under the medical authority. What is wanted is a large receiving hospital in the rear of the army, which would keep the cases of exhaustion and slight illness, take good care of them for a week or two, and send them back to the front. Mr. Olmsted telegraphed to-day, advising the Surgeon-General to send sufficient hospital accommodation, bedding, and medicines for six thousand men. This ought to be done. Meantime we lie here, and may fill this ship, which is now all in order, to-morrow.

Could you but see the lovely scene around me! We have had a little service of prayer and hymns in the cabin, and now we are all — the "staff," as we call ourselves — sitting at sunset on the deck, under an awning. We are anchored in the middle of the river, which is about three hundred yards wide at this point, and are slowly swinging at our anchor. We have dropped down the stream since morning. Scores of vessels — transports, mortar-boats, ammunition-barges—are close around us, and several gunboats. The regiments of Franklin's corps are camped along the banks; the bands playing on one side, "Hail Columbia!" and, farther down, "Glory, Hallelujah!" The trees which fringe the shore lean towards us, — locust, oak, and the lovely weeping-elm. One of the latter throws its shadow across my paper as we have slowly swung into it. I have told Mr. Olmsted that, now that I feel at home in the work, I am not tied to Mrs. Griffin, but consider the protection of the Commission sufficient, and that if he wants me, I will stay by the work as long as there is any. I like him exceedingly, autocrat and aristocrat that he is; I feel that he would protect and guard in the wisest manner those under his care. The other gentlemen on board are Mr. Frederick N. Knapp, second to Mr. Olmsted, in charge of the supplies; Dr. Robert Ware, chief-surgeon; Messrs. Charles Woolsey, George Wheelock, and David Haight, his assistants.

Direct to me in future to the care of Colonel Ingalls, Quartermaster's Department, Army of the Potomac — think of *that!*

✳ ✳ ✳

[aboard] "Spaulding,"
May 24 [1862].

Dear Mother, — I seize five spare moments for you, as I have not written for three days. Last night we half filled this ship with the worst cases from the shore hospital. She will probably fill up to-day from the "Elm City," and sail to-morrow. The men are mostly very sick, but no deaths occurred last night. Oh! what stories I shall have to tell you one of these days. Instances of such high unselfishness happen daily that, though I forget them daily, I feel myself strengthened in my trust in human nature, without making any reflections about it. Last night a wounded man, comfortably put to bed in a middle berth (there are three tiers, and the middle one incomparably the best), seeing me point to the upper berth as the place to put a man on an approaching stretcher, cried out: "Stop! put me up there. Guess I can stand l'isting better 'n him." It was agony to both.

There is great discussion among the doctors as to the character of the fever; some call it typhoid, others say it is losing that type and becoming malarial remittent. It matters little to me what it is; the poor fellows all look alike, — dry, bumed-up, baked, either in a dull stupor or a low, anxious delirium. They show little or no excitement, but are dull, weary, and sad. The percentage of sickness is thought to be small for an army on the march through such a region.

We are all well, and cheerful now that our work begins once more. Idleness depressed us a little. We now have over one hundred very sick men on board. Mrs. Griffin and I have just finished our morning's work below; Mrs. M. and Georgy have taken our places, and we have come on deck for a mouthful of fresh air. This morning, before I was up, I heard a crash and a cry, and the bowsprit of a large vessel, which the tide had swung upon us, glanced into the port-hole at the foot of my bed, tore through the partition, and, I believe, demolished the berth on the other side of it. The captain, who takes great pride in his ship, and has employed these leisure days in getting her painted, is now leaning over the side, looking at the defaced and splintered wood-work with a melancholy air.

Good-by. Called off.

GLOSSARY

berth: a shelf-like sleeping space, as on a ship, airplane or railroad car

blighted: destroyed, ruined; withered or decayed

caisson: a two-wheeled wagon, used for carrying artillery ammunition

cannonading: to attack continuously with or as if with a cannon(s)

carpet-bags: a bag for traveling, especially one made of carpeting; in this case, used as padding and covering for chairs

corps d'armee: French; army corps

foolscap: a type of inexpensive writing paper, especially legal-size, lined, yellow sheets, bound in tablet form

General Franklin: William B. Franklin, corps commander of the Army of the Potomac

General McClellan: George McClellan, one-time General-in-Chief of the Union Army and future presidential candidate

Mr. Olmsted: William Law Olmsted, noted landscape architect and head of the Sanitary Commission

overborne: past tense of overbear; to bear over or down by weight or force

remittent: abating for a time or at intervals; a remittent fever

rheumatic: pertaining to or of the nature of rheumatism (any disorder of the extremities or back, characterized by pain and stiffness)

sixes-and-sevenness: describes a state of confusion or disarray; British idiom

spurs: anything that goads, impels, or urges, as to action, speed, or achievement

sutlers: no longer in common use; a person who followed an army or maintained a store on an army post to sell provisions to the soldiers

whippoorwill: a bird; a nocturnal North American nightjar

verdure: greenness, especially of fresh, flourishing vegetation; vigor

Document Analysis

This analysis is based on three letters, from 1862, immortalized in Wormeley's book, *The Other Side of the War…*, the first a letter to her mother dated May 13, the second to a friend dated May 18 (although a only a section of the letter is referred to as the letter is very long), and the last to her mother again dated May 24. These letters cover a wide range of topics and are not, by any means, a complete cross-section of the letters to be found in Wormeley's book. But these letters seem best to aid a modern audience through their descriptions of the types of work and injuries Wormeley faced when she began work each day (which she called "Routine of Work"); how the Hospital Transport Service was run and how well it coped with the high number of casualties from the war (titled in her index "State of Affairs of the Hospital Transport Service"); and, finally, how the humanity of the soldiers and their ability to rise above their own injuries continued to amaze her (a part of a her letter labeled "Unselfishness of the Sick and Wounded" in the index). By analyzing these letters, a better understanding of Wormeley's work, to which she devoted her life, and the care she and others provided to the soldiers, should emerge.

In the Service of the Hospital Transport Service

A detailed description of Wormeley's specific daily routine in the Hospital Transport Service is provided in the first of her letters. The letter itself was written on her second day at her posting, but even in this short amount of time, Wormeley was able to explain what each day of service was going to look like. The descriptions of the injuries which each soldier is enduring or dying from is not the most helpful part of the letter; that comes from reading more deeply and understanding the services that Wormeley provided to the soldiers themselves. She clearly pays attention to each patient, but she also gives extra attention, which modern audiences would not expect from a nurse, such as her taking dictation and writing the lines thought of by a wounded poet. She and her fellows also spend time with the men, not simply bandaging wounds, but talking with them and keeping up morale. Her comments that the poet sat up in bed and wore some kind of voluminous garment "constructed for him by Miss Whetten out of an old green table-cloth" show each woman's attention to the men—for no other reason than out of a desire to see them well again.

More than simply entertaining the soldiers, Worme-

ley and the other women's daily routine included keeping watch, helping the soldiers prepare for the day and washing up, as well as serving breakfast. While these tasks do not seem out of place for nurses, they do suggest a shocking level of intimacy for 1800s women who are not married to the men in question. Since they were nursing the soldiers, it would have been considered shameful or looked down upon, but it was still highly out of the ordinary for upper-class women, such as these, to do tasks, even more so since the soldiers would rarely be men of equal social status. But even though Wormeley states that she is easily settling into the routine, just as the other women have, she is still horrified by some of the necessary tasks which she has to see and occasionally be involved. The doctors personally oversee the caring of wounds, but it is up to the nurses to soothe the men after they receive their care. Wormeley found this most difficult to endure as she had not yet built up any kind of tolerance to the pain and cries of the men.

The rest of that paragraph is dedicated to an outline of the tasks which she and the other nurses complete every day and how they spend their time while off duty. It is unsurprising that at the end of a shift the women chose to relax or write letters to friends and family—for these are the pastime which they would normally be engaged in, if they were still in their homes. Through this description, it is easy to see that these nurses make up an integral part of the Sanitary Commission machine, of which the Hospital Transport Service was a part. This is further described in Wormeley's second letter, in which she describes how the Sanitary Commission became such a prominent part of medical care in the Civil War. Simply stated, the government-run "Medical Department" was not sufficiently prepared for the huge number of dead and wounded which were produced by nearly every battle in the Civil War. From there, any boat or barge owned by the Sanitary Commission was put into service, loaded with nurses and patients and ordered to move soldiers from the field to somewhere where they were able to receive more comprehensive medical attention.

Wormeley continues her dialogue by explaining that while being treated properly is a must for any seriously wounded soldiers, some men were starting to take advantage of that fact, as is part of human nature and a justifiably fierce desire not to be killed in battle. While her words do not make her seem to be overly worried about the possibility of men abusing the system, even the fact that she brought up the topic at all in her letter lets audiences know that it is something which she and the other nurses must face. She clearly looks forward to the possibility of a large hospital following behind the army for less seriously sick or injured soldiers who would be able to return to their stations, but she also has a practical understanding of the government, the Sanitary Commission, and of the strains of war which make such an endeavor unlikely for the time being. Her disposition as she writes seems to be one of contentment, as she understands the reasons for the on-goings around her and her own place within them. Such ease of mind seems to be enviable in a time of much confusion and danger.

Wormeley's Patients

Wormeley's letters, however, not only show her ease in her place in the war and as a transport nurse, but also her pride in the soldiers whom she aids. In her letter to her mother, dated May 24, she gives some of the details of those whom she is currently tending while they recuperate from their wounds. While she had previously spoken of their wounds, their interactions, and sometimes even the amusement which they provide to the nurses, she had not before talked about the "instances of such high unselfishness" which occur, sometimes on a daily basis.

While she did not spend much time on the details of many instances in her letter, preferring instead to tell her mother about them in person, she does recount one instance at the end of the paragraph—a man giving up his bed in order that a more seriously injured fellow soldier could sleep there and volunteering to climb into a higher bed, even though it caused him great pain. While this does not seem to a modern audience like such a great sacrifice, it would be all too easy for a wounded man to think only of his own pain and ignore the plight of others. Wormeley reports that this is not the case and finds her own faith in humanity restored and "strengthened," even though she is surrounded by the proof of just how much damage men can do to one another. The importance of these moments to Wormeley are clearly demonstrated, as she writes about them almost immediately in her letter, with only a small opening greeting to her mother proceeding this information.

Wormeley cared deeply for her patients and about her own performance of her duties. This is apparent in each line of her letters and the detail which she includes, possibly to explain her choices to those who are not fellow volunteers in one of the bloodiest struggles in American history. She did not decide to help on a whim and then decide to go home when the job became too hard or too real. She, and many other women from similar backgrounds and subject to a similar drive to help, worked themselves to a state of pure exhaustion and sickness. In a time when doing very little or nothing pertaining to the Union's war effort would not have been considered unreasonable or excessively unusual, upper-class, wealthy, unmarried women left their homes, volunteered their time, and sacrificed their health in order to make some kind of difference for the men who risked their lives and limbs to reunite the country.

Essential Themes

Katherine Wormeley's book of letters has all but been relegated to the dusty shelf of the back part of a shuttered library and is only read and appreciated today by scholars researching her specific time period and occupation. But she should not be dismissed by ordinary readers, because her work is a shining example of what people are able to do when they decide to throw themselves into a cause. Wormeley's letters may not give the impression of being written by a woman who worked to shatter the glass ceiling of administration in the 1800s, but they provide invaluable details about the medical issues faced by staff and soldiers alike. They also provide minute descriptions of what nurses were required to do and how they lived upon transport ships, not an area of history that is otherwise widely known.

In the short-term, Wormeley influenced those around her by her actions as a nurse and those back home by keeping them informed of her activities and the happenings of the war. It would be a shame to underestimate how much those letters must have been treasured by the people who received them, for Wormeley had volunteered to put herself in harm's way in order to help the Union's cause and care for the injured and dying, instead of staying safe at home and, maybe, donating money or goods to the army. Long-term, her letters may have less obvious impact, but they are still vital parts of American history. The details in these letters help to create a whole picture of the Civil War, they flesh out the personalities of faceless soldiers, and they even give life to the administrators with whom she worked. Without such documentation, written history becomes nothing but a series of events without the power to draw in or impact modern audiences.

Anna Accettola, M.A.

Bibliography

Brockett, L. P. "Katherine Prescott Wormeley." *Women's Work in the Civil War: A Record of Heroism, Patriotism and Patience*. Tufts University, 1867. Web. 23 Aug. 2013.

"Hospital Transport Service." *Civil War Women*. The United States Army Heritage and Education Center, n.d. Web. 12 Sept. 2013.

Wormeley, Katharine Prescott. *The Other Side of the War: With the Army of the Potomac. Letters from the Headquarters of the United States Sanitary Commission during the Peninsular Campaign in Virginia in 1862*. Boston: Ticknor, 1889. Print.

Additional Reading

Diary of a Civil War Nurse, The. Smithsonian National Museum of American History, n.d. Web. 09 Sept. 2013.

Egenes, Karen J. "Nursing During the US Civil War: A Movement Toward the Professionalization of Nursing." Hektoen International: A Journal of Medical Humanities, Jan. 2009. Web. 09 Sept. 2013.

Favor, Lesli J. *Women Doctors and Nurses of the Civil War*. New York: Rosen, 2004. Print.

Smith, Adelaide W. *Reminiscences of an Army Nurse During the Civil War*. New York: Greaves, 1911. Print.

Straubing, Harold Elk. *In Hospital and Camp: The Civil War through the Eyes of Its Doctors and Nurses*. Harrisburg, PA: Stackpole, 1993. Print.

"The Shattered Remains of Lee's Army…"

Date: April 24, 1865 and April 25, 1865
Author: Andrews, Eliza Frances
Genre: diary; memoir

"The shattered remains of Lee's army are beginning to arrive. There is an endless stream passing between the transportation office and the depot, and trains are going and coming at all hours."

Summary Overview

This document, which is an excerpt from the diary of Eliza Frances Andrews' *War-Time Journal of a Georgia Girl: 1864-1865*, shows the Civil War from a point of view which is not often recorded or preserved for the modern audience. Eliza Andrews was an aristocratic, young, Southern female noncombatant, who witnessed much of the destruction which was wreaked on the South as the Confederate army was beaten back by the Union forces. She recorded these events both as they pertained to her and, in some cases, as they related to the whole Confederacy. Particularly interesting is that Andrews' father was a southern Unionist, while her brothers fully supported Georgian secession. This tension in the family, which was also a characteristic of the whole Civil War, is apparent in her diary, as she explains the workings of her daily life, the interactions of her family members, and the movements of the Union and Confederate troops in the South.

Defining Moment

In January of 1861, Georgia seceded from the Union and joined the Confederate States of America. As for the citizens of Georgia, they had been firmly placed on the southern side of the conflict between the states, which became the Civil War. This war was not fought solely because the Northerners were opposed to slavery and the Southerners depended on it for their econo-

my—it was also fought because the Southern states believed in a strong decentralized government, while the North preferred a larger federal government over individual state governments. While modern audiences tend to think of the South in a more negative light, documents such as this one written by Eliza Andrews show how these events cannot be viewed in such a strict, black and white light. Her father was a Unionist and a slave-owner. He owned nearly 200 slaves at the onset of the Civil War, but still he believed that secession was going to be detrimental to Georgia and the whole nation.

His belief was proved to be accurate in that nearly the whole South was decimated by the two armies which stormed through the land and wrought death in the fields. Firsthand accounts of these years show modern audiences how Southerners felt and were affected by the war, even if they did not support it at its outset. Printed years after the war had ended, Andrews' diary gives an inside look at those individuals who were swept along in the politics of the war without having a say about the direction in which their lives were heading. Since the Confederacy lost the Civil War, and perhaps especially because of this fact, it is important to understand the reasoning behind their secession and how they were affected after their defeat. History has long been known to be written by the victors, but the two sides of any conflict must be understood to gain full knowledge of any event. Documents such as the following provide the necessary missing links. Southern soldiers were not simply rebels who fought against a righteous North; they were friends, brothers, sons and husbands of good people who loved them. To dismiss them simply as the "losers" or those who were "wrong" is to undermine their entire way of life and belief system. From the entries in Andrews' diary, the soldiers are brought to life, as friends from her childhood and through her descriptions of her inability to turn away any in need, even though her family was deeply affected by the destruction rampant in the South.

Author Biography

Eliza Frances Andrews was born in 1840, on August 10, to a superior court judge in the Southern state of Georgia. From an upper-class family, Andrews was well educated and was assured in her station in life, due to her family's prominence and wealth. Her family was heavily involved in slavery and the cotton industry, which was typical of upper-class families of the time. But contrary to conventional thought, not all Southerners were pro-secession, which created a conflict in the Andrew's household. While her father was a Unionist, her brothers wished to secede.

Secession did come, however, and while the men of the Andrews family served their country to the best of their abilities, the women remained home (and eventu ally were forced to flee their home as the Confederate forces were overrun by those of the North). This time period is chronicled in Eliza Andrews' diary, *The War-Time Journal of a Georgia Girl, 1864-1865*, from which the above quote and the following excerpt have been taken. The forced desertion of the family home on account of General Sherman's army moving through Georgia in 1864 was a precursor to the eventual decline and ruin of the Andrews' family fortune and aristocratic prestige.

This loss was a turning point for Eliza Andrews, and she dedicated herself to a life path that was nearly unheard of for any high-born woman in that time period. She decided to support herself. Some of her other published works, such as *Journal of a Georgia Woman, 1870-1872 and A Family Secret*, show her growth as an independent woman and the beginnings of her career as an author. She spent the rest of her life writing articles and books about her own experiences and those of others. She also became a teacher and combined those skills along with her passion for botany to write two high school textbooks on botany in the early 1900s. Andrews spent the end of her life in Rome, Georgia, and passed away on January 21, 1931. She died having been honored by becoming the only American woman member of the International Academy of Literature and Science.

HISTORICAL DOCUMENT

April 24, Monday.

The shattered remains of Lee's army are beginning to arrive. There is an endless stream passing between the transportation office and the dépot, and trains are going and coming at all hours. The soldiers bring all sorts of rumors and keep us stirred up in a state of never-ending excitement. Our avenue leads from the principal street on which they pass, and great numbers stop to rest in the grove. Emily is kept busy cooking rations for them, and pinched as we are ourselves for supplies it is impossible to refuse anything to the men that have been fighting for us. Even when they don't ask for anything the poor fellows look so tired and hungry that we feel tempted to give them everything we have. Two nice-looking officers came to the kitchen door this afternoon while I was in there making some sorghum cakes to send to Gen. Elzeys camp They then walked slowly through the back yard, and seemed reluctant to tear themselves away from such a sweet, beautiful place. Nearly everybody that passes the street gate stops and looks up the avenue and I know they can't help thinking what a beautiful place it is. The Cherokee rose hedge is white with blooms. It is glorious. A great many of the soldiers camp in the grove, though Col. Weems [the Confederate commandant of the post] has located a public camping-ground for them further out of town. The officers often ask for a night's lodging, but our house is always so full of friends who have a nearer claim, that a great many have to be refused. It hurts my conscience ever to turn off a Confederate soldier on any account, but we are so overwhelmed with company – friends and people bringing letters of introduction – that the house, big as it is, will hardly hold us all, and members of the family have to pack together like sardines. Capt. John Nightingale's servant came in this afternoon – the "little Johnny Nightingale" I used to play with down on the old Tallassee plantation – but reports that he does not know where his master is. He says the Yankees captured him (the negro) and took away his master's horse that he was tending, but as soon as night came on he made his escape on another horse that he "took" from them, and put out for home. He says he don't like the Yankees because they "didn't show no respec' for his feelin's." He talks with a strong salt-water brogue and they laughed at him which he thought very ill-mannered. Father sent him round to the negro quarters to wait till his master turns up.

April 25, Tuesday.

Maj. Hall, one of Gen. Elzey's staff, has been taken with typhoid fever, so father sent out to the camp and told them to bring him to our house, but Mrs. Robertson had a spare room at the bank and took him there where he can be better cared for than in our house, that is full as an ant-hill already. I went round to the bank after breakfast to see Mrs. Elzey and inquire about him. The square is so crowded with soldiers and government wagons that it is not easy to make way through it. It is especially difficult around the government offices, where the poor, ragged, starved, and dirty remnants of Lee's heroic army are gathered day and night. The sidewalk along there is alive with vermin, and some people say they have seen lice crawling along on the walls of the houses. Poor fellows, this is worse than facing Yankee bullets. These men

were, most of them, born gentlemen, and there could be no more pitiful evidence of the hardships they have suffered than the lack of means to free themselves from these disgusting creatures. Even dirt and rags can be heroic, sometimes. At the spring in our grove, where the soldiers come in great numbers to wash their faces, and sometimes, their clothes, lice have been seen crawling in the grass, so that we are afraid to walk there. Little Washington is now, perhaps, the most important military post in our poor, doomed Confederacy. The naval and medical departments have been moved here – what there is left of them. Soon all this will give place to Yankee barracks, and our dear old Confederate gray will be seen no more. The men are all talking about going to Mexico and Brazil; if all emigrate who say they are going to, we shall have a nation made up of women, negroes, and Yankees.

I joined a party after dinner in a walk out to the general camping ground in Cousin Will Pope's woods. The Irvin Artillery are coming in rapidly; I suppose they will all be here by the end of the week – or what is left of them – but their return is even sadder and amid bitterer tears than their departure, for now "we weep as they that have no hope." Everybody is cast down and humiliated, and we are all waiting in suspense to know what our cruel masters will do with us. Think of a vulgar plebeian like Andy Johnson, and that odious Yankee crew at Washington, lording it over Southern gentlemen! I suppose we shall be subjected to every indignity that hatred and malice can heap upon us. Till it comes, "Let us eat, drink and be merry, for to-morrow we die." Only, we have almost nothing to eat, and to drink, and still less to be merry about.

Our whirlwind of a cousin, Robert Ball, has made his appearance, but is hurrying on to New Orleans and says he has but one day to spend with us.

The whole world seems to be moving on Washington now. An average of 2,000 rations are issued daily, and over 15,000 men are said to have passed through already, since it became a military post, though the return of the paroled men has as yet hardly begun.

GLOSSARY

Atlanta, GA: capital of the state of Georgia

Cherokee Rose: an evergreen climbing shrub with a white, fragrant rose; invasive in the United States

depot: station for the trains and other means of transportation; comes from French

General Arnold Elzey: Major General in the Confederate Army; performed mostly administrative work after being severely wounded at the Battle of Gaines's Mill in 1862.

heterogeneous: containing things which are all the same; in this case, households which all have people of the same race and background

sorghum: a type of grain, related to the sugar cane; used for food, fodder for animals, and to make alcoholic drinks

Washington, GA: a small town about 100 miles East of Atlanta; the setting of this excerpt and a place of refuge for many Confederate troops

Document Analysis

These journal entries, written by Eliza Frances Andrews, show not only the daily events in the life of a young Southern woman, but also the hardships which were faced by the civilians and how they interacted with troops, particularly in the final days of the Civil War. Instead of an abstract concept of loyalty to the Confederacy or fear for her family and friends, Andrews demonstrates her and her fellows' need to help the returning and defeated soldiers in any way that they are able. This is not because they have been defeated, but in spite of it, as a show of gratitude and loyalty for unknown men who risked their lives. Through an examination of the journal entries of April 24 and April 25, Andrews' account reveals how she herself and her family pushed through their own needs to attend to the soldiers and how she came to understand that her life was going to change and how drastically.

April 24, 1865

Eliza Frances Andrews' journal entry of April 24, 1865 begins with a description of General Robert E. Lee's army returning to the town in which Andrews and her family is currently residing. The "shattered remains" of the army evokes a fierce image of the once whole and proud army as broken down and despondent as the Civil War comes to its conclusion. Unlike previous entries which are largely concerned with the social visits and daily occurrences pertaining to Andrews' family, this entry focuses exclusively on the condition of the army as a whole and the individual soldiers, as well as the effects they have on the town and Andrews herself. It is at this time that Andrews becomes fully aware of the state of the war and the prospect that independence for the South is not likely to be the outcome of their attempt to secede.

Andrews continues her entry by describing a "state of never-ending excitement" aroused by the soldiers and the stories that they bring back with them from the front lines. This excitement is not positive or even some sense of hope about the outcome of the war, but more of an agitation of the spirit. They know that the war is coming to a close and the Union troops may be closing in on their town. Now they are just waiting for the end.

The trials with which the Andrews family have had to deal, namely, moving from their home to a safer part of the country and the lack of abundance to which they were accustomed, begin to fade when they are faced with the needs of the Confederate soldiers. She states that numerous soldiers pass by their home and take some momentary rest in the trees that line the street. The pain of the soldiers touches both Andrews and her family so that they feel compelled to help, even though they are not sure there is enough for themselves to eat. Such devotion to the soldiers shows that even though the South has been defeated and the soldiers are now part of a losing army, the loyalty of the citizenry is not abandoned. Even when the soldiers do not ask for something from the family, they do their best to make sure that as many hungry and tired soldiers are fed as possible.

The beauty of the house in which Eliza Andrews lived is in stark comparison to the downtrodden state of the soldiers and their camp outside of town. The two officers who Andrews says came to the house looking for a place to sleep clearly did not want to leave the beauty and luxury of the home. The Andrews family obviously was not left in complete squalor on account of the war, even though their family did suffer numerous financial and social downturns. But, having dealt with their own troubles, they opened their home as much as they could, until they were "pack[ed] together like sardines" and were forced to turn away anyone else who wished to stay. They did all they could in order to support anyone displaced by the war, even though they themselves were equally effected.

The final section of this entry has to do with Captain John Nightingale's servant, possibly his slave. While the story itself is light on particular details, it is representative of the status and class difference between the Andrews family and a "negro." While the Andrews family did not seem to be cruel to the man, he was also treated with a generally disinterested air, especially since he had arrived without his master. She did not even deign to give his name in the entry, even though his master is named very definitely. This does seem to represent any particular dislike of black individuals on the side of Andrews, but clearly demonstrates the social distinction between a white woman, whose family owned approximately 200 slaves before the war (information given earlier in the April 21st journal entry), and a slave. In the end the man was sent off to stay with the other black servants and slaves, not out of any contempt for his person but simply because it was the thing to do.

April 25, 1865

This entry contains a mix of war-focused and socially-focused elements, which blend together to show how life for Andrews became a clash of soldiers returning from war and the normal daily events of aristocratic social life. In her attempts to continue her social rounds, such as visiting with General Elzey's wife to inquire after the health of one of her husband's men or the brief visit of a cousin on his way to New Orleans, she had to carefully find a way to move through the central square of town, which had been overrun with soldiers. Her loyalty to the troops is now mixed with a general sense of distaste at having so many men loitering in the town. This is idea is emphasized by her description of the men as "the poor, ragged, starved, and dirty remains of Lee's heroic army." Even though she wants to help the soldiers in need, Andrews is still at heart a fastidious aristocratic woman.

A large portion of this entry deals with ideas of the future and what will become of the surviving Confederate sympathizers and soldiers once the war is officially concluded. Andrews has a front-row view of the partial contingents and administrative departments as they return to base after being destroyed in the field. There is no longer any hope for the Confederacy and this depression hangs over every aspect of Andrews' life. The talk in the town and the party she attends is directed by each individual's fears for the future—waiting either to flee to another country or be completely subjugated by President Andrew Johnson and the Union. One of Eliza Andrews' most pressing concerns, however, is related to her social station and the idea that some upstart northern men will be "lording it [their victory] over Southern gentlemen." Even with all hope of independence gone, Andrews is able to fall back upon her traditional southern ideals, firmly rooted in the superiority of some people over others, based on their family ties.

Essentially, this document shows the daily life of a southern aristocratic woman, her interactions with the soldiers in whom she dearly believed, and the social strata which defined her life. By reading such documents, very little new information about the Civil War as a dividing force is gleaned, but the details which make history more complete, the details about the human lives affected by events, become understandable. Confederate soldiers and sympathizers could be cast aside as simply the "losers" of the war, but there is much more to their story than that basic classification allows. Each civilian and each soldier had a story, a life, maybe a family who mourned their leaving, and should be remembered and respected for their sacrifice, even if in the end it was done in the service of a conquered people.

Essential Themes

The main purpose of this journal, as a whole, for a modern audience, if not for Eliza Frances Andrews herself, is as a chronicle of the trials and tribulations she and her family went through during the Civil War. This is an inside look into the lifestyle of an aristocratic family, especially during a time when they had been uprooted, moved in with family, and attempted to avoid becoming casualties themselves while the front lines of the war moved ever closer. These two entries, specifically, show how she and her family interacted with the soldiers and the loyalty she felt toward them, even after their defeat. Andrews does not waver in her support of the Confederate troops, which allows the modern reader to have a deeper and more complete understanding of the "other" side of the Civil War and the role patriotism played with Southern civilians, as well as the soldiers with whom she came into contact.

The chapter introductions also help to show how Andrews, many years later, was able to look back on her experiences and help to provide even more detail so that the later generations were better able to understand the context of her diary. Whether or not it was her main intention, Eliza Andrews' diary gives detailed information about aristocratic Southern life and the changes through which it was forced to go between the antebellum and Reconstruction periods of American history. This excerpt in particular highlights both her care and concern for the troops which are taking refuge with her family in Washington, Georgia, and also the conditions which the army, and the civilians who tried to aid them, faced once they were forced into retreat. To truly understand all aspects of such a war, it is not enough to know the dates and numbers of casualties on either side of the conflict. Each statistic comes from the suffering of a human being who was fighting for what he or she believed, and Eliza Andrews helps to give names and faces to those who could otherwise be lost or relegated to just one more piece of data.

Anna Accettola, M.A.

Bibliography

Andrews, Eliza F. "The War-Time Journal of a Georgia Girl, 1864-1865." *Documenting the American South.* University of North Carolina: Chapel Hill, 2004. Web. 23 Aug. 2013.

Henderson, Harris. "Summary of the War-Time Journal of a Georgia Girls: 1864-1865."*Documenting the American South.* University of North Carolina:

Chapel Hill, n.d. Web. 24 Aug. 2013. Rushing, S. Kittrell. "Eliza Frances Andrews (1840-1931)." *New Georgia Encyclopedia.* N.p., 29 July 2013. Web. 24 Aug. 2013.

Additional Reading

"Andrews, Eliza Frances (Fanny)." *Georgia Women of Achievement.* N.p., n.d. Web. 24 Aug. 2013.

Andrews, Eliza Frances. *A Family Secret.* Ed. S. Kittrell Rushing. Knoxville: U of Tennessee P, 2005. Print.

Andrews, Eliza Frances. *Botany All the Year Round: A Practical Text-book for Schools.* New York: American Book, 1903. Print.

Andrews, Eliza Frances. *Journal of a Georgia Woman, 1870-1872.* Ed. S. Kittrell Rushing. Knoxville: U of Tennessee P, 2002. Print.

Ford, Charlotte A. "Eliza Frances Andrews: A Fruitful Life of Toil." *The Georgia Historical Quarterly* 89.1 (2005): 25-56. JSTOR. Georgia Historical Society. Web. 24 Aug. 2013.

Garraty, John A. and Mark C. Carnes, eds. *American National Biography.* New York: Oxford University, 1999. Print.

Jones, Katherine M. *Heroines of Dixie: Confederate Women Tell Their Story of the War.* Indianapolis: Bobbs-Merrill, 1955. Print.

■ "Conquered, Submission, Subjugation ... "

Date: May 15, 1865
Author: Stone, Kate
Genre: diary; memoir

*"Conquered, submission, subjugation are words that
burn into my heart, yet I feel that we are doomed to
know them in all their bitterness."*

Summary Overview

Kate Stone's journal, from which the above quote and the following excerpt come, shows an inside look at the life of upper-class Southerners and the ordeals they faced during the war and as refugees. Stone's journal also shows the intense loyalty that many Southerners felt for those who fought in the war and their desire for a South independent from Northern influences and governmental control, evidenced by Stone's own words. By reading and understanding this document, modern audiences can gain a better perspective of the Southern point of view during the Civil War and the costs they bore; they can also come to understand how the war affected one girl who beforehand had faced very little conflict in her life. The changes through which she lived, as well as the hardships she faced, show the fervent hope of each Southerner and the decay of that hope as the war drew to a close.

Defining Moment

At the beginning of the Civil War, Kate Stone's journal expresses her hope and expectation, like that of many Southerners, that the South gaining its independence and becoming the Confederate States of America was inevitable. More than this, it is also a record of the daily life and movements of a typical southern aristocrat, which for a modern audience sheds light on one section of society that underwent drastic and extensive changes between their lives and statuses before the war and after its conclusion. While not always the most ex-

citing read, the journal of Kate Stone provides extensive evidence concerning the private and social lives of southern women.

Although the section which is highlighted in this analysis is more concerned with the reception of General Robert E. Lee's army as it was forced back and into submission toward the end of the Civil War, it is all too easy for modern audiences to forget that daily machinations of life continued on for those not directly involved with the fighting. This is not to say that Kate Stone, her family, and all of those around her were not aware of the on-goings of the war or that they lived their lives free from fear and doubt—from the entries in her journal, it can be seen that this is not so. For days before the entry of May 15, which begins, "Conquered, Submission, Subjugation," Stone describes the heavy nature of the household and the desultory and depressed moods of herself and her family members. But through this despair, they continued to meet with friends and family, have social visits, and continue their lives. These may no longer be joyful, or even cheerful, events, but they were a mandatory part of aristocratic life and this what not a part that could be put aside or completely left behind because the tide of the war was not to favor the South. Social traditions were, and are, strong in the South and must be conducted no matter the circumstances. Kate Stone's journal shows this peculiarity of Southern aristocratic life at the same time that it reveals information about General Lee's army near to the end of the Civil War.

Author Biography

Most of what is known about Kate Stone comes from the journal written by her own hand, an excerpt on which is the document to be discussed below. Beginning in 1861, when she was twenty years old, Kate Stone's life is chronicled as she moves from her simple life as a daughter of a Louisiana cotton plantation owner to a much more complex existence, dealing with the hardships that went hand in hand with civilian life during the Civil War. Her family owned the plantation Brokenburn, after which her journal is named, in Northern Louisiana and also owned about one hundred and fifty slaves. This was not uncommon in that part of the state, where African slaves outnumbered whites almost ten to one.

Throughout her journal, Kate Stone shows her incredible devotion to the Confederate States. She writes that her brother and uncle both joined the Confederate Army and her pride in their actions is matched only by her distain and scorn for any men of appropriate age who did not volunteer to go to war. But the war soon came home for Kate and, in 1862, her family was forced to move to Texas, taking up a sort of refugee status. This change in social status, from upper class to middle class, at best, was viewed as an indignity which she should not have to bear. This problem was only one that she would face, however, and when Lee's army started their retreat close to the end of the war, Kate was forced to realize that the Southern Independence which she had believed in so strongly was not to be.

Years later, Kate Stone commented on the journal entries that she had made during those turbulent war years. In 1900, after growing up and eventually having her own children, she recognized the error of her ways during her youth. She had been vain and lacked empathy and understanding for viewpoints other than her own. Fortunately, she eventually came to recognize the folly of her youth, prizing family and freedom over the material possessions that had meant so much to her at one time.

HISTORICAL DOCUMENT

May 9: Mamma is off with Capt. Buck to visit Mrs. Tooke. Several letters, one from Jimmy to Johnny describing his last visit to the river. One from Jimmy Carson and one from Missie Morris. The girls are having a lovely time in Homer with so many soldiers camped near. Most of them are Missourians. The tallest, handsomest men in the army come from Missouri. A regiment from that state is a splendid-looking body of men. But I do not believe those girls are having any nicer time than we are enjoying here in quiet little Tyler, Missie says there were no engagements and no marriages from the winter's campaign.

How comfortably our move was accomplished. Mamma gave general orders to the Corps d'Afrique to move all our "duds" to the new house. We have only the bare necessaries except servants. They are plentiful. Then Mamma seated herself to the perusal of Burns, Kate went to sewing, I went off calling, returned to dinner, and then went out again. Late in the afternoon Johnny and I went over to our new home to receive Mr. Moore, who had an engagement to call to say good-bye

as his furlough is out. Found everything in quite good order and not looking nearly as bare as we imagined it would. Said good-bye to Mr. Moore an hour, and then read until time for a walk, when Johnny went off to escort his bright particular star, Miss Lizzie Irvine. I went up to meet Mamma and welcome her to her new home, which we have named "The Rest" and which we intend to enjoy to the fullest until stern Fate again casts us out on the world. Lt. Holmes came to tea, though we had explained to him we would not be ready for visitors before Tuesday. He said he forgot our warning. He has a settled habit of coming every day. I suppose he could not break himself of it. Lt. Holmes and I went over to Mrs. Savage's to tea the other day taking Sister with us. Found everybody there utterly whipped, "routed horse, foot, and dragoons." Spent rather an uncomfortable evening. Mrs. Savage and Mrs. Carson amuse themselves spreading the news of my engagement to Lt. Holmes. But I cannot really blame them. When two people are as much together, such reports will arise, and it does no good to tell them, as we do, that there is no engagement. Have not an idea of marrying him or anyone else. We are friends, nothing more. Such reports die out after a time and meanwhile we see much pleasure and amusement together. Mrs. Savage, from being the hottest Rebel, is now "resigned, submissive, weak," and Mrs. Lily is an open and aggressive loyalist and most disagreeable. We were glad to get back and find Mamma and Lt. Dupre having a pleasant chat. Mrs. Tooke called in the morning accompanied by a new young man called Hardin, a rollicking fellow from Arkansas, an incessant talker. Mrs. Tooke invited us to go the following afternoon and call on a young lady visiting her, but on the evening in question first came Mollie Moore, Lizzie Irvine, and Mrs. Carson, and as they left Col. and Mrs. Bradforte and their train came to take tea, and then Dr. and Mrs. Walker. They had heard all kinds of discouraging reports, and they talked till we were all nearly desperate. In the morning we were wretched. Affairs seemed hopeless when Mrs, Savage and Mrs. Lily arrived harrowing us to the last pitch of endurance by their "I told you so" manner and their "I knew it all the time." Their covert abuse of our leaders and excuses for the Yankees were most exasperating. Mrs. Lily is a trial to me. I hope we will not see any of them again until things are settled and we know what to believe.

They left a few minutes before sunset. I hurried off in the carriage to keep the appointment with the girls. The sun was down when we left town, and when we drove up to Mrs. Tooke's door we saw them sitting at supper in the hall. They have only two rooms. But we made the best of it. Went in and chatted for a few minutes, refusing supper, I know to Mrs. Tooke's relief. Then home through the soft moonlight, we girls not at all afraid, though it was after eight when we reached home. We found Lt. Dupre and Lt. Holmes spending the evening and made an apology for our late arrival. We went to see Mrs. Gary, who looks very comfortable, and stopped to see Capt. Polys, who is improving.

Lucy is sick but Adeline fills her place acceptably. We have an excellent garden, though our neighbors said Warren was not doing a thing right in it. We can send salad to the hospital every day and soon other vegetables.

We find ourselves so comfortable that we are frightened. We fear it cannot last a pretty six-room house, nicely improved grounds and surroundings with the flowers in full bloom. We are thankful to be at rest once more.

I am busy embroidering a black velvet tobacco bag with scarlet fuchsias for Lt. Holmes.

May 15: Conquered, Submission, Subjugation are words that burn into my heart, and yet I feel that we are doomed to know them in all their bitterness. The war is rushing rapidly to a disasterous close. Another month and our Confederacy will be a Nation no longer, but we will be slaves, yes slaves, of the Yankee Government.

The degradation seems more than we can bear. How can we bend our necks to the tyrants' yoke? Our glorious struggle of the last four years, our hardships, our sacrifices, and worst of all, the torrents of noble blood that have been shed for our loved Country all, all in vain. The best and bravest of the South sacrificed and for nothing. Yes, worse than nothing. Only to rivet more firmly the chains that bind us. The bitterness of death is in the thought. We could bear the loss of my brave little brothers when we thought that they had fallen at the post of duty defending their Country, but now to know that those glad, bright spirits suffered and toiled in vain, that the end is overwhelming defeat, the thought is unendurable. And we may never be allowed to raise a monument where their graves sadden the hillside. There is a gloom over all like the shadow of Death. We have given up hope for our beloved Country and all are humiliated, crushed to the earth. A past of grief and hardship, a present of darkness and despair, and a future without hope. Truly our punishment is greater than we can bear.

Since Johnston's surrender the people in this department are hopeless. If we make a stand, it would only delay the inevitable with the loss of many valuable lives. The leaders say the country is too much disheartened to withstand the power of a victorious Yankee army flushed with victory. Still, many hope there will be a rally and one more desperate struggle for freedom. If we cannot gain independence, we might compel better terms.

By the twenty-fourth we will know our fate—Submission to the Union (how we hate the word!), Confiscation, and Negro equality or a bloody unequal struggle to last we know not how long. God help us, for vain is the help of man.

We hope President Davis is really making his way to this department, as we hear. His presence would give new life to the people. Poor Booth , to think that he fell at last. Many a true heart at the South weeps for his death. Caesar had his Brutus, Murat his Charlotte Corday, and Lincoln his Booth. Lincoln's fate overtook him in the flush of his triumph on the pinnacle of his fame, or rather infamy. We are glad he is not alive to rejoice in our humiliation and insult us by his jokes. The circumstance of his death forms a most complete tragedy. Many think Andy Johnson worse than Lincoln, but that is simply impossible. Added to our grief at the public calamity is our great anxiety about My Brother. He has had time to get here, if he was paroled, and we have not had a word from him. In the four-day fight before we gave up Petersburg, our army lost fifteen thousand men, and we tremble to think he may be among them. We hear that Tom Manlove is certainly dead, captured and died of his wounds.

Mamma is sewing with a heavy heart on a jacket for Lt. Holmes. Last week we made a heavy white suit for Lt. Dupre. It was an undertaking. A letter from Mrs. Amis to Mamma. She writes most despondently. Sunday Lt. Dupre, Lt. Holmes, Capt. Buck, Col. and Mrs. Bradforte, and Capt. Birchett all came up to discuss the gloomy outlook. We all meet now just to condole with each other. A more doleful crowd I never saw. Capt. Birchett says he is going to South America rather than live under Yankee rule. His father was president of an indignation meeting held in Vicksburg to pass resolutions of sympathy and regret on the death of Lincoln. Capt. Birchett is too disgusted for expression.

GLOSSARY

armistice: a temporary suspension of hostilities by agreement of the warring parties; a truce

Booth: referring to John Wilkes Booth, who assassinated President Abraham Lincoln in the Ford Theatre on March 18, 1865

Corps d'Afrique: another name for regiments of the United States Army composed of African American soldiers, the United States Colored Troops; also known as Buffalo Soldiers

dragoon: a member of a military unit formerly composed of cavalrymen; a mounted infantryman armed with a short musket

doleful: sorrowful; mournful; melancholy

furlough: a vacation or leave of absence granted to an enlisted person

rollicking: carefree and joyous; swaggering; boisterous

Trans-Mississippi Department: an administrative subdivision of the Confederate States of America, which were west of the Mississippi

Document Analysis

The journal of Kate Stone, from which the above excerpt is taken, shows the daily life of a Southern woman from an aristocratic family, who was forced out of her established life and home by the Civil War and forced to relocate, in this case to Texas. The journal covers a large time period, all of which is during the Civil War, but this excerpt, which includes several journal entries, comes from May 1865, specifically May 9 to May 15. While the title of this article, "Conquered, Submission, Subjugation," quotes the opening lines of Stone's May 15 entry, the entries from previous days are necessary foils to this specific record, allowing modern audiences to see how daily life for Southerners unfolded, what aspects they held most dear, and how the closing of the Civil War and the defeat of General

Robert E. Lee's Confederate army affected them.

Daily Life for Stone and her Family

Kate Stone's journal entry for May 9 starts off with several innocuous references to the daily events in which her family are participating. Her mother left to visit with a neighbor and three letters arrived. Even though none of this information is particularly ground shattering in its individuality or its pertinence to American history, it is a necessary and personal look at the parts of social life that were held dear by Kate Stone, specifically, and by the Southern populace, generally. She also continues her journal entry by repeating some of the information that came from a letter sent by Missie Morris, possibly either a friend or a relative. Her own point of view, that of a young, unmarried woman, is apparent in this section of the entry as she is interested in how the young women in Homer, Missouri are faring with the soldiers posted in the town. She compares their town to her own home in Tyler, Texas and remarks on how no weddings or engagements have been announced. Such remarks show her perception of the news and how life continues on even during war times—people visit, fall in love, get married—and Stone is very interested, like many girls her age, in keeping up with such information about the people whom she knows.

Stone goes on to explain about her family's relocation and how they are settling into their new home. If it had not already been known, her remark that servants are "plentiful," would surely give away her status as part of a wealthy family. Also, the following description of how each family member spent their free time for that day would show their status, as leisure was a luxury which few could afford, especially when just completing a household move to a different state. Kate Stone, herself, seems to be mostly at peace with her family's move, although her comment about the possibility of "stern Fate" casting them out into the world again shows that she is not happy to have been forced to leave her home, even if she supports the war which was the cause for the move.

Much of the rest of the journal entry consists of more details concerning her visits with family and neighbors, some of which occurred in the company of a Confederate soldier named Lieutenant Holmes. There is a generally positive tone to her words, even though her life is in some turmoil and she finds some of those with whom she visits to no longer have the zeal for independence that she herself feels. She is also forced to interact with some Union loyalists—whom she finds distasteful and tiresome. Part of this mentality comes from her own loyalties to the South and the Confederacy, but part of it may also be due to her own wish for a conclusion to the war. As she mentions in the last paragraph of this entry, she and her family are afraid. Their life is good momentarily, but they have no idea how fleeting it might be. Even though most of her entry seems to depict a quiet and peaceful life, the Civil War was an ever present worry in the minds of everyone, north or south, Unionist or Confederate.

Emotional Turmoil at the End of the War

From Stone's entries, it is apparent that she is very connected with the on-goings of the war, especially as members of her own family and one of her close friends, and possible romantic entanglement, Lieutenant Holmes, serve as soldiers. In her May 15 entry, however, her recitation of events shows the true depths of her emotions for any and all who fight for "her" side of the war and the horror that is the defeat of the Confederacy. Stone's dreams and struggles have now all been empty, as everything which she and her family have sacrificed for, including their move to another state and abandonment of many of their possessions, were given in vain. Stone is eloquent, but also nearly hysterical, in her journal as she relates this experience.

Kate Stone makes her feelings about the end of the war more than abundantly clear when she states, as dramatically as few other than a young woman can, that "we will be slaves, yes slaves, of the Yankee Government." Her grief at the loss of the war is amplified because, as she goes on to say, she has lost her brothers and now their death has been for nothing. They did not die for a new and free Confederate state, but in an abortive attempt to create a new government which has now been surrendered and abandoned. She does state, however, that many soldiers and civilians hold out hope that there will be another push against the Union or that surrender is not inevitable. But even as she writes those words, she knows that such a turn of events is not likely or even reasonable. The South was defeated and now all that is left to Stone is to try to reconcile herself with this outcome—one that she had seemingly never entertained before.

While surrender has not officially been announced or gone into effect, and would not until May 24, Stone is under no illusion about the state of war. The confusion of May 9 is now alleviated—as she states that there is no longer any hope for Southern independence in this war. In this same paragraph, she also describes her fears for what will happen now and how the war will affect her life—"…Submission to the Union…, Confiscation, and Negro equality…" While to modern audiences, equality for all men may seem to be a good outcome and one of the most famous consequences of the Civil War, it was one of the greatest fears for Southern men and women. It was also one that would irrevocably change Kate Stone's life and livelihood.

In Stone's second to last paragraph she spends some time talking about John Wilkes Booth, one of the most infamous men in American history. Instead of the most prevalent opinion, that Booth was a villain due to his assassination of President Abraham Lincoln, Stone clearly holds a different opinion. She is glad that he was able to end the life of the Union President and only despairs that Booth was not able to escape his own death. This may seem shocking to modern readers, but it works in conjunction with Stone's known hatred for all things northern or Union, most especially the President who would have stood victorious over the ruined Confederacy if he had not been killed. Such insights into Stone's mind aid modern audiences to be able to better understand the mentality which some Southerners held, especially through their defeat.

In Stone's last paragraph of her May 15 journal entry, she once again returns to a description of daily life—her mother sewing a jacket for Lieutenant Holmes and the receipt of a letter. These actions are clearly described with a heavy tone fitting with the idea that life continues to go on, even though the war has come to an unfavorable conclusion for those included in this journal. Stone and her friends and family have another social gathering, although the purpose of this one is "to condole with each other," instead of the more light-hearted gatherings described previously. Their lives are now taking another turn and they are trying to find a way to deal with the events that are to come—specifically regarding the consequences of being southern loyalists in a newly unified nation.

As stated, Kate Stone's journal holds information that is invaluable to those who would look into the daily life and times of an aristocratic girl who had to deal with the trials and tribulations of a civil war—especially one in which she was on the losing side. Her devastation shows how the Southern cause was no mere irritation at the rules of the Union, but a belief that the South should truly be a separate nation, with its own regulations and no overbearing central government. When this goal was no longer feasible, the people of the South were crushed and afraid. Kate Stone shows these emotions and brings life and personality to events that could too easily be lost. If those who are defeated in any conflict lose their voices, then it would be too easy for the same issues to be fought over again. With documents such as the writings of Kate Stone, hopefully, some life will be returned to the defeated so that they are not silenced in history.

Essential Themes

The lasting significance of this document may vary from person to person, scholar to scholar, reader to reader. This author, however, tends to see the significance in the fact that Kate Stone left a well-preserved and dedicated report of her life, times, and tribulations. By comingling the bland and basic every day details of her life with her more flowery and expressive views of the Civil War and her hope for an independent Confederacy, Kate Stone created an impression of a whole person memorialized in script. She did not include one part of her life and leave out another, nor did she focus on the war to the exclusion of more common occurrences, such as betrothals and social visits with family and friends.

Furthermore, Kate Stone was not a well-rounded and completely level-headed young woman. She was virulent in her opinions and beliefs that the South would win the war and become independent. So, by the end of the war when it was clear that Lee would be defeated and the Confederacy would once again be brought under the control of the Union, her outpouring of grief over the loss of that longed-for independence helps to understand the mood of the Confederate nation. At this point, she drops the proper Southern woman veneer and indulges in her fear of being subjugated again and hatred for those she perceives to be some kind of hated overlord. Such flair allows for modern audiences to bridge the gap between a woman from the 1800s south and the modern time, because this type of pain is universal, especially for young men and women who have had their desires and wishes overturned and made all for naught.

Anna Accettola, M.A.

Bibliography

Stone, Kate. "Brokenburn: The Journal Of Kate Stone." Ed. John Q. Anderson. Louisiana State UP, n.d. Web. 24 Aug. 2013.

Wilson, Edmund. *Patriotic Gore: Studies in the Literature of the American Civil War.* New York: Oxford UP, 1962. Print.

Additional Reading

Gallaway, B. P. *Texas, The Dark Corner of the Confederacy: Contemporary Accounts of the Lone Star State in the Civil War.* Lincoln: U of Nebraska P, 1994. Print.

"Kate Stone and Fan Butler: Transcript of Video." *Civil War Reconstruction: Mini Documentary.* PBS, n.d. Web. 24 Aug. 2013.

Marten, James Alan. *Texas Divided: Loyalty and Dissent in the Lone Star State, 1856-1874.* Lexington: UP of Kentucky, 1990. Print.

Sears, Stephen W., ed. *The Civil War: The Second Year Told By Those Who Lived It.* New York: Penguin, 2012. Print.

Simpson, Brooks D., ed. **The Civil War: The Third Year Told By Those Who Lived It**. New York: Penguin, 2013. Print.

Stone, Kate. *Brokenburn: The Journal of Kate Stone, 1861-1868.* Ed. John Q. Anderson. Baton Rouge: Louisiana State UP, 1955. Print.

"Texas During the Civil War." N.p., n.d. Web. 25 Aug. 2013.

THE DESTRUCTION OF SLAVERY

Though it seemed fairly straightforward for President Lincoln and many Americans to declare that slavery was a moral wrong, its abolition proved a much more complicated and perilous process. The Civil War was not begun to free the slaves, but to save the Union, a distinction that began to lose its meaning when slaves were freed as a matter of circumstance or necessity, or freed themselves when the Union Army came marching through. Though repeatedly protesting that the end of slavery, though much to be desired, was not the issue at hand, Northern political and military leaders quickly saw the need to clarify and then regulate the status of current and former slaves, and seek to provide a sustainable future for them.

The Confiscation Acts of 1861 and 1862 provided specific circumstances in which slaves were declared free, and these circumstances depended exclusively on military necessity (slaves were helping to free up more soldiers by keeping farms and businesses running in their absence) and property law (slaves, like cattle or horses, were forfeit if they were used in the service of the rebellion, or if it could be proven that they were owned by anyone in open rebellion). The 1863 Emancipation Proclamation, commonly perceived as the definitive moment when all slaves were free, was actually only a broadening of this—declaring that slaves only in rebellious states were free; border states where slavery was permitted, but which had not left the Union, were exempt. Their residents were loyal citizens, and so could not be deprived of their property rights.

As the war neared its end, discussions about slaves and former slaves broadened to include, first, the need for former slaves to serve in the Union Army, and the need to settle freed slaves who were attached to and relied on the army. In 1865, General William Sherman and Secretary of War Edwin Stanton met with a group of black leaders, all of them either ministers or connected to a church, and asked them what should be done. They were ready to be loyal citizens of the United States, they said, and ready to fight the Confederacy, but they needed land and they needed to be able to use their own labor for their own purposes. Grant's courtesy to this group is commented on, and soon after, he reallocated nearly 400,000 acres of land seized from Confederates to freed slaves, encouraging them to work up to forty acres, and to engage in trade under some level of protection by the military, if needed. Sadly, with the assassination of President Lincoln, the order was rescinded, returning many freed slaves to a landless, powerless status in former Confederate states. Indeed, Sherman himself, whom black leaders had called a gift from God, later stated that his order was only military, and did not apply in peacetime.

Bethany Groff

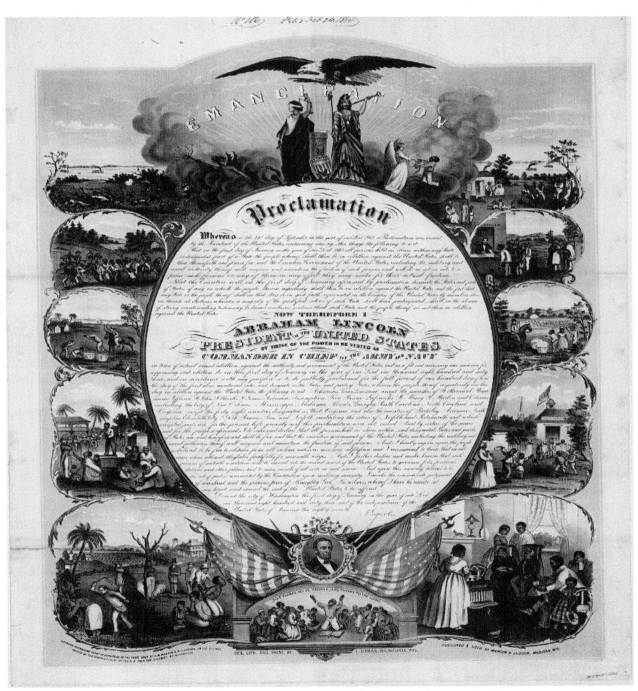

Lithograph print of the Emancipation Proclamation. Document on the Emancipation Proclamation appears on page 447.
Source: Library of Congress, Prints & Photographs Division, LC-DIG-pga-02040

■ The Confiscation Acts

Date: August 16, 1861; July 17, 1862
Author Name: Thirty-Seventh US Congress
Genre: law

*"All slaves . . . found on [or] being within any place
occupied by rebel forces and afterwards occupied by
the forces of the United States, shall be deemed
captives of war, and shall be forever free of their
servitude, and not again held as slaves."*

Summary Overview

The Confiscation Acts were laws passed by the Thirty-Seventh Congress of the United States that allowed Union soldiers to confiscate any property used by citizens or Confederate soldiers in furtherance of the war effort. In general, the Confiscation Acts were largely reformulations of standard wartime provisions calling for the confiscation of property used by opposing armies; however, the Confiscation Acts were controversial and unique in that they called for the removal of slaves from rebel citizens. The First Confiscation Act of 1861 gave Union generals and commanders the right to free slaves who had been used to aid the Confederate Army, though Abraham Lincoln and the US legislature had not committed to outlawing slavery as a whole throughout the South.

During the second session of the Thirty-Seventh Congress, a coalition of radical senators proposed a new version of the Confiscation Act that called for Union forces to confiscate—or, in essence, free—any slaves owned by rebels they encountered, even if these slaves were discovered away from any active arena of combat or were not used directly to aid the war effort. The more liberal, abolitionist version of the law was opposed by a conservative coalition in Congress that favored property rights and believed that slaves should be returned to their owners, as refusing to do so constituted theft

of property. A group of moderate senators intervened to reformulate the Second Confiscation Act in 1862 to create a compromise between these two opposing legislative positions. Ultimately, the Second Confiscation Act was ineffective at countering the rebel use of slaves during combat and was not a powerful tool for those seeking abolition. The importance of the Second Confiscation Act lies partly in the debate it raised in Congress regarding the rights of freedom and property, which ultimately led to the adoption of laws declaring that humans could not be considered property.

Defining Moment

The Thirty-Seventh Congress of the United States represented a major shift in legislative attitude regarding the continuation of slavery. In its final session, the previous Congress had proposed a constitutional amendment protecting the right to own slaves, and President Lincoln had promised in his inaugural address that he would not attempt to disrupt slavery where it already existed. Lincoln and the progressive Republicans were all abolitionists, but they were concerned that moving too quickly toward abolition would only strengthen secessionist sentiments and perhaps urge border states such as Missouri to join the Confederates. However, the realization that slavery provided a strong advantage to the disunionists convinced Lincoln and the members of the Thirty-Seventh Congress that legislative action was needed.

After the first major Union defeat of the Civil War, at the First Battle of Bull Run on July 21, 1861, Union commanders realized that slavery provided a major advantage to the Confederate war effort. Slaves aided Confederate forces by transporting food and equipment, and slave labor also allowed a greater number of citizens to join in the fighting, leaving their slaves to maintain family farms and businesses.

President Lincoln called a special session of Congress in July of 1861, the purpose of which was to discuss new legislative measures to penalize citizens who aided the rebellion and discourage popular support for the Confederates in the South. The First Confiscation Act, approved in August of 1861, gave Union commanders the power to seize any property, including slaves, being used to support "insurrectionary purposes." Abolitionists in Congress hoped to use the new law to further emancipation by encouraging Union commanders to liberate slaves. Practically, the law was a failure, as Union opinion regarding emancipation varied greatly between commanders, and many Union officers chose to return slaves to their owners rather than conduct confiscations.

A second special session of Congress was called in December of 1861 to discuss revisions to the Confiscation Act and other legislative efforts produced during the first session. Senator Lyman Trumbull led a coalition in Congress, then seen as radical, that called for a more explicit use of the Confiscation Act to free slaves utilized by insurrectionist forces. The desire to penalize the South ultimately built support for a more explicit policy that required Union forces to free slaves they encountered and provide a haven for slaves who escaped from Confederate territories. Conservative senators in the Thirty-Seventh Congress opposed the revised Confiscation Act, and the final version of the law resulted from a compromise devised by moderates in Congress.

The Confiscation Acts ultimately failed to deter popular support for the Confederate war effort in the South and also resulted in few "confiscations" of slaves. However, historians have pointed to the Confiscation Acts as important steps in the Union's increasing focus on emancipation. The congressional debates over the constitutional implications of the Confiscation Acts led to more aggressive legislative efforts to promote emancipation and, ultimately, to Lincoln's decision to issue the Emancipation Proclamation as an executive order.

Author Biography

The Thirty-Seventh Congress of the United States was in service from March 1861 to March 1863 and produced a variety of legislative decisions aimed at helping ensure Union victory during the Civil War. The legislature was called into special session by departing president James Buchanan in March of 1861 to address the threat of rebel secession, and it was still in session in April, when the Confederate attack on Fort Sumter occurred, officially marking the beginning of the Civil War.

Due to the large number of vacant seats representing states that had joined the secessionist effort, Congress was left with only two-thirds of its usual members, and the Republican Party enjoyed a majority in both the House and the Senate. The recent decline of the Whig Party and the Know-Nothing Party bolstered Republican Party support. At this point in history, the Republican Party was the more radical and liberal political organization, while the Democratic Party generally favored conservative policies.

The Thirty-Seventh Congress is remembered primarily for its legislation regarding emancipation, but it also passed a number of laws with far-reaching effects on American history. The Thirty-Seventh Congress passed the first ever revenue act, the Revenue Act of 1861, which was designed to fuel the Union war effort by collecting income tax from citizens. While the income tax was repealed after the Civil War, it was eventually reinstated and became the foundation of government funding in the United States. In addition, the Thirty-Seventh Congress passed the National Bank Act in 1864, a revision of the previous year's National Currency Act, which was initially meant to reject the proliferation of Confederate currency but also established a single accepted currency for the country as a whole.

The Thirty-Seventh Congress also played a major role in furthering the US public education system by passing the first of the Morrill Land-Grant Acts, which set aside more than fifteen million acres for the construction of trade and agricultural schools. This act, passed in 1862, was the beginning of the public university system in the United States and led to the establishment of many well-respected American universities, including the University of Berkeley and Cornell University.

Largely, the Thirty-Seventh Congress is remembered for its role in the abolition of slavery, though this did not occur until after the Thirty-Eighth Congress came into session. Illinois senator Orville Browning championed a bill that abolished slavery in the District of Columbia, and the arguments given in favor of this position would later be used to support nationwide abolition. The First and Second Confiscation Acts, in 1861 and 1862 respectively, were initially designed to prevent Confederate forces from utilizing slave labor to aid the war effort, but they became another important stepping-stone toward Lincoln's Emancipation Proclamation of 1863.

Illinois senator Lyman Trumbull was the leader of the abolitionist faction in the Thirty-Seventh Congress and one of the authors of the First Confiscation Act, which he hoped to use as a back-door approach to promoting the emancipation of Southern slaves. Trumbull was also one of the authors of the Thirteenth Amendment of the United States Constitution, accepted into law in 1864, which formally outlawed slavery throughout the United States. Maine senator William Fessenden was another abolitionist in the Thirty-Seventh Congress who helped to craft the Second Confiscation Act; he was largely responsible for the more direct attack on slavery in the second version of the law.

THE CONFISCATION ACTS

First Confiscation Act

CHAP. LX—An Act to confiscate Property used for Insurrectionary Purposes.

Be it enacted by the Senate and House of Representatives of the United States of America in Congress assembled, That if, during the present or any future insurrection against the Government of the United States, after the President of the United States shall have declared, by proclamation, that the laws of the United States are opposed, and the execution thereof obstructed, by combinations too powerful to be suppressed by the ordinary course of judicial proceedings, or by the power vested in the marshals by law, any person or persons, his, her, or their agent, attorney, or employé, shall purchase or acquire, sell or give, any property of whatsoever kind or description, with intent to use or employ the same, or suffer the same to be used or employed, in aiding, abetting, or promoting such insurrection or resistance to the laws, or any person or persons engaged therein; or if any person or persons, being the owner or owners of any such property, shall knowingly use or employ, or consent to the use or employment of the same as aforesaid, all such property is hereby declared to be lawful subject of prize and capture wherever found; and it shall be the duty of the President of the United States to cause the same to be seized, confiscated, and condemned.

SEC. 2. And be it further enacted, That such prizes and capture shall be condemned in the district or circuit court of the United States having jurisdiction of the amount, or in admiralty in any district in which the same may be seized, or into which they may be taken and proceedings first instituted.

SEC. 3. And be it further enacted, That the Attorney-General, or any district attorney of the United States in which said property may at the time be, may institute the proceedings of condemnation, and in such case they shall be wholly for the benefit of the United States; or any person may file an information with such attorney, in which case the proceedings shall be for the use of such informer and the United States in equal parts.

SEC. 4. And be it further enacted, That whenever hereafter, during the present insurrection against the Government of the United States, any person claimed to be held to labor or service under the law of any State, shall be required or permitted by the person to whom such labor or service is claimed to be due, or by the lawful agent of such person, to take up arms against the United States, or shall be required or permitted by the person to whom such labor or service is claimed to be due, or his lawful agent, to work or to be employed in or upon any fort, navy yard, dock, armory, ship, entrenchment, or in any military or naval service whatsoever, against the Government and lawful authority of the United States, then, and in every such case, the person to whom such labor or service is claimed to be due shall forfeit his claim to such labor, any law of the State or of the United States to the contrary notwithstanding. And whenever thereafter the person claiming such labor or service shall seek to enforce his claim, it shall be a full and sufficient answer to such claim that the person whose service or labor is claimed had been employed in hostile service against the Government of the United States, contrary to the provisions of this act.

APPROVED, August 6, 1861.

Second Confiscation Act

CHAP. CXCV.—An Act to suppress Insurrection, to punish Treason and Rebellion, to seize and confiscate the Property of Rebels, and for other Purposes.

Be it enacted by the Senate and House of Representatives of the United States of America in Congress assembled, That every person who shall hereafter commit the crime of treason against the United States, and shall be adjudged guilty thereof, shall suffer death, and all his slaves, if any, shall be declared and made free; or, at the discretion of the court, he shall be imprisoned for not less than five years and fined not less than ten thousand dollars, and all his slaves, if any, shall be declared and made free; said fine shall be levied and collected on any or all of the property, real and personal, excluding slaves, of which the said person so convicted was the owner at the time of committing the said crime, any sale or conveyance to the contrary notwithstanding.

SEC. 2. And be it further enacted, That if any person shall hereafter incite, set on foot, assist, or engage in any rebellion or insurrection against the authority of the United States, or the laws thereof, or shall give aid or comfort thereto, or shall engage in, or give aid and comfort to, any such existing rebellion or insurrection, and be convicted thereof, such person shall be punished by imprisonment for a period not exceeding ten years, or by a fine not exceeding ten thousand dollars, and by the liberation of all his slaves, if any he have; or by both of said punishments, at the discretion of the court.

SEC. 3. And be it further enacted, That every person guilty of either of the offences described in this act shall be forever incapable and disqualified to hold any office under the United States.

SEC. 4. And be it further enacted, That this act shall not be construed in any way to affect or alter the prosecution, conviction, or punishment of any person or persons guilty of treason against the United States before the passage of this act, unless such person is convicted under this act.

SEC. 5. And be it further enacted, That, to insure the speedy termination of the present rebellion, it shall be the duty of the President of the United States to cause the seizure of all the estate and property, money, stocks, credits, and effects of the persons hereinafter named in this section, and to apply and use the same and the proceeds thereof for the support of the army of the United States, that is to say:

First. Of any person hereafter acting as an officer of the army or navy of the rebels in arms against the government of the United States.

Secondly. Of any person hereafter acting as President, Vice-President, member of Congress, judge of any court, cabinet officer, foreign minister, commissioner or consul of the so-called confederate states of America.

Thirdly. Of any person acting as governor of a state, member of a convention or legislature, or judge of any court of any of the so-called confederate states of America.

Fourthly. Of any person who, having held an office of honor, trust, or profit in the United States, shall hereafter hold an office in the so-called confederate states of America.

Fifthly. Of any person hereafter holding any office or agency under the government of the so-called confederate states of America, or under any of the several states of the said confederacy, or the laws thereof, whether such office or agency be national, state, or municipal in its name or character: Provided, That the persons, thirdly, fourthly, and fifthly above described shall have accepted their appointment or election since the date of the pretended ordinance of secession of the state, or shall have taken an oath of allegiance to, or to support the constitution of the so-called confederate states.

Sixthly. Of any person who, owning property in any loyal State or Territory of the United States, or in the District of Columbia, shall here-after assist and give aid and comfort to such rebellion; and all sales, transfers, or conveyances of any such property shall be null and void; and it shall be a sufficient bar to any suit brought by such person for the possession or the use of such property, or any of it, to allege and prove that he is one of the persons described in this section.

SEC. 6. And be it further enacted, That if any person within any State or Territory of the United States, other than those named as afore-said, after the passage of this act, being engaged in armed rebellion against the government of the United States, or aiding or abetting such rebellion shall not, within sixty days after public warning and proclamation duly given and made by the President of the United States, cease to aid, countenance, and abet such rebellion, and return to his allegiance to the United States, all the estate and property, moneys, stocks, and credits of such person shall be liable to seizure as aforesaid, and it shall be the duty of the President to seize and use them as aforesaid or the proceeds thereof And all sales, transfers, or conveyances, of any such property after the expiration of the said sixty days from the date of such warning and proclamation shall be null and void; and it shall be a sufficient bar to any suit brought by such person for the possession or the use of such property, or any of it, to allege and prove that he is one of the persons described in this section.

SEC. 7. And be it further enacted, That to secure the condemnation and sale of any of such property, after the same shall have been seized, so that it may be made available for the purpose aforesaid, proceedings in rem shall be instituted in the name of the United States in any district court thereof, or in any territorial court, or in the United States district court for the District of Columbia, within which the property above described, or any part thereof, may be found, or into which the same, if movable, may first be brought, which proceedings shall conform as nearly as may be to proceedings in admiralty or revenue cases, and if said property, whether real or personal, shall be found to have belonged to a person engaged in rebellion, or who has given aid or comfort thereto, the same shall be condemned as enemies' property and become the property of the United States, and may be disposed of as the court shall decree and the proceeds thereof paid into the treasury of the United States for the purposes aforesaid.

SEC. 8. And be it further enacted, That the several courts aforesaid shall have power to make such orders, establish such forms of decree and sale, and direct such deeds and conveyances to be executed and delivered by the marshals thereof where real estate shall be the

subject of sale, as shall fitly and efficiently effect the purposes of this act, and vest in the purchasers of such property good and valid titles thereto. And the said courts shall have power to allow such fees and charges of their officers as shall be reasonable and proper in the premises.

SEC. 9. And be it further enacted, That all slaves of persons who shall hereafter be engaged in rebellion against the government of the United States, or who shall in any way give aid or comfort thereto, escaping from such persons and taking refuge within the lines of the army; and all slaves captured from such persons or deserted by them and coming under the control of the government of the United States; and all slaves of such persons found on [or] being within any place occupied by rebel forces and afterwards occupied by the forces of the United States, shall be deemed captives of war, and shall be forever free of their servitude, and not again held as slaves.

SEC. 10. And be it further enacted, That no slave escaping into any State, Territory, or the District of Columbia, from any other State, shall be delivered up, or in any way impeded or hindered of his liberty, except for crime, or some offence against the laws, unless the person claiming said fugitive shall first make oath that the person to whom the labor or service of such fugitive is alleged to be due is his lawful owner, and has not borne arms against the United States in the present rebellion, nor in any way given aid and comfort thereto; and no person engaged in the military or naval service of the United States shall, under any pretence whatever, assume to decide on the validity of the claim of any person to the service or labor of any other person, or surrender up any such person to the claimant, on pain of being dismissed from the service.

SEC. 11. And be it further enacted, That the President of the United States is authorized to employ as many persons of African descent as he may deem necessary and proper for the suppression of this rebellion, and for this purpose he may organize and use them in such manner as he may judge best for the public welfare.

SEC. 12. And be it further enacted, That the President of the United States is hereby authorized to make provision for the transportation, colonization, and settlement, in some tropical country beyond the limits of the

United States, of such persons of the African race, made free by the provisions of this act, as may be willing to emigrate, having first obtained the consent of the government of said country to their protection and settlement within the same, with all the rights and privileges of freemen.

SEC. 13. And be it further enacted, That the President is hereby authorized, at any time hereafter, by proclamation, to extend to persons who may have participated in the existing rebellion in any State or part thereof, pardon and amnesty, with such exceptions and at such time and on such conditions as he may deem expedient for the public welfare.

SEC. 14. And be it further enacted, That the courts of the United States shall have full power to institute proceedings, make orders and decrees, issue process, and do all other things necessary to carry this act into effect.

APPROVED, July 17, 1862.

GLOSSARY

abjudged: removed from, as through judicial decision

condemned: in the legal sense, appropriated for public use

countenance: to admit as acceptable, support, or accept the existence of

entrenchment: to dig or occupy a trench for the purpose of fortifying or defending a territory, or a trench or system of trenches used for fortification or defense

enacted: made into law or put into practice

insurrectionary: of or relating to an open revolt against a civil authority

proclamation: an official formal public announcement or the act of issuing such an announcement

rebels: those engaged in rebellion against the United States, used to refer to the individuals and states that joined the Confederates during the Civil War

Document Analysis

The text of the First Confiscation Act begins by announcing the purpose of the law, which is to "confiscate Property used for Insurrectionary Purposes." According to the primary provision of the law, "any property" used directly or indirectly for insurrection, or purchased with the goal of aiding insurrection or in support of an individual who then supported insurrection, would be, upon the authority of the president, "seized, confiscated, and condemned."

In legal terminology, the act of condemning property means to remove it from private ownership and place it within public use. In general, property that is condemned in this way is not transferred to public ownership but rather sold or converted so as to benefit the public. The Confiscation Act of 1861 gives state attorneys general the power to determine the method in which any seized property would be used but states that the use of such property must be for the good of the United States public.

Section 4 of the act specifically details that "any person claimed to be held to labor or service under the law" will be freed from these obligations, and the person claiming ownership of this labor or service will forfeit their rights. In essence, this section of the bill attacks labor contracts holding individuals in service to an employer who supports the insurrection; it calls for these contracts, however they came about, to be nullified by the use of labor to support rebellion.

At the time the First Confiscation Act was written, slaves were classified as property, and the provisions of the law calling for the confiscation of property were therefore considered to apply equally to slaves. The question remained of how the Union would handle the condemnation of the slaves, as the law called for property to be used to aid the public. The more liberal, abolitionist members of the Thirty-Seventh Congress, including Lyman Trumbull from Illinois, wanted slaves found aiding the Confederacy to be freed upon transfer to a state where slavery was prohibited. This aspect of the law was contrary to Lincoln's inaugural promise not to interfere with the legality of slavery and frightened many of the conservative and moderate members of Congress, who wished to avoid any act that might influence other states with powerful slave-owning lobbies to join with the Confederate secession.

The Confiscation Act of 1861 passed with a strong majority in both houses, though Lincoln was initially reluctant to sign the bill into law. What convinced Lincoln, and many of the members of Congress who took a more moderate stance on slavery, was the fact that slave labor allowed Confederate forces to bolster their armies. The Union defeat at the First Battle of Bull Run made this imbalance clear and called for strong legislative provisions. Ultimately, the Confiscation Act of 1861 was ineffective, as Union commanders made few confiscations and officers serving in border states like Missouri continued to return captured slaves rather than confiscating or freeing them as the law required.

Immediately after passing the Confiscation Act of 1861, a coalition of more liberal members of Congress began lobbying for a stronger version of the law, one that specifically targeted the institution of slavery. Lyman Trumbull and Maine senator William Fessenden, both of whom had strong personal commitments to abolition, spearheaded a new version of the bill that called for slaves to be freed wherever Union soldiers encountered them, even if the slaves in question were not being used directly to support the insurrection.

By 1862, it was clear that the dispensation of slaves was becoming an increasing problem. Slaves fled from their owners across Union lines as the Union Army advanced, hoping to find freedom. Union commanders differed in their approach to the problem, with some providing refuge to the fugitive slaves and others returning them to Confederate forces to be returned to their owners. In addition, slaves were still being used to bolster both the labor force and the military on the Confederate side, and this advantage was a continuing concern for Union commanders.

Trumbull and Fessenden's more radical version of the Confiscation Act was opposed by a coalition of

members of Congress who believed that the act violated constitutional rights. Specifically, opponents of the law were concerned that it called for the confiscation of property without due process in the courts. The debate continued until moderate members of Congress assisted in formulating a version of the law that was seen as a compromise between the two positions. The Confiscation Act of 1862 was adopted into law on July 17, though the final version was still seen as too radical by some in Congress.

The Confiscation Act of 1862 begins with the declaration that the law was formulated "to suppress Insurrection, to punish Treason and Rebellion, to seize and confiscate the Property of Rebels, and for other Purposes." The primary purpose of the law, provided in the next section, clearly states that "every person who shall hereafter commit the crime of treason against the United States, and shall be adjudged guilty thereof, shall suffer death, and all his slaves, if any, shall be declared and made free."

Orville Hickman Browning, who was strong supporter of abolition but took a moderate legislative stance on the issue, believed that the second act was unconstitutional because it allowed for the confiscation of property that legally belonged to individuals without first requiring that the individuals be found guilty by a court decision. In Browning's assessment, the constitutional rights guaranteed to all citizens must still protect citizens of the Confederate states, though they were currently participating in an insurrection. The Supreme Court upheld the constitutionality of the Confiscation Act of 1892, stating that extreme provisions are necessary in wartime that may violate the rights extended to the populace in other circumstances. Specifically, the Supreme Court ruled that in the case of the Civil War, the United States government, as manifested through the Union Army, had the rights both of a governing body and of a "belligerent," which is legally defined as a political party involved in warfare. As such, the Supreme Court ruled that the United States government was free to exercise its power in ways falling under either of these categories.

Sections 2 through 8 of the Confiscation Act of 1862 explain that the provisions of the law go into effect immediately but do not affect the prosecution or sentencing of any individuals arrested or convicted of treason before the passage of the law. In addition, these sections of the act state that the president of the United States has absolute discretion to command the seizure and condemnation of any and all property, items of value, or monetary holdings of any individual who takes part in rebellion against the United States. These sections had no direct bearing on the standing of slaves and were designed to send a message to any considering participating in the rebellion: the Union would consider their rights to property ownership forfeit and could, at any time thereafter, claim ownership of any properties and monetary holdings belonging to such individuals.

Sections 9 and 10 return to the issue of slaves directly and formally restate the position that all slaves confiscated will be freed and will not be, at any time, returned to slavery. Section 9 states that all slaves occupying areas utilized by rebel forces, even if not involved in assisting rebel armies, will be considered subject to confiscation and will be freed from slavery. Section 10 states that no Union commanders or soldiers will return escaped slaves to their former owners; it also states that slaves who escape their bondage and arrive in Union territory will also be freed from the conditions of slavery if commanding officers believe that the slaves were owned by soldiers or persons aiding the Confederate insurrection.

Sections 9 and 10 of the Confiscation Act are significant, in that they directly address the responsibilities of Union forces regarding escaped slaves and slaves owned by citizens engaged in the rebellion. In essence, these sections of the law are in keeping with the hopes of the abolitionists in Congress who wanted to use the Confiscation Acts to free slaves held by Confederate owners and provide a route through which slaves could earn their freedom by fleeing Confederate territories.

Section 11 of the Confiscation Act ascribes to the president the right to "employ" former slaves and all other persons of similar descent to serve in the military in furtherance of the Union cause. While this section of the law places limits on the freedom given to the former slaves, stating that they were required to serve in the Union Army at the president's discretion, the wording of the section is significant in that the law refers to these individuals as "persons of African descent." In her book *From Property to Person* (2005), historian Silvana Siddali sees this section as marking a turning point in the legal, legislative approach to slavery, in terms of viewing African Americans as people rather than property.

Section 12 of the Confiscation Act reflects differing opinions over what should be done with the former slave population after the conclusion of the war. While some envisioned former slaves as being integrated with the rest of the population, others, for various reasons, believed that this was not a tenable solution to the issue. Some felt that the slaves should be relocated, in a manner similar to that used to relocate Native Americans. Section 12 states that the president may "make provision for the transportation, colonization, and settlement, in some tropical country beyond the limits of the United States, of such persons of the African race . . . as may be willing to emigrate." Some in the government envisioned the United States transporting former slaves to the tropical islands of the Caribbean or other locations where former slaves had previously established colonies. While resettlement was not widely utilized after the Civil War, the members of the Thirty-Seventh Congress included the provision in the bill, planning for one of several potential measures that might be used to handle relocation of the former slave population.

The Confiscation Act of 1862 did not result in a large number of confiscations, and President Lincoln did not aggressively enforce adherence to the law among his military commanders. Historians have largely dismissed the provisions of the Second Confiscation Act as ineffective in addressing either the practical interests of those hoping to prevent the escalation of the conflict or the more radical goals of the abolitionists in Congress. Lincoln, for his part, was reluctant to support the law, and provisions were included in section 13 of the bill that allowed him to grant pardons to any individual whose property or assets had been seized as a result of the Confiscation Act. The moderate and conservative members of Congress considered the Confiscation Act to be a temporary initiative that would be repealed when the war was over, but the ultimate significance of the legislation came in the debate it stimulated in the legislature. The provisions of the law extending the rights of former slaves and the provisions that protected the rights of escaped slaves were significant and opened the door to an increasing exodus of slaves from the South. Ultimately, the failure of the act was twofold, in that it was not adequately enforced and it only granted freedom to slaves who were owned by "rebels," thus leaving considerable discretion to determine whether a slave should be freed.

What the Confiscation Act failed to achieve was ultimately accomplished by an executive order known as the Emancipation Proclamation, issued by President Lincoln in January of 1863. Utilizing his authority as commander in chief of the armed forces, Lincoln declared that all remaining slaves in Confederate territories were free in the eyes of the legitimate American government. What followed was a major exodus of slaves into Northern territories, weakening Confederate forces considerably. The achievements of the Emancipation Proclamation and the Thirteenth Amendment were largely the product of legislative and governmental debates that were initiated in the wake of the Confiscation Acts.

Essential Themes

The Confiscation Acts of 1861 and 1862, and the legislative efforts emerging from the Thirty-Seventh Congress, mark a historic point in American history. With these changes, the executive, legislative, and judicial branches of the government were forced to tackle the difficult issue of slavery and balance the need to unify the country with the overarching human-rights issues of the debate. Chief among these issues was the legal definition of slaves as property. The development of the Confiscation Acts provides a historic record of a substantial shift in the legislative approach to slavery. The first Confiscation Act makes no direct reference to slaves but considers them to be subject to confiscation because slaves were defined as property. The second Confiscation Act explicitly refers to slaves as "persons" who are to be freed from servitude. Between the two versions of the Confiscation Act, separated by a year of legislative debate, the beginnings of a new legislative position on the issue came about, ultimately leading to the legal position that no person can be considered property of another.

The total abolition of slavery was one of the most significant results of the Civil War and is perhaps the most important consequence of the war in terms of historical significance. Among abolitionists of the period, including Abraham Lincoln, it was initially believed that the Civil War would need to be settled before nationwide progress on abolition could be achieved. Interestingly, the fact that slave labor was a military benefit to the Confederate Army was one of the primary motivations behind the Union's decision to take a more affirmative stance on emancipation.

Throughout the nearly five years of the Civil War, numerous liberal military and legislative leaders attempted to institute local and state emancipation. In many cases, these legislative efforts were thwarted by senators and representatives who believed that an aggressive stance

on abolition would ultimately strengthen the Confederate cause. To provide one example, John C. Fremont, a Union general serving in Missouri, declared martial law after successfully defeating a pro-secession wing of the military in that state. Fremont decided to emancipate all slaves in the state, but he was removed from his post by President Lincoln, who feared that Fremont's emancipation law would urge citizens of Missouri to support the Confederate cause.

While the Confiscation Acts became a rallying point for legislators seeking to promote emancipation, they were also an example of the way that legislative bodies promote military victory by supporting legislation that can be used to either strengthen the power of military leaders or levy additional punishments and penalties against supporters of the enemy. The Confiscation Act was primarily produced to address Confederate ownership of slaves, but it also threatened those who supported the Confederacy with the potential loss of all property and monetary assets in the event of a Union victory. In this way, the Confiscation Acts can be seen as a legislative and legal threat to the Union's enemies. Though few Confederate supporters abandoned their positions as a result of the Confiscation Acts, the text of both laws serves as a prime example of legislation during wartime.

Micah Issitt

Bibliography

Hamilton, Daniel. *The Limits of Sovereignty: Property Confiscation in the Union and the Confederacy during the Civil War.* Chicago: U of Chicago P, 2007. Print.

Siddali, Silvana R. *From Property to Person: Slavery and the Confiscation Acts, 1861–1862.* Baton Rouge: Louisiana State UP, 2005. Print.

Syrett, John. *The Civil War Confiscation Acts: Failing to Reconstruct the South.* New York: Fordham UP, 2005. Print.

Additional Reading

Burlingame, Michael. *Lincoln and the Civil War.* Carbondale: Southern Illinois UP, 2011. Print.

Foner, Eric. *The Fiery Trial: Abraham Lincoln and American Slavery.* New York: Norton, 2010. Print.

Ranney, Joseph A. *In the Wake of Slavery: Civil War, Civil Rights, and the Reconstruction of Southern Law.* Santa Barbara: Greenwood, 2006. Print.

Rutherglen, George. *Civil Rights in the Shadow of Slav*

ery. New York: Oxford UP, 2013. Print.

Stokesbury, James L. *A Short History of the Civil War*. New York: Harper, 2005. Print.

Vorenberg, Michael. *Final Freedom: The Civil War, the Abolition of Slavery, and the Thirteenth Amendment*. New York: Cambridge UP, 2001. Print.

■ Treaty between the United States and Great Britain for the Suppression of the Slave Trade (Lyons-Seward Treaty of 1862)

Date: April 7, 1862
Author: Seward, William Henry
Genre: treaty

> *"The negroes who are found on board of a vessel condemned by the mixed courts of justice, . . . shall be immediately set at liberty, and shall remain free, the Government to whom they have been delivered guarantying their liberty."*

Summary Overview

By the mid-nineteenth century, efforts to end the transportation of slaves from Africa to various locations in the Western Hemisphere had been underway for decades. In 1807, Great Britain outlawed the slave trade within its empire, with a few exceptions in Asia, and the United States outlawed the importation of slaves in the same year, effective in 1808. In 1862, the United States was involved in the Civil War, a central cause of which was slavery. Great Britain and the United States had just come to an agreement regarding the *Trent* Affair, which dealt with stopping ships in international waters. Sensing that the time was right for further agreements, the British ambassador, Lord Richard Lyons, proposed to Secretary of State William Henry Seward an agreement that would expand efforts to totally eliminate the slave trade. This included allowing each country the freedom to board and inspect any ships suspected of being involved in the slave trade, not just their own. Within weeks, the two countries agreed, and without any senators from the Southern states, the treaty was quickly ratified.

Defining Moment

The relationship between the United States and Great Britain had fluctuated widely during the almost eighty years since the end of the Revolutionary War, but through the decades, ties had gradually become stronger. Agreements regarding the northern border of the United States and increased trade had brought the two countries into a more harmonious relationship. However, with the secession of the Southern states and the beginning of the American Civil War, the relationship between the two countries again became strained. The supply of American cotton to British mills was greatly diminished, and United States ships were intercepting British freighters as the Union blockade of the South tried to put economic pressure on the Confederates. To strengthen this effort, the American ships that had been patrolling near Africa to block the slave trade were withdrawn to American waters. The November 1861 *Trent* Affair, in which two Confederate emissaries were taken off the British ship RMS *Trent* in international waters, also put the British firmly at odds with the American government.

In addition to these elements, the British view of

the American secretary of state, William Seward, was highly negative. Seward had been the favorite to become the Republican nominee for president in 1860, but his strongly belligerent views on slavery and other issues diminished support for him, and the more moderate Abraham Lincoln was nominated. When Seward and others were convinced to take steps to relieve the tension with the British over the *Trent* Affair, the British ambassador to the United States, Lord Richard Lyons, came to change his opinion of Seward. After they had jointly solved one crisis, Lord Lyons pushed forward to address another issue related to the *Trent* Affair.

Although the international slave trade had been outlawed by most nations, it was still occurring. Based on understandings reached at the end of the War of 1812 and the *Trent* Affair, British naval officers would be taking a major risk by stopping any American ships in international waters. With the American navy focusing on the blockade in American coastal waters, many slave ships near Africa were flying the American flag to avoid being stopped by the British. Based on the common interest of the United States and Great Britain in ending the illegal slave trade, Lyons proposed a treaty to cooperate in apprehending ships and crews involved in the trade. Seward saw the treaty's advantage to the United States as well as to his own antislavery views. He and Lyons quickly negotiated the specifics of the treaty, and it was ratified by both countries.

Author Biography

Born May 16, 1801, to Samuel Sweezy Seward and Mary Jennings, William Henry Seward was one of five children in a strong and prosperous household in Florida, New York. He graduated from Union College with a law degree and began practicing law in 1821. He moved to Auburn, New York, to practice law with his fiancée's father. In 1824, he married Frances Adeline Miller, with whom he had five children. Having grown up in a household with slaves, he understood the inequality of the system. His wife was a strong abolitionist, pushing him further in that direction and opening their home to fugitive slaves.

During the 1830s, Seward entered politics, serving in the state Senate as a member of the Anti-Masonic Party. After losing a race to become governor of New York, Seward traveled throughout the state giving speeches, including one on the need for universal education. He was elected governor in 1838 and 1840 as a Whig. In 1849, he was chosen to be a US senator and led the antislavery wing of the Whig Party. Seward was reelected in 1855 and moved to the Republican Party, as most Whigs did when the Whig Party disintegrated. In 1858, he made a divisive and prophetic speech stating that the American system could not endure the split between slave and free states; he said it would become all one or the other. Seward was favored for the 1860 Republican nomination, and while he had the plurality on the first nominating ballet, his support rapidly dropped. He campaigned for the eventual nominee, Abraham Lincoln, and when Lincoln won the general election, Seward agreed to join his cabinet.

As secretary of state, Seward had an expansionist vision for America. Even during the Civil War, he spoke of expanding not just in North America but into the Pacific Ocean and the Caribbean. This, in addition to his aggressive nature, set him at odds with European leaders, who saw him as intruding into their areas. The most dangerous task that confronted him during the Civil War was the *Trent* Affair, when he had to work with the British to diffuse a situation that might have led to war with Britain. As this was handled very professionally, Seward's standing with British leaders increased, and they were willing to negotiate with him on a number of other matters, including ending the slave trade.

After the war, Seward's only acquisition was the purchase of Alaska. However, he strengthened relations with China and Japan, as well as helping establish a stronger American influence in Hawaii. He retired at the end of President Andrew Johnson's term of office and traveled widely until shortly before his death on October 10, 1872.

HISTORICAL DOCUMENT

Treaty between the United States and Great Britain for the Suppression of the Slave Trade. Concluded at Washington, April 7, 1862. Ratifications exchanged at London, May 25, 1862. Proclaimed by the President of the United States, June 7, 1862.

BY THE PRESIDENT OF THE UNITED STATES OF AMERICA: A PROCLAMATION.

Whereas a treaty between the United States of America and her Majesty the Queen of the United Kingdom of Great Britain and Ireland was concluded and signed by their respective Plenipotentiaries, at the city of Washington, on the seventh day of April last, which treaty is, word for word, as follows:

Treaty between the United States of America and her Majesty the Queen of the United Kingdom of Great Britain and Ireland, for the suppression of the African slave trade.

The United States of America and her Majesty the Queen of the United Kingdom of Great Britain and Ireland, being desirous to render more effectual the means hitherto adopted for the suppression of the slave trade carried on upon the coast of Africa, have deemed it expedient to conclude a treaty for that purpose, and have named as their Plenipotentiaries, that is to say:

The President of the United States of America, William H. Seward, Secretary of State;

And her Majesty the Queen of the United Kingdom of Great Britain and Ireland, the right honorable Richard Bickerton Pemell, Lord Lyons, a peer of her United Kingdom, a knight grand cross of her most honorable Order of the Bath, and her Envoy Extraordinary and Minister Plenipotentiary to the United States of America;

Who, after having communicated to each other their respective full powers, found in good and due form, have agreed upon and concluded the following articles:

ARTICLE I. The two high contracting parties mutually consent that those ships of their respective navies which shall be provided with special instructions for that purpose, as hereinafter mentioned, may visit such merchant vessels of the two nations as may, upon reasonable

grounds, be suspected of being engaged in the African slave trade, or of having been fitted out for that purpose; or of having, during the voyage on which they are met by the said cruisers, been engaged in the African slave trade, contrary to the provisions of this treaty; and that such cruisers may detain, and send or carry away, such vessels, in order that they may be brought to trial in the manner hereinafter agreed upon.

In order to fix the reciprocal right of search in such a manner as shall be adapted to the attainment of the object of this treaty, and at the same time avoid doubts, disputes, and complaints, the said right of search shall be understood in the manner and according to the rules following:

First. It shall never be exercised except by vessels of war, authorized expressly for that object, according to the stipulations of this treaty.

Secondly. The right of search shall in no case be exercised with respect to a vessel of the navy of either of the two Powers, but shall be exercised only as regards merchant-vessels; and it shall not be exercised by a vessel of war of either contracting party within the limits of a settlement or port, nor within the territorial waters of the other party.

Thirdly. Whenever a merchant-vessel is searched by a ship of war, the commander of the said ship shall, in the act of so doing, exhibit to the commander of the merchant-vessel the special instructions by which he is duly authorized to search; and shall deliver to such commander a certificate, signed by himself, stating his rank in the naval service of his country, and the name of the vessel he commands, and also declaring that the only object of the search is to ascertain whether the vessel is employed in the African slave trade, or is fitted up for the said trade. When the search is made by an officer of the cruiser who is not the commander, such officer shall exhibit to the captain of the merchant-vessel a copy of the before-mentioned special instructions, signed by the commander of the cruiser; and he shall in like manner deliver a certificate signed by himself, stating his rank in the navy, the name of the commander by whose orders he proceeds to make the search, that of the cruiser in which he sails, and the object of the search, as above described. If it appears from the search that the papers of the vessel are in regular order, and that it is employed on lawful objects, the officer shall enter in the log-book of the vessel that the search has been made in pursuance of the aforesaid special instructions; and the vessel shall be left at liberty to pursue its voyage. The rank of the officer who makes the search must not be less than that of lieutenant in the navy, unless the command, either by reason of death or other cause, is at the time held by an officer of inferior rank.

Fourthly. The reciprocal right of search and detention shall be exercised only within the distance of two hundred miles from the coast of Africa, and to the southward of the thirty-second parallel of north latitude, and within thirty leagues from the coast of the Island of Cuba.

ARTICLE II. In order to regulate the mode of carrying the provisions of the preceding article into execution, it is agreed—

First. That all the ships of the navies of the two nations which shall be hereafter employed to prevent the African slave trade shall be furnished by their respective Governments with a copy of the present treaty, of the instructions for cruisers annexed thereto, (marked A,) and of the regulations for the mixed courts of justice annexed thereto, (marked B,) which annexes respectively shall be considered as integral parts of the present treaty.

Secondly. That each of the high contracting parties shall, from time to time, communicate to the other the names of the several ships furnished with such instructions, the force of each, and the names of their several commanders. The said commanders shall hold the rank of captain in the navy, or at least that of lieutenant; it being nevertheless understood that the instructions originally issued to an officer holding the rank of lieutenant of the navy, or other superior rank, shall, in case of his death or temporary absence, be sufficient to authorize the officer on whom the command of the vessel has devolved to make the search, although such officer may not hold the aforesaid rank in the service.

Thirdly. That if at any time the commander of a cruiser of either of the two nations shall suspect that any merchant-vessel under the escort or convoy of any ship or ships-of-war of the other nation carries negroes on board, or has been engaged in the African slave trade, or is fitted out for the purpose thereof, the commander of the cruiser shall communicate his suspicions to the commander of the convoy, who, accompanied by the commander of the cruiser, shall proceed to the search of the suspected vessel; and in case the suspicions appear well founded, according to the tenor of this treaty, then the said vessel shall be conducted or sent to one of the places where the mixed courts of justice are stationed, in order that it may there be adjudicated upon.

Fourthly. It is further mutually agreed that the commanders of the ships of the two navies, respectively, who shall be employed on this service, shall adhere strictly to the exact tenor of the aforesaid instructions.

ARTICLE III. As the two preceding articles are entirely reciprocal, the two high contracting parties engage mutually to make good any losses which their respective subjects or citizens may incur by an arbitrary and illegal detention of their vessels; it being understood that this indemnity shall be borne by the Government whose cruiser shall have been guilty of such arbitrary and illegal detention; and that the search and detention of vessels specified in the first article of this treaty shall be effected only by ships which may form part of the two navies, respectively, and by such of those ships only as are provided with the special instructions annexed to the present treaty, in pursuance of the provisions thereof. The indemnification for the damages of which this article treats shall be paid within the term of one year, reckoning from the day in which the mixed court of justice pronounces its sentence.

ARTICLE IV. In order to bring to adjudication with as little delay and inconvenience as possible, the vessels which may be detained according to the tenor of the first article of this treaty, there shall be established, as soon as may be practicable, three mixed courts of justice, formed by an equal number of individuals of the two nations, named for this purpose by their respective Governments. These courts shall reside, one at Sierra Leone, one at the Cape of Good Hope, and one at New York.

But each of the two high contracting parties reserves to itself the right of changing, at its pleasure, the place of residence of the court or courts held within its own territories.

These courts shall judge the causes submitted to them according to the provisions of the present treaty, and according to the regulations and instructions which are annexed to the present treaty, and which are considered an integral part thereof; and there shall be no appeal from their decision.

ARTICLE V. In case the commanding officer of any of the ships of the navies of either country, duly commissioned according to the provisions of the first article of this treaty, shall deviate in any respect from the stipulations of the said treaty, or from the instructions annexed to it, the Government which shall conceive itself to be wronged thereby shall be entitled to demand reparation; and in such case the Government to which such commanding officer may belong binds itself to cause inquiry to be made into the subject of the complaint, and to inflict upon the said officer a punishment proportioned to any wilful transgression which may be proved to have committed.

ARTICLE VI. It is hereby further mutually agreed, that every American or British merchant-vessel which shall be searched by virtue of the present treaty may lawfully be detained, and sent or brought before the mixed courts of justice established in pursuance of the provisions thereof, if, in her equipment, there shall be found any of the things hereinafter mentioned, namely:

First. Hatches with open gratings, instead of the close hatches, which are usual in merchant vessels.

Second. Divisions or bulk-heads in the hold or on deck, in greater number than are necessary for vessels engaged in lawful trade.

Third. Spare plank fitted for laying down as a second or slave deck.

Fourth. Shackles, bolts, or handcuffs.

Fifth. A larger quantity of water in casks or in tanks than is requisite for the consumption of the crew of the vessel as a merchant-vessel.

Sixth. An extraordinary number of water casks, or of other vessels for holding liquid; unless the master shall produce a certificate from the custom-house at the place from which he cleared outwards, stating that a sufficient security had been given by the owners of such vessel that such extra quantity of casks, or of other vessels should be used only to hold palm oil, or for other purposes of lawful commerce.

Seventh. A greater number of mess-tubs or kids than requisite for the use of the crew of the vessel as a merchant-vessel.

Eighth. A boiler, or other cooking apparatus, of an unusual size, and larger, or capable of being made larger, than requisite for the use of the crew of the vessel as a merchant-vessel; or more than one boiler, or other cooking apparatus, of the ordinary size.

Ninth. An extraordinary quantity of rice, of the flour of Brazil, of manioc or cassada, commonly called farinha, of maize, or of Indian corn, or of any other article of food whatever, beyond the probable wants of the crew; unless such rice, flour, farinha, maize, Indian corn, or other article of food, be entered on the manifest as part of the cargo for trade.

Tenth. A quantity of mats or matting greater than is necessary for the use of the crew of the vessel as a merchant-vessel, unless such mats or matting be entered on the manifest as part of the cargo for trade.

If it be proved that any one or more of the articles above specified is or are on board, or have been on board during the voyage in which the vessel was captured, that fact shall be considered as *primâ facie* evidence that the vessel was employed in the African slave trade, and she shall in consequence be condemned and declared lawful prize; unless the master or owners shall furnish clear and incontrovertible evidence, proving to the satisfaction of the mixed court of justice, that at the time of her detention or capture the vessel was employed in a lawful undertaking, and that such of the different articles above specified as were found on board at the time of detention, or as may have been embarked during the voyage on which she was engaged when captured, were indispensable for the lawful object of her voyage.

ARTICLE VII. If any one of the articles specified in the preceding article as grounds for condemnation should be found on board a merchant-vessel, or should be proved to have been on board of her during the voyage on which she was captured, no compensation for losses, damages, or expenses consequent upon the detention of such vessel, shall in any case be granted either to the master, the owner, or any other person interested in the equipment or in the lading, even though she should not be condemned by the mixed court of justice.

ARTICLE VIII. It is agreed between the two high contracting parties, that in all cases in which a vessel shall be detained under this treaty, by their respective cruisers, as having been engaged in the African slave trade, or as having been fitted out for the purposes thereof, and shall consequently be adjudged and condemned by one of the mixed courts of justice to be established as aforesaid, the said vessel shall, immediately after its condemnation, be broken up entirely, and shall be sold in separate parts, after having been so broken up; unless either of the two Governments should wish to purchase her for the use of its navy, at a price to be fixed by a competent person chosen for that purpose by the mixed court of justice, in which case the Government whose cruiser shall have detained the condemned vessel shall have the first option of purchase.

ARTICLE IX. The captain, master, pilot, and crew of any vessel condemned by the mixed courts of justice shall be punished according to the laws of the country to which such vessel belongs, as shall also the owner or owners and the persons interested in her equipment or cargo, unless they prove that they had no participation in the enterprise.

For this purpose, the two high contracting parties agree that, in so far as it may not be attended with grievous expense and inconvenience, the master and crew of any vessel which may be condemned by a sentence of one of the mixed courts of justice, as well as any other persons found on board the vessel, shall be sent and delivered up to the jurisdiction of the nation under whose flag the condemned vessel was sailing at the time of capture; and that the witnesses and proofs necessary to establish the guilt of such master, crew, or other persons, shall also be sent with them.

The same course shall be pursued with regard to subjects or citizens of either contracting party who may be found by a cruiser of the other on board a vessel of any third Power, or on board a vessel sailing without flag or papers, which may be condemned by any competent court for having engaged in the African slave trade.

ARTICLE X. The negroes who are found on board of a vessel condemned by the mixed courts of justice, in conformity with the stipulations of this treaty, shall be placed at the disposal of the Government whose cruiser has made the capture; they shall be immediately set at liberty, and shall remain free, the Government to whom they have been delivered guarantying their liberty.

ARTICLE XI. The acts or instruments annexed to this treaty, and which it is mutually agreed shall form an integral part thereof, are as follows:

(A.) Instructions for the ships of the navies of both nations, destined to prevent the African slave trade.

(B.) Regulations for the mixed courts of justice.

ARTICLE XII. The present treaty shall be ratified, and the ratifications thereof shall be exchanged at London in six months from this date, or sooner if possible. It shall continue and remain in full force for the term of ten years from the day of exchange of the ratifications, and further, until the end of one year after either of the contracting parties shall have given notice to the other of its intention to terminate the same, each of the contracting parties reserving to itself the right of giving such notice to the other at the end of said term of ten years: And it is hereby agreed between them, that, on the expiration of one year after such notice shall have been received by either from the other party, this treaty shall altogether cease and determine.

In witness whereof the respective plenipotentiaries have signed the present treaty, and have thereunto affixed the seal of their-arms.

Done at Washington the seventh day of April, in the year of our Lord one thousand eight hundred and sixty-two.

[L. S.] *WILLIAM H. SEWARD.*
[L. S.] *LYONS.*

GLOSSARY

Cape of Good Hope: the site of the British Cape Colony in what is now South Africa, the principal settlement of which was Cape Town

mess-tubs or kids: large bowls or small tubs with rope handles, used for holding food

mixed courts of justice: the courts established by the treaty with judges appointed by both governments jointly overseeing the trial

plenipotentiaries: diplomatic officials with the power to represent a government on all issues

***primâ facie* evidence:** evidence "at first sight," sufficient to establish guilt without further examination unless disproved

Document Analysis

By 1862, the transportation of Africans to the Americas for the purpose of enslavement had existed for around 360 years. However, since 1836, no country had recognized participation in the international slave trade as a legitimate activity. Although slave trading had declined greatly since the end of the eighteenth century, the continued existence of slavery in several countries and colonies made it a profitable criminal endeavor for those who were willing to risk capture. With one of the major slaveholding countries in the midst of a civil war between the slaveholding and nonslaveholding sections, the opportunity existed to push for further steps to end the exploitation of Africans. Lord Lyons, envoy to the United States from Great Britain, and William Seward, US secretary of state, discussed this issue and drew up an agreement that, within a few years, effectively put an end to the transportation of slaves from Africa to the Americas.

Ever since the Portuguese began the practice in the fifteenth century, European and, later, American powers had sought economic gain via slave labor. However, beginning in the 1800s, slavery and the slave trade began to be examined from a human-rights perspective. As a result, both were slowly outlawed by the major Western powers. However, the legal changes outlawing both practices were not uniform, nor were they implemented at the same time in all places. Thus, as long as slavery was legal, the possibility for slave trade existed. Cuba, which allowed slavery until 1884, was the focal point for the Caribbean slave trade, including shipments to the United States, which were illegal after 1808. With the United States outlawing the participation of its citizens in slave trading between foreign countries in 1800, Great Britain's similar law in 1807, and the US ban on the importation of slaves going into effect in 1808, the international slave trade did decline. By the end of the 1830s, virtually all other European powers had similar laws, with enforcement varying from country to country. Under various treaties, the British fleet was the principal enforcement mechanism, and it posted numerous ships near the African coast.

In 1842, the United States signed the Webster-Ashburton Treaty, in which the United States promised to establish a fleet off the west coast of Africa to intercept slave ships flying the American flag. When the United States withdrew the ships to assist in the blockade of Southern ports in 1861, many slave ships began flying the American flag in order to avoid being stopped by the British. The British and most Union leaders wanted to end slavery, and they saw a treaty on the slave trade as one step toward that goal. Although the Lyons-Seward Treaty was signed and ratified, none of the Union leaders actually believed that ships were going to run the naval blockade of the South to bring in additional slaves. The last documented group of slaves illegally brought into the United States was in 1859. However, the treaty was a forceful statement of the American government's vision for the future.

The treaty itself is fairly straightforward, with provisions allowing for the conviction of slave traders even if no slaves were present. This means that anyone sailing a ship equipped to transport slaves was always at risk. Lyons and Seward tried to be as comprehensive as possible in drawing up the provisions under which a ship could be seized for participating in the slave trade. The opening of the treaty follows the traditional formulation of treaties by describing the nations involved and giving the credentials of those making the agreement. In line with the tradition established by President George Washington, references to the United States and its leaders are very simple compared to the British embellishments.

Having established the credentials of the negotiators, the twelve articles of the treaty outline three basic areas of agreement: who is authorized to undertake searches, the legal procedure for searches for evidence (including what constitutes evidence), and the adjudication of the treaty through "mixed courts of justice." Article 1 of the treaty begins with a statement reflecting these three themes of the treaty, as well as introducing the reason for the treaty's existence. The treaty "for the Suppression of the Slave Trade," as the formal title states, applies to the use of "their respective navies" to undertake the task. If a commercial vessel were suspected of having "been engaged in the African slave trade," then, as would be expected from democracies, the accused would "be brought to trial" and a verdict issued by a court. This summation of the treaty is then clarified throughout the remainder of the document, as well as through two annexes to the treaty, negotiated simultaneously with the formal treaty.

As to the first general principle of the treaty—who was authorized to undertake the mission to stop the slave trade—the ships authorized to undertake this mission are described in articles 1 and 2, as well as in annex A. In order for the goal to be reached, ships from either navy could stop commercial vessels from either country to inspect for signs of slave trading. (Prior to the treaty, only British naval vessels could stop British ships and American naval vessels, American ships.) However, in order to reduce any problems that might arise from possible interference with legitimate commercial enterprises, the treaty limits the scope of the search for slave traders in several ways. The first is by giving this task not to the whole navy but only to certain ships. Thus, as stated in article 1, only ships "authorized expressly for that object" were to undertake operations against suspected slave ships. The ship to be stopped had to be a private vessel; official (i.e., naval) ships of either country could not be stopped. In addition, the fourth section of article 1 delimits the geographical areas in which ships were subject to being searched. The northern border of the African search area was the thirty-second parallel north, which cuts approximately through the middle of the current nation of Morocco. Thus, the search area included essentially all the ocean adjacent to the entire west coast of Africa, as well as the area within thirty leagues of Cuba. Due to the success of the patrols, in 1863, the area within thirty leagues of Madagascar, Puerto Rico, and Santo Domingo (Hispaniola) was added to the search area.

In article 2, further clarification is given regarding those who were authorized to enforce the treaty. Naval vessels that were authorized to carry out the mission of stopping the slave trade were to be specifically named by their respective governments and given copies of the treaty, as well as the two annexes. While this would not be important when stopping a ship from their own country, having the document that authorized stopping a foreign ship would make discussions with the captain of the merchant ship easier. Naming specific ships made it easier to coordinate efforts. Section 2 of article 2 provides that ships assigned to this mission have as commander a person with at least the rank of lieutenant.

In annex A, not printed in this text, specific directions are given for the boarding of a ship suspected of participating in the slave trade. Anyone up to the commander of the naval vessel stopping the merchant ship could be part of the boarding crew. However, annex A tries to give assurance that a senior officer will participate in boarding the suspected ship and overseeing the search for evidence, stating that at least a lieutenant should be in charge of the boarding crew, or if the officer corps on board were depleted, then at least the "second in command of the ship" should participate in the search.

Most of the treaty deals with the procedure by which the search, and any evidence found, would be documented. This second aspect of the treaty, the procedure, was the first step to ensure that due process would be carried out in the investigation and in preparations for any possible trial. The third section of article 1 gives specific guidelines on the paperwork necessary when stopping and boarding a merchant ship. The captain of the naval vessel was to give a copy of his orders showing he was "authorized to search" to the captain of the merchant vessel. When someone other than the captain of the naval vessel did the actual boarding and search, this other officer also had to complete paperwork documenting his role in the action. This was to provide documentation regarding evidence to be used in any trial and to ensure that any innocent ship that was stopped had the necessary documents to explain its delay in transit and to make certain it was not stopped and searched by any other naval vessel. As previously mentioned, the treaty expresses a preference for an officer with at least the rank of lieutenant, with provisions for an exception in the unusual circumstance that no one with that rank or above was available. In order for the system to work correctly, the treaty states that the naval commanders should "adhere strictly to the exact tenor of the aforesaid instructions."

Annex A also states that the search was to "be conducted with the courtesy and consideration which ought to be observed between allied and friendly nations." Under provisions in article 2, if any ship in a convoy were suspected of being a slave ship, then the entire convoy would be stopped and the commander of the convoy would be allowed to participate in the search, along with the naval officials and the commander of the suspected ship. If nothing was found, then the ship would, as article 1 states, "be left at liberty to pursue its voyage." However, if sufficient evidence was found to cause the boarding party to take the merchant ship to be tried in court, three potential locations were given for this to happen. The naval commander was charged to take the merchant ship to the nearest or most easily reached court. Annex A gives stipulations as to how the merchant ship should be crewed during the trip to court. The merchant ship, and everyone and everything on it, was to be taken to the port, where a court could make a final ruling on the guilt or innocence of the captain and crew. It also directs the individual in charge of the search to draw up a document listing all the papers, people, and cargo found on the merchant ship.

As for the evidence necessary for the naval vessel to take the merchant ship to a court of justice, the most obvious piece of evidence would be Africans found on board en route to the Americas. However, as that was only possible on the westbound voyage, article 6 of the treaty lists ten items that were commonly identified as being integral to the slave trade. Thus, items such as "hatches with open gratings" or "a greater number of mess-tubs or kids than requisite for the use of the crew" could constitute enough evidence to take a ship into custody. As with many legal cases, there could be gray areas, such as how many mess-tubs a crew might need. This was the type of question for the court to rule on; a naval officer finding any of these items, or large enough quantities to raise questions, would be authorized to take possession of the merchant ship.

The "mixed courts of justice" were considered "mixed" because judges from both countries jointly presided at the trials. Annex B gives directions for the trials in line with its title, "Regulations for the Mixed Courts of Justice." Assuming that all the procedures had been correctly followed and one or more of the suspicious items listed in article 6 were found, even if a merchant captain and crew were found innocent, then there would be no compensation for the merchant or those shipping cargo on the vessel. However, if none of the suspicious items were found, then the naval officer and the nation that he served would be liable to pay compensation for delay and damages.

If the merchant captain and crew were found guilty of participating in the slave trade, then they were to be punished by the country whose flag they flew. Since both the United States and Great Britain had been signatories to an agreement to charge slave traders as pirates, the punishment would be similar. The ship itself would be destroyed, although provision was made for it to be purchased by one of the governments if it "should wish to purchase her for the use of its navy." Any cargo, except for persons from Africa being taken into slavery, became the property of the government whose flag the merchant vessel was flying. If it could be clearly proved that those shipping cargo on such a ship did not know of it being used for the slave trade, then they could get their cargo returned. The Africans on board a captured ship would "be immediately set at liberty, and shall remain free, the Government to whom they have been delivered guarantying their liberty." If Africans were found on board a slave ship, it might not be possible for them to be returned to their homes; however, the two countries did give the strongest assurances possible that those who might have become slaves would at least regain their freedom. The strength of the treaty lay in the fact that what might have been called circumstantial evidence in other cases was defined in the treaty as "*primâ facie* evidence" that the vessel was employed in the African slave trade.

Essential Themes

The Treaty for the Suppression of the Slave Trade was written in such a way as to follow as closely as possible the normal procedures of international law at the time. It includes provisions for compensation for those unjustly detained. However, the two countries' intent to end the slave trade could be seen in the list of prima facie evidence for conviction, which goes far beyond just finding chained Africans on board. The fact that shackles or extra sleeping mats could convict a slave trader made engaging in the slave trade a much more greater risk. While that could be avoided by stripping the ship when the slaves were sold and then reinstalling everything in the African port when new slaves were purchased, doing so negated the profits. As a result of this treaty, the transatlantic African slave trade finally came to an end. Although slavery lasted until the 1880s in Cuba and Brazil, there is no record of any people brought from Africa after the 1860s. The new era of closer US-British relations, which had started with the peaceful conclusion of the *Trent* Affair, was strengthened by the cooperation established by this treaty, often called the Lyons-Seward Treaty. These two individuals, who at the beginning of Abraham Lincoln's presidency seemed to be as far apart as their homelands, became effective partners in developing a close alliance. Even though there was still a long way to go toward full equality of all peoples, the successful suppression of the slave trade was a landmark on that path.

Donald A. Watt, PhD

Bibliography

"British-American Diplomacy: Treaty between United States and Great Britain for the Suppression of the Slave Trade; April 7, 1862." *Avalon Project*. Lillian Goldman Law Lib., 2008. Web. 18 Apr. 2013.

Goodwin, Doris Kearns. *Team of Rivals: The Political Genius of Abraham Lincoln*. New York: Simon, 2005. Print.

Jenkins, Brian. "The 'Wise Macaw' and the Lion: William Seward and Britain, 1861–1863." *University of*

Rochester Library Bulletin 31.1 (1978): n. pag. *River Campus Libraries: University of Rochester*. Web. 18 Apr. 2013.

Additional Reading

Ferris, Norman B. *Desperate Diplomacy: William H. Seward's Foreign Policy, 1861*. Knoxville: U of Tennessee P, 1976. Print.

Foreman, Amanda. *A World on Fire: Britain's Crucial Role in the American Civil War*. New York: Random, 2010. Print.

Hill, Walter B., Jr. "Living with the Hydra: The Documentation of Slavery and the Slave Trade in Federal Records." *Prologue* 32.4 (2000): n. pag. *National Archives and Records Administration*. Web. 18 Apr. 2013.

Jones, Howard. *Abraham Lincoln and a New Birth of Freedom: The Union and Slavery in the Diplomacy of the Civil War*. Lincoln: U of Nebraska P, 1999. Print.

Stahr, Walter. *Seward: Lincoln's Indispensable Man*. New York: Simon, 2012. Print.

Taylor, John M. *William Henry Seward: Lincoln's Right Hand*. New York: Harper, 1991. Print.

"Timeline of Atlantic Slave Trade." *ABCNews.com*. ABC News, 2 July 2000. Web. 18 Apr. 2013.

Van Deusen, Glyndon G. *William Henry Seward*. New York: Oxford UP, 1967. Print.

■ The Emancipation Proclamation

Date: January 1, 1863
Author: Lincoln, Abraham
Genre: legal document

> *"All persons held as slaves within any State or designated part of a State, the people whereof shall then be in rebellion against the United States, shall be then, thenceforward, and forever free . . ."*

Summary Overview

The Emancipation Proclamation has been a much-debated and much-misunderstood document. Many people believe it freed all the slaves, but it freed only those who lived in areas that were still in rebellion against the federal government as of the date of the proclamation, January 1, 1863. Although Abraham Lincoln had strong personal feelings against slavery, he initially had no plans to abolish it. But by the summer of 1862, he determined to free the slaves in the Rebel states because this would make it harder for the Confederacy to continue the war. He believed that his authority as commander-in-chief of the armed forces gave him the ability to do this; however, this military authority could not be applied to the slave states that had remained loyal to the Union. Therefore, the proclamation applied only to the states that were in rebellion against the federal government as of January 1, 1863.

Defining Moment

Despite Lincoln's personal abhorrence of slavery, he believed he had no constitutional authority to simply order an end to it, and he had promised in the 1860 presidential campaign not to interfere with slavery where it already existed. When the Civil War started, many Northerners saw the war primarily as a struggle to preserve the Union, but from the very beginning abolitionists saw the war as an opportunity to strike against slavery. In the summer of 1862, President Lincoln de-

cided that the time had come to issue a proclamation freeing the slaves in areas that were in rebellion against the federal government. Most of his cabinet members agreed when Lincoln first presented the idea of the proclamation on July 22, 1862. However, it was decided to wait until Union forces had won a significant victory, so that the proclamation would not look like an act of desperation.

After the Union victory at Antietam in September 1862, Lincoln believed the time had come. On September 22, 1862, he issued a preliminary emancipation proclamation, warning the rebellious states that if they did not return to the Union by January 1, 1863, their slaves would be declared "forever free." No rebelling state made any positive response, so on January 1 of the new year, Lincoln issued the formal Emancipation Proclamation. He was criticized at the time, and by some historians since, for not touching slavery where he could (in the loyal border states where slavery was legal), but announcing the freedom of slaves that were beyond his control. But Lincoln's view was precisely the opposite—he had no legal authority to end slavery in the loyal states—which were, by the fact of their loyalty, not subject to military control. But in the rebelling Confederate states, freeing their slaves was a war measure that would hamper their ability to prosecute the war by depriving them of much of their labor. The Emancipation Proclamation had a significant impact on the outcome of the war. It virtually ended any chance that the Confederacy would be recognized by or receive aid from Europe—as support for the South would imply support for slavery, which had been outlawed in Europe—and it made it clear that a Union victory would mean the end of slavery. It also authorized the enlistment of African Americans as soldiers in the Union military forces, and by the end of the war over 180,000 black troops had served—most of whom were freed slaves.

Author Biography

Abraham Lincoln rose from humble roots to become the president of the United States during a crisis that threatened the very existence of the nation. He was born in Hodgenville, Kentucky, on February 16, 1809. His mother died when he was a young boy. His father, Thomas Lincoln, was a frontier farmer who never prospered. In 1816, the family moved from Kentucky to Spencer County, Indiana, and in 1830 they moved to southern Illinois. As a young man, Lincoln clerked in a store in New Salem, Illinois, worked as a surveyor, and served as the town's postmaster. Lincoln, who had little formal education, studied law with a friend who tutored him and loaned him law books, and he was admitted to the Illinois bar in 1836. In 1837, Lincoln moved to Springfield, the new capital of Illinois. Over the next few years he developed a reputation as a highly capable lawyer.

Lincoln became involved in Whig Party politics, and served four terms as a member of the Illinois House of Representative. In 1846, he was elected to the House of Representatives, but served only one term. In 1856, Lincoln joined the new Republican Party, which had emerged in the crisis over the Kansas-Nebraska Act and the question of the potential extension of slavery into those territories. Lincoln said in later life that he did not remember a time when he was not opposed to slavery. The experience of seeing slaves when he was on a trip to New Orleans as a young man had made a deep impression upon him. In 1858, he ran as a candidate for the Senate against the incumbent, Stephen A. Douglas. Lincoln lost that election, but his series of seven debates with Douglas brought him to national attention, which opened the way for his nomination by the Republicans to run for the presidency in 1860. Although Lincoln was a moderate on the slavery issue within the context of the Republican Party (against allowing the westward expansion of slavery, but not an abolitionist), his election was seen by many Southerners as a threat to the existence of slavery. By the time Lincoln was inaugurated as president on March 4, 1861, seven Southern states had seceded from the Union. Lincoln led the nation through the Civil War but was assassinated just days after Robert E. Lee surrendered the main body of Confederate forces. He died in Washington, DC, on April 15, 1865.

HISTORICAL DOCUMENT

The Emancipation Proclamation
January 1, 1863
A Transcription
By the President of the United States of America:

A Proclamation.

Whereas, on the twenty-second day of September, in the year of our Lord one thousand eight hundred and sixty-two, a proclamation was issued by the President of the United States, containing, among other things, the following, to wit:

"That on the first day of January, in the year of our Lord one thousand eight hundred and sixty-three, all persons held as slaves within any State or designated part of a State, the people whereof shall then be in rebellion against the United States, shall be then, thenceforward, and forever free; and the Executive Government of the United States, including the military and naval authority thereof, will recognize and maintain the freedom of such persons, and will do no act or acts to repress such persons, or any of them, in any efforts they may make for their actual freedom.

"That the Executive will, on the first day of January aforesaid, by proclamation, designate the States and parts of States, if any, in which the people thereof, respectively, shall then be in rebellion against the United

States; and the fact that any State, or the people thereof, shall on that day be, in good faith, represented in the Congress of the United States by members chosen thereto at elections wherein a majority of the qualified voters of such State shall have participated, shall, in the absence of strong countervailing testimony, be deemed conclusive evidence that such State, and the people thereof, are not then in rebellion against the United States."

Now, therefore, I, Abraham Lincoln, President of the United States, by virtue of the power in me vested as Commander-in-Chief of the Army and Navy of the United States in time of actual armed rebellion against the authority and government of the United States, and as a fit and necessary war measure for suppressing said rebellion, do, on this first day of January, in the year of our Lord one thousand eight hundred and sixty-three, and in accordance with my purpose so to do publicly proclaimed for the full period of one hundred days, from the day first above mentioned, order and designate as the States and parts of States wherein the people thereof respectively, are this day in rebellion against the United States, the following, to wit:

Arkansas, Texas, Louisiana, (except the Parishes of St. Bernard, Plaquemines, Jefferson, St. John, St. Charles, St. James Ascension, Assumption, Terrebonne, Lafourche, St. Mary, St. Martin, and Orleans, including the City of New Orleans) Mississippi, Alabama, Florida, Georgia, South Carolina, North Carolina, and Virginia, (except the forty-eight counties designated as West Virginia, and also the counties of Berkley, Accomac, Northampton, Elizabeth City, York, Princess Ann, and Norfolk, including the cities of Norfolk and Portsmouth),

and which excepted parts are, for the present, left precisely as if this proclamation were not issued.

And by virtue of the power, and for the purpose aforesaid, I do order and declare that all persons held as slaves within said designated States, and parts of States, are, and henceforward shall be free; and that the Executive government of the United States, including the military and naval authorities thereof, will recognize and maintain the freedom of said persons.

And I hereby enjoin upon the people so declared to be free to abstain from all violence, unless in necessary self-defence; and I recommend to them that, in all cases when allowed, they labor faithfully for reasonable wages.

And I further declare and make known, that such persons of suitable condition, will be received into the armed service of the United States to garrison forts, positions, stations, and other places, and to man vessels of all sorts in said service.

And upon this act, sincerely believed to be an act of justice, warranted by the Constitution, upon military necessity, I invoke the considerate judgment of mankind, and the gracious favor of Almighty God.

In witness whereof, I have hereunto set my hand and caused the seal of the United States to be affixed.

Done at the City of Washington, this first day of January, in the year of our Lord one thousand eight hundred and sixty three, and of the Independence of the United States of America the eighty-seventh.

By the President: ABRAHAM LINCOLN
WILLIAM H. SEWARD, Secretary of State.

GLOSSARY

aforesaid: a reference to something previously stated in a document

emancipation: the act of setting a slave or slaves free

henceforward: from this point in time, into the future

parishes: Because of the French colonial heritage in Louisiana, what are called counties in other parts of the United States are called parishes in Louisiana

war measure: a measure to facilitate the conduct of a war, or to hamper the enemy's ability to carry on war; Lincoln believed the concept of the "war powers" of the president gave him authority to free the slaves in Rebel states as a war measure

Document Analysis

On September 22, 1862, shortly after the Battle of Antietam, President Abraham Lincoln issued what has become known as the "preliminary emancipation proclamation." This document was basically a warning to the Confederate states that if they did not end their war against the federal government by January 1, 1863, then on that date the slaves held in those rebellious areas would be set free. Lincoln had decided on this course of action by the midsummer of 1862, but members of his cabinet persuaded him to wait until a significant Union victory had been achieved before announcing the policy. Lincoln considered Major General George McClellan's victory over the Confederate forces at Antietam Creek, near Sharpsburg, Maryland, on September 17 to be that victory. Five days later he issued the preliminary statement. This document laid out what would happen if armed resistance to federal authority did not end by the close of the current year. The first two full paragraphs of the final proclamation that was issued on January 1, 1863, consist of quotations from the preliminary document of September 22, 1862. By giving the Confederate states nearly three months of warning, Lincoln hoped that some states might be induced to end their rebellion so that they might continue to be allowed to have slavery.

Provisions

Because Lincoln saw the Emancipation Proclamation as a war measure, aimed at limiting the power of the Confederacy to carry on the war, it would only take effect in areas that were in rebellion against the Union. Thus, the preliminary proclamation specifies how this status would be determined. If, by January 1, 1863, states had ended their rebellion and elected representatives to Congress, who had been chosen in elections in which the majority of eligible voters had taken part (thus indicating broad public support for any profession of loyalty by the state), then that state would no longer be considered to be in rebellion to the federal government. No Confederate state took any action to end their rebellion, so in the final form of the proclamation, Lincoln specified the states that were still in rebellion, excepting certain areas in Virginia and Louisiana that were already back under federal control.

Lincoln considered what he was doing in the Emancipation Proclamation to be primarily a war measure, and so he invoked "the power in me vested as Commander in Chief" of the military forces of the United States. Article 2, section 2 of the US Constitution provides that "the President shall be Commander in Chief of the Army and Navy of the United States." Lincoln states that he is taking this action at a "time of actual armed rebellion" against the government, and he believes it to be "a fit and necessary war measure." This concept of a "war measure" is crucial to an understanding of the Emancipation Proclamation and why it applied only where it did; it is also related to understanding why Lincoln did not take action to free the slaves earlier, or in some other fashion. Despite Lincoln's personal opposition to slavery, he believed that, constitutionally, he had no power to simply declare all slaves to be free. But the concept of "war powers" had evolved as an unwritten but generally accepted principle that in times of war a president might have extraordinary powers to take actions that would facilitate the prosecution of the war, or to hinder the ability of an enemy to carry on the war. Confiscation of the property of an enemy that was being used to support the war effort was considered a legitimate power of war, and some slaves had already been freed under the terms of the First Confiscation Act (August 1861) and the Second Confiscation Act (July 1862). Thus Lincoln believed that, as a war measure, he could order the freeing of the slaves in areas that were in rebellion against the legitimately established government. Slaves were often used to directly aid the Confederate forces, such as in building trenches and fortifications, or in other kinds of labor in and around military camps. Indirectly, slave labor kept much of the economy of the Confederacy running, and the presence of large numbers of slaves meant that a greater proportion of the white male population of the South was available for military service. For these reasons, Lincoln believed he could take action against slavery in the areas that were in rebellion. These arguments would not apply, however, to areas that had not rebelled—such as the border states, where slavery was legal, but which had nevertheless remained in the Union; these included Delaware, Maryland, Kentucky, and Missouri. Nor would it apply to areas where federal authorities had already retaken control—most prominently, the state of Tennessee.

Lincoln notes that this proclamation of January 1, 1863, is simply carrying out what he had warned the Confederate states that he would do when he issued the preliminary proclamation—all of this, he says, is "in accordance with my purpose to do so publicly proclaimed for the full period of one hundred days."

Francis Bicknell Carpenter was an artist commissioned to paint a picture memorializing the Emancipation Proclamation, and spent nearly six months at the White House in the spring and summer of 1864 working on this portrait. During this time Carpenter had many conversations with Lincoln, and Lincoln told him that when he issued the preliminary proclamation, he did not realize that it was precisely one hundred days from September 22, 1862, to January 1, 1863. Carpenter's painting, *First Reading of the Emancipation Proclamation of President Lincoln*, was unveiled to the cabinet on July 22, 1864—two years to the day from the occasion depicted in the picture.

The states identified in the proclamation as being in rebellion include all of the eleven states that had seceded and formed the Confederate States of America. Forty-eight western counties of Virginia had broken away from that state and in June 1863 were admitted to the Union as the new state of West Virginia. The proclamation would therefore not apply in western Virginia. Also, some counties along the Atlantic coast of Virginia had already been reoccupied by federal forces, and these specific counties are also listed as "excepted parts" where the proclamation would not apply. Likewise, in southern Louisiana, Union naval power had allowed federal forces to take control of a large region, and so specific parishes (counties) in Louisiana are also listed as excepted. In these excepted parts of Virginia and Louisiana, the situation was "left precisely as if this proclamation were not issued," meaning that the slaves in those regions were not set free. Contemporary accounts of the time when the final proclamation was issued tell of slaves reading the document or listening intently as it was read, to find out whether they were from areas that were considered in rebellion, and thus were freed by the document.

While slaves in loyal states or federally controlled portions of Rebel states were not affected by the proclamation, slaves in those areas that were declared to still be in a state of rebellion against the federal authority "are, and henceforward shall be free." Under the previous Confiscation Acts passed by Congress, there was the potential of court cases being filed later to determine whether the slaves freed under those laws had actually belonged to people supporting the Confederate war effort, or if those specific slaves had been used in ways that aided the war. But under the Emancipation Proclamation, no such claims by slave owners would be possible. If the state or part of a state in which they

lived was in rebellion against the government when the proclamation took effect, then the slaves in that area were freed—irrespective of the slave owners' loyalty or professed loyalty to the Union. Lincoln also pledged that the powers of the executive branch of the government, including the armed forces, would be used to see that the freedom of these former slaves is "recognized and maintained."

One of the issues that had been debated in connection with any potential policy that might free the slaves during the war was the possibility that the freed people might rise up in revenge against their former masters. Lincoln encouraged the freed slaves to refrain from any violence, unless it was necessary in legitimate cases of self-defense. Also, wherever they might have the opportunity to do so, they should "labor faithfully for reasonable wages." As it happened, there were very few incidents of violence by freed slaves. Their usual response to being set free was simply to leave the lands of their former masters; or, more precisely, the slaves freed themselves by leaving the farms and plantations where they had been enslaved and making their way to the lines of the Union Army. In 1865, Congress created the Freedman's Bureau, which was to try to help the freed slaves to make the transition to living as free people. The Freedman's Bureau—which was technically called the Bureau of Refugees, Freedmen, and Abandoned Lands—sought to provide schools for the freed slaves, and to negotiate contracts to see that the workers were paid reasonable wages for their labor.

Related Issues

The preliminary document that Lincoln issued in September 1862 was not only a warning of what would happen if the rebellion did not end by January 1, 1863. There were also suggestions of other potential actions that never materialized. Lincoln proposed suggesting to Congress laws that would give financial aid to any state that would undertake freeing their slaves on the state level. By this means, masters might be financially compensated for freeing their slaves. In the months leading up to the issuance of the Emancipation Proclamation, Lincoln had met several times with representatives of the loyal border states where slavery was legal. He urged them to consider voluntary emancipation, whether immediate or gradual, and suggested that federal money might be made available to aid them if they would do this. In May 1862, he warned the border state representatives he met with, "You cannot be blind to the signs of the times." None of the border states took this action before the Emancipation Proclamation was issued. Although the proclamation did not free the slaves in these loyal border states, some of these states—including Maryland, Missouri, and West Virginia—did adopt emancipation before the Thirteenth Amendment, which finally ended slavery everywhere in the United States, was ratified in December 1865.

Another issue that was proposed in the preliminary proclamation was aid for the colonization of freed African Americans outside of the United States. Like many antislavery advocates, Lincoln had initially supported colonization, but eventually meetings with representatives of free blacks in the North convinced him that the African American people were not, for the most part, interested in leaving the United States. In the final form of the Emancipation Proclamation, neither aid for states voluntarily freeing their slaves, nor any encouragement of colonization is mentioned. The time for such half-measures, Lincoln believed, had passed.

Another issue that was not mentioned in the preliminary document was the use of African American troops in the Union war effort. But in the final document, Lincoln declares that "such persons of suitable condition" (referring to the freed slaves mentioned in the previous paragraph), will be received into the US military "to garrison forts, positions, stations, and other places, and to man vessels of all sorts in said service." The question of using black troops, whether free men from the North or emancipated slaves, was controversial but had been discussed from the early days of the war. Freeing the slaves would take the laborers from the South that produced the agricultural products and other commodities essential to the Confederate economy. But beyond removing this source of support for the Confederacy, arming African Americans could add thousands of troops to the Union war effort.

Initially, Lincoln feared that freeing the slaves would alienate the border states and also some Northern voters. He also feared that using black troops would also upset some in the North. But by the end of 1862, Lincoln sensed that public opinion in the Northern states was changing on these issues. Freed slaves, who had escaped to Union lines or who had been confiscated as contraband of war, had already been aiding the Union war effort for some time. They were used as laborers in military camps, and as cooks, medical aides, and in other noncombatant positions. Some people in the North believed that the Confederacy might be on the verge of

arming the slaves to fight, promising them freedom if they served the Rebel military effort. (The Confederacy would embrace this idea toward the very end of the war, but the conflict ended before any black Confederate troops could be utilized to any significant extent).

Actually, blacks were serving in the US Navy even before the Emancipation Proclamation, as they had (in small numbers) ever since the American Revolution. During the Civil War, about eighteen thousand African Americans served in the US Navy, and by the end of the war, more than 180,000 served in the Union Army. Thousands of Northern blacks who had been free before the war served, but over half of all the black troops were freed slaves—so the Emancipation Proclamation had served to take people whose labor represented a valuable contribution to the Confederacy's rebellion and to turn them into soldiers fighting against the rebellion. Not all Northerners welcomed the use of black troops, and in some cases commanders were reluctant to have them doing anything other than occupation duty or manual labor in military camps. But when black troops fought, they performed admirably, and this lessened the prejudice against their use in combat. There was also initially some discrimination in pay and other issues, but eventually black troops were paid the same as any other Union soldiers.

Lincoln concluded the Emancipation Proclamation with a statement that he believed it to be "an act of justice, warranted by the Constitution, upon military necessity." Many abolitionists had argued from the very beginning of the war that the Confederacy, by taking up arms against the government, had forfeited any right to claim constitutional protections for slavery. They could not rebel against a constitutionally ordained government and at the same time invoke the protection of slavery under the Constitution. By the summer of 1862, Lincoln had come to see that if emancipation were undertaken as a war measure, "upon military necessity," then he could take action to free the slaves in the Rebel states. The phrase in which Lincoln invokes "the considerate judgment of mankind, and the gracious favor of almighty God" was suggested by Treasury Secretary Salmon P. Chase, but Lincoln no doubt heartily agreed with the sentiment expressed. Lincoln's personal religious beliefs are a complex issue; it might be said (perhaps too simply) that he had deist beliefs similar to many of the Founding Fathers. While he expressed belief in no particular religious group, he did believe in a Creator who exercised providence over the affairs of nations. While he was struggling with the question of what to do about freeing the slaves, Lincoln often spoke to others about feeling he was an instrument in the hands of this providential power, and he spoke of seeking to understand what the will of God might be for him in this matter.

Essential Themes

Even though it did not free all the slaves, the Emancipation Proclamation made it clear that the Civil War was not only a war to save the Union, but had been transformed into a conflict that would also spell the end of slavery in the United States. Lincoln said in his second inaugural address (in March 1865) that everyone knew that slavery was "somehow" the cause of the war. Yet in the beginning, neither side spoke much about the slavery issue. Confederate leaders talked of states' rights and sovereignty, while Union leaders spoke of the need to preserve the Union. But the issue of slavery could not be ignored, especially when advances of the Union Army into Confederate territory brought freed or runaway slaves under the control of federal forces. Slaves themselves, by running away to the Union lines, were raising the issue of what had to be done about slavery. Congress addressed this issue in the First and Second Confiscation Acts, which were the first official steps the federal government took toward the dismantling of slavery in Rebel areas.

Although Lincoln had a long-standing personal aversion to slavery, he felt the Constitution gave him no right to simply declare an end to the institution. But if a blow against slavery in the Rebel states was conceived of as a war measure, it might stand any possible legal challenges. A study of Lincoln's thought on the issue shows a clear progression from the beginning of the war to the summer of 1862, by which time he had decided to issue the proclamation. The Emancipation Proclamation did not free the slaves in loyal states, and in Confederate states it freed only those few who were in areas already controlled by Union forces. But it changed the nature of the war. Antislavery advocates in the North were given a new sense of purpose and direction, because the war now was clearly moving toward destroying slavery. Since no European nation wanted to be seen as propping up a government that sought to preserve slavery, the Proclamation effectively ended any chance of foreign intervention to aid the Confed-

eracy. Legal necessities dictated that the scope of the Proclamation be limited, in freeing only the slaves in areas in rebellion. Nevertheless, the Proclamation had a broad impact, and after it was issued, few doubted that eventually, further actions (including the Thirteenth Amendment) would insure that a Union victory would end slavery everywhere in the United States.

Mark S. Joy, PhD

Bibliography

Franklin, John Hope. *The Emancipation Proclamation.* New York: Doubleday, 1963. Print.

Guelzo, Allen C. *Lincoln's Emancipation Proclamation: The End of Slavery in America.* New York: Simon, 2004. Print.

Holder, Harold, Edna Greene Medford, and Frank J. Williams. *The Emancipation Proclamation: Three Views.* Baton Rouge: Louisiana State UP, 2006. Print.

Masur, Louis P. *Lincoln's Hundred Days: The Emancipation Proclamation and the War for the Union.* Cambridge: Belknap P of Harvard UP, 2012. Print.

McPherson, James M., and James K. Hogue. *Ordeal by Fire: The Civil War and Reconstruction.* 4th ed. Boston: McGraw, 2010. Print.

Paludin, Phillip Shaw. *The Presidency of Abraham Lincoln.* Amer. Presidency Series. Lawrence: UP of Kansas, 1994. Print.

Additional Reading

Belz, Herman. *Abraham Lincoln, Constitutionalism and Equal Rights in the Civil War Era.* New York: Fordham UP, 1998. Print.

Cox, LaWanda. *Lincoln and Black Freedom: A Study in Presidential Leadership.* Urbana: U of Illinois P, 1985. Print.

Goodwin, Doris Kearns. *Team of Rivals: The Political Genius of Abraham Lincoln.* New York: Simon, 2005. Print.

Oakes, James. *Freedom National: The Destruction of Slavery in the United States, 1861–1865.* New York: Norton, 2013. Print.

Perman, Michael. *Emancipation and Reconstruction.* 2nd ed. Wheeling: Harlan, 2003. Print.

"Primary Documents in American History: Emancipation Proclamation." *Library of Congress.* Lib. of Congress, 2013. Web. 7 May 2013.

■ War Department General Order 143

Date: 1863
Author: Stanton, Edwin M.
Genre: order

"No persons shall be allowed to recruit for colored
troops except specially authorized by the
War Department."

Summary Overview

Halfway through the Civil War, Union Army officials began to explore the possibility of enlisting black soldiers. Its ranks, which consisted only of white troops, had been thinned by casualties. In addition, the army's battlefield successes created a growing number of former slaves—freed according to the Emancipation Proclamation—able to fight for the Union. With the strong advocacy of African American activist Frederick Douglass, more black men came forward to enlist in the Union Army. In May 1863, the War Department, through War Department General Order 143, established the Bureau of Colored Troops. The bureau would be used to enlist and assign the growing number of black volunteers to established military units.

Defining Moment

In 1861, when Confederate forces captured Fort Sumter in South Carolina—effectively starting the Civil War—former slaves and other black Americans alike expressed their willingness to join the Union Army. As the war progressed, the number of additional white army volunteers began to dwindle. However, despite the benefit of increased manpower to the Union Army, the policy of enlisting black men was politically risky. President Lincoln understood that such a policy would enrage many public officials in states along the North-South border and upset white voters elsewhere in the Union. Nevertheless, the overwhelming number of available black volunteers would, in the minds of Lincoln, his military leaders, and Congress, help offset the declining number of white soldiers.

On July 17, 1862, Congress passed the Second Confiscation and Militia Act. The legislation freed slaves whose owners were members of the Confederate Army. The law also created an avenue whereby slaves—once the property of individuals who were now the enemies of the Union—could join the Union Army. Shortly thereafter, Lincoln unveiled his Emancipation Proclamation, which freed all slaves living in the Confederacy.

With the question of accepting black troops into the Union Army answered, the Union next turned to the recruitment, training, and assignment of black troops. This was a challenging process involving a great deal of administrative work and organizational management. Newly emancipated former slaves from the South, for example, would need to be treated differently than white volunteers. Union officers would need to take these differences into account when forming, training, and deploying regiments of black soldiers. Meanwhile, civil rights advocates such as Frederick Douglass pushed both the state and federal governments to accommodate black volunteers while calling upon more black people to join the Union Army.

This situation led the War Department to create a single office under the umbrella of the Adjutant General, the chief administrative officer of the army. Under the auspice of War Department General Order 143 and the orders of the secretary of war, the office became known as the Bureau of Colored Troops. The bureau was responsible for recruiting black soldiers, organizing their units, and securing white officers to oversee these units. The bureau, which at its height oversaw the activities of 180,000 troops, also served as a clearinghouse for information about the battlefield performance of these newly formed units.

Author Biography

Secretary of War Edwin Stanton drafted and disseminated War Department General Order 143. Stanton was born on December 19, 1814 in Steubenville, Ohio. His parents were physician David Stanton and Lucy Norman Stanton. An avid reader, he served as an apprentice to a local bookseller as a teenager. Stanton later attended Kenyon College in Gambier, Ohio, but financial limitations forced him to depart the college after only two years.

After returning to Steubenville, Stanton began practicing law at the office of a family friend. In 1835, he was admitted to the Ohio bar. By his early twenties, Stanton had established a reputation as an exceptional lawyer and become interested in politics. In 1837, while arguing before the Supreme Court on a patent issue regarding Cyrus Hall McCormick's mechanical grain reaper, he met Abraham Lincoln. In 1859, Stanton became the first attorney in United States history to use temporary insanity as a legal defense, using the argument while defending Daniel Sickles, who had been charged with murdering his wife's lover.

In 1860, President James Buchanan—whose administration was marred by corruption charges and the threat of Southern secession—tapped Stanton to be his attorney general. Stanton, a staunch antislavery activist, assailed the secessionist threat and successfully encouraged President Buchanan not to surrender at Fort Sumter in January 1861. When Lincoln became president in March, Stanton returned to his private legal practice, although he would continue to provide counsel for a number of Union officials, including Secretary of War Simon Cameron. Cameron's frequent missteps led Lincoln to move him to a different post in his administration. Lincoln, a Republican, turned to Stanton to take Cameron's place, despite the fact that Stanton was a Democrat.

Although he was often combative, outspoken, and stubborn as a cabinet official, Stanton became a close ally of Lincoln's, particularly on the issue of emancipation and recruiting former slaves into the Union Army. After Lincoln was assassinated, it was Stanton who uttered the famous words, "Now he belongs to the ages."

Stanton remained in the cabinet of President Andrew Johnson after Lincoln's death, but their relationship was tumultuous. Johnson repeatedly attempted to remove Stanton from his post, but he was rebuffed by Congress, which was responsible for removing government officials. Stanton eventually left his post in a compromise deal, returning to his private practice in 1869. However, that same year, President Ulysses S. Grant appointed him to the Supreme Court.

Before he was able to assume his position on the court, Stanton died from respiratory failure on December 4, 1869. He was survived by several children and his second wife, Ellen Hutchinson. Stanton is buried in Oak Hill Cemetery in Washington, DC.

HISTORICAL DOCUMENT

GENERAL ORDERS, No. 143 WAR DEPARTMENT, ADJUTANT GENERAL'S OFFICE, Washington, May 22, 1863.

I—A Bureau is established in the Adjutant General's Office for the record of all matters relating to the organization of Colored Troops. An officer, will be assigned to the charge of the Bureau, with such number of clerks as may be designated by the Adjutant General.

II—Three or more field officers will be detailed as Inspectors to supervise the organization of colored troops at such points as may be indicated by the War Department in the Northern and Western States.

III—Boards will be convened at such posts as may be decided upon by the War Department to examine applicants for commissions to command colored troops, who, on Application to the Adjutant General, may receive authority to present themselves to the board for examination.

IV—No persons shall be allowed to recruit for colored troops except specially authorized by the War Department; and no such authority will be given to persons who have not been examined and passed by a board; nor will such authority be given any one person to raise more than one regiment.

V—The reports of Boards will specify the grade of commission for which each candidate is fit, and authority to recruit will be given in accordance. Commissions will be issued from the Adjutant General's Office when the prescribed number of men is ready for muster into service.

VI—Colored troops may be accepted by companies, to be afterward consolidated in battalions and regiments by the Adjutant General. The regiments will be numbered seriatim, in the order in which they are raised, the numbers to be determined by the Adjutant General. They will be designated: "——Regiment of U. S. Colored Troops."

VII—Recruiting stations and depots will be established by the Adjutant General as circumstances shall require, and officers will be detailed to muster and inspect the troops.

VIII—The non-commissioned officers of colored troops may be selected and appointed from the best men of their number in the usual mode of appointing non-commissioned officers. Meritorious commissioned officers will be entitled to promotion to higher rank if they prove themselves equal to it.

IX—All personal applications for appointments in colored regiments, or for information concerning them, must be made to the Chief of the Bureau; all written communications should be addressed to the Chief of the Bureau, to the care of the Adjutant General,

BY ORDER OF THE SECRETARY OF WAR:
E. D. TOWNSEND, Assistant Adjutant General.

GLOSSARY

Adjutant General: chief administrative officer of an army

commissioned officer: military officer having the rank of lieutenant or above

non-commissioned officer: an enlistedman in a command position; corporal or sergeant or above

regiment: military group consisting of ten companies (approximately 1,000 troops and officers)

seriatim: one after another

Document Analysis

War Department General Order 143 sought to bolster the Union Army's troop numbers by recruiting black volunteers. The order established the Bureau of Colored Troops, a special office that was dedicated to organizing and managing the influx of black volunteers. The bureau was created to oversee the recruitment, training, and assignment of black troops in the Union Army. After the bureau was founded, it recruited soldiers according to Northern state designations. Outside of the free North, however, black volunteers were typically former slaves who required military training. The Bureau of Colored Troops, through the guidelines of War Department General Order 143, provided training, uniforms, and equipment for the Union Army's black regiments.

The recruitment and training of black troops under the bureau's management was considerably different from the Union Army's recruitment protocols for white volunteers. White Union Army recruits were organized through quotas. Recruiting stations were opened in cities and towns throughout the North. As the need for more troops arose during the war, the number of such stations increased, particularly in more populated municipal centers. White recruits could enlist in existing regiments at recruitment stations, or they could join new regiments that had not yet been deployed. Typically, the officers working at stations recruiting for already-formed regiments were themselves combat veterans. Newly forming regiments were often recruited by recently commissioned, less experienced officers.

For black Union recruits, the War Department deemed it necessary to create a single system of administration. Officers in charge of all aspects of the process, from recruitment to assignment, were required to adhere to a strict set of guidelines established by the Bureau of Colored Troops. Although the army (and indeed, its commander in chief, President Lincoln) believed in the value of recruiting black troops, the process was influenced by political forces and systemized racial prejudice. Black troops represented a boon for the Union Army's numbers, but many in North were reluctant, if not outwardly opposed, to accepting them. Once a recruitment policy was approved, it was critical that the army adhere to its strict protocols. The order was thus focused in such a way that only the entities and individuals assigned by the government could manage any part of the large recruitment operation.

The order calls for the establishment of the bureau within the adjutant general's office. The adjutant general served as the Union Army's chief administrative officer, managing all operations, supplies, and policies within its system. The centrality of the adjutant general ensured that all of the Union's operations were standardized and uniform. The Bureau of Colored Troops was incorporated into the overall purview of the army's central administrative office. The recruitment of black volunteers was handled by the federal government, without the participation of state governments.

Following the bureau's establishment, Major Charles W. Foster of Ohio was appointed commanding officer of administration by Adjutant General Lorenzo Thomas. Various field officers were appointed to oversee the organization and assignments of the Union Army's black recruits. Furthermore, several boards were convened to review the applications of white officers seeking command posts in black regiments and units.

The order manifests an acknowledgement of the fact that black soldier recruitment requires a specialized approach. Many of the protocols used for white soldiers were not applied to this group of soldiers. Many black soldiers hailed from the same regions as their white counterparts. However, a much larger number were former slaves who lacked formal education. The order clearly distinguishes black soldiers, not only as separate from white soldiers, but as a single, uniform group.

The boards established in section 3 of the order

played a pivotal role in the selection of officers. The expansion of the Union Army to include black regiments created opportunities for officers seeking command positions (and the pay increases that came with such posts). Army officials maintained that commanding officers assigned to black regiments should possess certain leadership qualities. The prevalent racial prejudices of the period gave rise to the notion that black soldiers should be trained differently from white troops, especially in light of the fact that so many black recruits were former slaves.

The board also served as the primary authority on who would be able to recruit these black troops. According to Order 143, the board established within the Bureau of Colored Troops would be solely responsible examining, approving, and denying those individuals who would recruit troops from the increasing number of black volunteers. Even if approved by the board, these recruiters would be limited in terms of the number of troops they recruited. The order states that a board-authorized army recruiter would only be allowed to raise one regiment's worth of men. A regiment consisted of about ten companies, each of which consisted of about one hundred men, including officers.

Under the guidelines of the order, troops recruited within the Bureau of Colored Troops system would first be assigned to companies. Those companies would be consolidated into either regiments or battalions (which consisted of between four and eight companies), a procedure administered by the Adjutant General. The regiments and battalions would then be ordered one after another ("seriatim") according to the chronological order by which they were raised. Each regiment and battalion would be given a special designation, identifying the grouping by its racial composition: Regiment of US Colored Troops.

Keeping in line with the strict protocols for the recruitment and assignment of black volunteers, the order states that the adjutant general would establish specialized recruiting stations and depots for this purpose. Each such depot and station would be managed by well-trained and government-sanctioned officers who would be responsible for mustering (formally gathering and organizing) and inspecting these troops as they came through the facility. This policy would facilitate the uniform application of army policies and practices.

A major theme found in the order focuses on the (white) officers. These individuals were responsible for the organization, training, assignment, and deployment of the newest members of the Union Army. It was critical, therefore, that the officers assigned to this duty were carefully screened and managed in order ensure the troops' top performance. The officers' ranks were of two kinds, noncommissioned and commissioned. The former—such as corporals and sergeants—were men given authority by commissioned officers (sometimes while in the field), often as a reward for their demonstrated leadership qualities. Commissioned officers were trained to become officers and included graduates of the United States Military Academy at West Point. This group received their commissions and promotions by sanction of the federal government.

The War Department did not see a reason to change the protocols for promoting those officers who were assigned to work with black regiments. As they were already officially screened by the Adjutant General and the aforementioned board within the Bureau of Colored Troops, the officers would continue to see promotions based on merit and valor. According to section 8 of Order 143, noncommissioned officers would continue to be rewarded with promotions based on their distinguishing character and actions. Likewise, commissioned officers would be eligible for promotions based on their own meritorious activity.

There was a difference for officers who received their command over a white regiment as opposed to a black regiment. As mentioned earlier, officers were assigned their command over white regiments according to necessity—an officer who distinguished himself during a battle might, for example, be promoted and reassigned to a command in a similar combat situation. Officers seeking promotion typically would gain the support of their political leaders, such as congressmen or other elected officers. On the other hand, officers who sought to become a part of a black regiment needed to apply for such slots. Most knew no political officials who would lobby the War Department on their behalf. These officers needed to pass an examination, for which they needed to study extensively in order to ensure that they were prepared for any situation as an officer of a black regiment.

An important omission from the order is any protocol permitting the promotion of black soldiers to officer rank. Systemized racism and political sensitivity prevented the promotion of any black man to a rank in which he could be a white man's superior officer.

There were already black regiments in existence—

which included black officers—by the start of the Civil War. Louisiana had in 1861 established the Native Guards to support the Confederacy, but these regiments were not used; any such regiment that was captured by the Union was simply dissolved. By 1863, black men were barred from holding any higher rank, with the rare exception of black medical doctors or chaplains who were given their ranks in title only and without any discernible authority.

Also absent from War Department General Order 143 is any description of the training black troops would receive upon recruitment. The inclusion of such information would have divulged elements of battlefield strategy. Black soldiers in the Union Army were involved in a wide range of activities contributing to the war effort. Many served noncombat roles, working as laborers, medical corps, and chaplains. Others were assigned to artillery and infantry units. In total, the bureau managed nearly 180,000 black troops, organizing them into 120 infantry regiments, twenty-two artillery batteries, and seven cavalry regiments.

In 1863, the Union Army was as reluctant to let black soldiers go into battle as they were to let them join the military at all two year prior. Yet, black regiments of the Union Army fought in forty-one major battles and countless smaller skirmishes during the latter half of the war. According to a wide range of accounts, the regiments performed bravely and heroically. Nevertheless, in comparison to white soldiers, black troops were used in limited fashion on the battlefield; the vast majority of black soldiers who died during the war were killed by disease, not as a result of combat.

War Department General Order 143 is illustrative of the prevailing prejudices and racist ideologies of the Civil War era. President Lincoln and his antislavery supporters in the Republican Party were successful in adopting the Emancipation Proclamation, but this victory did not immediately change America's deeply ingrained racist culture. The order itself displays racial prejudice, as it presumes black men—in light of a presumed lack of intellect and social skills—would require additional training and education that white men would not. In addition, the order takes pains to remind readers that black troops would only serve—their role was to follow orders and not to issue them.

Essential Themes
The decision to recruit black men into the Union Army was not an overwhelmingly popular one. Despite the

fact that slavery was outlawed in the North, racism and prejudice against black people remained prevalent. Nevertheless, the dwindling number of able-bodied white Union soldiers and recruits led the Union to begin recruiting from this sizable population. Because of the large volume of black volunteers seeking to join the army, the Union leadership determined it was important to carefully organize and manage the affairs of black recruits. War Department General Order 143 served as the vehicle for that endeavor.

By establishing the Bureau of Colored Troops and the rules pertaining to the recruitment, processing, and deployment of black soldiers, the order demonstrates that a carefully ordered system, one that was unlike the processes utilized for raising white soldiers, was necessary. The rules governing not just the recruits but the white officers overseeing these troops reflect the racial stereotypes maintained by the North and reflect the strength of political forces opposed to black recruitment altogether. The order's language is extremely precise on the protocols for black troop recruitment and organization. For example, it ensures that no black man would have authority over a white man, and maintains the compensation and promotion policies afforded to white officers who are assigned to black regiments.

Despite the fact that black volunteers, just like their white counterparts, came from more than one geographic and socioeconomic area, the order assumes each black volunteer to be of a social stratum beneath that of white Americans. All black troops in the Union Army were subject to the same rules and protocols. Furthermore, black regiments, with the exception of the commissioned and noncommissioned officers under whose command they operated, remained separate from white regiments as they went about their wartime duties.

In addition to the adjutant general, recruitment boards served as a secondary administrative authority in the recruitment of black volunteers, overseeing the troops sent through the bureau's recruitment system. These boards, found at each recruitment post, selected white officers for black regiments. Aspiring officers who looked for a command in a black regiment were required to apply for the position and pass an examination administered by the board. By carefully selecting the officers for each regiment, the boards were responsible for assigning the officers most capable of leading this special brand of Union soldier. They also ensured that officers so assigned would adhere to the strict protocols established by the bureau and enforced by the adjutant general.

Michael Auerbach, MA

Bibliography

"Biography: Edwin Stanton." *Freedom: A History of US.* Public Broadcasting Service, n.d. Web. 25 Apr 2013.

"The Civil War's Black Soldiers." *National Park Service.* US Department of the Interior, 2013. Web. 25 Apr. 2013.

"The Fight for Equal Rights: Black Soldiers in the Civil War."*National Archives.* US National Archives and Records Administration, n.d. Web. 25 Apr 2013.

Additional Reading

Berlin, Ira. *Freedom's Soldiers: The Black Military Experience in the Civil War.* Cambridge: Cambridge UP, 1998. Print.

Glatthaar, Joseph T. *Forged in Battle: The Civil War Alliance of Black Soldiers and White Officers.* Baton Rouge: Louisiana State UP, 2000. Print.

McPherson, James. *The Negro's Civil War: How American Blacks Felt and Acted during the War for the Union.* New York: Vintage, 2003. Print.

Roberts, Rita. "Black Soldiers in Blue: African American Troops in the Civil War Era." *Journal of American History* 90.4 (2004): 1455–57. Print.

■ General Sherman Interviews the Freedmen Ministers in Savannah

Date: January 12, 1865
Author: various
Genre: report

> *"The way we can best take care of ourselves is to have land, and turn it and till it by our own labor . . . to assist the Government, the young men should enlist. . . and serve in such manner as they may be wanted."*

Summary Overview

In late 1864 and early 1865, Union Army general William Tecumseh Sherman led his army on a brutal, destructive march through Georgia and the Carolinas. The aim of the campaign was to economically and psychologically cripple the Confederate States Army. Sherman's "hard war" tactics succeeded. Southern land and property was devastated, and Southern civilian resolve to continue with what had already been a difficult struggle began to falter. As a side effect of Sherman's March to Sea, tens of thousands of enslaved African Americans gained their freedom under the enforced tenets of the 1863 Emancipation Proclamation. Freedmen saw Sherman as a liberator, and thousands of refugees attached themselves to his army. Sherman, however, saw this unplanned addition of men as an impediment to his military mission. To discuss possible efforts to detach them from his army, he met with a group of black leaders in Savannah, Georgia. From this meeting arose what became known as the short-lived policy of "forty acres and a mule."

Defining Moment

Chattel slavery was a fact of life in the Americas from the first moment that Europeans arrived in the Caribbean in the late 1400s. The colonies of British North America incorporated slavery into their social and eco-nomic systems, although the institution always carried greater heft in the agricultural South. In South Carolina, for example, a black majority existed as early as the 1600s. After the United States declared independence in 1776, Northern states began passing laws abolishing slavery. In the early 1800s, Congress barred the trans-atlantic slave trade. At the same time, the Southern economy was becoming ever more closely tied to the use of slave labor to grow "king cotton," the economic heart of the regional economy.

By the mid-1800s, sectional divisions over slavery had intensified. Westward expansion made the spread of slavery an ongoing and highly controversial political question. Management of the issue occurred through piecemeal legislative measures that bandaged but did not heal the growing rift. In the Northern states, a shift in public opinion on the moral question of slavery towards abolition took place in the 1850s, setting the North and South at even greater odds. When Republican Abraham Lincoln, an affirmed opponent of the expansion of slavery, was elected as president in 1860, the pressure on the nation became too great to bear. South Carolina led the majority of its fellow slave states in declaring itself independent of the United States in December 1860.

The American Civil War began on April 12, 1861. The demand for soldiers stripped both North and South first of volunteer troops and then of white conscripts. The Union Army was further swelled in some instances by volunteer black regiments. Early Southern military victories proved that the rebellion could not be easily suppressed. In time, Union political leaders expanded the goals of the war from simple reunification to emancipation. By the time General Sherman led his forces on a purposely destructive march across the South, the Emancipation Proclamation had freed the slaves of the Confederacy by decree, if not yet in practice. Sherman's forces liberated slaves as they crossed Georgia, inflicting serious damage to the state's economy in the process. With no means to support themselves, these freed peoples attached themselves to Sherman's forces. By early 1865, the general had determined that he must free his military column of what he saw as civilian hindrances. After taking the city of Savannah, he requested a meeting to discuss the situation with black leaders there.

Author Biography

Both Union officials and Southern freedmen took part in the Savannah meeting between General Sherman and the regions black leaders. In addition to General Sherman, the Union side included Secretary of War Edwin M. Stanton. Born in Ohio in 1820, Sherman served in the Seminole War and Mexican-American War in his youth before retiring briefly to civilian life in the 1850s. The eruption of the Civil War had brought him back to the army—and the North—from a position at the Louisiana Military Seminary. He fought as part of the command of General Ulysses S. Grant in the western theater of the conflict, rising in time to become the commanding general of the Union Army in the west. In this role, General Sherman undertook his pivotal march, destroying Confederate property and freeing Southern human chattel. Yet Sherman was no special friend of the people his actions directly aided. Historical evidence instead paints him as a figure morally neutral on the issues of slavery and race relations. Other evidence depicts him as clearly racist toward the black population of the United States. It seems clear that his meeting with black Georgian leaders was motivated by military necessity rather than altruism.

Stanton, in contrast, was a behind-the-scenes force in a number of actions intended to end slavery and support the interests of the freedmen. As secretary of war, Stanton became an advocate of efforts to promote racial equality during the Civil War; he encouraged the issuance of the Emancipation Proclamation and urged Lincoln to arm Southern slaves so that they might mount an internal resistance to the Confederacy. Stanton and Sherman shared a deep desire to end the war and reunite the United States. They agreed on the necessity of hard-war tactics. Nevertheless, their outlooks on the issues caught up in the Civil War did not mesh well past that simple goal. As the war ended, for example, Stanton rejected the lenient terms of surrender negotiated by Sherman with Confederate General Joseph E. Johnston. Stanton later became an ally of the Radical Republicans in Congress, who sought to reconstruct the South along lines of political, social, and economic equality of the races, a concept anathema to Sherman's worldview.

HISTORICAL DOCUMENT

MINUTES OF AN INTERVIEW BETWEEN THE COLORED MINISTERS AND CHURCH OFFICERS AT SAVANNAH WITH THE SECRETARY OF WAR AND MAJOR-GEN. SHERMAN.

HEADQUARTERS OF MAJ.-GEN. SHERMAN, CITY OF SAVANNAH, GA., Jan., 12, 1865—8 P.M.

On the evening of Thursday, the 12th day of January, 1865, the following persons of African descent met by appointment to hold an interview with Edwin M. Stanton, Secretary of War, and Major-Gen. Sherman, to have a conference upon matters relating to the freedmen of the State of Georgia, to-wit:

One: William J. Campbell, aged 51 years, born in Savannah, slave until 1849, and then liberated by will of his mistress, Mrs. May Maxwell. For ten years pastor of the 1st Baptist Church of Savannah, numbering about 1,800 members. Average congregation, 1,900. The church property belonging to the congregation. Trustees white. Worth $18,000.

Two: John Cox, aged fifty-eight years, born in Savannah; slave until 1849, when he bought his freedom for $1,100. Pastor of the 2nd African Baptist Church. In the ministry fifteen years. Congregation 1,222 persons. Church property worth $10,000, belonging to the congregation.

Three: Ulysses L. Houston, aged forty-one years, born in Grahamsville, S.C.; slave until the Union army entered Savannah. Owned by Moses Henderson, Savannah, and pastor of Third African Baptist Church. Congregation numbering 400. Church property worth $5,000; belongs to congregation. In the ministry about eight years.

Four: William Bentley, aged 72 years, born in Savannah, slave until 25 years of age, when his master, John Waters, emancipated him by will. Pastor of Andrew's Chapel, Methodist Episcopal Church—only one of that denomination in Savannah; congregation numbering 360 members; church property worth about $20,000, and is owned by the congregation; been in the ministry about twenty years; a member of Georgia Conference.

Five: Charles Bradwell, aged 40 years, born in Liberty County, Ga.; slave until 1851; emancipated by will of his master, J. L. Bradwell. Local preacher in charge of the Methodist Episcopal congregation (Andrew's Chapel) in the absence of the minister; in the ministry 10 years.

Six: William Gaines, aged 41 years; born in Wills Co., Ga. Slave until the Union forces freed me. Owned by Robert Toombs, formerly United States Senator, and his brother, Gabriel Toombs, local preacher of the M.E. Church (Andrew's Chapel.) In the ministry 16 years.

Seven: James Hill, aged 52 years; born in Bryan Co., Ga. Slave up to the time the Union army came in. Owned by H. F. Willings, of Savannah. In the ministry 16 years.

Eight: Glasgon Taylor, aged 72 years, born in Wilkes County, Ga. Slave until the Union army came; owned by A. P. Wetter. Is a local preacher of the M.E. Church (Andrew's Chapel.) In the ministry 35 years.

Nine: Garrison Frazier, aged 67 years, born in Granville County, N.C. Slave until eight years ago, when he bought himself and wife, paying $1,000 in gold and sil-

ver. Is an ordained minister in the Baptist Church, but, his health failing, has now charge of no congregation. Has been in the ministry 35 years.

Ten: James Mills, aged 56 years, born in Savannah; free-born, and is a licensed preacher of the first Baptist Church. Has been eight years in the ministry.

Eleven: Abraham Burke, aged 48 years, born in Bryan County, Ga. Slave until 20 years ago, when he bought himself for $800. Has been in the ministry about 10 years.

Twelve: Arthur Wardell, aged 44 years, born in Liberty County, Ga. Slave until freed by the Union army. Owned by A. A. Solomons, Savannah, and is a licensed minister in the Baptist Church. Has been in the ministry 6 years.

Thirteen: Alexander Harris, aged 47 years, born in Savannah; free born. Licensed minister of Third African Baptist Church. Licensed about one month ago.

Fourteen: Andrew Neal, aged 61 years, born in Savannah, slave until the Union army liberated him. Owned by Mr. Wm. Gibbons, and has been deacon in the Third Baptist Church for 10 years.

Fifteen: Jas. Porter, aged 39 years, born in Charleston, South Carolina; free-born, his mother having purchased her freedom. Is lay-reader and president of the board of wardens and vestry of St. Stephen's Protestant Episcopal Colored Church in Savannah. Has been in communion 9 years. The congregation numbers about 200 persons. The church property is worth about $10,000, and is owned by the congregation.

Sixteen: Adolphus Delmotte, aged 28 years, born in Savannah; free born. Is a licensed minister of the Missionary Baptist Church of Milledgeville. Congregation numbering about 300 or 400 persons. Has been in the ministry about two years.

Seventeen: Jacob Godfrey, aged 57 years, born in Marion, S.C. Slave until the Union army freed me; owned by James E. Godfrey—Methodist preacher now in the Rebel army. Is a class-leader and steward of Andrew's Chapel since 1836.

Eighteen: John Johnson, aged 51 years, born in Bryan County, Georgia. Slave up to the time the Union army came here; owned by W. W. Lincoln of Savannah. Is class-leader and treasurer of Andrew's Chapel for sixteen years.

Nineteen: Robt. N. Taylor, aged 51 years, born in Wilkes Co., Ga. Slave to the time the Union army came. Was owned by Augustus P. Welter, Savannah, and is class-leader in Andrew's Chapel for nine years.

Twenty: Jas. Lynch, aged 26 years, born in Baltimore, Md.; free-born. Is presiding elder of the M.E. Church and missionary to the department of the South. Has been seven years in the ministry and two years in the South.

✳ ✳ ✳

Garrison Frazier being chosen by the persons present to express their common sentiments upon the matters of inquiry, makes answers to inquiries as follows:

First: State what your understanding is in regard to the acts of Congress and President Lincoln's [Emancipation] proclamation, touching the condition of the colored people in the Rebel States.

Answer—So far as I understand President Lincoln's proclamation to the Rebellious States, it is, that if they would lay down their arms and submit to the laws of the United States before the first of January, 1863, all should be well; but if they did not, then all the slaves in the Rebel States should be free henceforth and forever. That is what I understood.

Second—State what you understand by Slavery and the freedom that was to be given by the President's proclamation.

Answer—Slavery is, receiving by *irresistible power* the work of another man, and not by his *consent*. The freedom, as I understand it, promised by the proclamation, is taking us from under the yoke of bondage, and placing us where we could reap the fruit of our own labor, take care of ourselves and assist the Government in maintaining our freedom.

Third: State in what manner you think you can take care of yourselves, and how can you best assist the Government in maintaining your freedom.

Answer: The way we can best take care of ourselves is to have land, and turn it and till it by our own labor—that is, by the labor of the women and children and old men; and we can soon maintain ourselves and have something to spare. And to assist the Government, the young men should enlist in the service of the Government, and serve in such manner as they may be wanted. (The Rebels told us that they piled them up and made batteries of them, and sold them to Cuba; but we don't believe that.) We want to be placed on land until we are able to buy it and make it our own.

Fourth: State in what manner you would rather live—whether scattered among the whites or in colonies by yourselves.

Answer: I would prefer to live by ourselves, for there is a prejudice against us in the South that will take years to get over; but I do not know that I can answer for my brethren. [Mr. Lynch says he thinks they should not be separated, but live together. All the other persons present, being questioned one by one, answer that they agree with Brother Frazier.]

Fifth: Do you think that there is intelligence enough among the slaves of the South to maintain themselves under the Government of the United States and the equal protection of its laws, and maintain good and peaceable relations among yourselves and with your neighbors?

Answer—I think there is sufficient intelligence among us to do so.

Sixth—State what is the feeling of the black population of the South toward the Government of the United States; what is the understanding in respect to the present war—its causes and object, and their disposition to aid either side. State fully your views.

Answer—I think you will find there are thousands that are willing to make any sacrifice to assist the Government of the United States, while there are also many that are not willing to take up arms. I do not suppose there are a dozen men that are opposed to the Government. I understand, as to the war, that the South is the aggressor. President Lincoln was elected President by a majority of the United States, which guaranteed him the right of holding the office and exercising that right over the whole United States. The South, without knowing what he would do, rebelled. The war was commenced by the Rebels before he came into office. The object of the war was not at first to give the slaves their freedom, but the sole object of the war was at first to bring the rebellious States back into the Union and their loyalty to the laws of the United States. Afterward, knowing the value set on the slaves by the Rebels, the President thought that his proclamation would stimulate them to lay down their arms, reduce them to obedience, and help to bring back the Rebel States; and their not doing so has now made the freedom of the slaves a part of the war. It is my opinion that there is not a man in this city that could be started to help the Rebels one inch, for that would be suicide. There were two black men left with the Rebels because they had taken an active part for the Rebels, and thought something might befall them if they stayed behind; but there is not another man. If the prayers that have gone up for the Union army could be read out, you would not get through them these two weeks.

Seventh: State whether the sentiments you now express are those only of the colored people in the city; or do they extend to the colored population through the country? and what are your means of knowing the sentiments of those living in the country?

Answer: I think the sentiments are the same among the colored people of the State. My opinion is formed by personal communication in the course of my ministry, and also from the thousands that followed the Union army, leaving their homes and undergoing suffering. I did not think there would be so many; the number surpassed my expectation.

Eighth: If the Rebel leaders were to arm the slaves, what would be its effect?

Answer: I think they would fight as long as they were before the bayonet, and just as soon as soon as they could get away, they would desert, in my opinion.

Ninth: What, in your opinion, is the feeling of the colored people about enlisting and serving as soldiers of the United States? and what kind of military service do they prefer?

Answer: A large number have gone as soldiers to Port Royal [S.C.] to be drilled and put in the service; and I think there are thousands of the young men that would enlist. There is something about them that perhaps is wrong. They have suffered so long from the Rebels that they want to shoulder the musket. Others want to go into the Quartermaster's or Commissary's service.

Tenth: Do you understand the mode of enlistments of colored persons in the Rebel States by State agents under the Act of Congress? If yea, state what your understanding is.

Answer: My understanding is, that colored persons enlisted by State agents are enlisted as substitutes, and give credit to the States, and do not swell the army, because every black man enlisted by a State agent leaves a white man at home; and, also, that larger bounties are given or promised by State agents than are given by the States. The great object should be to push through this Rebellion the shortest way, and there seems to be something wanting in the enlistment by State agents, for it don't strengthen the army, but takes one away for every colored man enlisted.

Eleventh: State what, in your opinion, is the best way to enlist colored men for soldiers.

Answer: I think, sir, that all compulsory operations should be put a stop to. The ministers would talk to them, and the young men would enlist. It is my opinion that it would be far better for the State agents to stay at home, and the enlistments to be made for the United States under the direction of Gen. Sherman.

In the absence of Gen. Sherman, the following question was asked:

Twelfth: State what is the feeling of the colored people in regard to Gen. Sherman; and how far do they regard his sentiments and actions as friendly to their rights and interests, or otherwise?

Answer: We looked upon Gen. Sherman prior to his arrival as a man in the Providence of God specially set apart to accomplish this work, and we unanimously feel inexpressible gratitude to him, looking upon him as a man that should be honored for the faithful performance of his duty. Some of us called upon him immediately upon his arrival, and it is probable he would not meet the Secretary with more courtesy than he met us. His conduct and deportment toward us characterized him as a friend and a gentleman. We have confidence in Gen. Sherman, and think that what concerns us could not be under better hands. This is our opinion now from the short acquaintance and interest we have had. (Mr. Lynch states that with his limited acquaintance with Gen. Sherman, he is unwilling to express an opinion. All others present declare their agreement with Mr. Frazier about Gen. Sherman.)

Some conversation upon general subjects relating to Gen. Sherman's march then ensued, of which no note was taken.

GLOSSARY

batteries: military divisions in the artillery similar to a company; alternatively, the physical materials used to barrage a location

before the bayonet: forced through the threat of violence; at gunpoint

bondage: slavery

brethren: brothers; fellows

deportment: behavior

Providence: fate; divine intervention or direction

quartermaster: military officer responsible for managing supplies

yoke: metaphorically, a link to servitude or oppression

Document Analysis

In January 1865, Secretary Stanton, General Sherman, and a group of twenty African American freedmen identified as being community leaders of Savannah, Georgia, met at Sherman's request to discuss the situation facing recently freed African Americans in the South. Sherman, then in the midst of his March to the Sea, had liberated tens of thousands of slaves under the Emancipation Proclamation. Sherman was unwilling to use his army to shelter them indefinitely, but leaders in Washington recognized that they had a responsibility to ensure that the people who had at last attained freedom could also establish themselves as self-sufficient members of society. For a number of reasons, the discussion was an unusual one in the context of the time. African Americans—even free blacks in the more moderate North—lacked status as American citizens under an 1857 US Supreme Court decision (*Dred Scott v. Sandford*). Without citizenship, African Americans had no legal or political rights, including the right to vote, under the laws of the United States. With rare exceptions, white Americans considered their black counterparts to be of inferior social status. Therefore, the leaders called upon by Sherman to discuss ideas about what should be done with the thousands of refugees populating the South lacked even a semblance of political or social equality with the men whom they were being asked to advise.

The Condition of the Freedmen

How could such an unlikely meeting come to be? Centuries of slavery had created notable African American communities, particularly in Southern states with high slave populations, such as Georgia. Despite laws and customs limiting the actions and practices of enslaved African Americans, these communities organized along lines similar to those of all human civilizations; certain people emerged as spokespeople and leaders. Church organizations provided a unifying core. Indeed, of the African American leaders selected by Sherman to participate in the Savannah discussion, many were active ministers and all had connections to African American churches in the area. By the time Sherman and Stanton met these leaders, their need was great. Sherman wanted nothing more than to rid his forces of the freedmen refugees attached to it. Stanton—an advocate of African American advancement—surely wanted to ensure that Sherman's success in freeing large numbers of slaves would not result in mass starvation. Thus Sherman, at Stanton's urging, summoned the freedmen detailed in the first portion of the meeting minutes.

The freedmen were a diverse group, encompassing men as young as twenty-six and as old as seventy-two. Some had been born into freedom, and others obtained it in the years preceding the Civil War through owner manumission or through buying their freedom. Only the Emancipation Proclamation freed many others. Most of the Savannah leaders were natives of the city or its immediate environs, with a minority hailing from the Carolinas or even from as far away as the slave state of Maryland. The freedmen selected Garrison Frazier as their main representative. Frazier, a former slave, had successfully purchased his and his wife's freedom several years earlier and served for many years as a Baptist minister.

The topics of the meeting revolved around race relations and changes wrought by the Civil War that affected the African American populace. Much of the discussion focused on determining the freedmen's level of knowledge about the policies and events of the Civil War, presumably as a means of assessing African American knowledge of their situation. If the freedmen were poorly informed, Stanton, a man sympathetic to the African American cause, might have felt compelled to disregard their ideas on other matters. Thus, the discussion opens with questions about the 1863 Emancipation Proclamation and the freedom that it granted to those enslaved by people in rebelling states. (The Emancipation Proclamation, contrary to popular belief, did not free all slaves in the United States, only those contained within the borders of the Confederacy.) As part of their answer, the freedmen quite eloquently describe the difference between slavery and freedom, noting that slavery relies on compulsion by "irresistible power" to require labor from a person, while freedom requests that that same labor be given by consent. The freedmen further suggest that their liberty benefits everyone: they "reap the fruit of [their] own labor" even as they "assist the Government in maintaining their freedom."

Notable of the freedmen's answers to this series of questions is the high degree of accuracy and astuteness with which the men assess the historical, economic, and political factors at play in the execution of the Civil War. For example, the group correctly summarizes the tenets of the Emancipation Proclamation and gives a concise assessment of the progression of the Civil War. Although the president did not directly inform the rebellious states that they would be permitted to retain slavery if they gave up their rebellion, for example, the practical effect of a state rejoining the Union before the issuance of the Proclamation was just that. The men within the group had been behind enemy lines for years. By the nature of their background, they were unlikely to enjoy high levels of literacy. Nevertheless, they were well informed of national events. African Americans may have lacked citizenship and political rights, but the answers of the freedmen clearly suggest that they did not lack interest in or knowledge of the government and events of the nation that only reluctantly acknowledged their humanity. They were also willing to lend support to a government that had for many years permitted their enslavement. Having received their freedom under Lincoln, African Americans' dedication to the United States federal government was, the freedmen stated, very great, even though they understood that the Emancipation Proclamation was a result of the ongoing war and not one of inherent moral righteousness.

The Freedmen's Wishes

Much of the remainder of the conversation is split into two main sections. The first of these addresses how best African Americans could be organized into free communities, an act that would help ensure their long-term success outside of slavery and in the short term remove the thousands of followers from Sherman's army. The freedmen suggest a simple plan: they wish to farm to support themselves and their families. By having land, they suggest, they can use the labor that previously served their masters to maintain themselves. Although recently freed slaves obviously had no property of their own, there was a solution to this dilemma. The federal government had, in the past, implemented land redistribution schemes that resold lands confiscated from Confederate supporters to Union investors or area freedmen who could afford to purchase the property. The freedmen state that they "want to be placed on land until we are able to buy it"—that is, they wish to have tenancy to work the land for a period in order to save up the required funds to buy the land outright. This suggestion was indeed one that resonated with the Union leaders, for a scheme along these lines was instituted soon thereafter.

The leaders then ask the Savannah freedmen whether they wish to live in an integrated or segregated society. Frazier answers the question independently, stating that he prefers segregation because "there is a prejudice against us the South that will take years to get over." Nearly all the others agree with him, with only the freeborn Maryland native Lynch instead arguing for an integrated society, perhaps a reflection of his own roots in the more integrated urban society of Baltimore. This preference on the part of African Americans for segregation as the Civil War came to a close is perhaps surprising to modern readers. Certainly, the threat of racism and discrimination was intense for a people who had been enslaved and subject to great inequity for many centuries. The appeal of living in a society that would not have rejected their humanity, skills, or prospects for achievement merely because of their race must have appealed greatly to people who had experienced nothing but racism throughout their lives. The United States government, too, had previously considered formal policies of segregation. Earlier proposals had been put forth to create reservations not unlike later Native American reservations, but for freedmen in the South. Yet the actual effects of such policies were far from beneficial to African Americans as they faced enduring marginalization and discrimination through legal segregation in years to come.

The second major portion of the conversation focused on African American involvement with the Union and Confederate military. The freedmen firmly rejected the notion that enslaved African Americans would willingly fight for the Confederacy—the Confederacy did not in fact allow black soldiers into its army until later in 1865 due to internal resistance over the idea. The freedmen equally asserted that African Americans would willingly fight for the Union forces. This disparity is only logical. Although most in both the Union and the Confederacy accepted that any black soldier who fought for the Confederacy would likely need to be granted freedom as a result, it is hard to imagine that even those desperately longing for freedom would be enthusiastic volunteers in an army fighting for the right to keep others in their position in bondage. A Confederate victory aided by slaves would only perpetuate the institution. In contrast, the issuance of the Emancipation Proclamation had put the Union firmly on the side of liberty. With only a slight prodding from the ministers in their communities, African American men would willingly enlist in the Union cause. As the freedmen explained, many young men "have suffered so long from the Rebels that they want to shoulder the musket" against those oppressors.

Sherman's Attitude

The conversation next turned to the opinions of the African American populace about Sherman, who left the room for the duration of this part of the discussion. Stanton had valid reason to wonder about the black leaders' opinion of Sherman, whose stance on racial issues had been an apparent mass of contradictions. Sherman, a man of his time and society, was a firm and unquestioning believer in the natural superiority of whites over blacks. Although Sherman was certainly astute enough to recognize that political and cultural pressures were consigning the institution of slavery to history, he had expressed disgust with the antislavery or pro–African American rights views of both family members and political or military acquaintances in the past. His Northern ties made him a Union man during the Civil War, but Sherman approached the conflict as one supporting the authority of the federal government over the rebellious Confederacy, not one with a primary aim of spreading political and social rights for African Americans, enslaved or free. He refused to command African American soldiers even after Union laws changed to permit black Americans to enlist in the military, explaining that he neither believed black soldiers to be the equal of white soldiers in battle nor expected his existing troops, many of whom shared Sherman's racist outlook, to accept African Americans into their ranks. President Abraham Lincoln reminded Sherman that he, too, was subject to the laws of the United States, yet Sherman still resisted accepting black soldiers into his army, allowing African Americans only in supporting roles as camp laborers in much the same way that the Confederate Army employed black slaves. The general's personal views on African Americans were no secret.

Equally, Stanton and the allied congressional Radical Republicans did not wholeheartedly approve of Sherman's policies or beliefs. Writing in his memoirs, Sherman included a letter from a commander in the Union capital that informed him of accusations of his mistreatment of the African Americans freed by his march. According to this letter, Sherman had physically detached a large contingent of African American camp followers from his trail by driving them away and cutting down the bridges behind them; a Confederate cavalry then massacred the refugees. The letter asserts that Sherman must surely have undertaken this action in order to ease military operations and not as a result of any intentional ill will toward the refugees, and the general obviously agreed with this assessment or he would not have included what he said had been previously confidential correspondence in his personal memoirs. Stanton, Sherman acknowledged, was more than likely among the group who spoke poorly of Sherman over incidents such as these.

Yet Sherman's military victories significantly benefited the same Southern African Americans whom he personally did not like or respect as a group, and Sherman was fully aware of this fact. As the head of the western portion of the Union Army, Sherman oversaw the march across Georgia that enforced the Emancipation Proclamation by military might. Nine of the twenty freedmen gathered for the conversation had themselves been freed from bondage only with the arrival of the Union Army. In his memoirs, Sherman pointed to his army's success in securing liberty for so many freedmen, dismissing the idea that he was hostile to African Americans simply because he had refused to "[load] down my army by other hundreds of thousands of poor negroes" (Sherman 247). From Sherman's somewhat paternalistic perspective, he had helped deliver a great gift to the South's new freedmen, and his actions therefore were above reproach. Whether this position was truly valid is much more debatable, and the fact that Stanton bothered to ask the question suggests that he was far from confident in Sherman's treatment of African Americans and their reception to that treatment.

The freedmen of Savannah spoke highly of Sherman to Stanton when asked, asserting that he was "a man in the Providence of God" charged with freeing the slaves, an assessment that subtly compares Sherman with the biblical figure of Moses, who legendarily led the Jews from captivity in Egypt. They also lauded the general's personal conduct, noting that "it is probable he would not meet the Secretary [Stanton] with more courtesy than he met us," based on their early meetings with him. Some historians, however, have questioned whether this praise was truly the freedmen's thoughts or an effort to tell Stanton and, by association, Sherman, the answer that he wanted to hear (Fellman 164). Indeed, Lynch again refused to add his voice to the overall chorus of praise, and even the freedmen's strong statement was somewhat qualified by the comment that it was "our opinion now from the short acquaintance and interest we have had." Throughout his career, Sherman longed for respect and popularity. His discussion of the Savannah conversation in his memoirs focuses almost entirely on this last question of Stanton's, suggesting that the issue was one around which he felt the need to defend his record to foster that respect and popularity among the American public.

In all, the unlikely conversation between highly influential Union leaders and local African American freedman in Savannah was a notable one. It provided a rare opportunity for black leaders to express their wishes and views on their role in the post–Civil War South. Although the freedmen made no especially shocking requests given the situation in which they found themselves, the mere interest by the government in listening to the ideas of ordinary, nonvoting African Americans was in itself a remarkable action. That the government representatives did listen to and value the freedmen's input is clear, because the conversation directly informed military orders issued by General Sherman soon thereafter—orders that married the interests of the general with the advancement of African Americans. This uneasy alliance characterized many of the changes to the racial balance of power in the United States during and immediately after the Civil War.

Essential Themes

In their discussion with General Sherman and Secretary Stanton, the free ministers of Savannah set forth a number of basic desires on the part of black Americans that remained among the key goals of that group and their supporters for many decades to come. They sought acceptance as contributing members of society, as willing soldiers, self-supporting farmers, and dedicated citizens. They also sought the ability to control property, to provide for their families, and to overcome the racism made endemic by years of slavery. Of these points, Sherman and Stanton most directly acted upon the wish for land separate from that controlled by white Southerners. Just days after the Savannah meeting, Sherman issued Special Field Order No. 15, a military order commanding that a great deal of property controlled by rebel Southern landowners be confiscated and given to freed African American tenants for resettlement as farmers. The later addition of surplus military animals to aid in farming lent this resettlement program its popular designation of "forty acres and a mule." Over the ensuing months, some 40,000 freed slaves were granted parcels in this territory. However, in early 1866, President Andrew Johnson rescinded Sherman's order and restored the land to its original owners. The quest for land ownership would become one of the most basic struggles of Southern African Americans for many years to come. Without land, most former slaves and their descendents became sharecroppers or tenant farmers in conditions of economic and political repression that were little better than slavery. Nearly 150 years later, the promise of forty acres and a mule remained a key argument in the legal and political efforts by some African Americans to obtain reparations for slavery from the federal government.

Unspoken but apparent is a wish on the part of the freedmen to be simply treated as fully capable human beings. For centuries, white Europeans and Americans had dismissed black Africans and their descendents as inherently incapable of the same intellectual, emotional, and moral depths as white people. The same Thomas Jefferson who wrote of the equality of all people in the Declaration of Independence, for example, voiced doubts that black people could in fact be equal with their white counterparts. Yet the Savannah ministers display a keen understanding of the realities of the war, and a desire on the part of their people to have equality of opportunity in order to support themselves and their families. Although Reconstruction brought about efforts to ensure this equality of opportunity, discriminatory policies in the years following 1877 wiped out much of this progress. Whether all contemporary Americans enjoy equality of opportunity remains a topic of political and social controversy.

Vanessa E. Vaughn, MA

Bibliography

Fellman, Michael. *Citizen Sherman: A Life of William Tecumseh Sherman.* New York: Random, 1995. Print.

Lewin, Tamar. "Calls for Slavery Restitution Getting Louder." *New York Times.* New York Times, 4 June 2001. Web. 26 Apr. 2013.

McPherson, James M. "The Ballot and Land for the Freedmen, 1861–1865." *Reconstruction: An Anthology of Revisionist Writings.* Ed. Kenneth M. Stampp and Leon F. Litwick. Baton Rouge: Louisiana State UP, 1969. 132–55. Print.

Sherman, William Tecumseh. *Memoirs of William T. Sherman.* 2nd ed. New York: Appleton, 1889. Print.

Additional Reading

Berlin, Ira., et al., eds. *Freedom's Soldiers: The Black Military Experience in the Civil War.* New York: Cambridge UP, 1998. Print.

Foner, Eric. *A Short History of Reconstruction, 1863–1877.* New York: Harper, 1990. Print.

---. *Forever Free: The Story of Emancipation and Reconstruction.* New York: Knopf, 2005. Print.

Oubre, Claude F. *Forty Acres and a Mule: The Freedmen's Bureau and Black Land Ownership.* Baton Rouge: Louisiana State UP, 1978. Print.

■ Special Field Order No. 15: Forty Acres and a Mule

Date: January 16, 1865
Author Name: Sherman, William Tecumseh
Genre: order

". . . so that each family shall have a plot of not more than (40) forty acres of tillable ground. . ."

Summary Overview

In early 1865, Union general William Tecumseh Sherman, with the tacit approval of Secretary of War Edwin M. Stanton and President Abraham Lincoln, issued a field order that radically redistributed some 400,000 acres of Confederate agricultural lands owned by rebelling Southerners to newly freed African Americans. Sherman had recently embarked upon his psychologically and militarily shattering March to the Sea across Georgia, and a great number of emancipated slaves followed on the heels of his conquering army. Special Field Order No. 15 thus served a number of purposes: it resettled these refugees so that the army no longer had to protect them; it punished rebels in the very heart of the Confederacy; and it provided a potentially enduring means of support for newly freed slaves. Although this promise of "forty acres and a mule" proved short-lived, it carried lasting implications for both the reconstructed South and for African Americans.

Defining Moment

Lasting from 1861 until 1865, the Civil War was the bloodiest and most grueling conflict fought on US soil. The core cause of the war was the widespread practice of chattel slavery across the agricultural South, which relied on this cheap forced labor to support the large plantations that were the heart of its society and economy. The growth of abolitionist sentiment in the North and the election of a president who had avowed his unwillingness to see slavery expand into new US states and territories spurred some Southern leaders to secede from the United States. The resulting conflict at first focused mainly on the forcible reuniting of the sundered country, but in time it came to increasingly address the moral and political questions raised by slavery.

Although the conflict was less than three months from its end when Sherman issued Special Field Order No. 15 from his military headquarters in Savannah, Georgia, in January of 1865, its looming finality was not yet apparent to the governments, armies, and people of the divided United States. Union forces had made significant inroads into Confederate territory in recent months, with Sherman and his army inflicting incredible destruction in Georgia in a successful effort to show the Southern populace that war was a terrible machine from which their faltering Confederate government could not protect them. As Sherman's army crossed the South, it enforced the 1863 Emancipation Proclamation freeing enslaved African Americans in territories rebelling against the US federal government. Thus, Sherman's March to the Sea was also a march of liberation for the region's black residents, many of whom attached themselves to the trailing edge of Sherman's army.

These human additions to Sherman's marching force came to number in the thousands. Because the freed people had no money or possessions other than the clothes on their backs, they were entirely dependent on the Union Army to feed and shelter them. The pressure to care for a civilian populace in the midst of an intense military campaign was strategically unwelcome. Sherman and Secretary of War Edwin Stanton met with a group of African American ministers at the conquered city of Savannah, Georgia, in January of 1865 to discuss possible arrangements to detach the refugees from Sherman's army. A few days later, Sherman issued Special Field Order No. 15 in a direct response to this conversation.

Author Biography

Born in Lancaster, Ohio, in 1820, William Tecumseh Sherman spent much of his adult life involved with the US military. He attended the prestigious West Point military academy, graduating near the top of his class, and participated to in both the Seminole War in Florida and the Mexican-American War in California. After leaving the army in the mid-1850s, Sherman worked in banking and real estate for several years. With the outbreak of the Civil War, he became an officer in the Union Army and rose rapidly through its ranks. He fought alongside Ulysses S. Grant to take control of Confederate strongholds along the Mississippi River and became the head of the Army of the Tennessee after Grant assumed leadership of the war's western theater. The following year, Sherman took this position after Grant became the Union Army's general-in-chief.

In late 1864, Sherman launched a devastating campaign across Georgia and the Carolinas. He and his troops pillaged and destroyed land and property to un-

dermine civilian support for the Confederate Army and to show the futility of continued war. The combined psychological and physical warfare worked. Southern support for the Confederacy declined as Sherman's "hard war" raged on, and his so-called March to the Sea has been widely credited as a factor in the Union victory in the spring of 1865.

Sherman was neither an abolitionist nor a particular supporter of African American rights; like the wide majority of Americans of his era and social station, he believed that black people were inherently inferior to white people. His racial views informed his actions both before and during the war. Prior the conflict, Sherman had shown little interest in using the US political system to curtail the spread of slavery, and some evidence suggests that he sympathized to a degree with the Southern position regarding African Americans. Immediately before the conflict erupted, Sherman lived in the Southern state of Louisiana, where he actively sought to remain neutral on the controversial issue of slavery. As a military officer, he declined to allow black soldiers to serve under him, believing that they could not possibly be equal to white soldiers. His motivations in issuing Special Field Order No. 15 must therefore not be viewed as an effort to support the social, political, or economic interests of freed black slaves in whom Sherman had little interest and even less respect.

HISTORICAL DOCUMENT

1. The islands from Charleston south, the abandoned rice-fields along the rivers for thirty miles back from the sea, and the country bordering the St. John's River, Florida, are reserved and set apart for the settlement of the negroes now made free by the acts of war and the [Emancipation] proclamation of the President of the United States.

2. At Beaufort, Hilton Head, Savannah, Fernandina, St. Augustine, and Jacksonville, the blacks may remain in their chosen or accustomed vocations; but on the islands, and in the settlements hereafter to be established no white person whatever, unless military officers and soldiers detailed for duty, will be permitted to reside; and the sole and exclusive management of affairs will be left to the freed people themselves, subject only to the

United States military authority, and the acts of Congress. By the laws of war, and orders of the President of the United States, the negro is free, and must be dealt with as such. He cannot be subjected to conscription, or forced military service, save by the written orders of the highest military authority of the [War] department, under such regulations as the President or Congress may prescribe. Domestic servants, blacksmiths, carpenters, and other mechanics, will be free to select their own work and residence, but the young and able-bodied negroes must be encouraged to enlist as soldiers in the service of the United States, to contribute their share toward maintaining their own freedom, and securing their rights as citizens of the United States.

Negroes so enlisted will be organized into companies,

battalions, and regiments, under the orders of the United States military authorities, and will be paid, fed, and clothed, according to law. The bounties paid on enlistment may, with the consent of the recruit, go to assist his family and settlement in procuring agricultural implements, seed, tools, boots, clothing, and other articles necessary for their livelihood.

3. Whenever three respectable negroes, heads of families, shall desire to settle on land, and shall have selected for that purpose an island or a locality clearly defined within the limits above designated, the Inspector of Settlements and Plantations will himself, or by such subordinate officer as he may appoint, give them a license to settle such island or district and afford them such assistance as he can to enable them to establish a peaceable agricultural settlement. The three parties named will subdivide the land, under the supervision of the inspector, among themselves, and such others as may choose to settle near them, so that each family shall have a plot of not more than forty acres of tillable ground, and, when it borders on some water-channel, with not more than eight hundred feet water-front, in the possession of which land the military authorities will afford them protection until such time as they can protect themselves, or until Congress shall regulate their title. The quartermaster may, on the requisition of the Inspector of Settlements and Plantations, place at the disposal of the inspector one or more of the captured steamers to ply between the settlements and one or more of the commercial points heretofore named, in order to afford the settlers the opportunity to supply their necessary wants, and to sell the products of their land and labor.

4. Whenever a negro has enlisted in the military service of the United States, he may locate his family in any one of the settlements at pleasure, and acquire a homestead, and all other rights and privileges of a settler, as though present in person. In like manner, negroes may settle their families and engage on board the gunboats, or in fishing, or in the navigation of the inland waters, without losing any claim to land or other advantages derived from this system. But no one, unless an actual settler as above defined, or unless absent on Government service, will be entitled to claim any right to land or property in any settlement by virtue of these orders.

5. In order to carry out this system of settlement, a general officer will be detailed as Inspector of Settlements and plantations whose duty it shall be to visit the settlements, to regulate their police and general arrangement, and who will furnish personally to each head of a family, subject to the approval of the President of the United States, a possessory title in writing, giving as near as possible the description of boundaries; and who shall adjust all claims or conflicts that may arise under the same, subject to the like approval, treating such titles altogether as possessory. The same general officer will also be charged with the enlistment and organization of the negro recruits, and protecting their interests while absent from their settlements; and will be governed by the rules and regulations prescribed by the War Department for such purposes.

6. Brigadier-General R. Saxton is hereby appointed Inspector of Settlements and Plantations, and will at once enter on the performance of his duties. No change is intended or desired in the settlement now on Beaufort Island, nor will any rights to property heretofore acquired be affected thereby.

By order of Major-General W. T. Sherman,
L. M . Dayton, Assistant Adjutant-General.

GLOSSARY

blacksmith: person engaged in work shaping or repairing metal

bounties: bonuses or rewards paid for completing a certain action

prescribe: call for; establish

quartermaster: military officer responsible for managing supplies

tillable: able to be worked for agricultural purposes

vocations: jobs; occupations

Document Analysis

General William Tecumseh Sherman was far from a Radical Republican dedicated to the political, social, and economic equality of black and white Americans, but his Special Field Order No. 15 is among the most radical policies developed and implemented during the Civil War. Issued shortly before the war's end, primarily as a way to clear a growing African American civilian contingent away from Sherman's army and to weaken the Confederacy from within, the order instituted a policy of land redistribution that promised to dramatically reshape the economic and social position of freed African American slaves in the South in just a short time. The order punished Confederates by taking possession of valuable agricultural lands while assuring a base of Union support in the very heart of the Confederacy, not far from the place where the rebellion had begun years before with South Carolina's declaration of secession. Although Sherman had little personal interest in the lasting success of a group of people that his writings suggest he felt were vastly inferior to their white counterparts, his order redrew the South along racial lines not seriously discussed even by the more moderate wing of the Republican Party leading the Union at the time; property rights were, after all, among the most fundamental of the liberties assured under the US Constitution. The radical nature of the order may belie Sherman's intentions, but the lasting conversation that the action began influenced racial policies in the South well past the order's own brief period of efficacy.

Special Field Order No. 15 begins by outlining the lands affected by its directives. These included "the islands from Charleston south"—more commonly known as Georgia's Sea Islands—"the abandoned rice-fields" stretching along the coastline, and "the country bordering the St. John's River, Florida." In total, this area, which became known as "Sherman's Land" or "Sherman's Reservation," encompasses a thirty-mile swathe inland along the southeast's Atlantic coastline from Charleston, South Carolina, in the north to Jacksonville, Florida, in the south. Sherman's language is somewhat vague, however, on whether the order commandeered all of the land within the borders that he outlined or merely those lands actually abandoned by their occupants; earlier Congressional legislation had declared lands belonging to Confederate soldiers or supporters to be abandoned, however.

Containing hundreds of thousands of acres, this region had historically been the heart of the rice-growing industry and as such held great agricultural and economic value for those in possession of it. Because of its plantation-based economy, the region was already home to thousands of African Americans who had toiled in bondage on the very land that Sherman's order now reserved for them. The vast majority of these freedmen had only recently obtained liberty. Sherman's order specifically grants the lands to those African Americans who had been freed by the 1863 Emancipation Proclamation and other "acts of war," which particularly included Sherman's own March to the Sea. Sherman may not have supported African American equality, but he firmly believed that his army deserved recognition and respect for the role that it had played in executing the practical emancipation of the multitudes legally freed by the authority of a government not then recognized in the South.

The second section of the order contains three main points. First, freedmen living in specified cities were permitted to carry on as residents of those mixed-race cities along whatever lines they may already have envisioned. In contrast, the second key point formally racially segregates the remainder of the land, creating a black-only territory outside of local or state government authority. This order of segregation can be traced to the discussion that Sherman and Secretary of War Stanton had with African American leaders in Savannah several days before the issuance of Special Field Order No. 15. As part of this conversation, the Union leaders asked the freedmen of Savannah whether Southern African Americans would on the whole prefer to live in an integrated society or in separate black-only colonies. The leaders, citing the history of institutionalized racism that they believed would take many years to overcome, mostly argued for racial separation. Special Field Order No. 15 complies with that request—a seemingly odd one when viewed through the lens of the later civil rights movement to eradicate just these kinds of racial barriers—by expelling any white people then residing in the Sherman Reservation from its boundaries, excepting government or military personnel charged with the management of the land and its people.

Finally, the second section sets guidelines for the enlistment of freedmen in the army, including the payment of enlistment bonuses to family members on the Sherman Reservation in order to support their agricultural endeavors. Sherman's own refusal to employ African American soldiers in his army undermines the seeming magnanimity in this action. Although the Union Army had at first declined to allow black soldiers into its ranks, by early 1865 recruitment policies had changed. The Supreme Court decision stripping African Americans of citizenship still stood, and as such, black Americans could not be legally drafted into the army; they could, however, voluntarily enlist. Yet Sherman refused to allow black soldiers into his ranks, a clear reflection of his racist beliefs that black soldiers were simply not as good as white soldiers. Instead, he permitted African Americans only in support roles behind the lines. Although politicians in Washington— including President Lincoln—pressured Sherman to change his mind and follow the US laws allowing black soldiers into the army, Sherman resisted. Because of

this, the encouragement that he gives to young freedmen to enlist in the army actually had the effect of separating those recruits even further from his own ranks. Telling freedmen to enlist got those soldiers as far away from Sherman's army as he could possibly secure.

The order then lays out the specific details of the process of distributing land to the freedmen. Family groups were to settle in clusters, with three heads of households being required to apply together for permission to take control of an area of land. The government then granted the applicants an area of land that they were to divide among themselves, presumably so that larger families with more able hands could have larger plots than smaller families who were perhaps unable to manage a great deal of land. Land allotments were capped at forty acres per family, with further restriction preventing any one household from having access to more than 800 feet of waterfront. Forty acres was apparently an arbitrary division, but one that had been used before in planned Union subdividing and sale of confiscated lands; it became part of the Reconstruction-era rallying cry of "forty acres and a mule" commonly attributed to the promises of Special Field Order No. 15. This section further guaranteed freedmen settlers military protection on their forty acres "until such time as they can protect themselves, or until Congress shall regulate their title"—that is, until the communities were sufficiently established to be able to care for their own interests or until Congress made other arrangements to finalize their temporary situation. To this end, the official managing the settlement could use seized Confederate vessels to conduct trade between the agricultural settlements and the cities encompassed by the order.

Further to the tenets of taking possession is a series of directives permitting freedmen to retain their land claims without being physically present on the land under certain circumstances. Soldiers and army laborers, for example, could establish and maintain land claims without being present. Freedmen who had already received land allocations could retain those claims while on nearby waterways. But the order specifically forbade people not contained in the group of recently freed slaves—the very people that Sherman wished to detach from his army—from undertaking to make a land claim under the order.

Next, the order establishes a government position, the Inspector of Settlements and Plantations, to "visit the settlements, to regulate their police and general arrangement, and who will furnish personally to each head a family . . . a possessory title in writing . . . and who shall adjust all claims or conflicts" that may result from this land distribution. The inspector also oversaw the military enrollment of African American soldiers and helped manage their lands while they were fighting. Yet the emphasis in this section on the possessory nature of the title is the idea that proved most pivotal in time. Because the title granted possession, but not ownership, of the land to the freedmen settled there, it did not provide an entire legal guarantee that the residents could not be expelled. If their possessory titles were revoked, they lost all claim to the farms or homes that they had established there. It was in fact this usage of the possessory title that Sherman himself later pointed to as a justification for President Andrew Johnson's decision to rescind Special Field Order No. 15; because the titles were possessory, the actual land itself had not been given to its tenants, and returning possession to the original owners after the war was, by this logic, quite fair.

Whether this was the intention from the beginning remains debatable, however. On one hand, the order was issued in wartime by a military official and as such may be reasonably assumed to be effective largely as a function of that conflict; discussion of land redistribution throughout the war had mostly hinged on its use as a tool of war. On the other hand, Secretary of War Edwin Stanton, an ally of the Radical Republican wing of Congress and a proponent of African American rights, had a definite if somewhat unclear role in the reading and revising of Sherman's order. Using freedmen as an economic weapon only to discard them after the war had ended did little to further long-term Radical Republican goals.

The last section of Special Field Order No. 15 names Brigadier General Rufus Saxton as the official inspector of settlements and plantations and puts him in charge of administering the order's tenets. Saxton, a Massachusetts native and decorated Union officer, was a logical choice for this role, although Saxton's radical republicanism and personal beliefs made Sherman dislike him greatly (Fellman 165). Saxton was an abolitionist and supporter of African American political and economic advancement who could be expected to work diligently to execute Sherman's order because of these moral values. Saxton was also an experienced quartermaster with particular experience in the distribution of lands. In 1863, Lincoln had named Saxton one of the commissioners responsible for the

management of seized lands in South Carolina's Sea Islands, amounting to a little over 60,000 acres. The commission had auctioned off some of the lands, but a substantial acreage was earmarked for sale to African American families. In an effort to secure more of these lands for prospective African American landowners, Saxton had devised a plan to settle African Americans on plots of land earmarked for auction before the sale took place. This, Saxton hoped, would allow a greater number of freedmen the opportunity to buy land at an affordable price. Although Saxton's earlier efforts in the Sea Islands were not a success—much of the land sold for prices far higher than freedmen could pay—his belief in the vital importance of African American land ownership as an accompaniment to freedom was apparent (Oubre 8–11).

Indeed, Sherman seems to have felt confident that assigning this task—one that Sherman himself had essentially no interest in overseeing and little concern for its success beyond removing the unwanted civilian freedmen from his military machine—to Saxton would guarantee that the general could focus his attentions on the continued conquering of the South. Passing the job to Saxton also insulated Sherman from what he believed would be its inevitable problems, even as it made Sherman look like a great protector of an oppressed people. Although Sherman probably did not select Saxton in a real effort to help the freedmen succeed on their new lands, Saxton proved a strong advocate for the freedmen after Sherman appointed him to the task. Believing the government to have fallen through in its efforts to ensure land for freedmen in the past, he communicated with Stanton to ensure that the federal government would protect freedmen's rights to the lands that he allotted in the Sherman Reservation; with Stanton's assurance, Saxton distributed some 400,000 acres of land in less than six months' time. In fact, the recipients of that land had tenancy for only a short time, but this was not due to any action on the part of either Saxton or Stanton.

Special Field Order No. 15 contains a series of directives outlining the extent and execution of the land redistribution policy. What the order does not contain, however, is a direct listing of its causes and goals; this information must be inferred from the document, from historical evidence about Sherman, and from evidence about the other key events and figures involved in the order's creation. Ultimately, the policies promulgated in Special Field Order No. 15 served a number of purposes. For Sherman, the order rid him of the free black civilian population that he believed was weighing down his fighting force. It allowed him to make a strong move against the Confederate rebels that his army was in the midst of fighting on all fronts, while ensuring that the new residents of the Sherman Reservation were deeply supportive of that army. At the same time, the order appeased even the most radical of the Radical Republicans, a group with whom Sherman had clashed more than once in the past over what was generally perceived as his intense hatred of African Americans; Sherman later included a December 1864 letter in his memoirs referencing the "almost *criminal* dislike to the negro" that Republicans in the capital believed him to have shown in his actions to date (Sherman 247–48).

For Sherman, therefore, the order offered valuable military and political expedients that served his immediate aims in subduing the Confederacy and in streamlining his increasingly unwieldy army. Later, Sherman again used the freedmen as a way to improve his military operations, declaring that pack animals too strained for further military use be sent to the freedmen's farms where they could provide useful, lighter-duty agricultural service and recover their strength at the same time—the "mules" of "forty acres and mule." That the land redistribution established in Special Field Order No. 15 also greatly aided freed African Americans and provided a basis for the later work of Reconstructionists in establishing high levels of economic and political equality between the races in the South was, for Sherman, a side effect of these primary aims. Some historians have even speculated that Secretary of War Stanton, not Sherman, was the genesis of the land redistribution enacted by the order, in part because of this seeming disparity between Sherman's previous actions and the apparent goals and effects of Special Field Order No. 15. Yet the uneasy alliance of the furtherance of African American equality with the achievement of military and political aims was at the core of the Civil War, which was a conflict begun as a result of racial issues and as time progressed became tied to changing the way that African Americans lived.

Essential Themes

Within a short time of its issuance, the promises of Special Field Order No. 15 were interpreted by the nation's growing freed African American population to be "forty acres and a mule" in recompense for their time in bondage. Yet this interpretation quickly proved inaccurate. Although several thousand freedmen and their families were in fact settled on the lands seized and redistributed under Sherman's order, regime change in Washington, DC, changed the flavor of Reconstruction almost before it was truly underway. Lincoln, who was assassinated not long after Confederate general Robert E. Lee surrendered to Union general Ulysses S. Grant in an act that essentially ended the Civil War, was succeeded by the Southern-born Andrew Johnson. Johnson's policies toward the defeated former Confederacy were even more lenient than those proposed by Lincoln, and his actions discouraged many of the gains that freed Southern African Americans longed for.

Among these actions was the revocation of Sherman's order in the winter of 1866. As Johnson formally pardoned former Confederates, he restored confiscated lands to them and expelled the African American tenants who had taken possession under Sherman's Special Field Order No. 15. By this time, even Sherman had undertaken to provide justification for this decision. In an open letter to the president published by the *New York Times*, Sherman explained that the order had been one with military aims that gave freedmen only possession, and not ownership, of the land. With the war over and military influence in the South at least temporarily waning, the order therefore had lost its justification; after military governments took control of much of the South under the more radical Congressional Reconstruction plan, the promise of "forty acres and a mule" was not resurrected.

Yet the promise was also not forgotten. Special Field Order No. 15 serves as a lynchpin of the argument in favor of government reparations to the descendents of formerly enslaved African Americans. During the civil rights era some one hundred years later, Dr. Martin Luther King Jr. specifically called out Sherman's order as a broken promise to African Americans. The order was frequently cited during the unsuccessful legal and political attempts to secure reparations during the late twentieth and early twenty-first centuries. Supporters of restitution have argued that the legacy of slavery has unfairly taken wealth and property due to contemporary African Americans—a clear nod to the land granted and then rescinded from the freed African American population of 1865. Sherman's Special Field Order No. 15 thus carries lasting relevance for the country and its people despite losing its official authority to distribute land.

Vanessa E. Vaughn, MA

Bibliography

Buescher, John. "Forty Acres and a Mule." *Teachinghistory.org*. George Mason University, n.d. Web. 2 May 2013.

Fellman, Michael. *Citizen Sherman: A Life of William Tecumseh Sherman*. New York: Random, 1995. Print.

Foner, Eric. *A Short History of Reconstruction, 1863–1877*. New York: Harper, 1990. Print.

---. *Forever Free: The Story of Emancipation and Reconstruction*. New York: Knopf, 2005. Print.

Lewin, Tamar. "Calls for Slavery Restitution Getting Louder." *New York Times*. New York Times, 4 June 2001. Web. 2 May 2013.

Marszalek, John F. "William Tecumseh Sherman." *American National Biography Online*. Oxford UP, n.d. Web. 2 May 2013.

McPherson, James M. "The Ballot and Land for the Freedmen, 1861–1865." *Reconstruction: An Anthology of Revisionist Writings*. Ed. Kenneth M. Stampp and Leon F. Litwick. Baton Rouge: Louisiana State UP, 1969. Print.

Oubre, Claude F. *Forty Acres and a Mule: The Freedmen's Bureau and Black Land Ownership*. Baton Rouge: Louisiana State UP, 1978. Print.

Sherman, William Tecumseh. *Memoirs of William T. Sherman*. Vol. 2. New York: Appleton, 1891. Print.

Additional Reading

Cornish, Dudley Taylor. *The Sable Arm: Black Troops in the Union Army, 1861–1865*. Lawrence: UP of Kansas, 1987. Print.

Foner, Eric. *Reconstruction: America's Unfinished Revolution, 1863–1877*. New York: HarperCollins, 2002. Print.

Reid, Debra A., ed. *Beyond Forty Acres and a Mule: African American Landowning Families since Reconstruction*. Gainesville: UP of Florida, 2012. Print.

Trudeau, Noah Andre. *Southern Storm: Sherman's March to the Sea*. New York: HarperCollins, 2008. Print.

■ Fourteenth and Fifteenth Amendments to the Constitution

Date: July 9, 1868; February 3, 1870
Author: Fortieth and Forty-First Congresses of the United States
Genre: constitution; law

> *"No State shall make or enforce any law which shall abridge the privileges or immunities of citizens of the United States; nor shall any State deprive any person of life, liberty, or property, without due process of law."*

Summary Overview

At the conclusion of the Civil War, the United States government was saddled with the responsibility of rebuilding and restructuring a devastated South. Tasked with discerning how to deal with the political, economic, and population breakdown of half of the reunited nation, the government, dominated by Northern Republicans, began to propose and pass legislation to transform the Southern states. This period, known as Reconstruction, established profound legal change. In instituting unprecedented laws, acts, and constitutional amendments, the Fortieth and Forty-First Congresses not only redefined the citizenship status and legal rights of former slaves and other free blacks, but they also expanded the authority of the national government over the states. The redefinition of the federal and state relationship codified in the Fourteenth and Fifteenth Amendments was a highly controversial yet crucial aspect of Reconstruction that allowed the US government to institute and defend the newly established rights of black Americans.

Defining Moment

Signed in 1863, two years before the conclusion of the war, the Emancipation Proclamation declared the slave population of the Confederate states free from the bondage of slavery. In December 1865, the Thirty-Eighth Congress passed the Thirteenth Amendment, which abolished slavery throughout the rest of the Union, including the border slave states of Missouri, Kentucky, Delaware, and Maryland that had remained in the Union and were previously exempted from the dictates of the Proclamation. With almost four million newly freed African Americans, the majority of whom resided in Southern states that were hostile to their new status; the US government knew that a permanent solution was needed to ensure the rights of former slaves. The government became determined to enact new legislation to ensure that the rights of freedmen would not be immediately abridged as soon as Southern states were reintegrated into the Union.

The government was also facing the question of what criteria Confederate states would have to meet in order to be allowed back into the Union. At the conclusion of the Civil War, Union troops remained an occupying force in the Southern states and the South had no federal representation in Congress. The federal government was in a position to wield unprecedented power over the rebuilding of Southern state governments. Congress also had the power to dictate the conditions under which these states could receive reinstatement to full federal representation. Seen as an affront by some to the critical issue of state rights, much debate ensued concerning what proof of loyalty or other qualifications rebel states would have to meet to be fully readmitted to the Union. Another crucial question for Reconstruction legislators was how to enforce these legal changes and requirements on the states without violating the constitutional limitations on the federal government. The writing and passing of the Fourteenth and Fifteenth Amendments reflects the struggles and attempted solutions by the Reconstruction-era Congress to establish legal equality between blacks and whites in the United States. Beyond these immediate goals, however, the Reconstruction amendments redefined the balance of power between the individual states and the federal government.

Author Biography

The Thirty-Ninth through the Forty-First Congresses of the United States were convened during one of the most unstable and demanding times in American political history. The Union victory in the Civil War provided a remarkable opportunity for Congress to institute sweeping legal, social, and constitutional changes, not only over the defeated Southern states, but over the nation as a whole. The efforts to bring these changes to fruition, however, were disrupted and marred by a presidential assassination, uncooperative Southern states, and repeated presidential vetoes to their legislative efforts.

In the aftermath of the Civil War, the Thirty-Ninth Congress was composed only of representatives from states loyal to the Union; Alabama, Arkansas, Florida, Georgia, North Carolina, South Carolina, Texas, Virginia, and Mississippi were all denied federal representation. Tennessee, though having seceded from the Union during the Civil War, became the only Southern state to regain congressional seats during the session. The Thirty-Ninth Congress was only assembled for one month before Abraham Lincoln's assassination, which shook the foundation of the newly victorious federal government. Andrew Johnson, Lincoln's successor to the presidency, vetoed nearly every bill, act, and amendment proposed by the Congress. Despite these hurdles, however, the Thirty-Ninth Congress used a two-thirds majority vote to override Johnson's presidential vetoes

in order to pass landmark legislation. During its tenure, the Thirty-Ninth Congress debated and passed the Civil Rights Act of 1866, the Freedmen's Bureau Bill, and the Fourteenth Amendment to the Constitution. It would be an additional two years before the amendment was ratified.

The Fortieth Congress convened in March of 1867 and was populated largely by a political faction known as the Radical Republicans. The Radical Republicans pushed hard for the implementation of Reconstruction policies, which gave substantial civil rights to former slaves and doled out tough guidelines to govern Southern states. The Radical Republicans often clashed with President Andrew Johnson, who was much more conciliatory toward the ex-Confederate states. These tensions came to a head in 1868, when the Fortieth Congress impeached Johnson on charges of violating congressional policy (he was acquitted and finished his term). Despite these intragovernmental tensions, the Fortieth Congress was able to compose and pass three Reconstruction Acts and the Fifteenth Amendment to the Constitution, which would be ratified within the next year.

The Forty-First Congress convened in March of 1869 and contained the first African American member of Congress, Hiram Rhodes Revels from Mississippi, and the first African American member of the House of Representatives, Joseph H. Rainey from South Carolina. Ulysses S. Grant, the former Civil War general, was elected president of the United States during Congress's first session, and the following year, the four remaining Southern states were readmitted to the Union: Virginia (January), Mississippi (February), Texas (March), and Georgia (July) were once again granted federal representation.

Although the Fifteenth Amendment was passed by the Fortieth Congress one month before its final session, several states resisted ratification. The Forty-First Congress ruled, therefore, that in order for the remaining four Southern states to be readmitted to the Union, they had to accept both the Fourteenth and Fifteenth amendments, which, having no other choice, they eventually did. For many, this was the final step in Reconstruction.

HISTORICAL DOCUMENT

AMENDMENT XIV
Passed by Congress June 13, 1866. Ratified July 9, 1868.
Note: Article I, Section 2, of the Constitution was modified by Section 2 of the 14th amendment.

Section 1.
All persons born or naturalized in the United States, and subject to the jurisdiction thereof, are citizens of the United States and of the State wherein they reside. No State shall make or enforce any law which shall abridge the privileges or immunities of citizens of the United States; nor shall any State deprive any person of life, liberty, or property, without due process of law; nor deny to any person within its jurisdiction the equal protection of the laws.

Section 2.
Representatives shall be apportioned among the several States according to their respective numbers, counting the whole number of persons in each State, excluding Indians not taxed. But when the right to vote at any election for the choice of electors for President and Vice-President of the United States, Representatives in Congress, the Executive and Judicial officers of a State, or the members of the Legislature thereof, is denied to any of the male inhabitants of such State, being twenty-one years of age,* and citizens of the United States, or in any way abridged, except for participation in rebellion, or other crime, the basis of representation therein shall be reduced in the proportion which the number of such male citizens shall bear to the whole number of male citizens twenty-one years of age in such State.

Section 3.
No person shall be a Senator or Representative in Congress, or elector of President and Vice-President, or hold any office, civil or military, under the United States, or under any State, who, having previously taken an oath, as a member of Congress, or as an officer of the United States, or as a member of any State legislature, or as an executive or judicial officer of any State, to support the Constitution of the United States, shall have engaged in insurrection or rebellion against the same, or given aid or comfort to the enemies thereof. But Congress may by a vote of two-thirds of each House, remove such disability.

Section 4.
The validity of the public debt of the United States, authorized by law, including debts incurred for payment of pensions and bounties for services in suppressing insurrection or rebellion, shall not be questioned. But neither the United States nor any State shall assume or pay any debt or obligation incurred in aid of insurrection or rebellion against the United States, or any claim for the loss or emancipation of any slave; but all such debts, obligations and claims shall be held illegal and void.

Section 5.
The Congress shall have the power to enforce, by appropriate legislation, the provisions of this article.
Changed by Section 1 of the 26th amendment.

AMENDMENT XV
Passed by Congress February 26, 1869. Ratified February 3, 1870.

Section 1.
The right of citizens of the United States to vote shall not be denied or abridged by the United States or by any State on account of race, color, or previous condition of servitude.

Section 2.
The Congress shall have the power to enforce this article by appropriate legislation.

Proposal and Ratification of 14th Amendment
Ratification was completed on July 9, 1868.
The amendment was subsequently ratified by Alabama, July 13, 1868; Georgia, July 21, 1868 (after having rejected it on November 9, 1866); Virginia, October 8, 1869 (after having rejected it on January 9, 1867); Mississippi, January 17, 1870; Texas, February 18, 1870 (after having rejected it on October 27, 1866);

Delaware, February 12, 1901 (after having rejected it on February 8, 1867); Maryland, April 4, 1959 (after having rejected it on March 23, 1867); California, May 6, 1959; Kentucky, March 18, 1976 (after having rejected it on January 8, 1867).

Proposal and Ratification of 15th Amendment

The fifteenth amendment to the Constitution of the United States was proposed to the legislatures of the several States by the Fortieth Congress, on the 26th of February, 1869, and was declared, in a proclamation of the Secretary of State, dated March 30, 1870, to have been ratified by the legislatures of twenty-nine of the thirty-seven States. The dates of ratification were: Nevada, March 1, 1869; West Virginia, March 3, 1869; Illinois, March 5, 1869; Louisiana, March 5, 1869; North Carolina, March 5, 1869; Michigan, March 8, 1869; Wisconsin, March 9, 1869; Maine, March 11, 1869; Massachusetts, March 12, 1869; Arkansas, March 15, 1869; South Carolina, March 15, 1869; Pennsylvania, March 25, 1869; New York, April 14, 1869 (and the legislature of the same State passed a resolution January 5, 1870, to withdraw its consent to it, which action it rescinded on March 30, 1970); Indiana, May 14, 1869; Connecticut, May 19, 1869; Florida, June 14, 1869; New Hampshire, July 1, 1869; Virginia, October 8, 1869; Vermont, October 20, 1869; Missouri, January 7, 1870; Minnesota, January 13, 1870; Mississippi, January 17, 1870; Rhode Island, January 18, 1870; Kansas, January 19, 1870; Ohio, January 27, 1870 (after having rejected it on April 30, 1869); Georgia, February 2, 1870; Iowa, February 3, 1870.

Ratification was completed on February 3, 1870, unless the withdrawal of ratification by New York was effective; in which event ratification was completed on February 17, 1870, when Nebraska ratified.

The amendment was subsequently ratified by Texas, February 18, 1870; New Jersey, February 15, 1871 (after having rejected it on February 7, 1870); Delaware, February 12, 1901 (after having rejected it on March 18, 1869); Oregon, February 24, 1959; California, April 3, 1962 (after having rejected it on January 28, 1870); Kentucky, March 18, 1976 (after having rejected it on March 12, 1869).

The amendment was approved by the Governor of Maryland, May 7, 1973; Maryland having previously rejected it on February 26, 1870.

The amendment was rejected (and not subsequently ratified) by Tennessee, November 16, 1869.

GLOSSARY

abridge: diminish the extent of

due process: an established system of legal procedures that ensure compliance with accepted rules and ideologies

equal protection: the concept that principles of law must be applied equally in all comparable situations

immunities: exemptions

insurrection: an uprising against an established regime

ratification: formal confirmation

Document Analysis

Throughout the South during the Civil War, both the rumored and real proximity of Union forces often resulted in slaves refusing to work, abandoning their plantations, or demanding to be paid wages by their masters. Even in yet unoccupied areas, slaves began fleeing to the Northern lines in substantial numbers. Eventually runaway slaves were permitted to join the Union Army to assist in combat. Military service had long been understood in the United States as linked to rights of citizenship. In enlisting with Union forces, escaped slaves were manifestly claiming access to rights—an issue with which the federal government was soon forced to grapple. Simultaneously, the social philosophy and governmental theory of equal rights for slaves, long championed by abolitionist groups, was becoming increasingly influential in the halls of power. Many of the abolitionists' calls for equality under the law worked to inform the ideas ultimately contained in the Reconstruction amendments. Though a controversial and barely articulated goal at the start of the war, by the conclusion of the conflict, the freeing of slaves and the codification of their equal status became a defining objective of the Union forces as well as a political and legal goal of the US government. After the passage of the Thirteenth Amendment outlawing slavery, the Thirty-Ninth through the Forty-First Congresses set about writing and passing amendments to the Constitution that empowered the government to enact and enforce among all the states the equality of African Americans before the law. In doing so, the Reconstruction Congress expanded the definition of United States citizenship, the authority of the federal government over the states, and the legal status of African Americans.

The Fourteenth Amendment

The first section of the Fourteenth Amendment served to define the parameters of national citizenship. In 1857, the Supreme Court's decision in *Dred Scott v. Sandford* had classified people of African ancestry, slave or free, as noncitizens. Within the jurisdiction of the United States, blacks had no citizenship rights and enjoyed no constitutional protections. The Fourteenth Amendment directly refuted this decision by declaring all people born in the United States to be US citizens. Citizenship rights would henceforth be determined at the national level and the enumerated rights of citizens were to be considered unalterable by the states. This codification of citizenship was noted by Congressman

Wendell Phillips, who participated in its passage, as being a profound step for the United States, a country that had previously left undefined the parameters of what constituted a citizen. The clause guaranteeing the "privileges and immunities" of citizenship, however, had a contested meaning almost from the moment of its writing. Crafted by the Joint Committee on Reconstruction and principally authored by John Bingham, a representative from Ohio, the clause likely sought to constitutionally protect the Civil Rights Act, which dictated that rights extended to whites must likewise be extended to all citizens. By constitutionalizing the equal rights of citizens within states, Congress sought to prevent a repeal of the acts that enumerated the civil liberties states were required to provide for all of their citizens. The guarantees of "due process of law" and "equal protection under the law" were clauses that, at the time of their writing, were primarily concerned with guaranteeing that no citizen could be denied his or her liberty without just cause. Additionally, "just cause" could only derive from the applied rights and legal structures that operated equally for all citizens of the day.

The second section of the Fourteenth Amendment was written specifically to address the limitations on population representation in the Constitution's first article. When writing the original Constitution, Southern states were profoundly concerned that their seats in the House of Representatives could easily be overwhelmed by Northern states if they were prevented from including slave numbers into their overall population. As a result of vigorous negotiating over the manner in which populations should be calculated for the purpose of representation and taxation, Northern and Southern states came to a compromise regarding how to count Southern slaves. Article 1, section 2 of the Constitution states, "Representatives and direct Taxes shall be apportioned among the several States which may be included within this Union, according to their respective Numbers, which shall be determined by adding to the whole Number of free Persons, including those bound to Service for a Term of Years, and excluding Indians not taxed, three fifths of all other Persons." The section denoting "three fifths of all other persons" was a reference to slaves' inclusion in determining the amount of federal representation allowed to Southern states. Though every five slaves would count as three additional people in the South's representative populous, the slaves were barred from ever contributing to the selection of the representatives their numbers allowed. In the wake of the Civil War, the Fourteenth Amendment sought to reverse this constitutional edict. The second section of the amendment mandated that former slaves be counted as whole people. Additionally, the amendment dictated that if a state denied any men of voting age access to the vote, the number of representatives claimed by that state in Congress must likewise be reduced. This clause served the purpose of preserving federalism by keeping the right to create voting laws in the hands of the states while also attempting to prevent Southern states from instituting legislation specifically preventing former slaves from voting. According to the section, if states did institute such targeted discriminatory legislation, they would lose representation proportional to the population excluded from voting, thereby weakening their influence at the federal level.

The third section of the Fourteenth Amendment sought to deal with the reestablishment of Southern state governments as well as the reintegration of Southern delegates into the federal government. Of major concern to the Reconstruction Congress was the possibility of the immediate return of Confederate officials to positions of political and legal authority and thus a rapid return to the racial dynamics of Southern slavery and the immediate oppression of freedmen. Additionally, Congress feared that rebel leaders would escape punishment by simply retaking their positions of power without any apparent consequences for their betrayal of the Union. Congress' concern was well-founded: Andrew Johnson had already begun to assemble new state governments in the South that were replete with former Confederate leaders. To prevent a de-facto reenslavement of the African American population in the South, the Fourteenth Amendment precluded from holding office at the state or federal level those who had "engaged in insurrection or rebellion" against the government as well as those who had "given aid or comfort to [its] enemies."

The fourth section of the amendment expressed the commitment of the federal government to paying all Union debts and pensions, but it prohibited not only the federal government but also states from paying off debts to those who had supported the Confederacy. Most importantly, neither the government nor the states were permitted to reimburse former slaveholders for the value of their slaves. The majority of Southern wealth before the Civil War was located in the value of their slave population. When slaves were emancipated, the vast majority of the wealth held by

slaveholders was instantly eliminated. Early in the war, President Lincoln had proposed that slave states still in the Union participate in "compensated emancipation," in which slaves residing within Union borders would be gradually freed in exchange for the government providing slave owners monetary compensation for the freed slaves' value. Though Lincoln's proposal was rejected by the slaveholding border states, the concept of "compensated emancipation" continued to be debated by those concerned about the postwar decimation of the South's economy. The Fourteenth Amendment prevented either the federal government or the states from compensating former slave owners for the slaves that had been emancipated.

Finally, and considered of paramount importance by the Reconstruction Congress, the Fourteenth Amendment granted Congress the right to make compulsory the provisions of the amendment. The Fourteenth Amendment clearly located the political authority to generate and enforce civil rights laws in the hands of the federal government. Prior to the passage of the Fourteenth Amendment, states retained authority over all aspects of the general welfare, heath, and safety of those citizens who resided within its borders. The federal government's powers over state action were restricted exclusively to issues of commerce, taxation, interstate disputes, and foreign relations. All other powers were reserved for the states. The Fourteenth Amendment was a defining moment in which the federal government was given license to override any state law or action that violated the rights of national citizenship.

The Fifteenth Amendment

The Fifteenth Amendment addressed the issue of political citizenship rights that had been largely ignored not only by the Thirteenth and Fourteenth Amendments, but also by the Reconstruction bills Congress had passed during its Thirty-Ninth session. Although no legislation had been put into place guaranteeing freedmen's voting rights, a precedent had already been set by the federal government in making black suffrage a requirement for Southern states seeking readmission to the Union. The Fortieth congressional session, which was comprised of a significant number of Radical Republicans, first attempted to remedy this oversight by implementing a voting rights bill. Constitutional debates soon began, however, over the right of the federal government to dictate voting parameters that were widely understood to be reserved to the states. Additionally, questions concerning the second section of the Fourteenth Amendment, which allowed states to restrict voting rights as long as they abdicated the right to added representation, was understood to indicate that states retained the right to create parameters around what part of their state population was allowed to vote. As a result, the Congress turned once again to the task of making constitutional the political rights of former slaves.

In debating the form the amendment would take, several congressmen proposed including additional disenfranchised groups into the amendment's guarantee of voting rights. It was proposed that the amendment protect from voting discrimination the Irish, women, religious dissenters, nonpropertied citizens, and immigrants. There was also concern that if race were the only protection mentioned by the amendment, states could find indirect means of excluding blacks from voting, such as requiring educational tests or proof of property ownership—problems that would indeed arise after the era of Reconstruction ended. Despite these more comprehensive proposals, the final result was direct and succinct. The amendment simply prohibited the federal and state government from denying any citizen the right to vote on "account of race, color, or previous condition of servitude." Additionally, just as in the Fourteenth Amendment, the Fifteenth conferred on Congress the ability to enforce African American voting rights through legislation. Though soon to face massive resistance by state law and even the federal judiciary, the protection of voting rights by the Fifteenth Amendment gave freedmen full political rights for the first time in United States history.

Essential Themes

The Due Process Clause of the Fourteenth Amendment had a profound and long-term legal effect in protecting the rights of the people outlined in the Bill of Rights against infringement by the states. Additionally, as a result of the federal enforcement of the amendments and acts implemented during the era of Reconstruction, African Americans experienced unprecedented access to political participation in the South. By the end of the nineteenth century, however, the gains of citizenship rights for African Americans began to experience a rapid and devastating decline. The Jim Crow era of social and legal subordination of the black population of the South began to emerge in full force. Jim Crow laws effectively functioned to dismantle the authority of the Fourteenth and Fifteenth Amendments over

civil rights law in the South. The federal Congress and judiciary did little to prevent these racially discriminatory laws and, indeed, upheld many of their tenets. For example, the Supreme Court case of *Plessy v. Ferguson*, decided in 1896, made constitutional the doctrine of "separate but equal" and is an unambiguous example of just how quickly the Reconstruction amendments were taken apart through political and legal means. It would take nearly one hundred years for civil rights enforcement to receive federal support once more, and only as a result of mounting pressure from the activism of the civil rights movement.

Amanda Beyer-Purvis, MA

Bibliography

Benedict, Michael Less. "Preserving the Constitution: The Conservative Basis of Radical Reconstruction." *Journal of American History* 61.1 (1974): 65–90. Print.

Bergesen, Albert, "Nation-Building and Constitutional Amendments: The Role of the Thirteenth, Fourteenth, and Fifteenth Amendments in the Legal Reconstitution of the American Polity Following the Civil War." *Pacific Sociological Review* 24.1 (1981): 3–15. Print.

Currie, David P. "The Reconstruction Congress." *University of Chicago Law Review* 75.1 (2008): 383–495. Print.

Epps, Garrett. *Democracy Reborn: The Fourteenth Amendment and the Fight for Equal Rights in Post–Civil War America*. New York: Holt, 2006. Print.

Foner, Eric. "The Strange Career of the Reconstruction Amendments." *Yale Law Journal* 108.8 Symposium: Moments of Change: Transformation in American Constitutionalism (1999): 2003–9. Print.

Heiny, Louisa M. A. "Radical Abolitionist Influence on Federalism and the Fourteenth Amendment." *American Journal of Legal History* 49.2 (2007): 180–96. Print.

Mathews, John M. *Legislative and Judicial History of the Fifteenth Amendment*. New York: Da Capo, 1971. Print.

Meyer, Howard N. *The Amendment That Refused to Die: Equality and Justice Deferred: The History of the Fourteenth Amendment*. Lanham: Madison, 2000. Print.

Richards, David A. J. *Conscience and the Constitution: History, Theory, and Law of the Reconstruction Amendments*. Princeton: Princeton UP, 1993. Print.

Additional Reading

Foner, Eric. *Reconstruction: America's Unfinished Revolution, 1863–1877.* New York: Perennial, 2002. Print.

Goldstone, Lawrence. *Inherently Unequal: The Betrayal of Equal Rights by the Supreme Court, 1865–1903.* New York: Walker, 2011. Print.

McKitrick, Eric L. *Andrew Johnson and Reconstruction.* Chicago: U of Chicago P, 1960. Print.

Perry, Michael J. *We the People: The Fourteenth Amendment and the Supreme Court.* New York: Oxford UP, 1999. Print.

"Reconstruction: The Second Civil War." *American Experience.* PBS Online/WGBH, 2004. Web. 29 Apr. 2013.

A Contested Election: Report to Congress on the Activities of the Ku Klux Klan

Date: February 11, 1870
Author: United States House of Representatives
Genre: report

> *"The object of the Klan is to whip unarmed negroes,*
> *scare timid white men, break up elections, and*
> *interfere with the State government, and steal*
> *and plunder the goods of the people."*

Summary Overview

The activities of the newly organized Ku Klux Klan in Tennessee so disrupted the 1868 election in the Fourth Congressional District that Governor William Brownlow invalidated the election results and declared Republican candidate Lewis Tillman the winner. Conservative candidate C. A. Sheafe, who received the majority of votes, contested the decision and petitioned the US House of Representatives to reverse Brownlow's ruling. The House committee tasked with investigating the matter took extensive testimony, which revealed the nature and extent of the Klan's efforts to intimidate African Americans and their white supporters. As a result, the House of Representatives decided that Tillman should be awarded the seat in Congress. The committee's inquiry prompted widespread interest in Klan activities and was instrumental in the establishment of a joint committee of Congress to investigate the Klan's influence across the South.

Defining Moment

In August 1868 the Tennessee state legislature had initiated its own investigation into the activities of the Ku Klux Klan as part of an ongoing campaign by Radical Republican Governor William Brownlow to reactivate the Tennessee State Guard, a militia under his control.

The Guard was established in 1867 and used effectively to keep peace during elections that year; however, early in 1868 it was deactivated. Reports during the spring of 1868 of growing violence against African Americans and white Americans who supported Republicans made Brownlow fearful that congressional elections in November would be disrupted. Convinced that federal troops would be unavailable to stop Klan violence, Brownlow called a special session of the Tennessee legislature in July 1868 to push through legislation reactivating the Guard.

During the session, a joint military committee conducted an inquiry into Klan activities. Led by Tennessee state senator William J. Smith and state representative William F. Prosser, former Union officers and staunch supporters of Reconstruction, the committee took testimony from dozens of witnesses who told horrifying stories of intimidation, physical abuse, rape, and murder. The committee's report was printed in September 1868. To Brownlow's dismay, however, the bill authorizing reestablishment of the Guard did not pass in time for him to deploy troops to areas where Klan violence was likely to be highest during the November election.

Initial results in Tennessee's Fourth Congressional District indicated that conservative C. A. Sheafe defeated Republican Lewis Tillman by a comfortable majority. Governor Brownlow was convinced that Klan intimidation kept many of the district's nearly eight thousand African Americans from voting; he declared the results invalid and certified Tillman as the winner. Sheafe contested the decision, and in 1869 the matter was taken up in the US House of Representatives, which has the power to seat its members.

The House committee adjudicating Sheafe's claim heard testimony from individuals who had been subject to Klan intimidation. Also testifying was Tennessee state senator William J. Wisener, another member of the state legislature's joint military committee. Through him, extracts from the joint military committee's report were made part of the House investigation. The House committee also incorporated into its report information from an 1868 account of Klan activities in Tennessee submitted by Major General William P. Carlin, assistant commissioner of the Tennessee Freedmen's Bureau, to Major General Oliver O. Howard, commissioner of the Freedmen's Bureau in Washington, DC, as well as accounts from other bureau agents. Their reports confirmed the testimony of witnesses to both the Tennessee legislature in 1868 and the House committee in 1869 that the Ku Klux Klan was a growing menace, posing a serious threat to the restoration of democracy and the guarantee of equal rights in former Confederate states.

Author Biography

The principals in the 1868 election in Tennessee's Fourth Congressional District were little more than pawns in the chess game between Southerners intent on restoring the social and political order as it had existed before the war and Radicals bent on reconstructing the state in the image of its Northern neighbors. Ironically, Republican candidate Lewis Tillman was a Tennessee native who had spent his career in the state's court system and as a newspaper editor, while his conservative opponent, C. A. Sheafe, was an Ohioan who had served in the federal army before moving to Tennessee.

That the Ku Klux Klan played a role in keeping Tillman's supporters from the polls seems indisputable, yet it is in some ways remarkable. Founded in 1866, the Klan had no strong formal organization; many bands of miscreants rode through the countryside calling themselves Klansmen. While the perpetrators of violence were most often members of the working classes, a number of prominent Southerners had ties to the Klan, helping to protect other Klansmen accused of crimes. The Klan remained active throughout the South until the mid-1870s.

In Tennessee the fight against the Klan was led by William G. Brownlow. Born in 1805 in Virginia, Brownlow became a minister and was a traveling preacher throughout Appalachia before settling in Elizabethton, Tennessee, in 1836. Before the Civil War he was editor of a pro-Union newspaper. He left the state after Tennessee seceded but returned in 1863 when Union troops established an occupation force there. He was elected governor in 1865 and was reelected in 1867, largely on votes of his new constituency, freed slaves. Shortly after the 1868 elections, he began lobbying the legislature to appoint him US senator for Tennessee, a position he assumed in March 1869. After serving one term, he returned to Tennessee and resumed his newspaper career until his death in 1877.

Among the groups that gathered information on atrocities committed by the Ku Klux Klan and other reactionary groups in the South, none was more important than the Bureau of Refugees, Freedmen, and Abandoned Lands. Established by Congress in 1865, the Freedmen's Bureau, as it was popularly known, assisted freed slaves with a variety of economic and political issues. Led by Union General Oliver O. Howard, a native of Maine, the Bureau placed agents throughout the South to carry out its mission. These agents were often targets of Klan violence themselves, and their reports to the Bureau's headquarters in Washington, DC, provided further evidence of the difficulties African Americans faced in becoming fully integrated into postwar society.

HISTORICAL DOCUMENT

This pertains to the deposition of William H. Wisener in case of C. A. Sheafe vs. Lewis Tillman, contested election.

WM. GALBREATH, Mayor.

Report of the joint military committee of the two houses in relation to the organization of the militia of the State of Tennessee, submitted to the extra session of the thirty-fifth general assembly, September 2, 1868.

Mr. Speaker: Your committee to whom was referred that part of the governor's message relating to outrages perpetrated by an organization known as the Ku-Klux Klan, and the necessity of organizing the militia for the protection of the loyal people of the State of Tennessee, have had the same under consideration; and after summoning a great many witnesses before them, are satisfied that there exists an organization of armed men going abroad disguised, robbing poor negroes of their fire-arms, taking them out of their houses at night, hanging, shooting, and whipping them in a most cruel manner, and driving them from their homes. Nor is this confined to the colored men alone. Women and children have been subjected to the torture of the lash, and brutal assaults have been committed upon them by these night-prowlers, and in many instances, the persons of females have been violated, and when the husband or father complained, he has been obliged to flee to save his own life.

Nor has this been confined to one county or one section of the State alone. Your committee find, that, after a careful investigation of all the facts, that these depredations have been committed all over Middle and West Tennessee, and in some parts of East Tennessee; particularly has this been the case in Maury, Lincoln, Giles, Marshall, Obion, Hardeman, Fayette and Gibson Counties. In Lincoln County, they took Senator Wm. Wyatt from his house in the night, and inflicted all sorts of indignities upon him. They beat him over the head with their pistols, cutting a frightful gash, and saturating his shirt with blood, leaving him insensible. Senator Wyatt is a Christian gentleman, and sixty-five years of age; his only offense being that he is a Union man and a member of the State legislature.

We also find that the same spirit exists in Obion County; that it was rife there, indeed, one year and a half ago, when the disloyalists so inhumanly and brutally murdered Senator Case and his son. Since then, depredations have been committed all over the country that calls loudly for redress. No loyal man is safe in that country at the present time.

Your committee's attention has also been directed to Maury County. We find that a perfect reign of terror exists there; that some two hundred colored men have had to flee from their homes, and take refuge in the city of Nashville; afraid to return, although here they are destitute of food, or any means of subsistence. In this county, schoolhouses have been burned down, teachers driven away, and colored men shot, whipped, and murdered at will. Hon. S. M. Arnell, congressman from that district, was sought for, when he was at home on a visit, by members of the Ku-Klux Klan, who were thirsting for his blood.

In Fayette County, the teacher of colored children has been assaulted and driven away by the Ku-Klux Klan.

Your committee find, that to enumerate all the outrages committed by this organization of outlaws, would take more time than can be spared. They would most respectfully direct your attention to a synopsis of the evidence taken before your committee; remarking at the same time, that much valuable information is necessarily left out on account of the witnesses fearing to have their names mentioned in this report, lest they should hereafter, on account of their testimony, lose their lives.

One of the most brutal assaults perhaps, that had been committed, was on the person of a school teacher, in Shelbyville, Bedford County, Tennessee. Mr. Dunlap, a white instructor, was taken from his house in the night by the Ku-Klux Klan, and most inhumanly whipped; and for no other reason than he was a white man, teaching a colored school. One witness testified that he was a confederate soldier, a native Tennessean; has been with negroes all his life, and seen them whipped by different persons; but never saw any one beaten as this man, Dunlap, was. It is in evidence that Mr. Dunlap is a member of the Methodist Church, and a very quiet, inoffensive man. Attention is especially directed to the evidence in this case.

Your committee also find that there has been a determined effort and is still a determined purpose all over Middle and West Tennessee, to keep colored men from the polls, and thus secure the election to office of candidates of the democratic party. Very many of the outrages committed have been against men who were formerly soldiers in the national army. The proof shows that there is an eternal hatred existing against all men that voted the republican ticket, or who belong to the Loyal League, or are engaged in teaching schools, and giving instruction to the humbler classes of their fellow-men.

The committee are compelled to conclude, from the evidence before them, that the ultimate object of the Ku-Klux Klan is, to intimidate Union men, both black and white, keep them from the polls on election day, and, by a system of anti-lawry and terrorism, carry the State in November next for Seymour and Blair.

Your committee would again call the attention of the general assembly to the following synopsis of testimony, as better calculated to show the true condition of the country than anything your committee could say:

We are permitted to make the following extracts from the report of Major General Carlin to General Howard, for the month of June, 1868:

"General: I have the honor to submit the following report on the condition of affairs pertaining to this department, during the month of June last. It is with deep regret that I am compelled to begin this report with the statement, that, since my connection with the bureau, no such discouraging state of affairs has prevailed in Tennessee, during any one month, as that for the month of June last. I say discouraging, because it is totally beyond the powers of myself and subordinates to remedy evils that cry aloud for redress."

"In the counties of Marshall, Rutherford, Maury, and Giles, it may be said that a reign of terror has been established, and will doubtless remain, unless the State, or United States, should provide a military force to be stationed in those counties."

"The hostility of the implacable pro-slavery people to colored education has manifested itself in numerous instances of violence toward teachers of colored schools."

"Your attention is called especially to the case of Mr. Newton, who was assaulted and badly wounded at Somerville. He would doubtless have been slain if he had not escaped in time. The case was reported by the undersigned to Major General Thomas, commanding the department, and troops were asked for to protect the school and teachers. Mr. Newton was escorted back by them to his school-house, where he has continued to conduct his school."

"This affair is more particularly described in the extracts from the report of Lieutenant Colonel Palmer, sub-assistant commissioner of the sub-district of Memphis."

"There will doubtless be great excitement and frequent disturbances in the State during the present political canvass for President and State officers. Nearly every day furnishes additional evidence of the determination of the Ku-Klux Klan and their friends to bring about a state of affairs that will preclude the possibility of personal liberty for the colored people, and the active, out-spoken Union men. I doubt if any measure, short of martial law, will preserve peace and insure safety till after the next election."

A. H. Eastman, agent at Columbia, Tennessee, reports the following extracts:

"The Ku-Klux Klan appear to be on the 'war path.' Complaints of visitations by night, all over my district, of the breaking into of houses and assaults upon the inmates, are very frequent. The Klan went to the house of Joshua Ferrell, an old and quiet colored man, on the night of the 12th instant, called him from his bed, and, while he was unfastening the door, they jumped in upon him and beat his head with a pistol, cutting a gash half an inch wide, four inches long, and to the skull. Then they asked him for fire-arms, which he said he had not. They then took him into a field and whipped him so badly that it nearly killed him. They also tore up everything in the house, and then went to his son's house, took him from his bed, smashed a large looking-glass over the head of his sick wife, who was in bed. They then whipped the man with stirrup-straps and buckles, which cut long and deep gashes into the flesh, and all because, they said, he was a 'big-feeling nigger, voted for Brownlow, and belonged to the Union League.'

J. K. Nelson, agent at Murfreesboro, Tennessee, says the Ku-Klux Klan took from his house, about midnight, Bill Carlton, (colored) living in Middleton district, and beat him very severely, giving him, as he says, one hundred and fifty lashes with a heavy leather strap.

"On Thursday night last, the Klan went to the house of Minor Fletcher, living eight miles from here, on the Shelbyville pike, rode into his front and back porches on their horses, and called him out. They then proceeded to the house of D. Webb, about ten or twelve in number, and, as he reports, called to him to come out. This he refused to do, until they assured him that he should not be hurt, and threatened him with violence in case of his refusal. He went out; they then accused him of being a radical, and a Loyal Leaguer. He denied being a member of the league, but told them that he was a Union man and always had been. They called him a liar, and threatened to hang him, calling at the same time for a halter. His wife, who was in a critical condition, screamed and plead for him, and begged them to spare him on her account. They then told him to go back to his wife. He turned to go, when one of them caught him by the hair, jerked him to the ground, sprang upon him, and beat him in the face in a shocking manner, at the same time holding a pistol to his head, and threatening to shoot him. They then left him in an almost insensible condition, scarcely able to crawl to his house."

"More than half the outrages perpetrated by this Klan are not reported to me. The parties are afraid, or have a want of confidence in the bureau. There is a feeling of insecurity among the people (Unionists) that has not been equaled since 1861. I am so impressed with my own inability to fully understand the exact condition of affairs that I will be excused for not making the same comprehensible to you."

"This I do know, that I have been sleeping for months with a revolver under my pillow, and a double-barreled shot-gun, heavily charged with buck shot, at one hand, and a hatchet at the other, with an inclination to sell the little piece of mortality with which I am entrusted as dearly as possible. I have had to submit to insults, which make a man despise himself for bearing, and which I cannot submit to any longer. Many freedmen are afraid to sleep in their own houses. Many have already been driven from the country." . . .

Rev. H. O. Hoffman, Shelbyville, Tenn.:

"Have never seen any of the Klan, but that it exists in our county no one doubts. Several have been harmed by this secret organization. Mr. Dunlap and a colored man by the name of Jeff were badly whipped on the night of the 4th of July. His person was cut in great gashes, from the middle of his back to his knees. Mr. Dunlap's offense was teaching a colored school. I have been repeatedly threatened, and was told that the Ku-Klux Klan had a list made of men they designed driving from the country. Found the following note in my yard:

"In Ku-klux Council, July 24, 1868.
Rev. Mr. Hoffman: Your name is before the council. Beware! We will attend to you. You shall not call us villains—damn you.
Ku-Klux."

"I believe the object of the Klan is to whip unarmed negroes, scare timid white men, break up elections, and interfere with the State government, and steal and plunder the goods of the people." . . .

GLOSSARY

Blair: Francis Blair; politician, Union Army general, and unsuccessful candidate for vice president of the United States on the Democratic ticket in 1868

Galbreath, William: mayor of Shelbyville, Tennessee, in 1869

Mr. Speaker: DeWitt C. Senter, speaker of the Tennessee State Legislature in 1868

Radical: term generally used by Southerners after the Civil War to describe those who supported Reconstruction policies and equal rights for former slaves

Seymour: Horatio Seymour, two-term governor of New York (1853–1854 and 1863–1864) and unsuccessful Democratic candidate for president of the United States in 1868

stirrup-straps: leather loops attached to a saddle to assist riders in mounting

Thomas, George Henry: US Army major general, a career soldier and in 1868 commander of the Department of the Cumberland (Tennessee and Kentucky)

Document Analysis

The excerpt above is part of an official report of a committee of the US House of Representatives appointed in 1869 to investigate a contested election that took place the previous November in Tennessee's Fourth Congressional District. The committee was charged with making recommendations to the full House regarding a challenge filed by C. A. Sheafe, who had won the popular vote. Governor William Brownlow, determining that voter intimidation had been rampant in the district, certified Sheafe's opponent, Republican candidate Lewis Tillman, as the winner. The committee's report is contained in the Miscellaneous Documents of the Forty-First Congress (1869–71) under the title *Papers in the Contested Election Case of Sheafe vs. Tillman in the Fourth Congressional District of Tennessee*, which has an official printing date of February 11, 1870. The excerpted passages are taken from official reports and witness testimony that describe conditions in Tennessee during the spring and summer of 1868. The initial selection provides a summary and findings from a joint military committee appointed in August 1868 by the Tennessee legislature to investigate activities of the Ku Klux Klan. The Klan was thought to be responsible for an ongoing campaign of intimidation directed at re-cently freed slaves and their white supporters in order to keep those in the state supportive of Radical Republicans from voting or exercising other civil rights. Reports written by agents or managers of the Freedmen's Bureau provide information to superiors about the conditions of freed slaves in regions for which the agents were responsible. The brief excerpt from testimony by Reverend H. O. Hoffman describes his experience with the Klan.

Like most reports, the document prepared by the House of Representatives has a formal organization that reflects the conduct of the investigation. In the full report, transcripts of questions posed to each witness and witnesses' responses are recorded verbatim. Among those testifying before the House committee was Tennessee state senator William Wisener, who provided information about his own experiences with the Klan as well as information from reports he had received while serving as a member of the joint military committee. As a supplement to Wisener's testimony, the congressional committee authorized the printing of an appendix that offers further evidence of the scope and characteristics of activities being conducted by the Klan. The excerpts above are taken from this appendix, which provides graphic details of the Klan's activities throughout Tennessee.

Founded as a social club in Pulaski, Tennessee, the Ku Klux Klan quickly transformed into an agency of white supremacists and former secessionists disgruntled with Radical Republican efforts to give African Americans equal rights. At a meeting held in Nashville in 1867, former Confederate General Nathan Bedford Forrest was selected as national head of the organization. Despite some attempt to create a structure and hierarchy (complete with mysterious titles for leaders such as "Grand Wizard," "Grand Dragon," and "Grand Cyclops," to name a few), the Klan remained only loosely organized and its leaders had little control over individual groups operating locally under its aegis. In keeping with the secretive nature of the organization, Klan members tended to act at night and nearly always wore disguises. Many Southerners insisted that the Ku Klux Klan did not exist at all. Supporters claimed that much of the violence attributed to the Klan was imagined by its supposed victims, and that night riders who might have caused injury on occasion were simply vigilantes or misguided fun-seeking youth who meant no real harm.

The Testimony

The excerpts from the House of Representatives report represent a sampling of firsthand testimony describing encounters between the Ku Klux Klan and its many victims, and secondhand accounts from officials who routinely received reports of acts of violence. In the first passage, the authors of the joint military committee's report to the Tennessee legislature make clear that, despite protests from many white citizens that the Klan was not really dangerous, this "organization of armed men" posed a serious threat to the safety and well-being of the state's African American population. The summary statement that "poor negroes" were being robbed of their firearms, whipped, hanged, shot, and driven from their homes is based on testimony from numerous African American victims and from white Americans who either witnessed the atrocities or learned of them shortly after they occurred.

The committee seems to go out of its way to stress the widespread nature of the Klan's reign of terror. Traditionally, Tennesseans viewed their state as being divided into three broad regions. When talk of secession grew in 1861, West and Middle Tennessee, areas with many slaveholders, sided with the newly forming Confederacy. East Tennessee, populated by small farmers, was inclined to remain in the Union. While one

might have expected trouble in the western and middle regions of the state, the authors of the report make it explicit that all three sections were experiencing an upsurge of Klan violence. After claiming that the "depredations" caused by the Klan extended across the entire state, the committee lists specific counties in which violence was especially prevalent. This list actually served a second purpose: it provided Governor Brownlow a reason for declaring martial law in particularly troubled areas and for deploying troops from the Tennessee State Guard there. Although the governor was unable to send troops in before the November election, after the State Guard was finally reactivated early in 1869, Brownlow declared martial law in nine counties in February.

Particularly noteworthy, too, is the report's stress on the violence committed against white Americans in Tennessee who were working to advance the improvement of the African American population. Virtually every person identified in the excerpt from the joint military committee report is white, including numerous individuals teaching in African American schools who had been intimidated, beaten, or otherwise threatened simply for wanting to educate former slaves. The report's authors also play upon a fear common among Southerners, the desecration of the family ("women and children have been subjected to the torture of the lash") and especially of women ("the persons of females have been violated"). Though perhaps not intentional, there is a note of irony in this behavior. One of the principal arguments of white supremacists was that, if not checked, African Americans would take advantage of white women and adulterate the purity of the race.

Because the joint military committee report was being submitted to colleagues in the legislature, the authors include incidents in which elected officials have suffered at the hands of Klansmen who have no respect for the law or those sworn to uphold it. The extensive description of the treatment of the aging Senator William Wyatt is intended to make fellow legislators realize that the danger posed by the Klan could easily be visited upon them. The allusion to State Senator Almon Case and his son would have also caused consternation among Radical legislators. Case was murdered in January 1867, his son four months earlier. Case's assailant was known but escaped prosecution because he enjoyed the protection of white Americans sympathetic to the Klan's activities. The committee may have been looking toward the upcoming congressional elections when they cited the case of Samuel M. Arnell, who had been elected to the US House of Representatives in a contested election a year earlier. Arnell's experience makes it clear that even members of Congress had much to fear from Klansmen "thirsting" for their blood.

Reports from various officials of the Freedmen's Bureau corroborate the testimony of witnesses before the joint military committee and the congressional committee investigating the contested election. The Freedmen's Bureau was established as the Civil War was coming to a close by President Abraham Lincoln, who foresaw that former slaves would need assistance in becoming independent citizens. Designed to provide legal, medical, educational, and economic aid, the Bureau established offices and deployed agents throughout the South. Their efforts met with stiff resistance from the white population, and many agents found themselves subjected to harassment and intimidation similar to that suffered by the clients they were supposed to be serving. Major General William Carlin's report on conditions in West Tennessee highlights several cases of brutality that had occurred recently in this region, among them the ongoing hostility toward education for African Americans exhibited by "pro-slavery people," by which he means former secessionists who had adopted the mantle of white supremacists. Throughout the South, many white Americans were fearful that, once educated, African Americans would become a powerful political force in communities where they outnumbered white people, and therefore posed a threat to their former masters. Few in the South believed that the races could coexist harmoniously; white Americans especially feared that educating and arming the African American population would inevitably lead to a revolution aimed at wiping out all white people.

Undoubtedly many of the attacks on African Americans perpetrated by the Klan were launched randomly against any African American unfortunate enough to be spotted by night riders out to cause mayhem and create terror. As the reports by agents A. H. Eastman and J. K. Nelson indicate, however, some African Americans were targeted for their political activity. Both Joshua Ferrell and D. Webb were told they were chosen by the Klan because they supported the Union League or the Loyal League, held Radical sympathies, or voted for the Radical Republican candidate for governor in the most recent election. The activities of the Union League (sometimes called the Loyal League) were particularly vexing to former secessionists and white suprema-

cists. Founded in 1862 in Northern cities to support the Union cause, the Union League organized chapters in the South after the war to promote the Republican political agenda and to encourage African Americans to vote and become involved in politics. Many former slaves joined the Union League even if they were not political activists.

As every witness testifies, the Klan's actions ranged from simple intimidation to significant physical violence, sometimes resulting in murder. In many cases threats alone were enough to cause white and African Americans alike to submit to the Klan's will. One intimidation technique typical of many groups of Klansmen is described by the Reverend H. O. Hoffman, who reports having received threats himself, including one delivered in a fashion typical of Klansmen at the time: a note left in his yard warning him that his "name is before the Council" and that the Klan "will attend to you." Such notes alone were often sufficient to deter whites from continuing to support African Americans, and in some cases caused them to leave the region rather than face the prospect of reprisal for their actions.

A number of whites were forced to submit to public insult, which, coupled with secondhand reports of violence, caused them to behave like agent J. K. Nelson, who slept with firearms nearby. Many African Americans, fearing for their lives and wishing to keep themselves and their families safe from Klan attacks, simply fled to what they perceived to be safer regions. As the joint military committee report indicates, this posed new problems: the "two hundred colored men" who fled to Nashville ended up "destitute of food, or any means of subsistence." This early instance of African American flight to urban centers is a harbinger of what would come for many who left the harsh life of the segregated rural South only to end up no better off in crowded cities, where they remained victims of inequality and prejudice.

Language and Rhetoric

Some of the hyperbolic language in these excerpts can be attributed to a general tendency during the nineteenth century for Americans to assume an oratorical posture in their writing. A comparison of these reports with contemporary sermons might reveal striking similarities. Words such as "outrage," "depredation," and "reign of terror" appear regularly in written communications from this period, particularly in newspapers. While some accounts are emotionally charged and may be exaggerated, the sheer volume of reporting makes it evident that the Klan's campaign of terror was effective in keeping freed slaves and their white supporters from exercising their civil rights.

The inclusion of lengthy descriptions of specific acts of mayhem and torture, however, would have had immediate impact on readers of these reports, and would have convinced even the most skeptical to agree that strong countermeasures were required to curb the Klan's activities. Reverend Hoffman's description of the injuries suffered by the "colored man by the name of Jeff," agent Eastman's testimony about the treatment Joshua Ferrell received simply because he supported Governor Brownlow and the Union League, and the manhandling of Minor Fletcher and D. Webb described by agent J. K. Nelson contain little overblown rhetoric. Instead, the graphic language used in a series of declarative sentences filled with strong action verbs conveys without exaggeration the horror of the circumstances in which these men found themselves. The detail with which incidents of brutality are described is clearly intended to provoke both fear and outrage. The elderly Senator Wyatt was pistol-whipped so badly that he suffered a "frightful gash, saturating his shirt with blood, leaving him insensible." Joshua Ferrell, also old and apparently harmless, was similarly beaten, the pistol "cutting a gash half an inch wide, four inches long" into his skull. Little is left to the imagination except the unstated conclusion that incidents like these will continue to occur unless the Klan is neutralized.

Also common among these reports is the tendency to establish clear political and moral differences between perpetrators and victims in the attacks. For example, Senator Wyatt is described as "a Christian gentleman" and "a Union Man." The schoolteacher Dunlap is "a member of the Methodist Church," quiet and inoffensive. Many of the victims are former members of the Union Army. Those who threaten these honest, lawabiding, loyal citizens of the United States are violent, lawless bands intent on sedition. The attack on Senator Case indicates to the writers of the joint committee report that "no loyal man" is safe at present. Additionally, there is a sense running through these reports that these individual groups of "night-prowlers" are part of a larger, sinister organization that was creating a "system of anti-lawry and terrorism" for political motives: to deliver votes in the upcoming presidential election to the Democratic ticket.

The testimony recorded in these reports displays the power of anecdotal evidence in supporting an argument for government support of victims. The specific action sought by both state and federal officials was armed intervention. In his June 1868 report, Carlin makes it clear that Freedmen's Bureau agents were powerless to "remedy" the "evils that cry out for redress," and he predicts exactly what Governor Brownlow feared. The level of Klan activity in the early months of 1868 strongly suggested that "frequent disturbances" would continue to occur during the fall campaigns for president and seats in Congress. The Klan's activities were certain to "bring about a state of affairs that will preclude the possibility for the colored people, and the active, outspoken Union men" to vote in the November election. Carlin is clear in his belief that nothing short of martial law "will preserve the peace and insure safety." No doubt in the summer of 1868 Governor Brownlow was pleased to see this kind of support for his own position against the Klan. For members of Congress receiving this report in 1870, the message was equally clear: some definite action was needed to ameliorate or eliminate Klan violence, or the country as a whole might slip back into anarchy and civil strife.

Essential Themes
The importance of congressional investigations into the activities of the Ku Klux Klan during the first decade following the end of the Civil War can hardly be overstated. Between 1866 and 1870 the Klan had spread to virtually every state in the former Confederacy. Its brutal campaign to intimidate the African American population in those states not only affected the political climate, but also caused many former slaves to fear for their lives and their property. The ability of Klansmen to act with impunity, knowing that sympathetic white officials in law enforcement and government would do little to prosecute them for any crimes they committed, created a virtual state of anarchy that many then and later would equate with terrorism. Although it is impossible to speculate on what might have happened, many scholars agree with those who witnessed Klan violence that the United States may well have slipped back into civil war had the Klan's activities not been checked. Hence, reports that document the Klan's systematic assault on equal rights were instrumental in bringing about action at the federal level to suppress the organization and restore order and the rule of law in the South.

Various investigations led to decisions that influenced the future of the nation. Undoubtedly the 1868 report prompted Tennessee legislators to reestablish the State Guard. In 1870 the House of Representatives was convinced by its committee's report that the African American population in Tennessee had been denied their civil rights; it voted to allow Tillman to retain the disputed Fourth District seat in Congress. Widespread accounts of Klan violence such as the ones documented in the House committee's report were instrumental in generating further action at the federal level. In 1871, Senator John Scott of Pennsylvania convened a congressional committee to investigate Klan activities in the South. The extensive testimony presented before Smith's committee was published in thirteen volumes in 1872 as *Report of the Joint Select Committee Appointed to Inquire in to the Condition of Affairs in the Late Insurrectionary States*. It became the most important contemporary document outlining the nature and extent of Klan violence during the early years of Reconstruction. The report also prompted passage of a stronger law allowing the federal government to counter Klan activities, which were identified as supporting a specific political agenda, that of the Democratic Party.

As a result of strong enforcement by President Ulysses S. Grant, the Ku Klux Klan's influence was almost completely nullified by 1877, when Reconstruction ended and former Confederate states were once again allowed to participate as full partners in the national government. Unfortunately, once free to act without federal supervision, many Southern states enacted laws that brought about the same result that the Klan had sought through violence: a segregated society in which African Americans remained separate and decidedly unequal.

Laurence W. Mazzeno, PhD

Bibliography

Alexander, Thomas B. *Political Reconstruction in Tennessee*. Nashville: Vanderbilt UP, 1950. Print.

Coulter, E. Merton. *William G. Brownlow: Fighting Parson of the Southern Highlands*. Chapel Hill: U of North Carolina P, 1937. Print.

Katz, William L. *The Invisible Empire: The Ku Klux Klan Impact on History*. Washington: Open Hand, 1986. Print.

Queener, Verton M. "A Decade of East Tennessee Republicanism, 1867–1876." *East Tennessee Historical Society's Publications* 14 (1942): 59–85. Print.

Severance, Ben H. *Tennessee's Radical Army: The State Guard and Its Role in Reconstruction, 1867–1869*. Knoxville: U of Tennessee P, 2005. Print.

Trelease, Allen W. *White Terror: The Ku Klux Klan Conspiracy and Southern Reconstruction*. New York: Harper, 1971. Print.

Additional Reading

Bergeron, Paul H., Stephen V. Ash, and Jeanette Keith. *Tennesseans and Their History*. Knoxville: U of Tennessee P, 1999. Print.

Budiansky, Stephen. *The Bloody Shirt: Terror after Appomattox*. New York: Viking, 2008. Print.

Foner, Eric. *Reconstruction: America's Unfinished Revolution, 1863–1877*. New York: Harper, 1988. Print.

Horn, Stanley F. *Invisible Empire: The Story of the Ku Klux Klan, 1866–1871*. Cos Cob: Edwards, 1969. Print.

Martinez, J. Michael. *Carpetbaggers, Cavalry, and the Ku Klux Klan: Exposing the Invisible Empire during Reconstruction*. Lanham: Rowman, 2007. Print.

Newton, Michael. *The Ku Klux Klan: History, Organization, Language, Influence, and Activities of America's Most Notorious Secret Society*. Jefferson: McFarland, 2007. Print.

Patton, James Welch. *Unionism and Reconstruction in Tennessee 1860–1869*. Chapel Hill: U of North Carolina P, 1980. Print.

Rable, George C. *But There Was No Peace: The Role of Violence in the Politics of Reconstruction*. Athens: U of Georgia P, 2007. Print.

Randel, William P. *The Ku Klux Klan: A Century of Infamy*. Philadelphia: Chilton, 1965. Print.

Summers, Mark W. *A Dangerous Stir: Fear, Paranoia, and the Making of Reconstruction*. Chapel Hill: U of North Carolina P, 2009. Print.

■ Letter to Senator Joseph C. Abbott on the Ku Klux Klan

Date: May 24, 1870
Author: Tourgée, Albion W.
Genre: letter

> *"The habit of regarding the South as simply a laboratory, where every demagogue may carry on his reconstructionary experiments at will, and not as an integral party of the Nation itself, has led our Government to shut its eyes to the atrocities of these times."*

Summary Overview

After the murder of North Carolina state senator John Walter Stephens, radical Republican and district judge Albion W. Tourgée sent Joseph Carter Abbott a detailed letter outlining atrocities committed by the Ku Klux Klan in central North Carolina. A former general in the Union Army, Abbott had moved to North Carolina after the war and was then serving as a US senator. Concentrating on acts of violence committed against African Americans, poor whites, and Republican politicians, Tourgée presents grim statistics of murder and mayhem as evidence for his compelling argument that swift action by the federal government was necessary to stop the violence. Copies of the letter were sent to several prominent politicians, including North Carolina governor William Woods Holden. That summer, it was published in the *New York Tribune*, bringing national attention to the Klan's activities and rousing the public and Congress to take action against the secret society.

Defining Moment

Albion Tourgée's letter outlining the atrocities committed by the Ku Klux Klan in North Carolina was prompted by the murder of his friend and protégée John W. Stephens. A native North Carolinian, Stephens had worked as a tobacco trader and agent for the American Bible and Tract Society. During the Civil War, he had served the Confederacy, but after the South surren-

dered, he became a Republican and worked to advance the enfranchisement of African Americans and assure them equal treatment. Tourgée, a district judge, mentored Stephens in his law studies, enabling Stephens to become a justice of the peace in Caswell County, a hotbed of Ku Klux Klan activity in 1869 and 1870. Conservatives were outraged at Stephens's activities in support of African Americans, and he quickly became a target for the Klan.

On May 21, 1870, Stephens attended a Democratic political meeting at the Caswell County Courthouse in Yanceyville. There, he met former Democratic sheriff Frank Wiley, whom he hoped to convince to run again for the office as a Republican. Wiley, a member of the Klan, lured Stephens into the basement of the courthouse. There, a group of Klansmen stabbed him, leaving his body in a locked storage room, where it was discovered the next day.

Tourgée must have learned of the murder almost immediately, as his letter to Senator Abbott was written only a few days after the event. Stephens's murder was far from anomalous, however; it was simply the latest is a long list of outrageous violations committed by the Klan against African Americans and their white supporters. In his letter, Tourgée provides a catalog of some of these crimes, which include murders, beatings, rapes, and property damage. Tourgée calls for the federal government to take swift, specific action to curb the violence occurring in North Carolina and elsewhere throughout the South.

It is worth noting that others besides Tourgée were moved to act against the Klan after Stephens was killed. Most notable among them was Governor William Holden, who, in June 1870, cited a list of criminal activities similar to those described in Tourgée's letter as justification for calling out the state militia to quell Klan violence. Holden was given a copy of Tourgée's letter, and he likely arranged its publication in the *New York Tribune*, then one of the most widely read papers in America.

Author Biography

Albion Winegar Tourgée was born May 2, 1838, in Williamsfield, Ashtabula County, Ohio, and raised on his father's farm. He enrolled at the University of Rochester in 1859 but was forced to leave for financial reasons in 1861. He worked briefly as an educator in New York before enlisting in the Twenty-Seventh New York Volunteers in April 1861. Injured during the Battle of Bull Run in July, he left active service to recuperate but returned to duty with the 105th Ohio Volunteers. Because of his exemplary service, the University of Rochester awarded him a bachelor's degree in 1862 and a master's degree in 1865. Tourgée married Emma Kilbourne, his longtime sweetheart, in May 1863. Harsh conditions in the western theater and several months in a prisoner of war camp exacerbated his prior injury, forcing him to resign his commission in late 1863.

After leaving the military, Tourgée completed studies in law and worked as an attorney, journalist, and teacher. In October 1865, he moved to Greensboro, North Carolina, where he set up a law practice. One of thousands of Northerners intent on reforming political, social, and economic conditions in the South, Tourgée proved a staunch radical Republican. In 1868, he was elected a district judge, a position he held for six years. That same year, he played a major role in drafting the state's civil code. Tourgée's six years on the bench were filled with controversy, as his consistent support of African Americans and fellow Republican reformers angered Southern conservatives, who referred to him and other transplanted Northerners as "carpetbaggers." He received numerous death threats from the secretive Ku Klux Klan and, for some time, found it necessary to carry arms when going out in public.

Tourgée moved back north in 1879 and became a writer and advocate for civil rights. His most widely read work, *A Fool's Errand by One of the Fools* (1879), is a fictionalized account of his experiences in North Carolina. Tourgée's 1880 nonfiction work *The Invisible Empire* exposes the reign of terror caused by the Ku Klux Klan.

In 1896, Tourgée filed a brief in the United States Supreme Court on behalf of the plaintiff in *Plessy v. Ferguson*, a landmark civil rights case that set the course for race relations in America for more than half a century. Tourgée argued for what he called "color-blind justice" that would guarantee equal rights to every American. The Supreme Court decided instead that "separate but equal" accommodations were sufficient.

In 1897, Tourgée was appointed US consul to Bordeaux, France, where he spent the last years of his life. He died on May 21, 1905, of complications from the wounds he had received during the Civil War.

HISTORICAL DOCUMENT

My Dear General:

It is my mournful duty to inform you that our friend John W. Stephens, State Senator from Caswell, is dead. He was foully murdered by the Ku-Klux in the Grand Jury room of the Court House on Saturday or Saturday night last. The circumstances attending his murder have not yet fully come to light there. So far as I can learn, I judge these to have been the circumstances: He was one of the Justices of the Peace in that township, and was accustomed to hold court in that room on Saturdays. It is evident that he was set upon by some one while holding this court, or immediately after its close, and disabled by a sudden attack, otherwise there would have been a very sharp resistance, as he was a man, and always went armed to the teeth. He was stabbed five or six times, and then hanged on a hook in the Grand Jury room, where he was found on Sunday morning. Another brave, honest Republican citizen has met his fate at the hands of these fiends. Warned of his danger, and fully cognizant of the terrible risk which surrounded him, he still manfully refused to quit the field. Against the advice of his friends, against the entreaties of his family, he constantly refused to leave those who had stood by him in the day of his disgrace and peril. He was accustomed to say that 3,000 poor, ignorant, colored Republican voters in that county had stood by him and elected him, at the risk of persecution and starvation, and that he had no idea of abandoning them to the Ku-Klux. He was determined to stay with them, and either put an end to these outrages, or die with the other victims of Rebel hate and national apathy. Nearly six months ago I declared my belief that before the election in August next the Ku-Klux would have killed more men in the State than there would be members to be elected to the Legislature. A good beginning has been made toward the fulfillment of this prophecy. The following counties have already filled, or nearly so, their respective "quotas:" Jones County, quota full, excess 1; Orange County quota full; excess, 1. Caswell County quota full; excess, 2; Alamance County quota full; excess, 1. Chatham County quota nearly full. Or, to state the matter differently, there have been twelve murders in five counties of the district during the past eighteen months, by bands of disguised villains. In addition to this, from the best information I can derive, I am of the opinion that in this district alone there have been 1,000 outrages of a less serious nature perpetrated by the same masked fiends. Of course this estimate is not made from any absolute record, nor is it possible to ascertain with accuracy the entire number of beatings and other outrages which have been perpetrated. The uselessness, the utter futility of complaint from the lack of ability in the laws to punish is fully known to all. The danger of making such complaint is also well understood. It is therefore not unfrequently by accident that the outrage is found out, and unquestionably it is frequently absolutely concealed. Thus, a respectable, hard working white carpenter was working for a neighbor, when accidentally his shirt was torn, and disclosed his back scarred and beaten. The poor fellow begged for the sake of his wife and children that nothing might be said about it, as

the Ku-Klux had threatened to kill him if he disclosed how he had been outraged. Hundreds of cases have come to my notice and that of my solicitor. . . .

Men and women come scarred, mangled, and bruised, and say: "The Ku-Klux came to my house last night and beat me almost to death, and my old woman right smart, and shot into the house, 'bust' the door down, and told me they would kill me if I made complaint;" and the bloody mangled forms attest the truth of their declarations. On being asked if any one knew any of the party it will be ascertained that there was no recognition, or only the most uncertain and doubtful one. In such cases as these nothing can be done by the court. We have not been accustomed to enter them on record. A man of the best standing in Chatham told me that he could count up 200 and upward in that county. In Alamance County, a citizen in conversation one evening enumerated upward of 50 cases which had occurred within his own knowledge, and in one section of the county. He gave it as his opinion that there had been 200 cases in that county. I have no idea that he exceeded the proper estimate. That was six months ago, and I am satisfied that another hundred would not cover the work done in that time.

These crimes have been of every character imaginable. Perhaps the most usual has been the dragging of men and women from their beds, and beating their naked bodies with hickory switches, or as witnesses in an examination the other day said, "sticks" between a "switch" and a "club." From 50 to 100 blows is the usual allowance, sometimes 200 and 300 blows are administered. Occasionally an instrument of torture is owned. Thus in one case two women, one 74 years old, were taken out, stripped naked, and beaten with a paddle, with several holes bored through it. The paddle was about 30 inches long, 3 or 4 inches wide, and 1/4 of an inch thick, of oak. Their bodies were so bruised and beaten that they were sickening to behold. They were white women and of good character until the younger was seduced, and swore her child to its father. Previous to that and so far as others were concerned her character was good.

Again, there is sometimes a fiendish malignity and cunning displayed in the form and character of the outrages. For instance, a colored man was placed astride of a log, and an iron staple driven through his person into the log. In another case, after a band of them had in turn violated a young negro girl, she was forced into bed with a colored man, their bodies were bound together face to face, and the fire from the hearth piled upon them. The K. K. K. rode off and left them, with shouts of laughter. Of course the bed was soon in flames, and somehow they managed to crawl out, though terribly burned and scarred. The house was burned.

I could give other incidents of cruelty, such as hanging up a boy of nine years old until he was nearly dead, to make him tell where his father was hidden, and beating an old negress of 103 years old with garden pallings because she would not own that she was afraid of the Ku-Klux. But it is unnecessary to go into further detail. In this district I estimate their offenses as follows, in the past ten months: Twelve murders, 9 rapes, 11 arsons, 7 mutilations, ascertained and most of them on record. In some no identification could be made.

Four thousand or 5,000 houses have been broken open, and property or persons taken out. In all cases all arms are taken and destroyed. Seven hundred or 800 persons have been beaten or otherwise maltreated. These of course are partly persons living in the houses which were broken into.

And yet the Government sleeps. The poor disarmed nurses of the Republican party—those men by whose ballots the Republican party holds power—who took their lives in their hands when they cast their ballots for U.S. Grant and other officials—all of us who happen to be beyond the pale of the Governmental regard—must be sacrificed, murdered, scourged, mangled, because some contemptible party scheme might be foiled by doing us justice. I could stand it very well to fight for Uncle Sam, and was never known to refuse an invitation on such an occasion; but this lying down, tied hand and foot with the shackles of the law, to be killed by the very dregs of the rebellion, the scum of the earth, and not allowed either the consolation of fighting or the satisfaction that our "fall" will be noted by the Government, and protection given to others thereby, is somewhat too hard. I am ashamed of the nation that will let its citizens be slain by scores, and scourged by thousands, and offer no remedy or protection. I am ashamed of a State which has not sufficient strength to protect its own officers in the discharge of their duties, nor guarantee the safety of any man's domicile throughout its length and breadth. I am ashamed of a party which, with the reins of power in its hands, has not nerve or decision enough to arm its own adherents, or to protect them from assassinations at the hands of their opponents. A General who in time of war would permit 2,000 or 3,000 of his men to be bushwhacked and destroyed by private treachery even in an enemy's country without any one being punished for it would be worthy of universal execration, and would get it, too. How much more worthy of detestation is a Government which in time of peace will permit such wholesale slaughter of its citizens? It is simple cowardice, inertness, and wholesale demoralization. The wholesale slaughter of the war has dulled our Nation's sense of horror at the shedding of blood, and the habit of regarding the South as simply a laboratory, where every demagogue may carry on his reconstructionary experiments at will, and not as an integral party of the Nation itself, has led our Government to shut its eyes to the atrocities of these times. Unless these evils are speedily remedied, I tell you, General, the Republican party has signed its death warrant. It is a party of cowards or idiots—I don't care which alternative is chosen. The remedy is in our hands, and we are afraid or too dull to bestir ourselves and use it.

But you will tell me that Congress is ready and willing to act if it only knew what to do. Like the old Irish woman it wrings its hands and cries, "O Lawk, O Lawk; if I only knew which way." And yet this same Congress has the control of the militia and can organize its own force in every county in the United States, and arm more or less of it. This same Congress has the undoubted right to guarantee and provide a republican government, and protect every citizen in "life, liberty, and the pursuit of happiness," as well as the power conferred by the XVth Amendment. And yet we suffer and die in peace and murderers walk abroad with the blood yet fresh upon their garments, unharmed, unquestioned and unchecked. Fifty thousand dollars given to good detectives would secure, if well used, a complete knowledge of all this gigantic organization of murderers. In connection with an organized and armed militia, it would result in the apprehension of any number of these Thugs *en masque* and with blood on their hands. What then is the remedy? *First*: Let Congress give to the U. S. Courts, or to Courts of the States under its own laws, cognizance of this class of crimes, as crimes against the nation, and let it provide that this legislation be enforced. Why not, for instance, make going armed and masked or disguised, or masked or disguised in the night time, an act of insurrection or sedition? *Second:* Organize militia, National— State militia is a nuisance—and arm as many as may be necessary in each county to enforce its laws. *Third:* Put detectives at work to get hold of this whole organization. Its ultimate aim is unquestionably to revolutionize the Government. If we have not pluck enough for this, why then let us just offer our throats to the knife, emasculate ourselves, and be a nation of self-subjugated slaves at once.

And now, Abbott, I have but one thing to say to you. I have very little doubt that I shall be one of the next victims. My steps have been dogged for months, and only a good opportunity has been wanting to secure to me the fate which Stephens has just met, and I speak earnestly upon this matter. I feel that I have a right to do so, and a right to be heard as well, and with this conviction I say to you plainly that any member of Congress who, especially if from the South, does not support, advocate, and urge immediate, active, and thorough measures to put an end to these outrages, and make citizenship a privilege, is a coward, a traitor, or a fool. The time for action has come, and the man who has now only speeches to make over some Constitutional scarecrow, deserves to be damned.

GLOSSARY

bushwhacked: attacked by a person or group waiting in hiding; "bushwhackers" was a term commonly used to describe Confederate irregulars

Chatham: Chatham County, North Carolina

Court House: the Caswell County Court House in Yanceyville, North Carolina

palings: boards sharpened at one end, used for fencing

XVth Amendment: Fifteenth Amendment to the US Constitution, guaranteeing voting rights to former slaves and people of color

Document Analysis

The murder of John W. Stephens, Albion Tourgée's close friend, served as the impetus for the long letter Tourgée wrote on May 24, 1870, to Joseph C. Abbott, then representing North Carolina in the United States Senate. The two men had similar backgrounds. Like Tourgée, Abbott was from the North, having been born and raised in New Hampshire, but remained in the South after the war. He served in the Union Army, rising to the rank of brevet brigadier general in 1865. Both men were delegates at North Carolina's 1868 constitutional convention. Tourgée no doubt felt confident that, in writing to Abbott, he was addressing a friend to whom he could lay out a series of complaints about activities of the Ku Klux Klan in North Carolina and ask for assistance in putting an end to them, lest the Klan's reign of terror undo the activities of Republicans to reform the Southern political system and guarantee civil rights for African Americans in the South.

Although cast in the form of personal correspondence, Tourgée's letter is actually a carefully crafted argument that lays out the case for federal intervention in North Carolina and other Southern states to end the atrocities being perpetrated by the Ku Klux Klan. As such, it is similar to the Declaration of Independence, in which Thomas Jefferson, writing for the committee appointed by the Second Continental Congress to draft the document, carefully delineates the specific offenses that justified the colonists' decision to break away from Britain. One important formal difference between the two documents may help highlight the difficulty Tourgée faced in making his case. The Declaration of Independence employs deductive logic and is organized as a formal syllogism. Jefferson first states as a major premise what he believes is a universal truth: when a ruler denies people their inalienable rights, those people are justified in rebelling. Jefferson follows this assertion with a list of facts (his minor premise) that explain how King George III has violated the colonists' rights. The conclusion that Americans are justified in their cause follows logically. Tourgée has no major premise from which to argue, or if he does, he leaves it unstated. Instead, he employs inductive logic to build his case, relying on the accumulation of specific evidence to convince Abbott that the federal government, especially the Republicans in Congress, should take immediate action to relieve the suffering of African Americans and their white Republican allies in the South. It should be noted, though, that while Tourgée relies on logic to lead Abbott (and others) to conclude that immediate relief is necessary, he peppers his letter with words that evoke strong emotions to supplement the logic of his appeal.

Tourgée's argument may be outlined as follows. The murder of state senator John W. Stephens, a hero in the cause of enfranchisement and equal rights for African Americans, is a high-profile example of what has been happening in North Carolina for some time. Statistics prove that Klan violence is widespread, and reports of specific incidents reveal that it is grotesque and sadistic. Government officials have so far been powerless or unwilling to stop the violence. Therefore, action is needed at the federal level to protect citizens and bring Klan members and their supporters to justice.

Tourgée begins by paying tribute to Stephens, whom he calls a "brave, honest Republican citizen" who "manfully refused to quit the field," even in the face of repeated threats from the Klan. Calling Stephens a Republican is a way for Tourgée to remind Abbott that Stephens had the same objectives as Abbott in his own political activities. In fact, Tourgée continues, Stephens was determined to remain with the African Americans who had elected him to office in order to end the "outrages" to which they were being subjected, or "die with the other victims of Rebel hate and national apathy." The last phrase is one to which Tourgée returns at the end of his letter, but first he describes the level and types of violence that prompt him to appeal to Abbott (and the United States Congress) for assistance.

Tourgée relies on two types of evidence to make his case: statistics that demonstrate the magnitude of the problem of unchecked Klan violence and graphic anecdotes of individual atrocities. For example, he notes "twelve murders in five counties of the district during the past eighteen months" and "1,000 outrages of a less serious nature." He reports that a source in Chatham County has evidence of more than two hundred similar events, while one in Alamance County has firsthand knowledge of fifty and strong evidence of nearly two hundred as well. He closes the first major section of his argument, the presentation of evidence of Klan atrocities, with a list of powerful statistics: in the district where Tourgée lives, there have been "twelve murders, 9 rapes, 11 arsons, 7 mutilations" confirmed, four to five thousand instances of property damage, and seven to eight hundred cases of beatings and other instances of maltreatment.

At the same time, Tourgée seldom misses an opportunity to present his statistics in a context aimed at generating strong emotional reaction from his reader. For example, pointing out that "3,000 poor, ignorant, colored Republican voters" had elected Stephens to the North Carolina Senate not only highlights the wide support Stephens had among the formerly disenfranchised portion of the local populace, but also reminds Abbott that the African Americans for whom people like himself and Tourgée had fought were the ones who were now being victimized again by Stephens's murder. Numbers provide specificity, and Tourgée makes good use of them in dramatizing the impact of the Klan's reign of terror. He details the way men and women, dragged from their beds, are beaten with sticks or switches, fifty to one hundred blows being the "usual allowance," although occasionally "200 and 300" are "administered." The use of neutral terms, such as "allowance" and "administered," creates a macabre counterpoint to the high number of blows given to these defenseless victims.

Perhaps the best example of Tourgée's ability to employ specific data for emotional effect is in his description of the beating of two women (one of them in her seventies) with a paddle. With the precision of a carpenter outlining measurements for the construction of a household item such as a cabinet or storage chest, Tourgée gives exact dimensions of this cruel "instrument of torture" that Klan members used to punish two white women "of good character." The point that Klan violence extends beyond the African American community would not have been lost on Abbott or on anyone else who might read Tourgée's impassioned plea for outside help.

While statistics may provide an indication of the scope of the problem on which Tourgée wishes to report, he relies on other rhetorical methods to engage Abbott emotionally so that he may be prompted to act against the Klan. One of Tourgée's most effective techniques is to relate specific anecdotes about the Klan's treatment of victims. The story of the two white women beaten with a paddle is one such example. Equally effective in rousing emotions of revulsion are examples used to support Tourgée's claim that there is "a fiendish malignity and cunning" in some of the Klan's activities. The simple sentence noting an attack on a black man in which "an iron staple [was] driven through his person into the log" is an example of understatement and circumlocution. The word "person" is used euphemistically: Abbott and other nineteenth-century readers would have understood that Tourgée was referring to the man's genitalia.

A longer anecdote recounts what might be the most horrific act Tourgée ascribes to the Klan, an attempt to murder a young African American couple by burning them alive in bed. The hideous unstated link between the heat of sexual passion and the literal heat of the fire may well have motivated this particular form of torture, as many Southern whites at this time believed African Americans were incapable of controlling sexual urges. Tourgée renders a graphic account of the young couple's plight as their attackers meticulously prepare them for what should have been certain death. That they escaped may be little short of miraculous, but their bodies forever bear the scars of the incident. To emphasize his point, Tourgée ends the paragraph with a monumental understatement: "The house was burned." The juxtaposition of this bald report of property damage stands in sharp contrast to the agony which the young man and woman have suffered and will continue to suffer at the hands of these night riders who depart the scene with "shouts of laughter."

Tourgée concludes this section of his argument with a typical rhetorical device, noting that he "could give other incidents of cruelty" and then citing two more specific examples. He says at this point "it is unnecessary to go into further detail" but follows his disclaimer with the list of statistics that provide a frightening summation of Klan violence. Having demonstrated to his satisfaction that a serious problem exists, Tourgée then moves the next section of his argument, a damning account of government inaction in the face of these atrocities.

"And yet the Government sleeps," Tourgée states. This jarring indictment is the lead-in for an emotional diatribe against all levels of government, which, to date, had been ineffective in quelling the Klan's activities. Chief among the targets of Tourgée's wrath is his own Republican Party, which he feels has abandoned brave souls like Stephens (and himself). Instead of receiving support from the national party, these "poor disarmed nurses" who "took their lives in their hands" to foster Republicanism are now being "sacrificed, murdered, scourged, mangled," Tourgée claims, because the party "scheme" to bring about Reconstruction gradually while placating Democrats (especially conservative Southerners) might be derailed should stronger actions be undertaken in their defense.

The language Tourgée employs in this section of his argument is particularly emotional. He claims to be "ashamed" of his state, which cannot protect its duly elected officials. Behind that statement is his knowledge that many in North Carolina, including some public officials, supported the Klan's objectives. He is especially "ashamed" of the Republican Party, which, despite holding the reins of political power, lacks "nerve or decision enough to arm its own adherents." That statement reveals Tourgée's radical stance, since arming "adherents" would have meant giving weapons to African Americans. Following through on such a plan would have infuriated Southern conservatives, who believed arming a large population of former slaves would lead to a much-feared black uprising that could wipe out all whites in the South.

To impress upon Abbott the seriousness of his complaint, Tourgée employs a military analogy that was sure to hit home with the former Union officer. "A General" who would permit thousands of his troops to be "destroyed by private treachery even in an enemy's country without any one being punished" would deserve "universal execration." Therefore, in times of peace, a government that permits similar "wholesale slaughter of its citizens" is even more detestable. Not to act on behalf of those being oppressed can only be attributed to "cowardice, inertness, and wholesale demoralization," Tourgée concludes. Certainly neither Abbott nor any Republican could have failed to be startled or even angered by such strong words.

Sadly, Tourgée continues, the sense of outrage that ought to be felt by every person of good moral character is absent, perhaps because four years of war had "dulled our Nation's sense of horror." Tourgée believes too many

Southern demagogues have been allowed to get away with outrageous behavior because Republicans have been unwilling to face up to their responsibilities to oppressed people in the region. At this pivotal point in the nation's history, Tourgée suggests, the Republican Party lacks leadership. Someone must step forward—a strong politician with the qualities of generalship that helped the North win the war, perhaps—to remedy these evils.

Abbott, the former commander-turned-politician, could see himself in both roles presented in Tourgée's comparison. In fact, the letter contains strong evidence that Tourgée wants Abbott to see himself as a military commander who must take decisive action against an enemy that is slaughtering his forces. A look back at the letter's salutation makes this point clear. Rather than addressing Abbott as "Senator," Tourgée addresses him as "My Dear General." Already reminded subtly of his role as a defender of the rights of African Americans and of Republican values, Abbott would have quickly grasped the point Tourgée was making. It was time for men of action like Abbott to take steps to bring the Klan to justice.

Tourgée is ready with specific suggestions for solving the problems he outlines in his missive. Rather than moaning and wringing their hands in uncertainty and indecision, the members of Congress should exercise their power to bring about change, using military force if necessary. Tourgée claims an effective remedy can be provided by implementing three specific strategies: making the activities of the Klan acts of "insurrection or sedition," punishable by federal, rather than state, law; organizing and employing the national military, not state militia, to enforce the new law; and employing detectives to identify those who are perpetrating atrocities.

Tourgée believes the Klan's activities are no different from those of the Southerners who attempted to secede nearly a decade earlier. The group's "ultimate aim is unquestionably to revolutionize the Government." In the most impassioned sentence in his letter, Tourgée concludes with a graphic description of the only plausible possibilities for his Republican colleagues should Congress not move to curb the Klan's activities. Failing the courage to act, Republicans should simply "offer our throats to the knife"—in other words, become sacrificial lambs, although there is no hope that the cause in which they will be sacrificed will be won. Republicans, including Tourgée, would thereby "emasculate" themselves, because failure to act would be unmanly. Worst of all, failure to act would make Republicans (and their followers) "a nation of self-subjugated slaves," reverting to the intolerable conditions that existed in America before the Civil War. The many hard-fought battles in which the party and its agents have engaged in the five years since the war's end will have been for naught, Tourgée warns, and as noted earlier in the letter, the Republican Party will have "signed its death warrant."

The care with which Tourgée took to craft his argument suggests that he knew the letter would become a public document at some time. Certainly he would have expected Senator Abbott to share it with others in Congress, whether by reading it or by using it as the basis for making a case for the government to intervene in affairs in North Carolina and elsewhere. In fact, the letter circulated on Capitol Hill during the summer of 1870, helping shape the opinion of members of Congress who initiated a series of laws to curb the Klan's activities. Additionally, although Tourgée was not pleased that the letter was published in *New York Tribune* on August 3, the document once again proved effective as a weapon against the Klan. In what was then among the most widely read papers in the country, Tourgée's missive was used to point out the nature and extent of the Klan's activities (although the published version may have exaggerated the statistical data Tourgée originally shared) and to highlight the difficulties state and local politicians were experiencing in trying to eliminate its pernicious influence.

Essential Themes

Written while Congress was deliberating legislation to restrict activities of the Ku Klux Klan, Tourgée's letter to Abbott may have influenced legislation that made much of what the Klan did a violation of civil and criminal law. Certainly his pleas and those of other Republicans living in the South prompted Congress to investigate the Klan's activities and enact a series of laws to protect civil rights for all citizens. The Enforcement Act of 1870 banned the use of force, intimidation, or other means of coercion to keep people from voting; the Enforcement Act of 1871 gave the federal government the right to oversee elections, and the Civil Rights Act of 1871 granted federal officials wide powers to enforce provisions of the Fourteenth Amendment. At the legislative level, these strong actions provided a framework to curtail the Klan's activities and guarantee the safety of African Americans and those who sympathized with their cause when these groups chose to exercise rights guaranteed to them under the Constitution. In the short term, these laws effectively negated the Klan's influence, and by 1872, the organization had disbanded.

Sadly, Tourgée's prophesy regarding the effects of Republican inactivity in vigorously promoting civil rights for African Americans proved devastatingly accurate. In 1877, Reconstruction came to an end, and the president withdrew federal troops that had been dispatched to the South specifically to assist in bringing former Confederate states into compliance with new laws designed to guarantee equal rights for former slaves. At the same time, federal oversight of state governments ended. With little interference from the federal government, Southern states were allowed to enact a series of repressive segregationist laws, known as Jim Crow laws, which affected African Americans' ability to receive the same education, hold the same jobs, or live in the same neighborhoods as whites.

Ironically, Tourgée was a principal participant in the Supreme Court case that effectively gave federal government sanction to segregation. In 1896, as lead member of the plaintiff's counsel, Tourgée filed a brief with the court on behalf Homer A. Plessy in his suit to overturn Louisiana's Separate Car Act (1890), which required passengers of different races to ride in separate rail cars. Tourgée's plea for what he called "color-blind justice" was passed over in favor of a decision that segregation was permissible as long as "separate but equal" facilities and services were provided to all citizens of a state. Worse, after World War I, the Klan reorganized and African Americans were once again subjected to intimidation and physical violence throughout the South. The Supreme Court decision permitting state-sponsored segregation stood for half a century until the civil rights movement of the 1950s and 1960s resulted in the passage of the Civil Rights Act of 1964, which eliminated legal segregation and paved the way for greater racial equality in the United States.

Laurence W. Mazzeno, PhD

Bibliography

Bradley, Mark L. *Bluecoats and Tar Heels: Soldiers and Civilians in Reconstruction North Carolina.* Lexington: UP of Kentucky, 2009. Print.

Elliott, Mark. *Color-Blind Justice: Albion Tourgée and the Quest for Racial Equality: From the Civil War to Plessy v. Ferguson.* New York: Oxford UP, 2006. Print.

Gross, Theodore L. *Albion W. Tourgée.* New York: Twayne,
1963. Print.

McIver, Stuart. "The Murder of a Scalawag." *American History Illustrated* 8 (1973): 12–18. Print.

Nye, Russel B. "Judge Tourgée and Reconstruction." *Ohio Archaeological and Historical Quarterly* 50 (1941): 101–14. Print.

Olsen, Otto H. *Carpetbagger's Crusade: The Life of Albion Winegar Tourgée.* Baltimore: Johns Hopkins UP, 1965. Print.

Tourgée, Albion W. "Letter to Senator Joseph C. Abbott (1870)." *Undaunted Radical: The Selected Writings and Speeches of Albion W. Tourgée.* Ed. Mark Elliott and John David Smith. Baton Rouge: Louisiana State UP, 2010. 47–51. Print.

Trelease, Allen W. *White Terror: The Ku Klux Klan Conspiracy and Southern Reconstruction.* New York: Harper, 1971. Print.

Additional Reading

Beckel, Deborah. *Radical Reform: Interracial Politics in Post-Emancipation North Carolina.* Charlottesville: U of Virginia P, 2011. Print.

Blight, David W. *Race and Reunion: The Civil War in American Memory.* Cambridge: Harvard UP, 2001. Print.

Escott, Paul D., ed. *North Carolinians in the Era of the Civil War and Reconstruction.* Chapel Hill: U of North Carolina P, 2008. Print.

Hume, Richard L. "Carpetbaggers in the Reconstruction South: A Group Portrait of Outside Whites and the 'Black and Tan' Constitutional Conventions." *Journal of American History* 64.2 (1977): 313–30. Print.

Katz, William L. *The Invisible Empire: The Ku Klux Klan Impact on History.* Seattle: Open Hand, 1987. Print.

Newkirk, Vann R. *Lynchings in North Carolina: A History, 1865–1941.* Jefferson: McFarland, 2009. Print.

Newton, Michael. *The Ku Klux Klan: History, Organization, Language, Influence and Activities of America's Most Notorious Secret Society.* Jefferson: McFarland, 2007. Print.

Parsons, Elaine Frantz. "Midnight Rangers: Costume and Performance in the Reconstruction-Era Ku Klux Klan." *Journal of American History* 92.3 (2005): 811–36. Print.

Randel, William P. *The Ku Klux Klan: A Century of Infamy.* Philadelphia: Chilton, 1965. Print.

Zuczek, Richard. "The Federal Government's Attack on the Ku Klux Klan: A Reassessment." *South Carolina Historical Magazine* 97.1 (1996): 47–64. Print.

■ *United States v. Cruikshank*

Date: 1874
Author: Bradley, Joseph P.
Genre: court case

> *"It is not the right to vote which is guarantied to all citizens. Congress cannot interfere with the regulation of that right by the states except to prevent by appropriate legislation any distinction as to race, color, or previous condition of servitude."*

Summary Overview

United States v. Cruikshank was an appeal to the United States Supreme Court, argued in 1875 and decided the following year, to overturn the conviction of several men arrested following a massacre in Colfax, Louisiana, on April 13, 1873. After the hotly contested election of 1872, a paramilitary group of white men overpowered and killed a group of black freemen and state militia members guarding the newly elected Republican government at the Grant Parish courthouse. Several of the white men were convicted of conspiracy under a federal act designed to enforce the US Constitution's Fourteenth and Fifteenth Amendment guarantees of equal rights regardless of color. The defendants challenged the conviction, arguing that Congress did not have the authority to criminalize individuals' behavior and could only legislate against government discrimination. In 1874, Supreme Court associate justice Joseph P. Bradley, serving as a circuit justice in the Louisiana circuit court, heard the defendants' appeal and ruled in their favor, thus sending the case on to the Supreme Court. The Supreme Court agreed with Bradley's ruling and overturned the convictions, paving the way for paramilitary white supremacist groups to control the Southern states through violence and intimidation against black men trying to exercise their rights.

Defining Moment

Racial tension in Louisiana was extremely high following the Civil War. The federal Reconstruction Act of 1867 required all states to grant black men the right to vote. Unfortunately, this led to violence and murder against those who attempted to exercise that right, as well as widespread election fraud on the part of whites who opposed black suffrage.

Initially, Louisiana governor Henry Clay Warmoth tried to provide racial balance in his community by appointing William Ward, a black Civil War veteran of the Union Army, to be a commanding officer of a black unit of the state militia. But shortly before the 1872 election Warmoth aligned with the Liberal Republicans, who sought to disenfranchise black citizens, and formed an alliance with the Democratic Party. This alliance supported Warmoth to become Louisiana's US senator and John McEnery to become the new governor of Louisiana.

Voter fraud was rampant, and the election board was split regarding which candidate had actually won. Much of the reelected board claimed that McEnery had won the governor's seat, but a minority of the board and the federal government claimed that Republican William Pitt Kellogg had won. McEnery and his party assumed control following the election, but with federal assistance, Kellogg was eventually certified as the Louisiana governor. When the newly elected Republicans took their offices in the Grant Parish courthouse, groups of free black citizens and the black state militia unit occupied the area outside the courthouse to protect the government against overthrow by white protestors. In late March of 1873, several white men formed an alliance to retake the courthouse and reinstate their preferred government. Supported by the Ku Klux Klan and armed with a cannon, approximately three hundred white men attacked the estimated one hundred black men surrounding the courthouse. Most of the black men were killed on the spot, many after surrendering, or else were executed later that night. The courthouse was burned.

In the weeks and months that followed, several members of the paramilitary group were tracked down and charged with criminal violations under the US Enforcement Act of 1870. This act was passed by Congress to enforce the newly ratified Fourteenth and Fifteenth Amendments guaranteeing black citizens equal rights and protection under the law. The defendants appealed the convictions on the grounds that the Enforcement Act was unconstitutional, and the appeal was heard by the US Supreme Court.

Author Biography

Joseph P. Bradley was born on March 14, 1813, in Berne, New York. At age twenty, he relocated to New Jersey to study divinity at Rutgers University, but eventually he decided to pursue law instead. He became a member of the New Jersey bar in 1839 and established a reputable and lucrative practice in the fields of patent and railroad law in the city of Newark. He earned a solid reputation for his trial work within the federal court system, and when the Judiciary Act of 1869 created a vacancy on the US Supreme Court, he secured a nomination from President Ulysses S. Grant. Justice Bradley took his oath of office and assumed his seat on March 21, 1870.

From April 4, 1870, to January 9, 1881, Justice Bradley served as the circuit justice for the US Circuit Court for the Fifth Circuit. While there, he wrote the opinion for the District of Louisiana case *United States v. Cruikshank et al.*, which narrowly construed Congress's authority under the Fourteenth and Fifteenth Amendments to the Constitution and sent the case on to the Supreme Court for judgment. The Supreme Court's decision ultimately paved the way for white supremacist groups to control the post–Civil War South. Bradley also became infamous for his concurring opinion in *Bradwell v. Illinois*, a Supreme Court case that held that the right of a woman to practice law was not constitutionally protected under the privileges and immunities clause of the Fourteenth Amendment. In writing separate from the majority, who had relied upon states' rights grounds to justify the decision, Bradley declared that "the paramount destiny and mission of women are to fulfill the noble and benign offices of wife and mother. This is the law of the Creator."

Justice Bradley also served in the Sixth Circuit, which covered Ohio, Kentucky, and Tennessee, from May 2 until May 17, 1881, and the Third Circuit, covering New Jersey, Delaware, and Pennsylvania, from January 10, 1881, until early 1892. His service in both the Supreme Court and the Third Circuit ended with his death in Washington, DC, on January 22, 1892, most likely of tuberculosis. Bradley was buried at the Mount Pleasant Cemetery in Newark, New Jersey.

HISTORICAL DOCUMENT

The main ground of objection is that the act is municipal in its character, operating directly on the conduct of individuals, and taking the place of ordinary state legislation; and that there is no constitutional authority for such an act, inasmuch as the state laws furnish adequate remedy for the alleged wrongs committed.

It cannot, of course, be denied that express power is given to congress to enforce by appropriate legislation the 13th, 14th and 15th amendments of the constitution, but it is insisted that this act does not pursue the appropriate mode of doing this. A brief examination of its provisions is necessary more fully to understand the form in which the questions arise. The first section provides that all citizens of the United States, otherwise qualified, shall be allowed to vote at all elections in any state, county, city, township, etc., without distinction of race, color or previous condition of servitude, any constitution, law, custom or usage of any state or territory to the contrary notwithstanding. This is not quite the converse of the 15th amendment. That amendment does not establish the right of any citizens to vote; it merely declares that race, color or previous condition of servitude shall not exclude them. This is an important distinction, and has a decided bearing on the questions at issue. The second section requires that equal opportunity shall be given to all citizens, without distinction of race, color or previous condition of servitude, to perform any act required as a prerequisite or qualification for voting, and makes it a penal offense for officers and others to refuse or omit to give such equal opportunity. The third section makes the offer to perform such preparatory act, if not performed by reason of such wrongful act or omission of the officers or others, equivalent to performance; and makes it the duty of inspectors or judges of election, on affidavit of such offer being made, to receive the party's vote; and makes it a penal offense to refuse to do so. These three sections relate to the right secured by the 15th amendment. The fourth section makes it a penal offense for any person, by force, bribery, threats, etc., to hinder or prevent, or to conspire with others to hinder or prevent, any citizen from performing any preparatory act requisite to qualify him to vote, or from voting, at any election. This section does not seem to be based on the 15th amend-

ment, nor to relate to the specific right secured thereby. It extends far beyond the scope of the amendment, as will more fully appear hereafter. The fifth section makes it a penal offense for any person to prevent or attempt to prevent, hinder or intimidate any person from exercising the right of suffrage, to whom it is secured by the 15th amendment, by means of bribery, threats, or threats of depriving of occupation, or of ejecting from lands or tenements, or of refusing to renew a lease, or of violence to such person or his family. The sixth section, under which the first sixteen counts of the indictment are framed, contains two distinct clauses. The first declares that "if two or more persons shall band or conspire together, or go in disguise upon the public highway, or upon the premises of another with intent (to violate any provision of this act), such persons shall be held guilty of felony." Of course this would include conspiracy to prevent any person from voting, or from performing any preparatory act requisite thereto. The next clause has a larger scope. Repeating the introductory and concluding words, it is as follows: "If two or more persons shall band or conspire together, or go in disguise upon the public highway, or upon the premises of another with intent to injure, oppress, threaten, or intimidate any citizen, with intent to prevent or hinder his free exercise and enjoyment of any right or privilege granted or secured to him by the constitution or laws of the United States, or because of his having exercised the same, such persons shall be held guilty of felony." Here it is made penal to enter into a conspiracy to injure or intimidate any citizen, with intent to prevent or hinder his exercise and enjoyment, not merely of the right to vote, but of any right or privilege granted or secured to him by the constitution or laws of the United States.

The question is at once suggested, under what clause of the constitution does the power to enact such a law arise? It is undoubtedly a sound proposition, that whenever a right is guaranteed by the constitution of the United States, congress has the power to provide for its enforcement, either by implication arising from the correlative duty of government to protect, wherever a right to the citizen is conferred, or under the general power (contained in *article 1, § 8. par. 18*) "to make all laws necessary and proper for carrying into execution the foregoing powers, and all other powers vested by this constitution in the government of the United States, or any department or officer thereof." It was on the principle first stated that the fugitive slave law was sustained by the supreme court of the United States. *Prigg v. Pennsylvania, 16 Pet. [41 U. S.] 539.* The constitution guarantied the rendition of fugitives held to labor or service in any state, and it was held that congress had, by implication, the power to enforce the guaranty by legislation. "They require," says Justice Story, delivering the opinion of the majority of the court, "the aid of legislation to protect the right, to enforce the delivery, and to secure the subsequent possession of the slave. If, indeed, the constitution guaranties the right, and if it requires the delivery upon the claim of the owner (as cannot well be doubted), the natural inference certainly is, that the national government is clothed with the appropriate authority and functions to enforce it. The fundamental principle applicable to all cases of this sort would seem to be, that where the end is required, the means are given; and, where the duty is enjoined, the ability to perform it is contemplated to exist on the part of the functionaries to whom it is entrusted. The clause is found in the national constitution and not in that of any state. It does not point out any state functionaries, or any state action to carry its provisions into effect. The state, therefore, cannot be compelled to enforce them, etc. The natural if not the necessary conclusion is, that the national government, in the absence of all positive provisions to the contrary, is bound, through its own departments, legislative, judicial, or executive, as the case may require, to carry into effect all the rights and duties imposed upon it by the constitution." To the objection that the power did not fall within the scope of the enumerated powers of legislation confided to congress, Justice Story answers: "Stripped of its artificial and technical structure, the argument comes to this, that, although rights are exclusively secured by, or duties are exclusively imposed upon, the national government, yet, unless the power to enforce these rights or to execute these duties can be found among the express powers of legislation enumerated in the constitution, they remain without any means of giving them effect by any act of congress, and they must operate solely proprio vigore,

however defective may be their operation; nay, even although in a practical sense, they may become a nullity from the want of a proper remedy to enforce them, or to provide against their violation. If this be the true interpretation of the constitution, it must, in a great measure, fail to attain many of its avowed and positive objects as a security of rights and a recognition of duties. Such a limited construction of the constitution has never yet been adopted as correct, either in theory or practice." *[Prigg v. Pennsylvania] 16 Pet. [41 U. S.] 618. . . .*

Again, "the citizens of each state shall be entitled to all the privileges and immunities of citizens in the several states." But this does not authorize congress to pass a general system of municipal law for the security of person and property, to have effect in the several states for the protection of citizens of other states to whom the fundamental right is guarantied. It only authorizes appropriate and efficient remedies to be provided in case the guaranty is violated. Where affirmative legislation is required to give the citizen the right guarantied, congress may undoubtedly adopt it, as was done in the case of the fugitive slave law and as has been done in later times, to carry into full effect the 13th amendment of the constitution by the passage of the civil rights bill, as will be more fully noted hereafter. But with regard to mere constitutional prohibitions of state interference with established or acknowledged privileges and immunities, the appropriate legislation to enforce such prohibitions is that which may be necessary or proper for furnishing suitable redress when such prohibitions are disregarded or violated. Where no violation is attempted, the interference of congress would be officious, unnecessary, and inappropriate.

The bearing of these observations on the effect of the several recent amendments of the constitution, in conferring legislative powers upon congress, is next to be noticed. The 13th amendment declares that neither slavery nor involuntary servitude, except as a punishment for crime, shall exist within the United States or any place subject to its jurisdiction, and that congress shall have power to enforce this article by appropriate legislation. This is not merely a prohibition against the passage or enforcement of any law inflicting or establishing slavery or involuntary servitude, but it is a positive declaration that slavery shall not exist. It prohibits the thing. In the enforcement of this article, therefore, congress has to deal with the subject matter. If an amendment had been adopted that polygamy should not exist within the United States, and a similar power to enforce it had been given as in the case of slavery, congress would certainly have had the power to legislate for the suppression and punishment of polygamy. So, undoubtedly, by the 13th amendment congress has power to legislate for the entire eradication of slavery in the United States. This amendment had an affirmative operation the moment it was adopted. It enfranchised four millions of slaves, if, indeed, they had not previously been enfranchised by the operation of the Civil War. Congress, therefore, acquired the power not only to legislate for the eradication of slavery, but the power to give full effect to this bestowment of liberty on these millions of people. All this it essayed to do by the civil rights bill, passed April 9, 1866 [14 Stat. 27], by which it was declared that all persons born in the United States, and not subject to a foreign power (except Indians, not taxed), should be citizens of the United States; and that such citizens, of every race and color, without any regard to any previous condition of slavery or involuntary servitude, should have the same right in every state and territory to make and enforce contracts, to sue, be parties, and give evidence, to inherit, purchase, lease, sell, hold, and convey real and personal property, and to full and equal benefit of all laws and proceedings for the security of persons and property, as is enjoyed by white citizens, and should be subject to like punishment, pains and penalties, and to none other, any law, etc., to the contrary notwithstanding.

It was supposed that the eradication of slavery and involuntary servitude of every form and description required that the slave should be made a citizen and placed on an entire equality before the law with the white citizen, and, therefore, that congress had the power, under the amendment, to declare and effectuate these objects. The form of doing this, by extending the right of citizenship and equality before the law to persons of every race and color (except Indians not taxed and, of course, excepting the white race, whose privileges were adopted as the standard), although it embraced many persons, free colored people and others, who were already citizens in several of the states, was necessary for the purpose of settling a point which

had been raised by eminent authority, that none but the white race were entitled to the rights of citizenship in this country. As disability to be a citizen and enjoy equal rights was deemed one form or badge of servitude, it was supposed that congress had the power, under the amendment, to settle this point of doubt, and place the other races on the same plane of privilege as that occupied by the white race.

Conceding this to be true (which I think it is), congress then had the right to go further and to enforce its declaration by passing laws for the prosecution and punishment of those who should deprive, or attempt to deprive, any person of the rights thus conferred upon him. Without having this power, congress could not enforce the amendment. It cannot be doubted, therefore, that congress had the power to make it a penal offense to conspire to deprive a person of, or to hinder him in, the exercise and enjoyment of the rights and privileges conferred by the 13th amendment and the laws thus passed in pursuance thereof. But this power does not authorize congress to pass laws for the punishment of ordinary crimes and offenses against persons of the colored race or any other race. That belongs to the state government alone. All ordinary murders, robberies, assaults, thefts, and offenses whatsoever are cognizable only in the state courts, unless, indeed, the state should deny to the class of persons referred to the equal protection of the laws. Then, of course, congress could provide remedies for their security and protection. But, in ordinary cases, where the laws of the state are not obnoxious to the provisions of the amendment, the duty of congress in the creation and punishment of offenses is limited to those offenses which aim at the deprivation of the colored citizen's enjoyment and exercise of his rights of citizenship and of equal protection of the laws because of his race, color, or previous condition of servitude. To illustrate: If in a community or neighborhood composed principally of whites, a citizen of African descent, or of the Indian race, not within the exception of the amendment, should propose to lease and cultivate a farm, and a combination should be formed to expel him and prevent him from the accomplishment of his purpose on account of his race or color, it cannot be doubted that this would be a case within the power of congress to remedy and redress. It would be a case of interference with that person's exercise of his equal rights as a citizen because of his race. But if that person should be injured in his person or property by any wrongdoer for the mere felonious or wrongful purpose of malice, revenge, hatred, or gain, without any design to interfere with his rights of citizenship or equality before the laws, as being a person of a different race and color from the white race, it would be an ordinary crime, punishable by the state laws only. To constitute an offense, therefore, of which congress and the courts of the United States have a right to take cognizance under this amendment, there must be a design to injure a person, or deprive him of his equal right of enjoying the protection of the laws, by reason of his race, color, or previous condition of servitude. Otherwise it is a case exclusively within the jurisdiction of the state and its courts. . . .

The real difficulty in the present case is to determine whether the amendment has given to congress any power to legislate except to furnish redress in cases where the states violate the amendment. Considering, as before intimated, that the amendment, notwithstanding its negative form, substantially guaranties the equal right to vote to citizens of every race and color, I am inclined to the opinion that congress has the power to secure that right not only as against the unfriendly operation of state laws, but against outrage, violence, and combinations on the part of individuals, irrespective of the state laws. Such was the opinion of congress itself in passing the law at a time when many of its members were the same who had consulted upon the original form of the amendment in proposing it to the states. And as such a construction of the amendment is admissible, and the question is one at least of grave doubt, it would be assuming a great deal for this court to decide the law, to the extent indicated, unconstitutional. But the limitations which are prescribed by the amendment must not be lost sight of. It is not the right to vote which is guarantied to all citizens. Congress cannot interfere with the regulation of that right by the states except to prevent by appropriate legislation any distinction as to race, color, or previous condition of servitude. The state may establish any other conditions and discriminations it pleases, whether as to age, sex, property, education, or anything else. Congress, so far as the 15th amendment is concerned, is limited to the one subject of discrimination—on account of race,

color or previous condition of servitude. It can regulate as to nothing else. No interference with a person's right to vote, unless made on account of his race, color or previous condition of servitude, is subject to congressional animadversion. There may be a conspiracy to prevent persons from voting having no reference to this discrimination. It may include whites as well as blacks, or may be confined altogether to the latter. It may have reference to the particular politics of the parties. All such conspiracies are amenable to the state laws alone. To bring them within the scope of the amendment and of the powers of congress they must have for motive the race, color or previous condition of servitude of the party whose right is assailed.

According to my view the law on the subject may be generalized in the following proposition: The war of race, whether it assumes the dimensions of civil strife or domestic violence, whether carried on in a guerrilla or predatory form, or by private combinations, or even by private outrage or intimidation, is subject to the jurisdiction of the government of the United States; and when any atrocity is committed which may be assigned to this cause it may be punished by the laws and in the courts of the United States; but any outrages, atrocities, or conspiracies, whether against the colored race or the white race, which do not flow from this cause, but spring from the ordinary felonious or criminal intent which prompts to such unlawful acts, are not within the jurisdiction of the United States, but within the sole jurisdiction of the states, unless, indeed, the state, by its laws, denies to any particular race equality of rights, in which case the government of the United States may furnish remedy and redress to the fullest extent and in the most direct manner. Unless this distinction be made we are driven to one of two extremes—either that congress can never interfere where the state laws are unobjectionable, however remiss the state authorities may be in executing them, and however much a proscribed race may be oppressed; or that congress may pass an entire body of municipal law for the protection of person and property within the states, to operate concurrently with the state laws, for the protection and benefit of a particular class of the community. This fundamental principle, I think, applies to both the 13th and 15th amendments. . . .

GLOSSARY

amenable: answerable or liable to

animadversion: criticism

indictment: a formal charge filed against an individual for committing a crime

privileges and immunities: a collection of rights that US citizens possess that stem from the existence of a federal government

proprio vigore: by its own force

Document Analysis

The massacre at the Grant Parish courthouse in Colfax, Louisiana, took place on April 13, 1873. In the weeks and months that followed, several members of the white paramilitary group that organized the attack were tracked down and tried for murder and conspiracy to deprive black individuals of their constitutionally guaranteed equal protection under the law. Their conviction was based on legislation signed into law on May 31, 1870, entitled "An act to enforce the Rights of Citizens of the United States to vote in the several States of this Union, and for other Purposes," commonly referred to as the Enforcement Act of 1870. The purpose of this legislation was to enforce upon the states the newly established Fifteenth Amendment to the US Constitution, which states that US citizens cannot be denied the right to vote on the basis of their "race, color, or previous condition of servitude."

The Enforcement Act consists of twenty-three sections, the first three of which are directly related to the rights granted by the Fifteenth Amendment. Section 1 provides that all US citizens must be allowed to vote in any election regardless of race, color, or previous condition of servitude and regardless of any state or local law enacted to the contrary. Section 2 provides that if there are any prerequisites to being allowed to vote, such as owning property or completing registration papers, all citizens must have an equal opportunity to meet those prerequisites without regard to race, color, or previous condition of servitude. Section 3 extends this protection to situations where an individual offers or attempts to complete those prerequisites but is prevented from doing so; this means that a state cannot, for example, refuse to accept an individual's properly completed voting paperwork because of his color.

The next three sections address the behavior of private individuals rather than government actions. Section 4 makes it a criminal offense for any individual to use force, bribery, or threats to prevent any citizen from performing an act prerequisite to being able to vote. Section 5 further makes it a criminal offense to prevent or attempt to prevent a person from exercising his right to vote by threatening his job or home or by threatening violence against his family. Section 6 establishes a felony offense for involvement in a conspiracy to violate any of the provisions of the act or deprive a person of any of his constitutional rights by using threats, intimidation, or violence.

The defendants in *United States v. Cruikshank* were convicted under the sixth section of the Enforcement Act. They were not acting officially on behalf of the government to prevent the black freemen and militia members from exercising their constitutionally guaranteed rights, but instead had formed a paramilitary group to accomplish this privately. They were charged with both violating the rights of the black citizens occupying the courthouse and forming a conspiracy to deprive them of those rights. To appeal their convictions, the defendants challenged the constitutionality of this section of the Enforcement Act. They did not contest Congress's authority to prevent states and municipalities from disenfranchising black voters, as those provisions are permissible under the necessary and proper clause of the US Constitution (article 1, section 8), which grants Congress the authority to pass any law deemed "necessary and proper" to carry out its constitutional mandates. This would include passing laws to enforce the rights guaranteed by the newly ratified Thirteenth, Fourteenth, and Fifteenth Amendments. However, the defendants argued that Congress lacked the authority to regulate the behavior of individuals acting in a non-official capacity, and therefore their convictions should be overturned because this portion of the law is invalid.

In his opinion for the US Circuit Court for the District of Louisiana, Justice Bradley writes that when a citizen has rights that are secured by the Constitution "only by a declaration that the state or the United States shall not violate or abridge them," then these rights are "not created or conferred by the constitution"; instead, it is only guaranteed that those rights "shall not be impaired by the state, or the United States." And since section 1 of the Fifteenth Amendment states that "the right of citizens of the United States to vote shall not be denied or abridged by the United States or by any State on account of race, color, or previous condition of servitude," Congress only has the power to ensure that neither the state nor federal government prevents such individuals from voting, as it is "not a guaranty against the commission of individual offenses." Any regulation of individuals' actions must fall to the state governments, which are responsible for establishing appropriate legislation. Bradley further notes that the privileges and immunities clause of the Constitution, which states that "the Citizens of each State shall be entitled to all the Privileges and Immunities of Citizens in the several States," also does not authorize Congress to pass a general system of laws within each individual state, only to regulate the states themselves.

Bradley contrasts the Enforcement Act, which is at the heart of *United States v. Cruikshank*, with the Civil Rights Act, which was passed on April 9, 1866, and established, as he says, "that all persons born in the United States . . . should be citizens of the United States; and that such citizens, of every race and color, without any regard to any previous condition of slavery or involuntary servitude," should have the same rights in all US states and territories. This law was passed in response to the ratification of the Thirteenth Amendment to the Constitution, which states that "neither slavery nor involuntary servitude . . . shall exist within the United States, or any place subject to their jurisdiction," and it establishes criminal penalties for individuals who violate the provisions of the law. Bradley states that because this is an affirmative prohibition of the condition of slavery, the Civil Rights Act is an appropriate exercise of Congress's power to enforce this amendment.

By contrast, the Fifteenth Amendment states that "the right of citizens of the United States to vote shall not be denied or abridged by the United States or by any State on account of race, color, or previous condition of servitude." Bradley holds that the difference in language between these two amendments means that in the case of the Fifteenth Amendment, Congress only has the authority to prevent the states from denying its citizens of color the right to vote; it cannot exercise any power over the actions of private individuals. Additionally, he emphasizes that federal jurisdiction over violations of the Civil Rights Act only exists if the deprivation of rights is racially motivated. In other words, if a person is murdered because he is black, then federal laws would apply, but if a person is murdered and it is merely a coincidence that he is black, state laws would govern.

Bradley notes that the Fifteenth Amendment is in some ways an extension of the Civil Rights Act and "is to be interpreted on the same general principles." However, he elaborates that "the right conferred and guarantied is not an absolute, but a relative one." In particular, the Fifteenth Amendment "does not confer the right to vote" but rather grants "a right not to be excluded from voting." As such, that is "all the right that congress can enforce." According to Bradley, it is the "prerogative of the state laws" to confer the right to vote, and the Fifteenth Amendment can only prevent states from interfering with that right.

The decision in *United States v. Cruikshank* was not unexpected in light of a number of other Supreme Court decisions around the same time. In *Prigg v. Pennsylvania*, the Supreme Court upheld the federal Fugitive Slave Act, which mandated the return of any fugitive slave found in a free state, when the act was challenged by a Pennsylvania law providing protection to escaped slaves who had taken up residence in the state. Additionally, in a group of cases known collectively as the Slaughter-House Cases, the Supreme Court held that regulation of slaughterhouses was a state matter, not a federal one, even if there was an alleged violation of the Fourteenth Amendment's guarantee of equal protection under the law. The Supreme Court's decision in these cases established that the federal government would accept only limited involvement in enforcing the rights enshrined in the Thirteenth, Fourteenth, and Fifteenth Amendments. By later affirming the circuit court's decision in *United States v. Cruikshank*, the Supreme Court made it clear that it would likewise selectively determine when it would step in to enforce these rights and when it would leave that enforcement to the states.

Finally, in a section not reproduced above, Bradley addresses the specific counts of the defendants' convictions. The first count alleges that the defendants formed a conspiracy to interfere with the right of the black freemen and militia to peaceably assemble at the courthouse, in violation of the First Amendment to the Constitution. Bradley notes that the language of the First Amendment merely prevents Congress from making laws that interfere with this right but says nothing about Congress's authority to prevent private individuals from interfering with the rights of other individuals.

The second count contains a similar allegation of conspiracy to interfere with the right to bear arms. Bradley holds that this count suffers from the same problem as the first; namely, that the Second Amendment prohibits the government from interfering with an individual's right to bear arms but does not authorize Congress to prevent a private individual from doing the same to another individual.

The third count charges the defendants with forming a conspiracy to deprive a group of black citizens of their constitutionally guaranteed right to life and liberty without due process of the law. Bradley dismisses this count by reasoning that every murderer deprives his victim of the right to life, but this alone does not give the federal government the authority to make and enforce a law criminalizing murder in every state.

Bradley also dismisses the fourth, fifth, and eighth counts—which allege further deprivation of constitutional rights—by stating that such deprivation perpetrated by a private individual is only a federal offense if it is racially motivated, but the complaint does not explicitly allege racial motivation. He admits that the defendants' actions probably were racially motivated, and even describes the fourth count as alleging that defendants deprived "certain colored citizens of African descent, of the free exercise and enjoyment of the right and privilege to the full and equal benefit of all laws and proceedings for the security of persons and property which is enjoyed by the white citizens." However, he dismisses the count anyway, stating that the prosecution should have been more explicit in claiming racial motivation for the defendants' actions.

The sixth and seventh counts specifically reference deprivation of the right to vote guaranteed under the Fifteenth Amendment. Bradley dismisses these on the grounds that only the states, and not Congress, have

the authority to make these actions a crime, as described earlier in the opinion. The final eight counts are dismissed by stating that they "are literal copies, respectively, of the first eight, so far as relates to the language on which their validity depends."

Ultimately, *Cruikshank* has been criticized for its seemingly inconsistent treatment of the Thirteenth, Fourteenth, and Fifteenth Amendments. Bradley puts forth several arguments as to why the law under which Cruikshank and his fellow defendants were charged should be declared unconstitutional and attempts to justify this reasoning by citing prior precedents. However, those arguments often seem contradictory. The opinion specifically states that "the war of race . . . is subject to the jurisdiction of the government of the United States" regardless of who commits the crime and that "this fundamental principle . . . applies to both the 13th and 15th Amendment." Yet when dismissing the actual charges against the defendants, Bradley ignores the clear racial motivation behind the defendants' actions and declares that there is no federal jurisdiction because "Congress surely is not vested with power to legislate for the suppression and punishment of all murders, robberies, and assaults committed within the states." While both may be true statements, the conclusion only makes sense if one ignores the racial motivation for the underlying crime.

Essential Themes

The circuit court's decision in *United States v. Cruikshank* ultimately hinges on the notion that the right to vote is not granted by the US Constitution itself but is instead provided by the states. According to Bradley's interpretation, the federal government only has the authority to prevent the states from disenfranchising its black citizens; it is powerless to act against private individuals who seek to accomplish the same end. Bradley's attempts to explain why Congress was allowed to criminalize private behavior in the Civil Rights Act but not in the Enforcement Act were met with skepticism and continue to be debated many years later.

This case, and others like it, highlighted the growing racial tension in the United States as the Civil War ended and the Reconstruction efforts began. The Northern states of the Union refused to help rebuild the Confederate states if those states would not ratify the equal protection amendments to the US Constitution. But the establishment in the Southern states strongly resented the forced change to their way of life, and their citizens found other ways to disenfranchise black voters, including murder, violence, and intimidation.

The Supreme Court's decision to uphold Bradley's ruling in *United States v. Cruikshank* was heavily criticized for its failure to protect the rights the government had supposedly granted to newly freed black citizens in the Southern states. The Enforcement Act of 1870 prohibited states from taking any official actions to prevent black citizens from voting, but *United States v. Cruikshank* left it in the hands of the states themselves to protect black voters from aggression perpetrated by private individuals. The Southern states had no desire to pass or enforce laws protecting black voters, and the so-called right to vote enshrined in the Fifteenth Amendment was one that could not be exercised without fearing for one's life and safety.

Ultimately, the Supreme Court's decision had the effect of encouraging the growth of paramilitary white supremacy groups in the South. Organizations such as the Ku Klux Klan knew that the states themselves would never charge them for violating a black man's rights and, in the wake of *United States v. Cruikshank*, they also knew that the federal government would not intervene on behalf of the states' black citizens. The Supreme Court reversed some parts of the decision in later years, but the impact on the Reconstruction efforts was enormous, and the status of black citizens in the Southern states was severely harmed by the federal government's refusal to intervene in racially motivated deprivations of rights.

Tracey DiLascio, JD

Bibliography

Goldstone, Lawrence. *Inherently Unequal: The Betrayal of Equal Rights by the Supreme Court, 1865–1903.* New York: Walker, 2011. Print.

Keith, LeeAnna. *The Colfax Massacre: The Untold Story of Black Power, White Terror, and the Death of Reconstruction.* New York: Oxford UP, 2008. Print.

Lane, Charles. *The Day Freedom Died: The Colfax Massacre, the Supreme Court, and the Betrayal of Reconstruction.* New York: Holt, 2008. Print.

Stuntz, William J. *The Collapse of American Criminal Justice.* Cambridge: Belknap P of Harvard UP, 2012. Print.

Additional Reading

Curtis, Michael Kent. *No State Shall Abridge: The Fourteenth Amendment and the Bill of Rights.* Durham: Duke UP, 1986. Print.

Hoffer, Williamjames Hull. *Plessy v. Ferguson: Race and Inequality in Jim Crow America.* Lawrence: UP of Kansas, 2012. Print

■ Exchange of Letters Between Horace Greeley and Abraham Lincoln

Date: August 19, 1862; August 22, 1862
Author: Greeley, Horace; Lincoln, Abraham
Genre: letter

> *"It seems to us the most obvious truth, that whatever strengthens or fortifies Slavery in the Border States strengthens also Treason, and drives home the wedge intended to divide the Union."*
>
> — Horace Greeley

> *"If I could save the Union without freeing any slave I would do it, and if I could save it by freeing all the slaves I would do it; and if I could save it by freeing some and leaving others alone I would also do that."*
>
> — Abraham Lincoln

Summary Overview

Conditions were less than ideal for President Abraham Lincoln in the late summer of 1862. The Union army was not having great success putting down the Southern rebellion, and the mood of the Northern people was quickly growing sour. Lincoln knew that one of the reasons for his election as president was his anti-slavery perspective, but he did not intend for his stance on abolishing slavery to destroy the Union itself. New York Tribune editor

Horace Greeley criticized Lincoln for not waging an abolitionist war through his open letter titled "The Prayer of Twenty Millions," Lincoln responded with a letter of his own, highlighting his priority for preserving the Union over his benevolent mission to free slaves.

The exchange between Lincoln and Greeley unfolded directly before the public. For the Americans who elected Lincoln, this public discussion was of utmost importance. Northerners were acutely aware of this correspondence, as Greeley had chosen the avenue of a New York-based newspaper editorial to voice his complaint with the president's policy on war and slavery. President Lincoln seemed unclear in terms of his personal feelings about slavery. Republicans grew weary waiting for Lincoln to take action against slavery, while Democrats and border state supporters of slavery hoped he never would. One month after Greeley's letter, following the "bloodiest single day" of the Civil War at the Battle of Antietam, Lincoln began his work penning the "Emancipation Proclamation." Although the letter to Greeley was a timely response to public criticism, Lincoln's goal for emancipating Southern slaves eventually came to fruition.

Defining Moment

The pressure that Greeley put on Lincoln accented what seemed to be an incongruity in Lincoln's policy toward Southern slaves. While he won the election on the premise of emancipation by way of the Republican Party, Lincoln, thought Greeley, must go beyond existing antislavery laws, including the First Confiscation Act; Lincoln had actually supported and enforced these laws. Lincoln had to make a decision whether to defend himself at length against Greeley's attack or to completely ignore the accusations of negligence.

This was a defining moment for Lincoln's presidency and his management of the war. Although still relatively early in the narrative of the Civil War, the late summer of 1862 was a high time for the Confederate army. General Robert E. Lee's Army of Northern Virginia formulated plans to move north into the border state of Maryland. At the same time that the hot rhetoric of suppressing the rebellion took place in the New York press, soldiers prepared for fighting near Antietam Creek. Lincoln, filling the roles of both consummate politician and commander-in-chief, found it necessary to evaluate and react to both situations.

Author Biography

President Abraham Lincoln remains one of history's most written-about subjects, with countless interpretations and reinterpretations of his life. He was 28 years old when he moved to Springfield, Illinois and had already served two terms in the legislature. His childhood exploits as a rail-splitter are literally the material of legend. He became a self-taught attorney and rose through the ranks of Illinois society, eventually making a foray into state politics. He served several terms as a Whig representative in the Illinois Legislature. Yet, the aspect of Lincoln's biography that is most important to the circumstance of the exchange with Horace Greeley is his political background.

While Lincoln's reputation solidly defined him as an "emancipation" advocate, it was his promotion of free labor ideology that made him particularly popular in the then "west." Free labor ideology held fast to the Jeffersonian agrarian ideal that when a man owns his personal land he can be a more virtuous citizen. This stood firmly in opposition to the slave labor ideology of the American South up to and during the Civil War. Lincoln's stance as a Whig, largely favoring domestic and internal improvements, put his personal politics in a popular position among his fellow westerners. Lincoln's debates with Stephen Douglas, the bastion of "popular sovereignty," were well-known and very public. By the time Lincoln won the 1860 presidential election he was no longer serving as a Whig, but rather as an exemplar of the emerging Republican Party, whose platform had merged the old line Whigs with a renewed emphasis from the abolitionist camp. Combining a desire for internal infrastructure and an end to insidious, costly slave labor propelled the Republican Party to national prominence with President Lincoln.

As President, Lincoln disappointed many in his first year on the job, including Horace Greeley. Where Lincoln's vision for the war always considered the possibility of reconciliation and reunion, many others wanted a harsh and immediate response to the southern Confederacy. This tension around Lincoln's approach to the issue of emancipation and managing the nation became an issue of national prominence through his correspondence with Greeley.

Horace Greeley was the editor of the *New York Tribune*, an influential national newspaper. His open letter to Lincoln was an intentionally inflammatory commentary geared toward the president's policy on the subject of slavery. Greeley called into question the role of the president regarding the emancipation of slaves in the United States. Greeley's politics, as evidenced in the letter and elsewhere, were far from apologetic in their support of the Republican Party and immediate emancipation of the slaves. Because of his political persuasion, Lincoln's public position on slavery seemed weak. The incendiary remarks from the editorial provoked a response from the president, revealing both Greeley's political clout and Lincoln's concern for setting the re-

HISTORICAL DOCUMENT

To ABRAHAM LINCOLN,
President of the United States

DEAR SIR: I do not intrude to tell you—for you must know already—that a great proportion of those who triumphed in you election, and of all who desire the unqualified suppression of the Rebellion now desolating our country, are sorely disappointed and deeply pained by the policy you seem to be pursuing with regard to the slaves of the Rebels. I write only to set succinctly and unmistakably before you what we require, what we think we have a right to expect, and of what we complain.

I. We require of you, as the first servant of the Republic, charged especially and preeminently with this duty, that you EXECUTE THE LAWS. Most emphatically do we demand that such laws as have been recently enacted, which therefore may fairly be presumed to embody the present will and to be dictated by the present needs of the Republic, and which, after due consideration have received your personal sanction, shall by you be carried into full effect, and that you publicly and decisively instruct your subordinates that such laws exist, that they are binding on all functionaries and citizens, and that they are to be obeyed to the letter.

II. We think you are strangely and disastrously remiss in the discharge of your official and imperative duty with regard to the emancipating provisions of the new Confiscation Act. Those provisions were designed to fight Slavery with Liberty. They prescribe that men loyal to the Union, and willing to shed their blood in her behalf, shall no longer be held, with the Nations consent, in bondage to persistent, malignant traitors, who for twenty years have been plotting and for sixteen months have been fighting to divide and destroy our country. Why these traitors should be treated with tenderness by you, to the prejudice of the dearest rights of loyal men, we cannot conceive.

III. We think you are unduly influenced by the counsels, the representations, the menaces, of certain fossil politicians hailing from the Border Slave States. Knowing well that the heartily, unconditionally loyal portion of the White citizens of those States do not expect nor desire that Slavery shall be upheld to the prejudice of the Union—(for the truth of which we appeal not only to every Republican residing in those States, but to such eminent loyalists as H. Winter Davis, Parson Brownlow, the Union Central Committee of Baltimore, and to The Nashville Union)—we ask you to consider that Slavery is everywhere the inciting cause and sustaining base of treason: the most slaveholding sections of Maryland and Delaware being this day, though under the Union flag, in full sympathy with the Rebellion, while the Free-Labor portions of Tennessee and of Texas, though writhing under the bloody heel of Treason, are unconquerably loyal to the Union. So emphatically is this the case, that a most intelligent Union banker of Baltimore recently avowed his confident belief that a majority of the present Legislature of Maryland, though elected as and still professing to be Unionists, are at heart desirous of the triumph of the Jeff. Davis conspiracy; and when asked how they could be won back to loyalty, replied "only by the complete Abolition of Slavery." It seems to us the most obvious truth, that whatever strengthens or fortifies Slavery in the Border States strengthens also Treason, and drives home the wedge intended to divide the Union. Had you from the first refused to recognize in those States, as here, any other than unconditional loyalty—that which stands for the Union, whatever may become of Slavery, those States would have been, and would be, far more helpful and less troublesome to the defenders of the Union than they have been, or now are.

IV. We think timid counsels in such a crisis calculated to prove perilous, and probably disastrous. It is the duty of a Government so wantonly, wickedly assailed by Rebellion as ours has been to oppose force to force in a defiant, dauntless spirit. It cannot afford to temporize with traitors nor with semi-traitors. It must not bribe them to behave themselves, nor make cheat fair promises in the hope of disarming their causeless hostility. Representing a brave and high-spirited people, it can afford to forfeit anything else better than its own self-respect, or their admiring confidence. For our Government even to seek, after war has been made on it, to dispel the affected apprehensions of armed traitors that their cherished privileges may be assailed by it, is to invite insult and encourage hopes of its own downfall. The rush to arms of Ohio, Indiana, Illinois, is the true answer at once to the Rebel raids of John Morgan and the traitorous sophistries of Beriah Magoffin.

V. We complain that the Union cause has suffered, and is now suffering immensely, from mistaken deference to Rebel Slavery. Had you, Sir, in your Inaugural Address, unmistakably given notice that, in case the Rebellion already commenced were persisted in, and your efforts to preserve the Union and enforce the laws should be resisted by armed force, you would recognize no loyal person as rightfully held in Slavery by a traitor, we believe the Rebellion would therein have received a staggering if not fatal blow. At that moment, according to the returns of the most recent elections, the Unionists were a large majority of the voters of the Slave States. But they were composed in good part of the aged, the feeble, the wealthy, the timid--the young, the reckless, the aspiring, the adventurous, had already been largely lured by the gamblers and negro-traders, the politicians by trade and the conspirators by instinct, into the toils of Treason. Had you then proclaimed that Rebellion would strike the shackles from the slaves of every traitor, the wealthy and the cautious would have been supplied with a powerful inducement to remain loyal. As it was, every coward in the South soon became a traitor from fear; for Loyalty was perilous, while Treason seemed comparatively safe. Hence the boasted unanimity of the South—a unanimity based on Rebel terrorism and the fact that immunity and safety were found on that side, danger and probable death on ours. The Rebels from the first have been eager to confiscate, imprison, scourge and kill: we have fought wolves with the devices of sheep. The result is just what might have been expected. Tens of thousands are fighting in the Rebel ranks to-day whose, original bias and natural leanings would have led them into ours.

VI. We complain that the Confiscation Act which you approved is habitually disregarded by your Generals, and that no word of rebuke for them from you has yet reached the public ear. Fremont's Proclamation and Hunter's Order favoring Emancipation were promptly annulled by you; while Halleck's No. 3, forbidding fugitives from Slavery to Rebels to come within his lines--an order as unmilitary as inhuman, and which received the hearty approbation of every traitor in America--with scores of like tendency, have never provoked even your own remonstrance. We complain that the officers of your Armies have habitually repelled rather than invited approach of slaves who would have gladly taken the risks of escaping from their Rebel masters to our camps, bringing intelligence often of inestimable value to the Union cause. We complain that those who have thus escaped to us, avowing a willingness to do for us whatever might be required, have been brutally and madly repulsed, and often surrendered to be scourged, maimed and tortured by the ruffian traitors, who pretend to own them. We complain that a large proportion of our regular Army Officers, with many of the Volunteers, evince far more solicitude to uphold Slavery than to put down the Rebellion. And finally, we complain that you, Mr. President, elected as a Republican, knowing well what an abomination Slavery is, and how emphatically it is the core and essence of this atrocious Rebellion, seem never to interfere with these atrocities, and never give a direction to your Military subordinates, which does not appear to have been conceived in the interest of Slavery rather than of Freedom.

VII. Let me call your attention to the recent tragedy in New Orleans, whereof the facts are obtained entirely through Pro-Slavery channels. A considerable body of resolute, able-bodied men, held in Slavery by two Rebel sugar-planters in defiance of the Confiscation Act which you have approved, left plantations thirty miles distant and made their way to the great mart of the South-West, which they knew to be the indisputed possession of the Union forces. They made their way safely and quietly through thirty miles of Rebel territory, expecting to find freedom under the protection of our flag. Whether they had or had not heard of the passage of the Confiscation Act, they reasoned logically that we could not kill them for deserting the service of their lifelong oppressors, who had through treason become our implacable enemies. They came to us for liberty and protection, for which they were willing to render their best service: they met with hostility, captivity, and murder. The barking of the base curse of Slavery in this quarter deceives no one—not even themselves. They say, indeed, that the negroes had no right to appear in New Orleans armed (with their implements of daily labor in the cane-field); but no one doubts that they would gladly have laid these down if assured that they should be free. They were set upon and maimed, captured and killed, because they sought the benefit of that act of Congress which they may not specifically have heard of, but which was none the less the law of the land which they had a clear right to the benefit of—which it was somebody's duty to publish far and wide, in order that so many as possible should be impelled to desist from serving Rebels and the Rebellion and come over to the side of the Union, They sought their liberty in strict accordance with the law of the land—they were butchered or re-enslaved for so doing by the help of Union soldiers enlisted to fight against slaveholding Treason. It was somebody's fault that they were so murdered—if others shall hereafter stuffer in like manner, in default of explicit and public directions to your generals that they are to recognize and obey the Confiscation Act, the world will lay the blame on you. Whether you will choose to hear it through future History and 'at the bar of God, I will not judge. I can only hope.

VIII. On the face of this wide earth, Mr. President, there is not one disinterested, determined, intelligent champion of the Union cause who does not feel that all attempts to put down the Rebellion and at the same time uphold its inciting cause are preposterous and futile—that the Rebellion, if crushed out tomorrow, would be renewed within a year if Slavery were left in full vigor—that Army officers who remain to this day devoted to Slavery can at best be but half-way loyal to the Union—and that every hour of deference to Slavery is an hour of added and deepened peril to the Union, I appeal to the testimony of your Ambassadors in Europe. It is freely at your service, not at mine. Ask them to tell you candidly whether the seeming subserviency of your policy to the slaveholding, slavery-upholding interest, is not the perplexity, the despair of statesmen of all parties, and be admonished by the general answer.

IX. I close as I began with the statement that what an immense majority of the Loyal Millions of your coun-trymen require of you is a frank, declared, unqualified, ungrudging execution of the laws of the land, more especially of the Confiscation Act. That Act gives freedom to the slaves of Rebels coming within our lines, or whom those lines may at any time inclose—we ask you to render it due obedience by publicly requiring all your subordinates to recognize and obey it. The rebels are everywhere using the late anti-negro riots in the North, as they have long used your officers' treatment of negroes in the South, to convince the slaves that they have nothing to hope from a Union success-that we mean in that case to sell them into a bitter bondage to defray the cost of war. Let them impress this as a truth on the great mass of their ignorant and credulous bondsmen, and the Union will never be restored-never. We cannot conquer Ten Millions of People united in solid phalanx against us, powerfully aided by the Northern sympathizers and European allies. We must have scouts, guides, spies, cooks, teamsters, diggers and choppers from the Blacks of the South, whether we allow them to fight for us or not, or we shall be baffled and repelled. As one of the millions who would gladly have avoided this struggle at any sacrifice but that Principle and Honor, but who now feel that the triumph of the Union is dispensable not only to the existence of our country to the well being of mankind, I entreat you to render a hearty and unequivocal obedience to the law of the land.

Yours,

Horace Greeley
New York, August 19, 1862

✳ ✳ ✳

Hon. Horace Greeley:

DEAR SIR: I have just read yours of the 19th, addressed to myself through the New-York Tribune. If there be in it any statements or assumptions of fact which I may know to be erroneous, I do not now and here controvert them. If there be in it any inferences which I may believe to be falsely drawn, I do not now and here argue against them. If there be perceptible in it an impatient and dictatorial tone, I waive it in deference to an old friend, whose heart

I have always supposed to be right. As to the policy I "seem to be pursuing," as you say, I have not meant to leave any one in doubt.

I would save the Union. I would save it the shortest way under the Constitution. The sooner the national authority can be restored the nearer the Union will be "the Union as it was." If there be those who would not save the Union unless they could at the same time save Slavery, I do not agree with them. If there be those who would not save the Union unless they could at the same time destroy Slavery, I do not agree with them. My paramount object in this struggle is to save the Union, and is not either to save or destroy Slavery. If I could save the Union without freeing any slave, I would do it, and if I could save it by freeing all the slaves, I would do it, and if I could save it by freeing some and leaving others alone, I would also do that. What I do about Slavery and the colored race, I do because I believe it helps to save this Union, and what I forbear, I forbear because I do not believe it would help to save the Union. I shall do less whenever I shall believe what I am doing hurts the cause, and I shall do more whenever I shall believe doing more will help the cause. I shall try to correct errors when shown to be errors; and I shall adopt new views so fast as they shall appear to be true views. I have here stated my purpose according to my view of official duty, and I intend no modification of my oft-expressed personal wish that all men, everywhere, could be free.

Yours,

A. LINCOLN.

GLOSSARY

malignant traitors: Southerners who stood violently in opposition to the Union, secessionists

border slave states: states that bordered the Confederacy were contested throughout the war, often locations of political unrest and guerilla fighting; they included Missouri, Kentucky, West Virginia, Maryland, and Delaware

paramount: primary

"The Union as It Was": anti-war slogan that emphasized a return to political life before the Civil War began, popular among pro-Union Democrats

official duty: responsibilities as President of the United States

Document Analysis

Horace Greeley's editorial and President Lincoln's letter in response were two elements of one public conversation rather than two separate documents. Both wrote with an intentional focus on making political statements as well as expressing personal visions for American society. Greeley sought to provoke a public response from President Lincoln. The president, on the other hand, replied in a way that would placate the most radical abolitionists without upsetting the people of the Union who did not agree with the Republican Party's rather progressive stance on abolishing slavery. In short, Greeley forced Lincoln into a precarious political position, which the president then used to generate one of the most quoted (and misinterpreted) passages of his tenure in office.

Horace Greeley's literary style in his editorial followed the conventions of nineteenth-century press commentary. He wrote with a perspective that was clear from beginning to end, focusing on the unsuccessful job of the president. In his rhetoric, Greeley accented what he perceived to be several injustices regarding the slaves in the nation as well as the traitors in the South. He wanted Lincoln to approach the rebellion with vigor; there should be no question, he argued, that Southerners were traitors and should be treated as such. Lincoln's political acumen, however contested, considered the possibility of reconciliation from the very beginning of the conflict. The President carefully considered the ramifications of his actions against slavery because he had a persistent eye toward potential postwar reconciliation. Lincoln's political awareness prevented him from following into the kind of vitriolic political gamesmanship that made the 1850s so terribly divisive.

Greeley criticized Lincoln primarily on three counts. First, he wanted Lincoln to be more actively abolitionist in the pursuit of the war. Second, he expressed a desire for Southerners to be treated as traitors. Third, Greeley hoped Lincoln would allow African Americans to help in the prosecution of the war, if not as soldiers then at least in other ways. These collective ideas were a direct affront to Lincoln's approach to the war overall. Lincoln, staid statesman that he was, had to respond with control and restraint while carefully addressing these concerns, which were certainly on the minds of more than just Horace Greeley.

Lincoln's letter in reply became famous primarily because of its openness to interpretation. Many have taken the document out of context, particularly the most famous line. Lincoln writes, "If I could save the Union without freeing any slave I would do it, and if I could save it by freeing all slaves I would do it; and if I could save it by freeing some and leaving others alone I would also do that." This initial comment seems as though Lincoln cares little for the freedom of slaves, which seems to go directly against his stance as a Republican. What Lincoln expressed in this document was his forthright intention to save the Union first and foremost. He did not want a fight for the emancipation of slaves to ultimately destroy the Union, which would defeat the purpose in the first place. However, he punctuated his letter with the heartfelt comment, even crafting it with the modifier "oft-expressed" that all men "could be free." Free labor ideology, as Lincoln and others attested, was not fundamentally about race or class, but about all men having equal access to the work of his own hands. The emancipation of African Americans served that eventual end of the freedom of all people.

The tension in this exchange was most evident between Greeley's idealism and Lincoln's pragmatism. Horace Greeley had an admittedly different role as a newspaper editor than as the president, but he still put forth an unrealistic ideal in his perspective on the issue of slavery. Greeley's comments cut deeply into Lincoln's strategy of preserving the Union over emancipating slaves. Greeley obviously hoped that emancipation would happen more quickly than it did, however, Lincoln's desire to preserve the nation trumped his desire to free slaves. Therefore, Greeley's idealistic perspective clouded his vision for the larger mission of the war overall as Lincoln perceived it. Greeley harped on the singular perspective of the necessity of making the war about freeing slaves and finishing the job. He posited that to leave slavery unresolved would spark another war "within a year" if it were left "in full vigor." He finished his letter with a powerful indictment on both the president and his political party, "We cannot conquer Ten Millions of People united in solid phalanx against us, powerfully aided by the Northern sympathizers and European allies. We must have scouts, guides, spies, cooks, teamsters, diggers and choppers from the Blacks of the South, whether we allow them to fight for us or not, or we shall be baffled and repelled." These comments highlighted the necessity of black labor for Union victory and sound almost prophetic given the actual historical evidence of black service in the war. Nevertheless, this idealistic vision was not something that Lincoln could then indulge the nation. It took a few more months of turmoil and the formal Emancipation Proclamation to put the president in a position to take such a drastic and important step to arm the freedmen for battle.

Lincoln's plan for emancipation was not concrete, but as of his reply to Greeley he still hoped to be able to accomplish it peacefully. He did not intend to instigate the war, but it emerged based on his election. By the time Lincoln took office, rebels already occupied several forts throughout the American South. The standoff at Fort Sumter was merely the fruition of policies and actions that had taken place for many months prior. Lincoln's plan was fundamentally pragmatic, and initially he attempted to hold the Union together. He wanted to preserve the Union first and foremost so that there would be a free country for the freedmen to occupy. If he followed Greeley's haughty and idealistic advice, he would have been left with a nation completely destroyed from the inside out. His decision to focus on winning the war seemed reductionist in Greeley's eyes, but was the perfect solution for Lincoln. He did not want to alienate the pro-slavery advocates in the Border States because doing so would potentially ruin his chances for winning the war.

Not only did Lincoln and Greeley have different jobs, but they also had different purposes for writing their letters. It was evident immediately in the writing style and length of both documents. Greeley wrote to sell papers and drum up political support for his cause. Lincoln wrote to respond, respectfully and succinctly to Greeley's criticism. Greeley's exhaustive argument was standard for nineteenth-century newspapers, spending several paragraphs developing an argument to make his readers fill with frustration toward the president. Lincoln, on the other hand, merely defended his own well-founded actions to prosecute and win the war. He did not develop his argument at length, rather briefly explained his longstanding position on the institution of slavery and his justification for conducting the war as he saw fit in the immediate circumstance. His writing was clear, concise, and to the point. This short passage was often debated in the years since its penning, with many wondering about Lincoln's dedication to emancipation and commitment to black Americans.

Essential Themes

The discussion about emancipation in the mid-nineteenth century remained contested well into the post–Civil War era. The discussions that defined the Reconstruction Amendments were just as controversial as these between Lincoln and Greeley. What existed in the Lincoln-Greeley exchange was truly a conversation of agreement that differed on the condition of form and expediency. Greeley misunderstood the necessity of Lincoln's plan to attempt to preserve the Union. Likewise, Lincoln could ill afford to heed to the will of a newspaper editor. Both declared their message and plans, while traveling in the same trajectory merely at different speeds.

Liberation for slaves in the rebellious Southern states came in the form of the Emancipation Proclamation in 1863, but those in the valuable and contested Border States waited until the 13th Amendment in 1865. Nevertheless, the fruit of the Lincoln-Greeley exchange was important in forming the final resolution of the Civil War. It was President Lincoln's controversial comments in his reply to Greeley that influenced many conversations among historians to define Lincoln's legacy. The uncertainty of Lincoln's commitment to end slavery was difficult for African Americans to comprehend, but nevertheless his eventual actions toward emancipation, whether as a war aim or as a gesture of benevolence, cemented his legacy as The Great Emancipator for generations of Americans and scholars. Recently historians have utilized this correspondence with Greeley as a context for reevaluating Lincoln, but it was his practical angle in attempting to save the Union that defined his comments here.

Lincoln had already decided to issue an emancipation proclamation when he wrote this letter, and was waiting for a Union victory to give it impetus and credibility: his letter was intended to prepare the public for that proclamation, by stating that what he did about slavery—which would turn out to be freeing some and leaving others alone, in the proclamation, he did because it would help preserve the Union. He knew that this cause united the Northern people, while emancipation divided them—hence his assertion that what he did about slavery, was done in the cause of Union.

Gregory Jones

Bibliography

Donald, David Herbert. *Lincoln.* New York: Simon and Schuster, 1996. Print.

Foner, Eric. *Free Soil, Free Labor, Free Men: The Ideology of the Republican Party before the Civil War.* Oxford UP, 1999. Print.

Foner, Eric. *The Fiery Trial: Abraham Lincoln and American Slavery.* New York: Norton , 2011. Print.

Additional Reading

Douglas, Stephen A. and Abraham Lincoln. *The Lincoln-Douglas Debates.* New York: Dover , 2004. Print.

Goodwin, Doris Kearns. *Team of Rivals: The Political Genius of Abraham Lincoln.*

New York: Simon and Schuster, 2006. Print.

Guelzo, Allen C. *Lincoln and Douglas: The Debates that Defined America.* New York: Simon and Schuster, 2008. Print.

Snay, Mitchell. *Horace Greeley and the Politics of Reform in Nineteenth-Century America.* Lanham: Rowan and Littlefield, 2011. Print.

■ "Men of Color, To Arms!"

Date: March 21, 1863
Author: Douglass, Frederick
Genre: broadside

> *"Remember that in a contest with oppression, the Almighty has no attribute which can take sides with oppressors. The case is before you. This is our golden opportunity. Let us accept it, and forever wipe out the dark reproaches unsparingly hurled against us by our enemies."*

Summary Overview

The central issue in the American Civil War was the states' right to determine the fate of slavery in both the existing states as well as the territory of expansion. In that heated and eventually violent discussion, several key voices emerged, including that of the self-educated escaped slave turned free man Frederick Douglass. His story, chronicled in his famous personal narrative, was evidence for abolitionists against the virulent racism that permeated both Northern and Southern consciousnesses. Douglass became a voice for African American men throughout the free and slave states, representing the articulation of black manhood and civilization.

Douglass worked from the start of the war to persuade white administrators and commanders to allow black soldiers to serve in the Union army. For many months these men were denied their opportunity to fight in a war that was deciding their fate. Douglass continued working with intellectuals like Thomas Wentworth Higginson and Anna Elizabeth Dickinson to persuade influential Republican politicians, who were the most sympathetic to the abolitionist crusade, to allow black men to fight for their country. Douglass and others articulated that it was indeed the point of black service to earn full citizenship for African Americans.

Beyond emancipation, they fought for equal rights under the American Constitution.

Defining Moment

The "Call to Arms" presented by Douglass was a mechanism for rallying African American men, particularly free blacks in the North, to join the Union army. After two years of unsuccessful fighting across the South, especially in Virginia, the Union army needed support to continue the war. The Union high command had several commanders including General Irvin McDowell and General Ambrose Burnside, but there were none that had yet found permanence in the overall command. Despite the strategic stalemate at the Battle of Antietam in the fall of 1862, there were few significant victories for the federal army. The passing of the Emancipation Proclamation in January of 1863 effectively freed the slaves living in the rebellious states. By doing so, all invading Union armies received droves of slave men attempting to join the ranks.

Additionally, the influx of new soldiers for the Union army proved to be beneficial to the Union cause. Estimates vary, but most historians agree that nearly 200,000 black men fought for the Union military, effectively supporting the Northern effort to win the war against slavery and to preserve the Union. Those soldiers fought with distinction at numerous battles, including Wilson's Wharf, the fight for Battery Wagner, and the Battle of the Crater in Petersburg, Virginia among others.

Author Biography

Frederick Douglass was born a slave but became a free man by escaping bondage. His *Narrative of the Life of Frederick Douglass* is one of the most important books in the nineteenth century. In that text, Douglass explains not only his process of becoming a free man, but also in fighting for his own education. Literacy, for Douglass, was the key to his success. While he did not have citizenship, literacy helped him communicate with others who could help him personally as well as his role as an intellectual in nineteenth-century American life. It was his desire to reflect egalitarian humanism, the belief in equality for all human beings regardless of race or sex, wherever possible.

Douglass was the most qualified person to make the call to arms for black troops. Although too old to fight himself, and better connected to the political realm, besides, Douglass presented the argument for why black men should fight for the Union army to defeat their former masters and push to define black citizenship in the United States. Douglass's tacit support for black soldiers helped to persuade influential politicians to involve African American soldiers in the fight.

HISTORICAL DOCUMENT

When first the rebel cannon shattered the walls of Sumter and drove away its starving garrison, I predicted that the war then and there inaugurated would not be fought out entirely by white men. Every month's experience during these dreary years has confirmed that opinion. A war undertaken and brazenly carried on for the perpetual enslavement of colored men, calls logically and loudly for colored men to help suppress it. Only a moderate share of sagacity was needed to see that the arm of the slave was the best defense against the arm of the slaveholder. Hence with every reverse to the national arms, with every exulting shout of victory raised by the slaveholding rebels, I have implored the imperiled nation to unchain against her foes, her powerful black hand. Slowly and reluctantly that appeal is beginning to be heeded. Stop not now to complain that it was not heeded sooner. It may or it may not have been best that it should not. This is not the time to discuss that question. Leave it to the future. When the war is over, the country is saved, peace is established, and the black man's rights are secured, as they will be, history with an impartial hand will dispose of that and sundry other questions. Action! Action! not criticism, is the plain duty of this hour. Words are now useful only as they stimulate to blows. The office of speech now is only to point out when, where, and how to strike to the best advantage. There is no time to delay. The tide is at its flood that leads on to fortune. From East to West, from North to South, the sky is written all over, "Now or never." Liberty won by white men would lose half its luster. "Who would be free themselves must strike the blow." "Better even die free, than to live slaves." This is the sentiment of every brave colored man amongst us. There are weak and cowardly men in all nations. We have them amongst us. They tell you this is the "white man's war"; that you will be "no better off after than before the war"; that the getting of you into the army is to "sacrifice you on the first opportunity." Believe them not; cowards themselves, they do not wish to have their cowardice shamed by your brave example. Leave them to their timidity, or to whatever motive may hold them back. I have not thought lightly of the words I am now addressing you. The counsel I give comes of close observation of the great struggle now in progress, and of the deep conviction that this is your hour and mine. In good earnest then, and after the best deliberation, I now for the first time during this war feel at liberty to call and counsel you to arms. By every consideration which binds you to your enslaved fellow-countrymen, and the peace and welfare of your country; by every aspiration which you cherish for the freedom and equality of yourselves and your children; by all the ties of blood and idetity which make us one with the brave black men now fighting our battles in Louisiana and in South Carolina, I urge you to fly to arms, and smite with death the power that would bury the government and your liberty in the same hopeless grave. I wish I could tell you that the State of New York calls you to this high honor. For the moment her constituted authorities are silent on the subject. They will speak by and by, and doubtless on the right side; but we are not compelled to wait for her. We can get at the throat of treason and slavery through the State of Massachusetts. She was first in the War of Independence; first to break the chains of her slaves; first to make the black man equal before the law; first to admit colored children to her common schools, and she was first to answer with her blood the alarm cry of the nation, when its capital was menaced by rebels. You know her patriotic governor, and you know Charles Sumner. I need not add more.

Massachusetts now welcomes you to arms as soldiers. She has but a small colored population from which to recruit. She has full leave of the general government to send one regiment to the war, and she has undertaken to do it. Go quickly and help fill up the first colored regiment from the North. I am authorized to assure you that you will receive the same wages, the same rations, the same equipments, the same protection, the same treatment, and the same bounty, secured to the white soldiers. You will be led by able and skillful officers, men who will take especial pride in your efficiency and success. They will be quick to accord to you all the honor you shall merit by your valor, and see that your rights and feel ings are respected by other soldiers. I have assured myself on these points, and can speak with authority. More than twenty years of unswerving devotion to our common cause may give me some humble claim to be trusted at this momentous crisis. I will not argue. To do so implies hesitation and doubt, and you do not hesitate. You do not doubt. The day dawns; the morning star is bright upon the horizon! The iron gate of our prison stands half open. One gallant rush from the North will fling it wide open, while four millions of our brothers and sisters shall march out into liberty. The chance is now given you to end in a day the bondage of centuries, and to rise in one bound from social degradation to the plane of common equality with all other varieties of men. Remember Denmark Vesey of Charleston; remember Nathaniel Turner of Southampton; remember Shields Green and Copeland, who followed noble John Brown, and fell as glorious martyrs for the cause of the slave. Remember that in a contest with oppression, the Almighty has no attribute which can take sides with oppressors. The case is before you. This is our golden opportunity. Let us accept it, and forever wipe out the dark reproaches unsparingly hurled against us by our enemies. Let us win for ourselves the gratitude of our country, and the best blessings of our posterity through all time. The nucleus of this first regiment is now in camp at Readville, a short distance from Boston. I will undertake to forward to Boston all persons adjudged fit to be mustered into the regiment, who shall apply to me at any time within the next two weeks.

GLOSSARY

walls of Sumter: this is a reference to Ft. Sumter, South Carolina, in Charleston Harbor, where the first shots of the Civil War were fired in April of 1861

sagacity: having sound judgment or wisdom

luster: shine, polish, or appearance

Nathaniel Turner: black minister who led a slave rebellion in Southampton County, Virginia in 1831; ge was executed for his revolt

John Brown: white abolitionist who led an ill-fated attack on the federal armory at Harper's Ferry, Virginia in 1859; he became a martyr for the cause of abolition

Document Analysis

Frederick Douglass's broadside message, "Men of Color, To Arms!" was a certain rallying cry to the black freedmen of the North. He provided a message from a black man to black men about the necessity of service. He implored that it was high time for slaves to respond to the injustices of their slaveholders. It was time for black men to respond to a call that they had felt for many years. His connection between the struggles of African American men and the promise of a new redefined Union were tangible. Douglass wanted the newly free African American men to realize that they had an opportunity to fight and earn acceptance in the eyes of the broader white American community.

Douglass repeated the theme that now, meaning the spring of 1863, was finally time for black men to take up arms. Many had tried to volunteer and were denied during the first two years of the war, but the Emancipation Proclamation opened the opportunity for black service. He wrote, "A war undertaken and brazenly carried on for the perpetual enslavement of colored men, calls logically and loudly for colored men to help suppress." The interesting point about that perspective was that Douglass featured the negative Confederate war effort rather than the positive Union effort. For these men that he called, it was not merely a fight for rights, but instead a fight to resist the tyranny of Southern slavery. Their freedom and the freedom of those still in bondage was on the line. Fighting, in this case for the Commonwealth of Massachusetts, was worth the sacrifice that

it might cost. His comments on the timeliness of the service were rooted in the restrictions of the past, but also the urgency of the moment. He added, "In good earnest then, and after the best deliberation, I now for the first time during this war feel at liberty to call and counsel you to arms." It was important that they serve in the moment that their country needed them.

Douglass asserted that fighting for their freedom, or to stop slaveholders, would ultimately garner black soldiers equality under American law. Speaking specifically of the conditions of fighting, he explained that black troops would be given equal pay. He wrote, "I am authorized to assure you that you will receive the same wages, the same rations, the same equipments, the same protection, the same treatment, and the same bounty, secured to the white soldiers." Douglass may have been "assured" of this, but it certainly never materialized for black troops. Not only were they chronically under paid, they were also forced to do "slave like" labor, such as fatigue duty, cutting trees, laying roads, hauling supplies, and burying the white dead. When black troops signed up to fight they followed the rallying cries of men like Douglass, only to find themselves doing grunt labor often far from the firing lines of the Army of the Potomac in the early part of their service. As circumstances changed and the war continued, black soldiers did see combat in a variety of contexts, including the now-famous assault on Battery Wagner, South Carolina, by the 54th Massachusetts Infantry, led by Colonel Robert Gould Shaw.

Douglass acknowledged division within the black community and spoke against the detractors to service. He mentioned that some warned black men would be "no better off after than before the war," but Douglass linked the efforts to fight directly to the expansion of rights for many within the nation. He said that it is "your hour and mine." Their service and sacrifice was not merely for themselves, largely free blacks reading the broadside. Rather, Douglass wanted these men to fight for their "enslaved fellow-countrymen" and generations to come. Douglass saw the Civil War as an opportunity to broaden access to democracy. If the use of force was necessary, he knew that the help of black men would only strengthen the Union cause. He rallied black men on the point not just of the color of their skin, but enlisting them in a liberation army for the good of the nation. His politics were violent, but at the behest of advancing a nation of freedom more than simply to seek vengeance in the face of former masters.

Douglass wanted the men to think of their cause beyond individual motives, pointing to the supernatural as an avenue of support. He described their cause in terms of ultimate good, writing, "Remember that in a contest with oppression, the Almighty has no attribute which can take sides with oppressors. The case is before you. This is our golden opportunity. Let us accept it, and forever wipe out the dark reproaches unsparingly hurled against us by our enemies." The combination of bellicose language and the support of the Almighty was typical of the era. It was important that Douglass give the African American men agency in fighting because many thought they did not have a right to fight back against their oppressors. Douglass gave them the rhetoric to explain and justify their violent actions in a way that blended nicely with the Protestant Christianity that was so common among African Americans at the time. Douglass contextualized his statement in terms of both "opportunity" and "wiping out ... darkness," with both providing a combination of urgency and completeness to the task at hand.

Douglass he hoped that soldiers would see themselves among a long line of men who offered resistance to white rule. In the broadside, Douglass made direct reference to the slave rebellion attempts of Denmark Vesey, Nathaniel Turner, and the two men who died martyrs fighting alongside radical abolitionist John Brown, Shields Green and Copeland. These men were not the types of names that were thrown around flippantly. By invoking their sacrifice, Douglass intention-

ally provoked the men into believing it was indeed time to strike. These earlier attempts for freedom were not successful, but Douglass wanted the men observing the broadside to have a personal and historical connection with the efforts of the war through the violent sacrifice of the past. This war was the consummation of all of the efforts of other brave men. It was time to stand up and fight for the legacy of black men. It was time to fight for the possibility of freedom, both that away from slaveholders and also that of new citizenship in the Union.

Essential Themes

Frederick Douglass's purpose in the broadside was obviously to motivate soldiers to fight for the Union, but he added other terminology regarding consequences beyond freedom of the individual, including citizenship, a sense of justice for the oppressors, and a sense of personal honor. This collection of ideologies was not unlike that of the white soldiers fighting, which was an intentional point for Douglass. By fighting against white Confederate opponents on the field of mortal combat, the black soldiers had an opportunity to earn respect and dignity, with hopes of citizenship, from the federal government.

Historically, even though black soldiers fought valiantly in numerous engagements throughout the war, they were not immediately granted the citizenship that Douglass imagined. Rather, they were granted nominal freedom with the 13th Amendment to the United States Constitution in 1865, but many African American men found themselves *de facto* disfranchised by the perpetuation of "slave laws" renewed as Jim Crow laws in the post–Civil War South. This did not change the historical significance of the broadside. It symbolized an opportunity for black men to stand and fight for their own freedom. It was more than a vote, but rather a sign of manliness (as many in the nineteenth century perceived it) to fight alongside and against white men.

In a similar sense, the dream of racial revenge and eventual reconciliation through the destruction of slaveholders' property was also less than satisfactory for Douglass and his companions. Despite General William Tecumseh Sherman's infamous "March to the Sea" and the successful burning of cities like Atlanta, Georgia, and Columbia, South Carolina, much of the South remained able to rebuild during the Reconstruction era. The influx of northern economic capital (much to the chagrin of Southern lawmakers) served to support a rebuilding and new industrialization of the New South. In that new order, the people left with the least amount of support were the former slaves, the people for whom Douglass's rallying broadside sought to help, found themselves doing slave-like labor in slave-like conditions through sharecropping. These common African Americans lacked the economic mobility to leave their station, instead celebrating the success they found through the Freedmen's Bureau in unifying families and establishing some basic economic success. Following the corrupt presidential election of 1877, which put Republican President Rutherford B. Hayes in the oval office, federal troops were removed from their occupation of the American South, effectively allowing the Jim Crow laws of the former Confederacy to dominate the political and social landscape of the New South.

This broadside directly influenced a chain of events through black enlistment that changed the cultural landscape of the United States. Not only did black soldiers fight for their own emancipation in securing victory for the Union, but they also helped to maintain a longstanding Republican rule that helped to establish the constitutional amendments that defined black citizenship. Douglass's work to rally the black men of the North into Civil War service helped to solidify his personal legacy as one of the important historical actors in both Civil War and Civil Rights history.

Gregory Jones

Bibliography

Cornish, Dudley M. *The Sable Arm: Black Troops in the Union Army, 1861-1865.* Lawrence: UP of Kansas, 1987. Print.

Douglass, Frederick. *Narrative of the Life of Frederick Douglass: An American Slave, Written by Himself* (Bedford Series in History and Culture). New York: Bedford/St. Martin's, 2002. Print.

Martin Jr., Waldo E. *Mind of Frederick Douglass.* Chapel Hill: U of North
Carolina P, 1986. Print.

Further Reading

Glatthaar, Joseph. *Forged in Battle: The Civil War Alliance of Black Soldiers and White Officers.* Baton Rouge: Louisiana State UP, 2000. Print

Manning, Chandra. *What This Cruel War Was Over: Soldiers, Slavery, and the Civil War.* New York: Vintage, 2008. Print.

McFeeley, William. *Frederick Douglass.* New York: Norton, 1995. Print.

McPherson, James M. *The Negro's Civil War: How American Blacks Felt and Acted During the Civil War.* New York: Vintage, 2003. Print.

■ General Patrick Cleburne Proposes Black Soldiers for the Confederacy

Date: January 2, 1864
Author: Cleburne, Patrick R.
Genre: petition

> *"We propose...that we immediately commence training a large reserve of the most courageous of our slaves, and further that we guarantee freedom within a reasonable time to every slave in the South who shall remain true to the Confederacy in this war."*

Summary Overview

As the Army of Tennessee shivered in its winter quarters around Dalton, Georgia, in December 1863, one of its most popular division commanders formulated a startling proposal. Major General Patrick R. Cleburne, like many others, had taken stock of the Confederacy's gradually diminishing chances for military success. He could see defeat in drawn faces of the soldiers in his own army. Cleburne discussed his proposal with anyone who would listen—including his close friend and fellow general, Thomas Hindman—and composed a "memorial" detailing the plan's reasoning and advantages. Before taking the plan to the army's leadership, Cleburne enlisted the support of the generals and colonels in his division, who quickly added their names to the document.

On January 2, 1864, Cleburne and his supporters presented the memorandum to the Army of Tennessee's other general officers, including its commander, General Joseph E. Johnston, with the hope of gaining their endorsement before sending it to the Confederate government in Richmond. While a few officers expressed support for Cleburne's proposal, many others violently rejected the idea. A "monstrous proposition," one called it; "treasonous," said another. The opposition to the proposal meant that it would get no further up the chain of command, but a copy was leaked to Richmond anyhow. Jefferson Davis, the Confederate president, and his cabinet considered the plan so inflammatory that they forbade Cleburne and his associates from discussing it further. The resistance to Cleburne's proposal is not surprising, for he had suggested nothing more than a complete reversal of the very cause the Confederacy fought for: he had proposed that the South free slaves and allow them to serve as soldiers in the struggling nation's army.

Defining Moment

Three years of pressing defeat drew Cleburne to this point. Though the Confederate military had experienced some inspiring successes on the battlefield in 1862 and 1863, the larger strategic situation appeared increasingly gloomy. The armies of the United States encroached on every point of the Confederate frontier. The Army of the Potomac, despite enduring the repeated blows of the Army of Northern Virginia, still hovered a few-day's march from Richmond. Ulysses Grant's Union forces had stormed down the Mississippi River in 1862 and by the following summer had opened not only that passageway, splitting the South in two, but along with the Union Army of the Cumberland, had largely cleared Tennessee of Confederate troops.

The Union navy and army likewise had captured New Orleans, and occupied great swaths of coastal territory around the Gulf Coast, Charleston, South Carolina, and a vast chunk of eastern North Carolina. The recent agony of Cleburne's own Army of Tennessee only accentuated the frustration of Confederate armies. Just four months before composing his memorial, the Army had squandered an unexpected victory at Chickamauga and followed-up by being ignominiously swatted away from Chattanooga by Grant's forces, thus permanently abandoning Tennessee, and the door to the heartland, to the invaders.

Beyond the dismal military situation, the ability of the Confederacy to maintain itself as a viable and independent state seemed ever more in doubt. Confederate leaders had long hoped for diplomatic recognition and military assistance from England and France. In fact, as the war lengthened, they considered intervention necessary to their success. Yet England and France not only did not move decisively to help the Confederacy, their hesitation to support a slaveholding power bespoke a larger condemnation of the Southern cause. England had emancipated slaves in its empire in 1833 and had since championed liberal politics and free-labor: two principles the Confederacy stood pointedly against. As hope from abroad faded, the domestic scene failed to offer any bright spots. Politics divided the Confederacy, as the Davis administration enacted policies to centralize authority in the Richmond government and opponents like North Carolina's governor Zebulon Vance and Georgia's governor Joseph Brown moved to oppose that power shift. Cabinet members and other policy makers could not strengthen the Confederate economy or unify its nascent industrial capacity in complete service to the war effort. All the while, inflation caused the price of food and other necessary items to skyrocket while shortages of everything plagued the Southern factory and home.

Less visible but more insidious threats to the Confederate nation loomed beyond the control of the nation's military and political leaders. Dissent by ordinary Southerners suggested eroding popular support for the war. Groups of poor women mobbed Confederate supply depots for food and cloth all over the South in the spring of 1863. The disaffection prompted a chronic desertion problem in the army as enlisted men decided that protecting their own families had priority over protecting a tenuous nation. A more ominous sign of disintegration was how quickly enslaved black people disobeyed their masters or fled altogether when the Union army ranged near. Confederates' rhetoric had insisted that black men and women would remain loyal to their white owners, presenting a united front against the interloping Yankees. But the speed at which blacks abandoned slavery in favor of freedom unnerved observant Confederates.

Cleburne's friend, Thomas Hindman, first raised the option of arming slaves for service in the army. But he did so anonymously in an open letter published in Georgia just weeks before Cleburne made his memorandum known. Thus Hindman became the first high-ranking Confederate (in either the army or the government) to seriously address the problem of manpower with the solution of slaves. Hindman's letter placed the problem front-and-center: the Confederacy had suffered setbacks, and the Union army would only grow stronger since it had begun recruiting black southerners into its ranks. Both Hindman and Cleburne, in his proposal, offered the first attempt to think through and publically discuss why, and more importantly, how, the Confederacy could turn on its founding principles and embrace the idea of black soldiers.

Author Biography

Patrick Ronayne Cleburne had come to his generalship by a unique path. Born in Ireland in 1828 to a Protestant gentry family, he idylled in the countryside and attended school until his father's unexpected death when Patrick was fifteen years old. His family's newly desperate circumstances forced Patrick to search out work. After a few years as an apprentice druggist, he joined the British army and served for three years as an enlisted man in a locally stationed regiment performing constabulary duties. At the height of the potato famine in 1848, Patrick and several of his brothers and sisters migrated to the United States. He landed first in Cincinnati but quickly found work as a store manager at a pharmacy owned by a pair of doctors in Helena, Arkansas.

In Helena, Cleburne's fortunes rose and he eventually co-owned the store and turned to the study of law. During his apprenticeship at law, Cleburne came under the influence of a politically ambitious and often-violent contemporary named Thomas C. Hindman. Cleburne became a lawyer, dealing principally in land transactions. His political mentorship at the hands of Hindman included an induction to Democratic party politics. Cleburne wrote and spoke against the Know-

Nothing party and in the process, imbibed the political rhetoric of states' rights and anti-abolitionism. At the secession of Arkansas, Cleburne raised a company of infantry and was quickly elevated to the rank of Colonel in command of his regiment and then Brigadier General in command of his brigade.

Cleburne did not possess an outsized personality like so many Confederate generals. In fact, the Irishman was known to be a shy man, uncomfortable and awkward in social situations. An officer on his staff observed, "He is quiet, has little to say, and any one to see and not know him would take him much sooner for a private than a Major Gen'l." Cleburne's introverted

nature, however, did not hide his considerable skill as a military commander. His devotion to the regular drill of his brigade, and later, division, ensured his command's exemplary performance on the battlefield. Cleburne's own discerning decisiveness under fire when so many of his peers blustered ineffectively underscored that hard work and competence, not fearless machismo, made successful generals. With the confidence and love of his soldiers, the esteem of the Army of Tennessee's leadership, and continued demonstration of battlefield prowess, Cleburne, by the Autumn of 1863 earned a nationwide reputation as one of the Confederacy's shining stars.

HISTORICAL DOCUMENT

Commanding General, The Corps, Division, Brigade, and Regimental Commanders of the Army of Tennessee

General:

Moved by the exigency in which our country is now placed we take the liberty of laying before you, unofficially, our views on the present state of affairs. The subject is so grave, and our views so new, we feel it a duty both to you and the cause that before going further we should submit them for your judgment and receive your suggestions in regard to them. We therefore respectfully ask you to give us an expression of your views in the premises. We have now been fighting for nearly three years, have spilled much of our best blood, and lost, consumed, or thrown to the flames an amount of property equal in value to the specie currency of the world. Through some lack in our system the fruits of our struggles and sacrifices have invariably slipped away from us and left us nothing but long lists of dead and mangled. Instead of standing defiantly on the borders of our territory or harassing those of the enemy, we are hemmed in to-day into less than two-thirds of it, and still the enemy menacingly confronts us at every point with superior forces. Our soldiers can see no end to this state of affairs except in our own exhaustion; hence, instead of rising to the occasion, they are sinking into a fatal apathy, growing weary of hardships and slaughters which

promise no results. In this state of things it is easy to understand why there is a growing belief that some black catastrophe is not far ahead of us, and that unless some extraordinary change is soon made in our condition we must overtake it. The consequences of this condition are showing themselves more plainly every day; restlessness of morals spreading everywhere, manifesting itself in the army in a growing disregard for private rights; desertion spreading to a class of soldiers it never dared to tamper with before; military commissions sinking in the estimation of the soldier; our supplies failing; our firesides in ruins. If this state continues much longer we must be subjugated. Every man should endeavor to understand the meaning of subjugation before it is too late. We can give but a faint idea when we say it means the loss of all we now hold most sacred — slaves and all other personal property, lands, homesteads, liberty, justice, safety, pride, manhood. It means that the history of this heroic struggle will be written by the enemy; that our youth will be trained by Northern school teachers; will learn from Northern school books their version of the war; will be impressed by all the influences of history and education to regard our gallant dead as traitors, our maimed veterans as fit objects for derision. It means the crushing of Southern manhood, the hatred of our former slaves, who will, on a spy system, be our secret police. The conqueror's policy is to divide the conquered into factions and stir up animosity among them, and in training an army of negroes the North no doubt holds this thought in perspective. We can see three great causes operating to destroy us: First, the inferiority of our armies to those of the enemy in point of numbers; second, the poverty of our single source of supply in comparison with his several sources; third, the fact that slavery, from being one of our chief sources of strength at the commencement of the war, has now become, in a military point of view, one of our chief sources of weakness.

The enemy already opposes us at every point with superior numbers, and is endeavoring to make the preponderance irresistible. President Davis , in his recent message, says the enemy "has recently ordered a large conscription and made a subsequent call for volunteers, to be followed, if ineffectual by a still further draft." In addition, the President of the United States announces that "he has already in training an army of 100,000 negroes as good as any troops," and every fresh raid he makes and new slice of territory he wrests from us will add to this force. Every soldier in our army already knows and feels our numerical inferiority to the enemy. Want of men in the field has prevented him from reaping the fruits of his victories, and has prevented him from having the furlough he expected after the last reorganization, and when he turns from the wasting armies in the field to look at the source of supply, he finds nothing in the prospect to encourage him. Our single source of supply is that portion of our white men fit for duty and not now in the ranks. The enemy has three sources of supply: First, his own motley population; secondly, our slaves; and thirdly, Europeans whose hearts are fired into a crusade against us by fictitious pictures of the atrocities of slavery, and who meet no hindrance from their Governments in such enterprise, because these Governments are equally antagonistic to the institution. In touching the third cause, the fact that slavery has become a military weakness, we may rouse prejudice and passion, but the time has come when it would be madness not to look at our danger from every point of view, and to probe it to the bottom. Apart from the assistance that home and foreign prejudice against slavery has given to the North, slavery is a source of great strength to the enemy in a purely military point of view, by supplying him with an army from our granaries; but it is our most vulnerable point, a continued embarrassment, and in some respects an insidious

weakness. Wherever slavery is once seriously disturbed, whether by the actual presence or the approach of the enemy, or even by a cavalry raid, the whites can no longer with safety to their property openly sympathize with our cause. The fear of their slaves is continually haunting them, and from silence and apprehension many of these soon learn to wish the war stopped on any terms. The next stage is to take the oath to save property, and they become dead to us, if not open enemies. To prevent raids we are forced to scatter our forces, and are not free to move and strike like the enemy; his vulnerable points are carefully selected and fortified depots. Ours are found in every point where there is a slave to set free. All along the lines slavery is comparatively valueless to us for labor, but of great and increasing worth to the enemy for information. It is an omnipresent spy system, pointing out our valuable men to the enemy, revealing our positions, purposes, and resources, and yet acting so safely and secretly that there is no means to guard against it. Even in the heart of our country, where our hold upon this secret espionage is firmest, it waits but the opening fire of the enemy's battle line to wake it, like a torpid serpent, into venomous activity.

In view of the state of affairs what does our country propose to do? In the words of President Davis "no effort must be spared to add largely to our effective force as promptly as possible. The sources of supply are to be found in restoring to the army all who are improperly absent, putting an end to substitution, modifying the exemption law, restricting details, and placing in the ranks such of the able-bodied men now employed as wagoners, nurses, cooks, and other employe[e]s, as are doing service for which the negroes may be found competent." Most of the men improperly absent, together with many of the exempts and men having substitutes, are now without the Confederate lines and cannot be calculated on. If all the exempts capable of bearing arms were enrolled, it will give us the boys below eighteen, the men above forty-five, and those persons who are left at home to meet the wants of the country and the army, but this modification of the exemption law will remove from the fields and manufactories most of the skill that directed agricultural and mechanical labor, and, as stated by the President, "details will have to be made to meet the wants of the country," thus sending many of the men to be derived from this source back to their homes again. Independently of this, experience proves that striplings and men above conscript age break down and swell the sick lists more than they do the ranks. The portion now in our lines of the class who have substitutes is not on the whole a hopeful element, for the motives that created it must have been stronger than patriotism, and these motives added to what many of them will call breach of faith, will cause some to be not forthcoming, and others to be unwilling and discontented soldiers. The remaining sources mentioned by the President have been so closely pruned in the Army of Tennessee that they will be found not to yield largely. The supply from all these sources, together with what we now have in the field, will exhaust the white race, and though it should greatly exceed expectations and put us on an equality with the enemy, or even give us temporary advantages, still we have no reserve to meet unexpected disaster or to supply a protracted struggle. Like past years, 1864 will diminish our ranks by the casualties of war, and what source of repair is there left us? We therefore see in the recommendations of the President only a temporary expedient, which at the best will leave us twelve months hence in the same predicament we are in now. The President attempts to meet only one of the depressing causes mentioned; for the other two he has proposed no remedy. They remain to generate lack of confidence in our final success, and to keep us moving down hill as heretofore. Adequately to meet the causes which are now threatening ruin to our country, we propose, in addition to a modification of the President's plans, that we retain in service for the war all troops now in service, and that we immediately commence training a large reserve of the most courageous of our slaves, and further that we guarantee freedom within a reasonable time to every slave in the South who shall remain true to the Confederacy in this war. As between the loss of independence and the loss of slavery, we assume that every patriot will freely give up the latter — give up the negro slave rather than be a slave himself. If we are correct in this assumption it only remains to show how this great national sacrifice is, in all human probabilities, to change the current of success and sweep the invader from our country.

Our country has already some friends in England and France, and there are strong motives to induce these nations to recognize and assist us, but they cannot assist us without helping slavery, and to do this would be in conflict with their policy for the last quarter of a century. England has paid hundreds of millions to emancipate her West India slaves and break up the slave-trade. Could she now consistently spend her treasure to reinstate slavery in this country? But this barrier once removed, the sympathy and the interests of these and other nations will accord with our own, and we may expect from them both moral support and material aid. One thing is certain, as soon as the great sacrifice to independence is made and known in foreign countries there will be a complete change of front in our favor of the sympathies of the world. This measure will deprive the North of the moral and material aid which it now derives from the bitter prejudices with which foreigners view the institution, and its war, if continued, will henceforth be so despicable in their eyes that the source of recruiting will be dried up. It will leave the enemy's negro army no motive to fight for, and will exhaust the source from which it has been recruited. The idea that it is their special mission to war against slavery has held growing sway over the Northern people for many years, and has at length ripened into an armed and bloody crusade against it. This baleful superstition has so far supplied them with a courage and constancy not their own. It is the most powerful and honestly entertained plank in their war platform. Knock this away and what is left? A bloody ambition for more territory, a pretended veneration for the Union, which one of their own most distinguished orators (Doctor Beecher in his Liverpool speech) openly avowed was only used as a stimulus to stir up the anti-slavery crusade, and lastly the poisonous and selfish interests which are the fungus growth of the war itself. Mankind may fancy it a great duty to destroy slavery, but what interest can mankind have in upholding this remainder of the Northern war platform? Their interests and feelings will be diametrically opposed to it. The measure we propose will strike dead all John Brown fanaticism, and will compel the enemy to draw off altogether or in the eyes of the world to swallow the Declaration of Independence without the sauce and disguise of philanthropy. This delusion of fanaticism at an end, thousands of Northern people will have leisure to look at home and to see the gulf of despotism into which they themselves are rushing.

The measure will at one blow strip the enemy of foreign sympathy and assistance, and transfer them to the South; it will dry up two of his three sources of recruiting; it will take from his negro army the only motive it could have to fight against the South, and will probably cause much of it to desert over to us; it will deprive his cause of the powerful stimulus of fanaticism, and will enable him to see the rock on which his so-called friends are now piloting him. The immediate effect of the emancipation and enrollment of negroes on the military strength of the South would be: To enable us to have armies numerically superior to those of the North, and a reserve of any size we might think necessary; to enable us to take the offensive, move forward, and forage on the enemy. It would open to us in prospective another and almost untouched source of supply, and furnish us with the means of preventing temporary disaster, and carrying on a protracted struggle. It would instantly remove all the vulnerability, embarrassment, and inherent weakness which result from slavery. The approach of the enemy would no longer find every household surrounded by spies; the fear that sealed the master's lips and the avarice that has, in so many cases, tempted him practically to desert us would alike be removed. There would be no recruits awaiting the enemy with open arms, no complete history of every neighborhood with ready guides, no fear of insurrection in the rear, or anxieties for the fate of loved ones when our armies moved forward. The chronic irritation of hope deferred would be joyfully ended with the negro, and the sympathies of his whole race would be due to his native South. It would restore confidence in an early termination of the war with all its inspiring consequences, and even if contrary to all expectations the enemy should succeed in over-running the South, instead of finding a cheap, ready-made means of holding it down, he would find a common hatred and thirst for vengeance, which would break into acts at every favorable opportunity, would prevent him from settling on our lands, and render the South a very unprofitable conquest. It would remove forever all selfish taint from our cause and place independence above every question of property. The very magnitude of the sacrifice itself, such as no nation has ever voluntarily made before, would appal [sic] our enemies, destroy his spirit and his finances, and fill our hearts with a pride and singleness of purpose which would clothe us with new strength in battle. Apart from all other aspects of the question, the necessity for more fighting men is upon us. We can only get a sufficiency by making the negro share the danger and hardships of the war. If we arm and train him and make him fight for the country in her hour of dire distress, every consideration of principle and policy demand that we should set him and his whole race who side with us free. It is a first principle with mankind that he who offers his life in defense of the State should receive from her in return his freedom and his happiness, and we believe in acknowledgment of this principle. The Constitution of the Southern States has reserved to their respective governments the power to free slaves for meritorious services to the State. It is politic besides. For many years, ever since the agitation of the subject of slavery commenced, the negro has been dreaming of freedom, and his vivid imagination has surrounded that condition with so many gratifications that it has become the paradise of his hopes. To attain it he will tempt dangers and difficulties not exceeded by the bravest soldier in the field. The hope of freedom is perhaps the only moral incentive that can be applied to him in his present condition. It would be preposterous then to expect him to fight against it with any degree of enthusiasm, therefore we must bind him to our cause by no doubtful bonds; we must leave no possible loop-hole for treachery to creep in. The slaves are dangerous now, but armed, trained, and collected in an army they would be a thousand fold more dangerous; therefore when we make soldiers of them we must make free men of them beyond all question, and thus enlist their sympathies also. We can do this more effectually than the North can now do, for we can give the negro not only his own freedom, but that of his wife and child, and can secure it to him in his old home. To do this, we must immediately make his marriage and parental relations sacred in the eyes of the law and forbid their sale. The past legislation of the South concedes that a large free middle class of negro blood, between the master and slave, must sooner or later destroy the institution. If, then, we touch the institution at all, we would do best to make the most of it, and by emancipating the whole race upon reasonable terms, and within such reasonable time as will prepare both races for the change, secure to ourselves all the advantages, and to our enemies all the disadvantages that can arise, both at home and abroad, from such a sacrifice. Satisfy the negro that if he faithfully adheres to our standard during the war he shall receive his freedom and that of his race. Give him as an earnest of our intentions such immediate immunities as will impress him with our sincerity and be in keeping with his new condition, enroll a portion of his class as soldiers of the Confederacy, and we change the race from a dreaded weakness to a position of strength.

Will the slaves fight? The helots of Sparta stood their masters good stead in battle. In the great sea fight of Lepanto where the Christians checked forever the spread of Mohammedanism over Europe, the galley slaves of portions of the fleet were promised freedom, and called on to fight at a critical moment of the battle. They fought well, and civilization owes much to those brave galley slaves. The negro slaves of Saint Domingo, fighting for freedom, defeated their white masters and the French troops sent against them. The negro slaves of Jamaica revolted, and under the name of Maroons held the mountains against their masters for 150 years; and the experience of this war has been so far that half-trained negroes have fought as bravely as many other half-trained Yankees. If, contrary to the training of a lifetime, they can be made to face and fight bravely against their former masters, how much more probable is it that with the allurement of a higher reward, and led by those masters, they would submit to discipline and face dangers.

We will briefly notice a few arguments against this course. It is said Republicanism cannot exist without the institution. Even were this true, we prefer any form of government of which the Southern people may have the molding, to one forced upon us by a conqueror. It is said the white man cannot perform agricultural labor in the South. The experience of this army during the heat of summer from Bowling Green, Ky., to Tupelo, Miss., is that the white man is healthier when doing reasonable work in the open field than at any other time. It is said an army of negroes cannot be spared from the fields. A sufficient number of slaves is now administering to luxury alone to supply the place of all we need, and we believe it would be better to take half the able-bodied men off a plantation than to take the one master mind that eco-

nomically regulated its operations. Leave some of the skill at home and take some of the muscle to fight with. It is said slaves will not work after they are freed. We think necessity and a wise legislation will compel them to labor for a living. It is said it will cause terrible excitement and some disaffection from our cause. Excitement is far preferable to the apathy which now exists, and disaffection will not be among the fighting men. It is said slavery is all we are fighting for, and if we give it up we give up all. Even if this were true, which we deny, slavery is not all our enemies are fighting for. It is merely the pretense to establish sectional superiority and a more centralized form of government, and to deprive us of our rights and liberties. We have now briefly proposed a plan which we believe will save our country. It may be imperfect, but in all human probability it would give us our independence. No objection ought to outweigh it which is not weightier than independence. If it is worthy of being put in practice it ought to be mooted quickly before the people, and urged earnestly by every man who believes in its efficacy. Negroes will require much training; training will require much time, and there is danger that this concession to common sense may come too late.

P.R. Cleburne, major-general, commanding division
D.C. Govan, brigadier-general
John E. Murray, colonel, Fifth Arkansas
G.F. Baucum, colonel, Eighth Arkansas
Peter Snyder, lieutenant-colonel, commanding Sixth and Seventh Arkansas
E. Warfield, lieutenant-colonel, Second Arkansas
M.P. Howrey, brigadier-general
A.B. Hardcastle, colonel, Thirty-second and Forty-fifth Mississippi
F.A. Ashford, major, Sixteenth Alabama
John W. Colquitt, colonel, First Arkansas
Rich J. Person, major, Third and Fifth Confederate
G.S. Deakins, major, Thirty-fifth and Eighth Tennessee
J.H. Collett, captain, commanding Seventh Texas
J.H. Kelly, brigadier-general, commanding Calvalry Division

GLOSSARY

exigency: An urgent want or pressing necessity.

desertion: To leave the army without permission.

subjugated: To be forcibly placed under the power of another

John Brown fanaticism: A Southern description of abolitionists that attempted to describe the latter as bloodthirsty marauders.

Document Analysis

Patrick Cleburne's memorial laid out his proposal for the arming of slaves with the rhetorical skills of an attorney. He presented the problem, offered a solution, countered potential critics, and finished with an appeal for action. In addition to the straightforward suggestion about arming slaves, Cleburne slyly and skillfully advocated a wholesale reconsideration of the Confederate cause—a reversal which advocates and opponents alike could not help but notice.

Cleburne began with a stark vision of the present and the probable future. He noted that the Confederacy has spent blood and treasure on the war effort but instead of standing victorious, its armies are "hemmed in." The chief cause of this calamity was the overwhelming numbers the Union army was able to command, and this fact was apparent to every Southern soldier. Confederates were "sinking into a fatal apathy," Cleburne noted. He then painted a vivid picture of the "black catastrophe" that awaited a defeated South. Our dead will be dishonored and our living will be despised. Our teachers will be vindictive Yankees, bent on imposing a hostile racial order. Our conquerors will turn our loyal slaves against us and engender a mood among them of animosity and suspicion. Cleburne reeled off a remarkably succinct list of "all we now hold most sacred" that would be sacrificed in defeat: "slaves and all other personal property, lands, homesteads, liberty, justice, safety, pride, [and] manhood."

He reiterated the potential cause of defeat—the numerical inferiority of Confederate armies and the inability to replenish its ranks with new recruits. Then Cleburne introduced a set of facts that did not accord with Southern rhetoric about the value of slavery and therefore had not been widely considered. The time had come, he insisted, to face the fact that slavery was not a strength but, in fact, a weakness. How so? First, the enemy has successfully turned our slaves against us by recruiting them into their armies and utilizing their skills as guides and spies in Confederate territory. Further, in occupied areas, loyal slave owners eagerly cooperate with Union forces because to do otherwise would ensure the destruction of their property and the escape of their slaves. Finally, slaves had shown a shocking willingness to throw off their shackles and flee to the Yankees whenever armies were near. Thus, Confederate military strategy had been hampered by a need to not just protect militarily important junctions or strike at Federal armies, but to guard all our "vulnerable points," which "are found where there is a slave to set free."

Cleburne considered the administration's plan to modify the exemption laws to squeeze a few more men into the army unworkable and merely "a temporary expedient." He then stated his audacious idea, "that we immediately commence training a large reserve of the most courageous of our slaves, and further that we guarantee freedom within a reasonable time to every slave in the South who shall remain true to the Confederacy in this war." The plan to arm and train blacks for Confederate service was one thing, but Cleburne directly embraced the wider implication of his plan: universal emancipation. An honest state, after all, had to honor dangerous service with the benefits of freedom (if not complete political equality.) Thus, by abandoning claims to slavery itself, Cleburne found benefits far beyond hundreds of thousands of potential Confederate soldiers. By toppling slavery from its position as chief reason for secession, the Confederacy could execute a brilliant rhetorical move that would completely undermine its enemies and earn it new friends.

Removing slavery as the Confederate *casus belli* would reveal what many Southerners considered the venal and greedy intent that lay behind the North's moral posturing, and thus clear-eyed people in America and Europe would immediately drop their support for the Union war effort. England and France would be relieved of their moral qualms and come to the South's rescue. Most importantly, Cleburne contended, the move would give Southern slaves a reason to fight for the Confederacy if they believed that doing so would ensure their freedom. After all, Cleburne reasoned, if a black man had to be free, would not he much rather fight with his family and home at stake than on behalf of insidious Northerners who did not truly know or care for him?

Cleburne understood that a cause predicated on wealthy men keeping other men in bondage could be interpreted as a fundamentally "selfish" idealism. He reasoned that slavery had been the issue that obscured potentially higher-minded and more widely acceptable reasons for Southern independence. Therefore, dropping the pretense of slavery meant that the South could then "place independence above every question of property."

The general pithily dismissed potential objections to his plan. To those who claimed that republicanism could not survive without slavery, he pointedly noted that a compromised republicanism was preferable to complete subjugation. To those who insisted that white men could not labor in the way black slaves did in hot Southern fields, Cleburne raised the example of Confederate soldiers digging trenches and marching along dusty roads in the summer heat. White men could indeed endure it. Would not the idea of arming slaves cause too much "excitement" in the Confederacy? Cleburne claimed that excitement would be better than the present apathy. Finally, if an opponent insisted that "slavery is all we are fighting for, and if we give it up we give up all," then he replied that the war had revealed that the North fought for "sectional superiority...a more centralized form of government, and to deprive us of our rights and liberty." Was not opposing them a higher principle?

Cleburne's memorial received a cool reception at the Army of Tennessee headquarters. Other generals and staff officers condemned it outright. General William Bate declared it "hideous and objectionable...the serpent of Abolitionism." Cleburne clearly understood the rhetorical and practical intricacies of slavery, but had misjudged the attachment of Southerners to slavery as the preferred method of racial control. Upon observing the virulent opposition to Cleburne's plan, Johnston decided that it should go no further, and ordered Cleburne to cease promoting it. Cleburne did not send it along to Richmond, but opponents, alarmed by the apparent treachery in the officer corps, sent it to the Confederate capital to raise an alarm.

Essential Themes

When a leaked copy of Cleburne's memorandum found its way to Richmond, Jefferson Davis and his cabinet insisted that it not be circulated. In fact, he ordered the proposal squelched, not even to be discussed further. The concept of arming slaves proved, in early 1864, to be too heretical a thought. Davis and many in the Confederacy still maintained a conviction that more white men could be found for the army; that a signal battlefield victory could turn back the Union tide; that England could intervene; and that the Southern nation could still weather its current setbacks. In January 1864, Confederate leaders looked to another summer of vigorous defense, not to a capitulation of their core convictions about race relations in the South.

Indeed, what Cleburne had suggested struck at the very heart of the Confederate racial ideology that had driven the Southern states to assert independence in 1861. Southern whites built their convictions about race relations on a self-deceiving and occasionally contradictory ideology, but one they held as observable fact. Slavery, for white Southerners, provided necessary government of how the races related to one another. It was a necessary relationship and ensured that whites remained dominant and blacks subservient, reflecting a God-ordained social order. Blacks, without the controlling influence of whites and allegedly unable to govern their passions or their society, would run rampant in an orgy of violence before succumbing to indolence-induced starvation. Thus whites, even non–slave owners, considered slavery the key to personal and political safety, and all worked tirelessly to ensure that blacks never occupied any position of equality to a white man. To do otherwise would lead to white people being subservient to black people, an exchange that Cleburne acknowledged in his proposal to be unconscionable to Southern whites.

Curiously, whites maintained that enslaved blacks enjoyed and appreciated their subservient status as slaves. Whites fervently believed the notion that blacks loved their masters, clung to them for safety, and would stand by them in times of crisis—a fiction, indeed, but one that most Southerners genuinely believed. Abolitionists, Southerners claimed, did not care for actual black people: their insistence on abolition clearly indicated that they wanted blacks to suffer and starve without the helpful guidance of white masters. No, abolitionists wanted simply to lord a false moral superiority over white Southerners and instigate a cataclysmic race war in the South in furtherance of a policy of political and cultural greed. Thus, when the Republican Abraham Lincoln won the Presidency in 1860, eleven slaveholding states acted to ensure the perpetuation of slavery and their own safety by removing themselves from the Union.

Politicians and editors in 1860 and 1861 trumpeted the fact that secession was first and foremost a move to maintain the existing relationship between whites and blacks, that of slavery. That is what made Cleburne's proposal so startling. Advocates and opponents of the black-soldier plan knew that despite the delicate parsing of rights and privileges afforded to proposed emancipated soldiers, the process would, in time, encompass two dangerous and unthinkable precedents: the eventual emancipation of all slaves and the elevation of blacks to implied equality with whites by service alongside one another in the ranks. In January 1864, few Confederates, who had seceded to prevent those very things, could countenance the idea.

Christopher Graham

Bibliography

Levine, Bruce. Confederate Emancipation: Southern Plans to Free and Arm Slaves during the Civil War. New York: Oxford UP, 2006. Print.

Symonds, Craig L. *Stonewall of the West: Patrick Cleburne and the Civil War. Lawrence: UP of Kansas, 1997. Print.*

Additional Reading

Daniel, Larry J. *Soldiering in the Army of Tennessee: A Portrait of Life in a Confederate Army.* Chapel Hill: U of North Carolina P, 1991. Print.

Dew, Charles B. *Apostles of Disunion: Southern Secession Commissioners and the Causes of the Civil War.* Charlottesville: U of Virginia P, 2001. Print.

Levin, Kevin M. "Confederate Like Me," *Civil War Monitor,* Vol. 3, No. 1 (Spring 2013). Print.

Oakes, James. *The Ruling Race: A History of American Slaveholders.* New York: Norton, 1998. Print.

■ Jefferson Davis on the Employment of Slaves

Date: November 7, 1864
Author: Davis, Jefferson
Genre: speech; message to Congress

*"My present purpose is to invite your consideration to
the propriety of a radical modification in the theory
of the law."*

Summary Overview

Confederate President Jefferson Davis returned from an October 1864 tour of the troubled Deep South states and the bloodied Army of Tennessee to compose an address for the opening of the Second Confederate Congress. Davis designed the address to boost the morale of a discouraged country. He admitted to difficult circumstances the nation faced. He discounted the recent loss of Atlanta, and while pointing to minor successes elsewhere, insisted that the Confederacy consisted of ideas much more important than physical localities. A strained reason for hope, indeed, but politically necessary. Davis also admitted to the chief Confederate weakness, the shortage of men eligible to be soldiers in the army, and declared that a tightening of exemption laws would produce enough men to repel the invaders. The number of white men could be boosted, Davis maintained, if the Confederate military had access to large numbers of slaves to serve as wagon drivers, cooks, and laborers, and even as pioneer and engineer troops. He lamented that a February 1864 impressment law designed to raise 20,000 slaves for that purpose had failed to produce the required number. Impressed slaves could only be used in limited capacities owing to the fact that slave owners protective of their investments had constrained how, and how long, the state might use them. Davis cast around for ideas on how to increase the number of slaves fully committed to Confederate service.

The president found a solution not by adjusting numbers (though he did increase the requisition to 40,000 men) or reconsidering the degree of political pressure on individuals and states. Instead, he invited Congress to consider "a radical modification in the theory of the law." Davis meant for the Confederate government to assume greater power to impress, retain, train, and utilize slave labor in larger capacities in the military effort. He stopped short of advocating the arming of slaves for service in the ranks, but claimed that should the Confederacy desire to do so, the move would be "justifiable, if necessary." Ten months before, Davis had squelched the discussion of arming slaves when it was raised by General Patrick Cleburne. Now, Davis himself initiated a heated public discussion by suggesting, essentially, the same thing.

Defining Moment

The military situation in the South had changed dramatically since Cleburne's suppressed memorandum. Atlanta, in the heart of the Confederacy, had fallen to the Union army of William T. Sherman and Ulysses Grant's Union forces hemmed Robert E. Lee's Army of Northern Virginia to the outskirts of Richmond and Petersburg. Further, Abraham Lincoln's reelection to the presidency of the United States dashed Confederate hopes that victory by his Democrat opponent would signal a national desire to make peace with an independent Confederacy. Assistance from abroad, once a key expectation of Confederate leaders, now appeared impossible to attain. Now, at the same time that Davis delivered his address, Sherman set off his Union army on its celebrated "march to the sea." At home, supplies for the army dwindled while inflation continued to soar.

The desperation of the Confederate situation had caused many Southerners to give up hope for independence. Some acted on this loss of will by joining the now-chronic flow of deserters from the army. Others advocated the return of the Southern states to the Union. A few thinkers inside the government and in the civilian world, so stunned at Confederate reversals, began to formulate innovative ways to salvage hope. The Confederacy's chief ordnance officer, Josiah Gorgas noted "there is no help except to use negroes, giving them their freedom." The Governor of Louisiana, Henry W. Allen said much the same, "we have in our negro slaves the means of increasing the number of available fighting men." The editor of the *Charlotte (N.C.) Democrat* flatly proclaimed "it will be necessary to take negroes [into the army as soldiers] or abandon the struggle for independence." Indeed, Davis' closest advisors urged him to reconsider his stance. Judah P. Benjamin, the Confederate Secretary of State, most forcefully advocated the use of slave soldiers in the president's cabinet.

Davis, though strongly convinced about the rightness of slavery and the conservative nature of the Confederate experiment, was under a considerable pressure to contemplate the idea. He proved a nimble enough thinker to reexamine his convictions and consider a new relationship between blacks and whites in the South.

Author Biography

Jefferson Davis was born to be a champion of the South's peculiar institution. A Kentucky-born Mississippi planter, Davis had access to the west's finest private preparatory schools and then attended the United States Military Academy at West Point. He served at various frontier forts along the Mississippi River for seven years before he resigned his commission, married the daughter of future President Zachary Taylor, and settled in Mississippi to take up the life of a cotton grandee where his new bride promptly died of malaria. Under his brother's tutelage, Jefferson Davis became a planter and in 1843 entered the world of Democratic politics as a candidate for the state legislature. He lost, but his star rose in Mississippi political circles. Mar

ried again, to Varina Howell, Davis continued both his work as a planter and a party operative. The Democrats rewarded him with a nomination to the United States House of Representatives and Davis won the election in 1846. Shortly thereafter, he re-donned the military uniform when he became Colonel of the First Mississippi Volunteers for the war with Mexico. In battle he and his regiment gained national attention for bravery and élan, so much so that when he returned to Mississippi, the governor appointed him to fill a vacant senatorial seat. Senator Davis served in that body until 1860, except for the four years he stood as the Secretary of War in the Franklin Pierce administration.

Jefferson Davis' farewell address to the United States Senate upon Mississippi's withdrawal from the Union, offers a revelatory view of his thinking on slavery, secession, and the cause of the fledgling Confederacy. On what he called "the saddest day of my life," Davis stepped to the Senate floor and explained that since Mississippi had seceded, he must depart. He took pains to delineate between nullification and secession, to defend both John Calhoun and Andrew Jackson, and to wish the remaining Senators good will. But he insisted that Mississippi's secession followed a legal and legitimate course. Standing on the principle of state sovereignty, Davis insisted that states had the right to remove themselves from the dangerous effects of hostile laws. The hostile laws emanating from increasingly dominant Northern representatives in Congress consisted of the idea that black people should occupy a place of equality with white people. Davis rejected this notion not on social grounds, as so many of his contemporaries would, but on Constitutional precedent. In reviewing the Declaration of Independence and the Constitution Davis noted that blacks "were not put upon the footing of equality with white men." To insist otherwise, as the emerging Northern majority did, would court the destruction of the great republic. Davis thus cast the sectional disagreement not as particularly about slavery—though even he cited no other reason—but about great constitutional principles. He pledged that by seceding, the Southern states acted upon the "high and solemn motive of defending and protecting the rights we inherited." Davis' facility with the constitutional argument presaged his reassertion of it in November 1864, albeit with a slightly altered interpretation.

HISTORICAL DOCUMENT

To the Senate and House of Representatives of the Confederate States of America:

It is with satisfaction that I welcome your presence at an earlier day than that usual for your session, and with confidence that I invoke the aid of your counsel at a time of such public exigency. The campaign which was commenced almost simultaneously with your session in May last, and which was still in progress at your adjournment in the minute of June, has not yet readied its close. It has been prosecuted on a scale and with an energy heretofore unequalled. When we revert to the condition of our country at the inception of the operations of the present year, to the magnitude of the preparations made by the enemy, the number of his forces, the accumulation, his warlike supplies, and the prodigality with which his vast resources have been lavished in the attempt to render success assured; when we contrast the numbers and means at our disposal for resistance, and when we contemplate the results of a struggle apparently so unequal, we cannot fail, while tendering the full need of deserved praise to our Generals and soldiers, to perceive that a Power higher than man has willed our deliverance, and gratefully to recognize the protection of a kind Providence in enabling us successfully to withstand the utmost efforts of the enemy for our subjugation.

At the beginning of the year, the State of Texas was partially in possession of the enemy, and large portions of Louisiana and Arkansas lay apparently defenceless. Of the Federal soldiers who invaded Texes, none are known to remain except as prisoners of war. In Northwestern Louisiana, a large and well appointed army, aided by a powerful fleet, was repeatedly defeated, and deemed itself fortunate in finally escaping with a loss of one-third of its numbers, a large part of its military trains, and many transports and gunboats. The enemy's occupation of that State is reduced to the narrow district commanded by the guns of his fleet. Arkansas has been recovered, with the exception of a few fortified ports, while our forces have penetrated into Central Missouri, affording to our oppressed brethren in that state an opportunity -- of which many have availed themselves -- of striking for liberation from the tyranny to which they have been subjected.

On the east of the Mississippi, in spite of some reverses, we have much cause for gratulation.[sic] The enemy hoped to effect, curing the present year, by concentration of forces, the conquest which he had previously failed to accomplish by more extended operations. Compelled, therefore, to withdraw or seriously to weaken the strength or the armies of occupation at different points, he has afforded us an opportunity of recovering possession of extensive districts of our territory. Nearly the whole of Northern and Western Mississippi, of Northern Alabama, and of Western Tennessee, are again in our possession and all attempts to penetrate from the coast line into the interior of the Atlantic and Gulf States, have been baffled. On the entire ocean and gulf coast of the Confederacy, the whole success of the enemy, with the enormous naval resources at his command, has been limited to the capture of the outer defences of Mobile Bay.

If we now turn to the results accomplished by the two great armies, so confidently relied on by the invaders as sufficient to secure the subversion of our Government and the subjection of our people to foreign domination, we have still greater cause for gratitude to Divine power. In Southwestern Virginia, successive armies which threatened the capture of Lynchburg and Saltville have been routed and driven out of the country, and a portion of Eastern Tennessee reconquered by our troops. In Northern Virginia; extensive districts formerly occupied by the enemy are now free from their presence. In the Lower Valley, their General, rendered desperate by his inability to maintain a hostile occupation, has resorted to the infamous expedient of converting a fruitful land into a desert, by burning its mills, granaries and homesteads, and destroying the food, standing crops, live stock and agricultural implements of peaceful non combatants. The main army, after a series of defeats in which its losseshave been enormous; after attempts by raiding parties to break up our railroad communications, which have resulted in the destruction of a large part of the cavalry engaged in the work; after constant repulse of repeated assaults on our defensive lines, is, with the aid of heavy reinforcements, but with, it is hoped, waning prospect of further progress in the design, still engaged in an effort, commenced more than four months ago, to capture the town of Petersburgh.

The army of Gen. SHERMAN, although succeeding at the end of the Summer in obtaining possession of Atlanta, has been unable to secure any ultimate advantage from this success. The same General who, in February last, marched a large army from Vicksburgh to Meridian with no other result than being forced to march back again, was able, by the aid of greatly increased numbers, and after much delay, to force a passage from Chattanooga to Atlanta, only to be for the second time compelled to withdraw on the line of his advance, without obtaining control of a single mile of territory beyond the narrow track of his march, and without gaining aught beyond the precarious possession of a few fortified points, in which he is compelled to maintain heavy garrisons, and which are menaced with recapture.

The lessons afforded by the history of this war are fraught with instruction and encouragement. Repeatedly during the war have formidable expeditions been directed by the enemy against points ignorantly supposed to be of vital importance to the Confederacy. Some of these expeditions have, at immense cost, been successful; but in no instance have the promised fruits been reaped. Again, in the present campaign, was the delusion fondly cherished that the capture of Atlanta and Richmond would, if effected, end the war, by the overthrow of our Government and the submission of our people. We can now judge by experience how unimportant is the influence of the former event upon our capacity for defence, upon the courage and spirit of the people, and the stability of the Government. We may, in like manner, judge that if the campaign against Richmond had resulted in success, instead of failure, if the valor of the army under the leadership of its accomplished commander, had resisted in vain the overwhelming masses which were, on the contrary, decisively repulsed; if we had been compelled to evacuate Richmond as well as Atlanta, the Confederacy would have remained as erect and defiant as ever. Nothing could have been changed in the purpose of its Government, in the indomitable valor of its troops, or in the unquenchable spirit of its people. The baffled and disappointed foe would in vain have scanned the reports of your proceedings, at some new

legislative seat, for any indication that progress had been made in his gigantic task of conquering a free people. The truth so patent to us must ere long be forced upon the reluctant Northern mind. There are no vital points on the preservation of which the continued existence of the Confederacy depends. There is no military success of the enemy watch can accomplish its destruction. Not the fall of Richmond, nor Wilmington, nor Charleston, nor Savannah, nor Mobile, nor of all combined, can save the enemy from the constant and exhaustive drain of blood and treasure which must continue until he shall discover that no peace is attainable unless based on the recognition of our indefeasible rights.

Before leaving this subject, it is gratifying to assure you that the military supplies essentially requisite for military defence will be found, as heretofore, adequate to our needs; and that abundant crops have rewarded the labor of the farmer, and rendered abortive the inhuman attempt of the enemy to produce, by devastation, famine among the people.

It is not in my power to announce any change in the conduct of foreign Powers. No such action has been taken by the Christian nations of Europe as might justly have been expected from their history, from the duties imposed by international law, and from the claims of humanity. It is charitable to attribute their conduct to no worse motive than indifference to the consequences which shake; only the Republican portion of the American continent; and not to ascribe to design a course calculated to insure the prolongation of hostilities.

No instance in history is remembered by me in which a nation pretending to exercise dominion over another, asserting its independence, has been the first to concede the existence of such independence. No case can be recalled to my mind in which neutral Powers have failed to see the example of recognizing the independence of a nation, when satisfied of the inability of its enemy to subvert its Government; and this, too, in case where the previous relation between the contending parties had been confessedly that of mother country and dependent colony; not, as in our case, that of co-equal States united by federal compact. It has never been considered the proper functions and duty of neutral Powers to perform the office of judging whether in point of fact, the nation asserting dominion is able to make good its pretensions by force of arms, and if not, by recognition of the resisting party to discountenance the further continuance of the contest. And the reason why this duty is incumbent on neutral Powers is plainly apparent, when we reflect that the pride and passion, which blind the judgment of the parties to the conflict, cause the continuance of active warfare, and consequent useless slaughter, long after the inevitable result has become apparent to all not engaged in the struggle. So long, therefore, as neutral nations fail by recognition of our independence to announce that, in their judgment, the United States are unable to reduce the Confederacy to submission, their conduct will be accepted by our enemies as a tacit encouragement of continue their efforts, and as an implied assurance that belief is entertained by neutral nations in the success of their designs. A direct stimulus, whether intentional or not, is thus applied to securing a continuance of the carnage and devastation which desolate this continent, and which they profess deeply to deplore.

The disregard of this just, humane and Christian public duty by the nations of Europe is the more remarkable from the fact that authentic expression has long since been given by the Governments of both France and England to the conviction that the United States are unable to conquer the Confederacy. It is now more than two years since the Government of France announced officially to the Cabinets of London and St. Petersburgh its own conclusion, that the United States were unable to achieve any decisive military success. In the answers sent by those Powers no intimation of a contrary opinion was conveyed; and it is notorious that in speeches, both in and out of Parliament, the members of her Brittanic Majesty's Government have not hesitated to express this conviction in unqualified terms. The denial of our right, under these circumstances, is so obviously unjust, and discriminates so unfairly in favor of the United States, that neutrals have sought to palliate the wrong of which they are conscious by professing to consumer, in opposition to notorious truth and to the known belief of both belligerents, that the recognition of our independence would be valueless without their further intervention in the struggle an intervention of which we disclaim the desire and mistrust the advantage. We seek no favor, we wish no intervention; we know ourselves fully competent to maintain our own rights and independence against the invaders of our country; and we feel justified in asserting that, without the aid derived from recruiting their armies from foreign countries, the invaders would, ere this, have been driven from our soil. When the recognition of the Confederacy was refused by Great Britain, in the Fall of 1862, the refusal was excused on the ground that any action on the part of Her Majesty's Government would have the effect of inflaming the passions of me belligerents and of preventing the return of peace. It is assumed that this opinion was sincerely entertained, but the experience of two years of unequal carnage shows that it was erroneous, and that the result was the reverse of what the British Ministry humanely desired. A contrary policy, a policy just to us, a policy diverging from an unvarying course of concession to all the demands of our enemies, is still within the power of Her Majesty's Government, and would, it is fair to presume, be productive of consequences the opposite to those which have unfortunately followed its whole course of conduct from the commencement of the war to the present time. In a word, peace is impossible without independence, and it is not to be expected that the enemy will anticipate neutrals in the recognition of that independence. When the history of this war shall be fully disclosed, the calm judgment of the impartial publicist will, for these reasons, be unable to absolve the neutral nations of Europe from a share in the moral responsibility for the myriads of human lives that have been unnecessarily sacrificed during its progress.

The renewed instances in which foreign powers have given just cause of complaint need not here be detailed. The extracts from the correspondence of the State Department, which accompany this message, will afford such further information as can be given without detriment to the public interest, and we must reserve for the future such action as may then be deemed advisable to secure redress.

Your special attention is earnestly invited to the report of the Secretary of the Treasury, submitted in conformity with law. The facts therein disclosed are far from discouraging, and demonstrate that, with judicious legislation, we shall be enabled to meet all the exigencies of the war from our abundant resources, and avoid, at the same time, such an accumulation of debt as would render at all doubtful our capacity to redeem it.

The total receipts into the Treasury for the two quarters ending on the 30th September, 1864, were $415,191,550, which sum, added to the balance of $308,282,722, that remained in the Treasury on the 1st April last, forms a total of $728,474,272. Of this total, not far from half, that is to say, $342,560,327, have been applied to the extinction of the public debt, while the total expenditures have been $272,378,505, leaving a balance in the Treasury on the 1st October, 1864, of $108,435,440.

The total amount of the public debt, as exhibited on the books of the Register of the Treasury, on the 1st October, 1864, was $1,147,970,208, of which $539,840,090 were funded debt, bearing interest; $283,880,150 were treasury notes of the new issue, and the remainder consisted of the former issue of treasury notes, which will be converted into other forms of debt, and will cease to exist as currency on the 31st of next month.

The report, however, explains that, in consequence of the absence of certain returns from distant officers, the true amount of the debt is less, by about $2,500,000 than appears on the books of the Register, and that the total public debt on the 1st of last month, may be fairly considered to have been $1,126,381,095.

The increase of the public debt during the six months from the 1st of April to the 1st of October, was $97,050,780, being rather more than $16,000,000 per month, and it will be apparent, on a perusal of the report, that this augmentation would have been avoided, and a positive reduction of the amount would have been effected, but for certain defects in the legislation on the subject of the finances, which are pointed out in the report, and which seem to admit of easy remedy.

In the statements just made, the foreign debt is omitted, It consists only of the unpaid balance of the loan known as the cotton loan. This balance is but £2,200,000, and is adequately provided for by about 250,000 bales of cotton owned by the Government, even if the cotton be rated as worth but sixpence per pound.

There is one item of the public debt not included in the tables presented, to which your attention is required. The bounty bonds promised to our soldiers by the third section of the act of 17th February, 1864, were deliverable on the 1st October. The Secretary has been unable to issue them by reason of an omission in the law, no time being therein fixed for the payment of the bonds.

The aggregate appropriations called for by the different departments of the Government, according to the estimates submitted with the report, for the six months ending on the 20th June, 1865, amount to $435,102,679, while the Secretary estimates that there will remain unexpended, out of former appropriations, on the 1st January, 1865, a balance of $467,416,504. It would, therefore, seem that former estimates have been largely in excess of actual expenditures, and that no additional expenditures are required for meeting the needs of the public service up to the 1st July of next year. Indeed, if the estimates now presented should prove to be as much in excess of actual expenditures as has heretofore been the case, a considerable balance will still remain unexpended at the close of the first half of the ensuing year.

The chief difficulty to be apprehended in connection with our finances, results from the depreciation of the Treasury notes, which seems justly to be attributed by the Secretary to two causes -- redundancy in amount and want of confidence in ultimate redemption; for both of which, remedies are suggested that will commend themselves to your consideration as being practicable as well as efficient.

The main features of the plan presented are substantially these: First -- That the faith of the Government be pledged that the notes shall ever remain exempt from taxation. Second -- That no issue shall be made beyond that which is already authorized by law. Third -- That a certain fixed portion of the annual receipts from taxation during the war, shall be set apart specially for the gradual extinction of the outstanding amount, until it shall have been reduced to $150,000,000; and Fourth -- The pledge and appropriation of such proportion of the tax in kind, and for such number of years after the return of peace, as shall be sufficient for the final redemption of the entire circulation. The detail of the plan, the calculations on which it is based, the efficiency of its operation, and the vast advantages which would result from its success, are fully detailed in the report, and cannot be presented in a form sufficiently condensed for this message. I doubt not it will receive from you that earnest and candid consideration which is merited by the importance of the subject.

The recommendations of the report for the repeal of certain provisions of the tax laws which produce inequality in the burden of taxation; for exempting all Government loans from taxation on capital, and from any adverse discrimination in taxation on income derived from them; for placing the taxation on banks on the same footing as the taxation of other corporate bodies; for securing the payment into the treasury of that portion of the bank circulation which is liable to confiscation because held by alien enemies; for the conversion of the interest-bearing treasury notes now outstanding into coupon bonds, and for the quarterly collection of taxation; all present practical questions for legislation, which, if wisely devised, will greatly improve the public credit, and alleviate the burdens now imposed by the extreme and unnecessary depreciation in the value of the currency.

The return of the Produce Loan Bureau are submitted with the report, and the information is conveyed that the Treasury Agency in the Trans-Mississippi Department has been fully organized, and is now in operation with promise of efficiency and success.

The provisions heretofore made to some extent for increasing the compensation of public officers, civil and military, is found to be in some places inadequate, to their support; perhaps not more so anywhere than in Richmond, and inquiry, with a view to appropriate remedy, is suggested to your consideration. Your notice is also called to the condition of certain officers of the Treasury, who were omitted in the laws heretofore passed for the relief of other public officers, as mentioned in the report of the Secretary of the Treasury.

The condition of the various branches of the military service is stated in the accompanying report of the Secretary of War. Among the suggestions made for legislative action, with a view to add to the numbers and efficiency of the army, all of which will receive your consideration, there are some prominent topics which merit special notice.

The exemption from military duty now accorded by law to all persons engaged in certain specified pursuits or professions, is shown by experience to be unwise, nor is it believed to be defensible in theory. The defence home, family and country is universally recognized as the paramount political duty of every member of society; and in a form of Government like ours, where each citizen enjoys an equality of rights and privileges, nothing can be more invidious than an unequal distribution of duties

and obligations. No pursuit nor position should relieve any one, who is able to do active duty, from enrollment in the army, unless his functions or services are more useful to the defence of his country in another sphere. But it is manifest this cannot be the case with the entire classes. All telegraph operators, workmen in mines, professors, teachers, engineers, editors and employees of newspapers, journeymen printers, shoemakers, tanners, blacksmiths, millers, physicians and numerous other classes mentioned in the laws, cannot in the nature of things be either equally necessary in their several professions, nor distributed throughout the country in such proportions that only the exact numbers required are found in each locality; nor can it be everywhere impossible to replace those within the conscript age by men older and less capable of active field services. A discretion should be vested in the military authorities, so that a sufficient number of those essential to the public service might be detailed to continue the exercise of their pursuits or professions, but the exemption from service of the entire classes should be wholly abandoned. It affords great facility for abuses, offers the temptation as well as the ready means of escaping service by fraudulent devices, and is one of the principal obstructions to the efficient operation of the conscript laws.

A general militia law is needful in the interest of her public defence. The Constitution, by vesting the power in Congress, imposes on the duty of providing "for organizing, arming and disciplining the militia, and for governing such part of them as may be employed in the service of the Confederate States." The great diversity in the legislation of the several States on this subject, and the absence of any provision establishing an exact method for calling the militia into Confederate service, are sources of embarrassment which ought no longer to be suffered to impede defensive measures.

The legislation in relation to the cavalry demands change. The policy of requiring the men to furnish their own horses has proven pernicious in many respects. It interferes with discipline, impairs efficiency, and is the cause of frequent and prolonged absence from appropriate duty. The subject is fully treated in the Secretary's report, with suggestions as to the proper measures for reforming that branch of the service.

The recommendation hitherto often made is, again

renewed, that some measure be adopted for the reorganization and consolidation of companies and regiments when so far reduced in numbers as to seriously impair their efficiency. It is the more necessary that this should be done, as the absence of the legislation on the subject has forced Generals in the field to resort to various expedients for approximating the desired end. It is surely an evil that a commanding officer should be placed in a position which forces upon him the choice of allowing the efficiency of his command to be seriously impaired, or of attempting to supply by the exercise of doubtful authority the want of proper legal provision. The regard for the sensibility of officers who have heretofore served with credit, and which is believed to be the controlling motive that has hitherto obstructed legislation on this subject, however honorable and proper, may be carried to a point which seriously injures the public good; and if this be the case, it can scarcely be questioned which of the two considerations should be deemed paramount.

The Secretary's recommendations on the subject of facilitating the acquisition of the iron required for maintaining the efficiency of railroad communication on the important military lines are commended to your favor. The necessity for the operation in full vigor of such lines is too apparent to need comment.

The question in dispute between the two Governments relative to the exchange of prisoners of war has been frequently presented in former messages and reports, and is fully treated by the Secretary. The solicitude for the relief of the captive fellow-citizens has known no abatement; but has, on the contrary, been still more deeply evoked by the additional sufferings to which they have been wantonly subjected, by deprivation of adequate food, clothing and fuel, which they were not even allowed to purchase from the prison-sutlers. Finding that the enemy attempted to excuse their barbarous treatment by the unfounded allegation that it was retaliatory for like conduct on our part, an offer was made by us, with a view of ending all pretext for such recriminations or pretended retaliation.

The offer has been accepted, and each Government is, hereafter, to be allowed to provide necessary comforts to its own citizens held captive by the other. Active efforts are in progress for the immediate execution of this agreement, and it is hoped that but few days will elapse before we shall be relieved from the distressing thought that painful physical suffering is endured by so many of our fellow-citizens, whose fortitude in captivity illustrates the national character as fully as did their valor in actual conflict.

The employment of slaves for service with the army as teamsters, or cooks, or in any way of work upon fortifications, or in the Government workshops, or in hospitals, and other similar duties, was authorized by the act of 17th February last, and provision was made for their impressment to a number not exceeding twenty thousand, if it should be found to be impracticable to obtain them by contract with the owners. The law contemplated the hiring only of the labor of the slaves and imposed on the Government the liability to pay for the value of such as might be lost to the owners from casualties resulting from their employment in the service.

This act has produced less result than was anticipated, and further provision is required to render it efficacious. But my present purpose is to invite your consideration to the propriety of a radical modification in the theory of the law.

Viewed merely as property, and therefore as the subject of imprisonment, the service or labor of the slave has been frequently claimed for short periods, in the construction of defensive works. The slave, however, bears another relation to the State -- that of a person. The law of last February contemplates the relation of the slave to the master, and limits the impressment to a certain term of service. But for the purposes enumerated in the act, instruction in the manner of encamping, marching and parking trains is needful, so that, even in this limited employment, length of service adds greatly to the value of the negro's labor. Hazard is also encountered in all the positions to which negroes can be assigned for service with the army, and the duties required of them demand loyalty and zeal.

In this aspect the relation of person predominates so far as to render it doubtful whether the private right of property can consistently and beneficially be continued, and it would seem proper to acquire for the public service the entire property in the labor of the slave, and to pay therefor due compensation rather than to impress his labor for short terms; and this the more especially as the effect of the present law would vest this entire property in all cases where the slave might be recaptured after compensation for his loss had been paid to the private owner. Whenever the entire property in the service of a slave is thus acquired by the Government, the question is presented, by what tenure he should be held. Should he be retained in servitude or should his emancipation be held out to him as a reward for faithful service, or should it be granted at once on the promise of such service; and if emancipated, what action should be taken to secure for the freed man the permission of the State from which he was drawn to reside within its limits after the close of his public service. The permission would doubtless be more readily accorded as a reward for past faithful service; and a double motive for zealous discharge of duty would thus be offered to those employed by the Government -- their freedom, and the gratification of the local attachment which is so marked a characteristic of the negro, and forms so powerful an incentive to his action. The policy of engaging to liberate the negro on his discharge after service faithfully rendered, seems to me preferable to that of granting immediate manumission, or that of retaining him in servitude. If this policy should recommend itself to the judgment of Congress, it is suggested that, in addition to the duties heretofore performed by the slave, he might be advantageously employed as a pioneer and engineer laborer; and, in that event, that the number should be augmented to forty thousand.

Beyond this limit and these employments it does not seem to me desirable, under existing circumstances, to go. A broad moral distinction exists between the use of slaves as soldiers in the defence of our homes and the incitement of the same persons to insurrection against their masters. The one is justifiable if necessary, the other is iniquitous and unworthy of a civilized people; and such is the judgment of all writers on public law, as well as that expressed and insisted on by our enemies in all wars prior to that now waged against us. By none have the practices of which they are now guilty been denounced with greater severity than by themselves in the two wars with Great Britain in the last and in the present century; and in the Declaration of Independence of 1776, when enumeration was made of the wrongs which justified the revolt from Great Britain, the climax of atrocity was deemed to be reached only when the English monarch was denounced as having "excited domestic insurrection among us."

The subject is to be viewed by us, therefore, solely in the light of policy and our social economy. When so regarded, I must dissent from those who advise a general levy and arming of the slaves for the duty of soldiers. Until our white population shall prove insufficient for the armies we require, and can afford to keep in the field, to employ as a soldier the negro who has merely been trained to labor, and as a laborer, the white man, accustomed from his youth to the use of fire-arms, would scarcely be deemed wise or advantageous by any; and this is the question now before us. But should the alternative ever be presented, of subjugation or of the employment of the slave, as a soldier, there seems no reason to doubt what should then be our decision. Whether our view embraces what would, in so extreme a case, be the sum of misery entailed by the dominion of the enemy, or be restricted solely to the effect upon the welfare and happiness of the negro population themselves, the result would be the same. The appalling demoralization, suffering, disease and death which have been caused by partially substituting the invaders' system of police, for the kind relation previously subsisting between the master and slave, have been a sufficient demonstration that external interference with our institution of domestic slavery is productive of evil only.

If the subject involved no other consideration than the mere right of properly, the sacrifices heretofore made by our people have been such as to permit no doubt of their readiness to surrender every possession in order to secure their independence. But the social and political question which is exclusively under the control of the several States, has a far wider and more enduring importance than that of pecuniary interest. In its manifold phases it embraces the stability of republican institutions, resting on the actual political equality of all its citizens, and includes the fulfillment of the task which has been to happily begun -- that of Christianizing and improving the condition of the Africans who have, by the will of Providence, been placed in our charge. Comparing the results of our experience with those of the experiments of others who have borne similar relation to the African race, the people of the several States of the Confederacy have abundant reason to be satisfied with the past, and to use the greatest circumspection in determining their course.

These considerations, however, are rather applicable to the improbable contingency of our need of resorting to this element of resistance than to our present condition. It the recommendations above made, for the training of 40,000 negroes for the service indicated, shall meet your approval, it is certain that even this limited number, by their preparatory training in intermediate duties, would form a more valuable reserve force in case of urgency than three-fold their number suddenly called from field labor; while a fresh levy could, to a certain extent, supply their places in the special service for which they are now employed.

The regular annual reports of the Attorney General, the Secretary of the Navy and the Postmaster-General are appended, and give ample information relative to the condition of the respective departments. They contain suggestions for legislative provisions required to remedy such defects in the existing laws as have been disclosed by experience, but none or so general or important a character as to require that I should do more than recommend them to your favorable consideration.

The disposition of this Government for a peace solution of the issues which the enemy has referred to the arbitrament of arms, has been too often manifested, and is too well known to need new assurances. But while it is true that individuals and parties in the United States have indicated a desire to substitute reason for force, and by negotiation to stop the further sacrifice of human life, and to arrest the calamities which now afflict both countries, the authorities who control the Government of our enemies have too often and too clearly expressed their resolution to make no peace except on terms of our unconditional submission and degradation, to leave us any hope of the cessation of hostilities until the delusion of their ability to conquer us is dispelled.

Among those who are already disposed for peace, many are actuated by principle and by disapproval and abhorrence of the iniquitous warfare that their Government is waging, while others are moved by the conviction that it is no longer to the interest of the United States to continue a struggle in which success is unattainable. Whenever this fast-growing conviction shall have taken firm root in the minds of a majority of the Northern people, there will be produced that willingness to negotiate for peace which is now confined to our side. Peace is manifestly impossible unless desired by both parties to this war, and the disposition for it among our enemies will be best and most certainly evoked by the demonstration on our part of ability and unshaken determination to defend our rights, and to hold no earthly price too dear for their purchase. Whenever there shall be on the part of our enemies, a desire for peace, there will be no difficulty in finding means by which negotiations can be opened but it is obvious that no agency can be called into action until this desire shall be mutual. When that contingency shall happen, the Government, to which is confided the treaty-making power can be at no loss for means adapted to accomplish so desirable an end.

In the hope that the day will soon be reached when, under Divine favor, these States may be allowed to enter on their former peaceful pursuits, and to develop the abundant natural resources with which they are blessed, let us then resolutely continue to devote our united and unimpaired energies to the defence of our homes, our lives and our liberties. This is the true path to peace. Let us tread it with confidence in the assured result.

JEFFERSON DAVIS.
RICHMOND, Nov. 7, 1864.

GLOSSARY

impressment: the act of forcibly taking for the public service

property: a thing that is owned; Southerners considered slaves as their property in the same way as they thought of a chair, a plow, or a wagon as their property

manumission: the act of an owner releasing a slave from bondage

incitement: a cause for action; Southerners considered incitement to be the actions that the Union Army and government took to encourage enslaved people to run away

Social economy: how social classes are expected to work together; in the South, the social economy referred to the relationship between master and slave

Document Analysis

The section of Davis' November 7 address under review is entitled "Employment of Slaves." He begins with a reminder that the Act of the previous February authorized the impressment of up to 20,000 slaves "if it should be found impracticable to obtain them by contract with owners." Davis noted the problem with implementation of the Act; slave owners still possessed title to the contracted or impressed slaves and insisted on limitations to how the government employed their bondsmen. Owners included in contracts limits on amounts of time a slave could be away, and limits on the duties he might perform, thus constraining the Confederate government from obtaining a maximum amount of work.

Here is where Davis proposed "a radical modification in the theory of the law." As property, slaves' employment could be severely constrained by their masters. But, Davis said, "the slave…bears another relation to the state—that of a person." This stance contradicted the pro-slavery finding by the United States Supreme Court in the Dred Scott decision that black men were of such "an inferior order, and altogether unfit to associate with the white race, either in social or political relations…that they had no rights which the white man was bound to respect." Davis's new interpretation allowed the state—the Confederacy—to recognize blacks as persons and therefore demand a greater commitment from them. In fact, he wrote, "in this respect the relation of person predominates so far as to render it doubtful whether the private right of property can consistently and beneficially be continued." In other

words, the Confederacy may interpret the law in such a way as to disregard the rights of the slave owner and elevate the status of the slave to that of a legal person. Once so interpreted, the state could then claim the ability to keep a black man in service longer, train him for skilled work, and assign him to dangerous posts—all previously forbidden by contracting masters. Davis recognized that if the state viewed the impressed slave as a person, it had an obligation to grant that slave certain rights and privileges associated with personhood. After all, would not a slave in service to the military be expected to express loyalty, endure hardship, and strive to accomplish difficult tasks? Southern states had a long tradition of rewarding faithful or valorous slaves with emancipation. The same would be expected of slaves serving the Confederacy. The promise of freedom would be "a double motive for a zealous discharge of duty." Davis did stop to note that any such emancipation would happen only *after* the service was rendered, not before (as Cleburne and other advocates had suggested).

Davis demurred, however, from advocating the use of black men as soldiers. "Beyond these limits and these employments," he wrote, "it does not seem to me desirable, under existing circumstances, to go." However, Davis insisted that such a use would be legitimate; at least more legitimate than the Union's use of freed slaves as soldiers , which he considered "insurrection against their masters." If the Confederacy used slaves as soldiers, the moral world could be satisfied that the slaves did so solely "in defense of their homes." Principle aside, Davis quickly reminded his hearers that he found the use of slaves as soldiers unnecessary so long as enough white men stood ready to fill the ranks. But should that day come when sufficient white men failed at their duty to enlist, "there seems no reason to doubt what should then be our decision."

Davis grasped at a rhetorical maneuver Cleburne had made when Davis wrote "If the subject [the war] involved no other consideration than the mere right of property [in slaves], the sacrifices heretofore made by our people have been such as to permit no doubt of their readiness to surrender every possession in order to secure their independence." Where the Jefferson Davis of 1861 had bound the preservation of slavery and the constitutional claim to independence into one impenetrable cause, the Jefferson Davis of late 1864 proved willing to pry them apart and elevate one over the other.

Davis' address in regard to the potential of slave labor reads less like a lawyer's brief and more like a man who was delicately reconsidering a fundamental belief and careful to cover his changes with plenty of caveats and conditions. Davis' thinking about the core values of the Confederacy, though evolving, remained fundamentally conservative. His address pressed policy makers to reconsider the states' ability to claim the labor and destiny of slave owners' property, certainly a significant departure from the original secessionists' protest that the state could not govern the relationship between master and slave. And though he denied that the Confederacy was so desperate as to actually need slave soldiers, he staked a claim to consider their use in the future. Such an admission stunned the Confederate political class and set off a season of vigorous debate on the topic of black men in arms .

Essential Themes

Despite Davis' complete rejection of Patrick Cleburne's memorial ten months before, the General's logic about recasting Confederate rhetoric found the president a ready advocate. Davis, after all, had long cloaked the cause of slavery in the language of constitutional principal. Davis had begun divorcing the two as early as July 1864 when he privately told two unofficial Northern emissaries that slavery "was only a means of bringing other conflicting elements to an earlier culmination. It fired the musket which was already capped and loaded." All it took for Davis to publically discuss the implications of the rhetorical devaluing of slavery was the desperate straights of the Confederacy in late 1864.

The furthest implication—the arming of slaves as soldiers and the potential for widespread emancipation—however, was something Davis had conceded only in principle, not as policy. Davis initiated the discussion with his delicate thinking, but Confederates followed with a robust discussion about the fundamental alteration in the nature of slavery.

Many Confederates disagreed with Davis. Prominent statesmen like Georgia's Howell Cobb and Virginia's R.M.T. Hunter had no compunction about claiming slavery as the *raison d'etre* for the Confederacy and enforcing that conviction by opposing all attempts to place blacks alongside whites in the ranks or reward them with emancipation. David Yulee of Florida directly challenged Davis' new legal configuration: "whenever the Confederate government treats Slaves in the States otherwise than *as property* a social revolution is begun in the South, the end of which may not be foreseen." One congressman elegantly described how the bonds forged between soldiers would become sundered, as "a chain which the electric spark of sympathy and mutual confidence can no longer traverse...the answering smile, the triumphant glance, the understood pledge of mutual devotion, heretofore transmitted from company to company [will be] all interrupted and destroyed." Just as the nation depended on slavery to govern its race relations, individual white men would not countenance emotional intimacy not based on explicitly understood inequality.

Aside from the horrifying prospect of social equality that black men in the ranks might suggest, opponents of the black soldier idea offered other reasons to be against it. To arm blacks would demonstrate to the world—particularly to England and France—how weak and desperate the Confederacy had become. Thus exposed as helpless, the Confederacy would be easy prey for manipulative and predatory nations. Other opponents spoke for the soldiers in the ranks and claimed that they would not fight alongside blacks. But opposition always came back around to the conviction that the plan was impossible to countenance let alone implement because it would betray the very reason for the Confederacy. One opponent lamented that the likely outcome of even limited emancipation and arming of slaves "would inevitably [be] the destruction of the institution of slavery, and the consequent ruin and degradation of the South."

The plan's proponents denied the charge that the proposal to arm and emancipate black men betrayed

Confederate ideals. Nothing that Davis had proposed, they observed, permitted anything but perpetual superiority of whites over blacks. Indeed, the Davis administration's embrace of a limited plan of service followed by emancipation suggests that advocates were clear-eyed about the tenuous future of slavery as it had existed, and were thinking feverishly about how to maintain white supremacy in a post-war world. Historian Bruce Levine has claimed that the proponents of black soldiers had made a "cold-blooded appraisal of the slaveholder's desperate situation and dwindling options after about the middle of 1863." But Davis and the realists had still to convince a fractious and skeptical nation.

Christopher Graham

Bibliography

Cooper, William J., Jr. *Jefferson Davis, American.* New York: Vintage, 2001. Print

Levine, Bruce. *Confederate Emancipation: Southern Plans to Free and Arm Slaves during the Civil War.* New York: Oxford UP, 2006. Print.

Additional Reading

Escott, Paul D. *After Secession: Jefferson Davis and the Failure of Confederate Nationalism.* Baton Rouge: Louisiana State UP, 1992. Print.

Levine, Bruce. *The Fall of the House of Dixie: The Civil War and the Social Revolution that Transformed the South.* New York: Random House, 2013. Print.

Martinez, Jamie Amanda. *Confederate Slave Impressment in the Upper South.* Chapel Hill: U of North Carolina P, 2013. Print.

Thomas, Emory M. *The Confederate Nation: 1861-1865.* New York: Harper, reprint, 2011. Print.

■ General Lee on Black Confederate Soldiers

Date: January 11, 1865; February 18, 1865
Authors: Lee, Robert E.
Genre: letters

> *"If it end in subverting slavery it will be accomplished
> by ourselves, and we can devise the means of
> alleviating the evil consequences to both races."*

Summary Overview

From the first year of the war, with General Robert E. Lee serving as Jefferson Davis' military aid, until the last year, with Lee as General-in-Chief of Confederate armies, President Davis had always turned to the general as a confidant and as a source for sound and competent advice. By 1865, Lee served as more than the president's closest advisor; he stood as the most widely trusted and admired man in the Confederacy. No other general or politician held the confidence of such a wide part of the population. Where Davis faced opposition and had to fight for every political gain, Lee's gravitas could sway public opinion and official policy with a stroke of his pen.

Davis, in his November 7, 1864 address to the Second Confederate Congress had cautiously proposed an expanded role for enslaved blacks in the Confederate military. While he spoke only of employing blacks in more dangerous positions with pioneer and engineer troops, the power to do so that he requested implied blacks' future right to consideration as regular soldiers in the service. While the Confederate's prospects for victory in the war appeared increasingly distant and more people began to favor Davis's position, the proposal still faced significant opposition in Congress and in the public mind. Therefore, when Davis and ever more strident proponents of arming slaves, like Secretary of State Judah B. Benjamin, found the proposal at a public impasse, they turned to Lee.

Defining Moment

Davis' equivocal November proposal met with widespread inaction outside of the small but growing coterie that advocated arming slaves. Even in that desperate moment, many clung to the hope that Southern armies would prevail, that the Lincoln administration would sue for a negotiated peace, or that even England and France would still intervene. But events over the next two months proved them wrong. Sherman's march through Georgia had ended with the capture of Savannah in late December just after Phillip Sheridan's Union forces crushed Confederates in the Shenandoah Valley, while Union armies elsewhere continued to encroach on territory and drain blood and resources from Confederate armies. French diplomats effectively foreclosed the idea of any assistance in the same month. Finally, Confederate hopes were ruined by the results of the Hampton Roads Conference in February 1865. At Hampton Roads, Confederate and Union military commissioners met to consider a negotiated end to the war. While Confederate emissaries hoped for independence, or at least a return to the Union with slavery intact, the Union representatives (including Lincoln himself) plainly stated that the South must return to the Union under the terms of the newly passed 13th Amendment that abolished slavery altogether. Anything short of that and Northern armies would continue marching. The dismayed and disappointed Confederates left Hampton Roads convinced that peace could not be had.

These events caused many Southerners to reconsider their stance on the idea of using slaves as soldiers. Georgia Congressman Warren Akin noted in December "a great change is going [on] in the public mind about putting negroes in the army." Yet the resistance of stalwarts who did not wish to alter slavery still remained, particularly in the House of Representatives and the Senate. The advocates surrounding Davis looked to solicit a public opinion from General Lee, who they knew to be sympathetic to the idea. Lee did so in conversations and in two letters to Confederate politicians.

Author Biography
As a son of the most prominent of Virginia planter families, born in 1807, and married into the family of even more famous and wealthy Virginians, Lee grew up in a world built on the foundations of unfree labor. The young Lee attended West Point, graduated in 1829, and served in the United States army as an engineer officer. He gained national fame for valorous service in the Mexican War but only first commanded troops when appointed Lt. Colonel of the Second United States Cavalry regiment in 1855. At the Lee home, Arlington House, in northern Virginia, his wife's family owned nearly 200 enslaved black people. There, the Lee family practiced what they imagined as an enlightened form of slaveholding. They saw to the spiritual welfare of their slaves; they permitted their black people to read and tend to their own gardens; and they granted them unusual lenience in leaving the Arlington estate to visit Washington City just over the Potomac. The Lees spoke frequently of their desire to keep married slave couples together with their children, even if they did not always hold to this precept. The Lee family slaveholding ethic disdained the outright violence and humanity inherent in the institution. Though the Lee family's self-conception as benevolent and Christian masters may have led

to some alleviation for their bondsmen, it was by no means a precursor to emancipation or racial equality. They imagined a day when the benevolent guidance of moral white people would make blacks ready for freedom. But that day remained a theoretical concept. Until then, the Lees continued to coerce black people, sell them away, and deny them privileges accorded to free people. Indeed, the ethic of slave owning that the Lee family practiced did not arise from a concern for black people as much as from their self-regard as Christians and self-protection from the charges of abolitionists who condemned slavery's inherent violence. When Lee chose to resign his United States army commission and serve Virginia and the Confederacy, he did so to fight for and protect the larger system of values and assumptions about the races exemplified by how he practiced slavery.

In Confederate service, Lee spent the first year of war organizing Virginia's defense and advising President Davis on the military condition of the South at large. Upon being appointed commander of the Army of Northern Virginia, he delivered the Union army then pressing Richmond a series of heavy blows before marching north to threaten the United States capitol. Lee also commanded a failed effort by a small Confederate army to recapture Western Virginia and then organized Confederate coastal defenses along the South Carolina and Georgia coast. The stunning victories Lee engineered in the summer of 1862, at the head of an audacious and high-spirited army of cavaliers and fighters, fixed his place in the public mind as the beau ideal of a soldier and the most revered man in the Confederacy. Even the disaster at Gettysburg could not shake the confidence the nation, or the President, had in him. When Judah P. Benjamin solicited Lee's opinion regarding the potential use of black troops, he could expect a reasoned and tempered answer.

HISTORICAL DOCUMENT

Headquarters Army of Northern Virginia
January 11, 1865
Hon. Andrew Hunter
Richmond, Va.:

Dear Sir:
I have received your letter of the 7th instant, and without confining myself to the order of your interrogatories, will endeavor to answer them by a statement of my views on the subject. I shall be most happy if I can contribute to

the solution of a question in which I feel an interest commensurate with my desire for the welfare and happiness of our people.

Considering the relation of master and slave, controlled by humane laws and influenced by Christianity and an enlightened public sentiment, as the best that can exist between the white and black races while intermingled as at present in this country, I would deprecate any sudden disturbance of that relation unless it be necessary to avert a greater calamity to both. I should therefore prefer to rely upon our white population to preserve the ratio between our forces and those of the enemy, which experience has shown to be safe. But in view of the preparations of our enemies, it is our duty to provide for continued war and not for a battle or a campaign, and I fear that we cannot accomplish this without overtaxing the capacity of our white population.

Should the war continue under the existing circumstances, the enemy may in course of time penetrate our country and get access to a large part of our negro population. It is his avowed policy to convert the able-bodied men among them into soldiers, and to emancipate all. The success of the Federal arms in the South was followed by a proclamation of President Lincoln for 280,000 men, the effect of which will be to stimulate the Northern States to procure as substitutes for their own people negroes thus brought within their reach. Many have already been obtained in Virginia, and should the fortune of war expose more of her territory, the enemy would gain a large accession to his strength. His progress will thus add to his numbers, and at the same time destroy slavery in a manner most pernicious to the welfare of our people. Their negroes will be used to hold them in subjection, leaving the remaining force of the enemy free to extend his conquest. Whatever may be the effect of our employing negro troops, it cannot be as mischievous as this. If it end in subverting slavery it will be accomplished by ourselves, and we can devise the means of alleviating the evil consequences to both races. I think, therefore, we must decide whether slavery shall be extinguished by our enemies and the slaves be used against us, or use them ourselves at the risk of the effects which must be produced upon our social institutions. My opinion is that we should employ them without delay. I believe that with proper regulations they can be made

efficient soldiers. They possess the physical qualifications in an eminent degree. Long habits of obedience and subordination, coupled with the moral influence which in our country the white man possesses over the black, furnish an excellent foundation for that discipline which is the best guaranty of military efficiency. Our chief aim should be to secure their fidelity.

There have been formidable armies composed of men having no interest in the cause for which they fought beyond their pay or the hope of plunder. But it is certain that the surest foundation upon which the fidelity of an army can rest, especially in a service which imposes peculiar hardships and privations, is the personal interest of the soldier in the issue of the contest. Such an interest we can give our negroes by giving immediate freedom to all who enlist, and freedom at the end of the war to the families of those who discharge their duties faithfully (whether they survive or not), together with the privilege of residing at the South. To this might be added a bounty for faithful service.

We should not expect slaves to fight for prospective freedom when they can secure it at once by going to the enemy, in whose service they will incur no greater risk than in ours. The reasons that induce me to recommend the employment of negro troops at all render the effect of the measures I have suggested upon slavery immaterial, and in my opinion the best means of securing the efficiency and fidelity of this auxiliary force would be to accompany the measure with a well-digested plan of gradual and general emancipation. As that will be the result of the continuance of the war, and will certainly occur if the enemy succeed, it seems to me most advisable to adopt it at once, and thereby obtain all the benefits that will accrue to our cause.

The employment of negro troops under regulations similar in principle to those above indicated would, in my opinion, greatly increase our military strength and enable us to relieve our white population to some extent. I think we could dispense with the reserve forces except in cases of necessity.

It would disappoint the hopes which our enemies base upon our exhaustion, deprive them in a great measure of the aid they now derive from black troops, and thus throw the burden of the war upon their own people. In addition to the great political advantages that would result to our cause from the adoption of a system of emancipation, it would exercise a salutary influence upon our whole negro population, by rendering more secure the fidelity of those who become soldiers, and diminishing the inducements to the rest to abscond.

I can only say in conclusion that whatever measures are to be adopted should be adopted at once. Every day's delay increases the difficulty. Much time will be required to organize and discipline the men, and action may be deferred until it is too late.

Very respectfully, your obedient servant,

R.E. Lee,
General

*** *** ***

Headquarters Confederate States Armies, February 18, 1865. Hon. E. Barksdale, House of Representatives, Richmond

Sir:
I have the honor to acknowledge the receipt of your letter of the 12th instant, with reference to the employment of negroes as soldiers. I think the measure not only expedient, but necessary. The enemy will certainly use them against us if he can get possession of them; and as his present numerical superiority will enable him to penetrate many parts of the country, I cannot see the wisdom of the policy of holding them to await his arrival, when we may, be timely action and judicious management, use them to arrest his progress. I do not think that our white population can supply the necessities of a long war without overtaxing its capacity and imposing great suffering upon our people; and I believe we should provide resources for a protracted struggle — not merely for a battle or a campaign.

In answer to your second question, I can only say that, in my opinion, the negroes, under proper circumstances, will make efficient soldiers. I think we could at least do as well with them as the enemy, and he attaches great importance to their assistance. Under good officers and good instructions, I do not see why they should not become soldiers. They possess all the physical qualifications, and their habits of obedience constitute a good foundation for discipline. They furnish a more promising material than many armies of which we read in history, which owed their efficiency to discipline alone. I think those who are employed should be freed. It would be neither just nor wise, in my opinion, to require them to serve as slaves. The best course to pursue, it seems to me, would be to call for such as are willing to come with the consent of their owners. An impressment or draft would not be likely to bring out the best class, and the use of coercion would make to their measure distasteful to them and to their owners.

I have no doubt that if Congress would authorize their reception into service, and empower the President to call upon individuals or States for such as they are willing to contribute, with the condition of emancipation to all enrolled, a sufficient number would be forthcoming to enable us to try the experiment. If it proved successful, most of the objections to the measure would disappear, and if individuals still remained unwilling to send their negroes to the army, the force of public opinion in the States would soon bring about such legislation as would remove all obstacles. I think the matter should be left, as far as possible, to the people and to the States, which alone can legislate as the necessities of this particular service may require. As to the mode of organizing them, it should be left as free from restraint as possible. Experience will suggest the best course, and it would be inexpedient to trammel the subject with provisions that might, in the end, prevent the adoption of reforms suggested by actual trial.

With great respect,

Your obedient servant,
R. E. Lee, General.

GLOSSARY

habits of obedience: whites thought that enslaved blacks had developed a particular skill for behaving in a deferential manner toward their owners and expected them to display the same in the army

our social institutions: In the South, a specific reference to the institution of slavery

bounty: a cash bonus for enlisting in the army

Document Analysis

Lee offered his position in two letters. The second letter, to influential Mississippi Congressman Ethelbert Barksdale, is considered here first, because it was released to the public, reprinted in newspapers across the South, and had the greatest public influence. Barksdale, after early opposition, had reconsidered his position on the slave-soldier plan and by 1865 he stood as one of the plan's proponents in Congress. Prompted by a query from Barksdale, Lee wrote intending his letter to be quickly and widely published.

Lee's letter to Barksdale is short and succinctly declares his support for the plan to emancipate and arm slaves . He declared up front, "I think the measure not only expedient but necessary." He offered three points to back up his assertion. First, he noted that the Union army recruited black soldiers from the South, and the more territory they captured, the more recruits they could access. Lee admitted that while the existing population of white Southern men might be enough to repel the enemy in a single battle or campaign, he insisted that the present reserve of men could not sustain the South in any protracted contest. To enlist black soldiers would both withhold those recruits from Federal service and support the service of white men in Southern armies. Second, Lee contended that blacks would make fine soldiers, owing to what he considered their "habits of obedience." This endorsement from the Confederacy's premier military commander likely alleviated the fears of many Southerners who did not think a former slave had the moral capacity to make a good soldier. Finally, Lee offered his opinion on the process of recruitment. He insisted that for a black soldier to be effective, he must demonstrate his devotion to the

cause of freedom by volunteering for service. A man coerced into service by his master, Lee thought, would not fight as hard.

In Lee's letter to Barksdale the general crafted a forceful but palatable political message for public consumption. The issue of freeing slaves to fight for the South, however, touched upon greater and more fundamental concerns—those of the future of slavery in the white republic. Lee deliberately sidestepped this issue in his public letter. That he had considered the larger ramifications of black soldiers is clear from an earlier missive to Virginia state senator Andrew Hunter.

To Hunter, Lee had been candid. He explained his expectation for an ideal form of slavery. He valued slavery "controlled by humane laws and influenced by Christianity and an enlightened public sentiment." That vision is one that he and his family had attempted to implement at Arlington. That was the form of slavery he desired, and "I would deprecate any sudden disturbance of that relation." All things considered, then, Lee would have preferred to leave slavery as it was, or at least as he had imagined that he had practiced it. But he, as clearly as any other man in the Confederacy, knew that the war had irrevocably changed slavery. Two choices faced the Confederacy and its chief institution: to lose the war and have universal emancipation forced upon the South by a vindictive conqueror, or to get ahead of the changing institution and take a direct hand in how it changed. Thus, when Lee said that he would prefer to see slavery confirmed as it was "unless it be necessary to avert a greater calamity," he meant that the South should take charge to ensure that slavery changed on Southern white people's terms, and not those of Southern blacks or Northern whites. "If it [the proposal] end in subverting slavery it will be accomplished by ourselves, and we can devise the means of alleviating the evil consequences to both races."

Lee's Virginia paternalism still expressed itself with his insistence that the best method of survival for blacks was in inferior positions to Southern whites. Offering limited emancipation to worthy blacks in the South was his solution. Only white Southerners could compose a "well-digested plan of gradual and general emancipation." Even Lee's paternalism could not shield him from the realization that tampering with the fundamental aspects of slavery would lead irresistibly to "general emancipation."

Lee rehearsed the points he would unveil in his letter to Barksdale. The Union army threatened to recruit even more black Southerners. We should act to prevent that by bringing blacks into our own army. They will be good soldiers. And he insisted that if such a plan were to be considered and passed by Congress, it must be done immediately.

Essential Themes

When Judah P. Benjamin solicited General Lee's opinion about the use of black soldiers, he also requested the views of the soldiers in the Army of Northern Virginia. This request set off a remarkable series of debates, meetings, and resolutions from corps commanders to enlisted men in the ranks. At the regimental and brigade levels, soldiers held meetings, elected committeemen, presented resolutions, and voted. For instance, the officers and men of General Joseph Davis' Brigade of Mississippians elected Private W. C. McDougall of the 26th Mississippi as chairman of their meeting. Private William F. Price of the 11th Mississippi submitted resolutions that were discussed and adopted. The preamble to the resolutions declared "the enemy...has stolen our negroes and placed them in his armies." It continued, "we, the soldiers of this brigade...believe the time has come when the war material of our country, regardless of color, should be fully developed." They resolved that blacks should be inducted as soldiers, that Congress be comforted in knowing "that it will create no dissatisfaction in our ranks," and that the legislature of Mississippi raise and equip a brigade of black soldiers immediately.

A slight majority of resolutions favored the use of black soldiers. Yet some did so with considerable hesitation. Soldiers of the 56th Virginia Infantry began their resolutions by affirming "that slavery is the normal con-

dition of the negro" and that the right to hold slaves was granted by the constitution and laws. They further reminded readers of their commitment to slavery by noting "involuntary servitude is as indispensable to the moral and physical advancement, prosperity and happiness of the African race as is liberty to the whites." After reiterating their paternalistic beliefs about the role of the races in society, they grudgingly admitted "if the public exigencies require that any number of our male slaves be enlisted in the military service in order to the successful resistance to our enemies...we are willing to make concessions to their [the slaves'] false and unenlightened notions of the blessings of liberty, and to offer to those, and those only who fight in our cause, perpetual freedom." These white soldiers witnessed enslaved people's enthusiasm for freedom and considered it misinformed and dangerous. But they were willing to go along if that enthusiasm was tapped to defend the Confederacy. Still, they advocated conditional freedom and deplored universal emancipation.

Despite the support the question elicited, some commands remained divided on the use of black soldiers. Cavalrymen in the 3rd Virginia recorded contradictory resolutions. At first, they maintained that a vigorous application of the law would produce enough white troops to sustain the war effort. Further, "we contemplate with anxiety and apprehension the proposition to enlist negro troops in our armies, seriously doubting both its expedience and practicability, [and] dreading its effects upon our social system." Like many opponents in the wider Confederacy, these troopers preferred to maintain the "social system" as it had been, even in the face of its certain destruction. But this resolution "elicited an animated and protracted discussion," resulting in the adoption of a competing resolution, "we are in favor of putting every man in the country between the ages of 17 and 45 in the army, and as many negroes, without changing their social status, as the Commander-in-Chief may deem necessary." They had succumbed to the reasoning of black soldier advocates, but could never allow that a black man could possess the freedom of a white man.

The details of these debates within the Confederacy, among its highest leadership and its lowliest soldiers, offer a unique view of how white Southerners adapted to the changing realities offered by war, and of how they adjusted their thinking—or not—about the reasons for which they fought in the first place. The success of Union armies and the obvious preference of enslaved black people for freedom within Union lines had driven many Confederates to the realization that slavery as they had known it was dead. Whether the brutal, violent, and exploitative slavery that existed in all parts of the South, or the supposedly benevolent slavery that the Lees practiced, the Confederacy went to war to maintain the "social system" in which whites maintained mastery over black people. The chief means of maintaining that mastery was the legal institution of bondage. But the war itself had unwittingly tampered with the system of slavery. Many Confederates, if they recognized this fact or not in 1865, insisted that slavery as it was, be preserved. And if it were not preserved, the Confederacy would not be worth fighting for. Those who did foresee the end of legal bondage worked hard in early 1865 to establish new conditions of race relations—whether in an independent Confederacy or a conquered South. They had been pushed unwillingly to this point and with a glimmer of hope, imagined that whatever the outcome, if they could not preserve slavery, they could at least preserve white mastery.

Christopher Graham

Bibliography

Gallagher, Gary. *The Confederate War: How Popular Will, Nationalism, and Military Strategy Could Not Stave Off Defeat.* Cambridge: Harvard UP, 1999. Print.

Levine, Bruce. *Confederate Emancipation: Southern Plans to Free and Arm Slaves during the Civil War.* New York: Oxford UP, 2006. Print.

Pryor, Elizabeth Brown. *Reading the Man: A Portrait of Robert E. Lee Through His Private Letters.* New York: Penguin, 2007. Print.

Further Reading

Clampitt, Bradley R. *The Confederate Heartland: Military and Civilian Morale in the Western Confederacy.* Baton Rouge: Louisiana State UP, 2011. Print

Escott, Paul D. *Military Necessity: Civil-Military Relations in the Confederacy.* Westport: Praeger, 2006. Print

Glatthaar, Joseph T. *General Lee's Army: From Victory to Collapse.* New York: Free Press, 2008. Print.

■ An Act to Increase the Military Force of the Confederate States

Date: March 23, 1865
Author: Barksdale, Ethelbert
Genre: law

"Nothing in this act shall be construed to authorize a change in the relation which the said slaves shall bear toward their owners."

Summary Overview

In March 1865 the Confederate Congress struggled with the administration of a faltering nation. Congress made adjustments to tax and financial policy, the organization of military commands, and how the government might extract scarce resources from a depleted countryside. On February 10, Congressman Ethelbert Barksdale of Mississippi rose to address the procurement of men for the army . He spoke in support of a bill designed to bring enslaved black men into the service. Barksdale laid out the bill's provisions and carefully noted that any pay the slave soldier might earn could be paid to the master, should the master desire it, and that the bill should not be "construed to authorize a change in the relation which the said slaves shall bear toward their owners as property." He added a jab at opponents, "are gentlemen unwilling to let the people have the privilege of contributing their slaves as a free-will offering to aid in repelling the savage foe?"

Congressman Williams Wickham of Virginia rose to oppose the bill. The veteran of many campaigns and battles with the Army of Northern Virginia, Wickham had a keen sense of sacrifices made for the cause. He declared, "the day that such a bill passes Congress sounds the death knell of this Confederacy," and added "the very moment an order goes forth from the War Department authorizing the arming and organizing of negro soldiers there was an eternal end to this struggle."

Many of his compatriots grumbled in agreement.

Defining Moment

The February 1865 Hampton Roads Conference had been an utter failure for the Confederates. Many in the government knew that the only hope for Confederate independence lay not on a battlefield reversal but on a negotiated peace with the Union. The Confederate delegation met with Union representatives, including Abraham Lincoln and Secretary of State William Seward aboard a steamboat in Hampton Roads, Virginia, on February 3. The Southerners expected to bargain for independence, but retained a hope that if peace included a return to the Union, that slavery could remain intact. Lincoln responded that only reunion—and reunion with the Emancipation Proclamation, and the pending 13th Amendment abolishing slavery, as settled facts—would be acceptable. To the Confederates Lincoln appeared intransigent, only willing to accept what they considered their utter humiliation and subjection. They made no deal. When the representatives returned to Richmond bearing the sobering news, all but the most disillusioned knew that their certain fate included military defeat, forcible return to the Union, the compulsory emancipation of all the slaves, and black people's elevation to social and political equality. The desperate news shocked many into accepting the necessity of a drastic proposal.

Many advocates of enrolling slaves as soldiers had previously insisted that an offer of freedom to the black soldier and his family would ensure diligent and loyal service. Barksdale's bill compromised on that conviction in order to mollify opponents who feared the general offer of emancipation for service would further undermine slavery. Only in the final version of the bill was language included that permitted states to conscript slaves if a sufficient number were not volunteered by their masters. Barksdale's bill passed the House of Representatives on February 20 with a vote of forty in favor and thirty-seven against. Despite the representatives' passage of the Barksdale bill, the endorsement of General Robert E. Lee, and the rapid change in public opinion toward favoring the use of black soldiers, the Confederate Senate decisively killed a version of the bill the following day.

At this impasse, the Virginia legislature stepped in. Politicians in Virginia, particularly Governor William Smith, had long advocated the use of black soldiers even if their Senators opposed any such proposal. On March 4, the legislature passed a resolution supporting the Barksdale bill, and instructed their Senators to vote in its favor. Reluctantly, Senators R.M.T. Hunter and Alan Caperton cast "yes" votes on a new Senate bill on March 8, bringing its supporters to nine against the eight of the opponents. The House of Representatives accepted the Senate version the following day and President Davis signed the bill into law on March 13.

Author Biography

The First Confederate Congress met in 1861 under an imprimatur of newness. The founding of a new nation had given the men collected in Montgomery, Alabama, and Richmond, Virginia, a sense of starting over, despite the fact that the structure of government closely resembled that of the old United States. Chief among the novelties of 1861 was a rejection of political parties and partisanship. Many blamed partisan fighting for the poisonous state of antebellum politics that lead to disunion. In the new nation, then, Congressmen pledged to discard partisan interests in favor of unified efforts to achieve national independence and happiness. This hopeful tone did not last.

Though organized political parties did not develop, factions had emerged and political strife colored contests for national and state offices in 1863. The factions did not boast political agendas, but coalesced broadly around opposition to, or support of, the Jefferson Davis administration. Anti-administration politicians took the president to task for a variety of imperfectly implemented policies that accrued power to the central government. They decried unfair conscription laws and condemned overbearing impressment measures to supply the army. They spoke out against the suspension of habeas corpus and considered Jefferson Davis a stubborn tyrant too wedded to war and political independence to take advantage of overtures of peace from the Northern states. Pro-administration men defended Davis' policies, and insisted that the exegesis of war demanded sacrifice and cooperation. Ironically, for a nation state dedicated to the conservative principles of limited federal power and sacredness of property rights, the Davis administration and its supporters proved adept at devising new ways to exercise central authority in the Confederacy.

Ethelbert Barksdale was a pro-administration man who one observer labeled "the leader of the Administration party in the House." The Mississippian had learned his political skills at a young age when he became an editor of the *Yazoo City Democrat* and later as editor of newspapers in the state capital, Jackson. While Barksdale entered elected office as a delegate to the Democratic national convention in Charleston and representative of Mississippi in the First Confederate Congress, his brother William became a renowned general, commanding a brigade in the Army of Northern Virginia and being killed in action at Gettysburg. The Congressman supported administration efforts to strengthen conscription and increase taxes, standing regularly to argue their necessity on the House floor. The idea introduced by Congressman Barksdale in March 1865 had many progenitors, from General Patrick Cleburne to Secretary of State Judah P. Benjamin and Jefferson Davis himself. Indeed, Barksdale had first opposed the idea. But after Jefferson Davis made the policy his own the previous November, Barksdale came around, and wrote the actual legislation and managed it through the deliberation process.

HISTORICAL DOCUMENT

ADJT. AND INSP. GENERAL'S OFFICE,

Richmond, Va., March 23, 1865.

GENERAL ORDERS, No. 14.

I. The following act of Congress and regulations are published for the information and direction of all concerned:

AN ACT to increase the military force of the Confederate States.

The Congress of the Confederate States of America do enact, That, in order to provide additional forces to repel invasion, maintain the rightful possession of the Confederate States, secure their independence, and preserve their institutions, the President be, and he is hereby, authorized to ask for and accept from the owners of slaves, the services of such number of able-bodied negro men as he may deem expedient, for and during the war, to perform military service in whatever capacity he may direct.

SEC 2. That the General-in-Chief be authorized to organize the said slaves into companies, battalions, regiments, and brigades, under such rules and regulations as the Secretary of War may prescribe, and to be commanded by such officers as the President may appoint.

SEC 3. That while employed in the service the said troops shall receive the same rations, clothing, and compensation as are allowed to other troops in the same branch of the service.

SEC 4. That if, under the previous sections of this act, the President shall not be able to raise a sufficient number of troops to prosecute the war successfully and maintain the sovereignty of the States and the independence of the Confederate States, then he is hereby authorized to call on each State, whenever he thinks it expedient, for her quota of 300,000 troops, in addition to those subject to military service under existing laws, or so many thereof as the President may deem necessary to be raised

from such classes of the population, irrespective of color, in each State, as the proper authorities thereof may determine: *Provided,* That not more than twenty-five per cent. of the male slaves between the ages of eighteen and forty-five, in any State, shall be called for under the provisions of this act.

SEC 5. That nothing in this act shall be construed to authorize a change in the relation which the said slaves shall bear toward their owners, except by consent of the owners and of the States in which they may reside, and in pursuance of the laws thereof.
Approved March 13, 1865.

II. The recruiting service under this act will be conducted under the supervision of the Adjutant and Inspector General, according to the regulations for the recruiting service of the Regular Army, in so far as they are applicable, and except when special directions may be given by the War Department.

III. There will be assigned or appointed for each State an officer who will be charged with the collection, enrollment, and disposition of all the recruits that may be obtained under the first section of this act. One or more general depots will be established in each State and announced in orders, and a suitable number of officers will be detailed for duty in the staff departments at the depots. There will be assigned at each general depot a quartermaster, commissary, and surgeon, and the headquarters of the superintendent will be at the principal depot in the State. The proper officers to aid the superintendent in enlisting, mustering, and organizing the recruits will be assigned by orders from this office or by the General-in-Chief.

IV. The enlistment of colored persons under this act will be made upon printed forms, to be furnished for the purpose, similar to those established for the regular service. They will be executed in duplicate, one copy to be returned to this office for file. No slave will be accepted as a recruit unless with his own consent and with the approbation of his master by a written instrument conferring, as far as he may, the rights of a freedman, and which will be filed with the superintendent. The enlistments will be made for the war, and the effect of the enlistment will be to place the slave in the military service conformably to this act. The recruits will be organized at the camps in squads and companies, and will be subject to the order of the General-in-Chief under the second section of this act.

V. The superintendent in each State will cause a report to be made on the first Monday of every month showing the expenses of the previous month, the number of recruits at the various depots in the State, the number that has been sent away, and the destination of each. His report will show the names of all the slaves recruited, with their age, description, and the names of their masters. One copy will be sent to the General-in-Chief and one to the adjutant and Inspector General.

VI. The appointment of officers to the companies to be formed of the recruits aforesaid will be made by the President.

VII. To facilitate the raising of volunteer companies, officers recruiting therefor are authorized to muster their men into service as soon as enrolled. As soon as enrolled and mustered, the men will be sent, with descriptive lists, to the depots of rendezvous, at which they will be instructed until assigned for service in the field. When the organization of any company remains incomplete at the expiration of the time specified for its organization, the companies or detachments already mustered into service will be assigned to other organizations at the discretion of the General-in-Chief.

VIII. It is not the intention of the President to grant any authority for raising regiments or brigades. The only organizations to be perfected at the depots or camps of instructions are those of companies and (in exceptional cases where the slaves are of one estate) of battalions consisting of four companies, and the only authority to be issued will be for the raising of companies or the aforesaid special battalions of four companies. All larger organizations will be left for future action as experience may determine.

IX. All officers who may be employed in the recruiting service, under the provisions of this act, or who may be appointed to the command of troops raised under it, or who may hold any staff appointment in connection with them, are enjoined to a provident, considerate, and humane attention to whatever concerns the health, comfort, instruction, and discipline of those troops, and to the uniform observance of kindness, forbearance, and indulgence to their treatment of them, and especially that they will protect them from injustice and oppression.

By order: S. COOPER,
Adjutant and Inspector General.

GLOSSARY

General-in-Chief: the military commander of Confederate forces. General Robert E. Lee

rations: clothing and compensation: food, uniforms, and pay of soldiers

quota: the share of a total that is owed by a state

Document Analysis

The preamble states the law's purpose—to authorize the president to "ask for and accept from the owners of slaves, the services of such number of able-bodied negro men…to perform military service in whatever capacity he may direct." In President Davis' November 7 address to Congress that tentatively asked for the use of blacks by the military, he suggested 40,000 men employed in engineering and pioneering positions. The Barksdale bill permitted the president to use slaves however he wished, but was specific in declaring what everyone knew—the enrolled slaves were to be used as soldiers in the line. Section two directed the General-in-Chief (General Lee) to organize the enrollees into "companies, battalions, regiments and brigades," the military formations of front line infantry units. The black recruits, further, were to receive the same allowance for clothing, rations, and pay that white soldiers received.

Section four of the law revealed that the bill's authors had little faith in the willingness of slave owners to give over their property. Should the president "not be able to raise a sufficient number of troops," he was authorized to "call on each State…for her quota of 300,000 troops." In short, if owners would not volunteer their slaves, the law granted the states power to conscript them, so long as that conscription did not take in "more than twenty-five per cent of the male slaves…in any State." This last provision meant to ensure that a sufficient number of slaves remained in the fields to produce foodstuffs for the Confederacy.

The critical Section five of the law showed nods to conservative sentiment. Whereas Davis, Lee, and the bill's many advocates had endorsed emancipation as a necessary feature of the plan to bring black men into the Confederate army, Barksdale did not go so far. "Nothing in this act," his bill stated, "shall be construed to authorize a change in the relation which the said slaves shall bear toward their owners." Thus, the onus for motivating slaves into the army shifted from the desire of the slave himself for freedom, to the master, who may, or may not, consent to the freedom of slaves the master volunteered to the army. In all the ways the war had compelled Confederates to adapt to changes in slavery, and even consider its end, the notion that the most sacred relationship in slavery was the power of a white man over a black man, could not be touched.

Essential Themes

The law's advocates had insisted that any black man who volunteered his service should receive his freedom in return. The problem in this stipulation was that it inserted the state—by the granting of emancipation—between a master and his slave. This sacred bond between a master and his slave was the most essential relationship in the Confederate mind. The Barksdale bill overcame this contradiction by granting the master himself (not the government) the right to free an enrolled slave, or not, before service. The bill did contain a provision that the state might intervene and conscript slaves should owners not be sufficiently forthcoming, but the administration refused to avail itself of that power. The military order implementing the law—General Order Number 14—deemed that the army would only accept slaves voluntarily freed by their masters. Few masters were willing to free their slaves to fight for Southern independence, seemingly proving the point that the Confederacy's only cause was that of maintaining slavery.

To implement the new law, authorities turned to officers in General Richard Ewell's Department of Richmond. Many enlisted men in the Army of Northern Virginia offered their services as officers of new black regiments, but General James Longstreet suspected the applicants were instead motivated by a desire for promotion and some time away from the Petersburg trenches. Ewell selected a few officers and men to recruit black soldiers in central Virginia, South Carolina, and Georgia. The recruiters faced a difficult task. They first had to convince a slave owner to give up his property. At the same time, the recruiter had to convince an enslaved black man that his personal degradation as a slave was a thing of the past, even if all knew that Confederates never intended to abandon the subordinate place of blacks in Southern society. To reinforce the alleged good will of whites, plan advocates and their allies announced that old habits must die—that whites in general should be ready to afford a black man the honor and respect as an equal that had always been summarily rejected. General Order Number 14 reinforced this tone by ordering "harshness and contemptuous or offensive language or conduct to them must be forbidden."

Rumors abounded of generous and willing masters across the South who stood poised to offer their slaves for service. Reality, however, failed to sustain these expectations. In Richmond, authorities accepted black recruits from among the employees at several military hospitals. They numbered not more than sixty, and were assigned to a local defense battalion consisting of convalescent soldiers from those hospitals. At a recruiting station in downtown Richmond, Major Thomas Turner took in between thirty and forty black men and began organizing them into a company. A few of those recruits came from Richmond's free black population. One bemused newspaper reporter, witnessing a drill by the new company, noted how one of them executed a brilliant "military movement" and fled camp, never to return. Efforts elsewhere in the South could not even boast the meager numbers that recruiters in Richmond had raised. No other recruiting station reported raising a single man for the service. The reality of black men's mistrust of Confederate authority and their longing for uncompromised freedom, along with the recalcitrance of slave owners unwilling to turn over their bondsmen, made a farce of administration hopes.

But that is not to say that the effort to arm blacks in the waning days of the war did not bear tangible fruits. Historian Bruce Levine contends that the proposals to arm slaves represented the evolutionary thinking of slave owners in the face of changes to the system forced from the outside. To arm slaves, offer them freedom, and even consent to universal emancipation were not efforts simply to grant freedom or achieve racial enlightenment. Those efforts, in fact, were the attempt by whites to maintain dominance over blacks in a turbulent and uncertain moment. In all the discussions that allowed for freedom for black people, white Southerners never once considered the potential for blacks as equal citizens or equal social actors. In the language proposals, freed blacks would still be bound by labor contracts and under the oversight of masterful whites and without access to government. Freedom, in the hands of Southern whites, would still contain many restrictions.

Though the plans to arm slaves for the army did not produce results, the reality of freedom with restrictions came about within the year in Southern state governments during Reconstruction. Historian Bruce Levine has called the efforts at Confederate emancipation "no mere isolated oddity or anomaly; it formed, instead, a phase of that longer struggle" between white proprietors and black laborers. The war had altered the terrain—no longer could whites use the force of law to control the lives and labors of black people, but they expected to still maintain a dominant position. In Black Codes written by Southern legislators across the former Confed-

eracy, freed peoples's ability to make contracts, gather together, live in abodes of their choice, carry firearms, or participate in politics were severely restricted. Whites had enacted much of what they expected to accomplish with their plans for emancipation.

In the continuing war of words after the military conflict had ended, many former Confederates pointed to the emancipation effort as proof that the war had never been about slavery, or that slavery itself had never been particularly objectionable. They reasoned that the emancipation efforts demonstrated whites' implicit trust in giving arms to enslaved people, and that blacks demonstrated unabashed loyalty to the Confederacy in their willingness to wield those arms. How then, could slavery have been as central or as evil as their Northern conquerors claimed? That both of these assertions could not be substantiated by facts overlooks the reality that Confederates in late 1864 and 1865 knew and demonstrated otherwise. They could see that blacks who had shaken off their shackles flooded to the Union army, not to their own Southern homes. And observers could not deny that Southern slave owners dutifully sent their own sons to serve in the army, but could not part with their slaves for any price.

Christopher Graham

Bibliography

Levine, Bruce. *Confederate Emancipation: Southern Plans to Free and Arm Slaves during the Civil War.* New York: Oxford UP, 2006. Print.

Yeams, Wilfred Buck. *The Confederate Congress.* Athens: U of Georgia P, reprint edition, 2010. Print.

Additional Reading

Foner, Eric. *Reconstruction: America's Unfinished Revolution, 1863-1877.* New York: HarperCollins, 1988. Print.

Manning, Chandra. *What This Cruel War Was Over: Soldiers, Slavery, and the Civil War.* New York: Knopf, 2007. Print.

McCurry, Stephanie. *Confederate Reckoning: Power and Politics in the Civil War South.* Cambridge: Harvard UP, 2010. Print.

Power, J. Tracy. *Lee's Miserables: Life in the Army of Northern Virginia from the Wilderness to Appomattox.* Chapel Hill: U of North Carolina P, 1998. Print.

Rable, George R. *The Confederate Republic: A Revolution Against Politics.* Chapel Hill: U of North Carolina P, 1994. Print.

POSTWAR: POLITICS OF RACE AND RECONSTRUCTION

Immediately following the cessation of hostilities at the end of the Civil War, the question of how freed slaves would be treated in the newly reunited nation was swiftly addressed by Congress. In the Fourteenth Amendment, African Americans were made whole, legally speaking. Under slavery, and even though they had no voting rights or representation, slaves counted as three-fifths of a person when calculating a state's number of seats in Congress. Now African Americans were full citizens with voting rights, although the voting laws were left in the hands of the states. Two years later, the Fifteenth Amendment forbade voting discrimination based on race or former servitude, and a number of acts following that increased protection for African American voters against force, intimidation, or other means of coercion to keep them from voting. It also greatly broadened the federal government's authority to intervene in elections.

Some states in the former Confederacy were very reluctant to agree with these new terms, and even after they had been readmitted to the Union, violence designed to intimidate voters was rampant and unchecked by some officials. In some cases, judges and local officials sympathetic to African American rights were murdered outright by the Ku Klux Klan. The outrageously violent actions of the Klan stood in sharp contrast to the support and protections promised to newly enfranchised African Americans in the South by the federal government. Witnesses to the whipping, rapes, torture, and murder of black Americans, Republican officials, and anyone seen to be aiding Reconstruction, including teachers, pleaded with the federal government to intervene. Though the Klan was eventually crushed, the brutality of their attacks, their hatred of the federal government, and the stripping away of the new rights of black citizens all flavored the new South after Reconstruction.

The Supreme Court, in *United States v. Cruikshank* (1876), made it clear that the balance was once again shifting toward states' rights, and declared it unconstitutional to pursue federal action against individuals charged with criminal acts linked to voting. In other words, if, as was the case with *Cruikshank*, an armed mob interfered with an election, it was a state issue. In some states, where the right of African Americans to vote was hotly contested, the state could decline to intervene on their behalf. This enabled paramilitary groups to continue to intimidate black voters, and turned the course of Reconstruction, which began with a promise of civil rights, away from guaranteeing full civil rights to African Americans living in the South. In addition, the Constitution was narrowly read to address only who could not be prevented from voting, rather than enforcing the right to vote. This decision was as confusing and convoluted then as now, and opened the door for many states to strip black voters of their rights.

Bethany Groff

"TIME WORKS WONDERS."

IAGO.(JEFF DAVIS.) "FOR THAT I DO SUSPECT THE LUSTY MOOR
HATH LEAP'D INTO MY SEAT: THE THOUGHT WHEREOF
DOTH LIKE A POISONOUS MINERAL GNAW MY INWARDS." —— OTHELLO.

Cartoon showing Jefferson Davis looking over his shoulder at Hiram Revels seated in the United States Senate. Source:
Library of Congress, Prints & Photographs Division, LC-USZ62-108004

■ Freedman's Bureau Bill

Date: March 3, 1865
Author: 39th U.S. Congress
Genre: legislation

"...the Secretary of War may direct such issues of provisions, clothing, and fuel...needful for the immediate and temporary shelter and supply of destitute and suffering refugees and freedmen and their wives and children..."

Summary Overview

The Freedman's Bureau Bill, enacted by the U.S. Federal Government approximately six weeks before the conclusion of the war, was pivotal in the transition of countless African Americans from a state of slavery to that of freedom. It was written and debated by the 39th Congress—the same seating of Congress that also dealt with the Fourteenth Amendment that which prohibited the denial of citizenship based on race. With the notable exception of the previous amendment to the Constitution—the abolition of slavery in the Thirteenth—the Fourteen was extremely eventful, and a monumental step forward for African Americans. This bill was another progression, one that aimed to assist those who before had known only oppression.

However, the bill was not looked upon with great enthusiasm by all, especially by those living within the Confederacy; and it did not take long for the organization it created to be mocked. The prevailing attitude toward the Freedman's Bureau, as it soon became known, was embodied in Southern literature in the refrain, "Forty Acres and a Mule"—which was intended to suggest a doomed dream of agrarian reform (by which former slaves would obtain property). What is significant is the bill itself and what it stood for in the eyes of a government that tried to do right by those countless men, women, and children subjected to a life of labor and cruelty.

Defining Moment

When historians begin to research a particular event or person, no matter the topic, it is vital that they appreciate the wider context, as well. In the case of the Freedman's Bureau Bill, it is notable that it was written on March 3, 1865, during the death throes of the Confederacy. This in itself is meaningful. Federal lawmakers were conscious that the South was at its knees, the Confederate army running low on able men and provisions and facing high number of desertions. It was understood that the war would not go on much longer. Furthermore, the Confederate government was cognizant of the conditions faced by the populace at large: inflation was rampant, and the blockade along the coastline of the American South meant that people in the South were desperate. Thus it happened that General Robert E. Lee ultimately surrendered to General Ulysses S. Grant on April 9—a little more than a month after the drafting of the Freedman's Bureau Bill.

The timing of the creation of the Freedman's Bureau Bill was sound. For nearly two years, African American soldiers and sailors proved themselves again and again in the heat of battle; the most famous of the black regiments, the 54th Massachusetts Volunteer Regiment, led by Bostonian Colonel Robert Gould Shaw, highlighted the wartime capabilities of African Americans in July 1863. With the end of the war in sight, and thousands upon thousands of men, women, and children set to be free at the close of it, it was imperative that the lawmakers develop a system for their transition, both for their immediate aid and for their direction and support once the guns stopped. The bill was, after all, "an act to establish a Bureau for the Relief of Freedmen and Refugees."

Author Biography

For the men who constructed this document, as well as those involved in the drafting of the Fourteenth Amendment, the timing was crucial. The war looked to be over shortly, and it was essential that proper steps be taken to alleviate any undue suffering postwar. The 39th Congress had much to contend with: new amendments on the destruction of slavery and resolutions on the treatment of former slaves. Though not dealt with in the Freedman's bill, Congress also had to consider what was to be done with the former Confederate states. This is an theme that appears in the second

that the war continues for them long after the South's surrender, particularly with the presence of Union soldiers and the apparently brainwashed former slaves being protected by both the government and the Freedman's Bureau.

Careful lines needed to be drawn on how to approach the welfare of former slaves—they would be in need of shelter and provisions, but also of longer term support or guidance for their new lives. The Freedman's Bureau Bill laid out how the lawmakers thought the new organization should be run: "the said bureau shall be under the management and control of a commissioner to be appointed by the President, by and with the advice and consent of the Senate…" An intriguing part of the legislation is the assertion that the commissioner of the bureau would be required to swear an oath—the text of which was unavailable; it is a shame that the proposed oath did not form the original text of the bill as it might have given further insight into what the bureau hoped to achieve.

HISTORICAL DOCUMENT

An Act to Establish a Bureau for the Relief of Freedmen and Refugees

Be it enacted by the Senate and House of Representatives of the United States of America in Congress assembled, That there is hereby established in the War Department, to continue during the present war of rebellion, and for one year thereafter, a bureau of refugees, freedmen, and abandoned lands, to which shall be committed, as hereinafter provided, the supervision and management of all abandoned lands, and the control of all subjects relating to freedmen from rebel states, or from any district of country within the territory embraced in the operations of the army, under such rules and regulations as may be prescribed by the head of the bureau and approved by the President. The said bureau shall be under the management and control of a commissioner to be appointed by the President, by and with the advice and consent of the Senate, whose compensation shall be three thousand

dollars per annum, and such number of clerks as may be assigned to him by the Secretary of War, not exceeding one chief clerk, two of the fourth class, two of the third class, and five of the first class. And the commissioner and all persons appointed under this act, shall, before entering upon their duties, take the oath of office prescribed in an act entitled "An act to prescribe an oath of office, and for other purposes," approved July second, eighteen hundred and sixty-two, and the commissioner and the chief clerk shall, before entering upon their duties, give bonds to the treasurer of the United States, the former in the sum of fifty thousand dollars, and the latter in the sum of ten thousand dollars, conditioned for the faithful discharge of their duties respectively, with securities to be approved as sufficient by the Attorney-General, which bonds shall be filed in the office of the first comptroller of the treasury, to be by him put in suit for the benefit of any injured party upon any breach of the conditions thereof.

Sec. 2. *And be it further enacted,* That the Secretary of War may direct such issues of provisions, clothing, and fuel, as he may deem needful for the immediate and temporary shelter and supply of destitute and suffering refugees and freedmen and their wives and children, under such rules and regulations as he may direct.

Sec. 3. *And be it further enacted,* That the President may, by and with the advice and consent of the Senate, appoint an assistant commissioner for each of the states declared to be in insurrection, not exceeding ten in number, who shall, under the direction of the commissioner, aid in the execution of the provisions of this act; and he shall give a bond to the Treasurer of the United States, in the sum of twenty thousand dollars, in the form and manner prescribed in the first section of this act. Each of said commissioners shall receive an annual salary of two thousand five hundred dollars in full compensation for all his services. And any military officer may be detailed and assigned to duty under this act without increase of pay or allowances. The commissioner shall, before the commencement of each regular session of congress, make full report of his proceedings with exhibits of the state of his accounts to the President, who shall communicate the same to congress, and shall also make special reports whenever required to do so by the President or either house of congress; and the assistant commissioners shall make quarterly reports of their proceedings to the commissioner, and also such other special reports as from time to time may be required.

Sec. 4. *And be it further enacted,* That the commissioner, under the direction of the President, shall have authority to set apart, for the use of loyal refugees and freedmen, such tracts of land within the insurrectionary states as shall have been abandoned, or to which the United States shall have acquired title by confiscation or sale, or otherwise, and to every male citizen, whether refugee or freedman, as aforesaid, there shall be assigned not more than forty acres of such land, and the person to whom it was so assigned shall be protected in the use and enjoyment of the land for the term of three years at an annual rent not exceeding six per centum upon the value of such land, as it was appraised by the state authorities in the year eighteen hundred and sixty, for the purpose of taxation, and in case no such appraisal can be found, then the rental shall be based upon the estimated value of the land in said year, to be ascertained in such manner as the commissioner may by regulation prescribe. At the end of said term, or at any time during said term, the occupants of any parcels so assigned may purchase the land and receive such title thereto as the United States can convey, upon paying therefor the value of the land, as ascertained and fixed for the purpose of determining the annual rent aforesaid.

Sec. 5. *And be it further enacted,* That all acts and parts of acts inconsistent with the provisions of this act, are hereby repealed.

GLOSSARY

Attorney General: James Speed (1812-1887); served as Attorney General under both Presidents Abraham Lincoln and Andrew Johnson

per annum: per year

President: President Abraham Lincoln; at this time, he officially began his second term in office

refugee: slaves freed from slavery

Secretary of War: Edwin M. Stanton (1814-1869); served as Secretary of War under both Presidents Abraham Lincoln and Andrew Johnson

Treasurer: William Fessenden (1806-1869); served as Secretary of the Treasury during the last years of President Lincoln's time in office; he was succeeded by Hugh McCullough (1808-1895).

Document Analysis

In his online essay devoted to The Freedman's Bureau, historian William Troost, of the University of British Columbia, succinctly captures the significance of the Bureau's foundation—especially once enacted; Troost writes: "…the entire social order of the region [the former Confederacy] was disturbed as slave owners and former slaves were forced to interact with one another in completely new ways (web)." The conclusion of the war meant that the social dynamics of the South had changed—masters no longer could hold legal sway over those in bondage. Enslaved husbands would no longer have to watch their wives sold on the auction block, or see their children bequeathed to far off relatives or their owners. Enslaved children, such as Frederick Douglass once was, would no longer be removed from their mothers, to be raised miles away from maternal eyes.

Literacy and Land Reform

The Freedman's Bureau Bill was not the sole idea of its kind; the months leading to the conclusion of the war saw the formation of a number of groups committed to the betterment of freed men and women. Historian James M. McPherson lists a number of organizations that went South to assist former slaves in ways similar to the officially sanctioned Freedman's Bureau, from those devoted to general and education needs to those focused on religious matters. These organizations included the American Missionary Association, the National Freedmen's Relief Association, the New England Freedmen's Aid Society, and the Western Freedmen's Aid Commission (709-710). Literacy was high on the list of priorities for many of those who came South to teach. To quote William Troost again:

> Prior to the Civil War it had been the policy in the sixteen states slaves states to fine, whip, or imprison those who gave instruction to blacks or mulattos…This lack of literacy created great problems for blacks in a free labor system. Freedmen were repeatedly taken advantage of as they were often unable to read or draft contracts

The Bureau, over the following few years, expanded the funds allocated to the education of former slaves and the founding of schools; by 1870, this endeavour produced approximately eighty-six thousand literate individuals.

While the Bureau's literacy operations were, unquestionably, vital for the progress of freed men and women following their release from slavery, another of the organization's legacies, that of land redistribution, remains probably better known to students of Reconstruction.

The phrase "Forty Acres and a Mule" is, indeed, one of the best known expressions from the time of the war's end and after. From whence did it come? A close inspection of the Freedman's Bureau Bill reveals the birth of this phrase in Section Four:

> *And be it further enacted,* That the commissioner…shall have authority to set apart, for the use of loyal refugees and freedmen, such tracts of land within the insurrectionary states as shall have been abandoned, or to which the United States shall have acquired title by confiscation or sale, or otherwise, and to every male citizen, whether refugee or freedman, as aforesaid, there shall be assigned not more than forty acres of such land…

In principle, the idea was sound, and must have been viewed as a godsend to those previously facing unending labor on someone else's land. It was a promise of independence, of the freedom of working one's own land and providing for one's own family. For African American men, especially, the assurance of an allotment of land held a number of meanings; it meant that they no longer would be under the dominion of another (white) man, that they could claim the status of head of household, that they could take advantage of the social ideal of a patriarchy within their own family. For African American women, they would now be their own mistresses, as it were, and would be in the prime position of raising their own children. Such women could now rest in their own homes, assured that the children they bore—and those of subsequent generations—would no longer be subject to the trials of slavery. So short a time before, a child's status as free or slave depended solely on the state of the mother; if the mother was not a slave, then her child would be free; however, if the mother was enslaved, then that status was imposed upon the baby as well. The Freedman's Bureau Bill, with its assurance of land, as well as its terms of support and direction, gave solidity to the African American family within its own walls.

Disillusionment with the Bureau and Southern Ridicule

As with many such grand endeavours, both before and since, the reality of the Freedman's Bureau did not measure up to the good intentions its creators had envisioned for it. The appropriation and distribution of land, in particular, was one of the most problematic areas. In his work on the Civil War, historian James M. McPherson observes that the pledge of land was "...a troublesome question..." in its implementation (842). It did not take long for news to travel regarding this vexing matter. Two years after the bill was written, the eminent former slave Frederick Douglass, in the summer of 1867, received a letter concerning the future of the Bureau, which read, in part, "there are a great many Persons that are of the opinion that the Freedman's Bureau (its *affairs*), are not conducted as they ought to be." (Foner. 33. 1955).

In Southern literary works, the Bureau is often mentioned with derision and contempt, most notably in the second half of Margaret Mitchell's renowned 1936 novel, *Gone with the Wind*. While strictly a piece of fiction, the novel, like all literature, can be an important window on society. The Civil War was still within living memory when Mitchell began writing during the 1920s—her family, friends, and other contemporaries throughout the South would have been familiar with the tales and social history surrounding the war and its aftermath. Characters within the novel, such as Tony Fontaine and Will Benteen, as well as Scarlett O'Hara and Rhett Butler themselves, make frequent comments on how the Bureau leads on the recently freed former slaves, inciting them to violence and insolence. In one scene, Scarlett and Tony Fontaine discuss the Bureau's endorsement, for example, of miscegenation (intimate relations between, in this case, white women and black men).

While the implementation of the measures overseen by the Freedman's Bureau may not have garnered much applause, the effort represented a step forward in the understanding that the United States government needed to have a plan in place for the thousands of freed men, women, and children. Those white former slave owners—or, even non-slaveholding whites—had to come to terms with the new social order, although this, too, led to increasing Black Codes and the eventual Jim Crow laws. The Bureau sought to assist those formerly in bondage in gaining stability, to gain the self-worth they had previously been denied, and perhaps the education they sought.

Essential Themes

In reading through the Freedman's Bureau Bill in its entirety, there is a distinct feeling of authority that the writers wished to impart in this piece of legislation. The idea of a sanctioned organization designed for the betterment of the previously enslaved population is strong. The writers make frequent use of the standard legal phrase *"Be it enacted"* (original emphasis) to bring added force to the document and to convey a seriousness regarding the effort. It is important to remember that at the start of the Civil War in April of 1861, lying behind the hostilities was the aim of preserving the country as a whole.

The official tone is reinforced with the description of the intended structure of the organization, as well as the chain of command. Emphasising the jurisdiction of the War Department (known now as the Department of Defence) stressed the gravity that the writers wished to impart to the Bureau. In this vain, the men of the 39th Congress sought to put in place a plan to ensure freed slaves' education and access to land and employment. The Bureau, in other words, was intended to provide stability now and in the future.

Jennifer L. Henderson Crane, BA, PgDip

Bibliography

Aynes, Richard L. "The 39th Congress (1865-1867) and the 14th Amendment: Some Preliminary Perspectives," *Akron Law Review* 42 (2009); Akron Research Paper No. 09-09. Print.

Foner, Philip S. *The Life and Writings of Frederick Douglass*: Volume IV—*Reconstruction and After*. New York: International Publishers, 1955. Print.

McPherson, James. M. *Battle Cry of Freedom: The Civil War Era*. New York: Oxford UP, 1988. Print.

Parker, Marjorie H. "Some Educational Activities of the Freedmen's Bureau," *The Journal of Negro Education* 23 1 (Winter 1954), p. 9-21. Print.

Troost, William, "The Freedmen's Bureau," EH.Net (Economic History Association). Web.

Additional Reading

Abbott, Martin. "The Freedmen's Bureau and Negro Schooling in South Carolina," *South Carolina Historical Magazine* 57 2 (Apr. 1956), p. 65-81. Print.

Bentley, George R. *A History of the Freedmen's Bureau*. Philadelphia: U of Pennsylvania P, 1955. Print.

Berlin, Ira. *Slaves Without Masters: The Free Negro in the Antebellum South*. New York: Pantheon Books,

1974. Print.

Berlin, Ira, Steven F. Miller, and Leslie S. Rowland, eds. "Afro-American Families in the Transition from Slavery to Freedom," *Radical History Review* 42 (1988), p. 89-121. Print.l

Cimbala, Paul A. and Randall M. Miller. *In the Freedmen's Bureau and Reconstruction: Reconsiderations.* New York: Fordham UP, 1999. Print.

Finley, Randy. *From Slavery to Uncertain Freedom: The Freedmen's Bureau in Arkansas, 1865-1869.* Fayetteville: U of Arkansas P, 1996. Print.

Hornsby, Alton. "The Freedmen's Bureau Schools in Texas, 1865-1870," *Southwestern Historical Quarterly* 76 4 (Apr. 1973), 397-417. Print.

Schlomowitz, Ralph. "The Transition from Slave to Freedman Labor Agreements in Southern Agriculture, 1865-1870," *Journal of Economic History* 39 1 (1979), p. 333-336. Print.

Williams, Heather Andrea. " 'Clothing Themselves in Intelligence': The Freedpeople, Schooling, and Northern Teachers, 1861-1871," *The Journal of African American History* 4 (Fall 2002), p. 372. Print.

■ Freedmen's Monument Speech

Date: April 14, 1876
Author: Douglass, Frederick
Genre: speech

"Though the Union was more to him than our freedom or our future, under his wise and beneficent rule we saw ourselves gradually lifted from the depths of slavery to the heights of liberty and manhood..."

Summary Overview

Frederick Douglass—the name immediately brings to mind the stalwart man who broke the chains of his own enslavement, a man who chose to speak out for his brethren, and was not deterred. On April 14, 1876, there was no one better suited than Douglass to deliver an address at the unveiling of the Freedmen's monument in Washington, D.C. The time, the location, the subject, and the speaker—all combined into a remarkable event, one that Douglass praises within his speech. His eloquence, an undeniable gift in a man once denied the right to an education, resounds from the page, and his voice is powerfully heard. He utilized the occasion of the event for reflection of past events, for the celebration of what had been accomplished, and for the veneration of a man, President Abraham Lincoln, whose life was cut short. Those who were present as Douglass delivered his address were in an enviable position. For, as powerful and evocative as his words are when read, they must have been even more so when heard directly from the man himself.

Defining Moment

The monument depicts a standing Abraham Lincoln, while at his feet a crouched, shackled slave looks imploringly up at the president. The image is highly suggestive even from a twenty-first-century perspective; a nineteenth-century interpretation could have inferred that the slave sat at Lincoln's feet, trusting him to break his bonds, to tear asunder the existence given him because of the color of his skin. The slave's kneeling position also physically highlights an element of subordination; he is physically far lower than the proudly standing Lincoln, who merely looks benevolently down at the man at his feet.

In the quote mentioned above, "Though the Union was more to him than our freedom or our future, under his wise and beneficent rule we saw ourselves gradually lifted from the depths of slavery to the heights of liberty and manhood," Douglass reveals that he is fully cognizant of Lincoln's imperfections. He recognises that, while the central aim of the Lincoln administration—up until midway through the Civil War—was not the abolition of slavery, there were enough changes, large and small, to illustrate to Douglass and countless others that Lincoln was on the right path. What changes did he mean? One giant step forward, the Emancipation Proclamation of 1863, had implications that would shift the battle cry of the Union Army from 'preservation' to 'freedom.' This piece of legislation maintained that, from then on, in the eyes of the federal government, slaves were "forever free (McPherson. 563. 1988)." Although the Proclamation was an immediate source of debate, it nevertheless displayed to the African American community, free and enslaved, that a promise of things to come had been made. There was also legislation that "sanctioned the enlistment of black soldiers and sailors in Union forces (563)." The opportunity to take an active role in the Civil War, particularly in light of the success of the first black regiment, the 54th Massachusetts, led by Bostonian Colonel Robert Gould Shaw, represented another great leap forward for the black community.

Author Biography

With the possible exceptions of Harriet Jacobs and Harriet Tubman, Frederick Douglass must still be *the* most well known former slave. He was born in 1818 to a slave woman, Harriet Bailey, and states in his autobiography that his father was, in fact, his (white) master. Historian Maurice S. Lee offers a useful quote from Douglass' autobiography:

> I was born in Tuckahow, near Hillsborough, and about twelve miles from Easton, in Talbot County, Maryland. I have no accurate knowledge of my age, never having seen any authentic record containing it. By far the larger part of the slaves know as little of their age as horses know of theirs, and it is the wish of most masters within my knowledge to keep their slaves thus ignorant. I do not remember to have ever met a slave who could tell of his birthday. They seldom come nearer to it than planting-time, harvest-time, cherry-time, spring-time, or fall-time (175. 2009).

In this passage, Douglass makes use of an animal analogy—a horse—to describe his (and others') level of awareness of the world as a slave. Even the basic right of knowing the date of one's birthday was one withheld from those in bondage.

Education, so fundamentally tied in the story of Frederick Douglass, was denied to him early on; literacy, in a slave, was virtually unthinkable, and could have serious negative consequences. Although a start in his education was given by the kind wife of his overseer, a Mrs. Auld, this was quickly stopped by her husband; Lee offers Douglass's words again:

> A [slave] should know nothing but to obey his master—to do as he is told to do. Learning will spoil [original emphasis] the best [slave] in the world. Now…if you teach that [slave] (speaking of myself) how to read, there would be no keeping him. It would forever unfit him to be a slave. He would at once become unmanageable, and of no value to his master. As to himself, it could do him no good, but a great deal of harm. It would make him discontented and unhappy (177).

Fortunately in this case, we know just how well educated Douglass eventually became.

Douglass' personal life led him to become both a husband and a father. He and his first wife, Anna, whom he married in 1838 at the approximate age of 20, had five children together. Frederick and Anna were married for roughly forty-four years, and he remarried—to a white woman, Helen Pitts—following Anna's death in 1882. Helen was at his side until his own passing in 1895.

HISTORICAL DOCUMENT

Friends and Fellow-citizens:

I warmly congratulate you upon the highly interesting object which has caused you to assemble in such numbers and spirit as you have today. This occasion is in some respects remarkable. Wise and thoughtful men of our race, who shall come after us, and study the lesson of our history in the United States; who shall survey the long and dreary spaces over which we have traveled; who shall count the links in the great chain of events by which we have reached our present position, will make a note of this occasion; they will think of it and speak of it with a sense of manly pride and complacency.

I congratulate you, also, upon the very favorable circumstances in which we meet today. They are high, inspiring, and uncommon. They lend grace, glory, and significance to the object for which we have met. Nowhere else in this great country, with its uncounted towns and cities, unlimited wealth, and immeasurable territory extending from sea to sea, could conditions be found more favorable to the success of this occasion than here.

We stand today at the national center to perform something like a national act — an act which is to go into history; and we are here where every pulsation of the national heart can be heard, felt, and reciprocated. A thousand wires, fed with thought and winged with lightning, put us in instantaneous communication with the loyal and true men all over the country.

Few facts could better illustrate the vast and wonderful change which has taken place in our condition as a people than the fact of our assembling here for the purpose we have today. Harmless, beautiful, proper, and praiseworthy as this demonstration is, I cannot forget that no such demonstration would have been tolerated here twenty years ago. The spirit of slavery and barbarism, which still lingers to blight and destroy in some dark and distant parts of our country, would have made our assembling here the signal and excuse for opening upon us all the flood-gates of wrath and violence. That we are here in peace today is a compliment and a credit to American civilization, and a prophecy of still greater national enlightenment and progress in the future. I refer to the past not in malice, for this is no day for malice; but simply to place more distinctly in front the gratifying and glorious change which has come both to our white fellow-citizens and ourselves, and to congratulate all upon the contrast between now and then; the new dispensation of freedom with its thousand blessings to both races, and the old dispensation of slavery with its ten thousand evils to both races — white and black. In view, then, of the past, the present, and the future, with the long and dark history of our bondage behind us, and with liberty, progress, and enlightenment before us, I again congratulate you upon this auspicious day and hour.

Friends and fellow-citizens, the story of our presence here is soon and easily told. We are here in the District of Columbia, here in the city of Washington, the most luminous point of American territory; a city recently transformed and made beautiful in its body and in its spirit; we are here in the place where the ablest and best men of the country are sent to devise the policy, enact the laws, and shape the destiny of the Republic; we are here, with the stately pillars and majestic dome of the Capitol of the nation looking down upon us; we are here,

with the broad earth freshly adorned with the foliage and flowers of spring for our church, and all races, colors, and conditions of men for our congregation — in a word, we are here to express, as best we may, by appropriate forms and ceremonies, our grateful sense of the vast, high, and preeminent services rendered to ourselves, to our race, to our country, and to the whole world by Abraham Lincoln.

The sentiment that brings us here to-day is one of the noblest that can stir and thrill the human heart. It has crowned and made glorious the high places of all civilized nations with the grandest and most enduring works of art, designed to illustrate the characters and perpetuate the memories of great public men. It is the sentiment which from year to year adorns with fragrant and beautiful flowers the graves of our loyal, brave, and patriotic soldiers who fell in defense of the Union and liberty. It is the sentiment of gratitude and appreciation, which often, in the presence of many who hear me, has filled yonder heights of Arlington with the eloquence of eulogy and the sublime enthusiasm of poetry and song; a sentiment which can never die while the Republic lives.

For the first time in the history of our people, and in the history of the whole American people, we join in this high worship, and march conspicuously in the line of this time-honored custom. First things are always interesting, and this is one of our first things. It is the first time that, in this form and manner, we have sought to do honor to an American great man, however deserving and illustrious. I commend the fact to notice; let it be told in every part of the Republic; let men of all parties and opinions hear it; let those who despise us, not less than those who respect us, know that now and here, in the spirit of liberty, loyalty, and gratitude, let it be known everywhere, and by everybody who takes an interest in human progress and in the amelioration of the condition of mankind, that, in the presence and with the approval of the members of the American House of Representatives, reflecting the general sentiment of the country; that in the presence of that august body, the American Senate, representing the highest intelligence and the calmest judgment of the country; in the presence of the Supreme Court and Chief-Justice of the United States, to whose decisions we all patriotically bow; in the presence and under the steady eye of the honored and trusted President of the United States, with the members of his wise and patriotic Cabinet, we, the colored people, newly emancipated and rejoicing in our blood-bought freedom, near the close of the first century in the life of this Republic, have now and here unveiled, set apart, and dedicated a monument of enduring granite and bronze, in every line, feature, and figure of which the men of this generation may read, and those of aftercoming generations may read, something of the exalted character and great works of Abraham Lincoln, the first martyr President of the United States.

Fellow-citizens, in what we have said and done today, and in what we may say and do hereafter, we disclaim everything like arrogance and assumption. We claim for ourselves no superior devotion to the character, history, and memory of the illustrious name whose monument we have here dedicated today. We fully comprehend the relation of Abraham Lincoln both to ourselves and to the white people of the United States. Truth is proper and beautiful at all times and in all places, and it is never more proper and beautiful in any case than when speaking of a great public man whose example is likely to be commended for honor and imitation long after his departure to the solemn shades, the silent continents of eternity. It must be admitted, truth compels me to admit, even here in the presence of the monument we have erected to his memory, Abraham Lincoln was not, in the fullest sense of the word, either our man or our model. In his interests, in his associations, in his habits of thought, and in his prejudices, he was a white man.

He was preeminently the white man's President, entirely devoted to the welfare of white men. He was ready and willing at any time during the first years of his administration to deny, postpone, and sacrifice the rights of humanity in the colored people to promote the welfare of the white people of this country. In all his education and feeling he was an American of the Americans. He came into the Presidential chair upon one principle alone, namely, opposition to the extension of slavery. His arguments in furtherance of this policy had their motive and mainspring in his patriotic devotion to the interests of his own race. To protect, defend, and perpetuate slavery in the states where it existed Abraham Lincoln was not less ready than any other President to draw the sword of the nation. He was ready to execute all the supposed guarantees of the United States Constitution in favor of the slave system anywhere inside the slave states.

He was willing to pursue, recapture, and send back the fugitive slave to his master, and to suppress a slave rising for liberty, though his guilty master were already in arms against the Government. The race to which we belong were not the special objects of his consideration. Knowing this, I concede to you, my white fellow-citizens, a preeminence in this worship at once full and supreme. First, midst, and last, you and yours were the objects of his deepest affection and his most earnest solicitude. You are the children of Abraham Lincoln. We are at best only his step-children; children by adoption, children by forces of circumstances and necessity. To you it especially belongs to sound his praises, to preserve and perpetuate his memory, to multiply his statues, to hang his pictures high upon your walls, and commend his example, for to you he was a great and glorious friend and benefactor. Instead of supplanting you at his altar, we would exhort you to build high his monuments; let them be of the most costly material, of the most cunning workmanship; let their forms be symmetrical, beautiful, and perfect, let their bases be upon solid rocks, and their summits lean against the unchanging blue, overhanging sky, and let them endure forever! But while in the abundance of your wealth, and in the fullness of your just and patriotic devotion, you do all this, we entreat you to despise not the humble offering we this day unveil to view; for while Abraham Lincoln saved for you a country, he delivered us from a bondage, according to Jefferson, one hour of which was worse than ages of the oppression your fathers rose in rebellion to oppose.

Fellow-citizens, ours is no new-born zeal and devotion — merely a thing of this moment. The name of Abraham Lincoln was near and dear to our hearts in the darkest and most perilous hours of the Republic. We were no more ashamed of him when shrouded in clouds of darkness, of doubt, and defeat than when we saw him crowned with victory, honor, and glory. Our faith in him was often taxed and strained to the uttermost, but it never failed. When he tarried long in the mountain; when he strangely told us that we were the cause of the war; when he still more strangely told us that we were to leave the land in which we were born; when he refused to employ our arms in defense of the Union; when, after accepting our services as colored soldiers, he refused to retaliate our murder and torture as colored prisoners; when he told us he would save the Union if he could with slavery; when he revoked the Proclamation of Emancipation of General Fremont; when he refused to remove the popular commander of the Army of the Potomac, in the days of its inaction and defeat, who was more zealous in his efforts to protect slavery than to suppress rebellion; when we saw all this, and more, we were at times grieved, stunned, and greatly bewildered; but our hearts believed while they ached and bled. Nor was this, even at that time, a blind and unreasoning superstition. Despite the mist and haze that surrounded him; despite the tumult, the hurry, and confusion of the hour, we were able to take a comprehensive view of Abraham Lincoln, and to make reasonable allowance for the circumstances of his position. We saw him, measured him, and estimated him; not by stray utterances to injudicious and tedious delegations, who often tried his patience; not by isolated facts torn from their connection; not by any partial and imperfect glimpses, caught at inopportune moments; but by a broad survey, in the light of the stern logic of great events, and in view of that divinity which shapes our ends, rough hew them how we will, we came to the conclusion that the hour and the man of our redemption had somehow met in the person of Abraham Lincoln. It mattered little to us what language he might employ on special occasions; it mattered little to us, when we fully knew him, whether he was swift or slow in his movements; it was enough for us that Abraham Lincoln was at the head of a great movement, and was in living and earnest sympathy with that movement, which, in the nature of things, must go on until slavery should be utterly and forever abolished in the United States.

When, therefore, it shall be asked what we have to do with the memory of Abraham Lincoln, or what Abraham Lincoln had to do with us, the answer is ready, full, and complete. Though he loved Caesar less than Rome, though the Union was more to him than our freedom or our future, under his wise and beneficent rule we saw ourselves gradually lifted from the depths of slavery to the heights of liberty and manhood; under his wise and beneficent rule, and by measures approved and vigorously pressed by him, we saw that the handwriting of ages, in the form of prejudice and proscription, was rapidly fading away from the face of our whole country; under his rule, and in due time, about as soon after all as

the country could tolerate the strange spectacle, we saw our brave sons and brothers laying off the rags of bondage, and being clothed all over in the blue uniforms of the soldiers of the United States; under his rule we saw two hundred thousand of our dark and dusky people responding to the call of Abraham Lincoln, and with muskets on their shoulders, and eagles on their buttons, timing their high footsteps to liberty and union under the national flag; under his rule we saw the independence of the black republic of Haiti, the special object of slave-holding aversion and horror, fully recognized, and her minister, a colored gentleman, duly received here in the city of Washington; under his rule we saw the internal slave-trade, which so long disgraced the nation, abolished, and slavery abolished in the District of Columbia; under his rule we saw for the first time the law enforced against the foreign slave trade, and the first slave-trader hanged like any other pirate or murderer; under his rule, assisted by the greatest captain of our age, and his inspiration, we saw the Confederate States, based upon the idea that our race must be slaves, and slaves forever, battered to pieces and scattered to the four winds; under his rule, and in the fullness of time, we saw Abraham Lincoln, after giving the slave-holders three months' grace in which to save their hateful slave system, penning the immortal paper, which, though special in its language, was general in its principles and effect, making slavery forever impossible in the United States. Though we waited long, we saw all this and more.

Can any colored man, or any white man friendly to the freedom of all men, ever forget the night which followed the first day of January, 1863, when the world was to see if Abraham Lincoln would prove to be as good as his word? I shall never forget that memorable night, when in a distant city I waited and watched at a public meeting, with three thousand others not less anxious than myself, for the word of deliverance which we have heard read today. Nor shall I ever forget the outburst of joy and thanksgiving that rent the air when the lightning brought to us the emancipation proclamation. In that happy hour we forgot all delay, and forgot all tardiness, forgot that the President had bribed the rebels to lay down their arms by a promise to withhold the bolt which would smite the slave-system with destruction; and we were thenceforward willing to allow the President all the latitude of time, phraseology, and every honorable device that statesmanship might require for the achievement of a great and beneficent measure of liberty and progress.

Fellow-citizens, there is little necessity on this occasion to speak at length and critically of this great and good man, and of his high mission in the world. That ground has been fully occupied and completely covered both here and elsewhere. The whole field of fact and fancy has been gleaned and garnered. Any man can say things that are true of Abraham Lincoln, but no man can say anything that is new of Abraham Lincoln. His personal traits and public acts are better known to the American people than are those of any other man of his age. He was a mystery to no man who saw him and heard him. Though high in position, the humblest could approach him and feel at home in his presence. Though deep, he was transparent; though strong, he was gentle; though decided and pronounced in his convictions, he was tolerant towards those who differed from him, and patient under reproaches. Even those who only knew him through his public utterance obtained a tolerably clear idea of his character and personality. The image of the man went out with his words, and those who read them knew him.

I have said that President Lincoln was a white man, and shared the prejudices common to his countrymen towards the colored race. Looking back to his times and to the condition of his country, we are compelled to admit that this unfriendly feeling on his part may be safely set down as one element of his wonderful success in organizing the loyal American people for the tremendous conflict before them, and bringing them safely through that conflict. His great mission was to accomplish two things: first, to save his country from dismemberment and ruin; and, second, to free his country from the great crime of slavery. To do one or the other, or both, he must have the earnest sympathy and the powerful cooperation of his loyal fellow-countrymen. Without this primary and essential condition to success his efforts must have been vain and utterly fruitless. Had he put the abolition of slavery before the salvation of the Union, he would have inevitably driven from him a powerful class of the American people and rendered resistance to rebellion impossible. Viewed from the genuine abolition ground, Mr. Lincoln seemed tardy, cold, dull, and indifferent; but

measuring him by the sentiment of his country, a sentiment he was bound as a statesman to consult, he was swift, zealous, radical, and determined.

Though Mr. Lincoln shared the prejudices of his white fellow-countrymen against the Negro, it is hardly necessary to say that in his heart of hearts he loathed and hated slavery. The man who could say, "Fondly do we hope, fervently do we pray, that this mighty scourge of war shall soon pass away, yet if God wills it continue till all the wealth piled by two hundred years of bondage shall have been wasted, and each drop of blood drawn by the lash shall have been paid for by one drawn by the sword, the judgments of the Lord are true and righteous altogether," gives all needed proof of his feeling on the subject of slavery. He was willing, while the South was loyal, that it should have its pound of flesh, because he thought that it was so nominated in the bond; but farther than this no earthly power could make him go.

Fellow-citizens, whatever else in this world may be partial, unjust, and uncertain, time, time! is impartial, just, and certain in its action. In the realm of mind, as well as in the realm of matter, it is a great worker, and often works wonders. The honest and comprehensive statesman, clearly discerning the needs of his country, and earnestly endeavoring to do his whole duty, though covered and blistered with reproaches, may safely leave his course to the silent judgment of time. Few great public men have ever been the victims of fiercer denunciation than Abraham Lincoln was during his administration. He was often wounded in the house of his friends. Reproaches came thick and fast upon him from within and from without, and from opposite quarters. He was assailed by Abolitionists; he was assailed by slave-holders; he was assailed by the men who were for peace at any price; he was assailed by those who were for a more vigorous prosecution of the war; he was assailed for not making the war an abolition war; and he was bitterly assailed for making the war an abolition war.

But now behold the change: the judgment of the present hour is, that taking him for all in all, measuring the tremendous magnitude of the work before him, considering the necessary means to ends, and surveying the end from the beginning, infinite wisdom has seldom sent any man into the world better fitted for his mission than Abraham Lincoln. His birth, his training, and his natural endowments, both mental and physical, were strongly in his favor. Born and reared among the lowly, a stranger to wealth and luxury, compelled to grapple single-handed with the flintiest hardships of life, from tender youth to sturdy manhood, he grew strong in the manly and heroic qualities demanded by the great mission to which he was called by the votes of his countrymen. The hard condition of his early life, which would have depressed and broken down weaker men, only gave greater life, vigor, and buoyancy to the heroic spirit of Abraham Lincoln. He was ready for any kind and any quality of work. What other young men dreaded in the shape of toil, he took hold of with the utmost cheerfulness.

"A spade, a rake, a hoe,
A pick-axe, or a bill;
A hook to reap, a scythe to mow,
A flail, or what you will."

All day long he could split heavy rails in the woods, and half the night long he could study his English Grammar by the uncertain flare and glare of the light made by a pine-knot. He was at home in the land with his axe, with his maul, with gluts, and his wedges; and he was equally at home on water, with his oars, with his poles, with his planks, and with his boat-hooks. And whether in his flat-boat on the Mississippi River, or at the fireside of his frontier cabin, he was a man of work. A son of toil himself, he was linked in brotherly sympathy with the sons of toil in every loyal part of the Republic. This very fact gave him tremendous power with the American people, and materially contributed not only to selecting him to the Presidency, but in sustaining his administration of the Government.

Upon his inauguration as President of the United States, an office, even when assumed under the most favorable condition, fitted to tax and strain the largest abilities, Abraham Lincoln was met by a tremendous crisis. He was called upon not merely to administer the Government, but to decide, in the face of terrible odds, the fate of the Republic.

A formidable rebellion rose in his path before him; the Union was already practically dissolved; his country was torn and rent asunder at the center. Hostile armies were already organized against the Republic, armed with the munitions of war which the Republic had provided for its own defense. The tremendous question for him to decide was whether his country should survive the crisis and flourish, or be dismembered and perish. His predecessor in office had already decided the question in favor of national dismemberment, by denying to it the right of self-defense and self-preservation — a right which belongs to the meanest insect.

Happily for the country, happily for you and for me, the judgment of James Buchanan, the patrician, was not the judgment of Abraham Lincoln, the plebeian. He brought his strong common sense, sharpened in the school of adversity, to bear upon the question. He did not hesitate, he did not doubt, he did not falter; but at once resolved that at whatever peril, at whatever cost, the union of the States should be preserved. A patriot himself, his faith was strong and unwavering in the patriotism of his countrymen. Timid men said before Mr. Lincoln's inauguration, that we have seen the last President of the United States. A voice in influential quarters said, "Let the Union slide." Some said that a Union maintained by the sword was worthless. Others said a rebellion of 8,000,000 cannot be suppressed; but in the midst of all this tumult and timidity, and against all this, Abraham Lincoln was clear in his duty, and had an oath in heaven. He calmly and bravely heard the voice of doubt and fear all around him; but he had an oath in heaven, and there was not power enough on earth to make this honest boatman, backwoodsman, and broad-handed splitter of rails evade or violate that sacred oath. He had not been schooled in the ethics of slavery; his plain life had favored his love of truth. He had not been taught that treason and perjury were the proof of honor and honesty. His moral training was against his saying one thing when he meant another. The trust that Abraham Lincoln had in himself and in the people was surprising and grand, but it was also enlightened and well founded. He knew the American people better than they knew themselves, and his truth was based upon this knowledge.

Fellow-citizens, the fourteenth day of April, 1865, of which this is the eleventh anniversary, is now and will ever remain a memorable day in the annals of this Republic. It was on the evening of this day, while a fierce and sanguinary rebellion was in the last stages of its desolating power; while its armies were broken and scattered before the invincible armies of Grant and Sherman; while a great nation, torn and rent by war, was already beginning to raise to the skies loud anthems of joy at the dawn of peace, it was startled, amazed, and overwhelmed by the crowning crime of slavery — the assassination of Abraham Lincoln. It was a new crime, a pure act of malice. No purpose of the rebellion was to be served by it. It was the simple gratification of a hell-black spirit of revenge. But it has done good after all. It has filled the country with a deeper abhorrence of slavery and a deeper love for the great liberator.

Had Abraham Lincoln died from any of the numerous ills to which flesh is heir; had he reached that good old age of which his vigorous constitution and his temperate habits gave promise; had he been permitted to see the end of his great work; had the solemn curtain of death come down but gradually — we should still have been smitten with a heavy grief, and treasured his name lovingly. But dying as he did die, by the red hand of vio-lence, killed, assassinated, taken off without warning, not because of personal hate — for no man who knew Abraham Lincoln could hate him — but because of his fidelity to union and liberty, he is doubly dear to us, and his memory will be precious forever.

Fellow-citizens, I end, as I began, with congratulations. We have done a good work for our race today. In doing honor to the memory of our friend and liberator, we have been doing highest honors to ourselves and those who come after us; we have been fastening ourselves to a name and fame imperishable and immortal; we have also been defending ourselves from a blighting scandal. When now it shall be said that the colored man is soulless, that he has no appreciation of benefits or benefactors; when the foul reproach of ingratitude is hurled at us, and it is attempted to scourge us beyond the range of human brotherhood, we may calmly point to the monument we have this day erected to the memory of Abraham Lincoln.

GLOSSARY

abhorrence: loathing, revulsion

fidelity: loyalty, commitment.

Grant: President Ulysses S. Grant (1822-1885); he was an eminent general for the Union Army during the Civil War

gratification: satisfaction, fulfillment

sanguinary: bloody, brutal, gruesome

Sherman: William Tecumseh Sherman (1820-1891), served as a prominent general during the Civil War; he is particularly remembered for his famous "March to the Sea"

temperate: moderate, calm; it can also refer to the quality of abstaining from alcohol

Document Analysis

The unveiling of the Freedman's Monument on that April day in 1876 was well timed, and in more ways than one. Firstly, it was the eleventh anniversary of Abraham Lincoln's assassination, over a decade since the dreadful night at Ford's Theater when Lincoln and his wife sat watching the play, *Our American Cousin* before John Wilkes Booth changed the course of history. Secondly, it was the year 1876, a year that saw countless celebrations in honour of the centennial of the United States of America. Given all that had transpired during the Civil War and after, the centennial was all the more venerated. Thirdly, it was fifteen years ago, in the month of April, that the first shots were fired at Fort Sumter in South Carolina, prompting President Lincoln to call for volunteers for the Union Army.

An Objective Stance on Lincoln

Douglass's choice of words in his speech are intriguing, and causes one to reflect on how racially mixed the audience was; he specifically mentions the white people present, and also addresses those of his own race. Douglass wrote:

> It must be admitted, truth compels me to admit, even here in the presence of the monument we have erected for his memory, Abraham Lincoln was not, in the fullest sense of the word, either our man or model. In his interests, in his associations, in his habits of thought, and in his prejudices, he was a white man.

There is truth in what Douglass wrote. At the start of the war, and for a time during its early years, the Lincoln administration was far more concerned with the preservation of the Union; slavery, at that time, was not the issue it would later become for Lincoln and his administration. There has been some argument amongst historians on when this change occurred; some have suggested that the turning point was Gettysburg, others have said it was the Emancipation Proclamation. Whenever it was, the delay does not appear to have detracted from the overall perception of Lincoln held by Douglass. He accepts the president for who he is. There is admiration in Douglass when he writes that Lincoln began his own life not in the lap of luxury but rather as one "born and reared among the lowly...compelled to grapple singlehanded with the flintiest hardship of life, from tender youth to sturdy manhood."

It is useful to ask why Frederick Douglass chose this occasion to speak of issues that did not necessarily gild the memory of the slain president. There are elements of harshness in his remembrances, even while most of what he says is justified. Douglass wrote:

> ...When he strangely told us to leave the land in which we were born; when he refused to employ our arms in defence of the Union; when, after accepting our services as colored soldiers, he refused to retaliate our murder and torture as colored prisoners; when he told us he would save the Union if he could with slavery...

There is pain in this recounting, and there is also truth. In the 1850s, African Americans were encouraged to leave the United States and emigrate to the African colony of Liberia. Historian Peter Kolchin discusses this in his work on American slavery. Kolchin writes that despite all the encouragement blacks received, this was not a widely accepted idea and that many "rejected the notion of emigrating to Africa, for they saw themselves as...quintessentially American and looked upon Africa as a distant and savage land (84-85. 1995)."

Although it has always been a source of admiration when one volunteers for military service, the thought that an African American would do so during the Civil War was a novel one and had potentially life-threatening consequences. The act of black enlistment within the Union Army was viewed by the South as the federal government's approval of mutiny; Southern slaves, it was thought, would be incited to rebel against their owners upon seeing the *uniformed* black Union soldiers. The very concept of regiments made up of both free and formerly enslaved men was foreign to the Confederacy, and something they intended to react to—through punishment—if men from such regiments were captured in battle. In her work *Mothers of Invention: Women of the Slaveholding South in the American Civil War*, historian Drew Gilpin Faust recounts the experiences of Southern women who witnessed the arrival of black troops:

> Mary Lee of Winchester, Virginia, came "near to fainting," when the troops appeared; she felt "more unnerved than by any sight I have seen since the war [began]." (60. 1996).

Lincoln's Assassination

The assassination of Abraham Lincoln, on that day back in 1865, was a dark day for everyone in the country. Douglass himself had the privilege not only of meeting with the president, but also of discussing the enlistment of black men as soldiers and sailors with him. The relevant passage from his autobiographical writings is rather long; however, it is significant and worth reading in relation to his Freedmen's Monument Speech. This meeting occurred in the summer of 1863, and was the first to which Douglass was treated:

The room bore the marks of business, and the persons in it, the president included, appeared to be much overworked and tired. Long lines of care were already deeply written on Mr. Lincoln's brow, and his strong face, full of earnestness, lighted up as soon as my name was mentioned. As I approached and was introduced to him, he rose and extended his hand, and bade me welcome. I at once felt myself in the present of an honest man... Proceeding to tell him who I was, and what I was doing, he promptly, but kindly, stopped me, saying, 'I know who you are, Mr. Douglass... Sit down. I am glad to see you.' I then told him the object of my visit; that I was assisting to raise colored troops; that several months before I had been very successful in getting men to enlist, but now it was not easy to induce the colored me to enter the service, because there was a feeling among them that the government did not deal fairly with them in several respects. Mr. Lincoln asked me to state particulars. I replied that there were three particulars which I wished to bring to his attention. First that colored soldiers ought to receive the same wages as those paid to white soldiers. Second, that colored soldiers ought to receive the same protection when taken prisoners, and be exchanged as readily, and on the same terms, as any other prisoners, and if Jefferson Davis should shoot or hang colored soldiers in cold blood, the United States government should retaliate in kind and degree without dely upon Confederate prisoners in its hands. Third, when colored soldiers, seeking the 'bauble-reputation at the cannon's mouth,' performed great and uncommon service on the battlefield, they should be rewarded by distinction and promotion, precisely as white soldiers are rewarded for like services.

In laying out these specifications for the treatment of black enlistees, Frederick Douglass was clearly demonstrating how equality had to work for soldiers, that race simply could not be a factor. The men, white or black, would both face the dangers on the battlefield; both endeavored to serve their country at the highest level possible. In the end, a large part of Douglass's own mourning for President Lincoln may have rested in the fact that Lincoln allowed him an audience to discuss the issue of black soldiers and sailors; the president did not have to speak with Douglass at all, or he could have chosen to restrict the discussion points.

In writing of the assassination, Douglass in his Freedmen's Monument address writes as though the issue is something he cannot quite get past, particularly because Lincoln was not allowed to die a natural death. If the latter had been the case, writes Douglass, "we should still have been smitten with a heavy grief, and treasured his name lovingly"—but perhaps with not so much sadness as now. Douglass felt that the assassination of Abraham Lincoln was all the more grievous because the country had only so recently come through a bloody war, one that had wreaked havoc upon nearly every family. Douglass writes that the assassination " was the simple gratification of a hell-black spirit of revenge."

At the conclusion of his speech, Douglass attempts to bring light to the darkness caused by Abraham Lincoln's absence, saying that the president's murder, if anything, was now forever associated with slavery and the rebellion—and in being so, allowed "a deeper love for the great liberator."

Essential Themes

Frederick Douglass, in his Freedmen's Monument Speech, makes recurring references to the event's date of April 1876 and its associations with Lincoln, as well as the fact that the event itself was being held in Washington, D. C., where Lincoln had once held office. For those of Douglass' generation, it must have been an association that would live on in them. The language regarding the assassination is strikingly different from the tones used earlier; the speaker's words are violent and powerful, displaying an undiminished anger toward the actions of Wilkes Booth eleven years after the fact. Douglass observes that

> It was on the evening of this day, while a fierce and sanguinary rebellion was in the last stages of its desolating power; while its armies were broken and scattered before the invincible armies of Grant and Sher-

man; while a great nation, torn and rent by war, was already beginning to raise to the skies loud anthems of joy at the dawn of peace, it was startled, amazed, and overwhelmed by the crowning crime of slavery—*the assassination of Abraham Lincoln.*

There is still a measure of disbelief in what had happened, a sense that, given all that they had faced during the war, the success of the Union could only be capped by the death of their leader—for contemporaries, the shocking truth must have been incomprehensible.

Having had the opportunity to meet with President Lincoln and openly discuss his vision for the black troops who paved the way for future African Americans in the armed services, delivering an address before a new monument to the fallen president must have been bittersweet for Douglass. He respected Lincoln for his opinions and his faults—he respected Lincoln for the man the president was; and, despite their differences, he did not allow his admiration to be marred by Lincoln's departure from life.

Jennifer L. Henderson Crane, BA, PgDip

Bibliography

Carlson, Peter. "Abraham Lincoln Meets Frederick Douglass," *American History* 45 6 (Feb. 2011), p. 28-29. Print.

Foner, Philip S. *The Life and Writings of Frederick Douglass, IV, Reconstruction and After.* New York: International Publishers, 1955. Print.

Kolchin, Peter. *American Slavery: 1619-1877.* London: Penguin Books, 1995. Print.

Lee, Maurice S. *The Cambridge Companion to Frederick Douglass.* Cambridge: Cambridge UP, 2009. Print.

Lincoln Institute. "Frederick Douglass." Mr. Lincoln and Freedom [project]. Web.

McPherson, James M. *Battle Cry of Freedom: The Civil War Era.* New York: Oxford UP, 1988. Print.

Additional Reading

Clark-Lewis, Elizabeth. *First Freed: Washington, D.C. in the Emancipation Era.* Washington, DC: Howard UP, 2002. Print.

Douglass, Frederick. *My Bondage and my Freedom.* New Haven: Yale UP, 2014. Print.

Oakes, James. *The Radical Republicans: Frederick Douglass, Abraham Lincoln, and the Triumph of Antislavery Politics.* New York: Norton, 2007. Print.

Stauffer, John. *The Black Hearts of Men: Radical Abolitionists and the Transformation of Race.* Cambridge, MA: Harvard UP, 2001. Print.

Stephens, George E. and Donald Yacovone. *A Voice of Thunder: A Black Soldier's Civil War.* Champaign: U of Illinois P, 1999. Print.

◼ Prospects of the Freedmen of Hilton Head

Date: Late 1865
Author: Delany, Martin
Genre: series of articles

"After these centuries of trial and experience, would these [Africans] have been continually sought after, had they not proven to be superior to all others as laborers in the kind of work assigned them? Let political economists answer."

Summary Overview

Celebrated by many as the father of black national-ism, Martin Robison Delany is among the leading black thinkers and leaders of the nineteenth century. Like his colleague Frederick Douglass, Delany achieved great things as he led the fight against slavery and created new opportunities for freedmen, including serving as the first black major in the Union army, writing scores of influential articles and books, gaining acceptance to Harvard Medical School, participating in conventions, meeting President Lincoln, and traveling to Africa. Yet Delany's celebration of black identity and his support of freedmen's emigration to Africa distinguish him clearly from leaders such as Douglass. At times, Delany dedi-cated his efforts to integration in the United States, but his personal experiences and frustrations with the persistence of racism led him, at other times, to call for separatism. Criticized by leaders during his time, Delany's prophetic vision as expressed in articles such as "Prospects of the Freedmen of Hilton Head" none-theless planted the seeds for the Black Power move-ment that emerged in the second half of the twentieth century.

Defining Moment

The year 1865 marked the end of the U.S. Civil War and promised great hope but also great uncertainty. Gen-eral Robert E. Lee's capitulation to Union commander Ulysses S. Grant on April 9, 1865, was the first major surrender and clearly signaled the war's impending con-clusion. The war's end, however, did not immediately resolve the issue of slavery, in part because Lincoln's Emancipation Proclamation of 1863 had declared free-dom only for slaves in the Confederacy. This exempted the slave-holding border states of Delaware, Kentucky, Maryland, and Missouri and the Union-controlled state of Tennessee as well as some other areas controlled by federal troops in parts of Louisiana and Virginia. It was only in December, 1865 that Congress formally abol-ished slavery by passing the Thirteenth Amendment to the Constitution. These events ushered in the period known as Reconstruction, which in part aimed to de-fine the legal status and rights of freed slaves and to manage the former Confederate states' transition to self-government and the status of their leaders. During Reconstruction, Congress passed numerous acts and constitutional amendments addressing these issues and created the Bureau of Refugees, Freedmen, and Abandoned Lands (the Freedmen's Bureau) to estab-lish the necessary institutions and resources for these transitions.

Martin Delany was the first black major in the Union army and later worked as an officer for the Freedmen's Bureau, but he knew that establishing political and economic opportunity for freed slaves required not only new laws and agencies but also a profound shift in culture. Southern planters would have to respect freed slaves as equal citizens with the right to contract fair labor, and building this respect would entail uprooting society's deep-seated ideology of white supremacy. Confronting the difficulty of changing this poisonous belief system, Delany wrote the seven articles of "Prospects of the Freedmen of Hilton Head" while he was working for the Freedmen's Bureau in Hilton Head, South Carolina in late 1865, just before the passage of the Thirteenth Amendment. Addressing both the cultural and practical challenges that lay ahead, the articles brilliantly reflect the high hopes and deep uncertainty of this moment in U.S. history in which legal and institutional ground shifted fundamentally in the context of profound cultural aspirations and resistance.

Author Biography

In his long and restless life of 73 years, Martin Robison Delany worked tirelessly for the cause of freedom and achieved countless distinctions. Born in 1812 in Charles Town, Virginia, to a free mother and an enslaved father, Delany moved to Pennsylvania in the 1820s with his mother when she fled authorities who tried to imprison her for educating her children. Delany studied with abolitionist leaders in Pittsburgh during the 1830s and began his distinguished career. Over the next two decades, he established his own medical practice, attended conventions, and became a prolific writer. His achievements during this time include editorial work with Frederick Douglass on the *North Star*, a highly influential African American newspaper, and his brief attendance at Harvard Medical School, which was cruelly cut short after white students protested his and other black students' presence.

Partly in response to his rejection at Harvard and to the Compromise of 1850, which strengthened the Fugitive Slave Act, Delany then wrote The Condition, Elevation, Emigration and Destiny of the Colored People of the United States, which promoted black emigration to Central and South America. In subsequent years, Delany backed up his words by organizing a convention for emigration, and he himself moved to Canada in 1856, where he consulted with abolitionist John Brown on a possible slave insurrection. In the late 1850s, he began to promote black emigration to Africa and even visited the Niger Valley, signed a treaty to establish a settlement in West Africa, and went on a speaking tour in England to raise funds for the effort. In 1859-1861, Delany published a novel and an account of his experiences in Africa, but he abandoned the emigration project after the king with whom he had signed the treaty reneged.

During the Civil War, Delany redirected his attention to the United States. He recruited black troops for the Union forces, became the army's first black major, and gained notoriety for meeting President Lincoln. He subsequently worked with the Freedmen's Bureau in South Carolina during Reconstruction, continued to write, and even ran for lieutenant governor of the state. Yet, as the failures of Reconstruction became increasingly clear in the 1870s, a disillusioned Delany once again began to promote emigration to Africa, and his late writings underscore a "Pan-African pride in blacks' historical, cultural, and racial ties to Africa" (Levine 2). This emphasis chiefly contributes to his place in history as the father of Black nationalism.

HISTORICAL DOCUMENT

I.

PROSPECTS OF THE FREEDMEN OF HILTON HEAD.

Every true friend of the Union, residing on the island, must feel an interest in the above subject, regardless of any other consideration than that of national polity. Have the blacks become self-sustaining? and will they ever, in a state of freedom, resupply the products which comprised the staples formerly of the old planters? These are questions of importance, and not unworthy of the consideration of grave political economists.

That the blacks of the island have not been self-sustaining will not be pretended, neither can it be denied that they have been generally industrious and inclined to work. But industry alone is not sufficient, nor work available, except these command adequate compensation.

Have the blacks innately the elements of industry and enterprise? Compare them with any other people, and note their adaptation. Do they not make good "day laborers"? Are they not good field hands? Do they not make good domestics? Are they not good house servants? Do they not readily "turn their hands" to anything or kind of work they may find to do? Trained, they make good body servants, house servants, or laundresses, waiters, chamber and dining-room servants, cooks, nurses, drivers, horse "tenders," and, indeed, fill as well, and better, many of the domestic occupations than any other race. And with unrestricted facilities for learning, will it be denied that they are as susceptible of the mechanical occupations or trades as they are of the domestic? Will it be denied that a people easily domesticated are susceptible of the higher attainments? The slaveholder, long since, cautioned against "giving a nigger an inch, lest he should take an ell."

If permitted, I will continue this subject in a series of equally short articles, so as not to intrude on your columns.

II.

This subject must now be examined in the light of political economy, and, for reasons stated in a previous article, treated tersely in every sentence, and, therefore, will not be condemned by the absence of elaboration and extensive proof.

America was discovered in 1492 — then peopled only by the original inhabitants, or Indians, as afterwards called. No part of the country was found in a state of cultivation, and no industrial enterprise was carried on, either foreign or domestic. Not even in the West Indies — prolific with spices, gums, dye-woods, and fruits — was there any trade carried on among or by the natives. These people were put to labor by the foreigners; but, owing to their former habits of hunting, fishing, and want of physical exercise, they sank beneath the weight of toil, fast dying off, till their mortality, in time, from this cause alone, reached the frightful figure of two and a half millions. (See Ramsay's History.)

The whites were put to labor, and their fate was no better — which requires no figures, as all are familiar with the history and career of Thomas Gates and associates at one time; John Smith and associates, as colonists in the South, at another; how, not farther than Virginia, — at most, North Carolina, — they "died like sheep," to the destruction of the settlements, in attempting to do the work required to improve for civilized life. Neither whites, as foreigners, nor Indians, as natives, were adequate to the task of performing the labor necessary to their advent in the New World.

So early as 1502 — but ten years after Columbus landed — "the Spaniards commenced bringing a few negroes from Africa to work the soil." (See Ramsay's History.) In 1515, but thirteen years afterwards, and twenty-three from the discovery of America, Carolus V., King of Spain, granted letters patent to import annually into the colonies of Cuba, Ispaniola (Hayti), Jamaica, and Porto Rico, four thousand Africans as slaves — people contracted with to "emigrate" to these new colonies, as the French, under Louis Napoleon, attempted, in 1858, to decoy native Africans, under the pretext of emigrating to the colonies, into French slavery, then reject international interference, on the ground that they obtained them by "voluntary emigration."

Such was the success of this new industrial element, that not only did Spaniards and Portuguese employ them in all their American colonies, but so great was the demand for these laborers, that Elizabeth, the Virgin Queen of England, became a partner in the slave trade with the infamous Captain Hawkins; and, in 1618, her successor to the throne, and royal relative, James I., King of England, negotiated for and obtained the entire carrying trade, thus securing, by international patent, the exclusive right for British vessels alone to "traffic in blood and souls of men," to reap the profits arising from their importation.

Was it the policy of political economists, such as were then the rulers and statesmen of Europe, to employ a people in preference to all others for the development of wealth, if such people were not adapted to the labor designed for them? Would the civilized and highly polished, such as were then the Spanish, French, and Portuguese nations, together with the English, still have continued the use of these people as laborers and domestics in every social relation among them, if they had not found them a most desirable domestic element? Would, after the lapse of one hundred and sixteen years' rigid trial and experience from their first importation, the King of England have been able — whatever his avarice as an individual — to have effected so great a diplomatic treaty, as the consent from all the civilized nations having interests here to people their colonies with a race if that race had been worthless as laborers, and deficient as an industrial element? Would, in the year of the grace of Jesus Christ, and the light of the highest civilization, after the lapse of two hundred and twenty years from James's treaty, the most powerful and enlightened monarchy have come near the crisis of its political career in its determination to continue the system, and for two hundred and forty-seven years the most powerful and enlightened republic that ever the world saw have distracted the harmony of the nations of the earth, and driven itself to the verge of destruction by the mad determination of one half of the people and leading states, to perpetuate the service of this race as essential to the development of the agricultural wealth of the land? After these centuries of trial and experience, would these people have been continually sought after, had they not proven to be superior to all others as laborers in the kind of work assigned them? Let political economists answer.

V.

As shown in my last article, these people are the lineal descendants of an industrious, hardy race of men — those whom the most powerful and accomplished statesmen and political economists of the great states of Europe, after years of trial and rigid experience, decided upon and selected as the element best adapted to develop in a strange and foreign clime — a new world of unbroken soil and dense, impenetrable forests — the industry and labor necessary to the new life. This cannot and will not be attempted to be denied without ignoring all historical authority, though presented in a different light — and may I not say motive? — from that in which history has ever given It.

These people are of those to retain whom in her power the great British nation was agitated to the point,

at as late a period as 1837-8, of shattering the basis of its political foundation; and, within the last four years, the genius of the American government was spurned, assaulted, and trampled upon, and had come well nigh its final dissolution by full one half of the states, people, and statesmen inaugurating a civil war, the most stupendous on record, for no other purpose than retaining them as laborers. Does any intelligent person doubt the utility of such a people? Can such a people now be worthless in the country? Does any enlightened, reflecting person believe it? I think not.

But this is an experiment. Have we no precedent, no example? What of the British colonies of the West Indies and South America? Let impartial history and dispassionate, intelligent investigation answer. The land in the colonies was owned by wealthy capitalists and gentlemen who resided in Europe. The "proprietors," or planters, were occupants of the land, who owned the slaves that worked it, having borrowed the capital with which to purchase them at the Cuba markets or barracoons and supply the plantations. In security for this, mortgages were held by those in Europe on "all estate, real and personal," belonging to the planters, who paid a liberal interest on the loans.

When the opposition in the British Parliament, led by Tories, who were the representatives of the capitalists, yielded to the Emancipation Bill, it was only on condition of an appropriation of twenty millions of pounds sterling, or one hundred millions of dollars, as remuneration to the planters for their slaves set free. This proposition was so moderate as to surprise and astonish the intelligent in state affairs on both sides of the ocean, as the sum proposed only amounted to the penurious price of about one hundred and twenty dollars apiece, when men and women were then bringing at the barracoons in Cuba from five to six hundred dollars apiece in cash; and the average of men, women, and children, according to their estimate of black mankind, were "worth" four hundred and fifty dollars. Of course the tutored colonial laborer would be worth still more.

After the passage of the Act of Emancipation by the Imperial Parliament, the complaint was wafted back by the breeze of every passing wind, that the planters in the colonies were impoverished by emancipation, and dishonest politicians and defeated, morose statesmen seized the opportunity to display their duplicity. "What will become of the fair colonial possessions? The lands will go back into a wilderness waste. The negroes are idle, lazy, and will not work. They are unfit for freedom, and ought to have masters. Where they do work, not half the crop is produced on the same quantity of land. What will the whites do if they don't get servants to work for them? They and their posterity must starve. The lands are lying waste for the want of occupants, and the negroes are idling their time away, and will not have them when offered to them. The social system in the West Indies has been ruined by the emancipation of the negroes." These, and a thousand such complaints, tingled upon the sensitive ear in every word that came from the British colonies, as the key-note of the pro-slavery British party, till caught up and reechoed from the swift current of the southern extremity of Brazil to the banks of the Potomac, the northern extremity of the slave territory of the United States. But alive to passing events, and true to their great trust, the philanthropists and people soon discovered, through their eminent representatives and statesmen in Parliament, that the whites in the colonies had never owned the lands nor the blacks which they lost by the Act of Emancipation. And when the appropriation was made by Parliament, the money remained in the vaults of the banks in Europe, being precisely the amount required to liquidate the claims of the capitalists, and to satisfy the mortgages held by those gentlemen against "all estates" of the borrowers in the colonies, both "real and personal."

The cause of the cry and clamor must be seen at a glance. The money supposed to be intended for the colonists, small as it was, instead of being appropriated to them, simply went to satisfy the claims of the capitalists who resided in Great Britain, not one out of a hundred of whom had ever seen the colonies. And the lands being owned in Europe, and the laborers free, what was to save the white colonists from poverty? All this was well known to leading pro-slavery politicians and statesmen in Europe as well as America; but a determination to perpetuate the bondage of a people as laborers — a people so valuable as to cause them, rather than loose their grasp upon them, to boldly hazard their national integrity, and set at defiance the morality of the civilized world in holding them — caused this reprehensible imposition and moral outrage in misleading to distraction their common constituency

VI.

Mr. Editor: This is my sixth article on the subject of the "Prospects of the Freedmen of Hilton Head" Island, which you have so generously admitted into the columns of The New South, and for which liberality towards a recently liberated people, I most heartily thank you. The time may come when they, for themselves, may be able to thank you. I hope to conclude with my next.

After what has been adduced in proof of their susceptibility, adaptation, and propensity for the vocations of the domestic and social relations of our civilization, what are their *prospects?* for that now must be the leading question, and give more concern to the philanthropist, true statesman, and Christian, than anything relating to their fitness or innate adaptation, since that I hold to be admitted, and no longer a question — at least with the intelligent inquirer.

What should be the prospects? Will not the same labor that was performed by a slave be in requisition still? Cannot he do the same work as a freedman that he once did as a slave? Are the products of slave labor preferable to free? or are the products of free labor less valuable than slave? Will not rice and cotton be in as great demand after emancipation as before it? or will these commodities cease to be used, because they cease to be produced by the labor of slaves? All these are questions pertinent, if not potent, to the important inquiry under consideration — the prospects of the freedmen of Hilton Head.

Certainly these things will be required, in demand, and labor quite as plentiful; but not one half of the negroes can be induced to work, as was proven in the West Indies, and is apparent from the comparative number who now seek their old vocations to those who formerly did the same work.

Grant this, — which is true, — and is it an objectionable feature, or does it impair the prospects of the freedman? By no means; but, on the contrary, it enhances his prospects and elevates his manhood. Here, as in the case of West India emancipation before emancipation took place every available person — male and female — from seven years of age to decrepit old age (as field hands) was put into the field to labor.

For example, take one case to illustrate the whole.

Before liberated, Juba had a wife and eight children, from seven to thirty years of age, everyone of whom was at labor in the field as a slave. When set free, the mother and all of the younger children (consisting of five) quit the field, leaving the father and three older sons, from twenty-five to thirty years of age, who preferred field labor; the five children being sent to school. The mother, now the pride of the recently-elevated freedman, stays in her own house, to take charge, as a housewife, in her new domestic relations — thus permanently withdrawing from the field six tenths of the service of this family; while the husband and three sons (but four tenths) are all who remain to do the work formerly performed by ten tenths, or the whole. Here are more than one half who will not work in the field. Will any one say they should? And this one example may suffice for the most querulous on this subject. Human nature is all the same under like circumstances. The immutable, unalterable laws which governed or controlled the instincts or impulses of a Hannibal, Alexander, or Napoleon, are the same implanted in the brain and breast of page or footman, be he black or white, circumstances alone making the difference in development according to the individual propensity.

As slaves, people have no choice of pursuit or vocation, but must follow that which is chosen by the master. Slaves, like freemen, have different tastes and desires — many doing that which is repugnant to their choice. As slaves, they were compelled to subserve the interests of the master regardless of themselves; as freemen, as should be expected and be understood, many changes would take place in the labor and pursuits of the people. Some who were field hands, among the young men and women of mature age, seek employment at other pursuits, and choose for themselves various trades — vocations adapted to their tastes.

Will this be charged to the worthlessness of the negro, and made an argument against his elevation? Truth stands defiant in the pathway of error.

VII.

I propose to conclude the subject of "THE PROSPECTS OF THE FREEDMEN OF HILTON HEAD" with this article, and believe that the prospects of the one are the prospects of the whole population of freedmen throughout the South.

Political economy must stand most prominent as the leading feature of this great question of the elevation of the negro — and it is a great question — in this country, because, however humane and philanthropic, however Christian and philanthropic we may be, except we can be made to see that there is a prospective enhancement of the general wealth of the country, — a pecuniary benefit to accrue by it to society, — the best of us, whatever our pretensions, could scarcely be willing to see him elevated in the United States.

Equality of political rights being the genius of the American government, I shall not spend time with this, as great principles will take care of' themselves, and must eventually prevail.

Will the negroes be able to obtain land by which to earn a livelihood? Why should they not? It is a well-known fact to the statisticians of the South that two thirds of the lands have never been cultivated. These lands being mainly owned by but three hundred and twelve thousand persons (according to Helper) — one third of which was worked by four millions of slaves, who are now freemen — what better can be done with these lands to make them available and unburdensome to the proprietors, than let them out in small tracts to the freedmen, as well as to employ a portion of the same people, who prefer it, to cultivate lands for themselves?

It is a fact — probably not so well known as it should be — in political economy, that a given amount of means divided among a greater number of persons, makes a wealthier community than the same amount held or possessed by a few.

For example, there is a community of a small country village of twenty families, the (cash) wealth of the community being fifty thousand dollars, and but one family the possessor of it; certainly the community would not be regarded as in good circumstances, much less having available means. But let this amount be possessed by ten families in sums of five thousand dollars each, would not this enhance the wealth of the community? And again, let the whole twenty families be in possession of two thousand five hundred dollars each of the fifty thousand, would not this be still a wealthier community, by placing each family in easier circumstances, and making these means much more available? Certainly it would, And as to a community or village, so to a state; and as to a state, so to a nation.

This is the solution to the great problem of the difference between the strength of the North and the South in the late rebellion — the North possessing the means within itself without requiring outside help, almost every man being able to aid the national treasury; everybody commanding means, whether earned by a white-wash brush in black hands, or wooden nutmegs in white: all had something to sustain the integrity of the Union. It must be seen by this that the strength of a country — internationally considered — depends greatly upon its wealth; the wealth consisting not in the greatest amount possessed, but the greatest available amount.

Let, then, such lands as belong to the government, by sale from direct taxation, be let or sold to these freedmen, and other poor loyal men of the South, in small tracts of from twenty to forty acres to each head of a family, and large landholders do the same, — the rental and sales of which amply rewarding them, — and there will be no difficulty in the solution of the problem of the future, or prospects of the freedmen, not only of Hilton Head, but of the whole United States.

This increase of the wealth of the country by the greater division of its means is not new to New England, nor to the economists of the North generally. As in Pennsylvania, many years ago, the old farmers commenced dividing their one hundred and one hundred and fifty acre tracts of lands into twenty-five acres each among their sons and daughters, who are known to have realized more available means always among them — though by far greater in numbers — than their parents did, who were comparatively few. And it is now patent as an historic fact, that, leaving behind them the extensive evergreen, fertile plains, and savannas of the South, the rebel armies and raiders continually sought the limited farms of the North to replenish their worn-out cavalry stock and exhausted commissary department — impoverished in cattle for food, and forage for horses.

In the Path Valley of Pennsylvania, on a single march of a radius of thirty-five miles of Chambersburg, Lee's army, besides all the breadstuffs that his three thousand five hundred wagons (as they went empty for the purpose) were able to carry, captured and carried off more than six thousand head of stock, four thousand of which were horses. The wealth of that valley alone, they reported, was more than India fiction, and equal to all of the South put together. And whence this mighty available wealth of Pennsylvania? Simply by its division and possession among the many.

The Rothschilds are said to have once controlled the exchequer of England, compelling (by implication) the premier to comply with their requisition at a time of great peril to the nation, simply because it depended upon them for means; and the same functionaries are reported, during our recent struggle, to have greatly annoyed the Bank of England, by a menace of some kind, which immediately brought the institution to their terms. Whether true or false, the points are sufficiently acute to serve for illustration.

In the apportionment of small farms to the freedmen, an immense amount of means is placed at their command, and thereby a great market opened, a new source of consumption of every commodity in demand in free civilized communities. The blacks are great consumers, and four millions of a population, before barefooted, would here make a demand for the single article of shoes. The money heretofore spent in Europe by the old slaveholders would be all disbursed by these new people in their own country. Where but one cotton gin and a limited number of farming utensils were formerly required to the plantation of a thousand acres, every small farm will want a gin and farming implements, the actual valuation of which on the same tract of land would be several fold greater than the other. Huts would give place to beautiful, comfortable cottages, with all their appurtenances, fixtures, and furniture; osnaburgs and rags would give place to genteel apparel becoming a free and industrious people; and even the luxuries, as well as the general comforts, of table would take the place of black-eye peas and fresh fish, hominy and salt pork, all of which have been mainly the products of their own labor when slaves. They would quickly prove that arduous and faithfully fawning, miserable volunteer advocate of the rebellion and slaveholder's rule in the United States, — the London Times, — an arrant falsifier, when it gratuitously and unbidden came to the aid of its kith and kin, declaring that the great and good President Lincoln's Emancipation Proclamation would not be accepted by the negroes; 'that all Cuffee wanted and cared for to make him happy was his hog and his hominy;" but they will neither get land, nor will the old slaveholders give them employment. Don't fear any such absurdity. There are too many political economists among the old leading slaveholders to fear the adoption of any such policy. Neither will the leading statesmen of the country, of any part, North or South, favor any such policy.

We have on record but one instance of such a course in the history of modern states. The silly-brained, foolhardy king of France, Louis V., taking umbrage at the political course of the artisans and laborers against him, by royal decree expelled them from the country, when they flocked into England, which readily opened her doors to them, transplanting from France to England their arts and industry; ever since which, England, for fabrics, has become the "workshop of the world," to the poverty of France, the government of which is sustained by borrowed capital.

No fears of our country driving into neighboring countries such immense resources as emanate from the peculiar labor of these people; but when worst comes to worst, they have among them educated freemen of their own color North, fully competent to lead the way, by making negotiations with foreign states on this continent, which would only be too ready to receive them and theirs.

Place no impediment in the way of the freedman; let his right be equally protected and his chances be equally regarded, and with the facts presented to you in this series of seven articles as the basis, he will stand and thrive, as firmly rooted, not only on the soil of Hilton Head, but in all the South, — though a black, — as any white, or "Live Oak," as ever was grown in South Carolina, or transplanted to Columbia.

GLOSSARY

barracoon: an enclosure or barracks used in the slave trade to confine slaves temporarily while they awaited transport to other locations

Black nationalism: a twentieth-century political and social movement emphasizing national identity on the basis of race, self-determination, and independence from European cultural, political, and economic control

Hannibal: a third-century BCE Carthaginian military leader who successfully invaded the Roman Empire but was ultimately defeated by the Roman leader Scipio Africanus

John Smith: English explorer who was one of the settlers in Jamestown, Virginia, in the early seventeenth century

Napoleon: Late eighteenth- and early nineteenth-century French emperor who ruled during the French Revolution and subjugated much of Europe during the conflicts known as the Napoleonic Wars

osnaburg: a heavy, course cotton fabric used for grain sacks and other utilitarian applications

political economy: a term for the relationship between economic production and its legal, cultural, and political contexts and institutions

Document Analysis

In August of 1865, Delany traveled to Hilton Head, South Carolina after a sudden change of plans. In May of that year, he had been ordered to begin recruiting men to serve in the 105th regiment of the United States Colored Troops, but the military withdrew the order in June when the war ended. On August 7, 1865, Major Delany was commanded to report to the Freedmen's Bureau in Hilton Head for a three-year period of service. There, Delany served as an assistant commissioner and worked to organize and educate freedmen about their new rights and responsibilities and to help them obtain fair labor contracts. Delany's articles submitted to the newspaper *The New South* (five of the seven remain in print) were part of his strategy to defend the freedmen and African Americans in general against certain criticisms and to promote his ideas for how to establish new labor structures in the South (Levine 396). The articles, however, reflect deep ambiguity about the nature of African Americans and their chances for progress. With impressive boldness, Delany asserts the notion of universal human nature and yet African American superiority, and his plan for the political and economic success of freed slaves expresses both belief in the possibility of integration and cynicism about whites' motivations. To be sure, Delany's life experiences inform the articles' contradictions, but it would be a mistake to dismiss these tensions as an intellectual flaw or the product of the writer's personal idiosyncrasies. Instead, we can best understand these inconsistencies as a vivid reflection of the deep ambivalence in the legal and cultural history of the nineteenth-century.

In the first article, Delany implies that he is responding to the charge that former slaves are not ready for freedom and have not demonstrated adequate self-sufficiency. He immediately acknowledges that freedmen are not yet self-sustaining but also points out their industriousness and desire to work. Then, he writes, "But industry alone is not sufficient, nor work available, except these command adequate compensation" (Rollin 230). With this, he announces his two primary concerns in the series: the worth of African Americans and the structures needed to organize fair labor. The first two articles address the nature and talents of his race in astonishing terms of "political economy," in which Delany argues that the Africans brought to America were in fact chosen because they were the only group capable of the backbreaking work in the New World. He begins with the date of 1492, describing America as a vast wilderness populated by Native Americans, who had not cultivated the land and thus could not survive the hard labor required when they "were put to labor by the foreigners" (Rollin 231). Here, Delany claims that two-and-a-half million Native Americans died "from this cause alone" (Rollin 231), i.e., inability to survive the working conditions imposed by the colonists. He then claims that white settlers suffered the same fate and cites the colonist John Smith as an example. The solution for the European colonists was

to import African slaves, whose unique capabilities convinced Queen Elizabeth to invest in the slave trade. Delany goes on to argue that the African slave trade flourished and eventually provoked a Civil War because the Africans themselves had rare abilities unmatched by either whites or Native Americans. In this way, he transforms slavery from an issue of the weak oppressed by the strong to one of demand for rare talent, which effectively subverts racist notions of African inferiority and establishes the high value of the freedmen's labor. Nonetheless, this celebration of African identity reinforces the notion of racial separateness and partly accounts for Delany's legacy as a Black Nationalist.

In the sixth article, Delany addresses the question of industriousness against a more specific charge, but here he appeals to an egalitarian notion of "human nature." The issue is that many freed people refuse to work in the fields as they had done as slaves, prompting charges of laziness and unsuitability for freedom. Yet Delany describes the change as a natural consequence of freedom. If a family is no longer forced to work in the fields, then it is only natural that a mother might choose to stay home to run her household and to send her children to school, which accounts for the reduction in field labor. Delany thus defends the worth of blacks by declaring, "The immutable, unalterable laws which governed or controlled the instincts or impulses of a Hannibal, Alexander, or Napoleon, are the same implanted in the brain and breast of page or footman, be he black or white, circumstances alone making the difference in development according to the individual propensity" (Rollin 237). Here, people of African descent are characterized no longer as exceptional but as acting according to universal human nature—a nature that makes no distinction between the most prestigious leaders and the least-respected laborers.

An analogous contradiction emerges when Delany turns to the actual prospects of the freedmen in the seventh article. This time, the tension lies between hope for an integrated society and Delany's cynicism toward those who control the labor economy. The cynicism is immediately apparent when he chooses to frame his argument in terms of political economy because, he states, "however Christian and philanthropic we may be" (Rollin 238), no one will want to support the elevation of blacks unless they can offer "a prospective enhancement of the general wealth of the country" (Rollin 238). With this, Delany flatly rejects the idea that anyone will support freedmen as deserving human rights per se; wealth is the only true motivation for supporting the newly free people.

At the same time, however, Delany proposes a plan that implies strong hope and even belief in the possibility of an integrated labor economy that respects the ideal of the common good. Delany first points out the availability of land, as two-thirds of land in the South remains uncultivated. He then claims that only 312,000 people have been landowners in the South and, citing Pennsylvania as a positive example, argues that a greater number of owners would increase the wealth of the community overall. His specific proposal is that both the government and large landowners should either lease or sell to freedmen its lands in portions of 20 to 40 acres. These freedmen would then create great demand for farming supplies and other goods, thereby stimulating the economy. Delany declares his faith in such a plan by rejecting those sources (such as the *London Times*) that deny the practical feasibility of freedom. And yet, he also considers the possibility of failure when he states at the conclusion that if the government and plantation owners in the United States refuse to employ free blacks, educated freemen of the North would be willing to negotiate "with foreign states on this continent, which would only be too ready to receive them and theirs" (Rollin 241). Here, Delany refers to the possibility of emigrating within the North American continent, suggesting his doubts about the success of his own plan.

Delany's fascinating contradictions reflect larger tensions in the legal and cultural history of the nineteenth century. The legal and constitutional approach to slavery was long dedicated to preserving the union rather than to addressing slavery exclusively as a moral issue. For example, the Mexican-American War (1846-48) resulted in vast new territories for the United States, provoking the key issue of whether the new lands would allow slavery. After significant conflict and debate, Congress passed the Compromise of 1850, which was a series of bills intended to placate parties on both sides of the debate in order to preserve the union and maintain peace, not to address the issue of slavery as a moral or human rights issue. Accordingly, the Compromise pleased abolitionists by admitting California as a free state and by banning the slave trade in the District of Columbia, and it placated pro-slavery people by protecting the *practice* of slavery in the District of Columbia and by offering a harsher Fugitive Slave Act. This Act required runaway slaves to be returned

to their owners and imposed heavy fines on negligent law-enforcement officials and both fines and imprisonment on those who aided runaway slaves. It also denied both slaves and free blacks trials and testimony, so that many free blacks became enslaved based on nothing more than a white person's affidavit. For these reasons, The Fugitive Slave Act of 1850 outraged abolitionists.

Likewise, the Emancipation Proclamation of 1863 was directed toward the cause of freedom, not least because it began to formalize what appeared to be the inevitable end of slavery, but it also strategically tolerated slavery for the sake of preserving the Union. The proclamation granted freedom to more than 3 million slaves in the Confederate states but denied it to hundreds of thousands of slaves in the border states, in Union-occupied Tennessee, and in other parts of federally controlled slave states. Lincoln's rationale for this partial gesture was that he needed the border slave states to remain in the Union so that he could garner as much support for the North as possible and weaken "the Confederacy by holding out to irresolute Southerners the possibility that they could return to the Union with their property, including slaves, intact" (Foner 4). This does not mean that Lincoln did not want to abolish slavery; the proclamation was an important part of Lincoln's progressive evolution on the slavery issue and in part ensured that abolition would indeed occur. Rather, the proclamation's partial liberation reveals politics, rather than justice, as Lincoln's chief priority.

These political and legal compromises did in fact lead to justice, with the passage of the Thirteenth Amendment and subsequent constitutional amendments and laws that were part of Reconstruction, which lasted until 1877. In the early years of Reconstruction, progressive citizens and politicians achieved a great deal, establishing voting rights and citizenship for freed slaves, setting up integrated governments in the South, and establishing educational and other institutions for the new black citizens. Most scholars agree, however, that Reconstruction ultimately failed for many different reasons, including the devastating economic fallout from the war on the Southern economy and the international economic depression that began in 1873. Yet perhaps the most important cause of failure was the racist belief system that persisted despite the South's defeat and the new federal laws and institutions that supported the former slaves' freedom. By the early 1870s, conservatives replaced progressive governments throughout the South, and many conservatives staunchly opposed Reconstruction and tolerated or even encouraged widespread violence against African Americans. As reactionary conservatives took control of the South and the North began to lose interest in Reconstruction, the stage was set for the Jim Crow era, which established African Americans as an underclass in the United States for the next century.

Martin Delany lived to see the failure of Reconstruction, but he wrote "Prospects of the Freedmen" earlier, in 1865. Nonetheless, Delany clearly understood the distance between politics and justice and between the law and culture. He had witnessed this gap in the legal compromises prior to and during the war. He also experienced it in his own life from his earliest days: his family's move from Charles Town to Pennsylvania occurred after his mother, who was free, was persecuted for teaching her children to read and write; later, Delany was admitted to Harvard Medical School, but its racist culture defeated his right to attend. These realities of white resistance to the law deeply inform Delany's writings and help us to understand his desire to exalt African Americans while arguing for equal opportunity as well as his impulse to imagine economic structures that would facilitate success for freedmen even as he harbored doubts and cynicism about the motives of whites. His shrewd observation and experience taught him that culture had the power to defeat the law. Sadly, the failure of Reconstruction would justify the lesson. Yet, in 1865, he valiantly resolved to redefine prevailing beliefs and to frame them as part of an economic plan that he hoped and believed could succeed.

Essential Themes

In an attempt to lend objectivity to his arguments, Delany organizes both his characterization of African Americans and his practical proposals under the theme of political economy. Against the popular notion of the former slaves' childlike nature, laziness, and inability to be self-sufficient, Delany shockingly declares the African slave trade as a unique success in the face of previous failures based on the cultural (and implicitly racial) inferiority of whites and Native Americans. He uses this stance to elevate people of African descent based on the economic success that only they could provide to the New World settlers. He then uses this strategy to bolster his plan to promote the economic opportunity and welfare of freedmen: it is in the United States' interest to support this uniquely talented group that ensured the country's prosperity. Yet in arguing for

equal opportunity, Delany can only take this claim so far, as demonstrated when he falls back on the notion of universal human nature to explain the reduced pool of field labor. Likewise, Delany proposes a plan that assumes the cooperation and integration of government, private landholders, and freedmen but that also reveals cynicism and doubts about the plan's likelihood. These themes of separatism versus unity and hope versus cynicism mirror the deeper patterns of ambivalence and compromise that were so prevalent in the laws and culture of nineteenth-century slavery and its subsequent abolition.

Ashleigh Imus, Ph.D.

Bibliography

Foner, Eric. *Reconstruction: America's Unfinished Revolution, 1863-1877.* New York: Harper & Row, 1988. Print.

Levine, Robert S. *Martin R. Delany: A Documentary Reader.* Chapel Hill: U of North Carolina P, 2003. Print.

Rollin, Frank A. *Life and Public Services of Martin R. Delany.* New York: Arno Press and the New York Times, 1969. Print.

Additional Reading

Adeleke, Tunde. *Without Regard to Race: the Other Martin Robison Delany.* Jackson: UP of Mississippi, 2003. Print.

Foner, Philip S. and Robert James Branham, eds. *Lift Every Voice: African American Oratory, 1787-1900.* Tuscaloosa: U of Alabama P, 1998. Print.

Levine, Robert S. *Martin Delany, Frederick Douglass and the Politics of Representative Identity.* Chapel Hill: U of North Carolina P, 1997. Print.

Sterling, Dorothy. *The Making of an Afro-American: Martin Robison Delany 1812-1885.* Garden City: Doubleday, 1971. Print.

Ullman, Victor. *Martin R. Delany: The Beginnings of Black Nationalism.* Boston: Beacon Press, 1971. Print.

■ Letters from Louisiana

Date: February 8, 1866, and December 17, 1866
Author: Highgate, Edmonia
Genre: letter

> *"There has been much opposition to the School. Twice*
> *I have been shot at in my room...The rebels here*
> *threatened to burn down the school and house in*
> *which I board before the first month was passed yet*
> *they have not materially harmed us."*

Summary Overview

Well before President Lincoln's Emancipation Proclamation in 1863 and the end of the Civil War, teachers and activists in both the North and the South began the arduous task of creating educational opportunities and institutions for freed slaves. This effort occurred as part of the legal and institutional changes that came with the end of slavery; for example, the Freedmen's Bureau, a relief agency, provided funds to set up schools and to compensate teachers in the South. Yet this educational project also occurred in spite of the government's woefully inadequate support and the resistance of racist groups who undermined and even terrorized teachers and students attending the new black schools. Edmonia Highgate's letters from Louisiana document a generation's attempt to negotiate this resistance. They also reveal the diversity of the communities where she worked as well as the talent and ambition of the teachers who sought to create a culture of education for freed slaves in a society that nonetheless denied Highgate and her peers equal opportunity.

Defining Moment

President Lincoln's Emancipation Proclamation of 1863, which freed slaves in the Confederacy, initiated a period of astonishing change for both Southerners and Northerners. To be sure, this change did not happen overnight as true freedom for the former slaves proved slow and daunting: the Civil War would not end officially until Confederate troops began to surrender in April of 1865, and in December of the same year, the Thirteenth Amendment to the Constitution abolished the institution of slavery and was formally adopted. In the years following, Congress enacted a series of reforms as part of the period known as Reconstruction (1865-1877). These reforms included the Reconstruction Acts of 1867 and 1868, which gave the vote to freedmen, required new constitutions for the states that had supported the Confederacy, and set up occupied military districts in the South to ensure compliance with the new laws. The Fourteenth Amendment, which acknowledged African Americans' rights to citizenship, was ratified in 1868, followed by the Fifteenth Amendment in 1870, which intended to eradicate racial restrictions to voting (Mjagkij xi-xii).

In addition to these legal reforms, important new educational opportunities emerged for newly freed slaves. During and after the Civil War, Northerners, including many women, traveled to the South to provide food, clothing, and medical care as well as to set up schools for millions of freedpeople. Northern churches and secular humanitarian groups initially sponsored these relief efforts and included the American Missionary Association, the Friends Associations of Philadelphia and

New York, and other societies. In 1865, Congress created the Bureau of Refugees, Freedmen, and abandoned Lands, more commonly known as the Freedmen's Bureau, to assist the work begun by churches and other organizations. The Bureau provided over 5 million dollars for freedmen's education, including transporting and compensating teachers and providing educational sup-, plies, buildings, and properties to set up schools. The American Missionary Association (AMA) sponsored its first teacher, Mary S. Peake, in Virginia in September 1861. In 1864, the Association sent Syracuse native Edmonia Highgate to her first teaching post in Norfolk, Virginia. She later taught in Louisiana, and her letters of February 8, 1866, and December 17, 1866, document the astonishing challenges she faced there and her formidable courage and success as a teacher and leader (Sterling 261 and Butchart 1).

Author Biography

Edmonia Goodelle Highgate was the first of six children born to Hannah Francis and Charles Highgate in 1844 in Syracuse, New York. Her mother Hannah was born in Virginia and may have been a slave. Charles Highgate hailed from Pennsylvania and worked as a barber. The Highgates lived in the black community of Syracuse, where Charles worked hard to ensure his children's education. Edmonia graduated with honors from Syracuse High School in 1861, evidently the only African American student in her class. Earning a teaching certificate but barred by racism from teaching in her hometown, she first taught in a black school in Montrose, Pennsylvania. After only term, she was hired as principal of another black school in Binghamton.

In January of 1864, Edmonia applied to the American Missionary Association to teach freed slaves in the South. She was accepted and, after a brief period of fundraising for the National Freedmen's Relief Association, began teaching in Norfolk, Virginia. Exhausted after several months, she recuperated in Syracuse and took the opportunity to speak at a prestigious black convention held in the city (Butchart 3-11).

Edmonia returned to teaching in 1865, this time in Darlington, Maryland, where she organized a school and later brought her mother and sister Willela to run it. Once the school was established, Edmonia headed to New Orleans to organize another school for freed slaves and the Louisiana Educational Relief Association, an organization to support the education and general welfare of black people. After racial violence and rioting occurred, Edmonia moved to Lafayette Parish to continue teaching. Although there was violence there as well, she continued undaunted in her work and returned to New Orleans in 1867 to open yet another school. Early in 1868, Edmonia joined her sister Caroline in Mississippi and opened a new school in the town of Enterprise. Other Highgate family members joined the sisters to establish other schools. In 1870, Edmonia returned to the North to raise money for her school. During this time, she spoke at the Massachusetts Anti-Slavery Society and began publishing her letters in various journals. While preparing to return to Mississippi, Edmonia fell in love with a white man named John Henry Vosburg, with whom she became pregnant. Sadly, Vosburg was already married to another woman and betrayed Edmonia, who died from complications related to an abortion in the fall of 1870.

HISTORICAL DOCUMENT

When her brother died, Highgate placed her mother as teacher in Darlington, and she accepted a more rewarding position in New Orleans. That the "men in the rooms" acquiesced to her arrangement and continued to take an interest in her welfare is an indication of the esteem in which she was held. As she explained in her letter to the Reverend Strieby who had been her pastor in Syracuse before becoming an AMA official, New Orleans' schools were supported by the Freedmen's Bureau until a cutback in February 1866.

Reverend M.E. Strieby
February 8, 1866
New Orleans, [Louisiana]

Dear Friend:

The schools of New Orleans have been sustained without aid from northern Associations. But commencing with this month, the government has withdrawn its pecuniary assistance. While the Freedmen's Bureau still retains its supervision i.e. regulation of tuition fees, provision of school houses and school property, yet the colored people must compensate the teachers by making an advance installment of $1.50 per mo. for each child they send. This plan was proposed by Maj. Gen. Howard because the Bureau owes an arrearage on teacher's salaries of four months standing. Consequently the number of teachers in the city which up to Feb'y 1st was 150 has been reduced to twenty-eight. I need scarcely inform you that something like 3000 children have been shut out of our schools because their widowed mothers are "too poor to pay." Their fathers being among the numbers "who made way for Liberty and died."

There is a class mostly Creoles, who have for years, paid an educational tax to support the schools of the whites, themselves deriving no benefit there from. They cannot afford to pay that tax and teachers also. I refer now to the poorer class of Creoles. Of course some of them are wealthy but do not feel in the least identified with the freed men or their interest. Nor need we wonder when we remember that many of them were formerly slaveholders. You know the peculiar institution cared little for the ethnology of its supporters.

The question is this dear sir, can the American Missionary Association pay several teachers under the F. Bureau's supervision? The people's fees will not warrant the salary of even the twenty eight teachers retained. The Fred. Douglass school of which I am principal, numbered 800 pupils, now it has but 127. Board and other expenses are exorbitant here. We still draw rations from the Government yet those who have to wait for so long for their salary are reduced to sad straits. It may perhaps amuse you to know that the building in which I teach was formerly a slave pen but now conveniently fitted up as a graded school.

Very truly yours,

Edmonia G. Highgate

* * *

On July 30, 1866, white rioters attacked white and black Unionists who were holding a constitutional convention in New Orleans. Forty-eight men were killed and 166 wounded. After the riot, Highgate left the city to teach in a country parish some 200 miles away. Her letter is one of the few reports on the black Creoles of rural Louisiana.

Rev. M.E. Strieby
December 17th, 1866
Lafayette Parish, Louisiana

Dear Friend:

After the horrible riot in New Orleans in July I found my health getting impaired, from hospital visiting and excitement so I came here to do what I could and to get stronger corporally. I have a very interesting and constantly growing day school, a night school, and a glorious Sabbath School of near one hundred scholars. The school is under the auspices of the Freedmen's Bureau, yet it is wholly self supporting. The majority of my pupils come from plantations, three, four, and even eight miles distant. So anxious are they to learn that they walk these distances so early in the morning as never to be tardy. Every scholar buys his own book and slate &c. They, with but few exceptions are French Creoles. My little knowledge of French is put in constant use in order to instruct them in our language. They do learn rapidly. A class who did not understand any English came to school last Monday morning and at the close of the week they were reading "easy lessons." The only church of any kind here is Catholic and any of the people that incline to any belief are of the denomination.

There is but little actual want among these freed people. The corn, cotton and sugar crops have been abundant. Most of the men women and larger children are hired by the year "on contract" upon the plantations of their former so called masters. One of the articles of agreements is that the planter shall pay "a five per cent tax" for the education of the children of his laborers. They get on amicably. The adjustment of relation between employer and former slaves would surprise our northern politicians.

Most all of them are trying to buy a home of their

own. Many of them own a little land on which they work nights and Sabbaths for themselves. They own cows and horses, besides raising poultry. The great sin of Sabbath breaking I am trying to make them see in its proper light. But they urge so strongly its absolute necessity in order to keep from suffering that I am almost discouraged of convincing them. They are given greatly to the sin of adultry. Out of three hundred I found but three couple legally married. This fault was largely the masters and it has grown upon the people till they cease to see the wickedness of it. There has never been a missionary here to open their eyes. I am doing what I can but my three schools take most of my time and strength. I am trying to carry on an Industrial School on Saturdays, for that I greatly need material. There are some aged ones here to whom I read the bible. But the distances are so great I must always hire conveyances and although I ride horse-back I can seldom get a horse. There is more than work for two teachers yet I am all alone.

There has been much opposition to the School. Twice I have been shot at in my room. My night scholars have been shot but none killed. The rebels here threatened to burn down the school and house in which I board before the first month was passed yet they have not materially harmed us. The nearest military protection is two hundred miles distant at New Orleans. Even the F. M. B^au agt [Freedmen's Bureau Agent] has been absent for near a month. But I trust fearlessly in God and am safe. Will you not send me a package of "The Freedmen" for my Sunday School? No matter how old they are for there has never been a Sunday School paper here.

Yours for Christ's poor

Edmonia Highgate

GLOSSARY

Creole: a person who has African and French or Spanish ancestors; also, a language based on French and that uses words from African languages

Frederick Douglass: an escaped slave who became a prominent activist, writer, and speaker for the cause of African American freedom

industrial school: in this context, a school to teach sewing

Northern associations: the American Missionary Association and other private religious and secular organizations that supported the establishment of schools in the South

parish: in Louisiana, a secular territory that corresponds to a county in other states

pecuniary: relating to or consisting of money.

Sabbath: for Christians, Sunday, which is observed as a day of rest and religious observance

slave pen: a holding area where slaves were kept to wait to be sold or transported to other trading locations

Document Analysis

We can best understand Edmonia Highgate's letters of February 8 and December 17, 1866, in the context of her entire career as a distinguished teacher as well as a speaker and writer whose impressive intellect attracted the attention of notable black thinkers. She first wrote to the American Missionary Association (AMA) on January 18, 1864, in a letter describing her desire to teach in the South or southwest, her experience of two-and-a-half years, her age of 20 years, and her good health.

In this letter, Highgate also asserts her moral virtue, stating confidently, "I know just what selfdenial, self-discipline [sic] and domestic qualifications are needed for the work and modestly trust that with God's help I could labor advantageously in the field for my newly freed brethren" (Sterling 294). The courage, directness, and confidence in these words characterize Highgate's subsequent achievements.

She responded with total dedication to her first teaching assignment in Norfolk, which began in March 1864. There, she reported being moved beyond words by the joy and thirst for knowledge she observed in the newly freed people. By the end of that summer, however, Highgate suffered a breakdown from overwork and returned briefly to recuperate in Syracuse. While home, she was one of only two women to speak at the National Convention of Colored Men, a prestigious meeting attended by leading Black thinkers of the day, including Frederick Douglass, who introduced Highgate's lecture. This impressive accomplishment achieved at only 20 years old reveals Highgate's intellectual talent and ambition, qualities that she exercised in her subsequent work. To raise relief funds for freedmen, she traveled around upstate New York during the remaining months of 1864 and early 1865, earning money by delivering lectures about her experiences (Sterling 294-96).

In March of 1865, she returned under the auspices of the AMA to teach in Darlington, Maryland, but she soon communicated her intention to resign because she considered the position beneath her abilities: "I do not conceive it to be my duty to stay here in the woods and teach thirty four pupils when I have an opportunity of reaching hundreds" (Sterling 297). Highgate gave her position in Maryland to her mother and was then placed by the AMA in New Orleans. The organization's willingness to fulfill this request suggests the leaders' deep respect for this young, ambitious teacher.

Established in New Orleans, Highgate wrote on February 8, 1866, to Reverend Strieby, the family's church pastor in Syracuse and subsequently an AMA official. In this letter, Highgate reports the extreme challenges she faced in teaching the free people who were so desperate for education. With her customary directness, her letter dispenses with niceties and immediately reports the financial straits of the New Orleans schools. The situation was this: the northern missionary and secular humanitarian organizations that supported and staffed other new schools for freedmen in the South had not been supporting New Orleans schools because the Freedmen's Bureau, a government agency established for similar purposes, had done so. Beginning in February, 1866, however, the Freedmen's Bureau could no longer support the New Orleans schools because they had run out of funds and were four months' behind in paying teachers' salaries. As a result, even though the government bureau still supervised the schools by regulating tuition and providing buildings and property, families had to pay an advance installment of $1.50 for each child. This fee, explains Highgate, was impossible for many families, in part because the mothers were widowed after their husbands had died as soldiers in the war. Highgate estimates that due to inability to pay, "something like 3000 children" (297) were barred from attending school, and the number of teachers declined from 150 to 28. These numbers document the severe poverty of many of the freed people as well as the participation and profound sacrifice of the many former slaves who died defending their freedom.

Next, Highgate offers more detail about the financial struggle of, in her words, "a class mostly Creoles" (297). This group, she explains, were forced to pay an educational tax to support schools for whites, "themselves deriving no benefit there from" (297). Thus, the tax was not used to support any schools for the Creole people who paid it, and they were barred from attending the white schools. Moreover, the poorer Creoles were unable to pay both the tax and the advance installment required to send their children to the new schools. Interestingly, Highgate in this explanation distinguishes between the poor Creoles and their wealthy counterparts, whose role in slavery she does not hesitate to criticize when she declares that it is no wonder that the wealthy Creoles do not identify with the freed people at all "when we remember that many of them were formerly slaveholders. You know the peculiar institution cared little for the ethnology of its supporters" (297). In this fascinating statement, Highgate asserts that the institution of slavery did not discriminate on the basis of ethnicity among slaveholders, so that the white holders of power allowed Creoles (who are by definition partly of African ancestry) to own slaves. This is a notable fact given that the system of slavery in the United States was largely created and justified precisely on the basis of race and thus, to a significant degree, on ethnicity as well. In making this distinction, Highgate shows her understanding of the irrational nature of slavery as an institution and offers a rare glimpse of the diverse situations that occurred in practice.

In the final part of this letter, Highgate turns her attention to a specific request, asking whether the AMA might compensate several teachers, under the Freedmen Bureau's supervision. She again underscores the school's dire situation, reporting that her own school's enrollment has declined from 800 to 127, and she mentions the city's high cost of living and the "sad straits" (298) of those teachers who work without a salary. Yet her final sentence changes tone abruptly and reveals her courage and tenacity of spirit when she tells the Reverend that he might be amused to learn that her school building was once a slave pen. With this concluding remark, Highgate achieves several effects: First, she shows that she remains undaunted in the face of the serious financial and other difficulties presented by her teaching assignment. In fact, she celebrates the triumph of using a former slave pen as a schoolhouse: the very edifices of slavery have become the means of liberation. Second, this courageous, triumphant tone serves to support her request: she is not merely complaining but is making the best of a daunting challenge that deserves the attention and support of the American Missionary Association.

The following July in New Orleans, an integrated constitutional convention took place in New Orleans, but white racists began a riot and attacked the attendees, killing 48 and wounding 166 people. Edmonia Highgate decided it would be wise to leave the city, so she went to teach in Lafayette parish, 200 miles away. From there, she wrote again to Reverend Strieby on December 17, this time documenting a rather different situation for her students, but constant courage and dedication on her part (Sterling 298).

Highgate begins the letter by explaining her move from New Orleans to Lafayette Parish, stating that after the riot, "I found my health getting impaired, from hospital visiting and excitement so I came here to do what I could and to get stronger corporally" (298). What Highgate could achieve despite her compromised health was quite impressive, as she reports running essentially three schools, a day school, a night school, and "a glorious Sabbath School of near one hundred scholars" (298). She explains that the Freedman's Bureau supervises but does not fund the school, which is evidently supported by tuition paid by the students and by a tax on plantation owners (see below for explanation). She also later mentions needing cloth so that she might start a fourth "Industrial School" (299) on Saturdays, by which she means a school to teach sewing.

Highgate reports her students in Lafayette Parish to be more fortunate than those she taught in New Orleans. Most of them are "french Creoles" (298) from plantations anywhere from three to eight miles away, and they are so eager to learn that they rise early each morning and are never late. These former slaves are spared the abject poverty of most other freedpeople. Highgate writes that most of the adults and older children work as contract laborers on the plantations of the men who formerly owned them. Particularly interesting is the five-percent tax she mentions, which, according to the labor contracts, plantation owners had to pay for the education of their laborers' children. This partly accounts for the success of Highgate's school, but she also reports abundant corn, cotton, and sugar crops, which have allowed students to purchase their own books and slates; many families own land and livestock and plan to buy their own homes.

Highgate dedicates much of this letter to the cultural differences she must negotiate with her students. We learn that Highgate's own education included at least some French as she reports using it to communicate with her Creole students, who learn English quickly: one class of students with no knowledge of English progressed to an "easy" reader in one week's time. She discovers that the only Christian church in the area is Catholic and that many of her students insist on working on Sundays (which she calls "Sabbath breaking") to survive, frustrating her efforts to convince them otherwise. She also reports her dismay at the people's practice of adultery, by which she means intercourse between unmarried people (as opposed to extramarital intercourse), as she reports finding only three legally married couples out of 300 people. She reports doing what she can, but "there is more than work for two teachers yet I am all alone" (299).

As in her letter from February of the same year, Highgate follows this frank admission with a vivid portrait of her bravery. Despite her students' relative comfort, rebels continue to terrorize them and their teacher. In the final paragraph, Highgate reports that she has received death threats, has been shot at twice, and her night school students have also been shot at. The lack of protection from both the military and the Freedman's Bureau makes the situation all the more dire, but she remains undaunted. She concludes her letter by requesting Sunday school materials for her religious education efforts, once again communicating both the reality of the danger and her intentions to overcome it.

Highgate's letter seems primarily descriptive as she reports basic facts about her students and her ongoing struggle to teach despite the opposition of racist rebels. Nonetheless, her words occasionally reveal valuable context and subtext. When she mentions former slave owners, for example, she refers to them as "so called masters" (298), which represents a pointed effort to challenge the very notion of slave owners' dominance; with this phrase, Highgate rejects the notion that such owners were ever masters of other human beings, despite their legal ownership. This is not simply rhetoric; rather, it represents Highgate's confrontation with the shards of a dehumanizing institution and her determination to subvert its ideology of dominance, which lives on in her students' psyches. We see this confrontation again when she blames "the masters" (299) for the freed slaves' practice of adultery. Here, too, she signals that her task is nothing less than the construction of a new culture.

This level of awareness and ambition distinguishes Highgate as much more than a selfless schoolteacher with remarkable courage. Refusing to settle for the easy stereotype of "strong black woman," Highgate proves that she is a thinker and an activist. This is perhaps most notable in her comment about the amicable relations between the planters and former slaves: "The adjustment of relation between employer and former slaves would surprise our northern politicians" (299). The precise context of this comment is unclear, but Highgate implies that Northern politicians had doubts about the prospects for peaceful adjustment between former slave owners and slaves. With this statement, Highgate claims the right to educate privileged men about the facts on the ground and displays the intellectual prowess that earned her a distinguished reputation as speaker, writer, and teacher in her brief life.

Essential Themes

The learning, ambition, and courage that shine through Edmonia Highgate's letters represent the lives of many African Americans in the nineteenth century. As Butchart claims, the impressive achievement of both Edmonia and her sister Caroline "symbolized a widespread black thirst for knowledge" (3), which began prior to emancipation and increased rapidly. This desire for learning was remarkable given that emancipated people in other cultures frequently chose either to embrace ignorance or to exalt traditional forms of wisdom rather than formal learning (Butchart 2). This desire

for learning prompted thousands of African American teachers, even before the end of the Civil War, to travel to the South to aid the freed slaves. As Highgate exemplifies, many of these teachers were not mere untrained volunteers but highly educated and qualified teachers, and they often endured financial and other hardships, including acts of terror.

It is unfortunate that these hardships also reveal betrayal as another central theme in African Americans' lives during this period. Highgate's letters show that, despite the legal progress that occurred with the Emancipation Proclamation and subsequent constitutional amendments, the government did not establish sufficient services for its newly freed people. The Freedmen's Bureau was a step in the right direction but proved inadequate for the task at hand and eventually lost its funding. Worse, when African Americans persisted despite lack of resources and set up their own schools, partly with the help of charitable organizations, white racists attempted to destroy their efforts and, in some cases, their lives. This attempt to undermine the building of new lives would endure long after Reconstruction as Jim Crow laws were established to maintain segregation and inequality. In these ways, Edmonia Highgate's life and her death, which occurred as a result of her white lover's betrayal, emerge as a powerful symbol of the social and political victories and losses of African Americans during and after Reconstruction

Ashleigh Imus, Ph.D.

Bibliography

Butchart, Ronald E. "Edmonia G. and Caroline V. Highgate: *Black Teachers, Freed Slaves, and the Betrayal of Black Hearts." Portraits of African American Life Since 1865.* Edited by Nina Mjagkij. Wilmington: Scholarly Resources, 2003. Print.

Mjagkij, Nina. *"Introduction." Portraits of African American Life Since 1865.* Edited by Nina Mjagkij. Wilmington: Scholarly Resources, 2003. Print.

Sterling, Dorothy, ed. *We Are Your Sisters: Black Women in the Nineteenth Century.* New York: Norton, 1984. Print.

Additional Reading

Butchart, Ronald E. *Schooling the Freed People: Teaching, Learning, and the Struggle   for Black Freedom, 1861-1876.* Chapel Hill: U of North Carolina P, 2010. Print.

Clark Hine, Darlene and Kathleen Thompson. *A Shining Thread of Hope: The History of Black Women in America.* New York: Broadway Books, 1998. Print.

Enoch, Jessica. *Refiguring Rhetorical Education: Women Teaching African American, Native American, and Chicano/a Students, 1865-1911.* Carbondale: Southern Illinois UP, 2008. Print.

Hodges, Graham Russell, ed. *African American History and Culture.* New York: Garland, 1998. Print.

Sernett, Milton C. *North Star Country: Upstate New York and the Crusade for African American Freedom.* Syracuse: Syracuse UP, 2002. Print.

■ Reconstruction Acts of 1867

Date: March 2, 1867; March 23, 1867; July 19, 1867
Author: 40th United States Congress
Genre: law; legislation

> *"Be it enacted...that said rebel States shall be divided into military districts and made subject to military authority of the United States as hereafter prescribed..."*

Summary Overview

Post–Civil War America was a hotbed of economic, social, and political turmoil. Although the Northern army had succeeded in maintaining the Union, at the end of the war the North and South were far from unified. The post-war presidency was faced with challenges that ranged from defining the status of newly freed slaves in the South, to grappling with how to deal with the Southern states that had formally seceded. While these issues undoubtedly found their roots in the end of Abraham Lincoln's presidency, the real struggle to establish rights for black freedmen and to define the new South gained momentum during Andrew Johnson's tenure (1865–1869).

While the period of American Reconstruction would reach through the presidency of Ulysses S. Grant in the 1870s, the questions surrounding black rights and the status of the former Confederacy essentially had their foundation in the Reconstruction Acts of 1867. It was these acts which would cause great tension between the Republican North and Democratic South, ultimately defining what it meant to be a postwar United States citizen.

Defining Moment

As a former Democratic representative from Tennessee (the only Southern state to ratify the Fourteenth Amendment in 1866 and be restored to representation in Congress), Johnson was immediately at odds with the heavily Republican postwar Congress. The aftermath of a war between opposing factions in the same nation had raised unprecedented questions about how to deal with the states that had attempted to secede from the Union. What necessary changes were needed in order for the South to be able to re-acclimate to American life? In particular, what did this mean for newly freed blacks in Southern states?

Initial approaches to Reconstruction in the later years of the war had included lofty goals such as the total abolition of slavery and the preservation of the Union—neither of which were easily fixed in the wake of a long, bloody national conflict. It became the task of Johnson and the 40th Congress to implement a plan of action that would allow the Southern states to rejoin the Union in a way that would both reaffirm a state-by-state commitment to reunification, and put policies in place to establish the rights of freed black slaves as equal U.S. citizens.

These noble goals for postwar America proved to be much more challenging in practice than in theory, and were met with consternation from all sides. As the Reconstruction Acts of 1867 show, Johnson and his Congress would never see eye to eye on Reconstruction legislation, which ultimately contributed to his impeachment in 1868. Likewise, new legal parameters were met with mixed feelings in the South, where strict regulations would impede the former Southern states' control over their local governments. Democratic

Southern fears also abounded with regard to the impact that the newly sanctioned black vote could have on the future of American politics, as black voters tended to side with their Republican backers, potentially adding serious weight to an already strong Republican ticket. As a result, Reconstruction would continue for another decade, with each new wave of legislation attempting to correct old imbalances.

Author Biography

The Fortieth Congress of the United States met from 1867 to1869 after being called by the Thirty-Ninth Congress into immediate action so as to take control of the Reconstruction away from the presidency. Comprised of forty-seven elected Democrats and one hundred and seventy-seven Republicans, the Congress was responsible for the institution of the four Military Reconstruction Acts in 1867 and 1868 (three of which are discussed here), as well as the impeachment and subsequent Senate acquittal of President Andrew Johnson.

The initial disproportion in party power within the Congress was in part due to the inability of formerly seceded Southern states to hold formal representational power in government. It would become the responsi

bility of these states to regain their independence, and with it, their congressional presence. Prior to the readmission of Southern states to the Union, disparities in Congress were often between Radical Republicans, led by Thaddeus Stevens in the House and Charles Sumner in the Senate, and Moderate Republicans and Democrats. The former were considered to be radical in both their views on race (especially with regard to the equality of freed blacks in America), and in their belief that the rebel states of the South had forfeited their rights by seceding, and thus should become territories under congressional rule.

It was the efforts of this Congress that pushed forward legislation on Southern restructuring and called for a return to social order—even when these efforts were in opposition to Johnson's proposals for Reconstruction. This congressional platform would call for black suffrage in addition to the disenfranchisement of some members of former Confederate states, with specific stipulations for how rebel states were to reenter the Union. It was these actions that would result in the reunification of the North and South, and the ratification of the Fourteenth and Fifteenth Amendments to the United States Constitution.

HISTORICAL DOCUMENT

First Reconstruction Act (passed March 2, 1867): An Act to Provide for the More Efficient Government of the Rebel States.

Whereas, no legal State governments or adequate protection for life or property now exists in the rebel States of Virginia, North Carolina, South Carolina, Georgia, Mississippi, Alabama, Louisiana, Texas, and Arkansas; and whereas, it is necessary that peace and good order should be enforced in said States until loyal and republican State governments can be legally established; Therefore -

Be it enacted by the Senate and House of Representatives of the United States of America in Congress assembled, That said rebel States shall be divided into military districts and made subject to the military authority of the United States as hereinafter prescribed; and for that purpose

Virginia shall constitute the first district; North Carolina and South Carolina the second district; Georgia, Alabama, and Florida the third district; Mississippi and Arkansas the fourth district; and Louisiana and Texas the fifth district.

Sec. 2. *And be it further enacted*, That it shall be the duty of the President to assign to the command of each of said districts an officer of the army not below the rank of brigadier general, and to detail a sufficient military force to enable such officer to perform his duties and enforce his authority within the district to which he is assigned

Sec. 3. *And be it further enacted*, That it shall be the duty of each officer assigned as aforesaid to protect all persons in their rights of person and property, to suppress insurrection, disorder, and violence, and to punish, or cause to be punished, all disturbers of the public peace and criminals, and to this end he may allow local civil tribunals to take jurisdiction of and to try offenders, or, when in his judgment it may be necessary for the trial of offenders, he shall power to organize military commissions or tribunals for that purpose, and all interference, under color of State authority, with the exercise of military authority under this act, shall be null and void.

Sec. 4. *And be it further enacted,* That all persons put under military arrest by virtue of this act shall be tried without unnecessary delay, and no cruel or unusual punishment shall be inflicted; and no sentence of any military commission or tribunal hereby authorized, affecting the life or liberty of any person, shall be executed until it is approved by the officer in command of the district, and the laws and regulations for the government of the army shall not be affected by this act, except in so far as they conflict with its provisions; Provided, That no sentence of death, under the provisions of this act, shall be carried into effect without the approval of the President.

Sec. 5. *And be it further enacted,* That when the people of any one of said rebel States shall have formed a constitution of government in conformity with the Constitution of the United States in all respects, framed by a convention of delegates elected by the male citizens of said State twenty-one years old and upward, of whatever race, color, or previous condition, who have been resident in said State for one year previous to the day of such election, except such as may be disfranchised for participation in the rebellion, or for felony at common law; and when such constitution shall provide that the elective franchise shall be enjoyed by all such persons as have the qualifications herein stated for electors of delegates; and when such constitution shall be ratified by a majority of the persons voting on the question of ratification who are qualified as electors for delegates; and when such constitution shall have been submitted to Congress for examination and approval, and Congress shall have approved the same; and when said State, by a vote of its legislature elected under said constitution, shall have adopted the amendment to the Constitution of the United States proposed by the Thirty-ninth Congress, and known as article fourteen; and when said article shall have become a part of the Constitution of the United States, said State shall be declared entitled to representation in Congress, and senators and representatives shall be admitted therefrom on their taking the oath

prescribed by law; and then and thereafter the preceding sections of this act shall be inoperative in said State; Provided, That no person excluded from the privilege of holding office by said proposed amendment to the Constitution of the United States shall be eligible to election as a member of the convention to frame a constitution for any of said rebel States, nor shall any such person vote for members of such convention.

Sec. 6. *And be it further enacted,* That until the people of said rebel States shall be by law admitted to representation in the Congress of the United States, any civil government which may exist therein shall be deemed provisional only, and in all respects subject to the paramount authority of the United States at any time to abolish, modify, control, or supersede the same; and in all elections to any office under such provisional governments all persons shall be entitled to vote, and none others, who are entitled to vote under the fifth section of this act; and no person shall be eligible to any office under any provisional governments who would be disqualified from holding office under the provisions of the third article of said constitutional amendment.

* * *

Second Reconstruction Act (passed March 23, 1867): An Act Supplementary to an Act Entitled "An Act to Provide for the More Efficient Government of the Rebel States," passed March 2nd, Eighteen Hundred and Sixty-Seven, and to Facilitate Restoration.

Be it enacted by the Senate and House of Representatives of the United States of America in Congress assembled, That before the first day of September, eighteen hundred and sixty-seven, the commanding general in each district defined by an act entitled "An act to provide for the more efficient government of the rebel States", passed March second, eighteen hundred and sixty-seven, shall cause a registration to be made of the male citizens of the United States, twenty-one years of age and upwards, resident in each county or parish in the State or States included in his district, which registration shall include only those persons who are qualified to vote for delegates by the act aforesaid, and who shall have taken and subscribed the following oath or affirmation: "I, _____, do solemnly swear, (or affirm), in the presence of Almighty God, that I am a citizen of the State of _____; that I have resided in said State for _____ months next preceding this day, and now reside in the county of _____, or the parish of _____, in said State, (as the case may be); that I am twenty-one years old; that I have not been disfranchised for participation in any rebellion or civil war against the United States, nor for felony committed against the laws of any State or of the United States; that I have never been a member of any State legislature, nor held any executive or judicial office in any State engaged in insurrection or rebellion against the United States, or given aid or comfort to the enemies thereof; that I have never taken an oath as a member of Congress of the United States, or as any officer of the United States, or as a member of any State legislature, or as an executive or judicial officer of any State, to support the Constitution of the United States, and afterwards engaged in insurrection or rebellion against the United States, or given aid or comfort to the enemies thereof; that I will faithfully support the Constitution and obey the laws of the United States, and will, to the best of my ability, encourage others so to do: So help me God"; which oath or affirmation may be administered by any registering officer.

Sec. 2. *And be it further enacted,* That after the completion of the registration hereby provided for in any State, at such time and places therein as the commanding general shall appoint and direct, of which at least thirty days public notice shall be given, and election shall be held of delegates to a convention for the purpose of establishing a constitution and civil government for such State loyal to the Union, said convention in each State, except Virginia, to consist of the same number of members as the most numerous branch of the State legislature of such State in the year eighteen hundred and sixty, to be apportioned among the several districts, counties, or parishes of such State by the commanding general, giving to each representation in the ratio of voters registered as aforesaid as nearly as may be. The convention in Virginia shall consist of the same number of members as represented the territory now constituting Virginia in the most numerous branch of the legislature of said State in the year eighteen hundred and sixty, to be apportioned as

afore said

Sec. 3. *And be it further enacted,* That at said election the registered voters of each State shall vote for or against a convention to form a constitution therefor under this act. Those voting in favor of such a convention shall have written or printed on the ballots by which they vote for delegates, as aforesaid, the words "For a convention", and those voting against such a convention shall have written or printed on such ballots the words "Against a convention". The persons appointed to superintend said election, and to make return of the votes given thereat, as herein provided, shall count and make return of the votes given for and against a convention; and the commanding general to whom the same shall have been returned shall ascertain and declare the total vote in each State for and against a convention. If a majority of the votes given on that question shall be for a convention, then such convention shall be held as hereinafter provided; but if a majority of said votes shall be against a convention, then no such convention shall be held under this act: Provided, That such convention shall not be held unless a majority of all such registered voters shall have voted on the questions of holding such convention.

Sec. 4. *And be it further enacted,* That the commanding general of each district shall appoint as many boards of registration as may be necessary, consisting of three loyal officers or persons, to make and complete the registration, superintend the election, and make return to him of the votes, list of voters, and of the persons elected as delegates by a plurality of the votes cast as said election; and upon receiving said returns he shall open the same, ascertain the persons elected as delegates, according to the returns of the officers who conducted said election, and make proclamation thereof; and if a majority of the votes given on that question shall be for a convention, the commanding general, within sixty days from the date of election, shall notify the delegates to assemble in convention, at a time and place to be mentioned in the notification, and said convention, when organized, shall proceed to frame a constitution and civil government according to the provisions of this act, and the act to which it is supplementary; and when the same shall have been so framed, said constitution shall be submitted by the convention for ratification to the persons registered under the provisions of this act at an election to be conducted by the officers or persons appointed, or to be appointed by the commanding general, as hereinbefore provided, and to be held after the expiration of thirty days from the date of notice thereof, to be given by said convention; and the returns thereof shall be made to the commanding general of the district.

Sec. 5. *And be it further enacted,* That if, according to said returns, the constitution shall be ratified by a majority of the votes of the registered electors qualified as herein specified, cast at said election, at least one-half of all the registered voters voting upon the question of such ratification, the president of the convention shall transmit a copy of the same, duly certified, to the President of the United States, who shall forthwith transmit the same to Congress, if then in session, and if not in session, then immediately upon its next assembling; and if it shall moreover appear to Congress that the election was one at which all the registered and qualified electors in the State had an opportunity to vote freely, and without restraint, fear, or the influence of fraud, and if the Congress shall be satisfied that such constitution meets the approval of a majority of all the qualified electors in the State, and if the said constitution shall be declared by Congress to be in conformity with the provisions of the act to which this is supplementary, and the other provisions of said act shall have been complied with, and the said constitution shall be approved by Congress, the State shall be declared entitled to representation, and senators and representatives shall be admitted therefrom as therein provided.

Sec. 6. *And be it further enacted,* That all elections in the States mentioned in the said "Act to provide for the more efficient government of the rebel States", shall, during the operation of said act, be by ballot; and all officers making the said registration of voters, and conducting said elections, shall, before entering upon the discharge of their duties, take and subscribe the oath prescribed by the act approved July second, eighteen hundred and sixty-two, entitled "An act to prescribe an oath of office"; Provided, That if any person shall knowingly and falsely take and subscribe any oath in this act prescribed, such persons so offending, and being thereof duly convicted, shall be subject to the pains, penalties, and disabilities which by law are provided for the punishment of the crime of willful and corrupt perjury.

Sec. 7. *And be it further enacted,* That all expenses incurred by the several commanding generals, or by virtue of any orders issued, or appointments made by them, under or by virtue of this act, shall be paid out of any moneys in the treasury not otherwise appropriated.

Sec. 8. *And be it further enacted,* That the convention for each State shall prescribe the fees, salary, and compensation to be paid to all delegates and other officers and agents herein authorized or necessary to carry into effect the purposes of this act, not herein otherwise provided for, and shall provide for the levy and collection of such taxes on the property in such State as may be necessary to pay the same.

Sec. 9. *And be it further enacted,* That the word "article" in the sixth section of the act to which this is supplementary, shall be construed to mean "section".

***

Third Reconstruction Act (passed July 19, 1867): An Act supplementary to an Act entitled "An Act to provide for the more efficient Government of the Rebel States," passed . . . March 2, 1867 . . . and the Act supplementary thereto, passed . . . March 23, 1867.

Be it enacted . . . That it is hereby declared to have been the true intent and meaning . . . [of the acts of March 2 and March 23, 1867] . . . that the governments then existing in the rebel States of Virginia, North Carolina, South Carolina, Georgia, Mississippi, Alabama, Louisiana, Florida, Texas, and Arkansas were not legal State governments; and that thereafter said governments, if continued, were to be continued subject in all respects to the military commanders of the respective districts, and to the paramount authority of Congress.

Sec. 2. *And be it further enacted,* That the commander of any district named in said act shall have power, subject to the disapproval of the General of the army of the United States, and to have effect till disapproved, whenever in the opinion of such commander the proper administration of said act shall require it, to suspend or remove from office, or from the performance of official duties and the exercise of official powers, any officer or person holding or exercising, or professing to hold or exercise, any civil or military office or duty in such district under any power, election, appointment or authority derived from, or granted by, or claimed under, any so-called State or the government thereof, or any municipal or other division thereof, and upon such suspension or removal such commander, subject to the disapproval of the General as aforesaid, shall have power to provide from time to time for the performance of the said duties of such officer or person so suspended or removed, by the detail of some competent officer or soldier of the army, or by the appointment of some other person, to perform the same, and to fill vacancies occasioned by death, resignation, or otherwise.

Sec. 3. *And be it further enacted*, That the General of the army of the United States shall be invested with all the powers of suspension, removal, appointment, and detail granted in the preceding section to district commanders.

Sec. 4. *And be it further enacted*, That the acts of the officers of the army already done in removing in said districts persons exercising the functions of civil officers, and appointing others in their stead, are hereby confirmed: provided that any person heretofore or hereafter appointed by any district commander to exercise the functions of any civil office, may be removed either by the military officer in command of the district, or by the General of the army. And it shall be the duty of such commander to remove from office as aforesaid all persons who are disloyal to the government of the United States, or who use their official influence in any manner to hinder, delay, prevent, or obstruct the due and proper administration of this act and the acts to which it is supplementary.

Sec. 5. *And be it further enacted*, That the boards of registration provided for in the act. . . [of March 23, 1867]... shall have power, and it shall be their duty before allowing the registration of any person, to ascertain, upon such facts or information as they can obtain, whether such person is entitled to be registered under said act, and the oath required by said act shall not be conclusive on such question, and no person shall be registered unless such board shall decide that he is entitled thereto; and such board shall also have power to examine, under oath. . . any one touching the qualification of any person

claiming registration; but in every case of refusal by the board to register an applicant, and in every case of striking his name from the list as hereinafter provided, the board shall make a note or memorandum, which shall be returned with the registration list to the commanding general of the district, setting forth the grounds of such refusal or such striking from the list: provided that no person shall be disqualified as member of any board of registration by reason of race or color.

Sec. 6. *And be it further enacted*, That the true intent and meaning of the oath prescribed in said supplementary act is, (among other things), that no person who has been a member of the legislature of any State, or who has held any executive or judicial office in any State, whether he has taken an oath to support the Constitution of the United States or not, and whether he was holding such office at the commencement of the rebellion, or had held it before, and who has afterwards engaged in insurrection or rebellion against the United States, or given aid or comfort to the enemies thereof, is entitled to be registered or to vote; and the words "executive or judicial office in any State" in said oath mentioned shall be construed to include all civil offices created by law for the administration of any general law of a State, or for the administration of justice.

Sec. 7. *And be it further enacted*, That the time for completing the original registration provided for in said act may, in the discretion of the commander of any district, be extended to . . . [October 1, 1867] and the boards of registration shall have power, and it shall be their duty, commencing fourteen days prior to any election under said act, and upon reasonable public notice of the time and place thereof, to revise, for a period of five days, the registration lists, and upon being satisfied that any person not entitled thereto has been registered, to strike the name of such person from the list, and such person shall not be allowed to vote. And such board shall also, during the same period, add to such registry the names of all persons who at that time possess the qualifications required by said act who have not been already registered; and no person shall, at any time, be entitled to be registered or to vote by reason of any executive pardon or amnesty for any act or thing which, without such pardon or amnesty, would disqualify him from registration or voting.

Sec. 8. *And be it further enacted*, That section four of said last-named act shall be construed to authorize the commanding general named therein, whenever he shall deem it needful, to remove any member of a board of registration and to appoint another in his stead, and to fill any vacancy in such board.

Sec. 9. *And be it further enacted*, That all members of said boards of registration and all persons hereafter elected or appointed to office in said military districts, under any so called State or municipal authority, or by detail or appointment of the district commanders, shall be required to take and to subscribe the oath of office prescribed by law for officers of the United States.

Sec. 10. *And be it further enacted*, That no district commander or member of the board of registration, or any of the officers or appointees acting under them, shall be bound in his action by any opinion of any civil officer of the United States.

Sec. 11. *And be it further enacted*, That all provisions of this act and of the acts to which this is supplementary shall be construed liberally, to the end that all the intents thereof may be fully and perfectly carried out.

GLOSSARY

14th Amendment: (1868) provides for the rights of citizenship and equal legal protection for U.S. citizens

disenfranchisement: the blocking or removal of the right to vote

oath: a formal promise

ratify: an agreement, often made official through voting

secession: withdrawing from a larger unified body

suffrage: the right to vote

Document Analysis

For many Americans, particularly those in the South, efforts to repair a broken post–Civil War nation raised concerns about social freedoms and the future of the American political system. For former slave owners, who equated the loss of their slave labor force with a loss of economic strength, the congressional push for abolition and the passage of the Fourteenth Amendment also prompted fears about the future economic conditions of an already impoverished postwar South. While newly freed blacks questioned their shifting role in society, white Northerners and Southerners alike wondered how the widespread impact of emancipation would affect American life. In an attempt to deal with these issues and the myriad other questions that arose at this time President Andrew Johnson and the Fortieth Congress worked in the postwar years to establish new systems of government and federal legislations on abolition in an effort to ease the nation from war to peacetime. The challenges raised by Reconstruction would create many points of contention between Congress and the president, as is particularly evident in the Reconstruction Acts of 1867 outlined below.

First Reconstruction Act

The Reconstruction Acts of 1867 were put into place by the Fortieth Congress of the United States to deal with the aftermath of the American Civil War. The first of these four legislations, also known as the Military Reconstruction Act, was passed on March 2, 1867 and divided rebel Southern states into five military districts (with the exclusion of Tennessee, which had already been readmitted to the Union upon passing the Fourteenth Amendment). The remaining ten former Confederate states were divided into the following districts: Virginia; North and South Carolina; Georgia, Alabama, and Florida; Mississippi and Arkansas; and Louisiana and Texas. Each of these districts was to be temporarily overseen by a commanding general who would be appointed by the president of the United States with the approval of Congress.

After postwar race riots and the refusal of Southern states to ratify the Fourteenth Amendment, the introduction of military leadership in the South seemed inevitable in the minds of many Republicans. There were Northerners and Southerners from both ends of the political spectrum however who were concerned about the use of military occupation on American soil. This raised questions about the extent to which the federal government should be allowed to control its citizens at the state level. From the perspective of Congress, the establishment of federally enforced military leadership would provide the Southern rebel states with stability, in order to combat the social and political unrest left in the wake of the war. The postwar South was particularly unsettled with regard to freed black slaves, who had struggled to find a place in Southern culture since Lincoln's Emancipation Proclamation of 1863. While President Lincoln's declaration had in essence freed slaves in the rebel Southern states, many slaveholders did not recognize federal authority at that time. Life was equally difficult for former slaves who had gained their freedom, but lacked a formal education and necessary means for survival, in addition to facing a hostile Southern culture that had long depended upon slave labor for economic cogency.

With these issues in mind, the First Reconstruction Act allowed for the eventual readmission of rebel states into Congress, with the stipulation that said states would follow the protocols for abolition and loyalty to the Union laid out for them. In this moderate approach the Southern states were expected to form their own "convention of delegates elected by...male citizens," aged twenty-one or older, without restrictions on race. This was a conscious effort by Congress to establish a precedent for black suffrage in the Southern states, despite the legislation only calling for a temporary right for blacks to vote.

The act also stipulated that disenfranchisement was enacted in any cases in which an individual was convicted of "participation in the rebellion or for felony at common law." This was meant to preclude Confederate leadership from having a voice in the Reconstruction process. When delegations were formed another election was to take place on the issue of the ratification of the fourteenth article to the United States Constitution—the Amendment calling for equal rights and le-

gal protection for all American citizens, regardless of race. The act promised Southern states that ratified the Amendment and agreed to abolition their readmission to the Union as fully participatory states with congressional representation.

Although President Johnson agreed that the Southern states should have the ability to rejoin the Union, he felt that the congressional mandates for reunification set forth in the Reconstruction Acts were too harsh. Perhaps it was the President's own Southern roots, or perhaps it was his desire to fulfill Lincoln's vision for Reconstruction that ultimately led him to veto Congress' legislation. President Johnson proposed instead a counter-plan for Reconstruction in which the former Southern states would automatically be restored to their prewar status, with the exception of slavery, and in which provisional civil governments would be granted leadership. In a move that would be repeated with regard to future Reconstruction Acts, Congress overrode the President's veto, enacting further legislation to control postwar power in the Southern states.

Second Reconstruction Act

In response to Johnson's attempt to overturn the legislation of the First Reconstruction Act, Congress put forth a second act on March 23 of the same year. This act served in many ways as an addendum to the first, addressing the gaps and ambiguities of the initial regulations that had been brought to light by Johnson's resistance. The Second Act became a platform from which the role of imposed Southern military leadership would be reiterated, and in some ways, restructured as a reaction to Southern resistance to the First Act.

Whereas the First Reconstruction Act had laid the groundwork for military control in the South, the Second Act was more concerned with reaffirming the role of military leaders. Generals placed in governing positions were to act as the enforcers of legitimate voter registration in the formation of congressional delegations and the Southern election process. Most notably, military leadership was granted the authority to remove those in power who were not following the provisions for legal postwar Southern government structures as outlined in the First Reconstruction Act.

Central to this process was a formal oath to be taken by all Southern voters in the presence of a witness so as to ensure the legality of Southern elections. In addition to the conditions for legal voting rights outlined in the First Act (male, U.S. citizens over the age of twenty-one, with no record of crime or history of rebellion against the Union), the Second Act included a solemn swearing "in the presence of Almighty God" that one had "not been disenfranchised for participation in any rebellion or civil war against the United States," nor taken oath for a position of congressional or state leadership after which they "engaged in insurrection or rebellion against the United States." Congress hoped that, through the strict enforcement of the new regulations, Southern delegations would not be comprised of rebellious Southern war leaders. The intended outcome of a cooperative delegation was to create an election atmosphere in which the Southern convention would create new constitutions and civil governments based on loyalty to the Union and to abolition, leading to Southern-wide ratification of the Fourteenth Amendment.

Johnson refused the measures outlined in the Second Reconstruction Act much as he had the first. In his estimation Southern dissenters should be required to take an oath of loyalty to the Union with the exclusion of those who had been in prewar positions of power, who he felt should have to be directly pardoned by the president. In another power struggle between the Senate and the presidency Congress once again overrode Johnson's attempts to veto the act.

Third Reconstruction Act

The Second Reconstruction Act, though more detailed than the First, was ultimately restricted in the extent to which military leadership was able to enforce its power. On July 19, 1867 Congress passed a Third Reconstruction Act, emphasizing that, "the rebel states" of the South that had been provisionally set up by Johnson "were not legal State governments; and that thereafter, if continued, were to be continued subject in all respects to the military commanders of the respective districts" under the "paramount authority of Congress." In other words, Congress was to have the final say in matters of Southern Reconstruction, with congressionally approved military leadership at the helm.

The Third Reconstruction Act, like the Second, reiterated the qualifications for Southern voting privileges, with the additional condition that "no person shall, at any time, be entitled to be registered or to vote by reason of any executive pardon or amnesty for any act or thing which, without such pardon or amnesty, would disqualify him from registration or voting," officially overruling Johnson's intentions after the Second Re-

construction Act to offer presidential forgiveness on a case by case basis. According to Congress the legality of the Southern voting body was to be determined only by military leadership. Johnson vetoed the legislations outlined in the Third Reconstruction Act, with the same Congressional response that he had received after his attempts to prohibit the passage of the preceding acts.

Conflicts addressed by the first three congressional pieces of legislation culminated in the Fourth (and final) Reconstruction Act in 1868. This final statute was created by Congress in reaction to the refusal of ratification by Alabama voters who were against congressional Reconstruction efforts. When less than half of eligible voters in Alabama took part in the election to ratify the new constitution, Congress mandated that a majority vote (regardless of voter turnout) was sufficient for ratification. This went against the earlier Reconstruction efforts of Congress to maintain a majority vote with regard to the number of eligible voters participating in an election. It was nonetheless a successful venture, reaffirming the legislative role that Congress played in Reconstruction during Johnson's administration.

Essential Themes

Congressional debates over restrictions on presidential power would also remain. Citing the Tenure of Office Act, which prevented the president from removing individuals in federal positions of power without Senate approval, Congress fought Johnson's desire to replace Lincoln's war secretary, Edwin M. Stanton, with someone who more closely shared his own views on Reconstruction. The Congressional response to this incident, in combination with Johnson's repeated refusals of the Reconstruction Acts led to his impeachment. In the subsequent trial in which the Senate acquitted Johnson by one vote, it was citied that the president should not be subject to impeachment merely because of differences of opinion with Congress.

The Reconstruction Acts of 1867 established a military-based Reconstruction that lasted until 1870, at which point all Southern states gained readmission to the Union by eliminating the institution of slavery and ratifying either the Fourteenth of Fifteenth Amendments. While the new constitutions of the Southern states helped freed blacks to gain political and legal rights, racially based social inequalities would linger for decades, as echoes of Reconstruction tensions continued to reverberate in the South.

Emily Bailey, PhD candidate

Bibliography

Dickerson, Donna L. *The Reconstruction Era: Primary Documents on Events from 1865-1877.* Westport: Greenwood, 2003. Print.

Dunning, William A. *Essays on the Civil War and Reconstruction.* New York: Harper & Row, 1 9 6 5 . Print.

Ferrell, Claudine L. *Reconstruction.* Westport: Praeger, 2003. Print.

White, John. *Reconstruction after the American Civil War.* London: Longman, 1977. Print.

Additional Reading

Blum, Edward J. and W. Scott Poole. *Vale of Tears: New Essays on Religion and Reconstruction.* Macon: Mercer UP, 2005. Print.

Foner, Eric. *Reconstruction: America's Unfinished Revolution, 1863-1877.* New York: Perennial, 2002. Print.

Richter, William L. *The ABC-CLIO Companion to American Reconstruction, 1862-1877.* Santa Barbara: ABC-CLIO, 1996. Print.

Simpson, Brooks D. *The Reconstruction Presidents.* Lawrence: UP of Kansas, 1998. Print.

Trefousse, Hans L. *Historical Dictionary of Reconstruction.* New York: Greenwood, 1991. Print.

Turkel, Stanley. *Heroes of the American Reconstruction: Profiles of Sixteen Educators, Politicians, and Activists.* Jefferson: McFarland, 2005. Print.

Reconstruction: The Second Civil War. Produced by Elizabeth Deane for WGBH Boston, 2004. DVD.

House of Representatives – Articles of Impeachment

Date: February 1868
Author: House of Representative, 40th U.S. Congress
Genre: constitution; legislation; political tract

"That said Andrew Johnson, President of the United States, unmindful of the high duties of his office, and of his oath of office, and in disregard of the Constitution and laws of the United States..."

Summary Overview

The articles of impeachment of President Andrew Johnson consist of eleven indictments, which were intended to remove him from the office of the president. The most important charges were based on the President having violated the Tenure of Office Act, a constitutionality questionable law. This was the first time the House of Representatives voted to impeach a president. The United States Senate conducted an impeachment trial, ending in a vote of 35-19, one vote short of the two thirds necessary for conviction; the Senate had rejected the House of Representatives' charges. Johnson went on to serve out the end of his term, which ended on March 4, 1869. By defying the Republican majority that had impeached him, Johnson had in effect repudiated the result of the 1864 election.

Defining Moment

The articles of impeachment's importance were greater than any individual words or thoughts contained within them. The impeachment process represented not only an effort to remove the president, but an attempt to effect a change in the results of the 1864 election.

Under normal circumstances Andrew Johnson would never have been on a national ticket with Abraham Lincoln, but 1864 was anything but an ordinary year. The Civil War was still in full swing at the time of the convention in June, and the end was still not in sight.

In June of 1864 Republicans and war Democrats met in convention as the "National Union" Party." The party easily nominated Abraham Lincoln for a second term as president, but the nomination for vice president was an open question. Johnson was an important leader among the war Democrats. The other major candidate was the incumbent vice president, Hannibal Hamlin. Johnson brought a couple of important advantages to the table. The fact that Johnson was a Democrat and from Tennessee created good balance both regionally and politically. At the time the election looked like it might be a close one, and the bipartisan nature of the ticket was a political bonus. Johnson was the biggest vote getter on the first ballot of the Convention, and with last-minute vote switching he ended up with 494 of the 521 votes cast. Still, there was little expectation that he would end up as president. Of the sixteen presidents up to that time, only two had acceded to the presidency on the death of their predecessor—and none through assassination. On Abraham Lincoln's assassination, however, Johnson rose to the presidency barely a month after becoming vice president.

Now President Johnson's relationship with Congress was rocky at best. Johnson was a Southerner and a Democrat, and while loyal to the Union he did not share the view of the Republicans in Congress on Reconstruction. He was seen as being too soft on the Southern states. His veto of the Civil rights Act of 1866, which was subsequently overridden, and his opposition to the Fourteenth Amendment, set him on course for a showdown with the Republicans in Congress. That contest came in the form of a debate over the Tenure of Office Act. Johnson intentionally violated the act and expected to test its constitutionality in the courts; instead, it became the centerpiece of an effort to have him removed from office.

Author Biography

The author of the articles of impeachment in this case was a select committee of the House of Representatives of the 40th Congress. The Committee was made up of George Boutwell, Thaddeus Stevens, John Bingham, James Wilson, John Logan, George Julian and Hamilton Ward. The most famous member of the committee was Thaddeus Stevens who also served on a committee of two that informed the Senate of the impeachment of the president, and he served as the chairman of the managers of the House's presentation of its case for conviction at the Senate trial.

The 40th Congress met from March 4, 1867, to March 4, 1869. At the time of the impeachment of President Johnson this Congress had a massive Republican majority in both houses. The House of Representatives was made up of 173 Republicans, 47 Democrats and 4 others. A majority of over 120 seats ensured that whatever the Republican members wanted would pass. A majority of this scale made the House of Representatives effectively veto proof with far more than the simple majority needed to impeach a president. The Senate of the 40th Congress at the time of the impeachment trial also had a lopsided majority in favor of the Republicans. The Senate was made up of 45 Republicans and 9 Democrats, these numbers include four "Unionist" members, two of whom were effectively Republican and two effectively Democrats. This wide margin made the Senate effectively veto proof as well, giving them far more than the two thirds necessary to override a veto or convict a president at an impeachment trial.

This Congress still excluded members from ten of the eleven states that seceded; only Tennessee had returned to full membership in the Union.

HISTORICAL DOCUMENT

Article I

That said Andrew Johnson, President of the United States, on the 21st day of February, in the year of our Lord 1868, at Washington, in the District Columbia, unmindful of the high duties of his office, of his oath of office, and of the requirement of the Constitution that he should take care that the laws be faithfully executed, did unlawfully, and in violation of the Constitution and laws of the United States, issue an order in writing for the removal of Edwin M. Stanton from the office of Secretary for the Department of War, said Edwin M. Stanton having been theretofore duly appointed and commissioned, by and with the advice and consent of the Senate of the United States, as such Secretary, and said Andrew Johnson, President of the United States, on the 12th day of August, in the year of our Lord 1867, and during the recess of said Senate, having suspended by his order Edwin M. Stanton from said office, and within twenty days after the first day of the next meeting of said Senate, that is to say, on the 12th day of December, in the year last aforesaid, having reported to said Senate such suspension with the evidence and reasons for his action in the case and the name of the person designated to perform the duties of such office temporarily until the next meeting of the Senate, and said Senate, there afterward, on the 13th day of January, in the year of our Lord 1868, having duly considered the evidence and reasons reported by said Andrew Johnson for said suspension, and having refused to concur in said suspension, whereby and by force of the provisions of an act entitled "An act regulating the tenure of certain civil offices," passed March 2, 1867, said Edwin M. Stanton did forthwith resume the functions of his office, whereof the said Andrew Johnson had then and there due notice, and said Edwin M. Stanton, by reason of the premises, on said 21st day of February, being lawfully entitled to hold said office of Secretary for the Department of War, which said order for the removal of said Edwin M. Stanton is, in substance, as follows, that is to say:

EXECUTIVE MANSION,
Washington, D.C., February 21, 1868.

SIR:

By virtue of the power and authority vested in me as President by the Constitution and laws of the United States you are hereby removed from office as Secretary for the Department of War, and your functions as such will terminate upon receipt of this communication.

You will transfer to Brevet Major General Lorenzo Thomas, Adjutant General of the army, who has this day been authorized and empowered to act as Secretary of War *ad interim,* all records, books, papers, and other public property now in your custody and charge.

Respectfully yours,

ANDREW JOHNSON

To the Hon. EDWIN M. STANTON,
Washington, D.C.

Which order was unlawfully issued with intent then and there to violate the act entitled "An act regulating the tenure of certain civil offices," passed March second, eighteen hundred and sixty-seven, and with the further intent, contrary to the provisions of said act, in violation thereof, and contrary to the provisions of the Constitution of the United States, and without the advice and consent of the Senate of the United States, the said Senate then and there being in session, to remove said Edwin M. Stanton from the office of Secretary for the Department of War, the said Edwin M. Stanton, being then and there Secretary for the Department of War, and being then and there in the due and lawful execution and discharge of the duties of said office, whereby said Andrew Johnson, President of the United States, did then and there commit, and was guilty of a high misdemeanor in office.

Article II

That on said twenty-first day of February, in the year of our Lord one thousand eight hundred and sixty-eight, at Washington, in the District of Columbia, said Andrew Johnson, President of the United States, unmindful of the high duties of his office, of his oath of office, and in violation of the Constitution of the United States, and contrary to the provisions of an act entitled "An act regulating the tenure of certain civil offices," passed March second, eighteen hundred and sixty-seven, without the advice and consent of the Senate of the United States, said Senate then and there being in session, and without authority of law, did, with intent to violate the Constitution of the United States, and the act aforesaid, issue and deliver to one Lorenzo Thomas a letter of authority in substance as follows, that is to say:

EXECUTIVE MANSION,
Washington, D.C., February 21, 1868.

SIR:

The Hon. Edwin M. Stanton having been this day removed from office as Secretary for the Department of War, you are hereby authorized and empowered to act as Secretary of War *ad interim,* and will immediately enter upon the discharge of the duties pertaining to that office.

Mr. Stanton has been instructed to transfer to you all the records, books, papers, and other public property now in his custody and charge.

Respectfully yours,

ANDREW JOHNSON

To Brevet Major General LORENZO THOMAS, Adjutant General U.S. Army, Washington, D.C.

Then and there being no vacancy in said office of Secretary for the Department of War, whereby said Andrew Johnson, President of the United States, did then and there commit, and was guilty of a high misdemeanor in office

Article III

That said Andrew Johnson, President of the United States, on the twenty-first day of February, in the year of our Lord one thousand eight hundred and sixty-eight, at Washington, in the district of Columbia, did commit and was guilty of a high misdemeanor in office in this, that, without authority of law, while the Senate of the United States was then and there in session, he did appoint one Lorenzo Thomas to be Secretary for the Department of War *ad interim*, without the advice and consent of the Senate, and with intent to violate the Constitution of the United States, no vacancy having happened in said office of Secretary for the Department of War during the recess of the Senate, and no vacancy existing in said office at the time, and which said appointment, so made by said Andrew Johnson, of said Lorenzo Thomas, is in substance as follows, that is to say:

EXECUTIVE MANSION,
Washington D.C., February 21, 1868.

SIR:

The Hon. Edwin M. Stanton having been this day removed from office as Secretary for the Department of War, you are hereby authorized and empowered to act as Secretary of War *ad interim*, and will immediately enter upon the discharge of the duties pertaining to that office.

Mr. Stanton has been instructed to transfer to you all the records, books, papers, and other public property now in his custody and charge.
Respectfully yours,

ANDREW JOHNSON.

To Brevet Major General LORENZO THOMAS, Adjutant General U.S. Army, Washington, D.C

Article IV

That said Andrew Johnson, President of the United States, unmindful of the high duties of his office and of his oath of office, in violation of the Constitution and laws of the United States, on the twenty-first day of February, in the year of our Lord one thousand eight hundred and sixty-eight, at Washington, in the District of Columbia, did unlawfully conspire with one Lorenzo Thomas, and with other persons to the House of Representatives unknown, with intent, by intimidation and threats, unlawfully to hinder and prevent Edwin M. Stanton, then and there Secretary for the Department of War, duly appointed under the laws of the United States, from holding said office of Secretary for the Department of War, contrary to and in violation of the Constitution of the United States, and of the provisions of an act entitled "An act to define and punish certain conspiracies," approved July thirty-first, eighteen hundred and sixty-one, whereby said Andrew Johnson, President of the United States, did then and there commit and was guilty of a high crime in office.

Article V

That said Andrew Johnson, President of the United States, unmindful of the high duties of his office and of his oath of office, on the twenty-first day of February, in the year of our Lord one thousand eight hundred and sixty-eight, and on divers other days and times in said year, before the second day of March, in the year of our Lord one thousand eight hundred and sixty-eight, at Washington, in the District of Columbia, did unlawfully conspire with one Lorenzo Thomas, and with other persons to the House of Representatives unknown, to prevent and hinder the execution of an act entitled "An act regulating the tenure of certain civil offices," passed March second, eighteen hundred and sixty-seven, and in pursuance of said conspiracy, did unlawfully attempt to prevent Edwin M. Stanton, then and there being Secretary for the Department of War, duly appointed and commissioned under the laws of the United States, from holding said office, whereby the said Andrew Johnson, President of the United States, did then and there commit and was guilty of a high misdemeanor in office.

Article VI

That said Andrew Johnson, President of the United States, unmindful of the high duties of his office and of his oath of office, on the twenty-first day of February, in the year of our Lord one thousand eight hundred and sixty-eight, at Washington, in the District of Columbia, did unlawfully conspire with one Lorenzo Thomas, by force to seize, take, and possess the property of the United States in the Department of War, and then and there in the custody and charge of Edwin M. Stanton, Secretary for said Department, contrary to the provisions of an act entitled "An act to define and punish certain conspiracies," approved July thirty-one, eighteen hundred and sixty-one, and with intent to violate and disregard an Act entitled "An act regulating the tenure of certain civil offices," passed March second, eighteen hundred and sixty-seven, whereby said Andrew Johnson, President of the United States, did then and there commit a high crime in office.

Article VII

That said Andrew Johnson, President of the United States, unmindful of the high duties of his office and of his oath of office, on the twenty-first day of February, in the year of our Lord one thousand eight hundred and sixty-eight, at Washington, in the District of Columbia, did unlawfully conspire with one Lorenzo Thomas with intent unlawfully to seize, take, and possess the property of the United States in the Department of War, in the custody and charge of Edwin M. Stanton, Secretary for said Department, with intent to violate and disregard the act entitled "An act regulating the tenure of certain civil offices," passed March second, eighteen hundred and sixty-seven, whereby said Andrew Johnson, President of the United States, did then and there commit a high misdemeanor in office

Article VIII

That said Andrew Johnson, President of the United States, unmindful of the high duties of his office and of his oath of office, with intent unlawfully to control the disbursements of the moneys appropriated for the mili-

tary service and for the Department of War, on the 21st day of February, in the year of our Lord 1868, at Washington, in the District of Columbia, did unlawfully and contrary to the provisions of an act entitled "An act regulating the tenure of certain civil offices," passed March 2, 1867, and in violation of the Constitution of the United States, and without the advice and consent of the Senate of the United States, and while the Senate was then and there in session, there being no vacancy in the office of Secretary for the Department of War, with intent to violate and disregard the act aforesaid, then and there issue and deliver to one Lorenzo Thomas a letter of authority in writing, in substance as follows, that is to say:

'EXECUTIVE MANSION.
Washington, D.C., February 21, 1868.

SIR:
Hon. Edwin M. Stanton having been this day removed from office as Secretary for the Department of War, you are hereby authorized and empowered to act as Secretary of War ad interim, and will immediately enter upon the discharge of the duties pertaining to that office.

'Mr. Stanton has been instructed to transfer to you all the records, books, papers, and other public property now in his custody and charge.

Respectfully, yours,

ANDREW JOHNSON.

To Brevet Maj. Gen. LORENZO THOMAS, Adjutant-General United States Army, Washington, D.C.

whereby said Andrew Johnson, President of the United States, did then and there commit and was guilty of a high misdemeanor in office.

Article IX

That said Andrew Johnson, President of the United States, on the twenty-second day of February, in the year

620 of our Lord one thousand eight hundred and sixty-eight,

of our Lord one thousand eight hundred and sixty-eight, at Washington, in the District of Columbia, in disregard of the Constitution and the laws of the United States duly enacted, as commander-in-chief of the army of the United States, did bring before himself then and there William H. Emory, a major general by brevet in the army of the United States, actually in command of the Department of Washington and the military forces thereof, and did then and there, as such commander-in-chief, declare to and instruct said Emory that part of a law of the United States, passed March second, eighteen hundred and sixty-seven, entitled "An act making appropriations for the support of the army for the year ending June thirtieth, eighteen hundred and sixty-eight, and for other purposes," especially the second section thereof, which provides, among other things, that "all orders and instructions relating to the military operations issued by the President of Secretary of War shall be issued through the General of the army, and, in case of his inability through the next in rank" was unconstitutional, and in contravention of the commission of said Emory, and which said provision of law had been theretofore duly and legally promulgated by General Order for the government and direction of the army of the United States, as the said Andrew Johnson then and there well knew, with intent thereby to induce said Emory in his official capacity as commander of the Department of Washington, to violate the provisions of said act, and to take and receive, act upon, and obey such orders as he, the said Andrew Johnson, might make and give, and which should not be issued through the General of the Army of the United States, according to the provisions of said act, and with the further intent thereby to enable him, the said Andrew Johnson, to prevent the execution of the act entitled "An act regulating the tenure of certain civil offices," passed March second, eighteen hundred and sixty-seven, and to unlawfully prevent Edwin M. Stanton, then being Secretary for the Department of War, from holding said office and discharging the duties thereof, whereby said Andrew Johnson, President of the United States, did then and there commit and was guilty of a high misdemeanor in office.

And the House of Representatives, by protestation, saving to themselves the liberty of exhibiting at any time hereafter any further articles or other accusa-

tion, or impeachment against the said Andrew Johnson, President of the United States, and also of replying to his answers which he shall make unto the articles herein preferred against him, and of offering proof to the same, and every part shall be exhibited by them, as the case shall require, DO DEMAND that the said Andrew Johnson may be put to answer the high crimes and misdemeanors in office herein charged against him, and that such proceedings, examinations, trials, and judgments may be thereupon had and given as may be agreeable to law and justice.

SCHULYER COLFAX, *Speaker of the House of Representatives.*
IN THE HOUSE OF REPRESENTATIVES UNITED STATES, March 3, 1868

Article X

The following additional articles of impeachment were agreed to, viz:

That said Andrew Johnson, President of the United States, unmindful of the high duties of his office and the dignity and proprieties thereof, and of the harmony and courtesies which ought to exist and be maintained between the executive and legislative branches of the government of the United States, designing and intending to set aside the rightful authority and powers of Congress, did attempt to bring into disgrace, ridicule, hatred, contempt and reproach the Congress of the United States, and the several branches thereof, to impair and destroy the regard and respect of all the good people of the United States for the Congress and legislative power thereof, (which all officers of the government ought inviolably to preserve and maintain,) and to excite the odium and resentment of all the good people of the United States against Congress and the laws by it duly and constitutionally enacted; and in pursuance of his said design and intent, openly and publicly, and before divers assemblages of the citizens of the United States convened in divers parts thereof to meet and receive said Andrew Johnson as the Chief Magistrate of the United States, did, on the eighteenth day of August, in the year of our Lord one thousand eight hundred and sixty-six, and on divers other days and times, as well before as afterward, make and deliver with a loud voice certain intemperate, inflammatory and scandalous harangues, and did therein utter loud threats and bitter menaces as well against Congress as the laws of the United States duly enacted thereby, amid the cries jeers and laughter of the multitudes then assembled and in hearing, which are set forth in the several specifications hereinafter written, in substance and effect, that is to say:

SPECIFICATION FIRST. In this, that at Washington, in the District of Columbia, in the Executive Mansion, to a committee of citizens who called upon the President of the United States, speaking of and concerning the Congress of the United States, said Andrew Johnson, President of the United States, heretofore, to wit, on the eighteenth day of August, in the year of our Lord one thousand eight hundred and sixty-six, did in a loud voice, declare in substance and effect, among other things, that is to say:

> So far as the Executive Department of the government is concerned, the effort has been made to restore the Union, to heal the breach, to pour oil into the wounds which were consequent upon the struggle, and (to speak in common phrase) to prepare as the learned and wise physician would, a plaster healing in character and coextensive with the wound. We thought, and we think, that we had partially succeeded; but as the work progresses, as reconstruction seemed to be taking place, and the country was becoming reunited, we found a disturbing and marring element opposing us. In alluding to that element, I shall go no further than your convention and the distinguished gentleman who has delivered to me the report of its proceedings. I shall make no reference to it that I do not believe the time and the occasion justify.

We have witnessed in one department of the government every endeavor to prevent the restoration of peace, harmony, and Union. We have seen hanging upon the verge of the government, as it were, a body, called, or which assumes to be, the Congress of the United States, while in fact it is a Congress of only a part of the States. We have seen this Congress pretend to be for the Union, when its every step and act tended to perpetuate disunion and make a disruption of the States inevitable. . . . We have seen Congress in a minority assume to exercise power which, allowed to be consummated, would result in despotism or monarchy itself."

SPECIFICATION SECOND. In this, that at Cleveland, in the State of Ohio, heretofore, to wit, on the third day of September, in the year of our Lord one thousand eight hundred and sixty-six, before a public assemblage of citizens and others, said Andrew Johnson, President of the United States, speaking of and concerning the Congress of the United States did, in a loud voice, declare in substance and effect among other things, that is to say:

> I will tell you what I did do. I called upon your Congress that is trying to break up the government."

> In conclusion, beside that, Congress had taken much pains to poison their constituents against him. But what had Congress done? Have they done anything to restore the union of these States? No: on the contrary, they had done everything to prevent it; and because he stood now where he did when the rebellion commenced, he had been denounced as a traitor. Who had run greater risks or made greater sacrifices than himself? But Congress, factious and domineering, had undertaken to poison the minds of the American people."

SPECIFICATION THIRD - In this, that at St. Louis, in the State of Missouri, heretofore, to wit, on the eighth day of September, in the year of our Lord one thousand eight hundred and sixty-six, before a public assemblage of citizens and others, said Andrew Johnson, President of the United States, speaking of and concerning the Congress of the United States, did, in a loud voice, declare, in substance and effect, among other things, that is to say:

"Go on. Perhaps if you had a word or two on the subject of New Orleans you might understand more about it than you do. And if you will go back - if you will go back and ascertain the cause of the riot at New Orleans perhaps you will not be so prompt in calling out 'New Orleans.' If you will take up the riot at New Orleans, and trace it back to its source or its immediate cause, you will find out who was responsible for the blood that was shed there. If you will take up the riot of New Orleans and trace it back to the radical Congress, you will find that the riot at New Orleans was substantially planned. If you will take up the proceedings in their caucuses you will understand that they there knew that a convention was to be called which was extinct by its power having expired; that it was said that the intention was that a new government was to be organized, and on the organization of that government the intention was to enfranchise one portion of the population, called the colored population, who had just been emancipated, and at the same time disfranchise white men. When you design to talk about New Orleans you ought to understand what you are talking about. When you read the speeches that were made, and take up the facts on the Friday and Saturday before that convention sat, you will there find that speeches were made incendiary in their character, exciting that portion of the population, the black population, to arm themselves and prepare for the shedding of blood. You will

also find that that convention did assemble in violation of law, and the intention of that convention was to supersede the reorganized authorities in the State government of Louisiana, which had been recognized by the government of the United States; and every man engaged in that rebellion in that convention, with the intention of superseding and upturning the civil government which had been recognized by the government of the United States I say that he was a traitor to the Constitution of the United States, and hence you find that another rebellion was commenced, *having its origin in the radical Congress.*

"So much for the New Orleans riot. And there was the cause and the origin of the blood that was shed; and every drop of blood that was shed is upon their skins, and they are responsible for it. I could test this thing a little closer, but will not do it here to-night. But when you talk about the causes and consequences that resulted from proceedings of that kind perhaps, as I have been introduced here, and you have provoked questions of this kind, though it does not provoke me, I will tell you a few wholesome things that have been done by this radical Congress in connection with New Orleans and the extension of the elective franchise.

"I know that I have been traduced and abused. I know it has come in advance of me here as elsewhere - that I have attempted to exercise an arbitrary power in resisting laws that were intended to be forced upon the government; that I had exercised that power; that I had abandoned the party that elected me, and that I was a traitor, because I exercised the veto power in attempting, and did arrest for a time, a bill that was called a 'Freedman's Bureau' bill; yes, that I was a traitor. And I have been traduced, I have been slandered, I have been maligned, I have been called a Judas Iscariot and all that. Now, my countrymen, here to-night, it is very easy to indulge in epithets; it is easy to call a man Judas and cry out traitor, but when he is called upon to give arguments and facts he is very often found wanting. Judas Iscariot - Judas. There was a Judas, and he was one of the twelve apostles. Oh! yes, the twelve apostles had a Christ. The twelve apostles had a Christ, and he never could have had a Judas unless he had had twelve apostles. If I have played the Judas, who has been my Christ that I have played the Judas with? Was it Thad. Stevens? Was it Wendell Phillips? Was it Charles Sumner? These are the men that stop and compare themselves with the Saviour; and everybody that differs with them in opinion, and to try to stay and arrest their diabolical and nefarious policy, is to be denounced as a Judas."

Well, let me say to you, if you will stand by me in their action, if you will stand by me in trying to give the people a fair chance - soldiers and citizens - to participate in these offices, God being willing, I will kick them out. I will kick them out just as fast as I can.

"Let me say to you, in concluding, that what I have said I intended to say. I was not provoked into this, and I care not for their menaces, the taunts, and the jeers. I care not for threats. I do not intend to be bullied by my enemies nor jeers. I care not for threats. I do not intend to be bullied by my enemies nor overawed by my friends. But, God willing, with your help, I will veto their measures whenever any of them come to me."

Which said utterances, declarations, threats, and harangues, highly censurable in any, are peculiarly indecent and unbecoming in the Chief Magistrate of the United States, by means whereof said Andrew Johnson has brought to high office of the President of the United States into contempt, ridicule, and disgrace, to the great scandal of all good citizens, whereby said Andrew Johnson, President of the United States, did commit, and was then and there guilty of a high misdemeanor in office

Article XI

That said Andrew Johnson, President of the United States, unmindful of the high duties of his office, and of his oath of office, and in disregard of the Constitution and laws of the United States, did, heretofore, to wit, on the eighteenth day of August, A.D. eighteen hundred and sixty-six, at the city of Washington, and the District of Columbia, by public speech, declare and affirm, in substance, that the thirty-ninth Congress of the United States was a Congress of the United States authorized by the Constitution to exercise a legislative power under the same, but, on the contrary, was a Congress of only part of the States, thereby denying, and intending to deny, that the legislation of said Congress was valid or obligatory upon him, the said Andrew Johnson, except in so far as he saw fit to approve the same, and also thereby denying, and intending to deny, the power of the said thirty-ninth Congress to propose amendments to the Constitution of the United States; and, in pursuance of said declaration, the said Andrew Johnson, President of the United States, afterwards, to wit, on the twenty-first day of February, A.D. eighteen hundred and sixty-eight, at the city of Washington, in the District of Columbia, did, unlawfully, and in disregard of the requirement of the Constitution, that he should take care that the laws be faithfully executed, attempt to prevent the execution of an act entitled "An act regulating the tenure of certain civil offices," passed March second, eighteen hundred and sixty-seven, by unlawfully devising and contriving, and attempting to devise and contrive means by which he should prevent Edwin M. Stanton from forthwith resuming the functions of the office of Secretary for the Department of War, notwithstanding the refusal of the Senate to concur in the suspension theretofore made by said Andrew Johnson of said Edwin M. Stanton from said office of Secretary for the Department of War; and, also, by further unlawfully devising and contriving, and attempting to devise and contrive means, then and there, to prevent the execution of an act entitled "An act making appropriations for the support of the army for the fiscal year ending June thirtieth, eighteen hundred and sixty-eight, and for other purposes," approved March second, eighteen hundred and sixty-seven; and, also, to prevent the execution of an act entitled "An act to provide for the more efficient government of the rebel States," passed March second, eighteen hundred and sixty-eight, at the city of Washington, commit, and was guilty of, a high misdemeanor in office.

SCHULYER COLFAX, *Speaker of the House of Representatives.*
Attest: EDWARD McPHERSON, Clerk of the House of Representatives

GLOSSARY

40th Congress: U.S. Congress which meet from March 4, 1867, to March 3, 1869

Andrew Johnson: 17th President of the United States from 1865 to 1869

articles of impeachment: House of Representative resolution wherein wrongdoing by an executive or judicial branch official is described

high crimes and misdemeanors: Constitutional description of the types of wrongdoing for which executive or judicial branch official can removed from office; the exact meaning is up to Congress to decide

impeach: to accuse (via the House of Representatives) an executive or judicial branch official with misconduct important enough to require removal from office; the term is also used to describe the whole process by which an executive or judicial branch official is removed from office

pocket veto: a veto put into effect by a president not signing a bill for 10 days (Sundays not included) and Congress adjourning; this veto cannot be overridden

regular veto: a veto caused by the president sending back a bill to the originating house of Congress with a list of reasons for having rejected it; this type of veto can be overridden by a two-thirds vote in each house of Congress

Tenure of Office Act: an act passed by Congress over the president's veto that required Senate permission to fire any official who had been confirmed by the U.S. SenateDocument Analysis

Document Analysis

The true significance of these articles of impeachment is not in the words themselves, but rather in why they were written and what happened to them.

Johnson was a Democrat elected vice president under a Republican president who many in the Republican Party thought was too soft on the South; yet Lincoln was, particularly after the successful conclusion of the war, the undisputed leader of his party. Lincoln's violent and sudden death at the hands of a Southern sympathizer not only thrust Johnson into the presidency but also dealt him a hard hand to play as he tried to carry out Reconstruction.

Andrew Johnson's relationship with Congress was anything but good. Congress considered the conditions of "Presidential Reconstruction" too soft and they moved to impose what became known as "Congressional Reconstruction." Johnson's strained relationship with Congress can be seen in his problems with having his vetoes upheld. Throughout his presidency 15 of his 29 vetoes were overridden (counting eight pocket vetoes which cannot be overridden). Thus, 15 of the 21 times Congress could defeat the president they did. As a point of comparison, both Presidents Harry Truman and Gerald Ford had 12 vetoes overridden, but that was out of 250 (70 pocket) and 66 (18 pocket) vetoes respectively.

During the period prior to his impeachment Congress overrode nine of Johnson's fourteen regular vetoes, including what is known as the Tenure of Office Act. The act required that any officer of the government requiring Senate approval for his appointment also required Senate approval for his removal, including the Cabinet. The act included fines and jail time for violating the law, which were important provisions when the efforts to impeach the president were brought forward.

The Tenure of Office Act left two important questions open. The first was, Was the act constitutional? This debate had been held in 1789, when the founders decided in favor of presidential discretion in this matter, a fact well known to the political leaders of the day. The other was, What constituted a presidential term? Cabinet members got to keep their office for 30 days after a president's term ended, but was that counted from the point when the president ceased to be president or from the end of the specific four-year cycle?

The Tenure of Office Act became law over the president's veto on March 2, 1867, by votes of 35-11 in the Senate and 138-40 in the House. It is worth noting that the final bill approved by the House differed markedly from the one initially passed by the Senate. The Senate bill specifically excluded the department heads, the cabinet, from its provisions. It was amended in the House of Representatives to include cabinet officers, and this amendment was central to the impeachment of the president.

This was not the first effort to impeach President Johnson. There had been an effort at impeachment that ended in December 1867. It failed primarily because it appeared to be based on policy disagreements between the Radical Republicans and the president. This failure was part of the development of an important aspect of the presidential impeachment philosophy. The president had to be guilty of an indictable offense; in other words, he had to commit a crime for which he could go to jail. This is where the provisions in the Tenure of Office Act that made its violation a crime punishable by jail time became important in the impeachment process.

The defining moment came when Johnson finally decided to fire Secretary of War Edwin Stanton. Johnson had suspended Stanton while the Congress was in recess, but this was not agreed to by the Senate. Finally on February 21, 1968, Johnson ordered General Lorenzo Thomas to take over the duties of the Secretary of War. Johnson's actions were meant as a test of the Tenure of Office Act but they gave his opponents an opportunity to move against him.

For a second time the idea of impeaching the president came to the fore, and the firing of Edwin Stanton played a central role. A formal resolution of impeachment was presented from the Committee on Reconstruction. During the debate on the resolution those in favor focused on the violation of the Tenure of Office Act. The president's defenders argued that the act itself was unconstitutional. In the end the resolution was passed by a vote of 128-47. The president had been impeached and a committee of seven was selected to write the formal articles of impeachment.

The first nine articles passed by the House on March 2, 1868, revolved around the idea that President Johnson had violated the Tenure of Office Act of 1867. Through a tortured use of language the House of Representatives found nine different ways to say the same thing: Johnson had fired Secretary Stanton and then moved to prevent him from carrying out the duties of his former office. The vote on each of the first nine articles was passed overwhelming by a Congress, dominated by Republicans. The smallest margin of victory was on article 9, which passed with a margin of 67 votes. On March 3rd the House added two further articles, article 10, charging the president with speaking against the Congress and bringing Congress into disrepute, and article 11 which was more of a summary of all of the charges against the president.

The debate on the articles led to a final solution of an important and not unrelated issue. Was Andrew Johnson the president of the United States, or was he the vice president acting as president? It was an important technicality. Did the House need to impeach the president or the vice president? Which office holder was being impeached? Using the precedents of both John Tyler in 1841 and Millard Fillmore in 1850 it was agreed in both houses of Congress that the vice president had become president on the death of his successor. Thus, the House had to impeach the president, not the vice president, as the latter position was now vacant.

The Senate prepared itself for the impeachment trial to be conducted by the House by adopting rules for the conduct of the trial on March 2 (rules, incidentally, that would lay the groundwork for the trial of Bill Clinton 130 years later). The Senate began the trial process on March 5, 1868, when the Chief Justice and senators took an oath to provide impartial justice in regards to the trial. The Senate of the 40th Congress in spring 1868 was made up of 54 Senators, 45 Republicans (including two Unconditional Unionists), nine more than the number required to convict and remove the president.

On March 13 the president's counsel asked for 40 days in which to prepare his defense, the request was denied and the Senate set March 23 as the day on which the resident needed to be prepared to respond to the charges. When the Senate reconvened, the question was raised whether it could act as a constitutional body while still excluding the members from ten of the eleven Southern states. The Senate determined it could by a vote of 40 to 2. The president's counsel then answered the House's charges.

The president's counsel gave Johnson's response to the charges to the Senate on March 23. He responded to article 1 by charging that the law itself was unconstitutional, thus Johnson could not have violated the law or the Constitution. To article 2 he responded that Johnson's actions were lawful as there was a vacancy at the war department as he had fired the Secretary of War. For article 3 the defense was that the reasons ex-

pressed in his argument for articles 1 and 2 applied to this article as well. His argument for article 4 was that there was no effort to intimidate anyone; the president simply authorized General Thomas to take over as interim Secretary of War using the normal executive power. His defense for articles 5 through 8 can be summed up by saying that Johnson was simply trying to carry out his duties as president of the United States. He argued in response to article 9 that the president had been expressing to others the same sentiments he had expressed to the House of Representatives about the constitutionality of limits that had been placed on his role as commander in chief. For article 10 the president denied that the events accurately depicted not only what was said, but the tone and tenor of what was said, and that it was his duty as president to warn Congress when he saw them headed on the wrong course regarding Reconstruction. The response to article 11 contained the blanket denial that Johnson had done anything that constituted a high crime or a misdemeanor.

The trial itself began on March 30 and lasted until May 16, 1868. The Senate chose to vote on article 11 first. By this point, though, the outcome could little be in doubt. Earlier procedural votes had shown that nineteen members, including seven Republicans, would vote not guilty. The final vote on article 11 took place on May 16, 35 voted guilty and 19 voted not guilty, one short of the required number for conviction. The Senate reconvened on May 26 to try again to convict the president. The votes on articles 2 and 3 were identical to article 9, 35 to 19. After this additional failure the Senate agreed to go into "adjournment without day," meaning that they would not meet again as an impeachment trial court, effectively ending the efforts to impeach President Johnson without voting on eight of the articles. Of the nineteen votes, ten came from elected Republicans but three came from those often considered Democrats for practical purposes. The Republicans who voted against their party were Senators William Fressenden, James Grimes, John Brooks Henderson, Edmund Ross, Joseph Fowler, Lyman Trumbull, and Peter Van Winkle.

The Senate result kept Johnson in office for the remainder of his term and set the precedent that the Congress does not remove presidents for policy differences but only for actual crimes. After the trial Johnson remained in office for only ten more months, but his presidency was indeed weakened by the trial and he was left with little opportunity to accomplish his goals.

The Tenure of Office Act would be kept on the books

until 1887 when it was finally repealed. The idea of a congressional veto over the presidential firing of executive branch officers was ended by the Supreme Court in 1926 when they decided *Myers v. United States.*

Essential Themes

The short-term impact of this process may be less than is often ascribed. When the process began in earnest there was slightly over one year left in the Johnson presidency, and when the trial ended there were only ten months left. Of that time Congress would be out of session for four months. So although Johnson was a weakened president, the same would have been true after he failed to get the Democratic nomination for president in 1868. The impeachment process did usher in a period of weakness in the presidency, but there is no way of knowing whether this might have occurred, or to what extent, under a Lincoln presidency in light of the diminishment of war powers.

The most important theme to come out of this document does not issue from the document itself but rather from events surrounding it and from its consequences. It is not uncommon in American history to hear the language of impeachment used against presidents who face a hostile majority in Congress. Johnson was not the first president to hear that impeachment was being discussed, but he was the first president to see the House of Representatives actually draft and pass articles of impeachment.

Two historical precedents were set by this action of the 40th Congress. The first is that the House of Representatives would impeach only for indictable offenses. The second is that the Senate would not convict on the grounds, merely, that they do not like a president or disagree with his policies.

Donald E. Heidenreich, Jr., PhD

Bibliography

Cannon, Clarence. *Cannon's precedents of the House of Representatives of the United States. Washington, D.C.: GPO, 1945. Print.*

Library of Congress. "A Century of Lawmaking for a New Nation: U.S. Congressional Documents and Debates." Web.

Nelson, Michael, editor. The Evolving Presidency: Landmark Documents, 1787-2010. Washington, D.C.: CQ Press, 2012. Print.

University of Missouri Kansas City Law School. "Famous American Trials: The Andrew Johnson Impeachment Trial, 1868." Web.

White, Horace. Life of Lyman Trumbull. New York: Houghton Mifflin, 1913. Print.

Additional Reading

Graf, LeRoy, and Ralph W. Haskins, eds. *The Papers of Andrew Johnson.* Knoxville: U of Tennessee P, 1967-1999. Print.

Leibowitz, Arnold H. *An Historical-Legal Analysis of the Impeachments of Presidents Andrew Johnson, Richard Nixon, and William Clinton: Why the Process Went Wrong.* Lewiston, N.Y.: Edwin Mellen Press, 2012. Print.

McKitrick, Eric L. *Andrew Johnson and* Reconstruction. New York: Oxford University Press, 1988. Print.

Republican National Convention. *Proceedings of the First Three Republican National Conventions of 1856, 1860 and 1864.* Minneapolis: C.W. Johnson, 1893. Print. *An Historical-Legal Analysis of the Impeachments of Presidents Andrew Johnson, Richard Nixon, and William Clinton: Why the Process Went Wrong.* Lewiston, N.Y.: Edwin Mellen Press, 2012. Print.

McKitrick, Eric L. *Andrew Johnson and* Reconstruction. New York: Oxford University Press, 1988. Print.

Republican National Convention. *Proceedings of the First Three Republican National Conventions of 1856, 1860 and 1864.* Minneapolis: C.W. Johnson, 1893. Print. *Andrew Johnson and* Reconstruction. New York: Oxford University Press, 1988. Print.

Republican National Convention. *Proceedings of the First Three Republican National Conventions of 1856, 1860 and 1864.* Minneapolis: C.W. Johnson, 1893. Print.

■ Various Selections of Black Codes in the South

Date: 1865-1886
Author: Southern state lawmakers from former Confederate states
Genre: law, legislation

> *"Every negro is required to be in the regular service
> of some white person, or former owner, who shall be
> held responsible for the conduct of said negro..."*

Summary Overview

The status of the African American emerged as the primary problem during Reconstruction, the decade immediately following the Civil War when four million slaves earned their freedom. The Thirteenth Amendment legally abolished the institution of slavery, but white lawmakers in the South were resolute in making sure African Americans did not encroach on their social, political and economic spheres. They passed related laws that thus aimed to thwart their desire for freedom and individual as well as community independence. Although the provisions of these laws differed by state, they had similar effects on former slaves and people of African descent.

Known as the Black Codes, these laws severely limited several aspects of African Americans' lives. They gave former slaves some legal rights such as the right to acquire personal property and to marry. However, African Americans were subject to vagrancy laws and employment stipulations included in them. The Black Codes also made interracial marriage illegal, and African Americans could not serve on juries. Although African Americans could be called as a witness in court, they could not testify against any white person. These laws exemplify the attitudes of Southern whites toward former slaves and those of African descent. Furthermore, they reveal how such racial attitudes persisted for centuries and would continued to do so for decades to follow. Finally, such laws demonstrate that the Reconstruction plan enacted by President Andrew Johnson

did not go far enough to rectify race relations in the South; institutional and structural racism would forever plague the South.

Defining Moment

In early 1865, after four years of bitter fighting, the Civil War finally came to an end. Although the struggle ended, the social system in the antebellum South had yet to be reconfigured. Both the federal government and white Southerners did not commit to the idea of equal rights for African Americans, which meant that former slaves and persons of African descent would struggle to obtain citizenship and the privileges it entailed. The needs of the four million former slaves became an afterthought, although Congress did create the Freedmen's Bureau prior to the end of the war to aid in the transition from slave life to being free. The Bureau provided food and medical services and it created public schools for freedmen. Its most important task was to help former slaves find a job and help protect them from exploitation. Nonetheless, by the end of 1865, states in the South refused to grant African Americans equality before the law.

- Only days after the Civil War officially ended, President Abraham Lincoln was assassinated. As a result, vice president Andrew Johnson was tasked with the job of reconstructing the country and reincorporating the south into the Union. As a Southerner, Johnson favored allowing the Southern states to rejoin the Union as soon as possible. He decided to appoint former Confederate leaders as military governors until new state governments could be organized. The Southern states resented both the presence of the Freedman's Bureau and military governors and wanted to become autonomous as quickly as possible. In the summer of 1865, many of the states held constitutional conventions to frame their new state governments. Because only white delegates could vote on matters, many laws were passed that limited the freedoms of former slaves. These laws were very similar to those in the antebellum period, as white lawmakers felt no reason not to continue the tradition of treating blacks in America unequally.

Johnson significantly altered President Lincoln's plans for Reconstruction by adding provisions that punished wealthy planters whom he blamed for the secession crisis and ensuing Civil War. Furthermore, he made it increasingly difficult for former Confederates to acquire citizenship, and he mandated that the Southern states repeal their ordinances to secede and ratify the Thirteenth Amendment in order to make slavery illegal throughout the country. While his plan appeared demanding, in reality it was far from onerous. He sought to punish former Confederates and elite planters in the South, but he did not demand that Southern states give citizenship to African Americans. Johnson's Reconstruction plan did not include the extension of suffrage to African Americans. Rather, only white males over the age of twenty-one retained the right to vote.

President Johnson convened a constitutional convention in 1865 to negotiate the matters of the abolition of slavery as well as the repeal of the secession ordinances demanded by the president in his Reconstruction plan in order to construct a new constitution. The convention concluded that secession ordinances would be nullified, although many of the delegates argued that they would concede only if former slave owners were repaid for their lost human property. Nonetheless, the institution of slavery was abolished not by consent but through sheer force. The language used by Southern delegates regarding the issue of slavery thus conveyed the idea that while slavery was by law made illegal, it had in fact not been destroyed. Most blacks believed that the Southern states would try to repress them into a status of quasi-slavery—which was what the Black Codes tried to do. When the convention ended, delegates from the South called for various state legislatures to withhold certain privileges from former slaves. According to the delegates, many were morally inferior

and were vagabonds and lawless. Such notions undergirded the crafting of the Black Codes, which paved the way for the Jim Crow laws that maintained a caste system not only during Reconstruction but for many subsequent decades.

The Black Codes were written only months after the Civil War ended. These series of laws were very similar to the state slave codes that were in place prior to the Civil War and emblematize the efforts of white Southerners to dictate the meaning of citizenship and freedom for former slaves and those of African descent. They reveal that whites intended for the condition of free blacks to be no different from when they were enslaved. Furthermore, they convey the fear whites had in a post-slavery society of black political influence in states where the black population outnumbered the white population. At the same time that these regressive laws were passed, white vigilante groups such as the Ku Klux Klan (KKK) formed throughout the South and terrorized African Americans in order to impede them from exercising their legal rights as free people. As a result, any progress made during the early years of Reconstruction was lost. As a result, blacks did not gain legal equality for another century.

Author Biography

President Andrew Johnson encouraged Southern lawmakers in state legislatures to pass laws that would help white Southerners become economically self-sufficient since the institution of slavery, the catalyst of the Southern plantation economy, had been disbanded. Many Southern white legislators who had a vested interest in keeping free blacks in a state of legal servitude took part in the drafting of the Black Codes in the former Confederate states. They did so to reestablish civil authority over the area and to ensure that white hegemony would persist. Furthermore, the Southern economy relied on plantation agriculture, so these legislators passed these laws not only to maintain their own wealth as planters but also to ensure that an agricultural economy in the South prevailed. To do so meant securing a cheap labor force very similar to the slave system.

In Mississippi, then Governor Benjamin Grubb Humphreys is attributed with pushing the bill through the state legislature despite the fact that he did not actual author the law. Humphreys was born on August 26, 1808 in Claiborne County, Mississippi. Humphreys served as a general in the Confederate army and was a native of Mississippi. Prior to the war, he briefly attended the U.S. Military Academy at West Point before getting expelled for his involvement in a boisterous altercation. As a result, he returned home to Mississippi and became a politician and a cotton planter. In 1865, at the beginning of the Reconstruction era, Humphreys was elected governor of Mississippi. The majority of the time in postwar sessions for the Mississippi legislature was occupied by debates over the laws that would become the Black Codes. The law was only approved when Governor Humphreys compromised with state legislators; some legislators wanted a more forceful

Reconstruction process while others demanded that the governor ignore the federal government's plan. As a cotton planter and politician, Humphreys benefitted from the Black Codes because he relied on cheap labor to subsist. While serving as a Democratic governor for Mississippi, he promoted Jim Crow laws and promulgated that even though blacks were free they were not entitled to citizenship or social and political equality. Once Congress took control of Reconstruction in 1868, Humphreys was physically removed from office by U.S. occupying forces.

HISTORICAL DOCUMENT

Mississippi Black Code

Apprentice Law

Section 1. *Be it enacted by the legislature of the state of Mississippi,* that it shall be the duty of all sheriffs, justices of the peace, and other civil officers of the several counties in this state to report to the Probate courts of their respective counties semiannually, at the January and July terms of said courts, all freedmen, free Negroes, and mulattos under the age of eighteen within their respective counties, beats, or districts who are orphans, or whose parent or parents have not the means, or who refuse to provide for and support said minors; and thereupon it shall be the duty of said Probate Court to order the clerk of said court to apprentice said minors to some competent and suitable person, on such terms as the court may direct, having a particular care to the interest of said minors:

> *Provided,* that the former owner of said minors shall have the preference when, in the opinion of the court, he or she shall be a Suitable person for that purpose.

Section 2. *Be it further enacted,* that the said court shall

be fully satisfied that the person or persons to whom said minor shall be apprenticed shall be a suitable person to have the charge and care of said minor and fully to protect the interest of said minor. The said court shall require the said master or mistress to execute bond and security, payable to the state of Mississippi, conditioned that he or she shall furnish said minor with sufficient food and clothing; to treat said minor humanely; furnish medical attention in case of sickness; teach or cause to be taught him or her to read and write, if under fifteen years old; and will conform to any law that may be hereafter passed for the regulation of the duties and relation of master and apprentice:

> *Provided,* that said apprentice shall be bound by indenture, in case of males until they are twenty-one years old, and in case of females until they are eighteen years old.

Section 3. *Be it further enacted,* that in the management and control of said apprentices, said master or mistress shall have power to inflict such moderate corporeal chastisement as a father or guardian is allowed to inflict on his or her child or ward at common law:

> *Provided,* that in no case shall cruel or

inhuman punishment be inflicted.

Section 4. *Be it further enacted,* that if any apprentice shall leave the employment of his or her master or mistress without his or her consent, said master or mistress may pursue and recapture said apprentice and bring him or her before any justice of the peace of the county, whose duty it shall be to remand said apprentice to the service of his or her master or mistress; and in the event of a refusal on the part of said apprentice so to return, then said justice shall commit said apprentice to the jail of said county, on failure to give bond, until the next term of the county court; and it shall be the duty of said court, at the first term thereafter, to investigate said case; and if the court shall be of opinion that said apprentice left the employment of his or her master or mistress without good cause, to order him or her to be punished, as provided for the punishment of hired freedmen, as may be from time to time provided for by law, for desertion, until he or she shall agree to return to his or her master or mistress:

> *Provided,* that the court may grant continuances, as in other cases; and *provided,* further, that if the court shall believe that said apprentice had good cause to quit his said master or mistress, the court shall discharge said apprentice from said indenture and also enter a judgment against the master or mistress for not more than $100, for the use and benefit of said apprentice, to be collected on execution, as in other cases.

Section 5. *Be it further enacted,* that if any person entice away any apprentice from his or her master or mistress, or shall knowingly employ an apprentice, or furnish him or her food or clothing, without the written consent of his or her master or mistress, of shall sell or give said apprentice ardent spirits, without such consent, said person so offending shall be deemed guilty of a high misdemeanor, and shall, on conviction thereof before the county court, be punished as provided for the punishment of persons enticing from their employer hired freedmen, free Negroes, or mulattoes.

Section 6. *Be it further enacted,* that it shall be the duty of all civil officers of their respective counties to report any minors within their respective counties to said Probate Court who are subject to be apprenticed under the provisions of this act, from time to time, as the facts may come to their knowledge; and it shall be the duty of said court, from time to time, as said minors shall be reported to them or otherwise come to their knowledge, to apprentice said minors as hereinbefore provided.

Section 7. *Be it further enacted,* that in case the master or mistress of any apprentice shall desire, he or she shall have the privilege to summon his or her said apprentice to the Probate Court, and thereupon, with the approval of the court, he or she shall be released from all liability as master of said apprentice, and his said bond shall be canceled, and it shall be the duty of the court forthwith to reapprentice said minor; and in the event any master of in apprentice shall die before the close of the term of service of said apprentice, it shall be the duty of the court to give the preference in reapprenticing said minor to the widow, or other member of said master's family:

> *Provided,* that said widow or other member of said family shall be a suitable person for that purpose.

Section 8. *Be it further enacted,* that in case any master or mistress of any apprentice, bound to him or her under this act shall be about to remove or shall have removed to any other state of the United States by the laws of which such apprentice may be an inhabitant thereof, the Probate Court of the proper county may authorize the removal of such apprentice to such state, upon the said master or mistress entering into bond, with security, in a penalty to be fixed by the judge, conditioned that said master or mistress will, upon such removal, comply with the laws of such state in such cases:

> *Provided,* that said master shall be cited to attend the court at which such order is proposed to be made and shall have a right to resist the same by next friend, or otherwise.

Section 9. *Be it further enacted,* that it shall be lawful for any freedman, free Negro, or Mulatto having a minor child or children to apprentice the said minor child or children as provided for by this act.

Section 10. *Be it further enacted,* that in all cases where the age of the freedman, free Negro, or mulatto cannot be ascertained by record testimony, the judge of the county court shall fix the age.

II.

Vagrancy Law

Section 1. *Be it enacted by the legislature of the state of Mississippi,* that all rogues and vagabonds, idle and dissipated persons, beggars, jugglers, or persons practising unlawful games or plays, runaways, common drunkards, common nightwalkers, pilferers, lewd, wanton, or lascivious persons, in speech or behavior, common railers and brawlers, persons who neglect their calling or employment, misspend what they earn, or do not provide for the support of themselves or their families or dependents, and all other idle and disorderly persons, including all who neglect all lawful business, or habitually misspend their time by frequenting houses of ill-fame, gaming houses, or tippling shops, shall be deemed and considered vagrants under the provisions of this act; and, on conviction thereof shall be fined not exceeding $100, with all accruing costs, and be imprisoned at the discretion of the court not exceeding ten days.

Section 2. *Be it further enacted,* that all freedmen, free Negroes, and mulattoes in this state over the age of eighteen years found on the second Monday in January 1966, or thereafter, with no lawful employment or business, or found unlawfully assembling themselves together either in the day or nighttime, and all white persons so assembling with freedmen, free Negroes, or mulattoes, or usually associating with freedmen, free Negroes, or mulattoes on terms of equality, or living in adultery or fornication with a freedwoman, free Negro, or mulatto, shall be deemed vagrants; and, on conviction thereof, shall be fined in the sum of not exceeding, in the case of a freedman, free Negro, or mulatto, 150, and a white man, $200, and imprisoned at the discretion of the court, the free Negro not exceeding ten days, and the white man not exceeding six months.

Section 3. *Be it further enacted,* that all justices of the peace, mayors, and aldermen of incorporated towns and cities of the several counties in this state shall have jurisdiction to try all questions of vagrancy in their respective towns, counties, and cities; and it is hereby made their duty, whenever they shall ascertain that any person or persons in their respective towns, counties, and cities are violating any of the provisions of this act, to have said party or parties arrested and brought before them and immediately investigate said charge; and, on conviction, punish said party or parties as provided for herein. And it is hereby made the duty of all sheriffs, constables, town constables, city marshals, and all like officers to report to some officer having jurisdiction all violations of any of the provisions of this act; and it shall be the duty of the county courts to inquire if any officers have neglected any of the duties required by this act; and in case any officer shall fail or neglect any duty herein, it shall be the duty of the county court to fine said officer, upon conviction, not exceeding $100, to be paid into the county treasury for county purposes.

Section 4. *Be it further enacted,* that keepers of gaming houses, houses of prostitution, all prostitutes, public or private, and all persons who derive their chief support in employments that militate against good morals or against laws shall be deemed and held to be vagrants.

Section 5. *Be it further enacted,* that all fines and forfeitures collected under the provisions of this act shall be paid into the county treasury for general county purposes; and in case any freedman, free Negro, or mulatto shall fail for five days after the imposition of any fine or forfeiture upon him or her for violation of any of the provisions of this act to pay the same, that it shall be, and is hereby made, the duty of the sheriff of the proper county to hire out said freedman, free Negro, or mulatto to any person who will, for the shortest period of service, pay said fine or forfeiture and all costs:

Provided, a preference shall be given to the employer, if there be one, in which case the employer shall be entitled to deduct and retain the amount so paid from the wages of such freedman, free Negro, or mulatto then due or to become due; and in case such freedman, free Negro, or mulatto cannot be hired out he or she may be dealt with as a pauper.

Section 6. *Be it further enacted,* that the same duties and liabilities existing among white persons of this state shall attach to freedmen, free Negroes, and mulattoes to support their indigent families and all colored paupers; and that, in order to secure a support for such indigent freedmen, free Negroes, and mulattoes, it shall be lawful, and it is hereby made the duty of the boards of county police of each county in this state, to levy a poll or capitation tax on each and every freedman, free Negro, or mulatto, between the ages of eighteen and sixty years, not to exceed the sum of s I annually, to each person so taxed, which tax, when collected, shall be paid into the county treasurer's hands and constitute a fund to be called the Freedman's Pauper Fund, which shall be applied by the commissioners of the poor for the maintenance of the poor of the freedmen, free Negroes and mulattoes of this state, under such regulations as may be established by the boards of county police, in the respective counties of this state.

Section 7. *Be it further enacted,* that if any freedman, free Negro, or mulatto shall fail or refuse to pay any tax levied according to the provisions of the 6th Section of this act, it shall be prima facie evidence of vagrancy, and it shall be the duty of the sheriff to arrest such freedman, free Negro, or mulatto, or such person refusing or neglecting to pay such tax, and proceed at once to hire, for the shortest time, such delinquent taxpayer to anyone who will pay the said tax, with accruing costs, giving preference to the employer, if there be one.

Section 8. *Be it further enacted,* that any person feeling himself or herself aggrieved by the judgment of any justice of the peace, mayor, or alderman in cases arising under this act may, within five days, appeal to the next term of the county court of the proper county, upon giving bond and security in a sum not less than $25 nor more than $150, conditioned to appear and prosecute said appeal, and abide by the judgment of the county court, and said appeal shall be tried *de novo* in the county court, and the decision of said court shall be final.

Civil Rights of Freedmen

Section 1. *Be it enacted by the legislature of the state of Mississippi,* that all freedmen, free Negroes, and mulattoes may sue and be sued, implead and be impleaded in all the courts of law and equity of this state, and may acquire personal property and choses in action, by descent or purchase, and may dispose of the same in the same manner and to the same extent that white persons may:

Provided, that the provisions of this section shall not be construed as to allow any freedman, free Negro, or mulatto to rent or lease any lands or tenements, except in incorporated towns or cities, in which places the corporate authorities shall control the same.

Section 2. *Be it further enacted,* that all freedmen, free Negroes, and mulattoes may intermarry with each other, in the same manner and under the same regulations that are provided by law for white persons:

Provided, that the clerk of probate shall keep separate records of the same.

Section 3. *Be it further enacted,* that all freedmen, free

Negroes, and mulattoes who do now and have heretofore lived and cohabited together as husband and wife shall be taken and held in law as legally married, and the issue shall be taken and held as legitimate for all purposes. That it shall not be lawful for any freedman, free Negro, or mulatto to intermarry with any white person; nor for any white person to intermarry with any freedman, free Negro, or mulatto; and any person who shall so intermarry shall be deemed guilty of felony and, on conviction thereof, shall be confined in the state penitentiary for life; and those shall be deemed freedmen, free Negroes, and mulattoes who are of pure Negro blood; and those descended from a Negro to the third generation inclusive, though one ancestor of each generation may have been a white person.

Section 4. *Be it further enacted,* that in addition to cases in which freedmen, free Negroes, and mulattoes are now by law competent witnesses, freedmen, free Negroes, or mulattoes shall be competent in civil cases when a party or parties to the suit, either plaintiff or plaintiffs, defendant or defendants, also in cases where freedmen, free Negroes, and mulattoes is or are either plaintiff or plaintiffs, defendant or defendants, and a white person or white persons is or are the opposing party or parties, plaintiff or plaintiffs, defendant or defendants. They shall also be competent witnesses in all criminal prosecutions where the crime charged is alleged to have been committed by a white person upon or against the person or property of a freedman, free Negro, or mulatto:
Provided, that in all cases said witnesses shall be examined in open court on the stand, except, however, they may be examined before the grand jury, and shall in all cases be subject to the rules and tests of the common law as to competency and credibility.

Section 5. *Be it further enacted,* that every freedman, free Negro, and mulatto shall, on the second Monday of January 1866, and annually thereafter, have a lawful home or employment, and shall have a written evidence thereof, as follows, to wit: if living in any incorporated city, town, or village, a license from the mayor thereof; and if living outside of any incorporated city, town, or village, from the member of the board of police of his beat, authorizing him or her to do irregular and job work, or

a written contract, as provided in Section 6 of this act, which licenses may be revoked for cause, at any time, by the authority granting the same.

Section 6. *Be it further enacted,* that all contracts for labor made with freedmen, free Negroes, and mulattoes for a longer period than one month shall be in writing and in duplicate, attested and read to said freedman, free Negro, or mulatto by a beat, city, or county officer, or two disinterested white persons of the county in which the labor is to be performed, of which each party shall have one; and said contracts shall be taken and held as entire contracts; and if the laborer shall quit the service of the employer before expiration of his term of service without good cause, he shall forfeit his wages for that year, up to the time of quitting.

Section 7. *Be it further enacted,* that every civil officer shall, and every person may, arrest and carry back to his or her legal employer any freedman, free Negro, or mulatto who shall have quit the service of his or her employer before the expiration of his or her term of service without good cause, and said officer and person shall be entitled to receive for arresting and carrying back every deserting employee aforesaid the sum of $5, and 10 cents per mile from the place of arrest to the place of delivery, and the same shall be paid by the employer, and held as a setoff for so much against the wages of said deserting employee:

Provided, that said arrested party, after being so returned, may appeal to a justice of the peace or member of the board of police of the county, who, on notice to the alleged employer, shall try summarily whether said appellant is legally employed by the alleged employer and his good cause to quit said employer; either party shall have the right of appeal to the county court, pending which the alleged deserter shall be remanded to the alleged employer or otherwise disposed of as shall be right and just, and the decision of the county court shall be final.

Section 8. *Be it further enacted,* that upon affidavit made by the employer of any freedman, free Negro, or mulatto, or other credible person before any justice of the peace or member of the board of police, that any freedman, free Negro, or mulatto, legally employed by said employer, has illegally deserted said employment, such justice of the peace or member of the board of police shall issue his warrant or warrants, returnable before himself, or other such officer, directed to any sheriff, constable, or special deputy, commanding him to arrest said deserter and return him or her to said employer, and the like proceedings shall be had as provided in the preceding section; and it shall be lawful for any officer to whom such warrant shall be directed to execute said warrant in any county of this state, and that said warrant may be transmitted without endorsement to any like officer of another county, to be executed and returned as aforesaid, and the said employer shall pay the cost of said warrants and arrest and return, which shall be set off for so much against the wages of said deserter.

Section 9. *Be it further enacted,* that if any person shall persuade or attempt to persuade, entice, or cause any freedman, free Negro, or mulatto to desert from the legal employment of any person before the expiration of his or her term of service, or shall knowingly employ any such deserting freedman, free Negro, or mulatto, or shall knowingly give or sell to any such deserting freedman, free Negro, or mulatto any food, raiment, or other thing, he or she shall be guilty of a misdemeanor; and, upon conviction, shall be fined not less than $25 and not more than $200 and the costs; and, if said fine and costs shall not be immediately paid, the court shall sentence said convict to not exceeding two months' imprisonment in the county jail, and he or she shall moreover be liable to the party injured in damages:

> *Provided,* if any person shall, or shall attempt to, persuade, entice, or cause any freedman, free Negro, or mulatto to desert from any legal employment of any person with the view to employ said

freedman, free Negro, or mulatto without the limits of this state, such person, on conviction, shall be fined not less than $50 and not more than $1500 and costs; and, if said fine and costs shall not be immediately paid, the court shall sentence said convict to not exceeding six months' imprisonment in the county jail,

Section 10. *Be it further enacted,* that it shall be lawful for any freedman, free Negro, or mulatto to charge any white person, freedman, free Negro, or mulatto, by affidavit, with any criminal offense against his or her person or property; and, upon such affidavit, the proper process shall be issued and executed as if said affidavit was made by a white person; and it shall be lawful for any freedman, free Negro, or mulatto, in any action, suit, or controversy pending or about to be instituted, in any court of law or equity of this state. to make all needful and lawful affidavits, as shall be necessary for the institution, prosecution, or defense of such suit or controversy.

Section 11. *Be it further enacted,* that the penal laws of this state, in all cases not otherwise specially provided for, shall apply and extend to all freedmen, free Negroes, and mulattoes.

IV.

Penal Code

Section 1. *Be it enacted by the legislature of the state of Mississippi,* that no freedman, free Negro, or mulatto not in the military service of the United States government, and not licensed so to do by the board of police of his or her county, shall keep or carry firearms of any kind, or any ammunition, dirk, or Bowie knife; and, on conviction *thereof in the county* court, shall be punished by fine, not exceeding $10, and pay the costs of such proceedings, and all such arms or ammunition shall be forfeited to the informer; and it shall be the duty of every civil and military officer to arrest any freedman, free Negro, or mulatto found with any such arms or ammunition, and cause him or her to be committed for trial in default of bail.

Section 2. *Be it further enacted,* that any freedman, free Negro, or mulatto committing riots, routs, affrays, trespasses, malicious mischief, cruel treatment to animals, seditious speeches, insulting gestures, language, or acts, or assaults on any person, disturbance of the peace, exercising the function of a minister of the Gospel without a license from some regularly organized church, vending spirituous or intoxicating liquors, or committing any other misdemeanor t e punishment of which is not specifically provided for by law shall, upon conviction thereof in the county court, be fined not less than $10 and not more than $100, and may be imprisoned, at the discretion of the court, not exceeding thirty days.

Section 3. *Be it further enacted,* that if any white person shall sell, lend, or give to any freedman, free Negro, or mulatto any firearms, dirk, or Bowie knife, or ammunition, or any spirituous or intoxicating liquors, such person or persons so offending, upon conviction thereof in the county court of his or her county, shall be fined not exceeding $50, and may be imprisoned, at the discretion of the court, not exceeding thirty days:

Provided, that any master, mistress, or employer of any freedman, free Negro, or mulatto may give to any freedman, free Negro, or mulatto apprenticed to or employed by such master, mistress, or employer spirituous or intoxicating liquors, but not in sufficient quantities to produce intoxication.

Section 4. *Be it further enacted,* that all the penal and criminal laws now in force in this state defining offenses and prescribing the mode of punishment for crimes and misdemeanors committed by slaves, free Negroes, or mulattoes be and the same are hereby reenacted and declared to be in full force and effect against freedmen, free Negroes, and mulattoes, except so far m the mode and manner of trial and punishment have been changed or altered by law.

Section 5. *Be it further enacted,* that if any freedman, free Negro, or mulatto convicted of any of the misdemeanors provided against in this act shall fail-or refuse, for the space of five days after conviction, to pay the fine and costs imposed, such person shall be hired out by the sheriff or other officer, at public outcry, to any white person who will pay said fine and all costs and take such convict for the shortest time. (Westport, Conn., 1972) Ark. Narr., Vol. 8, 175- 179.

Louisiana Black Code

Sec. 1. Be it ordained by the police jury of the parish of St. Landry, That no negro shall be allowed to pass within the limits of said parish without special permit in writing from his employer. Whoever shall violate this provision shall pay a fine of two dollars and fifty cents, or in default thereof shall be forced to work four days on the public road, or suffer corporeal punishment as provided hereinafter.

Sec. 3. No negro shall be permitted to rent or keep a house within said parish. Any negro violating this provision shall be immediately ejected and compelled to find an employer; and any person who shall rent, or give the use of any house to any negro, in violation of this section, shall pay a fine of five dollars for each offence.

Sec. 4. . . . Every negro is required to be in the regular service of some white person, or former owner, who shall be held responsible for the conduct of said negro. But said employer or former owner may permit said negro to hire his own time by special permission in writing, which permission shall not extend over seven days at any one time. . . .

Sec. 5. . . . No public meetings or congregations of negroes shall be allowed within said parish after sunset; but such public meetings and congregations may be held between the hours of sunrise and sunset, by the special permission in writing of the captain of patrol, within whose beat such meetings shall take place. . . .

Sec. 6. . . . No negro shall be permitted to preach,

exhort, or otherwise declaim to congregations of colored people, without a special permission in writing from the president of the police jury. . . .

Sec. 7. . . . No negro who is not in the military service shall be allowed to carry fire-arms, or any kind of weapons, within the parish, without the special written permission of his employers, approved and indorsed by the nearest and most convenient chief of patrol. . . .

Sec. 8. . . . No negro shall sell, barter, or exchange any articles of merchandise or traffic within said parish without the special written permission of his employer,

specifying the article of sale, barter or traffic. . . .

Sec. 9. . . . Any negro found drunk, within the said parish shall pay a fine of five dollars, or in default thereof work five days on the public road, or suffer corporeal punishment as hereinafter provided.

Sec. 11. . . . It shall be the duty of every citizen to act as a police officer for the detection of offences and the apprehension of offenders, who shall be immediately handed over to the proper captain or chief of patrol. . . .

GLOSSARY

apprenticeship: a system by which a person is bound by indenture to learn a craft or trade

chose in action: the right to sue

corporeal: bodily; material or tangible

indenture: a contract that bounds a person to service of some form of work to possibly pay off a debt

lewd: wicked or vile; lascivious; inclined to be lustful

Mulatto: a term used in reference to individuals who are of mixed race but usually specifically designates any person who has a black grandparent or parent

pauper: a term used to describe a very poor person

tippling shops: stores that sold liquor in bottles or by the glass that was to be drunk at that location

vagrancy: the state of being an idle person who possesses no means of support, such as a beggar

Document Analysis

Southern lawmakers passed Black Codes in order to place the status of blacks as a form of legal servitude. They did not embrace black freedom after the Civil War concluded, and their fears dictated the laws they desired to be put in place as a result of Union victory. In the minds of white Southerners, free African Americans posed a menacing threat because they might refuse to work or could not be trusted to perform the labor with which they were tasked. Furthermore, they posed serious threats against their former masters and other white landowners. Most evident in this regard is that economic motivations undergirded the Black Codes of the South, as the Codes clearly contradicted the free labor ideology that the North espoused. Moreover, it is clear that Southerners wanted to keep in place an economic system characterized by plantation agriculture in the postwar years. The Southern economy was fueled by free labor up into the nineteenth century, so white Southerners wanted to force former slaves to work for them under the terms that they themselves decided. They viewed the freed slaves in the same way they had viewed their slaves and were determined to dominate and control them in the same fashion. Emancipation dissipated the former ties between masters and slaves which incited fear and paranoia in white Southerners that their former slaves no longer considered themselves as savage and inferior, a prerequisite for their acceptance of the idea that they were human labor. Mississippi passed the harshest set of laws in its Black Code, and those laws are emblematic for what the Black Codes in the South sought to achieve. The Code is divided into three sections designed to limit the civil rights of African Americans, to force African Americans into unpaid labor, and to render them vagrants and thus subject to incarceration. These impulses reveal that white lawmakers sought to maintain political, economic, and social control over African Americans and mulattos because they feared them as a threat to white hegemony once slavery was dismantled by Thirteenth Amendment. It becomes clear that blacks still possessed no voice in the political system during the Reconstruction era following the Civil War, and that the South still viewed African Americans as inferior to the white populace. Such attitudes persisted not only throughout the Reconstruction era but in the decades that followed, laying the groundwork for the Jim Crow system which plagued race relations in the South well into the twentieth century.

All public laws such as the Black Codes are passed in order to mold the socioeconomic behavior in the public sphere and sometimes the private one. The denizens and visitors of those living in the Southern states where the Black Codes were passed thus were the intended audience for such laws that structured their social relations and socioeconomic structures. However, Southern residents, law officials, lawyers and even some judges most like did not read the entire text of the laws themselves. Nonetheless, the presence of the Black Codes shaped socioeconomic behaviors and fostered an environment of fear for the black population while ensuring that white hegemony remained, especially in the political and economic systems. They further reveal the structural racism embedded in the legal system in the South that has persisted from the inception of the United States into the Reconstruction era and the epochs thereafter. The identity of the South hinged on the notion of white hegemony while the character and nature of those of African origin were deemed inferior to

the character and nature of the white man. The Black Codes reflect the South's refusal to concede to a Northern conception of the black population that considered them a free people worthy of U.S. citizenship.

Through the Black Codes, white Southerners sought to control the labor of former slaves despite appearing to grant them some rights regarding property. African Americans possessed the right to buy and sell any property that was not real estate, meaning they could not own land and thus were forced to rent it out. In doing so, Southern lawmakers ensured that African Americans would remain dependent on them for both housing as well as labor. In Mississippi, African Americans were permitted to rent property in towns and cities only if local government officials allowed them to. Because local government often forbade them from renting property, African Americans were forced to live in the countryside where they would work as agricultural laborers. White Southerners believed that agricultural work befitted former slaves, who could not perform any other kind of work. This elucidates a powerful stereotype of former slaves that emerged after the war: that blacks belonged on the plantation.

Various other ways to control labor of African Americans appear in the Codes. African Americans were expected to have a legally valid address and some form of employment at the outset of every calendar year which would coincide with when labor contracts were negotiated and signed. These contracts offered them a degree of protection, but the language used in the Codes implicate that white Southerners still did not view former slaves as free. Black "servants" signed contracts in order to serve their "masters," and the contract would include a list of obligations the servant owed his or her master and mistress. The "servant" did not have the ability to break their contract, and if they did they would be prosecuted in court and would be forced to forfeit their wages. Such language reflects a powerful stereotype about ex-slaves that emerged after the war ended: blacks were naturally and inherently servile. Those who broke their contracts were treated in a very similar way to how runaway apprentices were treated by law enforcement. Some Black Codes even limited the occupations blacks could have to being a servant or farmer. If they sought any other occupation, they would be heavily fined. In doing so, it becomes clear that white Southerners were skeptical that African Americans could be trusted to perform their labor.

While controlling the labor of blacks remained the

primary focus of the Black Codes, they also regulated the social rights and power of African Americans and mulattoes. Slaves possessed the legal right to marry within their own race, but the Codes made it illegal for any person classified as black to intermarry with a white person. For clarification of who is considered black in the eyes of the law, the Codes define a black person as an individual who has a black great-grandparent. This stipulation reflects Southern desires to keep the white race pure, a sentiment that pervaded U.S. society into the twentieth century. States passed several anti-miscegenation laws that were not repealed until the 1950s. Such laws reflect the notion that African-American blood was inferior and would soil the purity of white blood and thus the white race. This view of the African American as biologically inferior despite being free further conveys Southern efforts to preserve white hegemony in a post-slavery society.

Other sections in the Codes outline the rights blacks have in the courts, and many of the stipulations reflect the provisions of the antebellum slave codes. Former slaves and mulattoes had the right to testify against each other, but they could not testify against a white person accused of committing a crime against a black person in any criminal proceedings. Finally, blacks were limited in their Second Amendment right to bear arms, as the Codes did not allow them to possess swords or firearms unless they possessed a license. If caught, they would receive physical punishment and could be forced to work. This provision of the Codes suggests the overriding fear white Southerners had of blacks owning guns and the possibility of mutiny or attack. As a result, the image of a black individual holding a gun rendered him or her as dangerous. This fear of blacks possessing guns in the public sphere persisted into the twentieth century. When in the 1960s members of the radical and militant civil rights group known as the Black Panthers protested on the streets wearing guns, they were immediately arrested. Many of them were convicted and put on death row for merely protesting while holding weapons. Thus, the legacy of the Black Codes can be seen through this public imagining of black people who own guns as a threat to society.

The most well-known part of the Black Codes pertains to the regulation of the relationship between a master and his apprentice, and it demonstrates that white Southerners sought to maintain slavery in some form even after it was outlawed. Blacks under the age of eighteen whose parents could not properly care for

them or who were orphans were required to become apprentices under persons who could competently and sufficiently take care of them. African American orphans received far inferior treatment to white orphans. The length of an orphan's apprenticeship was contingent upon his or her gender: female orphans served usually until the age of eighteen, while male juveniles were apprentices until the age of twenty-one. If apprentices ran away before serving their entire indenture, their masters possessed the authority to recapture and punish them accordingly. The Codes did allow, however, for apprentices to challenge the right of their masters to hold them against their own will. If the apprentice brought a good case to the court that validated that he or she had a right to end the apprenticeship early, then the court had the authority to release the apprentice and fine the master. This section clearly demonstrates the determination of white Southerners to force former slaves to work for them under the terms that they dictated. Such provisions unveil that white Southerners sought to keep former slaves in legal servitude, as these juveniles worked without pay. Slave labor thus continued to fuel the Southern economy even when slavery was outlawed.

The vagrancy laws included in the Black Codes further expose how white Southerners used broad and vague language as a way to legally control blacks and their daily activities. Through them, white Southerners sought to regain control over property that was once theirs. Vagrancy laws have historically targeted racial minorities in the United States because they were viewed as an undesirable caste. These laws demonstrate white Southerners' fears that former slaves refused to work and presented them as a menace to society unworthy of social, political or economic clout. They became a central tool to regulate black workers and force them to labor for their former masters. The laws defined and policed a racial landscape that remained in place for decades to follow. Signs of vagrancy included excessive drinking of alcohol, gambling, and juggling. All individuals who were not employed, were frivolous with their money, and did not take care of themselves or those who depend on them were classified as vagrants by law. However, employers retained the authority to deduct wages from any employee they found guilty of disobedience, destruction of property, theft, or truancy. Appeals would be heard by local courts or justices of peace, but African American employees accused seldom ever received a favorable ruling. Those convicted of being vagrants were subject to fines up to one hundred dollars, and if they could not pay their fines they would be forced to work them off. They also faced the possibility of imprisonment for a short amount of time. Thus, the possibility of being convicted of vagrancy kept black laborers from leaving their masters' plantations. Such provisions mirror the antebellum slave codes and reveal that white Southerners sought to keep former slaves in a state of legal servitude. Such provisions reveal how desperate white Southerners were for blacks to return to agricultural labor, and that white Southerners relied on vagrancy provisions to force former slaves to sign labor contracts.

These Black Codes ultimately fostered an environment of fear for the newly freed blacks. In the Louisiana code, section eleven states that all citizens have the duty to act as a police officer in order "for the detection of offences and the apprehension of offenders." This provision gives the authority to any citizen—implied to be a white person—to accuse and apprehend any person who violates the Codes. The heightened racial tensions meant that blacks were falsely charged and often punished because of the vague and broad language of the Codes. This environment of fear conveyed by white Southerners resulted in African Americans finding themselves in a situation that arguably rivaled slavery.

Essential Themes

While the Black Codes severely limited the freedoms of former slaves, African Americans did make some progress, albeit transient progress, during the Reconstruction era. The restraining nature and overtly racist undertones of the Codes sparked black resistance to their enforcement. Furthermore, many Northerners contended that the Codes violated the principles of free labor enshrined in the U.S. Constitution and reflected the Southern sentiment that blacks were still the natural property of whites. As a result, Congress took over the oversight of Reconstruction and passed the Civil Rights Act in 1866 despite President Johnson's veto. This act enumerated the rights of U.S. citizens, such as the right to hold property, the right to buy and sell property. However, Congress feared that the Supreme Court would invalidate the act and thus proposed the Fourteenth Amendment, which recognized African Americans as citizens and asserted that they could not be sold for money. As a result, white Southerners rioted against the encroachment of blacks into formerly all white institutions, which lead to Radical Reconstruction in the

South in 1867. During Radical Reconstruction, African Americans were enfranchised with the passage of the Fifteenth Amendment. Some blacks even won elections to enter Southern states' governments as well as U.S. Congress. Most egregious features of the Black Codes were suspended by the Freedman's Bureau even before the civil rights act was passed. The Black Codes thus produced some meaningful changes for blacks by inciting a response from the North and the U.S. federal government.

The passage of the Black Codes convey Southern lawmakers' unwavering commitment to ensure that white hegemony remained in the South as well as their desire to ensure that the plantation agriculture that fueled the Southern economy for centuries would survive. Support for Reconstruction declined into the 1870s because of the rise of white vigilante groups such as the KKK that used violence to keep African Americans from exercising the freedoms and rights accorded to them. By the end of Reconstruction in 1877, the social, political, and economic gains blacks had made were effectively undone as a result of the widespread efforts of white supremacists. The Black Codes thus remained intact in the majority of the Southern states. They paved the way for Jim Crow laws, as many provisions of the Black Codes served as the foundation for the Jim Crow system which remained intact until the 1960s. As laws that regulated everyday activity, the Black Codes served as a form of personal and collective discipline of the black population and functioned as an instrument in maintaining white supremacy. They ensured that "whiteness" was maintained in the Jim Crow era through the quotidian as well as the legal precedents sets. The personal and collective discipline of a certain sector of society forms one fact of the apartheid state, and thus the legacy of the Black Codes is evident well into the twentieth century.

Madeline Weissman, M.A.

Bibliography

"Black Codes." *History.com*. A&E Television Networks, n.d. Web. 04 Oct. 2013.

Kelley, Robin D. G., and Earl Lewis. *To Make Our World Anew: A History of African Americans*. Oxford: Oxford UP, 2000. Print.

Smith, Page. *Trial by Fire: A People's History of the Civil War and Reconstruction*. New York: McGraw-Hill, 1982. Print.

Wilson, Theodore Brantner. *The Black Codes of the*

South (Southern Historical Publications, number 6). University: U of Alabama P, 1965. Print.

Additional Reading
Cohen, William. *Negro Involuntary Servitude in the South, 1865-1940: A Preliminary Analysis.* New Orleans: Southern Historical Association, 1976. Print.
DuBois, William Edward Burghardt. *Black Reconstruction in America.* New York: Russell [and] Russell, 1968. Print.
Foner, Eric. *Reconstruction: America's Unfinished Revolution, 1863-1877.* New York: Harper & Row, 1988. Print.
Schurz, Carl. *Report on the Condition of the South.* Teddington, Middlesex, U.K.: Echo Library, 2006.
Stewart, Gary. "Black Codes and Broken Windows: The Legacy of Racial Hegemony in Anti-gang Civil Injunctions." *The Yale Law Journal* 107.7 (1998): 2249-279. Print.

■ "The North Owes the Colored Race a Deep Obligation"

Date: March 16, 1870
Author: Revels, Hiram
Genre: speech

"I rose to plead for protection for the defenseless race... the people of the North owe to the colored race a deep obligation which is no easy matter to fulfill... the colored race saved to the noble women of New England and the middle states men on whom they lean today for security and safety"

Summary Overview

Using vivid language and rhetoric in this speech to the president, Hiram Revels, the first African American to be elected to the U.S. Senate and the embodiment of the Fifteenth Amendment, presented himself as a representative of all free black men and women throughout the country. He passionately spoke about reinstating black lawmakers in Georgia who were forced out of office in 1868 by moderate white Republicans and Democrats. Revels argued that the North was obligated to support these black legislators because of all of the sacrifice blacks gave during the war in order to save the Union. Rather than engaging in bloody revolt against their former oppressors, African Americans exhibited responsible, loyal behavior. Thus, they deserved the right to vote and hold political office, which the federal and state law sanctioned.

Revels' entrance into the U.S. Senate marked him as the voice and leader of African Americans during this time period. He personified African American freedom and enfranchisement. Although he was a moderate politician who was embraced by both Republicans and Democrats, this portion of Revels' speech reveals that Revels unapologetically refused to be diplomatic on the issue of denying African Americans their basic rights as American citizens. It also reveals the historical trend within the counter-narrative of African American history that African Americans as well as other subaltern groups participated in war efforts in order to prove their loyalty and gain equal rights in an American society that privileged the white male.

Defining Moment

The conclusion of the Civil War ushered in a period known as Reconstruction in which the Union sought to reconcile with the Confederate states and reconstruct the South. Because President Abraham Lincoln was assassinated shortly after the Civil war ended, his vice president Andrew Johnson was put in charge of reintegrating the South back into the Union. Republicans dominated in the former Confederate states and would only allow Southern states to be readmitted into the Union if the Thirteenth and Fourteenth Amendments were ratified into the Constitution. Passed in 1865, the Thirteenth Amendment made it illegal to have people perform coerced work unless incarcerated while the Fourteenth Amendment, passed in 1868 under the first Reconstruction Act, recognized African Americans as citizens. This right had been denied to slaves in the Dred Scott U.S. Supreme Court decision, which stated that African Americans could not testify in court because they were not citizens. Under the Reconstruction

642

Act, new constitutions were drawn up in the Southern states, and the South was redrawn into five military districts and subject to martial law. Finally, in 1870, the Fifteenth Amendment was ratified and guaranteed the right to vote for African American men. It enabled African Americans to be elected into the U.S. House of Representatives and U.S. Senate and thus set the stage for Hiram Revels to be elected into the U.S. Senate early that year.

Congress took over Reconstruction from President Johnson in 1867 and implemented its own vision for rebuilding the South. This period differed from Presidential Reconstruction because Congress supported the political rights of former slaves while President Johnson neglected their well-being. During this period African Americans were elected into office, although several white Southern men refused to vote because they disliked that suffrage was extended to African American men. Over 600 African Americans were elected to state legislatures in the South; whites turned to both violent and nonviolent tactics to try and keep African Americans out of the government. Black Codes were enacted in the Southern states that limited the rights of African Americans such as the right to enter into contracts, live in cities or towns, and bear arms. Vigilante groups such as the Ku Klux Klan sprung up in order to terrorize blacks and prevent them from exercising their right to vote.

Despite the attempts of Southern Democrats to prevent the U.S. Senate from allowing Revels to be a senator, the majority Republicans in the Senate prevailed in seating him. In his first speech to the Congress, he spoke before a packed gallery and chamber filled with white lawmakers as well as black men and women and addressed a bill regarding readmitting the former Confederate state of Georgia back into the Union. The bill addressed the representation in the Union for Georgia that included an amendment that made it illegal for African Americans to hold state office. Revels contended that the Republican Party and the North owed the black legislators in Georgia their support. In 1868, voters in Georgia ratified a new state constitution that extended suffrage to African American men, a necessary step under the stipulations of Congressional Reconstruction to allow Georgia to be readmitted to the Union. In that same year, twenty-nine black legislators were elected into the state house of representatives and three to the Georgia senate. When the state legislature convened later that year, however, white legislators from both parties unseated the black lawmakers because they claimed that the state constitution did not allow African Americans to hold office. African in Americans in Georgia turned to the federal government to intervene and force Georgia to comply with the Fourteenth and Fifteenth Amendments. Revels spoke vehemently in favor of getting the black lawmakers reinstated as a prerequisite for Georgia to be readmitted. Eventually, a congressional mandate was agreed upon that reinstated the black lawmakers in order for Georgia to rejoin the Union in July 1870.

As the 1870s wore on, the North felt less inclined to support Reconstruction in the South because of the turmoil it was causing in the South. African American politicians and members of the Republican Party were being driven from their offices and murdered in their homes by disgruntled white Southerners. Northerners felt that peace could only be achieved if Southern whites won back control of both state governments and African Americans despite the fact that whites would dominate once again and undermine the notion of equal rights. White Democrats regained control of the South and enacted various measures to prevent African Americans from voting through poll taxes, property qualifications, and other means. Although Revels embodied the achievements of Reconstruction, those achievements were short-lived, as the Reconstruction acts were struck down and the status of African Americans soon resonated with their status in the antebellum period.

Author Biography

Hiram Revels was born on September 27, 1827 in Fayetteville, North Carolina a freeman to parents of European and African ancestry. Early on he received an education by an African American woman at an all-black school. In 1838 he moved to Lincolnton, North Carolina to live with his older brother where he worked as an apprentice in his brother's barbershop. He attended the Union Quaker Seminary in Indiana and then furthered his studies at a black seminary in Ohio. In 1845, Revels became a minister at African Methodist Episcopal Church and worked as a preacher and teacher throughout the Midwest states. Throughout his career as a religious teacher and preacher, Revels faced some opposition and was even imprisoned in 1854 for preaching the gospel to African Americans. In 1862, he served as a chaplain in the U.S. Army where he partook in the recruitment and organization of black regiments for the

Union during the Civil War in both Missouri and Maryland. When African Americans were allowed to fight for the Union in 1862, Revels served as a chaplain in various campaigns, most notably one in Vicksburg.

Revels' political career as a Republican took off during Reconstruction. In 1869, he was elected to Congress to represent Adams County in the state senate in Mississippi. Because less than one thousand free blacks in Mississippi received an education, Revels' entrance into politics because essential to the Republican Party to rally a new electorate after the war when blacks were enfranchised. Although reluctant to enter into politics out of fear of violent opposition, Revels was quickly embraced by both whites and blacks because he was moderate and held empathetic political beliefs. In 1870, Revels was overwhelmingly elected by the Mississippi state senate to finish out the last year of the term of a vacated U.S. Senate seat as a result of the Civil War, which made him the first African American to serve in the U.S. Congress when he was sworn in on February 25, 1870. Democrats opposed Revels filling the seat and pointed to the Dred Scott decision, which stated that African Americans could not testify in court because they were not citizens. Furthermore, they contended, no African American man was a citizen prior to the ratification of the Fourteenth Amendment in 1868,

which meant that Revels did not meet the requirement for holding political office that mandated that he had to be a U.S. citizen for at least nine years. Nonetheless, Revels was elected because Republicans dominated the U.S. Senate, and the vote split along party lines.

Once sworn into the Senate, Revels was assigned to the Committee on Education and Labor and the Committee on the District of Columbia. He became the voice and representative for all black men and women throughout the country, and he advocated for reinstating black legislators who were forced from office in Georgia by white Democrats in 1868. As a moderate, he also favored granting amnesty to former Confederates as long as they swore an oath of loyalty. Revels promoted civil rights for African Americans throughout the year he held a Senate seat. At the conclusion of his term, he declined various positions offered to him by President Ulysses Grant and opted to return to Mississippi and serve as the first president of Alcorn University, an all-black college. Revels retired in 1882 and died suddenly at a religious conference on January 16, 1901. Despite his limited success while he served the U.S. Congress, Revels was a symbol of Union victory in the Civil War as well as the idealism evident during Radical Reconstruction.

HISTORICAL DOCUMENT

I remarked, Mr. President, that I rose to plead for protection for the defenseless race who now send their delegation to the seat of government to sue for that which this Congress alone can secure to them. And let me say further. That the people of the North owe to the colored race a deep obligation which is no easy matter to fulfill. When the federal armies were thinned by death and disaster, and somber clouds overhung the length and breadth of the Republic, and the very air was pregnant with the rumors of foreign interference—in those dark days of defeat whose memories even yet haunt us as an ugly dream, from what source did our nation in its seeming death throes gain additional and new-found prayer? It was the sable sons of the South that valiantly rushed to the rescue, and but for their intrepidity and ardent daring many a northern fireside would miss today paternal

counsels of brotherly love.

Sir, I repeat the fact that the colored race saved to the noble women of New England and the middle states men on whom they lean today for security and safety. Many of my race, the representatives of these men on the field of battle, sleep in the countless graves of the South. If those quiet resting-places of our honored dead could speak today what a mighty voice, like to the rushing of a mighty wind, would come up from those sepulchral homes! Could we resist the eloquent pleadings of their appeal? Ah, sir, I think that this question of immediate and ample protection for the loyal people of Georgia would lose its legal technicalities, and we would cease to hesitate in our provisions for their instant relief. Again, I regret the delay on other grounds. The taunt is frequently flung at us that Nemesis more terrible than the Greek impersonation of the anger of the gods awaits her hour of direful retribution. We are told that at no distant day a great uprising of the American people will demand that the Reconstruction acts of Congress be undone and blotted forever from the annals of legislative enactment. I inquire, sir, if this delay in affording protection to the loyalists of the state of Georgia does not lend an uncomfortable significancy to this boasting sneer with which we so often meet? Delay is perilous at best; for us it is as true in legislation as in psychic, that the longer we procrastinate to apply the proper remedies the more chronic becomes the malady that we seek to heal.

The land wants such
As dare with rigor execute the laws.
Her festered members must be lanced and tented
He's a bad surgeon that for pity spares
The part corrupted till the gangrene spread
And all the body perish. He that's merciful
Unto the bad is cruel to the good.

GLOSSARY

annals: a record of events in a specific year or a record in a historical chronicle

ardent: passionate or intensely devoted

festered: full of pus; putrefied or rotten

gangrene: death of soft tissue that results in putrefaction

intrepidity: state of being fearless or undaunted

malady: a disease or disorder of the body

sable: the color black

sepulchral: pertaining to burial; funereal

Document Analysis

The Reconstruction era in the South offered a glimmer of hope for African Americans in the South to obtain equal rights as citizens and to be integrated into the political process. The Fourteenth and Fifteenth Amendments recognized African Americans as citizens under the law and enfranchised African American men, which opened up the doors for African American men to be elected into office. Although African American members symbolized a new democratic order in the United States, they did not achieve as much success as their white counterparts who held higher political positions during Reconstruction. Nonetheless, they had a significant role as advocates for America's newest citizens. On February 25, 1870, Hiram Revels, a highly educated and religious man, became the first black man to be elected into the U.S. Congress to finish out the term of former Mississippi senator. Revels embraced his role as an advocate for all African Americans and articulated his beliefs unapologetically in his maiden speech. In a poignant part of his speech, Revels argues that the North owed the "colored race" protection as free citizens because of their service to the Union during the Civil War. Fervent in his conviction, Revels uses vivid and descriptive language to paint African Americans as loyal saviors for this country during the most desperate and desolate times. He alludes to the fact that despite being free African Americans remain a "defenseless race" in need of protection by the federal government. Addressing a packed gallery and chambers composed of both white and black spectators for the first time, Revels delivered a passionate and eloquent plea to legislators to address and rectify the injustice that occurred in Georgia. Revels depicts himself as a staunch advocate for and representative of all African Americans throughout the country and conveys a sense of hope that the government would recognize and appreciate the sacrifices African Americans made in order to save the Union.

Despite the fact that African Americans were free and equal citizens by law, Revels characterizes them as a "defenseless race," which the expulsion of black lawmakers in Georgia clearly demonstrated. In November 1867, an election in Georgia was held under Congressional Reconstruction policy in order to create a new state congress who would draft a new state constitution. Both black and white voters participated, although many white voters abstained from voting because they were upset that African Americans had the right to partake in the elections. As a result, several black candidates were voted into office. However, by 1868 white legislators in Georgia concluded that the Reconstruction acts were unconstitutional and asserted that anyone with 1/8 African blood or more could not serve in the state legislature. As a result, twenty nine black lawmakers were forcibly removed from office. Congress did not intervene in Georgia, thereby allowing white lawmakers to infringe on the rights of black people preserved in Georgia's new state constitution. Although a moderate politician throughout his career, Revels felt obligated to address this injustice in his inaugural speech as a member of the Senate because he wanted to show that he would become the defender of justice for all African Americans in the federal government since they have never had one before.

Using vivid and emotion language, Revels imparts his belief that the North was in debt to African Americans because they helped secure a Union victory during the bleakest moments of the Civil War. During the war, many male slaves sought liberty by running away to the Union lines despite receiving harsh treatment by Union soldiers. At the outset of the war, the Union army put escaped slaves to work as cooks, construction workers, drivers and blacksmiths. In 1862, African American men were allowed to serve in the army because less white men wanted to serve in the Union army "thinned by death and disaster." Most African American soldiers were former slaves in the South, and they served in all-black regiments that faced unfair government policies such as lower pay and inferior weaponry. Many whites in the North did not think that African Americans were

fit or competent to fight because slavery rendered them servile and docile. However, once they began to fight, their white critics had a quick change of mind and were surprised how valiantly and courageously they fought. Revels stresses these qualities in his speech when he characterizes them as valiant and intrepid.

Revels cites how slaves quelled the looming threat of foreign interference to help the South win the war. President Lincoln issued the Emancipation Proclamation in 1863, which freed the slaves in Southern states but not in the border states. Lincoln believed that freeing the slaves would hasten the end of the war by breaking the South's resistance. Furthermore, it was a preemptive measure to safeguard against the possibility of Great Britain entering the war on the South's side because England depended on cotton produced in the South. Britain espoused an anti-slavery sentiment, so by freeing the slaves Lincoln was confident that England would stay out of the war and northern victory would ensue. As a result of their contributions once freed, the Union army ultimately prevailed against the Confederate army, which is why Revels believes the North owes the black legislators in Georgia protection.

Revels uses hyperbolic language in order to emphasize how indispensable African Americans were to the Union's victory and to convince his black spectators that he would fight to protect their rights while in office. The "sable son of the South" bravely came to rescue the Union, and without them many northern families would not have survived the war. He reiterates the fact that without the help of African Americans during the war, the white elite would have perished. It is ironically those "noble women of New England" and "men in the middle states" that African Americans saved are the very people that African Americans rely on for safety and security. However, they remain a defenseless race despite their contributions. Revels' assertion alludes not only to the injustice in Georgia but also to the reality that since emancipation former slaves faced unchecked violence by vigilante groups, white mobs and disgruntled Democrats. Violence or the threat of violence against African Americans was widespread and random. An age of lynchings commenced during Reconstruction whereby white Southerners would murder African Americans as a spectacle for the public to see. These heinous attacks occurred often with the participation of law enforcement officials, and the perpetrators were seldom punished or punished very lightly. The murder of African Americans was thus viewed not as murder in the eyes of the law but pushed into a separate legal category by a government undergirded by white hegemony. Furthermore, white vigilante groups formed in the South to terrorize African Americans and prevent them from exercising their rights as free people. Revels recognized the fabric of American society for African Americans changed very little years after emancipation, so he invoked hyperbolic language to depict the African American contributions during the Civil War as indispensable to saving both the lives of northerners as well as the Union itself.

Framing his plea for federal intervention in Georgia around the concepts of justice and injustice, Revels stresses that the loyalty shown and sacrifices made by African Americans during the Civil War must be rewarded. Countless black men lost their lives fighting to save the Union, and Revels declares that if they were alive they would plead to the federal government to help protect their civil rights that the U.S. Constitution promised to protect. Revels makes an emotional appeal to the U.S. Congress to not let those black men and women who protected them and preserved the Union die in vain. He represented their intermediary, and he felt an obligation to listen to their pleas for protection. Using the metaphor of illness to represent injustice, Revels suggests that if the federal government does not protect its loyal citizens in the state of Georgia then other states will follow in Georgia's footsteps and the disease of injustice would become more "chronic." It is this "malady" that the government sought to eradicate with the passage of the Fourteenth and Fifteenth Amendment. Revels' speech thus criticizes the apathy of the federal government to protect its loyal citizens in the face of racial injustice. This emotional plea to the government to stand up for African Americans suggests that because many African Americans died both during slavery times and during the war that Revels saw himself in his political role as the voice and representative of the black community. Many black members were in the audience and were hopeful that he would stand up and vouch for them, which Revels did so through this subtle critique and emotional appeal to lawmakers to recognize the African American man as their brother.

Essential Themes

As the first African American man to take a seat in the U.S. Senate, Hiram Revels emerged as a representative for all African Americans throughout the country. His speech illustrates the important theme that during the Reconstruction period as well as afterwards, Southern whites, former slave owners and white lawmakers resisted treating African Americans as free. Even if they reconciled themselves to the notion that African Americans were no longer slaves, Southern whites believed that African Americans were not equal citizens and thus should not be granted the same rights as privileges as whites. Certain racial stereotypes were perpetuated throughout the Reconstruction era in order to espouse this view. Black legislators in Georgia voted into office had their rights violated in 1868 because of these prevailing attitudes towards the African American community despite the fact that the Fourteenth and Fifteenth Amendments were ratified into both the U.S. Constitution as well as in Georgia's new state constitution. Although a moderate politician, Revels could not stay silent regarding the federal government's apathy toward the violation of civil rights that occurred there

Many times throughout U.S. history African Americans as well as other subaltern groups fought in wars in order to prove their loyalty and worthiness of citizenship and equal rights. Despite facing hardships, African Americans felt proud of their wartime contributions and felt that they earned freedom for their families and for themselves. Revels vividly reminds the audience that when it appeared that the Union was going to lose, African American men from the South courageously came to its rescue. He further emphasizes the loyalty and sacrifices African Americans made for the Union during the war in order to argue that they merited protection when their civil rights were so viciously trampled on thereafter. African Americans saw World War I as a good opportunity to prove themselves as Americans and believed that if they fought in the war they would be entitled to rights. The war thus ushered in the "New Negro" movement which revived a sense of expectation in the African American community not seen since emancipation during the Civil War. Revels convey a sense of hope and expectation that the U.S. government would reward its loyal citizens by protecting the oppressed for their oppressors.

Maddie Weissman, M.A.

Bibliography

Kelley, Robin D. G., and Earl Lewis. *To Make Our World Anew: A History of African Americans.* Oxford: Oxford UP, 2000. Print. Potts, Kenneth. "Hiram Rhoades Revels," in Jessie Carney Smith, ed., *Notable Black American Men.* Farmington Hills: Gale,

1999. Print.

U.S. House of Representatives, Office of the Historian. "Revels, Hiram Rhodes." U.S. House of Representatives, n.d. Web. 10 Oct. 2013.

Additional Reading

Du Bois, W.E.B. *Black Reconstruction in America.* New York: Harcourt, Brace, 1935. Print.

Foner, Eric. *Reconstruction: America's Unfinished Revolution, 1863-1877.* New York: Harper & Row, 1988. Print.

Goldman, Robert M. *Reconstruction and Black Suffrage: Losing the Vote in Reese and Cruikshank.* Kansas: UP of Kansas, 2001. Print.

Lawson, Elizabeth. *The Gentleman From Mississippi: Our First Negro Representative, Hiram R. Revels.* New York: The Author, 1960. Print.

Matthews, John M. "Negro Republicans in the Reconstruction of Georgia," in Donald G. Nieman, ed., *The Politics of Freedom: African Americans and the Political Process During Reconstruction.* New York: Garland, 1994. 253–268. Print.

■ Ulysses S. Grant: Letter to Daniel H. Chamberlain

Date: July 26, 1876
Author: Grant, Ulysses
Genre: letter

*"A government that cannot give protection to life,
property, and all guaranteed civil
rights...to the citizen is...a failure, and every energy
of the oppressed should be exerted...to regain lost
privileges and protections"*

Summary Overview

As both president and army general, Ulysses S. Grant played a significant role in keeping the Union together, completely eradicating slavery, and making sure that blacks in America obtained and exercised equal rights despite the salience of white supremacists and vigilantes using violence for obstruction. Grant had predicted that slavery would collapse prior to the Civil War, and the Union victory and passage of the Thirteenth Amendment confirmed his prediction. Throughout the Reconstruction period immediately following the war, Grant served as president Andrew Johnson's general-in-chief where he constantly had to deal with the problem of white terrorism against former slaves. As president, the racial hostilities as well as violence heightened, but Grant was hesitant to provide federal intervention in the South because of party politics. A letter written to South Carolina Governor Daniel Chamberlain in response to the governor's report on an incident of racial violence highlights Grant's hesitance. He uses colorful and blunt rhetoric to call for all Americans to accept the end of slavery in order for the nation to progress forward.

Furthermore, Grant's letter conveys a feeling of resignation that racial tensions would continue to plague the South and prevent it from moving forward. The letter indicates a sense of frustration that its author had failed to obtain and protect equal rights for blacks throughout the nation despite the passage of several laws that granted blacks social and political rights. While blacks made some progress during Reconstruction, the rise of white terrorism scaled back those gains and rendered African Americans second-class citizens for decades to follow.

Defining Moment

At the beginning of the Civil War in 1861, Union Army General Ulysses S. Grant predicted the destruction of slavery because the toll of military action would render the institution unviable. Although he hesitated to attack the institution of slavery because doing so would exacerbate the resistance of white Southerners, Grant concluded in 1862 that the collapse of slavery was a crucial component of the Union's war effort. Furthermore, the enlistment of black soldiers after their emancipation in 1863 became vital to the Union's eventual victory. Even though Grant embraced black liberation, the preservation of the Union remained the sole indication of victory.

Shortly after the Civil War ended in 1865, President Abraham Lincoln was assassinated. Vice president Andrew Johnson took charge in quickly putting in place a Reconstruction plan known as Presidential Reconstruction. Johnson desperately tried to repair the nation by convincing the Southern states to rejoin the Union. He pardoned the Confederate war generals, but stipulated that white Southerners living in Confederate states take loyalty oaths to the Union. Unlike the majority of Congress members, Johnson showed little regard for the status of former slaves because he believed that white Southerners should control them. In December 1865, however, the Thirteenth Amendment was passed and made slavery illegal throughout the United States.

Tensions grew between U.S. Congress and Johnson because he vetoed legislation that enumerated certain rights to former slaves. As a result, Congress took control of Reconstruction in 1867. A Republican Congress redrew the South into five military districts and subjected them to martial law, which upset many white Southerners. They passed the Fourteenth Amendment to the U.S. Constitution, which granted citizenship the African Americans and ensured that they would be counted in the population for the representative purposes in the House of Representatives. New state constitutions were drawn up in the Southern states. In 1867, the Freedmen's Bureau, a bureau intended to help African Americans adjust to free life by helping them find jobs and a suitable place to live, strengthened in the South. The bureau not only helped African Americans find jobs and homes, it also established the first public schools funded by the government in the South. The literacy of African Americans became necessary in order for them assimilate and successfully transition from the status of slave to U.S. citizen. In 1868, Grant was elected president. The Fifteenth Amendment was needed to give vote to blacks in all states, which the Fourteenth Amendment had not sought to do. Ratified in 1870, the Fifteenth Amendment granted blacks in the Union the right to vote. As a result, massive rioting by whites throughout the country occurred.

Grant pleaded to the American public to accept the freedom of blacks and called for them to treat blacks as equals. However, the presence of white terror groups such as the Ku Klux Klan made Grant's pleas futile. The Klan and other vigilante groups targeted both whites and African American men and their families who belonged to the Republican Party as well as white and African American school teachers. They also attacked black landowners and other blacks who did not act in deference to whites. Mob violence and lynching served as effective tools to control black behavior as well as prevent them from exercising their rights as citizens. White supremacists systematically waged violence

against Republicans and African Americans in order to persuade the North to return control of the South to the Democrats. Through such interactions with white Southerners, African Americans realized that their freedom despite emancipation would come after a long, arduous struggle.

Author Biography

Ulysses S. Grant was born on April 27, 1822 in Point Pleasant, Ohio, to Jesse Root Grant and Hannah Simpson Grant. As a child his parents expected him to fulfill all duties young men were expected to do such as collecting firewood, which developed his skills in dealing with horses. At the age of seventeen, a congressman nominated Grant for a position at the U.S. Military Academy at West Point, where he eventually attended. At West Point, although he did not excel in his academics, Grant developed a reputation as a dexterous and fearless horseman. He graduated in 1843 and remarked that leaving West Point was one of the best moments of his life; he intended to resign after serving out his minimum obligated term in the military. The army failed to notice how skilled he was with horses and instead commissioned him as a second lieutenant in an infantry division. Grant resigned from the army in 1854 but struggled for the subsequent seven years in various civilian jobs.

In 1861, Grant served as a military commander who eventually rose in the ranks to become a general in chief of the armies of the Union during the Civil War and helped collapse slavery and preserve the Union. As a general he was widely respected for his ability to remain calm and collected under fire as well as for his talent for improvising under difficult circumstances. He also knew how to properly interact with superior officers and understood both tactics in waging war and strategies used in order to win. He waged several successful military campaigns, including the capture of Vicksburg, Mississippi and its thirty thousand Confederate soldiers on the fourth of July in 1863 and his victory at Chattanooga in November that same year. Because of his success Grant was chosen to lead the military campaigns in 1864 in which he saw great success. Union military victories ultimately secured the reelection of President Abraham Lincoln.

Grant served as general in chief during Reconstruction where he sought to preserve justice for the nearly four million freed slaves in the South. He witnessed the severity of white terrorism against African Americans and their allies and sought to stop the racial violence. He supported extending suffrage to African Americans as a means of protecting themselves and becoming equal citizens in the nation. In 1868, Grant ran for president as a Republican in order to make sure that the Union would be preserved and to protect African Americans from becoming re-enslaved. As president, Grant ratified the Fifteenth Amendment which enfranchised African Americans. He initially favored using federal force to protect African Americans from white terrorism and halt white Southerners from staging coups against Republican state governments. While his policies were successful to an extent, a combination of factors such as apathy in the North and the dominance of Democrats in Southern states constrained what Grant could do to thwart white supremacy. Ultimately, by the end of his presidency in 1876 Grant was powerless to stop the recoiling from Reconstruction.

HISTORICAL DOCUMENT

Executive Mansion, Washington, D.C.
Governor Daniel Chamberlain

Dear Sir: I am in receipt of your letter of the 22d of July, and all the enclosures enumerated therein, giving an account of the late barbarous massacre at the town of Hamburg, S.C. The views which you express as to the duty you owe to your oath of office and to citizens to secure to all their civil rights, including the right to vote according to the dictates of their own consciences, and the further duty of the Executive of the nation to give all needful aid, when properly called on to do so, to enable you to ensure this inalienable right, I fully concur in. The scene at Hamburg, as cruel, blood-thirsty, wanton, unprovoked, and uncalled for, as it was, is only a repetition of the course which has been pursued in other Southern States within the last few years, notably in Mississippi and Louisiana. Mississippi is governed to-day by officials chosen through fraud and violence, such as would scarcely be accredited to savages, much less to a civilized and Christian people. How long these things are to continue, or what is to be the final remedy, the Great Ruler of the universe only knows; but I have an abiding faith that the remedy will come, and come speedily, and I earnestly hope that it will come peacefully. There has never been a desire on the part of the North to humiliate the South. Nothing is claimed for one State that is not fully accorded to all the others, unless it may be the right to kill negroes and Republicans without fear of punishment and without loss of caste or reputation. This has seemed to be a privilege claimed by a few

States. I repeat again, that I fully agree with you as to the measure of your duties in the present emergency, and as to my duties. Go on—and let every Governor where the same dangers threaten the peace of his State go on—in the conscientious discharge of his duties to the humblest as well as the proudest citizen, and I will give every aid for which I can find law or constitutional power. A government that cannot give protection to life, property, and all guaranteed civil rights (in this country the greatest is an untrammeled ballot) to the citizen is, in so far, a failure, and every energy of the oppressed should be exerted, always within the law and by constitutional means, to regain lost privileges and protections. Too long denial of guaranteed rights is sure to lead to revolution—bloody revolution, where suffering must fall upon the innocent as well as the guilty.

Expressing the hope that the better judgment and co-operation of citizens of the State over which you have presided so ably may enable you to secure a fair trial and punishment of all offenders without distinction of race or color or previous condition of servitude, and without aid from the Federal Government but with the promise of such aid on the conditions named in the foregoing, I subscribe myself, very respectfully, your obedient servant,

U.S. Grant.

GLOSSARY

caste: social group

dictates: authoritative commands or orders

Daniel Chamberlain: Republican governor of South Carolina during Grant's presidency

Massacre at...Hamburg: a racially charged outbreak of violence in Hamburg, South Carolina, on the fourth of July in 1876

wanton: unjust, unprovoked

Document Analysis

In 1868, Republican presidential candidate Ulysses S. Grant, the renowned general who led the Union army to victory, was sworn into office. Although he lacked political experience, Grant took office in order to advocate for and preserve the rights of African Americans as equal citizens to their white counterparts. He pushed through the Fifteenth Amendment in order to extend suffrage for African Americans. However, segregation and discrimination against African Americans prevailed, and an age of violence and lynching commenced during Reconstruction and for decades to follow. These lynchings were motivated by racism and racial stereotypes that developed during the antebellum period. Such violence occurred outside the due process of law and, indeed, law enforcement officials themselves often participated in the atrocities. President Grant wrote this letter in response to a report of violence against Republicans written by Republican South Carolina Governor Daniel H. Chamberlain in his state. His language indicates a level of frustration that the government has failed because it cannot protect its own citizens as well as a sense of resignation that he cannot stop the white supremacists from taking control over the South through the use of violence. This personal and collective discipline waged by white Southerners through the use of unlawful and heinous violence functioned to control the political and economic position of African Americans and to protect whites from the danger African Americans posed according to the prevailing stereotypes of the period.

On July 4, 1876, a black militia went to Hamburg, South Carolina, to celebrate the nation's centennial. South Carolina was the center of the South's Recon-

struction as well as the burgeoning black power movement, such as it was. A white farmer came to the celebration and demanded that the militia move to the side of the road so that his carriage could pass through. The militia conceded, but on the following day the farmer told a state justice that the head of that militia be arrested because he got in the way of his road. The next day the militia returned to Hamburg but encountered a large group of white men who captured the twenty-five militia members, murdering five of them immediately. African American shops and homes were also destroyed. This massacre widened the chasm between the Republican governor and Democrats in the state, paving the way for a Democratic challenger to oust the incumbent in the election in November. At the national level, Democrats considered the event a prime example of why Republicans should not control the South; such violent events occurred in states such as South Carolina, Louisiana, and Mississippi because Republicans were in charge. The South wanted autonomy rather than the federal government interfering in their affairs. The prevalence of such violence led Northerners to feel more apathetic about maintaining Reconstruction efforts. As a result, Grant showed a reluctance to authorize federal intervention in the South because he knew that Northerners grew weary of reports of violence and desired peace if that meant giving Democrats back control of the South. He assured the governor that the North did not intend to humiliate the South and thus he would not send troops to intervene in state affairs.

Grant expresses that he took issue with the senseless murder of African Americans in the South and asserts that no citizens have the right to kill them with impunity. The age of lynchings began in the post-Civil War era and reveals underlying stereotypes and myths perpetuated about African Americans to ensure that they did not enjoy their newfound freedom or become part of the U.S. polity. The victims of lynchings endured horrific violence such as being hung, dragged by a wagon, or having parts of their body disfigured or dismembered. The perpetrators engaged in such acts with impunity, as local and state courts did relatively little to pursue or punish them because of the prevailing idea that African Americans were somehow less than fully human. Lynchings were often big public affairs with thousands of white men, women, and children observing, indicating that lynching functioned as a quasi-legal means to contain and discipline blacks as well as to consolidate a dominant concept of "whiteness" that crossed gender, class, and generational lines. Such violence signaled the growing chasm between the Democrats and Republicans as a result of Reconstruction and the fact that Southern Democrats would not accept African Americans as equal citizens.

Despite these salient stereotypes, Grant conveys a hope that he can appeal to the greater sense of the American people to accept the outcome of the Civil War and recognize African Americans as equal citizens. Furthermore, he views white supremacists as the violent, dangerous, and subhuman caste, thereby subverting the prevailing stereotypes of black men and white men. Grant's language suggests that he does not want to intervene in Southern affairs but hopes that Southerners will move forward and adopt a progressive attitude rather then hold on to antebellum attitudes and ideas about African Americans. His frustrations are further evident when he appeals to "the Great Ruler of the universe" to produce the "final remedy" for fixing the inhumane treatment of African Americans in the South. Grant's tone indicates that he was dubious over whether Americans were ready for African Americans to be treated as equal citizens under the law; while the Union proved victorious in the Civil War and reconsolidated the nation and outlawed slavery, the meaning of freedom for American citizens was still unclear. Grant laments the inability of the government to protect the rights and lives of its own citizens. His lamentations reveal his lack of experience in American politics especially with regards to African Americans and race relations.

The language Grant uses to describe the massacre and its perpetrators invokes the salient stereotypes of African Americans in public discourse in order to depict the perpetrators and fellow white Southerners as embodying the worst of those they claim to fear. His depiction of Southern Democratic politicians as "savages" and uncivilized and unchristian implies that they should not be granted any political clout and do not deserve any legal authority because it is they who pose a threat to the well-being of postwar American society. By doing so, Grant subverts the image of the African American as a dangerous, subhuman savage and rather argues that the white supremacists themselves are subhuman and present a danger to American society and the ideals it represents. Although he uses vivid language that conveys his frustration and anger over the current condition of race relations in the South, his tone is subdued because he has very little control over what is happening at the local level in the southern United States. He addresses the governor in very deferential language, calling himself an "obedient servant" in order to appease him as well as encourage him to protect the rights of African American citizens in his state. While such language offers support to the Republican efforts in the Southern states, it becomes clear that Grant knows that the Democrats would prevail through their tactics of unapologetic violence and murder.

Grant concludes his letter with a resigned tone and expresses unrealistic hopes that white Southerners would accept African Americans as equal citizens. His hope to "secure a fair trial and punishment of all offenders without distinction of race" highlights his advocacy for African American rights and desire to minimize lawlessness in the South. The resignation evident in Grant's letter was merited. After his presidency, Reconstruction came to an end and Democrats dominated politics--and no subsequent president during the nineteenth and early twentieth century would advocate for African Americans as much as Grant did.

Essential Themes

Although scholars believe Grant weakened the office of the presidency, it is undisputed that he advocated for African American rights more than any other U.S. president did in the nineteenth century. He intended his presidency to serve all American citizens and tried to avoid the party politics that had so plagued American society. He greatly wanted to extend and protect African Americans' right to vote through the ratification of the Fifteenth Amendment. Unfortunately, the country turned its back on African Americans and opened itself instead to discrimination and segregation.

Grant's letter to the governor clearly conveys a strong sense of resignation over the fact that he could not protect blacks from white terrorism and a sense of frustration about blacks not being treated as equal citizens. He felt that a government that could not protect the rights of its own citizens was a failure. This sentiment reflects the dark reality that throughout American history, the standard for fitness of U.S. citizenship was related to one's race: one must be white to be considered fit for citizenship. The ideal citizen according to conventional republican ideology possessed rationality and self-possession; however, historically African Americans were not self-possessed because the institution of slavery rendered them unfit to rule themselves. Thus, racial assumptions are ingrained in the republican ideology on which the United States was founded and suggests that a link between race and citizenship has existed since the nation's inception. Even after full citizenship was extended to blacks with the Fourteenth Amendment in 1868, minority groups outside of the black-white paradigm sued courts for citizenship by attempting to prove their whiteness and disproving their blackness, given the historical disadvantages that the concept of blackness has for achieving full political status in the United States. These cases implicate the sad reality of the non-citizenship of blackness and the birth of the alien citizen. Thus, as Grant laments in his letter, even though blacks legally acquired full citizenship, they never received the protections and guarantees of full citizenship because of entrenched racism within U.S. politics and society.

In addition, institutionalized segregation in the form of the Jim Crow laws that were passed at the end of the nineteenth and early twentieth century further crippled the black population by forcing them to live in low-cost housing and by preventing them from access to social services provided by the state. The Supreme Court case decision known as *Plessy vs. Ferguson* in 1896 established the principle of "separate but equal" and institutionalized Jim Crow laws in the South. Segregation became a reality in the South and would define race relations there well into the twentieth century. The political status of blacks as full, legal citizens did little to alter the perceived inferiority of blacks in the eyes of the white population; furthermore, they were still viewed as a racial Other that threatened to destroy the purity of the white race well into the twentieth century. Grant's doubts that Americans were not prepared

to make equality under the law for all citizens a reality thus became confirmed by the establishment of Jim Crow.

Madeline Weissman, M.A.

Bibliography
"Black Codes." *History.com*. A&E Television Networks, n.d. Web. 04 Oct. 2013.
Jacobson, Matthew Frye. *Whiteness of a Different Color: European Immigrants and the Alchemy of Race*. Cambridge, Massachusetts: Harvard UP, 1999. Print.
Kelley, Robin D. G., and Earl Lewis. *To Make Our World Anew: A History of African Americans*.
Oxford: Oxford UP, 2000. Print.
Smith, Page. *Trial by Fire: A People's History of the Civil War and Reconstruction*. New York:
McGraw-Hill, 1982. Print.
Ngai, Mae M. *Impossible Subjects: Illegal Aliens and the Making of Modern America*. Princeton,
New Jersey: Princeton UP, 2004. Print.
Randall, J. G., and David Herbert Donald. *The Civil War and Reconstruction*. Boston: Heath, 1961. Print.

Additional Reading
Foner, Eric. *Reconstruction: America's Unfinished Revolution, 1863-1877*. New York: Harper
& Row, 1988. Print.
McPherson, James M. *Ordeal by Fire: the Civil War and Reconstruction*. Boston:
McGraw-Hill, 2001. Print.
McFeely, William S. *Grant: A Biography*. New York: Norton, 1981. Print.
Perret, Geoffrey. *Ulysses S. Grant: Soldier & President*. New York: Random House, 1997. Print.
Simpson Brooks D. *Let Us Have Peace: Ulysses S. Grant the Politics of War &
Reconstruction, 1861-1868*. Chapel Hill: U of North Carolina P, 1991. Print.

APPENDIXES

Chronological List

NORTH AMERICA	DATE	THE WORLD
Declaration of Independence ratified in 1776, which reads: "All men are created equal." Vermont is the first state to abolish slavery, 1777. The Fugitive Slave Act is passed by Congress, 1783. The Act Prohibiting Importation of Slaves is passed by Congress, 1807 The Missouri Compromise establishes the dividing line between free and slave states, 1820. Maine is admitted to the Union as a free state.	1775	Adam Smith publishes *Wealth of Nations,* in 1776, a major text in the field of Western economics. Napoleon Bonaparte elected as "Emperor of French," December 2, 1804. In the Treaty of Cordoba, Mexico gains independence from Spain, August 24, 1821.
The first issue of *The Liberator*, an abolitionist journal written by William Lloyd Garrison, is published, 1831 Nat Turner, a slave, leads a rebellion in Virginia, killing more than 50 whites. He is captured and hanged, 1831. *Narrative of the Life of Frederick Douglas* is published, 1845.	1825	The Java War between Dutch colonialist and Javanese, 1825-1830. France invades and occupies Algeria, 1830. The eleven year reign of President Simon Bolivar ends in Gran Colombia, 1830. Charles Darwin begins his voyage on the H.M.S. *Beagle,* December 27, 1831 Slavery abolished throughout the British Empire, 1833. Karl Marx publishes *The Communist Manifesto,* 1848.
Uncle Tom's Cabin by Harriet Beecher Stowe is published, 1852. The Kansas-Nebraska Act is passed by Congress, introducing the concept of popular sovereignty as each state decides the issue of slavery, 1854. The Supreme Court issues the *Dred Scott* decision, declaring that Scott is not an American citizen and does not hold the right to petition, 1857. Abolitionist John Brown attempts to incite rebellion at Harper Ferry, Virginia. He is captured and hanged, 1859.	1850	The Irish Potato Famine, resulted in approximately 1 million deaths 1845-1852. The Crimean War between the Russian Empire and the alliance of French, British, and Ottoman Empires, 1853-1856. The British Empire gains control of India following the Indian Rebellion of 1857. The Suez Canal is constructed, 1859-1869.
Abraham Lincoln is elected sixteenth president of the United States, 1860. South Carolina is the first state to secede from the Union, December 1860.	1860	Brazil, Argentina, and Uruguay invade Paraguay, 1864.
Mississippi, Florida, Alabama, Georgia, Louisiana, and Kansas secede, January 1861. The Provisional Constitution of the Confederacy is adopted. Jefferson Davis is elected President, February 1861. Fort Sumter is bombarded and captured by Confederate troops, April 13, 1861. The Civil War begins.	1861	The Emancipation Reform abolishes serfdom in Russia, 1861. Britain, France, and Spain invade Mexico, intervening in the Mexican civil war, 1861. Maximilian I establishes the Second Mexican Empire. Kingdom of Italy proclaimed, unifying all the territory of modern day Italy, 1861.

NORTH AMERICA	DATE	THE WORLD
Maj. Gen. Robert E. Lee is given the command of the Confederate forces, April 1861. Abraham Lincoln suspends writ of habeas corpus, July 1861. The suspension allows Lincoln to imprision Confederate sympathizers without due process of law guranteed in the Constitution. Maj. Gen. George B. McClellan is offered command of the Union army in November, 1861.	1861 (cont.)	Queen Victoria of England announces neutrality in the American Civil War, 1861. Brazil recognizes the Confederate States of America, 1861. In November and December, the Trent Affair is resolved between the Federal government and Great Britain, averting Britain's support of the Confederacy.
The Battle of Shiloh between the forces of Maj. Gen. Grant and Gen. Johnston, April 6, 1862. In the first major battle of the war, more than 13,000 Union and 10,000 Confederate were dead and wounded. A military draft is adopted in the Confederacy, April 15, 1862. The Battle of Antietam takes place on September 7, 1862. The single bloodiest day of the war, more than 12,000 Union and 14,000 Confederate casualties. The Confederate Congress passes a bill exempting from army service anyone owning 20 or more slaves, October 11, 1862. After the success of the Union Army at Antietam, Lincoln issues the Preliminary Emancipation Proclamation, September 22, 1862. After replacing an ineffective McClelland, Gen. Ambrose Burnside engages Lee at Fredericksburg, Virginia, November-December, 1862. A decisive victorty for Lee, the Union suffers heavy casualties of more than 10,000 men.	1862	Otto von Bismarck becomes Prime Minister of Prussia, later unifying Germany, 1862. France gains control of Vietnamese territories Vien Hoa, Gia Dinh, and Dinh Toung, 1862. Easter Island is invaded by Peruvian slave raiders, beginning a decade of destruction, 1862. Mexican General Ignacio Zaragoza defeats the French Army, 1862; thereafter, commemorated as "Cinco de Mayo." The Great London Expedition, the first international expedition, takes place in London, 1862.
The Emancipation Proclamation is passed, January 1, 1863. In the winter of 1862-63, Grant's multiple attempts to capture Vicksburg, Mississippi fail due to weather and high waters of the Mississippi River. Public opinion turns against Grant. After a long siege, Vicksburg falls to Grant's army on July 4, 1863. Congress passes the Habeas Corpus Suspension Act, March 3, 1863. Liincoln signs a federal draft act. While suffering heavy casualties, Lee outmaneuvers the Army of the Potomac under Hooker at the Battle of Chancellorsville, Virginia, April 30-May 6, 1863. Public opinion in the north turns against the war. Riots occur in New York City in protest of the draft, July 1863. Beginning in the winter of 1862-1863, Walt Whitman volunteers tending to the wounded soldiers in Washington military hospitals. A Union victory in the Chattanooga Campaign opens a path to the heart of the Confederacy, October-November, 1863.	1863	France annexes Cambodia, 1863. The January Uprising by Poles against the Russian Empire begins, 1863. The International Red Cross is founded in Geneva, 1863. Treaty of Hue is signed between Vietnam and the French Empire, 1863. The British Royal Navy bombards Kagoshima, Japan, 1863, in retaliation for an attack by samurai against British nationals the previous year.

NORTH AMERICA	DATE	THE WORLD
The Battle of Gettysburg, Pennsylvania, July 1-3, 1863. More than 46,000 casualties are suffered by both sides. Lincoln delivers his address, in dedication of the Soldiers' National Cemetery, on November 19. Ulysses S. Grant is made commander in chief of the Union Armies, March 9, 1864. He reorganizes the armies and takes command of the Army of the Potomac. In May, Grant engages Lee in the "Battle of the Wilderness," resulting in heavy casualties for the Union. In the Battle of Fort Pillow, Henning, Tennessee, surrendered Union African American troops are slaughtered by Confederate troops under Maj. Gen. Nathan Bedford Forrest, April 12, 1864. The Fugitive Slave Act is repealed by Lincoln, June 28, 1864. Lee's army soundly defeats Grant's Union forces at Cold Harbor, Virginia, resulting in more than 12,000 causualties. Anti-war sentiment in the north continues to grow. In July, Sherman begins his offensive against Atlanta in one of the major campaings in the war. On September 2, Sherman captures the city, news of which ensures Lincolns reelection. In November, Sherman begins "The March to the Sea" to Savannah, Georgia, capturing the city on December 21, 1865.	1864	The First Geneva Convention is adopted, 1864. A collection of treaties that define "rules of international law for the protection of victims in armed conflicts." Spain attempts to regain control of Peru and Chile in the Chincha Islands War, 1864-1866. Mariano Melagarejo seizes power in Bolivia in a coup, 1864. Karl Marx forms the International Workingman's Association (Fist International) in London, 1864. Fyodor Dostoyevsky publishes *Notes from Underground,* 1864. The Russian Empire defeats and expels ethnic Circassia's from the areas of North Caucasus, 1864.
The 13th Amendment is passed by Congress, abolishing slavery in the United States, passed January 31, 1865 (adopted December 6, 1865). Petersburg and Richmond, Virginia both fall to Union forces. Lee surrenders to Grant at Appomattox, Virginia, April 9, 1865. Abraham Lincoln is assassinated by John Wilkes Booth, April 14, 1865. President Andrew Johnson declares the end of the Civil War, May 9, 1865. Confederate president Jefferson Davis is arrested the next day in Abbeville, Georgia.	1865	Gregor Johann Mendel formulates his theory of genetics, 1865. Leo Tolstoy first serializes portions of his novel *War and Peace,* 1865

Web Resources

civilwar.org

The Civil War Trust: Saving America's Civil War Battlefields site is dedicated to preserving battlefields of the American Civil War for educational and historical value. More than 34,000 acres of battlefield land at 110 battlefields in 20 states have been preserved. The online resource is rich in documentation and multi-media on the major battles of the war.

civil-war.net

Provides a wide selection of primary source documents and images of the Civil War. The website is also provides detailed information on the armies serving from each of the north and south states.

housedivided.dickinson.edu

House Divided: The Civil War Research Engine is a resource for primary source documents and images of the Civil War. House Divided is dedicated to building a continually growing collection through several digitization projects at Dickinson College.

americanjourneys.org

Chronicles American exploration through over 18,000 pages of firsthand accounts of North American exploration. Visitors can read through the views of various historical figures from America's lively and momentous past.

docsouth.unc.edu

A digital publishing project that reflects the southern perspective of American history and culture. It offers a wide collection of titles that students, teachers, and researchers of all levels can utilize.

teachinghistory.org

A project funded by the US Department of Education that aims to assist teachers of all levels to augment their efforts in teaching American history. It strives to amplify student achievement through improving the knowledge of teachers.

ushistory.org/us

Contains an outline that details the entire record of American history. This resource offers historical insight and stories that demonstrate what truly an American truly is from a historical perspective.

teachingamericanhistory.org

Allows visitors to learn more about American history through original source documents detailing the broad spectrum of American history. The site contains document libraries, audio lectures, lesson plans, and more.

history.com/topics/american-history

Tells the story of America through topics of interest such as the Declaration of Independence, major wars, and notable Americans.

loc.gov/topics/americanhistory.php

Covers the various eras and ages of American history in detail, including resources such as readings, interactive activities, multimedia, and more.

si.edu/encyclopedia_si/nmah/timeline.htm

Details the course of American history chronologically. Important dates and significant events link to other pages within the Smithsonian site that offer more details.

docsteach.org

Centered on teaching through the use of primary source documents. This online resource provides activities for many different historical eras dating to the American Revolution as well as thousands of primary source documents.

smithsonianeducation.org

An online resource for educators, families, and students offering lesson plans, interactive activities, and more.

edsitement.neh.gov

An online resource for teachers, students, and parents seeking to further their understanding of the humanities. This site offers lesson plan searches, student resources, and interactive activities.

digitalhistory.uh.edu

Offers an online history textbook, Hypertext History, which chronicles the story of America, along with interactive timelines. This online source also contains handouts, lesson plans, e-lectures, movies, games, biographies, glossaries, maps, music, and much more.

havefunwithhistory.com

An online, interactive resource for students, teachers, and anybody who has an interest in American history.

history.org

Offers an array of resources for visitors, including information on people, places, and culture. There are also resources for teachers including e-newsletters and electronic field trips.

gilderlehrman.org

Offers many options in relation to the history of America. The History by Era section provides detailed explanations of specific time periods while the primary sources present firsthand accounts from a historical perspective.

masshist.org

Home to millions of rare and distinctive documents that are crucial to the course of American history, many of them being irreplaceable national treasures. Online collections, exclusive publications, and teacher resources are included.

historymatters.gmu.edu

An online resource from George Mason University that provides links, teaching materials, primary documents, and guides for evaluating historical records.

Bibliography

"Abraham Lincoln." *Library of Congress*. Lib. of Cong., 2013. Web. 24 Apr. 2013.

"Abraham Lincoln: A Resource Guide." *Library of Congress*. Lib. of Cong., 30 July 2010. Web. 16 Apr. 2013.

"Abraham Lincoln's Blind Memorandum and the 1864 Election." *Iron Brigader*. Iron Brigader, 12 Nov. 2012. Web. 10 Apr. 2013.

"Alexander Stephens." *GeorgiaInfo*. Digital Lib. of Georgia, n.d. Web. 10 Apr. 2013.

Alexander, Thomas B. *Political Reconstruction in Tennessee*. Nashville: Vanderbilt UP, 1950. Print.

"American President: Abraham Lincoln (1809–1865)." *The Miller Center*. U of Virginia, 2013. Web. 24 Apr. 2013.

"Background Document on the Lieber Code." *American Red Cross*. International Committee of the Red Cross, 2012. Web. 26 Apr. 2013.

"The Battle of Roanoke Island." *National Park Service*. National Park Service, n.d. Web. 29 Apr. 2013.

"The Battle of Roanoke Island." *North Carolina Civil War Experience*. North Carolina Historic Sites, 31 Aug. 2011. Web. 29 Apr. 2013. Web.

Bender, Thomas. *A Nation among Nations: America's Place in World History*. New York: Hill, 2006. Print.

Benedict, Michael Less. "Preserving the Constitution: The Conservative Basis of Radical Reconstruction." *Journal of American History* 61.1 (1974): 65–90. Print.

Bergesen, Albert, "Nation-Building and Constitutional Amendments: The Role of the Thirteenth, Fourteenth, and Fifteenth Amendments in the Legal Reconstitution of the American Polity Following the Civil War." *Pacific Sociological Review* 24.1 (1981): 3–15. Print.

Bernstein, Iver. *The New York City Draft Riots: Their Significance for American Society and Politics in the Age of the Civil War*. New York: Oxford UP, 1990. Print.

Beschloss, Michael, and Hugh Sidey. "Abraham Lincoln." *White House*. White House Historical Association, 2009. Web. 15 Feb. 2013.

"Biographies of the Secretaries of State: John Hay." *US Department of State—Office of the Historian*. United States Department of State, n.d. Web. 10 Apr. 2013.

"Biography: Abraham Lincoln." *American Experience*.

PBS: Public Broadcasting Service. WGBH Educ. Foundation, n.d. Web. 16 Apr. 2013.

"Biography: Edwin Stanton." *Freedom: A History of US*. Public Broadcasting Service, n.d. Web. 25 Apr 2013.

Birkhimer, William E. *Military Government and Martial Law*. Kansas City: Franklin, 1914. Print.

Blight, David W. "The Civil War in History and Memory."*Chronicle of Higher Education* 48.44 (2012): B7. Print.

"The Blockade of Confederate Ports, 1861–1865." *Office of the Historian*. US Department of State, n.d. Web. 24 Apr. 2013.

Bonner, M. Brem, and Peter McCord. "Reassessment of the Union Blockade's Effectiveness in the Civil War." *North Carolina Historical Review* 88.4 (2011): 375–95. Print.

Bosco, David. "Moral Principle vs. Military Necessity." *American Scholar*. Phi Beta Kappa, 2008. Web. 26 Apr. 2013.

Bradford, Adam. "Recollecting Soldiers: Walt Whitman and the Appreciation of Human Value." *Walt Whitman Quarterly Review* 27.3 (2010): 127–52. Print.

Bradley, Mark L. *Bluecoats and Tar Heels: Soldiers and Civilians in Reconstruction North Carolina*. Lexington: UP of Kentucky, 2009. Print.

"British-American Diplomacy: Treaty between United States and Great Britain for the Suppression of the Slave Trade; April 7, 1862." *Avalon Project*. Lillian Goldman Law Lib., 2008. Web. 18 Apr. 2013.

Brown, Alexis Giradin. "The Women Left Behind: Transformation of the Southern Belle, 1840–1880." *Historian* 6.4 (2000): 759–77. Print.

Brown, George W. "Trends toward the Formation of a Southern Confederacy." *The Journal of Negro History* 18.3 (1933): 256–81. Print.

Buescher, John. "Forty Acres and a Mule." *Teachinghistory.org*. George Mason University, n.d. Web. 2 May 2013.

Burden, Jeffrey C. "Battle of Vicksburg." *HistoryNet*. Weider History Group, n.d. Web. 8 Apr. 2013.

Burt, Richard W. "Captain Richard W. Burt: Civil War Letters from the 76th Ohio Volunteer Infantry." Ed. Larry Stevens. *Larry Stevens' Web Site*. Larry Stevens, n.d. Web. 8 Apr. 2013.

Burton, Harold H. "Two Significant Decisions." *American Bar Association Journal* (1955): 121–25. Print.

Burton, Vernon. "Lincoln's Last Speech." *College of Liberal Arts and Sciences, University of Illinois*. University of Illinois Board of Trustees, May 2009. Web. 20 Feb. 2013.

Campbell, Jaqueline Glass. *When Sherman Marched North From the Sea: Resistance on the Confederate Home Front*. Greensboro: U of North Carolina P, 2003. Print.

Carwardine, Richard. *Lincoln: A Life of Purpose and Power*. New York: Vintage, 2006. Print.

Caudill, Edward, and Paul Ashdown. *Sherman's March in Myth and Memory*. Lanham: Rowman, 2009. Print.

"The Civil War's Black Soldiers." *National Park Service*. US Department of the Interior, 2013. Web. 25 Apr. 2013.

Click, Patricia C. *Time Full of Trial: The Roanoke Island Freedmen's Colony, 1862–1867*. Chapel Hill: U of North Carolina P, 2001. Print.

Costa, Dora L., and Matthew E. Kahn. "Cowards and Heroes: Group Loyalty in the American Civil War." *Quarterly Journal of Economic History* 118.2 (2003): 519–48. Print.

Coulter, E. Merton. *William G. Brownlow: Fighting Parson of the Southern Highlands*. Chapel Hill: U of North Carolina P, 1937. Print.

Cross, Jerry L. "Zebulon Baird Vance." *NCPedia*. State Lib. of North Carolina, 2007. Web. 11 Apr. 2013.

Currie, David P. "The Reconstruction Congress." *University of Chicago Law Review* 75.1 (2008): 383–495. Print.

David, Shannon Clark. "Confronting the Reality of Changed Lives: Love and Loss for Women in Civil War America." *Voces Novae: Chapman University Historical Review* 1.2 (2010): 3–10. Web. 8 Apr. 2013.

"December 26, 1861: Possible War between US and Britain Is Averted." *This Day in History: Civil War, December 26*. History.com. A&E Television Networks, LLC, n.d. Web. 15 Oct. 2012.

Doyle, Charles. *Federal Habeas Corpus*. New York: Nova, 2007. Print.

Dueholm, James A. "Lincoln's Suspension of the Writ of Habeas Corpus: An Historical and Constitutional Analysis." *Journal of the Abraham Lincoln Association* 29.2 (2008): 47–66. Web. 16 Apr. 2013.

Duker, William F. *A Constitutional History of Habeas Corpus*. Westport: Greenwood, 1980. Print.

Durrill, Wayne K. "Ritual, Community, and War: Local Flag Presentation Ceremonies and Disunity in the Early Confederacy." *Journal of Social History* 39.4 (2006): 1105–22. Print.

Edwards, Owen. "Gettysburg Address Displayed at Smithsonian." *Smithsonian*. Smithsonian, Dec. 2008. Web. 18 Feb. 2013.

Ekelund, Robert B., Jr., and Mark Thornton. "The Union Blockade and Demoralization of the South: Relative Prices in the Confederacy." *Social Science Quarterly* 73.4 (1992): 890–902. Print.

Elder, Robert. "A Twice Sacred Circle: Women, Evangelicalism, and Honor in the Deep South, 1784–1860." *Journal of Southern History* 78.3 (2012): 579–614. Print.

Elliott, Mark. *Color-Blind Justice: Albion Tourgée and the Quest for Racial Equality: From the Civil War to Plessy v. Ferguson*. New York: Oxford UP, 2006. Print.

Epps, Garrett. *Democracy Reborn: The Fourteenth Amendment and the Fight for Equal Rights in Post–Civil War America*. New York: Holt, 2006. Print.

Faulkner, Ronnie W. "Secession." *North Carolina History Project*. John Locke Foundation, 2013. Web. 24 Apr. 2013.

Faust, Drew Gilpin. "Altars of Sacrifice: Confederate Women and the Narratives of War." *Journal of American History* 76.4 (1990): 1200–1228. Print.

Fellman, Michael. *Citizen Sherman: A Life of William Tecumseh Sherman*. New York: Random, 1995. Print.

Ferris, Norman B. *The Trent Affair: A Diplomatic Crisis*. Knoxville: U of Tennessee P, 1977. Print.

"The Fight for Equal Rights: Black Soldiers in the Civil War." *National Archives*. US National Archives and Records Administration, n.d. Web. 25 Apr 2013.

Flynn, Kevin Haddick. "'Where the Murderin' Cannons Roar…': The American Civil War." *History of Ireland* 20.5 (2012): 28–32. Print.

Folsom, Ed, and Kenneth M. Price. "Walt Whitman." *Walt Whitman Archive*. Ctr. for Digital Research in the Humanities at the U of Nebraska-Lincoln, n.d. Web. 5 Apr. 2013.

Foner, Eric. *Forever Free: The Story of Emancipation and Reconstruction*. New York: Knopf, 2005. Print.

---. *A Short History of Reconstruction, 1863–1877*. New York: Harper, 1990. Print.

---. "The Strange Career of the Reconstruction Amendments." *Yale Law Journal* 108.8 Symposium: Moments of Change: Transformation in American Constitutionalism (1999): 2003–9. Print.

"Fort Sumter." *Civil War Trust*. Civil War Trust, 2013. Web. 24 Apr. 2013.

"Francis Lieber: A Biography That Is a Thesis upon His Work and Influence." *New York Times*. New York Times, 27 Jan. 1900. Web. 26 Apr. 2013.

Franklin, John Hope. *The Emancipation Proclamation*. New York: Doubleday, 1963. Print.

"Gettysburg." *Civil War Trust*. Civil War Trust, 2013. Web. 15 Feb. 2013.

"The Gettysburg Address Text." Visit-Gettysburg.com. 2013. Web. 15 Feb. 2013.

Goldstone, Lawrence. *Inherently Unequal: The Betrayal of Equal Rights by the Supreme Court, 1865–1903*. New York: Walker, 2011. Print.

Goodwin, Doris Kearns. *Team of Rivals: The Political Genius of Abraham Lincoln*. New York: Simon, 2005. Print.

Gross, Jennifer Lynn. "'Good Angels': Confederate Widowhood in Virginia." *Southern Families at War: Loyalty and Conflict in the Civil War South*. Ed. Catherine Clinton. Cary: Oxford UP, 2000. 133–54. Print.

Gross, Theodore L. *Albion W. Tourgée*. New York: Twayne, 1963. Print.

Guelzo, Allen C. *Lincoln's Emancipation Proclamation: The End of Slavery in America*. New York: Simon, 2004. Print.

---. *Abraham Lincoln as a Man of Ideas*. Carbondale: Southern Illinois UP, 2009. Print.

---. *Abraham Lincoln: Redeemer President*. Grand Rapids: Eerdmans, 1999. Print.

Gwin, Minrose. Introduction. *A Woman's Civil War: Reminiscences of the War, from March 1862*. By Cornelia Peake McDonald. Madison: U of Wisconsin P, 1992. 3–18. Print.

Hamilton, Daniel. *The Limits of Sovereignty: Property Confiscation in the Union and the Confederacy during the Civil War*. Chicago: U of Chicago P, 2007. Print.

Hargrove, Hondon B. *Black Union Soldiers in the Civil War*. Jefferson: McFarland, 1988. Print.

Harper, Douglas. "Habeas Corpus in the Civil War." *Etymonline*. Harper, n.d. Web. 11 Apr. 2013.

Harris, Leslie M. *In the Shadow of Slavery: African Americans in New York City, 1626–1863*. Chicago: U of Chicago P, 2003. 279–88. Print.

Hay, John. "The Mormon Prophet's Tragedy." *Atlantic Monthly* Dec. 1869: 669–78. *Utah Lighthouse Ministry*. Jerald and Sandra Tanner, n.d. Web. 10 Apr. 2013.

Heidler, David S., and Jeanne T. Heidler, eds. *Encyclopedia of the American Civil War: A Political, Social,* *and Military History*. 5 vols. New York: Norton, 2000. Print.

Heiny, Louisa M. A. "Radical Abolitionist Influence on Federalism and the Fourteenth Amendment." *American Journal of Legal History* 49.2 (2007): 180–96. Print.

"History of the Federal Judiciary: Ex parte *Merryman* and Debates on Civil Liberties during the Civil War." *Federal Judicial Center*. Federal Judicial Center, n.d. Web. 2 May 2013.

Holder, Harold, Edna Greene Medford, and Frank J. Williams. *The Emancipation Proclamation: Three Views*. Baton Rouge: Louisiana State UP, 2006. Print.

Holzer, Harold. *Lincoln at Cooper Union: The Speech That Made Abraham Lincoln President*. New York: Simon, 2004. Print.

Horwitz, Tony. *Confederates in the Attic: Dispatches from the Unfinished Civil War*. New York: Vintage, 1998. Print.

Hsu, David. "Walt Whitman: An American Civil War Nurse Who Witnessed the Advent of Modern American Medicine." *Archives of Environmental and Occupational Health* 65.4 (2010): 238–39. Print.

Jaffa, Harry, and Robert Johannsen, eds. *In the Name of the People: Speeches and Writings of Lincoln and Douglas in the Ohio Campaign of 1859*. Columbus: Ohio State UP, 1959. Print.

Jenkins, Brian. "The 'Wise Macaw' and the Lion: William Seward and Britain, 1861–1863." *University of Rochester Library Bulletin* 31.1 (1978): n. pag. *River Campus Libraries: University of Rochester*. Web. 18 Apr. 2013.

"John Milton Hay." *The World of 1898: The Spanish-American War*. Library of Congress, 22 June 2011. Web. 10 Apr. 2013.

Johnson, William H. *Autobiography of Dr. William Henry Johnson, Respectfully Dedicated to His Adopted Home, the Capital City of the Empire State*. Albany: Argus, 1900. Print.

Juncker, Clara. "Women at War: The Civil War Diaries of Floride Clemson and Cornelia Peake McDonald." *Southern Quarterly* 42.4 (2004): 90–106. Print.

Katz, William L. *The Invisible Empire: The Ku Klux Klan Impact on History*. Washington: Open Hand, 1986. Print.

Keith, LeeAnna. *The Colfax Massacre: The Untold Story of Black Power, White Terror, and the Death of Reconstruction*. New York: Oxford UP, 2008. Print.

Kerber, Linda K. "Separate Spheres, Female Worlds, Woman's Place: The Rhetoric of Women's History."

Journal of American History 75.1 (1988): 9–39. Print.

Kobre, Sidney. *Development of American Journalism.* Dubuque: Brown, 1972. Print.

Lane, Charles. *The Day Freedom Died: The Colfax Massacre, the Supreme Court, and the Betrayal of Reconstruction.* New York: Holt, 2008. Print.

Lankford, Nelson D. "Virginia Convention of 1861." *Encyclopedia Virginia.* Virginia Foundation for the Humanities, 5 Apr. 2011. Web. 24 Apr. 2013.

Latimer, Christopher P. *Civilian Liberties and the State: A Documentary and Reference Guide.* Santa Barbara: Greenwood, 2011. Print.

"Lesson 3: The Gettysburg Address (1863)—Defining the American Union." *National Endowment for the Humanities.* National Endowment for the Humanities, n.d. Web. 15 Feb. 2013.

Lewin, Tamar. "Calls for Slavery Restitution Getting Louder." *New York Times.* New York Times, 4 June 2001. Web. 26 Apr. 2013.

Lincoln, Abraham. "Abraham Lincoln's War Address." Furman U, n.d. Web. 16 Apr. 2013.

---. "First Inaugural Address—Final Text." *The Collected Works of Abraham Lincoln.* Ed. Roy Prentice Basler. Vol. 4. New Brunswick: Rutgers UP, 1953. Print. 262–71.

"Lincoln, Abraham." *Biographical Directory of the United States Congress.* Biographical Directory of the United States Congress, n.d. Web. 15 Feb. 2013.

Livingston, Rebecca. "Civil War Cat-and-Mouse Game: Researching Blockade-Runners at the National Archives." *Prologue Magazine* 31.3 (1999): n. pag. Web. 3 Mar. 2013.

"Louisiana and Black Suffrage." *Mr. Lincoln and Freedom.* Lincoln Institute, 2002–13. Web. 20 Feb. 2013.

Marszalek, John F. "William Tecumseh Sherman." *American National Biography Online.* Oxford UP, n.d. Web. 2 May 2013.

Masur, Louis P. *Lincoln's Hundred Days: The Emancipation Proclamation and the War for the Union.* Cambridge: Belknap P of Harvard UP, 2012. Print.

Mathews, John M. *Legislative and Judicial History of the Fifteenth Amendment.* New York: Da Capo, 1971. Print.

McDonald, Cornelia Peake. *A Woman's Civil War: Reminiscences of the War, from March 1862.* Ed. Minrose C. Gwin. Madison: U of Wisconsin P, 1992. Print.

McDonald, William N. *A History of the Laurel Brigade.* Ed. Bushrod C. Washington. Baltimore: Sun Job, 1907. Print.

McGuire, Judith White Brockenbrough. *Diary of a Southern Refugee, during the War.* 3rd ed. Richmond: Randolph, Print. 1889.

McIver, Stuart. "The Murder of a Scalawag." *American History Illustrated* 8 (1973): 12–18. Print.

McPherson, James M. "The Ballot and Land for the Freedmen, 1861–1865." *Reconstruction: An Anthology of Revisionist Writings.* Ed. Kenneth M. Stampp and Leon F. Litwick. Baton Rouge: Louisiana State UP, 1969. Print.

---. *Battle Cry of Freedom: The Civil War Era.* New York: Oxford UP, 1988. Print.

---. "Lincoln, Abraham." *American National Biography Online.* American Council of Learned Societies, Feb. 2000. Web. 10 Apr. 2013.

---. *The Negro's Civil War: How American Black Felt and Acted during the War for the Union.* New York: Vintage, 2003. Print.

McPherson, James M., and James K. Hogue. *Ordeal by Fire: The Civil War and Reconstruction.* 4th ed. Boston: McGraw, 2010. Print.

McPherson, James M., Henry Davis, and Patricia R. McPherson, eds. *Lamson of the Gettysburg: The Civil War Letters of Lieutenant Roswell H. Lamson, US Navy.* New York: Oxford UP, 1997. Print.

Metcalfe, N. H. "Military Influence upon the Development of Anaesthesia from the American Civil War (1861–1865) to the Outbreak of the First World War." *Anaesthesia* 60.12 (2005): 1213–17. Print.

Meyer, Howard N. *The Amendment That Refused to Die: Equality and Justice Deferred: The History of the Fourteenth Amendment.* Lanham: Madison, 2000. Print.

Miller, Charles Dana. *The Struggle for the Life of the Republic: A Civil War Narrative.* Ed. Stewart Bennett and Barbara Tillery. Kent: Kent State UP, 2004. Print.

Miller, Randall M., ed. *Lincoln and Leadership: Military, Political, and Religious Decision Making.* New York: Fordham UP, 2012. Print.

Mindich, David T. Z. "Raymond, Henry Jarvis." *American National Biography Online* (2010): 1. *Biography Reference Center.* Web. 2 Apr. 2013.

Mintz, Steven. *Huck's Raft: A History of American Childhood.* Cambridge: Harvard UP, 2004. Print.

Mitchell, Martha. "Hay, John." *Encyclopedia Brunoniana.* Providence: Brown University Library, 1993.

Web. 10 Apr. 2013.

Moore, Frank, ed. *The Rebellion Record*. Vol. 10. New York: Putnam, 1867. *Google Book s*. Web. 11 Apr. 2013.

Morgan, Chad. "Alexander Stephens (1812–1883)." *The New Georgia Encyclopedia*. Georgia Humanities Council, 2 July 2012. Web. 10 Apr. 2013.

Neely, Marc. *The Fate of Liberty: Abraham Lincoln and Civilian Liberties*. Oxford: Oxford UP, 1991. Print.

Norton, Mary Beth. *Liberty's Daughters: The Revolutionary Experience of American Women, 1750–1800*. Boston: Little, 1980. Print.

Nye, Russel B. "Judge Tourgée and Reconstruction." *Ohio Archaeological and Historical Quarterly* 50 (1941): 101–14. Print.

Olsen, Otto H. *Carpetbagger's Crusade: The Life of Albion Winegar Tourgée*. Baltimore: Johns Hopkins UP, 1965. Print.

Ott, Victoria E. *Confederate Daughters: Coming of Age during the Civil War*. Carbondale: Southern Illinois UP, 2008. Print.

Oubre, Claude F. *Forty Acres and a Mule: The Freedmen's Bureau and Black Land Ownership*. Baton Rouge: Louisiana State UP, 1978. Print.

Paludin, Phillip Shaw. *The Presidency of Abraham Lincoln*. Amer. Presidency Series. Lawrence: UP of Kansas, 1994. Print.

Peterson, Carla L. *Black Gotham: A Family History of African Americans in Nineteenth-Century New York City*. New Haven: Yale UP, 2011. Print.

Plumly, Stanley. "Whitman's Compost." *Virginia Quarterly Review* 88.2 (2012): 13–16. Print.

Powell, William S. "Zebulon Baird Vance, 13 May 1830–14 Apr. 1894." *Documenting the American South*. U of North Carolina, 2004. Web. 11 Apr. 2013.

Price, Angel. "Whitman's Drum Taps and Washington's Civil War Hospitals." *American Studies at the University of Virginia*. University of Virginia, n.d. Web. 5 Apr. 2013.

Queener, Verton M. "A Decade of East Tennessee Republicanism, 1867–1876." *East Tennessee Historical Society's Publications* 14 (1942): 59–85. Print.

Redkey, Edwin S., ed. *A Grand Army of Black Men: Letters from African-American Soldiers in the Union Army, 1861-1865*. New York: Cambridge UP, 1992. Print.

Richards, David A. J. *Conscience and the Constitution: History, Theory, and Law of the Reconstruction Amendments*. Princeton: Princeton UP, 1993. Print.

Risley, Ford. "The South's Capital Dilemma." *New York Times*. New York Times Co., 21 Mar. 2011. Web. 17 Oct. 2012.

Roper, Robert. "Collateral Damage." *American Scholar* 78.1 (2009): 75–82. Print.

Schecter, Barnet. *The Devil's Own Work*. New York: Walker, 2005. Print.

Schultz, Jane E. "The Inhospitable Hospital: Gender and Professionalism in Civil War Medicine." *Signs* 17.2 (1992): 363–92. Print.

Severance, Ben H. *Tennessee's Radical Army: The State Guard and Its Role in Reconstruction, 1867–1869*. Knoxville: U of Tennessee P, 2005. Print.

Sherman, William Tecumseh. *Memoirs of William T. Sherman*. Vol. 2. New York: Appleton, 1891. Print.

Siddali, Silvana R. *From Property to Person: Slavery and the Confiscation Acts, 1861–1862*. Baton Rouge: Louisiana State UP, 2005. Print.

Smith, John David, ed. *Black Soldiers in Blue: African American Troops in the Civil War Era*. Chapel Hill: U of North Carolina P, 2002. Print.

Smith-Rosenberg, Carroll. "The Female World of Love and Ritual: Relations between Women in Nineteenth-Century America." *Signs* 1.1 (1975): 1–29. Print.

Stephens, Alexander H. *Recollections of Alexander H. Stephens*. Ed. Myrta Lockett Avary. Baton Rouge: Louisiana State UP, 1998.

Stuntz, William J. *The Collapse of American Criminal Justice*. Cambridge: Belknap P of Harvard UP, 2012. Print.

Syrett, John. *The Civil War Confiscation Acts: Failing to Reconstruct the South*. New York: Fordham UP, 2005. Print.

Talbott, John. "Combat Trauma in the American Civil War." *History Today* 46.3 (1996): 41. Print.

Tourgée, Albion W. "Letter to Senator Joseph C. Abbott (1870)." *Undaunted Radical: The Selected Writings and Speeches of Albion W. Tourgée*. Ed. Mark Elliott and John David Smith. Baton Rouge: Louisiana State UP, 2010. 47–51. Print.

Trelease, Allen W. *White Terror: The Ku Klux Klan Conspiracy and Southern Reconstruction*. New York: Harper, 1971. Print.

Trudeau, Noah Andre. *Southern Storm: Sherman's March to the Sea*. New York: Harper, 2009. Print.

United States Senate. *Speech of Senator Charles Sumner on the Trent Affair*. Washington: US Senate, n.d.

Web. 6 May 2013.

"USS *Lamson*." *Destroyer History Foundation*. Destroyer History Foundation, 2013. Web. 3 Mar. 2013.

"Vance, Zebulon Baird (1830–1894)." *Biographical Dictionary of the United States Congress*. US Congress, n.d. Web. 11 Apr. 13.

"Vicksburg." *Civil War Trust*. Civil War Trust, n.d. Web. 8 Apr. 2013.

Weigley, Russell F., et al. *Philadelphia: A 300-Year History*. New York: Norton, 1982. Print.

Whitman, George Washington. Letter to Louisa Van Velsor Whitman. 6 Mar. 1864. *Walt Whitman Archive*. Ctr. for Digital Research in the Humanities at the U of Nebraska-Lincoln, n.d. Web. 9 Apr. 2013.

Wise, Stephen R. *Lifeline of the Confederacy: Blockade Running During the Civil War*. Columbia: U of South Carolina P, 1991. Print.

Wish, Harvey. "Slave Disloyalty under the Confederacy." *The Journal of Negro History* 23.4 (1938): 435–50. Print.

Witt, John Fabian. "Lincoln Changes the Rules of War." *American History* 47.6 (2013): 60–65. Print.

"Wound Dresser." *Revising Himself: Walt Whitman and Leaves of Grass*. Lib. of Cong., 16 Aug. 2010. Web. 5 Apr. 2013.

Ziegler, Philip. *Addington: A Life of Henry Addington, First Viscount Sidmouth*. New York: Collins, 1965. Print.

Index

Frederick City, Maryland 303
Fredericksburg, Virginia 287, 288, 290, 324, 327,
   336, 343, 390, 660
free blacks 35, 51, 63, 256, 265, 372, 376, 379, 453,
   466, 479, 525, 529, 595, 629, 644
Freedmen's Bureau 376, 452, 470, 478, 480, 488,
   492, 494, 495, 530, 573, 574, 586, 587, 593,
   597, 598, 599, 600, 601, 603, 628, 650, 668
Freedmen's Bureau Bill 480
Freeport Doctrine 98
free states 3, 5, 24, 40, 50, 71, 72, 147, 148, 175, 439
Fremont, John C. 436
Fugitive Slave Act 24, 147, 182, 245, 513, 587, 595,
   659, 661
fugitive-slave law 29

G

gag rules 21
gangrene 304, 308, 309, 393, 394, 395, 645
Garrison, William Lloyd 372
General Order Number 14 565
General Orders No. 100 Instructions for the Govern-
   ment of Armies of the United States in the
   Field 193, 202
Georgia Convention 138
Georgia Declaration of Causes of Secession 138
Gettysburg Address (Lincoln) 365, 370
Gettysburg, Battle of 365
Gettysburg, Pennsylvania 167, 221, 277, 278, 279,
   280, 281, 282, 283, 284, 285, 287, 290, 293,
   302, 303, 304, 305, 310, 312, 336, 345, 358,
   362, 365, 366, 367, 368, 369, 370, 397, 398,
   401, 403, 555, 562, 583, 657, 658, 661, 665,
   666, 667
Golden Rule 105
Gorgas, Josiah 542
Governor's Message on the Suspension of Writ of Ha-
   beas Corpus to the General Assembly of North
   Carolina (Vance) 211, 217
Grant, Ulysses S. 130, 178, 203, 221, 256, 267, 282,
   284, 290, 293, 294, 298, 317, 329, 363, 381,
   385, 456, 462, 472, 477, 480, 496, 507, 569,
   582, 586, 605, 649, 650, 652, 654, 661
Great Britain, relations with US 177, 185
Greeley, Horace 516, 517, 520, 522, 524

H

Habeas Corpus Suspension Act 226, 232

Hamburg, South Carolina 652
Hampton Roads Conference 554, 561
Hancock, Winfield Scott 290
Hardee, William J. 318
hardtack 273
Hard War (Sherman) 203, 210
Harper's Ferry 101, 103, 104, 259, 528
Harris, Thomas L. 79, 91
Hawks, Esther Hill 337
Hayes, Rutherford B. 530
Hay, John 218, 221, 224, 664
Higginson, Thomas Wentworth 102, 525
Highgate, Edmonia Goodelle 598
Hill, A.P. xix
Hilton Head, South Carolina 587, 593
Hindman, Thomas 531, 532
Holden, William Woods 498
Hood, John Bell 204
hospitals 204, 274, 288, 302, 308, 311, 321, 331,
   332, 334, 335, 336, 341, 344, 389, 390, 393,
   395, 404, 405, 408, 548, 566, 660
Hospital Transport Service 410, 412
House Divided 48, 66, 72, 75, 98, 100, 110, 118, 121
Howe, Julia Ward 106
Humphreys, Benjamin Grubb 629
Hunter, Andrew 555, 558
Hunter, R.M.T. 552, 562

I

Illinois Republican Convention 98
impeachment 51, 227, 605, 606, 613, 615, 616, 620,
   624, 625, 626, 627
Indian Wars 319
inequality 8, 88, 105, 143, 178, 247, 252, 439, 494,
   546, 552, 603
infantry 260, 268, 272, 276, 289, 292, 293, 294, 298,
   319, 528, 559, 664
injuries 143, 194, 198, 410, 495
international law 60, 61, 177, 179, 182, 183, 184,
   194, 446, 544, 661

J

Jackson, Thomas Stonewall 345
Jefferson Davis
Jefferson, Thomas 46, 116, 135, 136, 139, 331, 332,
   335, 470, 501
Jim Crow laws 485, 505
Jim Crow segregation 311